ROGUES' GALLERY

247 Professional Criminals of 19th-Century America

ROGUES' GALLERY

247 Professional Criminals of 19th-Century America

THOMAS BYRNES
POLICE INSPECTOR AND CHIEF OF DETECTIVES (1880-1895)
NEW YORK CITY

INTRODUCTIONS BY
ARTHUR M. SCHLESINGER, jr.
S. J. PERELMAN

CHELSEA HOUSE PUBLISHERS
NEW YORK CITY

PREFACE.

A S crimes against property are of so frequent occurrence in the cities and towns of this country, it was suggested to my mind that the publication of a book describing thieves and their various ways of operating would be a great preventive against further depredations. Aware of the fact that there is nothing that professional criminals fear so much as identification and exposure, it is my belief that if men and women who make a practice of preying upon society were known to others besides detectives and frequenters of the courts, a check, if not a complete stop, would be put to their exploits. While the photographs of burglars, forgers, sneak thieves, and robbers of lesser degree are kept in police albums, many offenders are still able to operate successfully. But with their likenesses within reach of all, their vocation would soon become risky and unprofitable.

Experience has shown me, during the twenty-three years of my connection with the Police Department of the City of New York, and especially the period in which I have been in command of the Detective Bureau, that bankers, brokers, commercial and business men, and the public, were strangely ignorant concerning the many and ingenious methods resorted to by rogues in quest of plunder.

With the view of thwarting thieves, I have, therefore, taken this means of circulating their pictures, together with accurate descriptions of them, and interesting information regarding their crimes and methods, gathered from the most reliable sources. Many mysterious thefts are truthfully explained, and the names of the persons credited with committing them are revealed; but as information merely, without corroborative proof, is not evidence, it would be valueless in a legal prosecution. In the following pages will be found a vast collection of facts illustrative of the doings of celebrated robbers, and pains have been taken to secure, regardless of expense, excellent reproductions of their photographs, so that the law-breakers can be recognized at a glance. By consulting this book prosecuting officers and other officials will be able to save much time and expense in the identification of criminals who may fall into their hands. In the compilation of this work, information obtained from newspapers and police officials of other cities was of great assistance to me, but all the matter and data were verified before being used.

Hoping that this volume will serve as a medium in the prevention and detection of crime, I remain, respectfully,

THOMAS BYRNES.

NEW YORK, September, 1886.

Police Department,
of the City of New York,
300 Mulberry Street,
New York, June 15ᵗʰ 1886

Inspector Thomas Byrnes,

Detective Bureau.

Dear Sir:

At a meeting of the Board of Police held this day, it was "Resolved That the application of Inspector Thomas Byrnes, for permission to publish a work entitled "Professional Criminals of America", be and is hereby granted."

Very respectfully,

Wm F. Kipp

Chief Clerk.

CONTENTS.

CONTENTS.

Yours truly
Thomas Byrnes

THE BUSINESS OF CRIME

BY ARTHUR M. SCHLESINGER, JR.

"THE land is full of bloody crimes, and the city is full of violence." This was
Ezekiel several centuries before Christ expressing a conviction put forth with
some regularity by moralists every generation since. Each generation, moreover,
cherishes the notion that its own age is the most depraved of all. We do this today, and
we may well be right. The streets of our affluent society seem far more perilous than
those same streets thirty years ago in the despair of the Great Depression. Yet we
should not forget that forty years ago President Hoover, speaking five weeks after the
Wall Street crash, with the economy tumbling down around him and the world on the
road to war, gravely pronounced "the volume of crime of all kinds and the growth of
organized crime in our country" to be "the most serious issue before our people." And
a quarter century before that President Theodore Roosevelt told Congress, "I call
your attention and the attention of the Nation to the prevalence of crime among us."

I

Efforts have been made from time to time to shuffle off the blame for crime on such
external abstractions as heredity and environment. Yet, while heredity and environment
obviously play their role, most philosophers through history have tended to agree with
Ezekiel that, in the end, the criminal instinct lies in the heart of man and would survive
all eugenic or social reform. "Want is not the sole incentive to crime," wrote Aristotle;
"men also wish to enjoy themselves and not to be in a state of desire—they wish to
cure some desire, going beyond the necessities of life, which preys upon them . . . and
therefore they commit crimes." Freud saw this inner restlessness as evidence of the
"desire for aggression" that he reckoned a fundamental part of the instinctual endow-
ment of all human beings.

> The result is that their neighbor is to them not only a possible helper or sexual object, but
> also a temptation to them to gratify their aggressiveness on him, to exploit his capacity for work
> without recompense, to use him sexually without his consent, to seize his possessions, to humiliate
> him, to cause him pain, to torture and kill him. . . . Culture has to call up every possible reinforce-
> ment in order to erect barriers against the aggressive instincts of men.

It is true, for all this, that crime has not always been a major American issue.
Colonial days, in the main, saw only relatively minor offenses—drunkenness, assault
and battery, petty thievery, sexual derelictions. Killing was rare—at least killing
white men. In Pennsylvania less than 40 persons were convicted of murder in the entire period from the first settlement to the Declaration of Independence. Yet Freud's
"barriers against the aggressive instincts" found themselves under constant and in-
creasing strain as men pushed ahead into the American wilderness.

XIII

John Winthrop, the first Governor of Massachusetts Bay Colony, wrote in the seventeenth century that "strict discipline . . . was more needful in plantations than in a settled state." The grounds for this contention were plain enough. The "settled state" the colonists had left behind in England was a stratified society where individual behavior was controlled, to some degree, by a web of law and custom. When economic change began to disrupt that web in eighteenth-century England, a contagion of lawlessness ensued. In the colonies the feudal controls never had a chance. It was clearly every man for himself in the wilderness. Equality of individual right and opportunity—at least for white men—soon became the heart of the American creed; and individualism *à l'outrance* could elevate man above positive law in a variety of ways. So Scotch-Irish squatters in eighteenth-century Pennsylvania argued that they were right to seize other people's land because "it was against the laws of God and nature, that so much land should be so idle while so many Christians wanted it to labor on." So traditional restraints began to give way, and individualism itself became a source of lawlessness.

Racism further nourished the aggressive impulse. A people who began by killing red men and enslaving black men must have buried a propensity toward violence deep in their institutions, their folkways and their psyche. "The whole commerce between master and slave," wrote Jefferson of the relationship between white man and black man, "is a perpetual exercise of the most boisterous passions, the most unremitting despotism on the one part, and degrading submissions on the other . . . The man must be a prodigy who can retain his manners and morals undepraved by such circumstances." Nor was the relationship between white man and red man conspicuously more conducive to self-restraint.

Habits of lawlessness found easy expression on the frontier. "There, remote from the power of example and check of shame," wrote Crèvecoeur in his *Letters from an American Farmer*, "many families exhibit the most hideous part of our society." Law did not exist much in the wilderness anyway; and, as my father put it in *Paths to the Present*, "From taking the law into one's hands when it could not function it was but a step to taking the law into one's hands when it did not function as one wanted it to." Men in the West lived and died by the gun; and the posse, the vigilante, and the lynch mob did not necessarily transform a taste for execution into a system of justice. In a period of 15 months during the decade before the Civil War, Los Angeles County, with a population of 8,000, had 44 murders—more than the total number of convictions for murder in Pennsylvania in the 90 years before independence. (If New Yorkers killed one another at the same rate today, there would have been 35,000 murders in New York City in 1968 instead of a paltry 904). Of 24 graves in the early cemetery of Wasatch, Utah, 23 were occupied by victims of homicide.

The frontier was the first great crucible of American crime; and the invention of the dime novel in 1860 soon produced the gun fighter—Wild Bill Hickok and Texas Jack—and later the desperado—Jesse James and Billy the Kid—as national heroes. In time the "other side," the forces of law and order, were strengthened by new dime novel stars—Deadwood Dick, Old Cap Collier, and Old Sleuth. But civilization was fast on the heels of the trapper and the cowboy; and soon, with the spreading domestication of the West and the growth of cities in the East, crime was finding a new home in the polyglot urban environment. Indeed, the shift from the frontier to the city as the center of American crime may perhaps be dated with precision—between, say, the rout of the James Brothers when they tried to knock over the bank at Northfield, Minnesota, on September 7, 1876, and the robbery by the urban gang of Jimmy Hope of nearly $3 million from the Manhattan Savings Institution in New York City on October 27, 1878. As the balance of power between frontier and city changed, the dime novel responded by coming up with the great urban avenger, Nick Carter.

II

Crime in the cities sprang initially out of the slums. Districts like the Five Points in lower Manhattan had long enjoyed notoriety and were part of the standard tour for foreign notables. Charles Dickens in the eighteen forties noted the "leprous houses" of the Five Points and decided that "in respect of filth and wretchedness" the area "may be safely backed against Seven Dials" in London. After the Civil War every growing city tended in emulation to develop its own Misery Row or Murderers' Alley. From such noisome places petty crooks made sorties into the larger community. But, despite impressions to the contrary, not all the post-Civil War rogues came out of the slums. A good many were born in respectable middle-class families in small towns or on farms. Reared on the dream of success, they now drifted to the cities in the hope of accelerating the Horatio Alger cycle from rags to riches. *Professional Criminals of America*, published eight years after the Manhattan Savings Institution caper, is an early and diverting report on the thieves and blackguards of urban America.

Its author, Inspector Thomas Byrnes, then Chief of Detectives in New York City, was a formidable figure. Born in Ireland in 1842, he had come to New York as a child. He received little education and was trained as a gas-fitter. When the Civil War broke out, he signed up with Ellsworth's Zouaves and fought at the First Battle of Bull Run. After two years' service, he joined the New York City police force in 1863 as a patrolman. His evident competence and determination soon lifted him from the ranks. In 1868 he was made a roundsman, in 1870 a captain. He broke the Manhattan Savings Institution case and in 1880 became head of the Detective Bureau.

New York City after the Civil War revelled in criminality. In 1868 nearly 80,000 crimes had been reported; no one knows how many more went unreported. Four years later William Evarts observed that there was more crime in New York than there was in London which had three times the population. In the early seventies, according to A. B. Callow, Jr., in his recent study *The Tweed Ring*, the city had 30,000 professional thieves and 2,000 gambling dens. But Byrnes, plunging in with a will, rapidly made the Detective Bureau the most expert operation of its sort in the country. There had been talented American detectives before, like George Reed of Boston, whom the *Boston Post* described upon his death in 1840 as "the most celebrated rogue catcher in the United States." But Reed and his generation of sleuths were loners. Byrnes ran an organization. By the time he was writing *Professional Criminals*, the Detective Bureau,

located in police headquarters at 300 Mulberry Street, consisted of two regular sergeants, 40 detective-sergeants and 14 patrolmen detailed for detective duty.

The Inspector was a robust, broad-shouldered man, just under six feet, with a great
jaw, a powerful neck and piercing eyes. He was erect in bearing, immaculate in appearance, meditative in manner; and he puffed constantly on a cigar. He compiled an astonishing record of arrests—3300 before he was through. In 1894 he boasted that as
head of the Bureau he had "obtained more years of convictions against crimes than the
detective forces of Scotland Yard, Paris and New Jersey put together, nearly 10,000
years."

He made this record in a variety of ways. He began by training his men to become
connoisseurs of criminal technique. "They know the style of work of every professional
thief in the country," a contemporary observer wrote, "and when a robbery and the
circumstances attending it are reported they can generally name the operator to whom
it should be credited." *Professional Criminals* is filled with aesthetic judgments: "Billy
Ogle is a good general thief"; Kid Affleck "cannot be called a first-class [confidence]
man, still he manages to obtain considerable money"; Joseph Forman "is one of the
smartest pickpockets in America, and a man well worth knowing"; "Chauncy Johnson
is one of the oldest and cleverest bank and general sneaks in America, and has stolen
more money collectively than any man in his line."

But the signature on the crime was only the beginning. Byrnes evidently conceived his mission as, above all, that of stopping depredations against the wealthy and
powerful in New York City. To accomplish this purpose he developed a complex system of treaties with the underworld by which, in effect, crooks would agree to practice
their craft outside New York City or outside plush areas within the city. He built a
network of informers whose interest it was to report on those who broke his rules; and,
when the treaties were violated or proved inadequate for the solution of particular
cases, the Inspector had no hesitation about resorting to the third degree. Thus he
cracked the Manhattan Savings Institution case by patient inquiry in the underworld
until he accumulated enough scraps of information to move in on the malefactors and
extract their confessions.

A characteristic example of his method was his establishment of a *cordon sanitaire*
around the financial district. For years, sneak-thieves, forgers and pickpockets had
preyed happily on Wall Street. In March 1880, soon after his installation as Chief of
Detectives, Byrnes laid down his famous Dead Line. Thereafter, known criminals ven-
turing south of Fulton Street were dead: i.e., they were picked up on sight and, if they
could not explain themselves, were packed off to Blackwell's Island. Crooks with legitimate business took the precaution of getting a pass from one of Byrnes's men before
setting off downtown. The system was good though not, apparently, infallible. When
the president of the Stock Exchange, in recognition of the Inspector's initiative, made
him a ceremonial presentation of a gold watch, some impious scoundrel made off with
the president's new fur-lined overcoat. In due course, men in Wall Street—especially
Jay Gould after Byrnes tracked down a rogue who was threatening the financier's
life—found further means of showing gratitude by giving the Inspector tips on stocks

and real estate.

Byrnes was content to have thieves do their thing elsewhere—in London or Chicago or San Francisco—so long as they acknowledged his control in New York and enabled him to carry out his chosen mission. Awed bankers told young Lincoln Steffens of the *Evening Post* that, when their houses were burgled, Byrnes would listen to their complaints in silence for a moment and then say, "Enough. Your diamonds will be delivered at your house within three days." On the third day—not the second or the fourth—the diamonds would be returned "with the compliments of the Inspector." When a pickpocket lifted Steffen's pay envelope, Byrnes asked how the envelope was addressed, how much was in it, and what car lines Steffens had taken to go home; then he said, "All right. I'll have it for you Monday morning." He knew the pickpockets who were working the particular car line and sent word through the detectives watching them that they had robbed a friend of the Chief's. On Monday morning Byrnes handed back the envelope with the money just as Steffens had received it from the newspaper.

On another occasion Byrnes, in a mood of unwonted perplexity, told Steffens he had just arrested a pickpocket who in the past had always been straight with him. "He operates all the big cities that I have no arrangement with: St. Paul, Seattle, 'Frisco, Los Angeles." But he had never worked in New York. "He keeps his woman here, and when he has made a pile he comes to town. . . . He calls on me to report and get permission; he promises not to do a thing here, and I have always let him have his vacation. Never has he broken faith. He has never given me any information; he's no use to me; but he has been on the level till here the other day he was caught in a crowded surface car with a fine gold watch in his hand. . . . Why?" Byrnes suggested that Steffens talk to the man and find out.

The rascal told Steffens he had noticed a man wearing a watch with a new type of thief-guard. Before he knew what he was doing, he was seized by the desire to see whether he could lift the watch. "I didn't mean to steal the watch," the thief said; "I got caught putting it back." When Byrnes returned, he asked, "What are we up against?" "An artist," Steffens replied, ". . . a poor helpless artist." When a man was master of his craft, Steffens said, he would sometimes practice it when he should not; whether painter or writer or thief, he could not help it. Byrnes ruminated for a moment; then said to the prisoner, "All right. You can go. Only remember, New York is no place for artists. Get me?"

In such ways Byrnes maintained relations with the underworld—relations he was quick to exploit when he wanted to solve a crime. "The detective's trade," Steffens concluded, "consists not in pursuing but in forming friendships with criminals." And, when the Inspector's reading of a crime and the reports from his intelligence network narrowed down the range of suspects, he then employed the most direct possible methods to encourage confession. The term "third degree" came into use when Byrnes was Chief of Detectives, and he remained an unabashed defender of the practice. "I believe in any method of proving crime against a criminal," he told an interviewer shortly before his death. When a reporter once asked him whether he had seen many tears flow, Byrnes replied, "Oceans of them. Some break my heart, some annoy me, and some amuse me." Then he added, a trifle ominously, "But all the crying is not done by the fair sex."

The last remark suggests that the Inspector, underneath his urbanity, was a tough customer. Indeed, by current standards, he repeatedly violated the constitutional rights of suspected criminals.* His presence alone was often enough to do the job. "His very manner," as a writer put it in *Collier's*, "the size of him, the bark in his voice, his menacing shoulders and arms would terrorize the average crook." In more complicated cases Byrnes used subtler means to play on the suspect's anxieties. Jacob A. Riis, the brilliant reporter of the undercity, wrote, "He would beat a thief into telling him what he wanted to know. . . . But when he had to do with men with minds he had other resources." Then he liked to put the suspect, as Byrnes described it himself, "into the state of mind of the man in Poe's story of 'The Telltale Heart,' wherein he can't help believing that proof of his guilt has been discovered and that his cross-examiners are mocking him by pretending not to be aware of it." On occasion, it was said, he would even produce wax figures of murder victims, complete with bloody wounds, and use them to break suspects down. In retrospect Byrnes looked back on beating and torture as "not only rude and brutal, but ineffective in the majority of cases." The third degree, he insisted, "should be a psychic rather than a physical process."

His attitude was strictly authoritarian. After his death in 1910, a writer in *Harper's Weekly* described him as "an autocrat, beneficent and ruthless. His reign meant security of life and property in the highest degree attainable under American laws; yet he was still the autocrat, absolute in authority, who never tolerated opposition, never imagined the possibility of any one doubting, much less disobeying, his orders." If he was a tyrant, wrote Riis, it was "because he was set over crooks, and crooks are cowards in the presence of authority."

III

On public display Byrnes sounded like a detective out of late 19th century romantic fiction. When he described the solution of crimes, he rarely mentioned underworld informers or the third degree; it was all a triumph of ratiocination. "There is a fascination about a mystery that human nature cannot resist," he told one interviewer. "My business is shrouded in mystery, and the more difficult it is to unravel the harder I work. . . . The man whose heart and soul is in his work never lets it wholly escape. I do not dream of my work, but I go to bed and lie there for hours studying a case. When I get a clue I go to sleep and follow it up for the next day. If it is one on which I have failed for the tenth time, I review each mistake and out of the corrections evolve the eleventh."

He was a consummate showman. "The [newspaper] boys called him a great faker," Riis wrote, "but they were hardly just to him in that. I should rather call him a great

*Even perhaps by writing this book. Perhaps some readers will be distressed to find miscreants bearing their family names in the Byrnes gallery. I can only report my own mixed feelings when I came across Bertha Schlesinger, the Confidence Queen, who used to plot her villainies "at the leading hotels" where she always went "attended by a maid or a man servant."

actor, and without being that no man can be a great detective." Steffens recalls him, when announcing one arrest, spinning a yarn so full of clues, thoughts, night reflections and acute reasoning, "in brief, so perfectly modelled upon the forms of the conventional detective story, that the cynical police reporters would not write it." Steffens, who was not above a bit of romanticization himself, even claims to have found Byrnes's secret cache of detective stories: "I read [them] and recognized in them the source of his best narratives. Thus I discovered that instead of detectives' posing for and inspiring the writers of detective fiction, it was the authors who inspired the detectives."

Byrnes's romantic proclivities found considerable play in *Professional Criminals*. Drama lurked everywhere in the interstices of his sketches. There is, for example, the cautionary tale of Franklin J. Moses, a Columbia graduate who served as Speaker of the House and then, from 1872-1874, as Governor of South Carolina before he took up a career as forger and swindler, mostly for trivial sums. One of his victims was Thomas Wentworth Higginson ($34). There is the lurid saga of Little Joe Elliott, the forger, and his marriage with the actress Kate Castleton, not to mention his escape with Charlie Becker from prison in Constantinople. There is Hungry Joe Lewis, the banco steerer, who tried to cheat Oscar Wilde, only to have Wilde stop payment on the check. There is Old Bill Connelly, 70 years old in 1886, a hotel thief who once robbed some French naval officers in America for the Yorktown celebration and who, it was sadly said, had worked of late years "generally in the small cities, on account of being so well known in the larger ones." There is Hugh L. Courtenay, alias Lord Courtney, alias Lord Beresford, alias Sir Harry Vane or Her Majesty's Lights, apparently the son of a former lodge-keeper of the Earl of Devon, who insinuated himself so successfully into society, particularly female, in Baltimore, Richmond, and Newport. There is John Larney, the pickpocket, who as a boy used to disguise himself as a match girl and was thereafter known as Mollie Matches; during the Civil War, he was a spectacular bounty-jumper and claimed to have enlisted in, and deserted from, 93 Ohio, Pennsylvania, Massachusetts, and New York regiments. There is Charley Ward, who enjoyed "the distinction of being the only man in his line who can play the confidence game successfully on women"; alas, chivalry evidently led the Inspector to withhold the detail of Ward's successes.

For all his posing and his brutality, Byrnes was highly shrewd and, in his way, humane. Riis thought him "quite without moral purpose or the comprehension of it, yet with a streak of kindness in him that sometimes put preaching to shame." He was, Riis concluded, a "big policeman." After he left, the reporter thought New York would not see his like again, and he found that both good and bad. "He was unscrupulous— he was for Byrnes. . . . But he made the detective service great. He chased the thieves to Europe, or gave them license to live in New York on condition that they did not rob there. He was a Czar, with all an autocrat's irresponsible powers, and he exercised them as he saw fit. If they were not his, he took them anyhow; police service looks to results first." Above all, the Inspector was a figure. "He made life in a mean street picturesque while he was there, and for that something is due him."

IV

Professional Criminals of America, as its title implies, begins with the assumption that crime in the United States has become a social institution. "Robbery," Byrnes said, "is now classed as a profession, and in the place of the awkward and hang-dog looking thief we have to-day the intelligent and thoughtful rogue." Perhaps "business" might have been a more precise word than "profession"; and certainly Byrnes wrote about criminals in language which might have been taken from the didactic tracts of the day praising contemporary millionaires and telling how they made their money. Thus, discussing the young crook making his way to the top:

> If he cannot strike out for himself by the force of his own genius some new line of forgery, confidence operations, embezzlements, or others of the class of crimes dependent upon brains, adroitness, and address for their success, he must enter on the broad level as a general thief. . . . From that level he may rise, partly by the force of his own increased knowledge . . . partly by his natural adaptability for especial methods of preying upon the community, partly by the advice and co-operation of older criminals. . . . From a petty general sneak thief he may become one of a gang of pickpockets, and from a pickpocket, in course of time, may suddenly come to the front with distinction. . . . The professional bank burglar must have patience, intelligence, mechanical knowledge, industry, determination, fertility of resources, and courage—all in high degree. . . . He is a man of brains, possessed of some executive ability.

And so on.

One cannot know whether the Inspector was being consciously satiric. But in a sense the criminal system tends to be a parody, as reflected in a crazy mirror, of the existing business system; and Byrnes was writing about American society toward the end of the era of the individual entrepreneur. Things were already beginning to change. What Professor Robert H. Wiebe has called "the search for order" was nerving business leaders to attack the hazards and unpredictabilities of the competitive economy. The "bureaucratic orientation" was starting to rationalize and control economic life. Businessmen were organizing combines and trusts and seeking alliances with and protection from government.

The free enterprise era was passing in crime too. Byrnes acknowledged this to a degree. He noted, for example, that the professional bank burglar could not utilize his skills "unless he can find suitable associates or gain admission to one of the already organized gangs." These gangs were no longer the large collections of miscellaneous rowdies who had streamed out of the Five Points or the Bowery in the middle years of the century, and, calling themselves such names as "Plug Uglies" or "Dead Rabbits," rioted against abolitionists or English actors, beat up anti-Tammany voters and edified foreign travelers. The new gangs were small units of specialists, working as a team to rob a bank or to pass counterfeit notes or to pull off ingenious swindles. *Professional Criminals* contains illuminating accounts of some of these emerging forms of integrated crime.

But the book also has its unaccountable lacunae. For the distinguishing feature of the new organized crime lay not alone in the fact that crooks were banding together, nor even in the rise of specialization; it lay essentially in the developing relationship between the new specialized bands and the civic authority. As in the case of business itself, the more complex the planning, the more elaborate and vunerable the administrative structure, the heavier the capital investment, the greater the felt need for order and for protection. Gambling and prostitution were the first great fields of organized criminal enterprise; later, liquor, drugs, industrial racketeering, and other illegal activities entered the corporate phase.

Gambling, vice, saloons, and even opium-smoking were relatively flourishing industries in New York after the Civil War. "Startling as is the assertion," as one reformer said of prostitution, "it is nevertheless true, that the traffic in female virtue is as much a regular business, systematically carried on for gain, in the city of New York, as is the trade in boots and shoes, dry goods and groceries." One corporate activity in search of security needed another. In the late sixties the Tweed Ring began the process of mutual-defense pacts between politicians and the underworld, one partner receiving payoffs, the other protection; and the investigation of New York crime by a committee of the state assembly in 1875 following the Ring's collapse documented emerging patterns of police-criminal cooperation. The center was the area between 24th and 40th Streets and Fifth and Seventh Avenues. When Police Captain A. S. Williams, known as "Clubber" because of his genial view that law came out of the end of a police club, was promoted from an assignment in the boondocks to West 30th Street, he said, "I've been having chuck steak ever since I've been on the force, and now I'm going to have a bit of tenderloin." The name stuck.

Yet Inspector Byrnes tells us very little about gambling or prostitution or the opium traffic or the Tenderloin. One cannot at this distance say why. Perhaps, like businessmen of the day, he was too much a product of the laissez-faire era to make easy adjustment to the new world of trusts and syndicates. There is no indication that Byrnes himself was anything other than an honest cop or that his own detectives took bribes. Perhaps, like other honest cops in other times, Byrnes decided that he had better get other people out of his business, stay out of their business and keep his nose clean.

Certainly the New York police system was not organized in a way to encourage even a Chief of Detectives to widen his scope. On top was a board of four civilian commissioners; then a superintendent as the operating head of the force; then four inspectors; then the precinct captains. The commissioners controlled promotions and appointments, mostly according to the behest of Tammany Hall; the inspectors controlled the captains, and the captains the precincts. G. W. Walling, who retired as superintendent in 1885, described his position as "that of a mere figure-head." With this hopeless division of responsibility and authority, many things occurred "which did not come under the immediate notice of the superintendent, and only reached his ears after some lapse of time." For example, Walling said, "The suppression of gambling, under the present form of police government, does not, by any means, lie with the superintendent. It is wholly and solely within the power of the captains of the various precincts." Walling declared himself "morally convinced" that the great majority of gambling establishments "pay for the privilege of being allowed to conduct their business without being molested."

Walling somewhat resented Byrnes's appointment as Chief of Detectives, because this removed the detective force from his command. But he conceded that Byrnes's duties "differed materially" from those of the other inspectors; "the captains of the various precincts, therefore, did not feel under any special responsibility to him, as no analogy exists between the work of the detectives and that of the general patrol force." And, in addition to his isolated position within the force, Byrnes had to cope with political pressures exerted through the board of commissioners. A letter addressed in 1879 to the head of the Society for the Prevention of Crime and signed "A Heart-broken Wife" pleaded for action to break up the gambling halls in Bleecker Street; "Captain Burns [sic] of the Police says he can't break them up as they have political influence behind them."

For whatever reason, *Professional Criminals* concentrated on free-enterprise villainy. No one reading Byrnes's book in 1886 would have been prepared for the crusade against organized crime in New York City which the Reverend Charles H. Parkhurst of the Madison Square Presbyterian Church launched in 1892. Parkhurst, touring the Tenderloin in disguise to collect evidence for his charges, made it a particular point to expose the corrupt relations between the crooks and the police.

A few weeks after Parkhurst began his crusade, Byrnes was made Superintendent. At first the reformers welcomed the appointment. Byrnes made a valiant effort to close down the saloons on Sunday, but very little happened. He then called in the inspectors and said, "Gentlemen, did I not command you last Monday on this very spot in this same office to enforce to the letter the laws regulating the saloons in this city?" Steffens, who was present and always fascinated by Byrnes's tendency under pressure to lapse from his meticulous English into his native Irish, reports that Byrnes, crouching low at them and balling his fists, then cried, "Well, and what I want to know now is did youse did it?"

But Byrnes's virtue, Parkhurst soon concluded, was "spasmodic." Undoubtedly the new Superintendent was angered by what he considered indiscriminate blasts against the police. Superintendent Walling well expressed the psychology:

> To such an extent is the public demoralized that they no longer consider the policeman in his true light, that of a preserver of the peace; but actually, and with some degree of justice, deem him a public enemy. This, of course, inevitably reacts on the police force itself, until a policeman very naturally comes to consider himself not unlike an armed soldier in the midst of a hostile camp. Further, the police are by no means supported by the authorities in the enforcement of the law.

Byrnes's loyalty to the force and his sense of the unfairness of some of the charges soon led him, with equal or greater unfairness, to challenge Parkhurst's motives and methods. Either Byrnes "was acquainted with the character of the police force at that time," Parkhurst concluded, "or he was not acquainted with it. If he was not acquainted with it he stands thereby convicted of base negligence or of colossal incompetence. If he was acquainted with it, his assault upon our efforts to improve the force was sneaking, vicious and malignant."

By 1894 Parkhurst's disclosures forced the state legislature to appoint a committee under the chairmanship of Senator Clarence Lexow to investigate the police department. In 1895 the Lexow Report burst over the city like a bombshell. It showed cops receiving monthly stipends from gamblers, saloonkeepers, and madams; one proprietor of a chain of bordellos testified that her annual payment to the law was $30,000. It showed cops even demanding percentages of the take from such petty operators as pickpockets and whores. It showed the police commissioners making promotions in the police force in response to bribes and appointments in Tammany Hall. It unveiled a fantastic network of commissioners, policemen, judges, politicians, and businessmen in squalid alliance with the major and minor crooks of the city. The report produced the resignation of Boss Croker, the leader of Tammany Hall, and the election in the autumn of a reform administration. One of the first acts of the new mayor was to fire the board of police commissioners and appoint a new board under the presidency of the young reformer Theodore Roosevelt.

Though the police commissioners were the primary target of the reformers, Superintendent Byrnes was inevitably in the line of fire. The Lexow Committee questioned him for four hours while he explained how, with the assistance of Jay Gould and others, he had acquired some $350,000 in securities and real estate. Though no personal corruption was demonstrated, the spell was broken. Jacob A. Riis, who became Theodore Roosevelt's personal brain truster, later wrote of Byrnes, "Twice I held Dr. Parkhurst from his throat, but in the end I had to admit that the Doctor was right."

Roosevelt, taking charge of what he called "the most important, and the most corrupt, department in New York," was convinced that Byrnes had to go. The reformer did not like the Superintendent's friendship with politicians and financiers nor his protection of his underworld informers; most of all, he knew that he would not have a free hand with so powerful a personality as the operating head of the police. "I think I shall move against Byrnes at once," he wrote Henry Cabot Lodge shortly after taking office. "I thoroughly distrust him, and cannot do any thorough work while he remains." Two weeks later he wrote his sister, "I am getting the Police Department under control; I forced Byrnes and Williams out, and now hold undisputed sway." He told Seth Low, "It was absolutely necessary that Byrnes should go. In the detective force he will be hard to replace, but as Chief of Police his loss will not be felt in the least."

Steffens remembers the day of Byrnes's departure as "memorable." A banker, who seemed really frightened, said, "What will happen to us now I dread to think." The thieves came too, Steffens wrote, and were more frightened than the honest men. One fellow sat on the steps of the police station, his head in his hands, his elbows on his knees. Steffens asked the doorman who he was. "Oh, just an old dip that the old man was good to sometimes. Thinks the world is coming to an end." Riis summed up the meaning of Byrnes's resignation. "There was not one of us all who had known him long," he wrote, "who did not regret it, though I, for one, had to own the necessity of it, for Byrnes stood for the old days that were bad. But, chained as he was in the meanness and smallness of it all, he was yet cast in a different mold. . . . I believed that, untrammeled, Byrnes might have been a mighty engine for good, and it was with sorrow I saw him go. He left no one behind fit to wear his shoes."

Byrnes now retired on a pension of $3000 a year and became general manager of the burglary-insurance department of the United States Casualty Company. He lived in a rambling brown house along the Shrewsbury River in Red Bank, New Jersey. He handled occasional problems for wealthy families, like the Goulds; he sailed his catboat in the Red Bank Yacht Club regattas; he mused in his drawing-room, where all the rugs and hangings were golden, and denounced the incompetence of the New York Police Department. His successors at Mulberry Street retaliated in kind. "It was a little town when Byrnes ran it," his one-time protegé Superintendent Michael McCafferty used to say, "and not so many different races up against you. It's a different situation now. He couldn't cope with it." No doubt Byrnes lived beyond his time. He died in New York City of stomach cancer on May 7, 1910.

V

McCafferty's crack—"not so many different races up against you"—invites another line of speculation about *Professional Criminals*. For, ever since Daniel Bell's now classic article "Crime as an American Way of Life" appeared in the *Antioch Review* in 1953, historians have begun to consider the role of crime as "one of the queer ladders of social mobility in American life." As a predominantly white Anglo-Saxon Protestant society, America has traditionally resisted the invasion of established citadels of power by people with odd names, accents, and backgrounds. This has meant that the more recent immigrant groups, as they began their own rise in American life, found most respectable gates closed. Those who had particular talents or who wanted wealth and status at once therefore turned to various marginal occupations. So, in the late 19th century when politics was in disrepute, the Irish with their special gifts seized on that as a quick road to power. Entertainment too has served as a social escalator for talented non-WASPs. Sports has been another such escalator; one can trace in the names of boxing champions the progression of ethnic groups using and then abandoning pugilism as their way to the top—first the Irish, then the Jews and Italians, then the Negroes.

The idea that crime was an immigrant monopoly has been expressed since almost the beginning of the republic. Mrs. Trollope, writing of America in the eighteen twenties, repeated with evident relish a statement she had heard that "very nearly all the white men who had suffered death [by capital punishment] since the Declaration of Independence had been Irishmen." When the Hungarian liberals and friends of Kossuth, Ferenc, and Theresa Pulszky, visited Boston in 1852, they were told that three-quarters of all the arrests by Boston police and nearly three-quarters of the commitments to the county jail involved immigrants, again mostly Irish. In later times Eastern European Jews, Italians, and Negroes were successively considered the bearers of the crime wave.

It is not clear at all that crime in America can be thus exclusively traced to foreigners. Very few immigrants, for example, got off the boat and headed directly to Wasatch, Utah. The desperadoes of the West mostly had splendid old American names. James Truslow Adams stated the case ingeniously forty years ago:

> It is impossible to blame the situation on the "foreigners." The overwhelming mass of them were law abiding in their own lands. If they became lawless here it must be largely due to the American atmosphere and conditions. There seems to me to be plenty of evidence to prove that the immigrants are made lawless by America rather than that America is made lawless by them. If the general attitude towards law, if the laws themselves and their administration, were all as sound here as in the native lands of the immigrants, those newcomers would give no more trouble here than they did at home.

Adams no doubt underestimated the disorienting effect of the immigration experience, but he had a point nevertheless.

Certainly *Professional Criminals* does not bear out any facile identification of crime with immigration. The great majority of Inspector Byrnes's acquaintances would appear to be WASPs, followed at some distance by Irish, Germans, and Jews. Byrnes mentions very few Italians, though Sicilian longshoremen in New Orleans were already being organized by an early version of the Mafia; eleven of them, after the murder of the Irish chief of police, were lynched in 1891. And black nationalists will no doubt be indignant to note that the main gallery—"Descriptions and Records of Professional Criminals"—includes no Negroes at all (Nigger Baker turns out to have been so called because of his "very dark complexion"), though some are listed at the back of the book under "Executions in the Tombs Prison." Feminists, on the other hand, should be gratified at the generous representation the Inspector has given to lady crooks. One wishes that the Inspector had offered his own assessment of a proposition of Superintendent Walling's about politics and crime: "All the sneaks, hypocrites and higher grade of criminals, when questioned upon the subject, almost invariably lay claim to be adherents of the Republican party; while, on the other hand, criminals of the lower order—those who rob by violence and brute force—lay claim in no uncertain terms to being practical and energetic exponents of true Democratic principles." Walling hastily added: "Of course, it is far from my intent to say that every Republican is a sanctimonious sneak, hypocrite or forger; or that every Democrat is a burglar, footpad, pimp or rough."

Professional Criminals catches crime as an American escalator at a rather early stage. This does not invalidate the Bell thesis, however. Many of Byrnes's Anglo-Saxon crooks were undoubtedly seeking short cuts to what sociologists call upward mobility. And, when one considers that they were soon enough replaced by the Red Rocks Farrells, Dion O'Banions, and Bugs Morans, who were then jostled by the Arnold Rothsteins, Legs Diamonds, and Lepke Buchalters, who in their turn were shouldered aside by the Lucky Lucianos, Frank Costellos, and Vito Genoveses, one must conclude that a coming generation of aspiring black criminals will probably do more to destroy the Mafia than the F.B.I. is likely to do.

Professional Criminals in America, in short, offers its cross-section of crime at the time when individual enterprise was beginning to yield to corporate endeavor, and old-fashioned Americans to more recent immigrants. The view from Byrnes's desk remains fascinating for all that. And the reader, before he settles down to exorcise the terrors of the present by contemplating these presumably more innocent scoundrels of the past, should remember that the victims of Inspector Byrnes's acquaintances did not find them all that benign. He should recall, too, the wise reminder of Dr. Karl Menninger: "The crime and punishment ritual is part of our lives. . . . We need criminals to identify ourselves with, to envy secretly, and to punish stoutly. They do for us the forbidden, illegal things we wish to do and, like scapegoats of old, they bear the burdens of our displaced guilt and punishment."

DON'T BLAME INSPECTOR BYRNES

BY S. J. PERELMAN

WHENEVER, in a somber mood, I start totting up the many experiences denied me in my lifetime, I think of four above all that I am sure would have been enormously enriching. I never met James Joyce. (A luncheon date in 1934 was cancelled bec ue e   e to it he had lost several chapters of *Finnegans Wake* in a cab.) I arrived   te to see Peking, and I never danced with that tigress star of Elinor   *eeks*, Aileen Pringle, the memory of whose voluptuous balcony has na ited me from youth. The fourth deprivation, while nowhere as acute, was profession-al: I never was a cub reporter assigned to cover police news, and consequently never knew any working criminals. In later years, however, I did encounter two who had re-tired, if only by their own deposition. The first was Mike O'Dowd, a local real-estate agent in the Pennsylvania boondocks where I reside. Mike was the prototype of the stage Irishman, a fellow of infinite jest and gift of the gab, who at one time had been a celebrated fur thief. His specialty, singular enough to have been immortalized in a study published by the University of Chicago, was the theft of women's fur coats from various New York department stores. He usually entered them just before closing, clad in a capacious ulster or balmacaan, and locked himself straightaway in a pay toilet. After the watchmen had made their rounds, Mike would emerge, select a hand-some mink or broadtail from the racks, and saunter out when the store reopened, wear-ing the booty under his coat. Even more striking, however, was Mike's disposition of the proceeds of his loot. A philosophical anarchist, he contributed all but the merest fraction to persons needier than himself. When the police ultimately caught up with him, they were so baffled by his altruism that they had him adjudged insane, but he beat the rap and ended his days on the steps of our country postoffice, chewing BL Cut Plug and discussing the theories of Kropotkin.

I met my second *gonif*, and an equally eminent one, at the Kentucky Derby in 1952. On the morning of the race, I was strolling along the main street of Louisville with Dr. David Maurer, this country's ranking authority on underworld slang and the author of that monumental treatise on the mores and speech of the confidence trick-ster, *The Big Con*, as well as of countless monographs on the argot of safecrackers, card sharps, junkies, and carnival folk. Through his research in linguistics, Maurer had de-veloped a wide acquaintance among such rapscallions, and I was absorbed in the ac-count of his scholarship when he broke off abruptly. Poised at the traffic light opposite, he whispered, was one of the most expert cannons, or pickpockets, in the business. I expected to meet a furtive character in a gooseneck sweater, the dismal stereotype familiarized by Thomas Burke's *Limehouse Nights* and the novels of Frank L. Packard. Instead, I was introduced to a personable, charming fellow on the order of Jack Dona-hue, the dancer, who met my gaze unflinchingly as we shook hands and made no move in the direction of my wallet. He chatted genially in an undertone with my companion for several minutes, and after his departure, Maurer provided a few discreet details. Herschel Downs, he said, cloaking him in an obvious pseudonym, had been for some years the head of a whiz mob, or group of pickpockets, a pursuit that earned him a snug annual income in excess of $35,000. Unfortunately, a discarded mistress had planted a gun on his person, resulting in a rap out of all proportion to his misdeeds. He was now engaged in selling vacuum cleaners from door to door and doing so well, it appeared, that he doubted he would ever return to lifting pockets. To me, in that atmosphere of easy money, it was a stunning demonstration of the wisdom of rectitude, of the superiority of good over evil, and for the first in my life, when I checked out of the hotel the next day, I didn't steal a single towel.

To any layman as ignorant of the grift and its denizens as myself, therefore, this compendium of thievery by Inspector Byrnes will come as a primer, a cornucopia, and a museum piece. Apart from its rogues' gallery of more than two hundred malefactors —so far as I know, the only attempt on record to publicize such malefactors—it contains a vast quantity of precise information about the criminal methods of the period, together with endless fascinating anecdotes and trivia that run the gamut from pilferage to murder. I use the word "primer" advisedly; the procedures employed in bank burglary, fraud, check-raising, pickpocketry, and every form of larceny short of chicken-stealing are so explicit that one speculates about their impact on the young back in 1886. I wonder how many youths, sneaking a cubeb behind the barn, pored over these pages and dreamed of swindling a chump one day or cracking a crib. Here, for instance, is an excerpt from the Inspector's chapter on safeblowing:

> While some bank thieves use the spirit lamp and blow-pipe to soften the hardened metals and take the temper out of the steel vault doors or cases . . . others, who do not care to spend time manipulating the intricate combination, use simple sort of machines, technically called the "drag" and "jackscrew." The former, simple as it looks, is extremely powerful—and so quiet. By means of a bit a hole is bored through a safe door; a nut is set "inside"; the point of the screw passes through the nut, which rests inside the surface that has been bored; then the screw is turned by a long handle, which two men can operate . . . . The "jackscrew" is rigged so that by turning it will noiselessly force into the crack of a safe door a succession of steel wedges; first, one as thin as a knife-blade; soon, one as thick as your hand; and they increase in size until the hinges give way.

And should the student be a dolt incapable of evolving these instruments, he is supplied with a further helpful tip: "Some burglars make their own outfit, but almost any blacksmith will make any tool he is called upon for."

The same emphasis on minutiae is manifest in a less glamorous but similarly knotty technique, that of rifling a hotel room. Says the Inspector: "A slight push may let him (the thief) enter the apartment, or it may be necessary to use a gimlet and a small piece of crooked wire to slide back the bolt, or a pair of nippers to turn the key on the inside of the lock, from the corridor . . . The much boasted of chain-bolt (the speaker's contempt verges on derision) can now be drawn back from the outside with only a piece of silk thread having a match tied to one end of it."

Turning to another category of the boost, we find this invaluable pointer for ladies bent on sneak theft: "The cloak is also a useful article of attire for the shoplifter, and record is kept of women who have concealed inconceivable quantities of goods under a sweeping outer garment. Large rolls of cloth, costly dresses, and sealskin sacques have been withdrawn from such repositories." Nowadays, of course, fashion has largely invalidated such devices. The fair shoplifter, all too sketchily clad in a mini-skirt and blouse with a plunging neckline, might manage to secrete a paper of hairpins or a stolen hankie under her wig, but if the present trend toward nudity continues, the poor thing is doomed to obsolescence.

Although Inspector Byrnes, as a peeler, frowns on lawbreakers and proffers their careers as an object lesson, he time and again yields to admiration for their artistry. "Bank sneak thieves," he admits, "are all men of education, pleasing address, good personal appearance, and are faultless in their attire." Of the fraternity that specializes in kiting checks, he says: "The professional forger is a man of great ability and naturally a cunning and suspicious sort of individual." One might bestow a like compliment on Junius Pierpont Morgan and Commodore Vanderbilt, who possibly would also merit the praise given hotel and boarding-house thieves: "The successful ones are men of respectable appearance, good address, and cool and daring fellows." And when, on occasion, Byrnes comes across a truly outstanding personality, a man of signal accomplishment like Thomas Ballard, dubbed the King of the Counterfeiters, his voice becomes almost lyrical: "He was a superior engraver, and the fine work on some of his bills was so cleverly and artistically executed as to deceive even the banks and the government." Cynic though he clearly was, I'll bet there was a suspicious moisture in the Inspector's eye the day Ballard went up the river for thirty years.

The rhetoric of the mid-Victorian era was not notable for its self-restraint; lady novelists and poets were wont to indulge in rhapsodical flights that dizzied the reader and left him as bilious as if he had eaten a boxful of marzipan. By and large, *Professional Criminals of America* is prosaic and factual, but when its author gets around to the weaker sex, he really soars. Though he attributes the following description of Doras Doyen, the victim of a mysterious murder, to "an able writer," I suspect it was his own handiwork:

> She was a shade below the middle height, but of a form of exquisite symmetry, which, though voluptuously turned in every perceptible point, was sufficiently dainty in its outline to give her the full advantage of a medium stature to the eye. Her complexion was that of a clear brown, bearing in it all the voluptuous ardor of that shade.

This is exactly as I would have described Miss Aileen Pringle, my afore-mentioned heartbeat with the physique of a pouter pigeon, were I gifted enough; and I'm positive never could have equalled the ensuing passage:

> Her features were not what might be termed regular, but there was a harmony in their expression which was inexpressibly charming; the nose was rather small, which was a fault; the mouth was rather large, but the full richness of its satin lips and the deep files of ivory infantry which crescented within their rosy lines redeemed all its latitudinal excess; while her large, black, steady

eyes, streaming now with glances of precocious knowledge, and anon languishing with meditation or snapping with mischievousness, gave the whole picture a peculiar charm which entitled it to the renown of one of the most fascinating faces that ever imperilled a susceptible observer.

The conjunction of "satin lips" with "deep files of ivory infantry" is, I contend, sheerest genius—a marriage of Jacqueline Susann and dentistry blessed by the U.S. Army Manual. What a pity Inspector Byrnes wasted twenty-three years sleuthing for the New York Police Department. Today he might have been a best-selling novelist, pontificating away on David Susskind's program and twinkling in the starry firmament with Irving Wallace, Harold Robbins, and Henry Sutton.

Regrettably, the flowers the Inspector has woven into his garland are too numerous, and their fragrance too heady, to be sniffed one-by-one, but among them are two more worthy of mention. The chapter entitled "Adventurers and Adventuresses" lists a variety of minor and rather harmless rackets being perpetrated at that time—quack medicine sales, influence-peddling, literary blackmail, etcetera. A couple of new phenomena, however, seemed to be emerging—the gigolo and the artist's model, both of them viewed with ill-concealed alarm. "A certain young man," the text reports breathlessly, "has for some time past devoted himself almost exclusively to playing the cavalier to a very old and very rich widow, whom he accompanies everywhere. Apropos, it may be remarked that this dancing attendance to dowagers who are rich is growing into quite an 'institution' . . . Is it a sign of the times?" As for the propensity of females to expose themselves in their birthday suits, it is ascribed to pure economic necessity. Quoted in support is the case of a young lady of birth, education, and refinement who, only because she and her mother were faced with starvation, became a model in a life class and earned "about $10 a week." Obviously, the wages of shame in the mid-eighties were far below the union scale of today. But, continues the text with prim disapproval: "Occasionally in our better classes, ay, even in our best society, it is rumored that ladies do not hesitate to serve as partial models for the bust or arms or for classic poses, to please popular artists or to gratify their own vanity. . . ." It is probably just as well that the writer of those words was not endowed with clairvoyance. Had he been able to look ahead eighty-three years into the future at the didoes currently observable in "Oh, Calcutta" and "I Am Curious Yellow," it's six, two, and even that he would have had a cardiac arrest.

"Opium Habit and Its Consequences," another chapter that repays browsing, is a cautionary tale annotated by the Inspector but related by an anonymous victim of the drug, whose descent into Avernus, naturally, took place in a Chinese laundry. Chinese laundries classically have been associated with evil; as little as a year ago a young and (I thought) worldly matron whom I was escorting home from a dance in Philadelphia shuddered visibly as we passed one. "Do you see that place?" she asked. "That's the center of the white slave trade for the whole eastern seaboard." In whatever case, the account herein contained of the experiences of this slave of the poppy, of the *Sturm und Drang* he underwent, is a lollapaloosa, exhuming such clichés as will render every reader of dime novels boozy with nostalgia. The Inspector throws in a few for good measure, as when he declares: "Few white men can run a 'joint' successfully. A Chinaman is meek, pretends not to understand when anything insulting is said to him, and so long as he gets paid for the opium does not care what the patrons do." His final word on the subject, additionally, must qualify as the understatement of all time about addiction: "My advice is to keep away from opium in all forms, as no good comes of it."

All in all, *Professional Criminals of America* is a gas, a vade-mecum for the amateur historian, the detective-story writer in quest of plots, and lovers of morbositá generally. If for no other reason, they should be captivated by the aliases of the rogues in the author's gallery, a few of which I cull at random:

Aleck the Milkman, Piano Charley, Brummagem Bill, English Paddy, Mary K. Hansen alias Klink (an unfortunate choice), Old Man Herring, Grand Central Pete, Funeral Wells, Hungry Joe, Marsh Market Jake, Yen Hock Harry, Kehoe the Mourner, Little Tip, Milky McDonald, Old Mother Hubbard, Three-Fingered Jack (a forerunner of Three-Fingered Brown?), Paper Collar Joe, The Peoria Kid, Sheeny Sam, The Student, and Worcester Sol.

A colorful crew, and if they invade your dreams, don't blame Inspector Byrnes. After all, he warned you.

METHODS

OF

PROFESSIONAL CRIMINALS OF AMERICA.

BANK BURGLARS.

THE ways of making a livelihood by crime are many, and the number of men and women who live by their wits in all large cities reaches into the thousands. Some of the criminals are really very clever in their own peculiar line, and are constantly turning their thieving qualities to the utmost pecuniary account. Robbery is now classed as a profession, and in the place of the awkward and hang-dog looking thief we have to-day the intelligent and thoughtful rogue. There seems to be a strange fascination about crime that draws men of brains, and with their eyes wide open, into its meshes. Many people, and especially those whose knowledge of criminal life is purely theoretical, or derived from novels, imagine that persons entering criminal pursuits are governed by what they have been previously, and that a criminal pursuit once adopted is, as a rule, adhered to ; or, in other words, a man once a pickpocket is always a pickpocket ; or another, once a burglar is always a burglar. Hardly any supposition could be more erroneous. Primarily there are, of course, predisposing influences which have a certain effect in governing choice.

A man of education, refined habits, and possibly a minimum of courage, would not be likely to adopt the criminal walks requiring brute force and nerve. Such a one would be far more likely to become a forger or counterfeiter than a highway robber. Still, under certain circumstances—opportunity and the particular mode of working of those who were his tutors in crime—he might be either, foreign as they would be to his nature. Criminal occupation, however, is, like everything else, progressive. Two things stand in the way of the beginner in crime attaching himself to what he may view—taking them in the criminal's own light—as the higher walks of predatory industry, the top rungs of the criminal ladder. The first is, naturally, lack of experience and skill ; the second, lack of confidence in him or knowledge of him by the older and more practiced hands, whose co-operation would be necessary.

Hence, if he cannot strike out for himself by the force of his own genius some new line of forgery, confidence operations, embezzlements, or others of the class of crimes dependent upon brains, adroitness, and address for their success, he must enter on the broad level as a general thief—one of the class who will steal anything that they can get away with, from a needle to a ship's anchor. From that level he may rise, partly by the force of his own increased knowledge of the practice of crime, partly by his natural adaptability for especial methods of preying upon the community, partly by the advice and co-operation of older criminals with whom he comes in contact, whether at liberty or doing time in a prison. From a petty general sneak thief he may become one of a gang of pickpockets, and from a pickpocket, in course of time, may suddenly come to the front with distinction even as a first-class bank burglar.

Cracksmen of this class head the list of mechanical thieves. It requires rare qualities in a criminal to become an expert bank-safe robber. Thieves of this high grade stand unrivaled among their kind. The professional bank burglar must have patience, intelligence, mechanical knowledge, industry, determination, fertility of resources, and courage—all in high degree. But, even if he possess all these, they cannot be utilized unless he can find suitable associates or gain admission to one of the already organized gangs. Sometimes the arrest of a single man out of a gang will put a stop to the operations of the remainder for a long time, simply because they need another man, and can find nobody they can trust. Bank burglars have been known to spend years in preparation—gleaning necessary information of the habits of bank officials, forming advantageous acquaintances, and making approaches to the coveted treasure all the time, but with the patience to wait until the iron is fully hot before striking a blow.

The construction of a massive bank safe, provided, as they now are, with electric alarms, combination and time locks, and other protective appliances, is such, that none but a mechanical genius can discover its weak points and attack it successfully. There is not a safe in use to-day that is absolutely burglar-proof, notwithstanding the fact that many manufacturers advertise and guarantee those of their build as such. Every now and then safe makers quietly alter the internal construction of their vaults, and these changes are brought about by the doings of some scientific robber. Just as soon as the safe builder becomes aware of the fact that burglars have unearthed a defect in vaults of his make, he sets his mechanics at work upon some new design, in the hope of thwarting thieves and making his vaults the more secure.

The wrecking of every safe, therefore, reveals a blemish, and necessitates alterations, which, of course, later on, make the work of the vault-opener more difficult. Hundreds of safes are turned out of the factories in the several cities weekly, and a calculating burglar, when he has discovered a defect in a certain pattern, will delay exposing his secret to the manufacturer until thousands of the seemingly strong, yet frail, vaults have been made and are in use. That insures him something to operate upon, for he well knows that after his first success, and the fact is reported at the safe factory, improvements will be in order.

The proficiency attained by our bank burglars, and the apparently comparative ease with which they secure the contents of massive vaults, is the result of constant and careful study of the subject. All the resources, ingenuity and cunning of the cracksman who makes bank-wrecking a specialty are put to the test in an undertaking of that sort, and plans follow plans until one is matured which circumstances may warrant as safe, feasible, and profitable. Then the accomplishment of the nefarious scheme only depends upon nerve, daring, and mechanical tools.

Some burglars make their own outfit, but almost any blacksmith will make any tool he is called upon for, if its construction is within his capacity, without asking any questions about the uses to which it is to be put, provided he gets his price for it. It is, of course, more than probable that he guesses the use for which it is intended, but that, he thinks, is not his business. The making of such implements is, as a rule, confined to those mechanics who are actually in league with the criminals who expect to use them. The heavy and unwieldy tools of years ago have been abandoned by the modern bank robber, with his new inventions. While some bank thieves use the spirit lamp and blow-pipe to soften the hardened metals and take the temper out of the steel vault doors or cases, others use only a small diamond-pointed drill. Then again, others, who do not care to spend time manipulating the intricate combination, use simple sort of machines, technically called the "drag" and "jackscrew." The former, simple as it looks, is extremely powerful—and so quiet. By means of a bit a hole is bored through a safe door; a nut is set "inside;" the point of the screw passes through the nut, which rests inside the surface that has been bored; then the screw is turned by a long handle, which two men can operate. As the screw turns, the nut is forced forward, farther and farther. It is a power that hardly any construction of a safe can resist. Either the back or the front must give way.

The "jackscrew" is rigged so that by turning it will noiselessly force into the crack of a safe door a succession of steel wedges; first, one as thin as a knife-blade; soon, one as thick as your hand; and they increase in size until the hinges give way. Where the size or location of the safe or vault to be forced precludes the use of these machines, and an explosion becomes necessary, dynamite and nitro-glycerine are used with the greatest skill, and with such art in the deadening of sound that sometimes an explosion which rends asunder a huge safe cannot be heard twenty yards away from the room in which it takes place.

The patient safe robber is aware of several ingenious ways of picking combination locks. In following their nefarious calling these men attain a delicacy of feeling by which they are able to determine to a nicety the exact distance necessary to raise each tumbler of the lock. The burglar masters a combination with almost mathematical accuracy, and manipulates its complex machinery with the same dexterity and precision that a music-teacher touches the keys of a piano. He is trained to detect one false note in a swelling chorus produced by the click of reverberating ratchets within the lock, and marks the period and duration of the drops. When they come across some new kind of lock, they will manage to get possession of one, whatever its cost, and whatever roundabout means may be necessary to get hold of it, and, taking it apart, will study its construction until they know its strong and weak points, and how to master it, just as well as its inventor or maker could. They are always on the alert to utilize for their purposes every new appliance of power.

The combination-safe picker is the cleverest of all the fraternity of lock workers. His is a life of study and careful experimenting. He proceeds to fathom the mystery of a new and intricate piece of mechanism with the same enthusiastic, yet patient, attention and study that actuates a scientist in search of more useful knowledge. Having acquired mastery over any combination, the burglar guards his secret jealously. Gaining access to the bank or building, he can tell at once the character of the combination he has to deal with, and that with him is tantamount to opening the safe or vault. Having rifled the safe of its contents, he closes the door, and begins to make arrangements to deceive the officials of the institution and the detectives. The crevices of the door are closed with putty, with the exception of a small orifice in the upper or horizontal crevice, through which powder is blown into the safe by means of a small bellows. The hole is then closed, a slow fuse which is inserted into the crack is set fire to, and the building is vacated. Half an hour or so later the fuse ignites the powder, and the safe door is shattered from its strong fastenings.

For fifteen years the manner in which a celebrated combination lock was picked by thieves was involved in mystery, during which time many honest bank employés suffered in reputation, and not a few were unjustly incarcerated. The criminals who operated so mysteriously upon the safes never took all the money or valuables. In many cases they helped themselves to but a small percentage of the proceeds, and it was this ruse that threw the officials off their guard and brought the employés into disrepute. The burglars familiarized themselves with the make and patterns of the locks, and then bored a hole within a short distance of where a spindle held the tumblers. With the use of a common knitting-needle the tumblers were dropped and the safe door opened.

The secret of another ingenious method of opening safes at last leaked out. The paying teller of an Eastern bank having been absent at lunch, returned earlier than was his wont, and discovered a strange man on his knees tampering with the dial of the combination. The man turned out to be "Shell" Hamilton, one of the Mark Shinburn gang. His arrest was the means of leading to the knowledge of the fact that the gang had been systematically picking a patent combination lock by removing the dial and placing a piece of paper behind it, so that when the safe was opened the combination registered its secret upon the paper. The thieves next watched their opportunity to gain possession of the paper, and the difficulty was at once overcome of opening the safe and gaining possession of its valuable contents.

Every gang of bank burglars has its recognized leader, whose word is law. He is a man of brains, possessed of some executive ability, sleek and crafty. The care with which, perhaps for years before the consummation of a crime, he arranges the plans for getting at the vault, illustrates the keenness of his perception and his depth of thought. Every little detail is considered and followed, so as to allay suspicion and permit him to get the closer to his prize. Bank burglaries invariably date back, and in some cases it has been known that the interior drawings of the building and plans of the vaults made at the time of their erection have for twenty years passed through the hands of several gangs as the sole legacy of some crafty leader. If provided with such important information, when, at last, the plundering of some institution is intended, the standing of the concern and the value of the securities kept in the vault must first be ascertained. Should these prove satisfactory, the conspiracy gets under way. Next, some inquiries are necessary as to the mechanical part of the work to be done. The name of the maker of the vault, the size of the lock by which it is protected, and if electric appliances guard it, must all be known, and are very easily learned.

The burglars generally hire a store adjoining the institution, from which they can operate the better, and in some instances they have gone so far as to rent the basement of the bank, or rooms overhead. They may fit up the place as an oyster saloon, billiard room, shoemaker's, barber's or tailor's shop, or start a dental establishment. The leader of the gang will for a long time employ none but the best workmen, sell A1 goods, pay his rent regularly, seem anxious for custom, be pleasant to all, and make himself a most desirable tenant; and his landlord has in several instances been the very president of the bank that this bland and good-natured tenant was secretly plotting against.

The leader of the burglars, after a few weeks' steady attention to business, will pass much of his spare time in conversation with the bank clerks, and thereby manages to gain their confidence. Being a rather good judge of human nature, he is thus able to survey the institution, secure all the inside information he desires, and probably gain an important ally in his nefarious undertaking. If he can tamper with or corrupt one of the clerks or watchmen, then the job is plain sailing. As soon, however, as the scheme becomes known to an outsider, the leader, fearing treachery, hastens matters as rapidly as possible. Should the mechanical part of the work have been figured down, and the combination be at the mercy of the robbers, the final work is generally completed between Saturday night and Sunday morning.

By cutting through the dividing partition wall, ceiling, or floor, the bank burglar and his assistants find no difficulty in getting into the bank. Then the wrecking of the vault begins, and in a short time the treasure that it contains is in the possession of the cracksmen. The task complete, the burglars carry their booty into the adjoining store, or perhaps the basement below the ransacked institution, and at the proper time remove it to a much safer place. When it is discovered that the bank vault was really not as secure as it was supposed to be, the affable business man who ran the oyster saloon or billiard room next door, or made change in the barber's or shoemaker's shop in the basement, or superintended the drawing of teeth overhead, has suddenly abandoned his expensive fixtures and light stock, and has left for parts unknown. He has realized thousands for every dollar that he invested, and in most cases he leaves in the lurch the mean tool who betrayed his trust in the hope that he would reap a rich reward by revealing to a professional robber the secrets of the institution where he was employed.

Some bank burglars devote most of their time and attention to the cashier of the bank that they have made up their minds to rob. They track him to his home, gain access to his sleeping-room at night, either by collusion with one of the servants, picking the door-locks or springing a window and gaining the keys, and take impressions in wax. Duplicates are easily made from these casts, and at the first opportunity the bank can be safely plundered. Should, however, the cashier be disturbed by the intrusion of the cracksmen into his apartment, the burglars would be forced to make an attempt upon the bank that night. Securing possession of the keys by threats, a couple of men would be left to guard the cashier while the other members of the band would proceed to the bank and rob it. In several instances the desperate robbers, under threats of instant death, have compelled the cashier whom they have surprised to accompany them to the bank and open the vault, so that they could rifle it.

The names of many expert bank burglars who have gained much notoriety by their criminal deeds will be found in the annexed list :

Charley Adams, alias Langdon W. Moore (22).—Jim Burns, alias Big Jim Burns (165).—George Bliss (see records of Nos. 20, 70, 80, 89, 110, 176).—Tom Biglow (see records of Nos. 20, 131).—Charles Bullard, alias Piano Charley (see records of Nos. 22, 176).—William Robinson, alias Gopher Bill (see record of No. 89).—George Havill, alias Joe Cook, alias Harry Thorn (15).—John Hope, alias Young Hope (19).—James Hope, alias Old Man Hope (20).—Harry Howard, alias English Harry (see record of No. 22).—Ed. Johnson (see record of No. 50).—William Kelly (see records of Nos. 19, 90).—Mike Kerrigan, alias Johnny Dobbs (64).—Mike Kerwin, alias Barney Oats (see record of No. 68).—Ira Kingsland (see record of No. 70).—Peter Emmerson, alias Pete Luthy, alias Banjo Pete (90).—Ned Lyons (70).—John Larney, alias Mollie Matches (11).—George Leslie, alias George Howard (see records of Nos. 50, 74, 80).—Charles Lowery (see record of No. 68).—John Leary, alias Red Leary (see record of No. 110).—Frank McCoy, alias Big Frank (89).—George Mason, alias George Gordon (24).—Joe Moran (see record of No. 8).—Ike Marsh (see records of Nos. 21, 22, 50, 89).—William Morgan, alias Bunker (see record of No. 21).—Frank McCrann, alias Big Frank (see record of No. 68).—Tom McCormack (201).—Sam Perris, alias Worcester Sam (199).—Jack Rand (see record of No. 22).—Patrick Shevlin (see records of Nos. 19, 28, 90). —James Simpson (see record of No. 21).—Charles Sanborn (see record of No. 21).—Mark Shinburn (176).—Robert S. Scott (see record of No. 50).—Mose Vogel (see records of Nos. 24, 50).—Gilbert Yost (see record of No. 74).—Adam Worth.—Joe Killoran, alias Joe Howard.—Daniel Dyson, alias Dan Noble.—Jim Brady, alias Big Jim.

See general index for further information.

BANK SNEAK THIEVES.

FOR many years bank sneak thieving flourished to an alarming extent in New York City, and under the old detective systems it seemed impossible to put a stop to that form of robbery. Notorious thieves in those days were permitted to loiter about the street, and on more than one occasion it was alleged that well filled cash boxes disappeared from bankers' safes while detectives were on watch outside. It was also openly insinuated that there was collusion between the police and the rogues, and numerous changes were made, but it was afterwards discovered that the accusations were groundless. While it may have been true that the detectives in some cases were not as vigilant as they might have been, subsequent developments have demonstrated that the financial quarter of the city was in the past but poorly protected. Well known thieves no longer haunt that prescribed locality, and since the establishment of a sub-detective bureau in Wall Street, six years ago, not a dollar has been stolen from any of the wealthy concerns in the great money centre by professional criminals. The inauguration also of a patrol service by experienced detectives during business hours, and the connecting by telephone of all the banking institutions have been the means of putting a stop to the operations of that particular class of rogues known as bank sneak thieves. Still, in the other cities of the country, where these precautions which have proved such a great preventive against the perpetration of crime have not been adopted, these thieves succeed in carrying on their depredations and reap rich rewards. Bank sneak thieves are all men of education, pleasing address, good personal appearance, and are faultless in their attire. With astonishing coolness these determined fellows commit the most daring thefts. The handful of successful rogues who have attained such exalted rank in the criminal profession despise the thousands of other robbers who live by the commission of small crimes. Aware of their superiority, these men are overbearing when chance brings them in contact with thieves of a lower degree. This is most noticeable in their manner of conducting themselves while serving out sentence in prison. As their exploits must necessarily occur in daylight and in public places, these robbers are really more daring than the bank burglar, who prefers to work under cover of night. The bank sneak is not an adept with the pick-lock, but great presence of mind, a quick eye, and wonderful nerve are the essentials he must possess to become a success.

Generally not more than three or four of these thieves are engaged in any robbery, and each of them has his allotted part to perform in the conspiracy. One may be a careful lookout, another must be an interesting conversationalist, and the third, generally a small-sized man, is the sneak, who stealthily steals behind the counter and captures the cash box or a bundle of bonds. While some robberies are carried out in a few minutes after the conception of the scheme, others have been planned months beforehand. The rogues who prowl about bankers' and brokers' offices day after day are ever on the watch for an opportunity to make a daring dash for plunder. Their appearance is so like that of the honest merchant or stock speculator that they have no difficulty in deceiving those who have no suspicion as to their real character or calling. They have also a faculty of worming themselves into the best society, and they spend their evenings in the lobbies of the leading hotels or other places where those foremost in financial circles are in the habit of assembling to discuss the events of the day. Information gathered in chance chats afterwards proves of valuable assistance to the cunning sneak thief in the carrying out of his operations. It is during those brief conversations that the robbers ascertain the topic that will most interest their intended victim. All men have their hobbies, and just as soon as the bank thief becomes aware of the fact that a certain banker, broker, paying teller or cashier has a failing for discussing any one thing in particular, they devote considerable time studying the subject until they are able to talk upon it properly and interestingly. This is one of the preliminary steps in a planned robbery. Next the thieves make themselves familiar with the manner in which business is conducted in the bank or office they are plotting to pillage. They never neglect any point, no matter how small it may be. The exact time that the clerks are in the habit of leaving their desks for dinner, the restaurants they dine at, and the time they are allowed for meals, are all noted. These are necessary for the success of the undertaking, and when at last all the plans have been perfected, the prize is captured at a time when there are but few persons in the banking institution. There have been exceptions to this rule, however, and cash boxes have been successfully spirited away just at the moment of the receipt of some astounding financial intelligence, and while the office was thronged with merchants and brokers discussing the startling news. Thefts of that sort require but a moment, and have been executed as rapidly as the occasion presents itself.

Here is a genuine instance of the great presence of mind of these criminals, from the record of one of the leading and most successful sneak thieves : There was a heated discussion in a broker's office one day about the location of a town in Ohio. The noted robber slipped into the place just in time to overhear several of the gentlemen declaring that the town was in different counties in that State. While the argument progressed the thief hit upon a plan that would enable him to capture the cash box, which temptingly rested in the safe, the door of which was open. He left as quickly as possible, and, meeting his confederate outside, sent him to a stationery store, telling him to buy several maps, and one especially showing the counties and towns in Ohio. Then the rogue returned to the broker's office to await his opportunity. A few minutes later he was followed by his companion in the rôle of a map peddler. Being at first told that no maps were wanted, the cunning accomplice, in a loud voice, said :

"Can I show you a new map, giving the boundaries of all the towns and counties in Ohio?"

The appeal was overheard by one of the men who had been involved in the recent discussion. He told the peddler to stop, at the same time saying, "Now, boys, I'll bet whatever you like that the town is in the county I said, and as chance has brought us a map, the bets can be settled without delay." Several bets were made, and for a few minutes the broker's office was in a much greater state of excitement than it ever had been before, even in panic days. As the peddler slowly unrolled his bundle of maps the brokers and the clerks gathered about him, anxious to learn the result. The sneak took advantage of the excitement and made his way, unnoticed, to the safe. He captured the cash box, containing $20,000, and escaped with it while his confederate was selling the map.

Another professional sneak, known as a man of great coolness and determination, and possessed of no small degree of courage, is credited with having entered a bank early in the morning and going behind the desk, divested himself of his coat, and, donning a duster, installed himself as clerk. He coolly waited there some time watching for a chance to seize a roll of greenbacks, bonds, or anything valuable that he could lay his hands on. One of the clerks requested the intruder to leave, but the wily thief retorted by telling the former to mind his own business, and also intimating that as soon as his friend, the president, arrived, he would have what he pleased to call a meddlesome fellow punished. The clerk, however, insisted upon the rogue's vacating the desk, and he finally did so under protest. In a seemingly high state of indignation the robber left the place, and later on the cashier, to his surprise, discovered that he had suddenly and mysteriously become $15,000 short. Of course the thief never called a second time to explain the mystery.

A bundle of bonds vanished from one of the rooms in a Safe Deposit vault in an Eastern city, recently, and the theft was not discovered until three months after the robbery had been committed. One of the depositors had called at the place for the purpose of clipping off his coupons. He had taken his box out of the compartment in which it was kept, and had gone into a side room with a table to do the coupon cutting. There was no one in the apartment excepting himself, but just as he had finished a man whom he believed to be one of the clerks entered the chamber for a second. The visitor tapped the old gentleman on the shoulder and instantly said, "Excuse me, sir, I have made a mistake," and passed out again. While the aged depositor had turned to see who it was had tapped him on the left shoulder, the supposed clerk, who was a professional sneak, picked up the bundle of bonds, which lay near the former's right hand. It happened that the lid of the tin box was down, and having no suspicion, and supposing that he had replaced the bonds, the old man returned the empty box to his compartment. Three months later, when the depositor again called at the Safe Deposit vaults to clip another set of coupons, he discovered that his bonds were missing and no one was able to account for their disappearance.

The robbery, it has been asserted, was effected in this way. In the Safe Deposit vaults was employed a clerk who was in the habit of wearing a buff-colored duster, much bedabbled with ink. On the day of the robbery the clerk was sent out on an errand and was away from his desk for nearly half an hour. During his absence a sneak thief of his build, and somewhat like him in appearance, and wearing an ink-stained duster, ran quickly down the steps, and without exciting any suspicion passed the watchman on guard at the entrance to the Safe Deposit vaults. No one paid any particular attention to the robber as he passed through the several rooms, supposing him to be the clerk. After he had captured the roll of bonds from which the coupons had been freshly cut, the man in the buff duster, unnoticed, passed out with the booty.

In robbing country banks, where the clerks are few, and generally during the dinner hour the cashier or paying teller is the only man left in the institution, sneaks have a simple and easy scheme for plundering. One first enters the bank and engages the cashier or teller in conversation, upon a subject in which the latter becomes deeply interested. While this is going on a carriage halts at the door, and the driver is sent in to tell the official inside that a gentleman who has hurt his leg and is unable to walk, desires to speak to him outside. The unsuspecting cashier or teller excuses himself to his first visitor and goes out to speak to the injured man, and in his absence the bank is ransacked. Robberies of this kind are committed quite frequently, and gangs of sneaks travel all over the country with a circus or wild beast show. In the towns and small cities the parade of the performers creates considerable excitement, and when the cavalcade happens to pass a bank the clerks, cashiers and paying tellers seem to forget themselves and run to the windows to look out. The sneak thieves take advantage of the opportunity and quietly slip into the institution. In a twinkling their work is complete, and before the procession has passed they have escaped with whatever they could lay hands on.

If, while watching about a bank a large check is cashed and the customer turns aside to a desk to count the money, the rogues generally succeed in getting a portion of the cash. The thief will drop a bill upon the floor, and just as the man has arranged his pile of notes the criminal will politely tell him that he has dropped some of his money. When the former stoops down to pick up the greenback, the sneak will steal a portion of the cash upon the desk, and walk off unquestioned. They are not greedy in ventures of that sort, but they secure enough, with almost comparative safety, and are content. Heated arguments invariably follow thefts of this sort. After counting his money, the depositor goes back to the teller and insists that he is short. The teller is equally positive that he paid out the proper amount, and in most cases a disruption of commercial relations is the culmination of the dispute.

Bank sneak thieves are not, however, confined to these systems. They are men of adaptability, and act at all times according to circumstances. They have been known to rob messengers in the street while on their way to bank to make a deposit. Some messengers always carry the bank book in their hand, with the bills folded between the covers. The ends of the greenbacks may extend beyond the length of the book, and these will instantly catch the quick eye of an experienced rogue. While the messenger is passing through a crowd, he will be thrown off his guard by a start of surprise, or a laughable remark. During that moment the entire amount in the book has been abstracted, and when the man reaches the bank and finds the cash gone, he cannot imagine how it was that he lost it.

The best safeguard against the bank-sneak thief is to be able to recognize him at sight, and be sure of his real character. The annexed list contains many of the names of the leading rogues who operate in that line, and whose photographs are to be found in the book:

Frank Buck, alias Bucky Taylor (27).—Jim Burns, alias Big Jim Burns (165).—Billy Burke, alias Billy the Kid (162).—Bill Bartlett (see records of No. 71 and George Wilkes).—Bill Baker (165).—George Carson, alias Heywood (3).—William Coleman, alias Billy Coleman (9).—John Curtin (169).—John Carroll, alias The Kid (192).— Charlotte Dougherty, stall for bank sneaks (see records of Nos. 25, 1, 179).—John Duffy (see record of No. 50).—Charles Fisher, alias Purdy (41).—Billy Forrester (76).—Billy Flynn (see records of Nos. 3, 50, 95, 165).—Eddie Guerin (see records of Nos. 11, 187).—Horace Hovan, alias Little Horace (25).—Robert Hovan (179).—Charley Hicks (see record of No. 8).—John Jourdan (83).—Thomas Leary, alias Kid Leary (6).—Ned Lyons (70).—Rufe Minor, alias Pine (1).—Emanuel Marks, alias Minnie Marks (187).—John O'Brien, alias The Kid (see record of No. 22).— Phillip Phearson, alias Philly Pearson (5).—C. J. Everhardt, alias Marsh Market Jake (38).—Joe Parish (84).—John Price (see records of Nos. 1, 9, 54).—Bill Vosburg (4).—Joe McClusky (see records of Nos. 8, 50).—Walter Sheridan (8).— Jim Brady, alias Big Jim.

See regular index for further information.

FORGERS.

A DISTINGUISHED and learned criminal jurist tersely described forgery as "the false making or materially altering, with intent to defraud, any writing which, if genuine, might apparently be of legal efficacy in the foundation of a legal liability." The crime, in a general sense, is the illegal falsification or counterfeiting of a writing, bill, bond, will, or other document, and the statutes generally make the uttering or using the forged instrument essential to the offense. The uttering is complete, however, if an attempt is made to use the fraudulent paper as intended, though the forgery be discovered in season to defeat the fraud designed. The intent to deceive and defraud is often conclusively presumed from the forgery itself. If one forge a note, or name, word or even figure upon a note, and cause it to be discounted, it is no defense whatever to the charge of forgery that he intended to pay the note himself, and had actually made provisions that no person should be injured. Forgery, attended as it is with such ruinous consequences, is easily perpetrated, and detected with much difficulty. It was one of the capital offenses years ago, and at the present time the punishment is severe, the Penal Code of the State of New York making the sentence, upon a second conviction for forgery in the first degree, imprisonment for life.

As compared with the other criminal classes the number of professional forgers in the United States is very small. All told there are not more than two dozen expert penmen and engravers who prostitute their talents by imitating the handwriting and workmanship of others. Few as are these swindlers, occasionally they suddenly launch forth some gigantic scheme, flooding the principal cities with their spurious and worthless paper. The operations of the forger are not by any means confined to this country and Canada. The bankers of Europe have been fleeced by them, and conspiracies hatched here have almost caused financial panics in England and on the Continent. But little was really known about the ingenious plottings and secret schemes of forgers and counterfeiters until the celebrated international criminal, Wilkes, made a confession of his doings. The statement made by the shrewd rascal while in prison in Italy, a few years since, is the most interesting document of its kind in existence. It covers a long period—nearly twenty years—and tells the inner history of one of the greatest bands of forgers that has ever been organized. The notorious penman's confession is given in full in another part of this book.

The professional forger is a man of great ability, and naturally a cunning and suspicious sort of an individual. Cautious in the extreme, he prefers to work in secret, and probably never more than two of his most intimate companions know what he is about until the counterfeits he has produced are ready to be put in circulation. So guarded is he, in fact, that while imitating the signature of a banking firm, duplicating the bonds or securities of a large corporation, or printing the delicately executed notes and currency of a country, he never permits any of his friends to enter his secret workshop. It is the proud boast of one of the most notorious of these swindlers, that while at his nefarious work no man, woman, or child ever saw him with a pen in his hand.

Some of the most prominent forgers are chemists, and by the aid of a secret mixture of acids, they are able to erase figures in ink from the face of notes without destroying or damaging the paper. Thus genuine orders upon banks or brokers for a few dollars are easily raised up into the thousands. Others, having a talent for imitating handwriting, especially autographs, fill out blank checks and notes to suit themselves. Photography has also recently been successfully applied as a means for transferring fine tracing, delicate engravings, and even signatures.

Away in the background, although plotting and planning daring work for others to execute, the forger runs but few risks by following a system calculated to protect himself against the annoyance of arrest or the danger of conviction. He keeps aloof from the several members of his band, and in most cases is only known to his manager, the go-between and guiding spirit of the gang. This is one of his best safeguards, and no matter what slip there may afterwards be in the effort to secure money upon his spurious paper, he is able to baffle all attempts to fasten the foundation of the crime upon himself. He employs as his manager only a man in whom he has the utmost confidence to conduct the negotiations, and the latter is generally a person of such notoriously bad character, that no jury would accept his uncorroborated testimony should he prove unfaithful. There have been instances, however, in which the manager has also been the capitalist and leading plotter. Such men are to be found in the best walks of life, and although having a good social standing their means of existence is a mystery to many. These are the most careful go-betweens, and they also have guarded ways of putting the forged notes into the hands of the agents of the "layers down," the title by which those who finally dispose of the fraudulent paper are known.

The organization of a forger's gang is unlike that of any other class of thieves. It has many subdivisions, all working in concert, and still but few of the operators have any acquaintance with the leading spirits in the vast conspiracy. The poor tools who risk their liberty never know the penman or engraver whose work they handle, and the forger, on the other hand, does not wish an acquaintance with them. He knows them simply by reputation as a good or ordinary "layer down," just as their standing may be. Then there are the quiet agents, who gather information and rarely appear in any criminal proceeding. These have a wide circle of acquaintances, many of whom are reputable merchants and brokers. During pleasant chats in the bar and reading rooms of hotels and at fashionable resorts, much useful information necessary for the carrying out of large plans is gleaned.

A banker's clerk, fond of billiards or horse-racing, and living above his salary, while in bad luck meets an agreeable friend at the track or around the green baize table. The forger's secret and most dangerous agents grasp the situation at a glance, and hidden behind their apparent good-nature is a plot for plunder. The clerk's losses make him desperate, and he never declines the proffered loan. It may be only a small sum, but it is the first step towards his downfall. He has become entangled in the clutches of a sharper, and at short acquaintance stands ready to follow the advice of his generous friend. When it is suggested that blank checks, or better still, ones filled out if procured by him, no matter the means he resorts to to get them, will bring him in a supply of ready cash, he grasps the opportunity. Rarely does the firm suspect, when at last the forgeries are scattered broadcast, that their fast-living clerk is really responsible for the counterfeits. The reckless young man, tainted by the success of others, will in a short time attempt to imitate signatures himself. Not having served a proper apprenticeship in ways that are wicked, the forgery is apparent. Caught in the act, he is sent to prison, and forever afterwards is an outcast from society.

The clerk's experience demonstrates but one of the insidious methods of the crafty forger and his agents. He has other schemes, most prominent among which is using the dishonest broker. Under cover of a legitimate business they dispose of considerable worthless bonds and securities. It often happens that stolen, forged, and counterfeit bonds are hypothecated for loans by some tottering firm, and are never redeemed. Bankers duped in that way, rather than make public the fact that they have been taken in, prefer to bear their losses and make no effort to prosecute the swindler.

The men who for a small percentage dispose of forged paper or handle counterfeits are mostly ex-convicts or novices in crime. Some of the check passers operate according to system and others depend upon circumstances. Several of the principal means taken by those who utter the spurious paper can be briefly explained. A forger, only one of whose notes was ever refused, always furnished his operators with duplicate drafts. One of these simply endorsed upon the back would at first be presented at the bank by the "layer down." The latter being a stranger, the teller would naturally decline to honor the note without proper identification. Then the "layer down," after remarking that he was not well acquainted with financial matters, would take the check and leave the institution. The second note, properly certified and endorsed with the signature of the firm whose genuine check had been imitated, would be handed to the operator by an accomplice on the street. After a brief absence the man would return to the bank and get the money, the teller supposing the identification to be freshly written. The presentation of the identified check first would not have been regular, and the wily leader never permitted any of his tools to run such risks.

The forger has another plan for depleting the bank account of a firm whose name he is using without authorization. It is to have at least three layers down. The rule is, if the first man comes out all right a second is sent in, and if he succeeds the third follows. Here the operations end for the day, and afterwards a watch is kept upon the bank until it is closed, and also upon the broker's office, the signature of which firm is being forged. Should no unusual commotion be observed at either place, it is taken for granted that the victim's account is large enough to be drawn from still further. A day or two later other checks previously prepared are presented in the same way. Upon the slightest sign of discovery the "layer down" and his lookouts disappear as quickly as possible, one covering the escape of the other. In the selection of the men who cash the notes old favorites are sent in first, as the chances of detection are then at a minimum. As the account drawn upon may give out at any moment, and then there would be questions to answer, the last men are required to possess plenty of nerve. The amount of a firm's account in bank is always a matter of guess-work, and therefore risky, though the forger's rule is to select wealthy concerns, leave a wide margin and work up gradually.

The forger has but little trouble getting the numbers for the checks he intends using. Just before the close of business on a Saturday afternoon one of his agents calls at the broker's office and sells some genuine bonds, and in payment asks that he be given at least two checks, explaining that he desires to send them by letter into the country or some other place. They are never refused, and therefore the forger thus manages to get the last numbers of the checks issued by the firm. This gives him all day Sunday to fix the figures on the forgeries, and he is ready to operate without fear of detection from that source first thing on Monday morning. The genuine checks several days later reach the bank through some reputable business firm, but in the meantime they have passed through so many hands that it is next to an impossibility to trace them.

A common, yet dangerous scheme, which has been carried out many times with success by check raisers, is like this : A member of the gang is first sent to purchase two drafts payable at a bank in another city. One is made out for a small amount and the other for a considerable sum. In a few days the purchaser returns the large check to the bank saying that he was unable to use it as he had intended. The amount it calls for is refunded to him and the redeemed check in most instances destroyed. Then, having a clear field before him, the forger forwards the small draft raised to correspond in number, date and amount to the large one to some distant city for collection. As the genuine draft has in the meantime been torn up, there is rarely any difficulty in getting the raised one cashed, and sometimes the deceit is not discovered at the bank of issue. Many cashiers have spent hours going over their books on account of a shortage, and all the trouble and annoyance was due to a raised check.

The photo-lithographic process of check counterfeiting first came to light in this city a few years ago. The checks were presented by a smart lad who invariably succeeded in cashing them. He was caught at last laying down one of the worthless notes, and had it not been for an accident he might then have escaped. The cashier to whom it was presented, while examining the draft, noticed that it was blurred, and on submitting it to experts, his suspicions were confirmed. It had been prepared with such accuracy that the stamp on it could not be distinguished from an authentic one. The forger, however, had not been satisfied with his work, and essayed an improvement by the use of chemicals, which in the warmth of the carrier's hand, had blurred and discolored the paper. The lad when cornered made a clean breast of it, and said that his brother-in-law had employed him to procure genuine checks and carry forged paper to the bank.

A man who appeared to be prudent, careful, conducting his transactions after the best methods, and on the strictest business principles, opened an account, a few years back, with one of the city banks under the name of Clarke.   He soon won the confidence of the bank authorities.   At first depositing moderate sums of money he created the belief that he was engaged in legitimate commerce, and he only called in his deposits as might any ordinary merchant.   He always kept a balance in the bank and seemed in no hurry to push his affairs to extremities.   The money on deposit was in certified checks of another bank, and Clarke and his credit was established, to all appearances, on a very comfortable basis.   Suddenly the notes began to assume an alarming magnitude.   They came, too, in unusually rounded figures, $4,500 and $6,500 looming up on their faces.   The suspicion of the cashier was aroused and an inquiry was set on foot.   Clarke's dealings were discovered to have jumped to such an altitude that it was at once decided that something must be wrong.

The authorities at the second bank were consulted, the checks were examined and at once their real nature became apparent, and they were pronounced forgeries.   Both banks were amazed.   Their consternation increased the more closely they tested the checks.   Each additional discrepancy discovered proved that the forgeries were not ordinary ones, and it was more than likely that they were being perpetrated on other institutions and probably for large amounts.   These checks, so many of which had passed current at the bank of certification, had been printed and stamped on specially manufactured paper and signed with a regularly prepared ink.   The writing was done in a bold, free hand that challenged detection by its freedom and similarity to that of the treasurer of the Western Union Telegraph Company.   They were lithographed imitations of the genuine checks of the bank, with a slight difference in the safety test, the numbering and the ink, but in rush of business these trifling defects could not be remarked.   The forgeries were admitted clever beyond all experience, and no fault was found with the teller for certifying them as genuine.   In those cases the layer down was a poor youth the bogus merchant had employed in his sham office at a salary of a few dollars per week.

Forgers who make a practice of defrauding the banks of the smaller cities, first establish confidence with the officials of the institution they intend to plunder.   This is done in a very simple manner, but one that generally proves successful.   Several weeks before the forgery is attempted the advance agent of the gang hires and opens an insurance or real estate office in the vicinity of the bank.   At the latter place he makes a number of bona fide deposits and has some business transactions, which are simply the transfer of money from one city to another.   Then when he is beyond suspicion he lays down for collection a draft for a large sum, which bears the forged signature of a genuine depositor at a bank in a distant city.   Upon the presentation of the paper the officials telegraph to the bank it is drawn upon, inquiring if the person or firm whose forged signature it bears is a depositor in good standing there.   The answer being satisfactory, at least three-fourths of the amount called for by the check is willingly advanced by the bank of deposit, to the forger's trusted agent.   In due time the counterfeit is forwarded for collection through the regular business channels, and when it finally reaches its destination its character is discovered.   The insurance or real estate office has in the meantime collapsed, and the forger and his tools have vanished.   A smart gang, with a dozen or more advance agents, have been known to dupe in a single year over forty banks throughout the country, netting, with a small outlay, about $160,000 by their operations.

Storekeepers and business firms have been swindled time and again by a peculiar class of forgers who seem to be satisfied with a few hundred dollars, and sometimes less. In all large cities these men succeed in operating extensively with raised or worthless checks. After a small purchase the forger presents the draft in payment, and should he be questioned, generally gives some ready reference. In his off-hand way of dealing with his victims the layer down is careful not to give an inkling of his true character till they have fallen a prey to his deceptions. When one of these criminals is run down as many as one hundred and fifty complainants appear to prosecute him.

Sometimes it happens in altering checks that the chemicals leave a blur upon the paper that cannot be erased. As the notes, although for small amounts, are genuine, the forger not willing to lose money even in experimenting, has been known to burn off the portion of the paper that he had unsuccessfully tampered with. Then one of his friends writes to the bank by which the draft was issued, stating that it had accidentally been partially burned, giving the date of issue and the amount it called for, and requesting that a duplicate be forwarded to the writer. To confirm the accident story, the fragments of the check are enclosed in the envelope. The duplicate asked for is generally received by return mail.

The craftiness and audacity of the professional forger may be better understood by the recital of the following actual occurrence :

Six years ago a band of international criminals left this city for the purpose of robbing foreign bankers with the aid of a large supply of well-executed counterfeit circular notes. The men were scarcely upon the high seas before the conspiracy became known here. Without delay cablegrams were flashed across the ocean warning the European authorities of the entire plot, and giving the names and accurate descriptions of all the operators. Notwithstanding the warning, the forger and his assistants landed without detection, and made their headquarters in one of the largest cities. In the course of a few days after his arrival the chief conspirator, who was traveling as an American tourist, desirous of becoming familiar with the faces and workings of the detectives, secured a letter of introduction to the Chief of the Bureau or Department of Criminal Investigations. He was well received, all the workings of that branch of the police service were explained to him, and he was pleasantly entertained for half an hour or more by the head of the force himself. During the chat the conversation turned apparently incidentally to forgers and counterfeiters. The detective, thrown completely off his guard, unbosomed himself to the bogus tourist. On the desk before the former lay the important message sent from New York concerning the band of forgers. It was an official secret, but the detective had no scruples in confiding it to his visitor. Telling the latter that his department was in communication with similar institutions in the United States, the Chief of one of the largest detective forces in Europe picked up the message and read it from beginning to end to the sham tourist. It was startling and unexpected news to the forger, but he controlled his alarm and resumed the conversation. At its close the noted criminal shook the hand of the police official who had unconsciously and gratuitously furnished him with so much information, and drove back to his hotel. The forger and his band disappeared from the city that night.

The counterfeiting of bonds and securities, for some unaccountable reason, seems to be at a standstill at present, and there is no likelihood that it will be resumed for some time to come. It is also a significant fact that all the leading spirits in that line in this country now devote their time and talents defrauding banks and brokers by forged drafts. They have tired most probably of the stupendous schemes which took years of constant study to perfect. It is well to remember, too, that all the recent attempts to flood the foreign market with forged paper have proved disastrous failures, in consequence of the timely warnings sent abroad from this city. The fabrication of the Brazilian and French bank-notes, the Missouri State Soldiers' pay securities, the Central Pacific and Morris & Essex Railroad bonds, are the latest conspiracies frustrated. Spurious greenbacks are not as numerous now as they were a few years ago, and coin counterfeiting has entirely passed out of the hands of the professional coiner.

The genuine and false names of the forgers who occupy a high rank in that illicit calling will be found in the annexed list :

Charles O. Brockway, alias Vanderpool (14).—Charles Becker (18).—William E. Brockway (32).—R. S. Ballard, alias Bullard (35).—Robert Bowman, alias Hogan (39). —Colonel A. C. Branscom (97).—George Bell (193).—Lester Beach (17).—George Havill, alias Joe Cook (15).—Edward Condit (42).—Hugh L. Courtenay, alias Lord Courtenay (58).—Joe Chapman (see records of Nos. 16, 18, 202, and George Wilkes). —Henry Cleary (see records of Nos. 37, 193, and George Wilkes).—Isaac Hooper (see record of No. 172).—Edward Darlington (36).—J. B. Doyle (see records of Nos. 31, 32).—Charles Denken (see records of Nos. 38, 41).—C. J. Everhardt, alias Marsh Market Jake (38).—Joe Elliott, alias Joe Reilly (16).—George Engles (see records of No. 18 and George Wilkes).—Charles Fisher, alias Purdy (41).—Charles Farren (see records of Nos. 13, 193.)—Robert Fox (see record of No. 37).—Valentine Gleason (see records of Nos. 8, 55, and George Wilkes).—Andy Gilligan (see record of No. 13).—Bertha Heyman (122).—John Hughes, alias John O'Neil, alias Jason Smith (60).—Charles Ward, alias Hall (104).—James Lee (108).—George Little, alias Tip Little (172).—Luther R. Martin, alias Martin Luther (31).—William H. Lyman (see record of No. 39).—Franklin J. Moses, alias ex-Governor Moses (98). —Steve Raymond, alias Marshal (55).—John Pettengill (198).—Charles Williamson, alias Perrine (202).—Walter Pierce, alias Porter (see records of Nos. 38, 41).— Augustus Raymond, alias Gus Raymond (26).—Walter Sheridan, alias Ralston (8).— Andrew L. Roberts (see records of Nos. 8, 55, and George Wilkes).—Freddie Reeves (see record of No. 112).— Charles Smyth, alias Doc. Smyth (112).—Charles R. Titus, alias Dr. Thompson (40).—Albert Wilson, alias Al. Wilson (37).—D. S. Ward, alias Capt. Ward (57).—George Edwards, alias Lynch (see record of No. 16). —Nathan B. Foster.—William E. Grey.—Clement Herring, alias Old Man Herring.— Louis Siscovitch.—Ivan, alias Carlo Siscovitch, alias Adams.—Elijah Alliger.—Susan R. Buck.—Charles B. Orvis.—G. W. Pontez.—George Wilkes.

See regular index for further particulars.

HOTEL AND BOARDING–HOUSE THIEVES.

THE class of thieves devoting themselves to robbing rooms in hotels and in fashion-able boarding-houses operate according to circumstances and always have their wits about them for any unexpected emergency. The successful ones are men of respectable appearance, good address, and cool and daring fellows. Some follow their nefarious vocation only in the morning, others in the afternoon, and still others operate at night. In their methods of procedure each of these subdivisions has other dis-tinguishing peculiarities. A great deal of ingenuity in getting into rooms is not infrequently shown by these men who in working run all sorts of risks and take desperate chances.

Until he has accomplished his purpose the hotel thief pursues his prey from one establishment to another with a persistency that knows no faltering. He makes it a specialty to scan the newspapers carefully, and keeps himself posted on the latest arrivals, the rooms they occupy and other data of interest. The coming and going of professionals, particularly female theatrical stars, salesmen, bankers, and bridal parties, and all persons likely to carry valuable jewelry and trinkets or a large amount of money, in this way are noted and are objects of special importance and solicitude.

When the unsuspecting prey fatigued by travel gives proof of his unconsciousness by deep, stertorous breathing, the hotel thief steals silently from his hiding-place. A slight push may let him enter the apartment, or it may be necessary to use a gimlet and a small piece of crooked wire to slide back the bolt, or a pair of nippers to turn the key left on the inside in the lock, from the corridor. Sometimes as many as a dozen rooms in the same hotel have been plundered in one night and none of the watchmen saw or heard the thief. The old style of climbing through transoms or unkeyed windows is at present not much in vogue. The hotel thief can carry his entire outfit in his vest pocket and can laugh in his sleeve at the common bolts and bars. The much boasted of chain-bolt can now be drawn back from the outside with only a piece of silk thread having a match tied to one end of it.

The shooting back of the old-fashioned slide-bolt from the outside of the apart-ment was for many years a bewildering mystery. As there were no marks to be found on the door in most cases when a robbery was reported, the hotel proprietor would frown and the clerk leer ; both facial contortions being meant to express suspicion and incredulity. Many times the unfortunate victim has been turned away as a cheat and a fraud, who wanted to swindle the hotel out of his board bill or else to bring a suit for damages on a trumped up charge. The result has been that strangers who had also been robbed under such conditions were afraid to report the case lest they too should be regarded with suspicion and treated with insult. In all of these robberies the bolt which had been shot back so mysteriously was located either above or underneath the common key-lock. A piece of crooked wire inserted through the keyhole by the nimble rogue made the bolt worthless, and a turn of the knob was all that was required to open the door.

It does not take over a few minutes for an expert hotel thief to enter a room. After he has reached the door of the apartment in which the weary traveler is sleeping soundly, he takes from his pocket a small nippers, a bent piece of wire, and a piece of silk thread. These are the only tools some men use. Inserting the nippers in the keyhole, he catches the end of the key. Then a twist shoots back the lock bolt, and another leaves the key in a position from which it can easily be displaced. Should the slumber of the occupant of the room be disturbed by the falling of the key on the carpet or floor, time is given him to fall asleep again. By pressing on the door the thief next locates the bolt. A piece of thread is attached to the bent point of the wire, making a sort of bow; and after crooking the wire to suit, it is pushed through the keyhole and carried up or down to the bolt. The looped head throws the pin of the bolt into place; the string is moved sideways until it grapples the pin, and then the bolt is slid back out of the nosing. The door yields to a slight pressure, and the completion of the task is deftly and expeditiously performed. Some thieves always stop to lock the room door behind them.

At their leisure these thieves spend their time "fixing" rooms in hotels. This is necessary in first-class establishments, where the room doors are protected by improved locks. One of these, known as the "thumb bolt," requires to be tampered with beforehand. While the shrewd robber occupies the room which, it may not be until months afterward, he intends to rob, he prepares the lock so that it will aid him in his future operations. Removing the screws, he takes off the thumb-plate and files a slot in the spring-bar. Then he replaces the plate and screws, and marks on the outside of the door by a slight indentation in the woodwork, or by a raising made by a brad-awl from the inside, the exact point at which to strike the filed slot when the door is locked. Returning on the night of the robbery with the only tools necessary—a common brad-awl and a pair of nippers—he pierces the soft wood at the proper point, and then by pushing the awl further in strikes the slot, and is able to noiselessly turn the bolt; he then uses his nippers to unlock the door. As many as a dozen rooms in a single hotel are "fixed" in this way, and the thief, by occasionally keeping his eye upon the register, awaits his prey. If some well known character in the habit of wearing costly jewels is registered as the tenant in one of the "fixed" rooms, then the thief engages an apartment on the same floor, and during the night-time consummates the long planned crime.

Another plan, and the one that is generally adopted by rogues who prowl about hotel corridors in the daytime, is to draw the screws of the nosing of the bolt and lock. By boring the screw-holes larger and moistening the screws, the latter are replaced and maintain a sufficient grip not to be displaced by the ordinary jar. As the wood becomes dry the door at the proper time can without trouble or danger from noise be easily forced in.

The boarding-house thief, always a smooth and entertaining talker, makes acquaintances in new quarters in short order. Generally in a pleasant sort of a chat with the inquisitive landlady, before he has been many hours there, he succeeds in gleaning all the information about the other guests in the house that he desires to know. Most women have the foolish fondness of making a display of their jewels and valuables in the parlor or dining-room of the fashionable boarding-house. While amusing his newly-made acquaintances with his laughable stories, the astute robber is at the same time making a thorough survey. His covetous eyes never miss the flash of diamonds, and should he be in doubt as to the genuineness of the sparklers, he has only to speak of them to one of the friends of the wearer, and he will be told when and where they were bought and the price paid for them.

After the cunning rogue has secured a full inventory of the jewels and valuable trinkets kept in the several rooms of the house he is ready for business. While the other guests are at breakfast or dinner the thief remains up-stairs, and the thorough manner in which he rummages the several apartments in such short time is really surprising. Before his victims have finished their morning or evening chat the thief's work is complete, and with well filled valise, unnoticed he slips out of the house. Probably before the robbery is discovered, the professional criminal is aboard of a train and on his way to some other city to dispose of his plunder and resume his profitable exploits. Thieves of this class are troublesome to track, but when run down at last there is no end to the number of complainants that come forward to prosecute them.

The names of several first-class hotel and boarding-house thieves, and of a number of rogues who have plundered the residences of physicians, will be found in the following list :

William Connelly, alias Old Bill (51).—Frank Auburn (46).—William Brooks, alias Fale (43).—Jim Blake (see record of No. 50).—Dave Cummings, alias Little Dave (50).—Albert Cropsey, alias Williams (54).—William Carter, alias Three-Fingered Jack (see record of No. 44).—Edward Fairbrother, alias Dr. West (48).—George W. Gamphor (49).—Charles Hylebert, alias Cincinnati Red, alias Red Hyle (44).—Edward Hyatt, alias Sturgess (45).—Doctor Long, alias Pop White (94).—William Miller, alias Billy Miller (53).—Charles McLaughlin, alias McClain (59).—Billy Pease (52).—Edward Rice, alias Big Rice (12).—Emile Voegtlin (47).—Charles Williams, alias Williams, alias Hoyt (194).—John Cannon, alias Old Jack (101).—Thomas White, alias Montreal Tom (see record of No. 101).—George Stacy, alias The Peoria Kid (see record of No. 101).—John B. Towle (106).

See regular index for further information.

SNEAK AND HOUSE THIEVES.

THE housebreaker and sneak are the most numerous of the thieving fraternity.   It is from the slums that the lower grade are recruited, but the successful robber must combine superior qualifications to make him an adept at the business.   Still the former are not devoid of ingenuity.   Locks and bolts cannot be relied upon as a rampart against these men.   There are but few dwellings in this city or country that are proof against the assaults of the burglar and sneak thief.   Some people believe their homes secure when they have fastened the doors and windows.   The average sneak thief laughs at the flimsy barriers, and can undo every one of them with a few simple instruments which he carries in his vest pocket.   Even the chain-bolt, which has been considered so formidable, is of no protection at all when pitted against the skill and science of this class of rogues.   When the massive bank vault offers no serious obstacles that the trained and experienced burglar cannot overcome, how can it be expected that the ordinary contrivances should be effectual.   While the operations of the former class of criminals are comparatively few and infrequent, on account of the multiplied risks and difficulties to be encountered, the well organized army of sneak thieves and housebreakers carry on their operations with a confidence born of repeated success.

Some housebreakers are daring and desperate rascals.   These are the ones that enter dwellings in the night-time in search of plunder and with masks on their faces and murder in their heart.   Sometimes night robberies are planned beforehand, but many have been committed at hap-hazard.   From servants or others employed in or about a residence, confederates of these thieves collect the information they desire. The manner of entering the premises depends upon its internal arrangements.   In some cases the front basement door is entered by a false key, in others the rogues climb up the front of the house and enter the second-story window, and still in others an entrance is effected from the rear.   Once inside, the burglar ransacks the apartments in which he expects to obtain the most booty.   He works expeditiously, going through an occupied chamber as carefully as he would an unoccupied one. Often these criminals disturb the sleeper, but the latter is so frightened at the presence of the robber that he lies still and offers no resistance.   Naturally housebreakers are not brave, and it is only when cornered they become bold and desperate in their anxiety to evade a long sentence.   The noise made by rats has on more than one occasion scared burglars away from silverware worth hundreds and thousands of dollars, which they abandoned after collecting and packing up for removal.

Three or four of these men have been known to band themselves together, but a desperate man would rather work on his own hook. "Long John" Garvey, who was killed by falling through a house in Brooklyn, a few years since, for years before his death took no one into his confidence, but planned and executed his own robberies. He gathered all the information that he desired from the columns of the morning newspapers. He made a specialty of robbing young married couples of their jewels and wedding presents. A marriage notice or a report of a wedding was the only news that Garvey wished to read, and he gloated over the announcement that the pair had received costly presents from their friends. When the robber ascertained where the pair had taken up house, either while they were off on their wedding trip or had returned to housekeeping, Garvey, by hiring an attic room on the same block, would pay them a midnight visit. He invariably secured the prize he was in quest of, but after a long career of thievery he died as most thieves do, a violent death. Becoming reckless at his successes, he undertook to ransack a house while in a state of intoxication. He secured property worth several thousand dollars, and as he was carrying it over the roof-tops he fell through a new building into the cellar. The groans of the thief attracted attention, and Garvey was found with the stolen jewelry in his possession. He was seriously injured and was removed to an hospital, where he died next day.

Another well known housebreaker was in the habit of attending all the fashionable balls. He never went there for pleasure, but always on business. The rogue, with envious eyes, watched the ladies bedecked with expensive jewelry and wearing necklaces and pins set with brilliants. He had but little difficulty ascertaining the names and addresses of the wearers of the diamonds. When the ball was over he would, with the assistance of a companion, dog his intended victim to their homes. He would keep a constant watch upon the house or its inmates for several days, and if in the meantime the jewels had not been taken to a Safe Deposit vault, the robber would conclude that the lady was in the habit of keeping her valuables in the house. When the opportunity offered, the thief, under some pretext or other, would make his way into the premises in search of the diamonds or jewelry he had first seen in the ballroom, and he generally succeeded in getting them.

The men who make it a business ransacking flats, first watch the occupants, and learning that a certain suite of rooms is rented by two or three persons reputed to be wealthy, they ascertain and note their habits. Should several of them pass the day at business, when the lady goes out shopping and the rooms are locked up, the thieves boldly enter the house, and, with the aid of a pick-lock, make their way into the apartments, which they ransack in the absence of the tenants. "Second-story" thieves, after locating a house that they intend to rob in the early evening, watch until the tenants in a private residence are down stairs at dinner. Then a young man, with the agility of a cat, crawls up the front of the dwelling, and enters the second-story window. He rifles all the rooms in the upper part of the house in a few minutes, and with the booty noiselessly descends the stairs and leaves the house by the front door. In several cases, however, the robber has been known to drop the property out of a front window to his confederates on the street. This is only done when he has become alarmed by hearing footsteps on the stairs, and is forced to retreat in the same manner that he had entered the premises.

Other thieves, who also pillage houses during the supper hour, pick the lock of the front door and steal in without making any noise. They wear rubbers or woolen shoes, and succeed at intervals in making large hauls. Private residences are easily plundered by these rogues during the summer months, while the occupants are in the country. Then there are the several types of sneaks who, under all sorts of pretexts, manage to get inside of a dwelling for a few minutes without attracting any attention, and remain just long enough to steal whatever they can lay their hands upon. Some of these go about as pedlers, piano tuners, health and building inspectors, book canvassers, sewing machine, life and fire insurance agents, and in various other rôles. They do not confine their operations to apartment houses or dwellings, but also rob business buildings in the daytime. Cash, jewelry, and valuables is the plunder most sought by the leading professional rogues of this class, but those of the lower grades seem to be satisfied with more bulky plunder. Young men make the most daring house thieves, but in the ranks may be found old criminals, who have passed the best years of their life operating in that way.

The names of a number of those who are classed as the most expert sneaks and house workers will be found in the following list:

David C. Bliss, alias Doctor Bliss (2).—B. B. Bagley (163).—Jim Burns, alias Big Jim (165).—William Wright, alias Roaring Bill (174).—Charley Bennett (188).— George Bell, alias Williams (193).—Tom Biglow (see records of Nos. 20, 131).— Bill Bartlett (see records of No. 71 and George Wilkes).—Dan Hunt, alias George Carter (71).—John Curtin, alias Reynolds (169).—Henry Cline, alias Weston (177).— Joe Colon (178).—Tommy Connors (61).—Dave Goldstein, alias Sheeny Dave (30). —Dave Mooney, alias Little Dave (173).—Joe Dubuque (see records of Nos. 74, 12, and Sam Perry).—John Duffy (see record of No. 50).—Stephen Dowd (see record of No. 190).—C. J. Everhardt, alias Marsh Market Jake (38).—Charles Fisher, alias Purdy (41).—Billy Forrester (76).—Billy Flynn (see records of Nos. 3, 50, 95, 165).— Eddie Guerin (see records of Nos. 11, 187).—Andy Gilligan (see record of No. 13).— Tom Gorman (see record of No. 146).—Horace Hovan, alias Little Horace (25).— Robert Hovan (179).—William Hague, alias Curly Harris (196).—Charles Williams, alias Woodward, alias Hoyt (194).—John Jourdan (83).—Thomas Leary, alias Kid Leary (6).—Ned Lyman (102).—Sophie Lyons, alias Levy (128).—Freddie Louther (161).—Tip Little (172).—Matthew Lane (see record of No. 2).—Rufus Minor, alias Rufe Pine (1).—John Mahaney, alias Mahoney, alias Jack Shepperd (62).—Billy Morgan (72).—Tilly Martin, alias Pheiffer (125).—John McGuire, alias Shinny McGuire (155).—John Murphy, alias Riley (166).—Emanuel Marks, alias Minnie Marks (187).—Tommy Mulligan (see record of No. 8).—Joe McCluskey (see records of Nos. 8, 50).—Eddie McGee (see record of No. 169).—Joe Otterberg, alias Oatsey, alias Stern (69).—Tim Oats (136).—Johnny O'Brien, alias The Kid (see record of No. 22).—Phillip Phearson, alias Philly Phearson (5).—Joe Parish (84).—Paul Wilson, alias Little Paul (29).—John Price (see records of Nos. 1, 9, 154).—Augustus Raymond, alias Gus Raymond (26).—Joe Real, alias Hoggy Real (67).—Ed. Rice, alias Big Rice (12).—Walter Sheridan, alias Ralston (8).—Frank Shortell (168).—Frank Stewart (see record of No. 12).—Christopher Spencer (see record of No. 69).—

Charles H. Dorauss, alias Jack Strauss (see records of No. 92 and Sam Perry).—William Russell, alias The Student (see records of Nos. 136, 171).—John T. Sullivan (see records of Nos. 163, 168).—John Tracy, alias Big Tracy (28).—John B. Towle (106).—Bill Vosburg, alias Old Bill (4).—Joe Whalen, alias Wilson (65).—William Ogle, alias Billy Ogle (13).—Westley Allen, alias Wess. Allen (164).—Albert Wise, alias Jake Sondheim, alias Al. Wilson (203).—Theodore Wildey, alias The. Wiley (171).—John Larney, alias Mollie Matches (11).—Jim Brady, alias Big Jim.—James Hoey, alias Orr.

See regular index for further information.

STORE AND SAFE BURGLARS.

A MAJORITY of the heavy store and safe burglaries perpetrated in this country have been committed between Saturday night and Monday morning. Thus the cracksmen had plenty of time, a day and two nights, to wrestle with the intricate combination of a strong vault, or select, gather and pack up for removal the most costly goods. These rogues are but a grade below the bank burglar, and an expert store-safe robber is always looked upon as a most important acquisition by those men who band themselves together for the purpose of plundering the coffers of moneyed institutions. Some store burglars are men of fair education, but those who spend their lifetime operating in the lower degrees in that line are coarse and dull, still in planning and executing a theft they display considerable shrewdness. Thieving to this class seems to be simply a natural trait, and they are not at all anxious to rise to the higher grades of crime.

When the store-safe burglar ascertains that a certain business firm is in the habit of keeping a large sum of money in their safe he determines to rifle it. Before the establishment closes on Saturday, one or two members of the band manage to conceal themselves in an empty room or packing-box on the premises, and when the building has been closed for the night the men leave their hiding-place and admit their confederates. The door is locked again and the cracksmen lose no time getting to work upon the stock or safe. These robbers vary in their manner of operating. Some prefer to steal silks or velvets, others have a fondness for silverware, jewelry and diamonds, and still others have a preference for only coin or greenbacks. The sort of plunder taken indicates the standing of the thieves. In the carrying off of bulky booty great risks are run, but the men who steal cash have but little to fear except discovery just as they are leaving the scene of their crime. This rarely happens, and should they be afterwards arrested for the burglary there is but little chance of ever legally fastening the offense upon them. The most reckless of the safe robbers use explosives, but the patient and careful operator either manipulates the combination or noiselessly wrecks the vault by leverage. The men who resort to explosives are known to their associates as "blowers." They are daring and desperate fellows and acquainted with the use of the drill and high explosives. It is a hazardous undertaking to shatter a safe in a large city, for the noise which follows an explosion makes the "blower's" chances of success slim and detection many. In sleepy country towns, where there is no police patrol system, these men still manage, however, to make an occasional haul.

The rattle made by a train on the Third Avenue Elevated railroad one night.

seven years ago, deadened the noise made by the blowing off the doors of two safes in a post-office station along that line. The noise made by the jolting of empty milk-cans on a cart, which was purposely driven through a down-town street, led to like results. In a neighboring city, but a few years ago, on a Fourth of July, a gang of "blowers" undertook to shatter a safe in a jewelry store, while a confederate was exploding several packs of large fire-crackers for the amusement of a number of children who had assembled in front of the place. Too large a charge of powder had been placed in the safe, and when the fuse had been ignited a tremendous explosion followed. The panes of glass were blown out of the front windows and the vault was badly wrecked. The explosion, which was louder than expected, instantly attracted attention, and the robbers ran away in the hope of escape. They were pursued and captured.

The "breaker" requires in his work a number of tools, and as they are all made of the hardest steel, a complete outfit is quite expensive. He is generally a cool, calculating criminal, who quietly and deliberately perfects his plans, and, after securing the booty, takes great pains to destroy all evidence that might lead to his detection. With the aid of diamond-pointed drills he is able to bore holes into the hardest known metals. Through these small openings he inserts the pick, but if the lock cannot be sprung in that way, the cutter or crook of a ponderous jimmy is next inserted. Then the tearing begins, and the leverage being immense, the safe is unable to stand the strain and finally yields. Some of the leading store-safe burglars use tools known as the "puller" and the "hydraulic jack." A gang of "breakers" made many thousand dollars last winter robbing post-office and store safes in all parts of the country. Their manner of operating demonstrated that they were expert cracksmen. In all their robberies they drilled a small hole through the door of the safe near the combination, and through the narrow opening they inserted some instrument which never failed to slide the bolts back. The entire operation was marvelous for its neatness and dispatch.

Concerning the doings of that class of criminals who make a business of manipulating combinations, this has been said of a successful offender at present serving out a term of imprisonment in an Eastern prison: "Give him but twenty minutes alone with a safe and he can open the most intricate lock that ever was devised, and if you will tell him merely the name of the safe maker, he will tell you instantly all the parts in the lock and give you a diagram of its mechanism. He never breaks a lock; he simply finds out inside of twenty minutes the combination in which it sits, opens the safe, and takes out what he wants and relocks it, and when the owner returns he finds the safe apparently just as he left it. To accomplish his work he needs, in addition to his quick wit and mechanical knowledge, three ordinary wires, which he forces into the lock about the handle in such a way that the number of the combination is reduced to twenty-four. He reasons that all persons in locking a safe make a certain number of moves, and a knowledge of this fact enables him to further reduce its probable combinations to two or three movements. These two or three movements he finds out by actual trial, which consumes the greater part of his twenty minutes. In the case when the safe is in an apartment that is in full view of the street, he drops a little quicklime on the floor, pours water on it, and the steam that arises effectually cloaks the windows.

In three instances he unlocked safes, abstracted the contents, relocked them, and made off in the time that the men who were in charge of them were at their dinner."

In several of the principal cities of this country there are old offenders who have tired of operating and occupy their time experimenting and teaching young thieves the art of safe robbing. These men are practical machinists who have learned the mysteries of the craft and the weak points of safes while in the employ of money-vault manufacturers. They plan many, if not all, of the out-of-town jobs, sometimes months before they are executed. Upon a percentage of the proceeds of the nefarious work they are able to live well and keep beyond the reach of the law. They never permit any of their pupils to operate in the city in which they dwell, but direct their movements throughout the surrounding country. Whatever plunder the young rogues secure has to be converted into cold cash before they are allowed to return to their old haunts. There are other men who spend their time taking impressions of store locks, and for a duplicate key to a business establishment demand a percentage of the plunder. One of these men in a simple sort of a way, some years ago, made the robbing of a broker's safe quite an easy matter, and yet a deep mystery. He learned that the confidential clerk employed in the place was infatuated with gambling, and made his acquaintance at the green baize table. One night the crafty rascal said that he had forgotten his keys and was anxious to unlock the drawer of a desk in the place. On the top of the desk lay a sheet of blotting paper that had been saturated with water. He borrowed the bunch of keys from the unsuspecting clerk, and while the latter was interested in the deal the fellow pressed the flat part of the key into the blotting paper, and also pressed it sideways. In that manner he secured a perfect impression of the key and also its thickness. Then he handed the keys back to the clerk, who thought no more of the matter. From the impression thus secured a duplicate key to the safe was manufactured, and with it, a month or so later on, the vault was easily plundered. A large haul was secured in that case, and for years suspicion pointed to the gambling confidential clerk as the thief. He was not arrested, however, and it was not until years after that the robber, while boasting about the theft, revealed the manner in which the duplicate key had been obtained. The clerk was then questioned, and he recalled the incident of loaning his keys to open a drawer in a desk in the gambling saloon.

The burglars who steal velvets, silks and silverware, take considerable time planning the robberies before they undertake the task of plundering the establishment. In some cases they scrape up an acquaintance with an employé, or send a confederate to price the most costly goods in stock. In that way they learn the shelf or shelves upon which the articles they are in search of are kept, and when at last they feloniously enter the premises they know just the place where they will find the most valuable goods.

The names and aliases of a number of the most expert store and safe thieves will be found in the following list :

John Anderson, alias Little Andy (see record of No. 63).—Martin Allen (see record of No. 164).—Thomas Kelly, alias Blink (66).—Fred. Benner, alias Dutch Fred (81).—Wm. Beatty, alias Burke (85).—James Burns, alias Big Jim (165).—Joe Rickerman, alias Nigger Baker (195).—Louis Brown, alias French Louie (204).—Oscar

Burns (151).—Jimmy Brown (see record of No. 4).—Brummagen Bill (see record of No. 196).—Dave Cummings, alias Little Dave (50).—George Lockwood, alias Cully (75).—John Curtin (169).—Patsey Carroll (see record of No. 66).—James Campbell, alias Shang (107).—John Connors, alias Liverpool Jack (see record of No. 86).— Denny Carroll, alias Big Slim (147).—Jack Cannon (101).—Daniel Watson, alias Dutch Dan (23).—Dave Mooney, alias Little Dave (173).—Pete Emmerson, alias Banjo Pete (90).—Charles Fisher, alias Purdy (41).—Billy Forrester (76).—Frank Russell, alias Little Frank (see record of No. 75).—Gustave Kindt, alias Marechal, alias French Gus (77).—John Green (see record of No. 80).—Fred. P. Grey (73).—Geo. Havill, alias Cook (15).—Robert Hovan (179).—Wm. Hague, alias Curly Harris (196).—Frank Reilly, alias Harrison (79).—Michael Hurley, alias Pugsey (88).—Geo. Hall, alias Porter (see record of No. 23).—Andy Hess (see record of No. 85).—John T. Irving, alias Old Jack (86).—Michael Kurtz, alias Sheeny Mike (80).—John Love, alias Wells (68).—Ned Lyons, (70).—Andrew McGuire, alias Fairy McGuire (78).—Thos. McCarty, alias Tommy Moore (87).—Eddie McGee (167).—John McMahon (170).— Bill Morris, alias Gilmore (see record of No. 23).—John McKeon, alias Kid McKeon (see record of No. 61).—Milkey McDonald (see record of No. 61).—Wm. Ogle, alias Billy Ogle (13).—Wm. O'Brien, alias Billy Porter (74).—Pete Lamb, alias Dutch Pete (181).—August Palmer (63).—Joe Parish (84).—Herman Palmer, alias Dutch Herman (189).—John Pettengill (198).—Wm. Pettibone (see record of No. 61).—Michael Quinn, alias Shang (82).—Joe Real, alias Hoggy Real (67).—Joe Otterberg, alias Oatsey (69).—John Tracy, alias Big Tracy (28).—John Talbot, alias The Hatter (see record of No. 66).—Joe Whalen, alias Wilson (65).—John Williams (see record of No. (24).—John Wilson, alias Dutch Chris. (see record of No. 80).—James Wilmont (see record of No. 80).—Gilbert Yost (see record of No. 74).—Westley Allen, alias Wess. Allen (164).

See regular index for others.

SHOPLIFTERS AND PICKPOCKETS.

HOLIDAY week is the shoplifters' harvest. The ladylike and gentlemanly pilferers of the city know this. They feel that Christmas comes but once a year, and before and after opportunities for spoliation are most abundant. So the shoplifter sallies forth and the pickpocket wends his way with keen eyes and ready hand among the throng—wends her way perhaps it should be put, for of the shoplifters who infest the city the large majority are females. There are various reasons for this. The work of shoplifting is comparatively easy, it is sometimes remunerative, and above all it is congenial. There are few ladies to whom the visitation of the shops and the handling of the wares are not joys which transcend all others on earth. And the female shoplifter has that touch of nature left in her which makes a clothing store, variety bazaar or jewelry establishment the most delightful spot to exercise her cunning.

In the last few years professionals of this order have wonderfully multiplied in this city, but their increase has been no more than commensurate with that of the metropolitan bazaars. That tells its own story. It is these very places which are most preyed upon and in which the temptation to larceny is most freely offered. The general exposure of the goods of the house on counter or on floor, the throng which is ever stirring about, the constant diversion for the eye or ear of watchers—all serve to prepare an easy way for the shoplifter.

The clerk's duties are generally manifold. He has to take down and sort his wares for customers; he has to answer a thousand idle queries; he has to puff up the goods, summon the cash boy and see to the account and change, while all that time the throng are whirling past him, and he has no eyes for an individual lounger. Women who, above all others, infest these places cannot but see how ample are the chances offered them, and such as are of the light-fingered community, and even some who are simply not strong in resisting the temptations to which their sex are most subject, are only too liable to pick up some stray trinket or bundle they have been handling and walk away with it. During the holidays many a jacket and dolman, and many a sealskin sack as well, could tell a curious tale of the odds and ends that were huddled beneath it.

It is true that articles of value are seldom captured by the shoplifter. It is generally pieces of dry goods, lingerie or cheap jewelry that are collected. But it is in the number of such petty larcenies that the losses to shopkeepers chiefly lie. Only recently a woman was arrested on whose person were found articles from nearly all of the variety stores on Broadway and Sixth Avenue. The ordinary female dress may be skilfully constructed so as to be an expansive receptacle for loot of all kinds, and the regular professional takes care that she is prepared for her trip with just such available provisions. That is how some of the stores where floor-walkers are employed are sometimes boldly plundered. The shoplifter gathers in her booty, safely stores it, and if detected in picking it up she becomes indignant, boldly subjects herself to an immediate search and nine times out of ten the employé, who is not familiar with criminal methods, misses the false pockets and is forced to admit the offender's innocence in spite of the evidence of his own senses. The cloak is also a useful article of attire for the shoplifter, and record is kept of women who have concealed inconceivable quantities of goods under a sweeping outer garment. Large rolls of cloth, costly dresses and sealskin sacques have been withdrawn from such repositories, and it is remembered at the Central Office that one clever professional carried under her arms a number of articles of various sizes which it would puzzle a man to bear about with his outstretched arms. A woman was noticed on Fourteenth Street leaving one of the bazaars with a big dolman on her, and a moment later a clerk came out saying that a number of valuable bonnets were missing. A detective elbowed his way through the crowd and overtook the amply clad woman. He feared to make a mistake and subject himself to merited censure by making an improper arrest, so he conceived the ruse of stumbling, apparently accidentally, and raising up one of the suspected stranger's arms. The trick worked admirably. The arm went up like a flash, and the ground forthwith was strewn with bonnets. She had nearly $200 worth in the collection.

Of course there are occasions when the shoplifter need not convert herself into a migratory storehouse. She sometimes has a confederate. She of the ready fingers and fluent tongue makes the circuit of the counters. The other presses along after her, gazing vacantly around and keeping severely distant from any of the wares exposed. When her confederate has slipped something out of sight she conveys it adroitly to the other, and the pair go on again. If the more clever operator be detected, no more than a single article will be found on her, and she can generally brazen her way out of its possession by alleging an absent mind or some distraction elsewhere in the store.

There are generally but two classes of shoplifters—the regular criminal professional and the kleptomaniac. The very poor classes seldom take a hand in it. Poverty is held by the world to be the badge of crime, and the poor slattern who enters a store is sure to be so carefully watched that larceny is next to impossible. The shoplifter is always a person of fair apparel and she generally has a comfortable home. If she be a professional she may be one of a criminal community and her home may be shared by some other engaged in equally evil ways. If she be a kleptomaniac—and in shoplifting the word has peculiar significance—she is possibly a woman whose life in other respects is exemplary. It does seem strange that a wife and mother whose home is an honest one, who attends religious service regularly, and who seems far removed from the world of crime, should be so carried away by her admiration of some trinket or knick-knack as to risk home, honor, everything to secure it. But the annals of metropolitan offenses are full of instances of just this kind. It is the sex's fondness for finery that nine times out of ten gets them into trouble. A woman who has left a home happy and well provided for goes shopping. She buys the necessary article she first started to procure after a good deal of selecting and chaffering. Then she has time to look about her and goes counter-gazing. That is the fatal moment. Some taking article—it may only be a trifle—catches her eye and absorbs her. She has already spent the contents of her purse, and she cannot honestly possess it. But the object every moment gains new fascination. She must have it. Then comes the temptation. It is so exposed. There is no one about. It would be such a simple thing to take it and conceal it. Conscience stifled by cupidity is dormant, and the lust of possession is all that possesses her. A moment more and the article is under her cloak, and all of a tremble she is edging away, half frightened, half regretful, yet wholly swayed by the securing of the moment's idol. Then comes detection. Everything about her rises to betray her—her frightened glance, her sneaking attitude, the closer clutch she has upon her cloak. She is accosted, questioned, and then every thought of home, family and the disgrace that threatens rises before her, and she summons all the pluck there is in her poor, fluttering heart, and denies.

Fatuous soul! She forgets that the sanctity which a moment since surrounded her as an honest woman is now stripped from her. She is searched. The stolen article is found upon her, and she stands there drooping and despairing—a proven thief.

Every year, repeated over and over again, is this sad scene produced. Kleptomania is a by-word applied to Heaven knows how many forms of crime. But among the shoppers of New York there are more women who have had a passion for larceny bred in them than perhaps anywhere else in the world.

Of the real criminal set of shoplifters there are some who extend their operations and embrace picking pockets in the part they play. They are a dangerous class, for at no place are opportunities for plying their arts more frequent than in a shopping bazaar. Attention is engaged by articles that have a greater lure for female eyes than anything else in the world. There is a constant excitement and ripple of conversation. Minds are full of purchases and heedless of pockets. Satchels and purses are laid carelessly upon the counter. The shoplifter sees all this and is ready to act upon it. Not long since a lady placed on a counter beside her a well filled purse. A moment after she mechanically picked it up again and prepared to pay for a purchase. She opened it. There was a bundle of paper in it. She looked at it again. It was not her own, but one that had been adroitly substituted for it.

An unusually cunning shoplifter successfully operated for several years by means of a scheme that he had devised himself. He traveled through England, France, and other European countries, leaving a trail of mysterious thefts behind him. Upon his return to the United States he was detected in the act of committing a robbery, and his plan was exposed. Cloth and silk houses were the scenes of his crimes. The fellow was aided in his thieving by a large-sized valise. The bottom of the bag, which parted in the middle, was hinged to the sides. Near the handle was a spring arrangement which connected with the movable bottom. The shoplifter was in the habit of entering a store while the clerks were engaged in the rear. Going boldly up to a counter he would seemingly carelessly set down his valise upon a pile of goods. As he did so he would spring the bottom, and thus bag a roll of silk or fine cloth. That done he might make a small purchase, or ask one of the clerks for the address of another firm in the same line of business.   His appearance was such that it would not cause the slightest suspicion, and the thief, until his way of working was discovered, always managed to leave the store with his gripsack full of plunder.

Two or three shoplifters have been known to enter large cloth dry goods or ostrich feather establishments in the morning just before business opening time, and while the porter or clerk was sweeping out.   On some pretext or another one of the rogues engages the single guardian of the store in conversation, and invariably succeeds in luring the unsuspecting man to the rear of the place.   This is the thieves' opportunity, and when the porter's or clerk's back is turned to them the shoplifter's confederates are busy.   In a twinkling they conceal whatever goods they are able to capture in false pockets upon their person.   Then the first man tells his dupe that he will call again, and leaves the store after his associates.

By what is known as "substitution," a few skillful male and female shoplifters occasionally succeed in making rich hauls.   They operate solely in jewelry stores, and have a fondness for handling and pricing diamond rings and pins.   A lapidary who manufactures paste rings and pins is next visited.   He is employed to make a substitute for the piece of jewelry which the shoplifter intends stealing.   A good description of the article wanted is furnished him, and it is soon finished.   When the duplicate has been secured, two or three of the shoplifters acting in concert call at the jewelry store. While the diamonds are again being examined, the spurious article is deftly substituted for the genuine one.   After an extended examination the supposed purchase is deferred, the case is returned to the safe, and it is often days before the fact is discovered that a costly ring or pin has been stolen and a paste one left in its place.   The shoplifters who make a practice of stealing uncut diamonds sometimes substitute spurious stones to cover the theft.   They have been known to swallow the gems, and when arrested on suspicion were able to escape conviction on account of the clever manner in which the trick was performed.   This class of thieves are not numerous, and but few have operated in the metropolis within the last ten years.   Of late they have plied their vocation with considerable success in several European cities; and it is a well known fact that an ex-official of New York City went to Europe in connection with two of this class of thieves, and he is credited with receiving the proceeds of their plunder and shipping it to this country.

But while the shoplifter's depredations have made people wary and led to considerable losses to the storekeepers—not so much from very costly articles, but from a quantity whose number aggregates a goodly sum—their practices have frequently led to the injuring of clear reputations and the subjecting of tender feelings to great suffering.   Most of the large jewelry establishments and great bazaars employ detectives, the rest floor-walkers.   Many of these do not possess the intelligence and cunning they require, and deplorable mistakes occur.   Ladies of position have time and again been accused of larcenies of which they were guiltless.   And some really absent minded have carried some article away from the counter utterly unconscious of it.   Of course it would require an adept in psychological arts to tell the really absent minded woman from the one who pleads it in extenuation of an actual crime, and that makes shoplifting and its consequences all the more deplorable.   The guilty have again and again secured immunity from punishment by a well concocted story of forgetfulness.   And, perhaps as often, the truly innocent has suffered for the guilty.

There seems no immediate relief for this.   But the employment of intelligent and discriminating watchers, and the painstaking investigation of cases of shoplifting are all that can be done to facilitate an apportioning of punishment to the offender, and the saving of the unintentional transgressor from the unhappy consequences of a moment's distraction.

PICKPOCKETS.

Pickpockets are an interesting class of thieves, and among the men and women who pursue that particular phase of crime there is much diversity of standing.   The male operators all dress well and display considerable jewelry, but the females, while pillaging, generally appear in humble attire.   Professional pickpockets are naturally great rovers and are continually traveling over the country to attend large gatherings.   It is in crowds that these dexterous rascals successfully practice their nefarious calling.   They are to be found one day among the assemblage present at the inauguration of the President of the United States, another at the funeral obsequies of some distinguished person, and the next at a country fair.   A year ago members of the light-fingered fraternity flocked from all parts of the country to New York City, expecting to reap a rich harvest among the immense gathering at the funeral of ex-President Ulysses S. Grant.   The perfect police arrangements, however, frustrated the plans of these rogues, and notwithstanding the fact that there were hundreds of thousands of people that day along the route of the funeral procession, not a single watch or pocket-book was stolen.   Never before in the history of the Police Department had there been such a clean record.   The day before the funeral all the professional pickpockets then in the city were arrested upon suspicion, and the police magistrates, when the precautionary scheme was explained to them, concurred in the flank movement against the rogues and held the prisoners. The alarm was then raised, and just as soon as the news had spread beyond the limits of the city, the hundreds of criminals on their way to New York gave up the project, left the trains and scattered in another direction.   A few, however, who were reckless enough to attempt to reach the metropolis, found detectives awaiting them at the several depots.   They were taken in charge and were kept safely housed at the Police Central Office, the various precinct station-houses and the Tombs prison until the funeral was over and all the strangers had departed for their homes.   When there was no one to prey upon the disgusted rogues were liberated.   The effort made to thwart the many bands of pickpockets upon that occasion was truly a bold one, but the end certainly justified the means.

Of professional pickpockets there are several types, and their peculiarities and characteristics are imperfectly understood by the general public.   Odd are the notions that some people entertain of the personal appearance of criminals of that class.   Some believe them to be a forbidding and suspicious-looking set, but the photographs in this book will convince them that they are not unlike ordinary individuals, and that unless their faces are known, their appearance or dress would not excite curiosity.   Still between the several classes of operators there is a vast and striking difference.   The pickpocket, either male or female, who dexterously abstracts a purse or captures a watch or diamond pin on any of the principal thoroughfares, in a street car, train or church, does not in any way resemble the person who will perform the same operation in a side street or at an enthusiastic gathering. Various as are the dispositions of these robbers also are their methods in getting possession of a pocket-book or valuables. Those who seek only large plunder are entertaining conversationalists and easy in their manners. They are generally self-possessed fellows, and are dexterous and cautious operators. Women make the most patient and dangerous pickpockets. Humble in their attire, and seemingly unassuming in their demeanor, without attracting any notice or particular attention, they slip into an excited crowd in a store or in front of a shop-window. A quick eye or a delicate touch will locate for them without difficulty the resting-place of a well filled purse. That discovered, they follow the victim about until the proper opportunity presents itself and they capture the prize. Sometimes they go off on thieving excursions in pairs, but an expert female pickpocket invariably prefers to work alone. The latter class are difficult to run down because of their craftiness and closeness. Men, after committing a large theft, are in nearly all instances extravagant and reckless, but women have no such reputation. On the contrary, they are careful of the money they have stolen, and have been known to remain concealed for a long time.

There is on record the case of a female pickpocket who after capturing a wallet containing many thousand dollars in greenbacks, aware that she was suspected, succeeded in eluding arrest until the only witness against her had died. The day following the robbery the woman, who was well advanced in years and was possessed of an excellent education, under an assumed name entered a religious institution. Being an apparently genial and good-natured person, and after telling a plausible and sad story of her unhappy marriage to a drunkard, she had no trouble in gaining admission to the home. Her conduct there was exemplary, and in the course of a short while she was given an easy position. There she remained for months and years, but when at last she read of the death of the wealthy lady whose pocket-book she had stolen, the cunning pickpocket, aware that the danger of conviction for the larceny had passed, soon vanished from the home and returned to her old trade. There are other instances illustrative of the care with which women avoid detection that are on a par with the one mentioned.

The pickpockets who pursue their calling under the cover of a shawl or overcoat carried carelessly over one arm, invariably the left one, take a seat in the car on the right side of the person they intend robbing, and operate under the coat, shawl, or newspaper. In case the pocket is high or too small to admit the hand freely, a sharp knife is used to cut the side of the dress or pantaloons of the victim. Others of the light-fingered fraternity wear light overcoats with the large pockets removed. Entering a crowded car, the thief, while standing up, selects a woman who, while paying her fare, has displayed a well filled purse. The man, when the opportunity occurs, carelessly laps his coat over her dress. Then by inserting his hand through the outside opening of his false pocket, quietly proceeds to do his work. Female pickpockets who operate in cars, stages and boats invariably use cloaks, which shield them while stealing. They press against the person whose pockets they are rifling, and the cloak completely hides the movements of their hands.

Some expert pickpockets ply their vocation alone. One of this class succeeded in stealing a valuable timepiece from the vest pocket of a distinguished jurist some time since while the latter was viewing a procession from in front of a leading hotel. Another class of pickpockets are to be found in churches and at funerals. Women generally do the stealing, and they pass the plunder to their male confederates, who disappear with the watch or pocket-book the moment it has been captured. The men as a rule are old thieves who have lost their nerve and are unable to work themselves. Those that operate in conjunction with an assistant always require the latter to do the pressing or engage the attention of the intended victim while his pocket is being plundered. A "mob" is always composed of not less than three men working in harmony. Just as soon as a watch or pocket-book has been stolen by one of these men the thief hands the plunder to his accomplices, who passes it to the third or fourth man, as the case may be. This style of thieving is to protect the rogue, and only yields small profits on account of the number engaged in the crime. Should the victim discover on the spot that his pocket had been picked and cause the arrest of the robber standing alongside or in front of him, the failure to find the plunder upon the prisoner would create a serious doubt as to his guilt. Cunning old professionals, veritable Fagins, are the brains of these "mobs." They delegate a daring young man with quick hands to do the stealing, and the instant the purse, timepiece or jewel has been passed to them they disappear. If it is a purse that has been taken, it is promptly rifled and the "leather" thrown into an ash-barrel or sewer. The veteran first divides with himself the lion's share of the booty, and afterwards splits up the remainder with the other members of the gang. Serious trouble resulting in bloodshed at intervals occur over quarrels concerning the spoils. Should a newspaper item announce that the stolen pocket-book contained a large sum of money when the leader of the gang had said he found but a few dollars in it, co-partnership would be dissolved by a sanguinary affray, the cause of which, for the protection of the others, would not be revealed.

"Sidewalk committees" at the time of military parades or political processions have a couple of young men who are known as pushers. These go in advance of the thief and locate the whereabouts of the plunder for him. They rush and push to and fro in the crowd, or at a street crossing, jostling against every one they come in contact with advancing in an opposite direction. When the pusher discovers the pocket that plunder is sure to be found in, the fellow signals to the pickpocket indicating the victim and just where the purse or wallet is carried. Then the robbery follows. Some nervous people, while carrying large sums, betray themselves to a shrewd thief by their actions, and afterwards think it strange that the rogue should have known the very pocket that they had the roll of greenbacks in. If they had remained cool while riding in a car or passing through a crowd, and had not clapped their hand every few minutes on the outside of the pocket in which they carried the money, to feel if it was still there, they would doubtless have avoided their loss. Pickpockets, like other individuals, are not gifted with second sight, and watch for signs to guide them in their operations. If their mode of working was better understood by the public and properly guarded against, the vocation of the pickpocket would in a short time become unprofitable.

The favorite method of robbery by the men who operate upon trains has been described in this way. When a mob of pickpockets start out to "work a crowd" on a train they break into twos. The part of one is to ascertain the location of his victim's money. He gets alongside the man whose pocket is to be picked, and with rapid movement he dexterously passes his fingers over every pocket. His touch is so delicate that it enables him to locate the prize, and to ascertain its character, whether a roll, a purse, or a pocket-book. The surging of the crowd, especially on a railroad train, accounts to the suspicious traveler for the occasional jostling he receives. It is found that the most common receptacle for the pocket-book is the left trousers pocket. When the victim is selected, the second man plants himself squarely in front of him, while the other crowds up behind him on the right side. The operator in front, under cover of a newspaper or coat thrown over his arm, feels the pocket, and if the victim is a straight-backed man, in standing position, he finds the lips of the pocket drawn close together. In such a case it is dangerous to attempt the insertion of the hand. A very low-toned clearing of the throat, followed by a gutteral noise, is the signal for his confederate to exert a gentle pressure upon the victim's right shoulder. This is so gradually extended that the traveler yields to the pressure without knowing it, and without changing the position of his feet. This throws the lips of the pocket conveniently open for the operator in front, who does not insert his hands to draw the book out, but works upon the lining. He draws it out a little at a time, without inserting his fingers more than half way. Should this process of drawing the contents of the pocket to its mouth be felt by the victim, another low clearing of the throat gives the sign to the confederate, and the game is dropped. If the victim's suspicions are not aroused, the pickpocket continues at his work of drawing the lining out until the roll of bills or pocket-book is within reach of his deft fingers. The successful completion of the undertaking is indicated by a gentle chirrup, and the precious pair separate from their victim to ply the same tricks upon the next one.

The stealing of watches and pins is made a specialty of by the gangs of pickpockets who ride in street cars. In the taking of a timepiece the system of jostling and crowding is resorted to while the "wire" (one who actually does the work) is stealing the watch. He raises the timepiece out of the pocket by means of the chain with his left hand, which is concealed by a coat or shawl. After the watch has been taken from the pocket the thief drops it into the palm of his right hand, and by a quick turn of the wrist the ring is twisted off. Another method is to resort to the usual jostling, and the man who actually does the stealing, when the opportunity presents itself, raises his left arm, which is generally covered by a coat or shawl, about as high as the victim's shoulders, while with the right hand he deftly abstracts the watch, letting it drop into palm of his hand. Then, with the use of the thumb and forefinger, he twists the ring from the watch. The chain, which is seldom taken, is quietly allowed to drop down, and usually the first intimation a person has that his watch is gone, is when the thief's victim's attention is called to his dangling chain. The moment that the timepiece has been stolen the man who takes it passes it to an associate, who leaves the car at once, and the others comprising the gang ride a square or two before getting out.   Some people wonder how the pickpockets succeed in stealing a watch without first unscrewing the snap at the end of the chain, not knowing that the ring has been twisted out. To capture a diamond pin the method is slightly different.   Rogues of that class while at work, it has been said, generally lift one arm above the height of the pin, and while the owner's attention is attracted by something started for the purpose, the jewel is abstracted by an exceedingly quick and clever movement of the thumb and forefinger of the other hand.   As the pin starts from its place it is caught in the palm of the thief's hand, and before the owner has discovered his loss the jewel has passed out of the possession of the man who stole it.   Persons carrying large sums of money or valuables should not allow their attention to be diverted by seeming disturbances or other distractions, as these occurrences are gotten up for the purpose of robbing them.

The annexed list gives the names and aliases of a number of the leading professional shoplifters and pickpockets whose records will be found in the book:

SHOPLIFTERS.—Kate Armstrong, alias Mary Ann Dowd (132).—Annie Mack, alias Brockie Annie (130).—Jake Sondheim, alias Al. Wilson, alias Al. Wise (203).— Margaret Brown, alias Old Mother Hubbard (117).—Mary Busby (126).—Harry Busby (135).—Mary Ann Connelly, alias Irving (120).—Eddie Miller, alias Dinkleman (7). —Dave Goldstein, alias Sheeny Dave (30).—Sophie Elkins (see record of No. 128).— Eddie Kelly, alias Little Eddie (see record of No. 184).—Sheeny Erwin (182).— Louise Jourdan, alias Little Louise (131).—Julius Klein, alias Young Julius (191).— Lena Kleinschmidt (119).—Sophie Levy, alias Lyons (128).—Peter Lamb, alias Dutch Pete (181).—Rudolph Lewis, alias Young Rudolph (184).—George Levy, alias Lee (185).—Kate Leary, alias Red Kate (see record of No. 128).—Bell Little (see record of No. 172).—Eddie McGee (167).—Johnny Curtin, alias Reynolds (169).—Anna B. Miller (see record of No. 7).—Tilly Miller (see record of No. 38).—Andy McAllier (see record of No. 75).—Jack McCormack, alias Big Mack (see record of No. 184).—Billy Perry (175).—Walter Price (197).—Frank Watson, alias Big Patsey (see records of Nos. 184, 190, 191).—Christene Mayer, alias Kid Glove Rosey (118).—Nellie Barns, alias Bondy (see record of No. 130).—Grace Daly, alias Big Grace (see record of No. 130).

See regular index for others.

PICKPOCKETS.—Jimmy Anderson, alias "Jimmy the Kid" (142).—Westley Allen, alias Wess. Allen (164).—Kate Armstrong, alias Mary Ann Dowd (132).—John Anderson (see record of No. 135).—Fred Benner, alias Dutch Fred (81).—Margaret Brown, alias Old Mother Hubbard (117).—Mary Busby (126).—Harry Busby (135).— George Harrison, alias Boston (144).—Thomas Burns, alias Combo (148).—Joe Rickerman, alias Nigger Baker (195).—Oscar Burns, alias Harley (151).—George Bell, alias Williams (193).—William Brown, alias Burton (see record of No. 164).—Brummagen Bill (see record of No. 196).—Mary Ann Connelly, alias Irving (120).—Joe Gorman (146).—Jim Casey, alias Big Jim (91).—Mary Connors (see record of No. 139).— Samuel Casper (see records of Nos. 152, 153).—Eddie Miller, alias Dinkleman (7).— Dick Morris, alias Big Dick (141).—Thomas Price, alias Deafy Price (158).—Billy

Darrigan (180).—William Dougherty, alias Big Dock (186).—Joe Dubuque (see records of Nos. 12, 80, and Sam Perry).—William Davis (see record of No. 157).—Alexander Evans, alias Aleck the Milkman (160). — Tom Fitzgerald, alias Phair (139).—Bridget Fitzgerald, alias Phair (see record of No. 139).—Abe Greenthal, alias The General (152).—Herman Greenthal (153).—John Gantz (see record of No. 81).—Molly Holbrook, alias Hoey (116).—Frank Reilly, alias Harrison (79).—James Johnson, alias Jersey Jimmie (145).—James Wilson, alias Pretty Jimmie (143).—William Kennedy (see records of Nos. 161, 194).—Louise Jourdan, alias Little Louise (131).—Sophie Levy, alias Lyons (128).—Terrence Murphy, alias Poodle (134).—George Milliard (138).—John McGuire, alias Shinny McGuire (155).—John Riley, alias Murphy (166).—Patrick Martin, alias English Paddy (133).—Frank Mitchell (see record of No. 133).—Tommy Matthews (156).—Jimmy Murphy (see record of No. 150).—James Lawson, alias Nibbs (137).—Freddie Louther (161).—Timothy Oats, alias Tim Oats (136).—James Price, alias Jimmy Price (154).—Billy Peck (157).—William Perry (175).—Walter Price (197).—Kate Ryan (129).—Annie Riley (see records of Nos. 166, 171).—James Campbell, alias Shang Campbell (107).—William Scott, alias Scotty (183).—Bill Sturgess, alias Old Bill (see record of No. 22).—Edward Tully, alias Broken Nose Tully (140).—James Wells, alias Funeral Wells (150).—Alonzo Henn, alias Alonzo.—Charley Allen.—Charley Douglass, alias Curley Charley.—James Wilson, alias The Bald Face Kid.—James McKitterick, alias Oyster Jim.

See regular index for further information.

CONFIDENCE AND BANCO MEN.

————

A GRASPING nature is a serious blemish that many men of standing and respectability unfortunately possess. The temptation to take a chance in a seemingly innocent lottery is one that can scarcely be resisted by people with the failing mentioned, and therefore the names of authors, politicians, divines, and even famous generals of America and Europe are to be found on the list of those who have been fleeced by confidence and banco operators. It is an innate desire on the part of the stranger to beat the sharper at his own game that leads the former on to his ruin. The accomplished operator hunts his dupe among those of high life, while an inferior set of these criminals select the ignorant and especially the gullible countryman for their victims. While the rustic may be a trifle suspicious in his dealings with thieves, men of culture and long experience, on the other hand, are easily taken in by the glib-tongued, nattily dressed young man, who shakes hands with them effusively on the street corners. The leading confidence and banco operators are an industrious set. They are also men of education, possessed of plenty of assurance, gifted with a good knowledge of human nature and a fair amount of ingenuity. The few who are proficient in all these attainments find no difficulty in helping themselves to other people's money.

Their form of roguery has been said to be the safest, pleasantest, and most amusing way for a shrewd thief to make his living. There certainly must be a strange fascination about these methods of swindling, for in the ranks of the sharpers has been discovered an ex-Governor and many others, who have at one time figured in good society. These nefarious professions are divided up into specialties. Some ply their vocation in the vicinity of hotels and railroad depots, and others along the river front, particular attention being paid to steamers about departing for Europe. Of all the different types of rogues a successful confidence or banco man is the most accomplished; they are really criminal callings that an unpolished man cannot attempt to follow. The success of the confidence game entirely depends upon the skill with which it is played, and in the selection of a victim all the powers of penetration of the cunning operator are brought into play. Few of the gangs of these men exceed four in number, and the majority of them do not exceed three. The operators are very careful in their personal appearance, and avoid anything remarkable in their dress, and endeavor to attain an easy respectability in effect, rather than the assumption of a man of fashion. Professional confidence men have more than once declared that a tinge of gray in their side whiskers would be a great advantage to them, and a bald head a fortune. The man who loiters about the offices and corridors of the principal hotels awaiting his prey, appears as the best-natured person in the world. He is invariabiy to be found with a smile on his face, and in moving out of the way of the guests and porters passing to and fro, politely bows at every turn. Eagerly he scans the freshly written name in the register, and when that has been secured he awaits the chance to practice his threadbare tricks upon the new arrival. He greets the latter in the street and in a few minutes gains his confidence. Then at a preconcerted signal a confederate appears upon the scene, who is either collecting or anxious to settle a bill. The first confidence man will then ask his newly-made friend to advance him the sum demanded for a few minutes, or else favor him for cash in lieu of a check. In ninety-nine out of every one hundred cases the stranger is anxious and happy to accommodate the confidence man. The money is handed over to the second operator and he quickly vanishes. Not long afterwards the affable hand-shaker disappears, and then the stranger discovers that the check he cashed is worthless, or that the money he loaned has gone forever. Those who operate on the river fronts or at railroad depots are invariably in search of a man to take charge of their stock farm, etc.; the method of obtaining the victim's money varies as the circumstances require. These are a few of the numerous ways that the confidence man has of defrauding his victims. Their varied schemes have been exposed by the newspapers, and it seems strange that these men on that account should be able at all to eke out a livelihood. But it must be admitted that they do, and a good one too, and these rogues have been often heard to boast that a fool is born every minute, and that they are able to find more subjects than they can safely operate upon. A veteran confidence man who died recently in an Eastern prison, was credited with having made during his long career of swindling over a million dollars. His wonderful cheek and coolness may be best illustrated by the mention of the manner in which he twice succeeded in robbing the same man. Early in his criminal life the confidence man realized $30,000 upon some worthless notes which he induced a wealthy and casual acquaintance to cash. Thirty years later the sharper returned in the rôle of a penitent, and promised to make restitution to his old victim for his past misdeeds. So well did he manage to gain the confidence of his old friend anew, that in the course of a few days he again borrowed $3,000 on another set of worthless notes.

It is in an out-of-the-way street that the banco men have the rooms where they practice their nefarious tricks. They generally hire a furnished apartment on a lower floor, and in nearly all cases there is no question as to the nature of the business they intend to carry on in the place. The payment of a week's rent in advance seems to satisfy the average landlord, and for the first week, at least, everything is all right. Probably the operators will only occupy the room for a day or two, having in the meantime managed to fleece some one. When a suitable apartment and location has been secured the criminals are ready for business. The hand-shaker then sallies forth, and at the first opportunity grasps a prosperous looking stranger by the hand and exclaims: "Well, Mr. Brown, how are all my friends in Greenville?" The stranger, surprised with the good nature and unexpected friendliness of the reception, invariably responds: "You've made a mistake, sir. I'm Mr. Jones, of Austin, Texas." Then the roper-in apologizes, hurries off and reports to the steerer, who pulls a book out of his pocket and hunts up Austin. The book is what is known as a bank-note reporter, and gives a complete list of all the banks in the country. From the list the banco man finds that Mr. Thomas is the president of the Austin bank, and that Messrs. Black and White are among its directors. Then he follows Mr. Jones, accosts him in the street, shakes hands with him, calls him by name, and saying he is Mr. Thomas's nephew, asks about the health of the Blacks, Whites and other prominent people. The stranger is flattered by the attentions of the bank president's stylish nephew, and it does not take long to decoy him into the room where the boss banco man is waiting to play his part. There are desks and maps in the apartment which, to all appearances, is the office of some commercial concern. The dupe is lured to the banco men's shop by the usual story about a book or a painting drawn in a lottery, then the cash prize and the rest of it. The stranger usually bites in a few minutes; he is anxious to get $500 for $100; puts down his wad of bills, and the operators capture it, and he walks out in a brown study, not knowing exactly how he was done up, but quite sure he has been swindled. The banco men leave their office a minute or two after. The victim does not complain to the police, because he is ashamed to tell how green he was, and fears that if he makes any complaint the newspapers will learn of the robbery and then all his friends will hear of his experience in the metropolis.

With a few slight changes "banco" is the old English game of "eight dice cloth." It was introduced into this country some thirty years ago by a noted sharper who operated throughout the West. He re-christened the game lottery, notwithstanding the fact that there is no vestige of lottery about it at all. The old game with the new name is so simple, and apparently honest, that even the shrewdest are readily induced to take a hand, and are thus fleeced. There are forty-three spaces upon a banco lay-out; forty-two are numbered, and thirteen contain stars also (no prizes); one is blank, and the remaining twenty-nine represent prizes ranging from two to five thousand dollars. The game can be played with dice or cards. The latter are numbered with a series of small numbers ranging from one to six, eight of which are drawn and counted, the total representing the number of the prize drawn. Should the victim draw a star number he is allowed the privilege of drawing again by putting up a small amount of money. He is generally allowed to win at first, and later on the game owes him from one to five thousand dollars. This is when he draws the conditional prize, No. 27. The conditions are that he must put up five hundred dollars, or as much as the dealer thinks he will stand. This is explained to him as necessary to save what he has already won, and entitle him to another drawing. He draws again, and by skillful counting on the part of the dealer he draws the "blank," and loses all. Sharp as was Oscar Wilde when he reaped a harvest of American dollars with his curls, sun-flowers, and knee-breeches, he could not refrain from investing in a speculation against which he was "steered" by the notorious Hungry Joe. The latter boasted that his plunder amounted to thousands of dollars, and Oscar, when asked about it, maintained a painful silence. Another equally notorious character succeeded in swindling an Episcopal clergyman. The banco man handed the Rev. Mr. Blank a forged letter of introduction from another minister in Cleveland, whose name he had discovered in a church almanac. Mr. Blank said that he was glad to meet the Rev. Mr. Watts's brother. The letter read : " My brother is buying books for me. Please honor his draft for $100, and thereby do me a great favor." The preacher thought it was all right, and put up his check for $75 when it was asked for.

Banco men seem to take a fiendish delight in outwitting men illustrious in all the walks of life. One of them, in conversation recently with a reporter, smilingly said : " The prettiest banco is when we land a big fish. Talk about trout-fishing ! Just think of the fun hooking a man that's worth anywhere from $500 to $5,000 ! Of course, it takes a man of education and refinement to do this sort of business, but there are several college graduates among our fellows."

Many confidence and banco men who have been found loitering about the hotels and streets, waiting for victims, have been arrested as vagrants. When, however, a complainant comes forward, these offenders are vigorously prosecuted. The gold-brick swindle, which is fully described elsewhere, is really a part of the confidence game.

The names of a number of the men foremost in the line of confidence and banco operators will be found in this list :

Joe Bond, alias Paper Collar Joe (200).—Hod Bacon (see record of No. 94).— Charles Mason, alias Boston Charley (92).—Dr. J. E. Coons (see record of No. 122). —James Fitzgerald, alias Red Fitz (113).—Frank Hammond, alias Western Frank (see record of No. 91).—Tip Farrell (see record of No. 93).—George Gifford (see record of No. 99).—Bertha Heyman (122).—Charles Ward, alias Hall (104).—George Hall, alias Porter (23).—Joe Howe (see record of No. 91).—Joe Lewis, alias Hungry Joe (95).—Peter Lake, alias Grand Central Pete (93).—Edward Lillie (100).—Edward Lyman (102).—George, alias Tip Little (172).—Doctor Long, alias Pop White (94).— Edward Rice, alias Big Ed. Rice (12).—Dave Swain, alias Old Dave (99).—Ike Vail, alias Old Ike (10).—Jim Casey, alias Big Jim (91).—Joe Eaton (Gold Brick).—Nathan White, alias Nat White (Gold Brick).—Ellen Peck.

See regular index for others.

RECEIVERS OF STOLEN GOODS.

WITHOUT a safe market for his ill-gotten property the avocation of the rogue would be unprofitable. The buying of stolen goods is therefore not a crime of recent origin, but dates back to the very beginning of thievery. It is really the root of the evil, but the suppression of receivers of stolen goods in the State of New York, owing to existing laws, has been made almost an impossibility. Receivers have their grades and classes. Some make it a business to purchase bonds, securities, diamonds or silks. The receiver in the habit of handling stolen paper, could not be induced to risk a speculation in bulky plunder. These offenders are extremely careful in their negotiations with professional rogues. They seem to place but little faith in the word of a thief, and are naturally suspicious of all persons with whom they have any dealings. After a large robbery the burglars do not, as is generally supposed, cart the plunder to the house or store of the receiver. Instead, they quietly remove it to a safe place of storage in some neighboring city or town. The wives of criminals undergoing imprisonment are invariably the custodians of loot. The burglars have confidence in these women, and so have the receivers. The booty is conveyed to their apartments in trunks and does not attract any attention. When it has been placed in charge of the wife of an imprisoned confederate, the "fence" is notified and samples of the goods furnished. Should the receiver desire an examination of the property he sends his trusted appraiser to look it over, and should it prove to be as represented, a settlement is effected and the trunks are reshipped to the rooms of another thief's wife. The latter's unlucky husband was perhaps a favorite with the receiver, and the woman is always a willing party to transactions of this sort. Receivers, while they rarely pay more than one-quarter of the value of the stolen article, run no risks. They never make a settlement with the thieves until the proceeds of the robbery have been removed a second time, and to a place the location of which the gang they are dealing with knows nothing about. There are two reasons why the purchaser is so careful. One is because he fears treachery at the hands of the robbers, and the other because he does not desire to incur any loss. In event of the stolen goods being seized in transit from the storage place of the thieves to that of the receiver, the loss falls upon the former. The reason why the rogues are kept in ignorance of the final hiding-place is to prevent them, should there be any bickering as to the price, from betraying the buyer. The simple testimony of the self-confessed thief that he sold the stolen goods to a certain person, would be of no value in a legal sense without the corroborative proof of the seizure of the plunder. On account of the receiver's guarded manner of doing business this is never possible, and the moment that the goods come into his possession all tags and marks that would lead to their identification are removed and destroyed.

Under the cover of some legitimate business, receivers in the large cities are able to conduct their nefarious transactions without much danger of detection. To conceal their shady speculations they run a fancy goods or jewelry store, on apparently a square basis and in a business district. These are the class that purchase from shoplifters, pickpockets, and dishonest employés. To watch their patrons would be a task that would bear but little results. Persons known as professional criminals shun these places, and the men and women who sell the proceeds of their pilferings there are only petty thieves. While seemingly purchasing some article, they are really making a bargain for its sale, and never carry on their negotiations in the presence of a stranger. The goods bought under such conditions are never offered for sale in these places, but are disposed of to unscrupulous shopkeepers who delight in peddling them, and are all the time boasting of their honesty and, perhaps, quoting Scripture.

There are many people to be found in cities who are constantly on the lookout for bargains, and possess a fondness for other people's property. To this class of receivers pickpockets and sneak thieves safely dispose of stolen watches and trinkets. The establishments of pawnbrokers, who advance loans on jewelry and clothing, are the places patronized by young rogues. Old rogues, by melting watch-cases, run but little chance of detection, and net quite a large profit by the sale of the metal to reputable firms. A smart receiver, who deals in stolen jewelry, as a rule makes it a habit after a purchase to reduce all small articles into metal, just as soon as bought. The most annoying class are the second-hand dealers, who buy and sell stolen wearing apparel. They invariably have friends in another city, so that as soon as plunder has been bought it is shipped away to be disposed of elsewhere.

All phases of crime excepting this one—the worst of all—are, in the State of New York, amply and clearly covered by the statutes. On more than one occasion the guilt of several persons, notorious as purchasers of the proceeds of robberies to the police and the public, has been morally certain ; still, in a legal sense, it was impossible to secure their conviction, because the law seemed to especially protect them from punishment. Among the many things to make out a case upon which a conviction might be expected, it is necessary to establish the fact that the receiver knew that the property he had bought had been stolen or appropriated wrongfully. This clause is therefore a serious stumbling-block in the way of prosecution, and serves as a shield for the buyer of booty, no matter how notorious he or she may be. All indictments and trials in this section of the country must be framed and conducted in accordance with the provisions and requirements of the Penal Code. Chapter 550 applies to receivers of stolen goods, and this section of the law was doubtless intended to put a stop to the buying of what thieves call "swag ;" but the peculiar construction of the statute has completely upset the intention of the law makers. The chapter mentioned is as follows :

"A person who buys or receives any stolen property or any property which has been wrongfully appropriated in such a manner as to constitute larceny according to this chapter, knowing the same to have been stolen or so dealt with, or who corruptly, for any money, property, reward or promise or agreement for the same conceals, withholds or aids in concealing or withholding any property, knowing the same to have been stolen or appropriated wrongfully in such a manner as to constitute larceny under the provisions of this chapter, if such misappropriation had been committed within the State, whether such property were so stolen or misappropriated within or without the State, is guilty of criminally receiving such property, and is punishable by imprisonment in a State prison for not more than five years or in a county jail for not more than six months, or by a fine of not more than two hundred and fifty dollars, or by both such fine and imprisonment."

The opinion of one of the leading prosecuting officers of New York City shows how difficult it is under the present law to establish the guilt of a receiver of stolen goods. What he has said on the subject, and the suggestions he has made, are interesting and important. They are as follows:

"The law requires proof of guilty knowledge—that is, it must be proven to the satisfaction of a jury that the party receiving the goods knew at the time of their receipt that they were stolen. Such guilty knowledge must be proved by facts and circumstances, and it is difficult to collect such facts and circumstances as will satisfy the jury beyond reasonable doubt of the defendant's guilt.

"Even where the thief himself becomes a witness for the State, it is the practice of the courts to warn the jury that it is unsafe to deprive a man of his liberty upon the unsupported testimony of either a confessed or a convicted criminal.

"I am of the opinion that the law on this subject should be more stringent. It might, for instance, make it presumptive proof of guilt, sufficient, in the absence of explanation, to convict the defendant, that the goods were immediately after the theft found in his possession. There is, of course, a presumption to that effect as the law now stands, but it is only a presumption and is not sufficient to found a conviction upon unless the jury are satisfied from all the evidence beyond all reasonable doubt that the defendant is guilty."

If the suggestions of the learned prosecutor were embodied in the law, I feel satisfied that they would materially assist the authorities in ridding the community of this class of offenders.

TRICKS OF SAWDUST MEN.

THE murder recently of a well-known sawdust swindler has had a detrimental effect upon the other men who made their living in the same way. The old methods had to be abandoned, but recent reports from all parts of the West show that they have flooded a good many towns with new circulars. The popular form of swindle, up to last August, was by working the "panel game." The first move of sawdust men is to secure the list of the names of people who were regular subscribers to lotteries and various gift-book concerns. People who go into those things will be pretty sure to bite on another scheme. When the list has been duly studied, agents are sent out all over the country to look up the history of the most promising ones. This done, a circular is mailed to each man, which runs something as follows :

Mr. ———.

DEAR SIR : I will confide to you through this circular a secret by which you can make a speedy fortune. I have on hand a large amount of counterfeit notes of the following denominations : $1, $2, $5, $10 and $20. I guarantee every note to be perfect, as it is examined carefully by me as soon as finished, and if not strictly perfect is immediately destroyed. Of course it would be perfectly foolish to send out poor work, and it would not only get my customers into trouble, but would break up my business and ruin me. So, for personal safety, I am compelled to issue nothing that will not compare with the genuine. I furnish you with my goods at the following low price, which will be found as reasonable as the nature of my business will allow :

For $1,200 in my goods (assorted) I charge...............$100
For   2,500 in my goods (assorted) I charge............... 200
For   5,000 in my goods (assorted) I charge............... 350
For 10,000 in my goods (assorted) I charge............... 600

Then follows advice to the verdant reader, impressing upon his mind that the gates of State prison are yawning for him, and that he must be very careful. He must send word two days before his expected arrival in this city, go to a hotel which is named and remain in his room until the manufacturer called upon him. This done, an agent sends up his card and devotes an hour to sounding the man, to see if he is fair game or an emissary from the police in disguise. If all promises well the man leaves, appointing the next day as the time for the bargain. On the day appointed the first caller drops in to the hotel and leads the stranger to the "factory."

In a roughly furnished office, before a high desk at the wall, sits the principal operator, busily counting out a huge pile of crisp bills. They are fresh from the Government Treasury, and of all denominations. The countryman is introduced, explained the process by which the money can best be disposed of, and given general directions of how to avoid suspicion. Then the bills are exhibited. The man always protests that they are poor counterfeits and would never deceive him, but on the whole thinks they will do. The amount desired is carefully counted out and handed to the stranger to recount. They are then nicely done up in packages, each denomination by itself, and the whole carelessly tossed into a small leather gripsack. This done, the bag is laid on the top of the desk, while the "manufacturer" holds the attention of the stranger and lifts the lid of the desk in front of the bag. Half a dozen bonds are shown as a specimen of good counterfeiting, and the suggestion is made that after the money has been used the customer may take a fancy to handle some bonds also. While the two men are busy looking at the bonds, a confederate in the next room opens a slide or panel at the back of the desk and substitutes another satchel in the place of the one with the greenbacks. The customer is then handed the bag and hurries away, and the swindler closes up his office for a month or so and moves to another similarly equipped establishment.

Since the panel trick became known the sawdust men have been forced to invent another device. Within the past few months they have issued a long circular, which contains a clipping supposed to be cut from a New York newspaper announcing that a full set of dies and plates has been stolen from the Sub-Treasury. This is the basis on which the circular is framed, and it claims that the writer has obtained stolen plates, from which the greenbacks are being struck off. The interesting circular ends with the following : "The slip will show you our officials in high standing have used them for their own purpose and benefit, and why not every one in need ? Address, in confidence," etc.

The purpose of the letter is to lead the one addressed to believe that the money offered is really genuine, being printed from the plates claimed to have been stolen from the Treasury. The same old scheme of conducting a man to a hotel and then to the "office" is used, but the panel trick is no longer worked. Instead, the "beer" or "horse-car" game is made use of. In the first case the purchaser is introduced to the sawdust man on the street, and to conclude the bargain the party adjourn to the nearest saloon. Stepping into a private room they take seats at a table and the money is exhibited. This done, the amount demanded is paid, and as the operator rolls the "goods" into a little red package and snaps an elastic band around it he calls for beer. But before they are handed over the appearance of the waiter alarms the sawdust man and he drops the package into his lap, with a wink at the customer. While the beer is being brought another red package is substituted from under the table, and the trick has been played. If the countryman is suspicious the greenbacks are dumped into a little leather satchel marked with a cut or scratch, and after being duly locked the key is handed to him. The party then board a car and in a few moments a clerical-looking gentleman gets on, and with a bag precisely similar in marks, etc., to the one containing the "goods." Of course the bags are changed and the purchaser is swindled. After the change has been made the sawdust men disappear.

Another scheme is explained by the following circular :

New York, June 11, 1886.

Dear Sir : No doubt when you receive this letter you will say it is some trap set for you to get you into trouble ; but such is not the case. I promise you this, as true as there is a God in heaven, I obtained your name through a friend of mine who passed through your place, as this is all I know of you ; and on my solemn oath I speak the plain, candid truth ; and I swear before the Almighty God in heaven, my purpose is far from harming you either in word, look or action ; and should you make up your mind to answer this letter, I will give you my word and honor that no person, man, woman or child, shall ever hear from my mouth the least thing that ever passed between us, and I will keep this promise as sacred as I would my oath before God in heaven.

I will be plain with you. I am dealing in articles, paper goods, 1s, 2s, 5s, 10s and 20s—(do you understand ?) I cannot be plainer until I know your heart is true to me, then I will send you full and plain particulars that I mean you right, and will satisfy and convince you that I can furnish you with a fine, safe and profitable article, that can be used in any manner and for all purposes, and no danger. Now understand me fair and square ; I ask no money in advance nor do I want it. I want to give you plain and positive proofs that, should I give you my assistance, I can and will help you out of any money or business troubles you may be in, and no matter to what extent ; and no power on the face of God's earth need ever be the wiser for it unless you betray me ; and as my intentions are square and upright to you, and as I never have or will harm you by word, look or action, I ask you before heaven, as a man of honor and principle, not to expose or betray me. And if I have made a mistake in sending you this letter, I ask you to forgive me, and let the matter rest where it is, for my intentions are as upright to you as heaven itself, for a man can have honor and principle no matter what his business may be in this world, so do not harm me, for my motto in this life is and always has been, if you can't do a fellow-being some good, do him no harm, no matter what his calling may be.

Now a word of advice in regard to this business. There are some unprincipled men in this city advertising goods the same as mine. But before God and man they are far from it. They will send you circulars and promise all kinds of things, and should you be foolish enough to send them money, that is the last you will hear of them or your money, and there are other firms here dealing in green goods of a very poor quality and not safe to handle. Now I am not writing this letter through malice or selfishness to get your trade, but to warn you against them should you at any time receive their circulars (as these people have their agents going from one State to another, getting storekeepers' names, and in fact names of people in all kinds of business), and should make up your mind to write and place confidence in me, with a view of trading with me, I will take it as matter of honor and strict friendship between us, if you will notify me if these people send their circulars to you, as I will prove they are not reliable men to trade with, and this is the Almighty God's honest truth, as I am the only person who can furnish you with a safe and profitable article that will stand a critical test, and I will prove each and every promise I have given you before I will expect or receive one dollar.

I will as a test of honor and confidence on your part request the return of this letter. I will then know you mean me no harm, for I will not answer any communications unless it is returned to me.

I will not deviate from this rule, and on my sacred oath and honor, before God and man, I will return yours.

Yours in honor and friendship.

Since 1869, the sawdust business has grown and prospered. The operators work carefully, their only fear being lest some detective be entrapped. The police have tried over and over again to get at the swindlers, and although they are known it is next to impossible to obtain proof against them. The victims refuse to appear against them, for the very fact of having had dealings with the sawdust men closes their mouths, for fear the transaction would be made public. In this way the sawdust business goes on.

FRAUDS IN HORSE SALES.

SHARPERS who sell worthless animals at fabulous prices constitute a class of criminals often exposed. They keep barely within the letter of the law, and so escape punishment. When some one remarked that a man would cheat in a horse trade who would scorn to steal an umbrella, he showed a deep knowledge of the ethics of the human family. Light and trivial though the latter offense may be, judged by the great American race, it is weighty indeed when compared to that of driving a sharp bargain over a roadster or racer. "Trust neither your brother nor your pastor if he is trying to sell you a horse," is the wisdom of a man of experience who has learned the irresistible temptation which lies in the mouth of the man with a horse to sell.

Dishonest horse dealers flourish in New York. They are the confidence operators of the horse trade, and are not to be confounded with the dealers who may neglect to point out some of the defects of their living stock in trade. Their purpose is robbery pure and simple, with just enough tinge of trade in it to give it a color of respectability and to keep out of State prison. They conduct their business much after the fashion of the banco men, sending "steerers" out to the railroad stations, the ferries, and the big horse sales, to bring unsuspecting countrymen to their lairs. They also reach victims, like the fortune-telling cheats and many other forms of metropolitan swindlers, through the advertising columns of the daily newspapers.

It is not difficult to pick out the advertisements of the skin dealers, or "gypsies," from any issue of the newspapers. The favorite dodge is the "death of the owner," or the "family going to Europe" pretext for selling a magnificent animal for a song. Here is a sample advertisement which may be regarded with suspicion :

"A family going abroad will sacrifice immediately very speedy roadster and stylish, gentle family horse ; also quiet pet horse, used by ladies ; lady's phaeton, sidebar top buggy, extension top family phaeton, harness, etc., in superb order. Owner's private stable."

The oft-repeated announcement of a firm well known to the police reads as follows :

"A bargain to immediate purchaser—handsome pair coach mares, tender in the feet, suitable for country use, $60 for both ; 3 strong young horses, suitable for general business use ; price from $50 to $100 each ; sold separately ; trial allowed. Owner's private stables."

It will be seen that great leeway is allowed here for infirmities of almost any character.

Perhaps it is a lady who has a turnout to sell, and who will conduct the negotiations through a trusty "groom" in her own private stables, or a gentleman suddenly called out of town. They may be expected to woo you in some such wise as these :

"A lady offers her turnout for sale ; handsome cob, 15 hands, seven years old, warranted sound and kind ; elegant top phaeton, harness, etc.; sold separate."

"A gentleman suddenly called away must sell a beautiful brown horse, 16 1-4 hands high ; fast traveler ; safe and perfectly sound ; suit family, doctor, coupé or business."

There is nothing suspicious in the language of these offers, and man or woman in search of a bargain will find nothing suspicious in the commodious stable to which he is directed or in the glib-tongued, horsey-looking man he finds there. The rascals simply use the machinery of a reputable business to carry on their nefarious operations, trusting to the always good crop of credulous individuals to furnish them with a supply of victims.

The confidence game, which is often worked in the "skin stables," is as old as the hills. While the agent of the wealthy owner, gone to heaven or to Europe, is engaged in showing off the "points" of his racer, a confederate rushes in and displays uncommon anxiety to purchase the horse.

"No," says the agent, "you are a dealer and my principals will not allow me to sell to a dealer. The horse is too valuable. You know very well that they do not care for the money. What they wish is to be assured that the animal falls into good hands."

Pretty soon the alleged "dealer" gets an opportunity to whisper to the victim a word of temptation.

"I must have that horse," he says ; "if you will buy him for me I will give you $50 commission ; but don't give me away to the agent."

Tickled to death over this opportunity to make money so easily, Mr. Greenhorn swallows the hook, line, bob and sinker ; purchases the horse and leads him away to a specified corner where he is to meet the "dealer." Needless to say, this worthy does not appear, and the victim finds himself most unwillingly possessed of a piece of rope with something in the shape of a horse at the other end of it. As a party to a little deception he has no case against the man who sold him the worthless animal.

The police wage constant war upon these stables, and often make things very uncomfortable for the owners, but the latter are so well grounded in the law and so careful to keep inside the legal fence in their transactions that the police are heavily handicapped in trying to deal with them.

"Horse sharps," although frequently arrested, are rarely convicted. The last conviction was on May 28, 1881, when Samuel Watson was sent to Sing Sing prison for two and a half years. Jeremiah W. Strong, a Justice of the Peace of Hartford, Conn., bought an elegant roadster from Watson at a stable on Fifteenth Street, near Sixth Avenue. Strong started to drive away, but the animal, on reaching the corner of Fourteenth Street, dropped dead. Watson was convicted, but his brother swindlers made up a big purse and carried the case to the Court of Appeals. That court finally decided against him.

WHY THIEVES ARE PHOTOGRAPHED.

WHERE, it does not matter, but in a place of amusement which blazed with light and was radiant with the shimmer of silks, the flash of jewels, and the artificial glories with which wealth and fashion surround themselves, a tall, well dressed man was standing, with a lady on his arm, waiting till the outgoing throng gave him exit. There was a judge of the Supreme Court just behind him, and he was elbowed by a banker whose name is mighty on "the street." Suave manners, a face massive and intelligent, apparel in unexceptionable taste—he had them all, and yet there was something about the man that recalled to a reporter who saw him there, other and strangely remote associations. It certainly was not the dress or attitude or air that seemed familiar. Nor was it the quick, sharp eyes that lighted and seemed indeed the most notable features of the countenance. Nor could it be the neatly trimmed whiskers or the somewhat sallow cheeks they covered. No, it was none of these. And certainly no suggestion of recognition could lie in the thin hair, carefully brushed back from a forehead that bulged out into two knobs and was crossed by some deep lines. But yet as that same forehead was bowed for a moment, what was there in it that recalled something—a man or a statue or a picture? Something that memory certainly did not bring to mind as the seat of a living man's brain, a part of a living man's face; but something that had been seen fixed, immovable, with unchanging profile and unvarying lines.

In a moment the head was erect again, the face smiling, and in the change the fancied familiarity melted, but did not die away. It was still there, and for a moment it was intensified as a sudden look of recognition, a look that had a flash of malice in it, came into the sharp eyes. But without any salutation being given they dropped, and the face was turned away. This passed almost in the fraction of a second; but the reporter noticed the look and turned to see where it was directed. What he saw quickened his interest. A man was standing near the entrance watching the very face which had caught his attention. And this man was a Central Office detective.

"That man's face seems familiar to me," remarked the reporter, indicating the retreating figure. "You know him, do you not?"

"I? Yes, I know him."

"I wonder where I have seen him."

"He is seen sometimes about town."

"But I think I've seen him under some peculiar circumstances."

"He has been visible under peculiar circumstances," said the detective. "He is a professional criminal, and was last sentenced for burglary."

A burglar! This prim, genteel, thoughtful looking personage? He would be a minister or merchant or physician on the first flash to nine men out of ten. Here in the flare of the gaslight, in the heart of fashion, with a judge at his back and a millionaire at his elbow—a burglar? Not low browed, sullen, with stealthy glance and hunted air—not at all as fancy and romance have pictured him. But holding his head as high as the next. And with that, memory, faithful to the impression that bulging forehead and its deep lines had wrought, raked out of the past a wooden frame in a mysterious chamber and a picture it enclosed of a bowed, distorted face, through whose half closed eyelids two small specks seemed to glare maliciously, and a forehead with two knobs and some black lines upon it. That was it. The picture was this man's portrait, and the mysterious chamber where it hung was the Rogues' Gallery.

Sitting there the next day the reporter spoke of the impression made by the picture, and how, amid surroundings so misleading and under appearances so altered, the bowed forehead and its dark lines in the gallery of malefactors had flashed out in the gay and fashionable throng, calling attention to their owner, as Cain's mark had done of old. The conversation which ensued is correctly given by the reporter in the following words :

"In that," said Inspector Byrnes, "does the usefulness of the Rogues' Gallery lie. There are people who look at the pictures and say :—'Of what good can these twisted and unnatural faces be? Were their owners met in the streets their countenances would be composed. They would be altogether free of these distortions, by which they have tried to cheat the purpose of the police in photographing them. No one would know them then.' Well, that is all wrong. The very cleverest hands at preparing a false physiognomy for the camera have made their grimaces in vain. The sun has been too quick for them, and has imprisoned the lines of the profile and the features and caught the expression before it could be disguised. There is not a portrait here but has some marked characteristic by which you can identify the man who sat for it. That is what has to be studied in the Rogues' Gallery—detail. A general idea of the looks of a person derived from one of these pictures may be very misleading. The person himself will try to make it so by altering his appearance. He can grow or shave off a beard or mustache, he can change the color of either, he may become full faced or lantern jawed in time. But the skilled detective knows all this and looks for distinguishing marks peculiar to his subject. You understand me. It was a forehead drew your attention. The lines of the forehead would probably be a detective's study in that burglar's case. It did not matter much what disguise he assumed. That feature would remain a tell-tale."

"Have detectives frequently succeeded in singling out by their portraits men who have tried to deceive the camera?"

"Quite frequently. The very men who have gone to the most trouble to make their pictures useless have been betrayed by them. Look at 'Pop' Tighe, over there, with his phiz screwed up like a nut-cracker; he thought that he could play the sneak without any one getting on to him from that likeness. But he made a mistake, like the rest. So did 'Bill' Vosburgh, and even 'Jim' Reynolds, who is grinning down from the corner there, with his head away back and his features all distorted, could not get the best of the sun, and the camera caught enough of him to satisfy his victims."

"Then the pictures must not be considered merely as portraits when a criminal is to be identified by them?"

"In some cases they are quite sufficient. You see there is not much of that old dodge of distorting the features attempted nowadays. When we have a man with a strong case against him he knows that his portrait in some shape or other must be added to the gallery, and he is shown that it is absurd to try and defeat the purposes of justice. That makes him resigned to his fate, and all our recent artistic acquisitions are good ones. A point is made to have the best we can get, for of late photography has been an invaluable aid to the police. In the Federal service and in all the big cities they are following our example. But this is probably the most complete criminal directory in the country. I say in some cases because there are numbers of instances where a criminal appears in public under circumstances far different from those under which he is brought here. You yourself have seen what a swell cracksman may look like when he has the means and the taste to dress himself. Well, there are scores of men and women whose appearance in the streets gives no hint to their character. Deception is their business, and they have to study its arts carefully. It is true there are criminals brought here who even in sitting for a photograph in the Rogues' Gallery show a weakness to appear to advantage. I have seen women especially whose vanity cropped out the moment the muzzle of the camera was turned on them. But that is infrequent, and you must look for the faces you see here in other shapes and with other accompaniments when you catch sight of them in public."

"Do the general run of offenders, then, put on style?"

"They all have their weaknesses. Of course the lower class of them spend their money in the way their instincts dictate. Some are slovenly hulks of fellows who pride themselves on shabbiness. To some shabbiness is a part of their business. Then there are others of the flashy order who run into extremes in dress, and copy the gamblers and variety theatre performers in their attire. But there are many—and they are of the higher and more dangerous order of criminals—who carry no suggestion of their calling about with them. Here is where the public err. Their idea of burglars and all that have been gathered from books, and they look for Bill Sykeses and Flash Tobby Crackitts, whereas the most modest and most gentlemanly people they meet may be the representatives of their very characters. Remember that nearly all the great criminals of the country are men who lead double lives. Strange as it may appear, it is the fact that some of the most unscrupulous rascals who ever cracked a safe or turned out a counterfeit were at home model husbands and fathers. In a great many cases wives have aided their guilty partners in their villainy, and the children, too, have taken a hand in it. But in as many all suggestion of the criminal's calling was left outside the front door. There was George Engles, the forger. His family lived quietly and respectably, mingled with the best of people and were liked by all they met. George Leonidas Leslie, alias Howard, who was found dead near Yonkers, probably made away with by his pals, was a fine-looking man, with cultured tastes and refined manners. 'Billy' Porter and 'Johnny' Irving were not so spruce, but they would pass for artisans, and Irving is said, in all his villainy, to have well provided for his old mother and his sisters. 'Johnny the Greek' paid for his little girls' tuition at a convent in Canada, and had them brought up as ladies, without ever a suspicion of their father's business reaching them. I know this same thing to be done by some of the hardest cases we have to contend with. One of the most noted pickpockets in the country had children whose dress and manners won them general admiration. There is nothing to mark people of that stamp as a class."

"Is physiognomy any guide?"

"A very poor one. Judge for yourself. Look through the pictures in the Rogues' Gallery and see how many rascals you find there who resemble the best people in the country. Why, you can find some of them, I dare say, sufficiently like personal acquaintances to admit of mistaking one for the other. By the by, that is no uncommon occurrence, and the more you consider it the more readily you will come to appreciate how easy it is for a detective to pick up the wrong man. Time and again I have seen victims of thieves when called upon in court to identify a prisoner seated among a number of on-lookers pick out his captors, or a court clerk, or a reporter as the offender."

"Is it usual for criminals to be so trim?"

"No, not many of them. You see thieves must dress up to their business. I do not mean that they should indicate their business by their dress. No, no; just the opposite. They attire themselves so as to attract the least attention from the class of people among whom they wish to operate. To do this they must dress like this class. If they are among poor people, they dress shabbily. If among well-to-do folks, put on style. If among sporting men, do the flash act. It is a great thing to escape notice, and some men have a good deal of trouble to do it. There is 'Wess.' Allen. The scar on his cheek and the missing eye would mark him anywhere, but he manages to be so sober in his dress that no one notices him. 'Deafy' Price, a railroad pickpocket, is a capital fellow for gaining confidence and leaving scant recollection of his dress and features. Kehoe, 'the Mourner,' and his wife had faces thoroughly adapted for their business, which was to pick pockets at wakes and funerals. They were the most solemn looking pair you ever saw."

"You then consider the popular idea of criminals' appearance is all wrong?"

"I will not say that. River thieves and low burglars are as hard-looking brutes as can be found. So are a good many of the more desperate fellows. 'Ned' Farrell, the butcher-cart thief, is a type of the bully—big and brawny and wicked-looking. 'Big Frank' McCoy had all the inches he required, but although there was a sinister flavor about him, he could look the gentleman. Nugent, the Manhattan Bank burglar, carried a good deal of his old business of a butcher about with him in his appearance, but there was something about him that suggested the criminal. There are numbers of the confidence men, too, who in spite of their gentlemanly dress and conversational powers, look the very incarnation of sharpers. In fact, it is a bad thing to judge by appearances, and it is not always safe to judge against them. Experience of men is always needed to place them right."

DESCRIPTIONS AND RECORDS

OF

PROFESSIONAL CRIMINALS OF AMERICA.

1

RUFUS MINOR, alias RUFE PINE.

BANK SNEAK.

DESCRIPTION.

Forty-eight years old in 1886. Born in United States. Married. No trade. Stout build. Height, 5 feet 5½ inches. Weight, 160 pounds. Brown hair, gray eyes, round face, dark complexion. Very bald. Has a clerical appearance at times. Can grow a heavy beard (dark brown) in a short time; generally wears it when committing crime, and removes it shortly after. Has a dot of India ink on the back of left hand.

RECORD.

RUFE MINOR, alias PINE, is no doubt one of the smartest bank sneaks in America. His associates are Georgie Carson (3), Horace Hovan (25), Johnny Jourdan (83), Billy Burke, alias "Billy The Kid" (162), Johnny Carroll, alias "The Kid" (192), Emanuel Marks, alias Minnie Marks (187), Big Rice (12), Mollie Matches (11), Billy Flynn, Big Jim Burns (165), Charley Cummisky, George Howard, alias Killoran and other clever men. He is a very gentlemanly and intelligent man, and is known in a number of the principal cities. He is no doubt one of the best generals in his line; he comes of a good family, and it is a pity he is a thief.

Minor was arrested on March 23, 1878, at Petersburg, Va., in company of George

Carson, Horace Hovan, and Charlotte Dougherty (Horace's wife), charged with the larceny of $200,000, in bonds and securities, from the office of James H. Young, No. 49 Nassau Street, New York City, on January 2, 1878. They were all brought north, on a requisition, but no case was made out against them, and they were discharged. He was arrested again in New York City on November 14, 1880, with Johnny Jourdan and Georgie Carson, charged with the larceny of a tin box containing $8,500 in money and $56,000 in bonds from the vault of the Middletown Savings Bank, at Middletown, Conn., on July 27, 1880. Horace Hovan, who was previously arrested in this case, was taken to Connecticut. Minor, who was not identified, was held in New York City, charged with being the party who stole $28,000 in bonds from a safe in the office of Merritt Trimbal, in the Coal and Iron Exchange Building on Courtlandt Street, New York, on October 15, 1879. The bonds were found in possession of the Third National Bank of New York City, having been hypothecated by a notorious bond negotiator and insurance agent. No case was made out against Minor, and he was discharged. Rufe Minor and Billy Burke are credited with obtaining $17,000 from the Commercial National Bank of Cleveland, O., in the fall of 1881. Burke was arrested in this case in Buffalo, N. Y., but Minor escaped. Minor was no doubt the principal man in the following robberies: the First National Bank of Detroit, Mich., $3,200; the Middletown National Bank of Connecticut, $73,500; Bank of Cohoes, N. Y. (attempt), $100,000; Brooklyn (N. Y.) Post-office robbery, $3,000; Providence (R. I.) Gas Company robbery, $4,000; Guarantee Trust and Safe Deposit Company's vaults, at Philadelphia, Pa., $71,000; Rufus Rose Insurance Agent's safe, at Albany, N. Y., $3,800; the Safe Deposit vaults on State Street, Boston, Mass, $25,000; the Bank of Baltimore, Md. (bonds), $12,000. Minor was also credited with sneaking $114,000 in bonds from the Erie County (N. Y.) Savings Bank, on April 30, 1882. The bonds were returned to the bank by a well known Baltimore lawyer, who received $25,000 for them.

He was arrested again in New York City on June 25, 1883, and delivered to Marshal Frey, of Baltimore, for the larceny of $12,000 in bonds from the Bank of Baltimore, on September 25, 1882. For this he was tried and acquitted by a jury on November 1, 1883. Minor and Johnny Price were arrested in Boston, Mass., on February 1, 1884, and given one hour to leave the city. He was arrested again in New York City on June 28, 1884, for the authorities of Augusta, Ga. Minor, Price and Billy Coleman sneaked a package containing $2,700 in money from a bank safe in Augusta, Ga. Billy Coleman and Price were arrested two days afterward, tried, convicted, and sentenced to seven years each in State prison, on May 7, 1884. Minor was taken to Augusta and discharged, as he could not be identified as the third party in the robbery.

He was arrested again in New York City on January 12, 1886, charged with the larceny of $130 from the pocket of one Samuel Henze, in the office of the "Evening Journal," in Jersey City, N. J. He gave the name of William Jackson, and was taken to New Jersey by requisition on January 17, 1886. In this case he was tried in the Hudson County (N. J.) Court, and acquitted on April 21. 1886. Minor's defense was an alibi. See records of Nos. 9, 25, and 83.

Rufe Minor's picture is an excellent one.

2

DAVID BLISS, alias DOCTOR BLISS.

SNEAK.

DESCRIPTION.

Thirty-nine years old in 1886. Born in United States. Married. Doctor. Slim build. Height, 5 feet 8½ inches. Weight, 135 pounds. Light colored hair, turning gray. Gray eyes, long face, light complexion. Has a hole on the right side of his forehead.

RECORD.

The "Doctor" has a fine education, and is a graduate of a Cincinnati Medical College. He is a southerner by birth, and at one time held a prominent government position. He was caught stealing, however, and was sentenced to a long term of imprisonment. Through the influence of his friends he was pardoned, but again drifted back to evil ways. He is pretty well known in most of the eastern cities, and is considered a very clever sneak thief.

He was arrested in New York City on the arrival of the steamer Providence, of the Fall River Line, from Boston, on December 21, 1880, in company of one Matthew Lane, another thief. They had in their possession a trunk containing $2,500 worth of silverware, etc., the proceeds of several house burglaries in Boston, Mass. They were both taken to Boston by requisition on December 31, 1880, and sentenced to two years each in the House of Correction there.

Bliss was arrested again in New York City on April 7, 1883, for the larceny of a package containing $35,000 in bonds and stocks from a safe in an office at No. 757 Broadway, New York City. After securing the package of bonds he started down stairs, and on his way dropped into another office, the door of which was standing open, and helped himself to $100 in money that was lying on one of the desks. All of the bonds and stocks were recovered, after which the "Doctor" pleaded guilty, and was sentenced to two years in Sing Sing prison on April 12, 1883. His time expired on January 11, 1885.

Bliss's picture is an excellent one.

3

GEORGE CARSON, alias HEYWOOD.

BANK SNEAK.

DESCRIPTION.

Thirty-one years old in 1886. Born in United States. Clerk. Can read and write. Married. Medium build. Height, 5 feet 5½ inches. Weight, 155 pounds. Hair, brown. Eyes, hazel. Complexion, florid. Dot of India ink on right hand. Blonde color mustache.

RECORD.

CARSON is a very clever bank sneak, an associate of Rufe Minor (1), Horace Hovan (25), Johnny Carroll (192), Cruise Cummisky, and other first-class men. He was arrested at Petersburg, Va., on March 23, 1878, in company of Rufe Minor, Horace Hovan, alias Little Horace, and Charlotte Dougherty (Horace's wife), charged with the larceny of $200,000 in bonds and securities from the office of James H. Young, No. 49 Nassau Street, New York City. They were all brought to New York, and subsequently discharged.

Carson was arrested in New York City on November 15, 1880, for robbing the Middletown Bank of Connecticut, on July 27, 1880, of $8,500 in money and $56,000 in bonds. Johnny Jourdan, Horace Hovan and Rufe Minor were also arrested for this robbery. Carson was tried in Connecticut, proved an alibi, and the jury failed to agree, and he was discharged on April 26, 1881. He then traveled around the country with Charley Cummisky, alias Cruise, and was picked up in several cities, but was never convicted. He was again arrested in Brooklyn, N. Y., on August 2, 1883, with Billy Flynn (now in jail in Europe), and committed to the penitentiary for vagrancy. He was discharged on a writ by the Supreme Court on September 11, 1883. Carson and Flynn were seen in the vicinity of Raymond Street Jail on the night of July 31, 1883, when Big Jim Burns, the Brooklyn Post-office robber, escaped. This celebrated criminal has been concerned in several other large robberies, and has been arrested in almost every city in the United States and Canada. He is now at liberty, but may be looked for at any moment. Carson's picture is a very good one, taken in 1885.

4

WILLIAM VOSBURG, alias OLD BILL.

SNEAK AND STALL.

DESCRIPTION.

Fifty-seven years old in 1886. Born in United States. Can read and write. Married. Stout build. Height, 5 feet 10 inches. Weight, 170 pounds. Hair, dark, mixed with gray. Gray eyes. Light complexion. Generally has a smooth-shaven face.

RECORD.

VOSBURG is one of the oldest and most expert bank sneaks and "stalls" in America, and has spent the best portion of his life in State prisons. He was formerly one of Dan Noble's gang, and was concerned with him in the Lord bond robbery in March, 1886, and the larceny of a tin box containing a large amount of bonds from the office of the Royal Insurance Company in Wall Street, New York, several years ago. Vosburg was arrested in New York City on April 2, 1877, for the Gracie King robbery, at the corner of William and Pine streets. He had just returned from serving five years in Sing Sing prison. In this case he was discharged. On April 20, 1877, he was again arrested in New York City, and sent to Boston, Mass., for the larceny of $8,000 in bonds from a man in that city. He obtained a writ in New York, but was finally sent to Boston, where they failed to convict him. On June 10, 1878, he was arrested in New York City, charged with grand larceny. On this complaint he was tried, found guilty, and sentenced to fifteen months in the penitentiary, by Recorder Hackett, on December 28, 1878. He did not serve his full time, for on May 3, 1879, he was again arrested in New York City, with one John O'Brien, alias Dempsey, for an attempt at burglary at 406 Sixth Avenue. In this case he was admitted to bail in $1,000 by the District Attorney, on May 17, 1879. The case never was tried, for on September 23, 1879, he was again arrested, with Jimmy Brown, at Brewster's Station, New York, on the Harlem Railroad, for burglary of the post-office and bank. For this he was tried, convicted, and sentenced to four years in State prison at Sing Sing, on February 19, 1880, under the name of William Pond, by Judge Wright, at Carmel, New York. Brown never was tried.

After his release he claimed to be playing cards for a living, when in fact he was running around the country "stalling" for thieves. He was arrested in Washington, D. C., on March 4, 1885, at President Cleveland's inauguration, for picking pockets. Through the influence of some friends this case never went to trial. He then started through the country with Johnny Jourdan (83), Philly Phearson (5), and Johnny Carroll, alias The Kid (192). On April 1, 1885, the party tried to rob a man in a bank at Rochester, N. Y., but failed. They followed him to a hotel, and while he was in the water-closet handled him roughly and took a pocket-book from him, but not the book with the money in it. Phearson and Carroll escaped, and Vosburg and Jourdan were arrested, and sentenced to two years and six months each for assault in the second degree, by Judge John S. Morgan, on June 15, 1885, at Rochester, N. Y.

Vosburg's picture is a good one, taken in March, 1885.

5

PHILLIP PHEARSON, alias PHILLY PEARSON, alias Peck.

BANK SNEAK.

DESCRIPTION.

Fifty-four years old in 1886. Height, 5 feet 5½ inches. Weight, 135 pounds. Hair mixed gray. Eyes, blue. Complexion, sallow. Ink marks : Eagle wreath, American flag, square and compass, an Odd Fellow's link, also "J. Peck," with face of woman underneath the name, all the above on left fore-arm ; star and bracelet on left wrist ; star between thumb and forefinger of left hand ; figure of woman on right fore-arm ; above the elbow is a heart, with "J. P." in it ; shield and bracelet with letters "W. D." on same arm.

RECORD.

PHEARSON, or PECK (which is his right name), is one of the oldest and smartest sneak thieves in this country. He has obtained a good deal of money in his time, for which he has done considerable service in State prisons. He comes from a respectable Quaker family of Philadelphia.

Phearson, Chas. Everhardt, alias Marsh Market Jake (38), and George Williams, alias Woodward (194,) were arrested in Montreal, Canada, in 1876, for sneaking a package containing $800 in money from a safe in that city. Williams gave bail and jumped it, and Phearson and Everhardt stood trial, and were sentenced to three years and six months in prison. On June 16, 1879, shortly after his release in Canada, he was arrested in New York City for the larceny of a $1,000 4-per-cent bond from a clerk of Kountze Brothers, bankers, in the general Post-office building. To this offense he pleaded guilty, and was sentenced to three years and six months in State prison, on June 26, 1879, under the name of George W. Clark. Phearson was again arrested in New York City in October, 1885, for the larceny of $85, on the till-tapping game. He claimed to be a health officer, and while he had the proprietor of the store in the yard, his accomplice carried away the drawer. For this offense he was tried, convicted, and sentenced to five years in State prison by Judge Cowing on November 5, 1885, under the name of Daniel Kennedy.

Phearson's picture is an excellent one, taken in 1885.

6

THOMAS LEARY, alias KID LEARY,
alias BRIGGS, alias WALTER H. KIMBALL.

BANK SNEAK.

DESCRIPTION.

Thirty years old in 1886. Medium build. Height, 5 feet 6 inches. Dark red hair. Eyes, bluish gray. Complexion, light. Born in New Orleans. Weight, 120 pounds. Married.

RECORD.

"KID" LEARY, alias GEORGE R. BRIGGS, was arrested in New York City on October 24, 1877, in company of Langdon W. Moore, alias Charley Adams, charged with being implicated in the robbery of the Cambridge National Bank of Cambridge, Mass., September 26, 1877, when bonds and securities amounting to $50,000 were stolen. He was not returned to Massachusetts in this case, for lack of identification, but was held in New York for the larceny of a trunk containing gold and silver jewelry. The facts were that on May 12, 1877, the firm of Alling Brothers & Co., of Worcester, Mass.. shipped a trunk containing $9,000 worth of jewelry from Worcester to Hartford, Conn., to their agent, who discovered that the checks had been changed and the trunk stolen.

It was traced from Hartford to a New York hotel, and from there to Baltimore, Md., where it was found empty. Leary was identified as the party who received the trunk at the hotel and shipped it to Baltimore. A portion of the contents was found in the house where Leary was arrested, in New York City. His case was set down for trial on November 8, 1877, but was adjourned until November 20, 1877, when he was convicted and sentenced to five years in State prison for the offense. See record of No. 26.

Leary was again arrested in Baltimore, Md., on October 5, 1881, charged with robbing the South Baltimore Permanent Mutual Loan and Savings Association. He was found guilty and sentenced to five years in State prison on October 21, 1881, under the name of Walter H. Kimball. Allowing him his full commutation time, he was discharged on December 21, 1885.

His picture is a good one, taken some eight years ago. He has filled out more now.

7

EDWARD DINKELMAN, alias EDDIE MILLER,
alias Hunter, alias Bowman.
PICKPOCKET, SHOPLIFTER, AND HOTEL THIEF.

DESCRIPTION.

Forty-one years old in 1886. Born in Germany. Height, 5 feet 4 inches. Stout build. Dark hair, dark eyes, round face, dark complexion. Dresses well, and is very quick in his movements. Weight, about 150 pounds.

RECORD.

Eddie Miller, the name by which he is best known, is a celebrated New York shoplifter. He generally works with his wife, Anna B. Miller. He is also a clever sneak, and occasionally turns his hand to hotel work. He was in prison in Chicago, Syracuse, and Canada, and is known in all the principal cities of America.

Miller was arrested in New York City on March 23, 1880, for the larceny of three gold chains, valued at $100, from a jewelry store at 25 Maiden Lane. For this offense he pleaded guilty in the Court of General Sessions, New York, and was sentenced to two years in State prison on April 16, 1880, under the name of William Hunter. After his conviction and sentence he asked to be allowed to visit his home, on Sixth Avenue, for the purpose of getting some clothes and giving his wife some instructions in relation to his affairs. An officer of the court was sent with him, and while the officer was speaking to Miller's wife, Miller sprang through an open doorway, cleared a flight of stairs in a few jumps, reached the street, and escaped. He was afterwards arrested in Chicago, Ill., and returned to New York to serve his sentence.

Miller was arrested again in New York City for grand larceny, and sentenced to ten years in State prison, on May 16, 1884, under the name of William Bowman. His time will expire on September 16, 1890. Miller's picture is a very good one.

8

WALTER SHERIDAN, alias RALSTON,
alias KEENE.

BANK SNEAK, FORGER AND COUNTERFEITER.

DESCRIPTION.

Fifty-five years old in 1886. Born in New Orleans, La. Married. No trade. Height, 5 feet 7½ inches. Weight, about 165 pounds. Light brown hair, dark eyes, Roman nose, square chin. Generally wears blonde whiskers. He is a good-looking man, and assumes a dignified appearance.

RECORD.

WALTER SHERIDAN is an accomplished thief, a daring forger, bank sneak, hotel thief, pennyweight-worker and counterfeiter. He is also one of the most notorious criminals in America. Among his aliases are Stewart, John Holcom, Chas. Ralston, Walter Stanton, Charles H. Keene, etc. When a boy, Sheridan drifted into crime and made his appearance in Western Missouri as a horse thief. He finally became an accomplished general thief and confidence man, but made a specialty of sneaking banks. In 1858 he was arrested with Joe Moran, a noted Western sneak thief and burglar, for robbing a bank in Chicago, Ill., and was sentenced to five years in the Alton, Ill., penitentiary, which time he served. He was afterwards concerned in the robbery of the First National Bank of Springfield, Ill., with Charley Hicks and Philly Phearson (5). Sheridan engaged the teller, Hicks staid outside, and Phearson crawled through a window and obtained $35,000 from the bank vault. Hicks was arrested and sentenced to eight years in Joliet prison. Philly Phearson escaped and went to Europe. Sheridan was arrested in Toledo, O., shortly afterwards with $22,000 in money on him. He was tried for this offense but acquitted. He next appeared in a "sneak job" in Baltimore, Md., in June, 1870, where he and confederates secured $50,000 in securities from the Maryland Fire Insurance Company. After this he secured $37,000 in bonds from the Mechanics' Bank of Scranton, Pa. He was also implicated and obtained his share of $20,000 stolen from the Savings and Loan Bank of Cleveland, O., in 1870. He was arrested in this case, but secured his release by the legal technicalities of the law.

Sheridan's most important work was in the hypothecation of $100,000 in forged bonds of the Buffalo, New York and Erie Railroad Company to the New York Indemnity and Warehouse Company, in 1873, for which he obtained $84,000 in good hard cash. It took months to effect this loan. He took desk room in a broker's office on the lower part of Broadway, New York, representing himself as a returned Californian of ample means. He speculated in grain, became a member of the Produce Exchange, under the name of Charles Ralston, and secured advances on cargoes of grain. He gained the confidence of the President of the Indemnity and Warehouse

1

RUFUS MINOR,
ALIAS RUFE PINE,
BANK SNEAK.

2

DAVID C. BLISS,
ALIAS DOCTOR BLISS,
SNEAK.

3

GEORGE CARSON,
ALIAS HEYWOOD,
BANK SNEAK.

4

WILLIAM VOSBURG,
ALIAS OLD BILL
BANK SNEAK AND STALL

5

PHILLIP PHEARSON,
ALIAS PHILLY PHERSON,
BANK SNEAK.

6

THOMAS LEARY,
ALIAS KID LEARY. ALIAS BRIGGS
BANK SNEAK.

7

EDWARD DINKLEMAN,
ALIAS EDDIE MILLER—HUNTER—BOWMAN,
PICKPOCKET,
SHOP LIFTER AND HOTEL THIEF.

8

WALTER SHERIDAN,
ALIAS RALSTON—KEENE,
BANK SNEAK, FORGER AND
COUNTERFEITER.

9

WILLIAM COLEMAN,
ALIAS BILLY COLEMAN,
BURGLAR AND BANK SNEAK.

10

IKE VAIL,
ALIAS OLD IKE,
CONFIDENCE.

11

JOHN LARNEY,
ALIAS MOLLIE MATCHES,
BANK SNEAK AND BURGLAR.

12

EDWARD RICE,
ALIAS BIG RICE,
CONFIDENCE AND HOTEL SNEAK.

13

WILLIAM OGLE,
ALIAS BILLY OGLE—FRANK SOMERS,
BURGLAR AND FORGER.

14

CHAS. O. VANDERPOOL,
ALIAS CHAS. O. BROCKWAY,
FORGER AND COUNTERFEITER.

15

JOSEPH COOK,
ALIAS GEO. HAVILL—HARRY THORN,
BANK BURGLAR, SNEAK AND FORGER.

16

FREDERICK ELLIOTT,
ALIAS JOE ELLIOTT—JOE REILLY,
FORGER.

17

LESTER BEACH,
FORGER.

18

CHARLES BECKER,
ALIAS CHARLEY BECKER,
FORGER.

19

JOHN HOPE,
ALIAS WATSON,
MANHATTAN BANK BURGLAR.

20

JAMES HOPE,
ALIAS OLD MAN HOPE,
BANK BURGLAR.

21

JOHN CLARE,
ALIAS GILMORE,
BANK BURGLAR.

22

LANGDON W. MOORE,
ALIAS CHARLEY ADAMS,
BANK BURGLAR.

23

DANIEL WATSON,
ALIAS DUTCH DAN—KANE,
BURGLAR AND TOOL MAKER.

24

GEORGE MASON,
ALIAS GORDON,
BANK BURGLAR.

Company, telling him that his mother in California had a large amount of railroad bonds which she wanted to obtain a loan upon, to buy real estate. Sheridan gave him the bonds ($125,000), and received a certified check for $84,000, which he cashed at once and divided with his accomplices, Andy Roberts, Valentine Gleason, and Charles B. Orvis; after which he and Martha Hargraves went to Europe, taking with them 200 of the same $1,000 forged bonds to place in the European market.

They went to Switzerland, and put up at the house of a well known English ticket-of-leave man. In their absence, one day, the daughter of this ex-convict stole the bonds from Sheridan's trunk. When accused of the theft she said that she heard that the police were coming to the house to search it, and had burned them, when in fact she had given them to her father, who afterwards realized considerable money from them. Sheridan and Martha returned to America, and Sheridan was shortly after arrested in Washington, D. C., for this forgery, brought to New York, tried, convicted, and sentenced to five years in Sing Sing prison, for forgery in the third degree, on March 6, 1877. Roberts and Gleason were also arrested in this case, and were confined in Ludlow Street Jail, New York, for years.

Sheridan was an associate of Horace Hovan (25), Johnny Jourdan (83), Billy Burke (162), George Carson (3), Tommy Mulligan, Joe McCloskey, Dave Cummings (50), and other first-class men.

Sheridan was arrested again in Philadelphia, Pa., for a "pennyweight job"—a box of diamonds—and sentenced to three years in the Eastern Penitentiary and fined $500, on October 6, 1881. His time expired early in 1884.

He was arrested again in St. Louis, Mo., on November 19, 1884, under the name of John Holcom, by the United States authorities, for having three counterfeit $500 bills in his possession, and sentenced to two years in State prison in the latter part of November, 1884.

See record of George Wilkes, also.

Sheridan's picture is a good one, taken in 1876.

9

WILLIAM COLEMAN, alias BILLY COLEMAN.

BURGLAR AND BANK SNEAK.

DESCRIPTION.

Thirty years old in 1886. Born in United States. Married. No trade. Slim build. Height, 5 feet 11½ inches. Weight, 155 pounds. A fine, tall, smooth-faced fellow. Brown hair, blue eyes, fair complexion; wears a No. 9 shoe. Has W. C. and N. Y. in India ink on right arm, slight scar on the right side of face, mole in the centre of his back.

RECORD.

Billy Coleman was born in New York, and is well known in all the principal cities in America, especially in Chicago, where he has lived.

He was arrested in Poughkeepsie, N. Y., and sentenced to Sing Sing prison for five years, on October 14, 1869, for burglary in the third degree. He escaped from Sing Sing on a tugboat on August 17, 1871. After his escape he went South, and was convicted and sentenced to three years in Pittsburgh, Pa., and served his time in the Western Penitentiary.

He was arrested again in New York City for attempting to pick pockets, and sentenced to one year in the penitentiary in the Court of Special Sessions, New York, on January 22, 1876, under the name of Thomas Moriarty. After his discharge he went West, and the record shows that he was arrested in Chicago, Ill., and sentenced to one year in Joliet prison on March 9, 1882. His time expired in January, 1883.

Coleman then started around the country with Rufe Minor (1) and Johnny Price, sneaking banks. Coleman and Price were arrested in Augusta, Ga., on March 26, 1884, for sneaking a package of money, $2,700, from a safe in that city. After abstracting $150 from the package and dividing it, Coleman, Rufe Minor and Price parted for a few days. Two days afterwards Price and Coleman were arrested, and shortly afterwards tried and convicted; they were sentenced to seven years in State prison each on May 7, 1884. Rufe Minor came north and was arrested in New York City on June 28, 1884, and taken to Augusta, Ga., by a requisition. Coleman has been arrested and convicted of several other robberies throughout the country, under aliases. This fact makes it difficult to give data correctly.

He still owes time in Sing Sing prison, N. Y.

His picture is a good one.

10

ISAAC VAIL, alias OLD IKE.

CONFIDENCE.

DESCRIPTION.

Fifty-one years old in 1886. Born in United States. Married. Slim build. Height, 5 feet 11 inches. Weight, 178 pounds. Gray hair, brown eyes, light complexion, gray whiskers. Generally wears a goatee. A tall, thin, gentlemanly-looking man.

RECORD.

IKE VAIL is well known from Maine to California. Of late years he has confined himself to the eastern cities, and the confidence man may be seen almost any morning around railroad depots or steamboat landings in search of victims. He has done service in several prisons, and his history would fill an ordinary sized book. I will simply give one or two of his later convictions, to assist in convicting him should he fall into the meshes of the law again.

Vail was arrested in New York City on February 20, 1880, for swindling one Levi P. Thompson, a Justice of Peace of Evensville, Minn., out of $60, by the confidence game. He pleaded guilty in this case, in the Court of General Sessions, New York City, and was sentenced to eighteen months in State prison by Judge Cowing, on February 26, 1880.

Vail was arrested several times afterwards in Boston, New York, and other cities, and again in New York City on August 30, 1885, for attempting to ply his vocation on the steamer Glasgow, lying at Pier 20, North River. For this offense he was sentenced to six months in the penitentiary on Blackwell's Island, on a complaint of vagrancy, as he had obtained no money from his victim. He was, however, discharged by Judge Van Brunt in the Supreme Court, on a writ on September 4, 1885.

Vail's picture is an excellent one, taken in 1880.

11

JOHN LARNEY, alias MOLLIE MATCHES.

PICKPOCKET, BANK BURGLAR, ETC.

DESCRIPTION.

Forty-seven years old in 1886. Born in United States. Married. No trade. Stout build. Height, 5 feet 7½ inches. Weight, 160 pounds. Brown hair, hazel eyes. Wears a No. 7 shoe, and generally wears a full dark beard. He has two upper teeth out on right side ; also a small India-ink mark between thumb and forefinger of left hand. Straight nose. Part of an anchor on one arm.

RECORD.

" MOLLIE MATCHES," or JOHN LARNEY, which is his right name, although a talented thief, was always an outspoken one. He makes his home in Cleveland, O.; wears fine clothes, which is his weakness ; seldom indulges in liquor, never to excess ; he has an aversion to tobacco. When he settled down in Cleveland, in 1875, he said he was going to live honestly if the police would let him. For some reason or another he failed to do so. The great fault with Mollie was the freedom with which he talked of his affairs, to which failing he ultimately owed his downfall. The act that made Larney notorious and gave him his alias was on the occasion of a large celebration in New York City, when he was a boy. He disguised himself as a match girl, and, basket in hand, mingled with the crowds in the streets. Being slight in form and having delicate features, the boy had no difficulty in carrying out the deception. His day's work, it is said, netted him over $2,000, and the nickname of " Mollie Matches." During the war Mollie attained great eminence as a bounty jumper. He says that he enlisted in ninety-three Ohio, Pennsylvania, Massachusetts and New York regiments. Being of a frugal disposition, and having an eye to comfort in his old age, he invested in property in Toronto and Silver Creek, Canada, which he still holds under the name of John Dolan. Later he bought real estate in Cleveland, O. Mollie Matches has become pretty well known all over the United States. At the age of thirty-three years he had served eleven years in various reformatories and penal institutions, and was still indebted twelve years' time to others from which he had escaped. He still owes six years to a Massachusetts State prison where he was sentenced to for seven years. He staid there just nine months; he had the freedom of the jail-yard on account of his eyesight failing him; he finally recovered his liberty and eyesight both. About seven years after his escape he was again sent to the same prison, which was in Salem, and served a sixteen months' sentence without being recognized. The adventures through which this man passed are wonderful. He is believed to have realized by his tricks about $150,000, a large portion of which he has paid out lately to lawyers.

Mollie was convicted at Galesburg, Ill., for robbing the Farmers' and Mechanics' Bank of that city, and was sentenced to ten years in State prison at Joliet, Ill., on July 17, 1882. At a trial in Cleveland, O., on January 14, 1885, the above bank obtained a judgment of $12,000 against Mollie. An associate of his, Eddie Guerin, testified on this trial as follows: "After I had concluded that the Galesburg Bank was an easy one to work, I sent for 'Mollie Matches' and two others. They agreed with me. One of them went to a neighboring town and hired a horse and wagon containing a large dry goods box. We hitched the team near the bank about noon. 'Mollie' watched the president and treasurer go out of the bank, and immediately entered it and went to the cashier and proceeded to buy a New York draft, with small silver, making much noise. Another man stood near by holding up a paper that screened the third man, who sneaked in and took $9,600 off the desk alongside the cashier, while Mollie was arguing with him about the draft. Mollie admitted to the cashier that he had made a mistake as to the amount of money he had with him, and gathering up what he had, said he would go for some more. Once outside, the 'look-out,' the sneak and Mollie (the 'stall') jumped into the wagon, and were driven by the fourth man to the railroad depot, and all escaped. It was months afterwards that Mollie was arrested in Cincinnati, O., on December 21, 1881, and taken back to Galesburg for trial.

His picture is a fair one, although a copy.

12

EDWARD RICE, alias BIG RICE.

CONFIDENCE AND HOTEL MAN.

DESCRIPTION.

Forty-eight years old in 1886. Stout build. Height, 5 feet 10 inches. Weight, about 180 pounds. A fine, large, well-built man. Very gentlemanly appearance. Born in United States. Married. Brown hair, light brown beard, light complexion.

RECORD.

BIG RICE, as he is familiarly called, is well known in all the principal cities in the United States. He is a very clever general thief, a good "stall," confidence man and "pennyweight" and hotel worker. He has traveled from the Atlantic to the Pacific at the expense of others, and has served at least twenty years in State prison during his life, ten years of which was in one sentence. Rice, in 1870, was implicated in a bank robbery in Halifax, N. S., with Horace Hovan and another man; the latter two were arrested, and Rice escaped and finally sent back the $20,000 stolen from the bank vault, and Hovan and the other man were discharged.

Rice was arrested in New York City, on April 24, 1878, for complicity in the robbery of the National Bank of Cambridgeport, Mass., which occurred in September, 1877. He gave the name of Albert C. Moore. He was discharged in New York City on April 31, 1878, the Governor of Massachusetts refusing to grant a requisition for him. He was immediately arrested by the Sheriff of New York on a civil process, the bank having commenced a civil action against him for the recovery of the money stolen from the bank, about $12,000. On May 8, 1878, Judge Pratt, of Brooklyn, N. Y., vacated the order of arrest and removed the attachment off his house on Thirteenth Street, Brooklyn, N. Y., and he was discharged. He was at once arrested on a requisition from Massachusetts, one having been obtained during his confinement on the civil charge, and he was taken to Cambridgeport, Mass., for trial, which never came off, on account of there not being sufficient evidence to convict him. Rice was also charged with robbing the Lechmere National Bank of East Cambridge of $50,000, on Saturday, March 16, 1878. When arrested he had in his possession a number of United States bonds of $1,000, and a bogus check for $850.

Ed. Rice, Joe Dubuque, and a party named Frank Stewart were arrested in Rochester, N. Y., on April 29, 1881, by officers from Detroit, Mich., charged with having early in April, 1881, stolen $728 worth of diamonds and jewelry from a jewelry store in that city. They were also charged with the larceny of $5,000 in money from the banking-house of Fisher, Preston & Co., of that city, in July, 1880.

Rice was taken back to Detroit on a requisition, when an additional charge was made against him of complicity in the robbery of the First National Bank. He was bailed out in September, 1881, and forfeited it. He was re-arrested in Syracuse, N. Y., in July, 1885, and taken back to Detroit, and in an effort to save himself from punishment in this case, he accused one Joseph Harris, who was keeping a saloon in Chicago, of it. Harris was arrested in Chicago, on July 29, 1885, and taken to Detroit for trial. Rice was discharged after an examination by a magistrate on September 1, 1885. He was arrested again on a requisition from Ohio the same day, but discharged in a few days on a writ of habeas corpus.

Rice was arrested again in Boston, Mass., on June 11, 1886, where he had just arrived from Canada, and delivered to the Cincinnati police authorities, who wanted him for a burglary committed in that city in the fall of 1883. Paddy Guerin, who was with him in this burglary, was arrested and sentenced to four years in State prison.

Rice's picture is a very good one.

13

WILLIAM OGLE, alias BILLY OGLE,

alias FRANK SOMERS.

BURGLAR AND FORGER.

DESCRIPTION.

Thirty-two years old in 1886. Born in New York. Medium build. Married. Height, 5 feet 7½ inches. Weight, 148 pounds. Brown hair, brown eyes, fair complexion. Wears sandy mustache and sometimes side whiskers.

RECORD.

BILLY OGLE is a good general thief. He fell in with Charles Vanderpool, alias Brockway, some years ago, and worked with him up to the Providence job in August, 1880. He does not confine himself to any particular kind of work. He is a handy burglar, good sneak, and first-class second-story man.

Ogle was arrested in Chicago with Charles Vanderpool, alias Brockway, in 1879, for forgery on the First National Bank of that city. Brockway was bailed in $10,000, in consequence of some information he gave to the authorities, and the case never was tried. Ogle was also finally discharged. He was arrested shortly after, in 1879, in Orange, N. J., for an attempt at burglary, and on a second trial he luckily escaped with six months' imprisonment. Ogle was again arrested in New York City and convicted for uttering a forged check for $2,490, drawn on the Phœnix Bank of New York, purported to be signed by Purss & Young, brokers, of Wall Street, New York City. He was sentenced to five years in State prison by Judge Cowing, on June 14, 1880. His counsel appealed the case, and Judge Donohue, of the Supreme Court, granted him a new trial, and he was released on $2,500 bail in July, 1880. Andy Gilligan and Charles Farren, alias the "Big Duke," were also arrested in connection with this forgery. While out on bail in this case, Ogle was again arrested in Providence, R. I., on August 16, 1880, with Charles O. Brockway and Joe Cook, alias Havill, a Chicago sneak, in an attempt to pass two checks, one on the Fourth National Bank for $1,327, and the other, of $1,264, on the old National Bank of that city. He was convicted for this offense, and sentenced to three years in State prison on October 2, 1880, under the name of Frank Somers. His time expired in August, 1883. He was arrested again in the spring of 1884 for a "second-story job," with John Tracy, alias Big Tracy. They robbed the residence of John W. Pangborn, on Belmont Avenue, Jersey City Heights, of diamonds and jewelry valued at $1,500. He was convicted for this offense on June 26, 1884. His counsel obtained a new trial for him in July, 1884, upon which he was tried and acquitted. Big Tracy was also discharged, and they both went West. In the fall of 1885 Ogle was arrested in Tennessee, and sentenced to ten years in the penitentiary for house work. He shortly afterwards made his escape from a gang while working out on a railroad, and is now at large.

Ogle's picture is a good one, taken in 1880.

14

CHARLES O. VANDERPOOL, alias BROCKWAY.

FORGER AND COUNTERFEITER.

DESCRIPTION.

Fifty-one years old in 1876. Born in United States. Married. Medium build. Dark curly hair, blue eyes, sallow complexion. Height, 5 feet 9¼ inches. Weight, 160 pounds. Black beard.

RECORD.

CHARLES O. BROCKWAY, whose right name is Vanderpool, is one of the cleverest forgers in America. He has no doubt been responsible for several forgeries that have been committed in America during the past fifteen years. He at one time kept a faro bank in partnership of Daniel Dyson, alias Dan Noble, who is now serving twenty years in Europe for forgery. He subsequently branched out as a counterfeiter, and served two terms in State prison for it. The last one, of five years, was done in Auburn, New York, State prison. His time expired there in 1878. He afterwards went West, and was arrested in Chicago, Ill., with Billy Ogle, in June, 1879, for forgery on the First National Bank of that city. At the time of his arrest a full set of forgers' implements was found in his room. He made a confession, and charged an ex-government detective with having brought him to Chicago and picked out the banks for him to work. This statement was corroborated by a subsequent confession of Billy Ogle. The authorities indicted the ex-detective, and Brockway was admitted to bail in $10,000. The case never went to trial for lack of other evidence to corroborate Brockway and Ogle, who were both men of bad character.

Brockway came back to New York, where he was credited with doing considerable work. The following banks are said to have been victimized through him : The Second National Bank, the Chemical National Bank, the Bank of the Republic, the Chatham National Bank, the Corn Exchange Bank, and the Phœnix National Bank.

He was finally arrested at Providence, R. I., on August 16, 1880, with Billy Ogle (13) and Joe Cook, alias Havill (15), a Chicago sneak, in an attempt to pass a check on the Fourth National Bank for $1,327, and another on the old National Bank for $1,264. Brockway pleaded guilty to two indictments for forgery, and was sentenced to eight years in State prison at Providence, R. I., on October 2, 1880.

His time will expire, allowing full commutation, on August 26, 1886. See commutation laws of Rhode Island.

Brockway's picture is a good one, taken in 1880.

15

JOSEPH COOK, alias GEO. HAVILL,
alias HARRY THORN.
FORGER AND SNEAK.

DESCRIPTION.

Thirty-nine years old in 1886. Born in Canada. Slim build. Height, 5 feet 8 inches. Weight, 145 pounds. Light hair, blue eyes, light complexion.

RECORD.

"COOK," or HAVILL, which is his right name, is a Chicago sneak thief. He came East with Brockway in 1869. Brockway used him in a few transactions in New York, and afterwards in Providence, R. I., where he was arrested with Brockway and Billy Ogle on August 16, 1880, for attempting to pass two forged checks, one on the Fourth National Bank and another on the old National Bank of that city. Havill was convicted under the name of Joseph Cook for this offense, and was sentenced to four years in State prison at Providence, R. I., on October 2, 1880. His time expired March 14, 1884.

Havill was arrested near Elmira, N. Y., on February 14, 1885, in company with John Love (68), Charles Lowery, Frank McCrann and Mike Blake, for robbing the Osceola Bank of Pennsylvania, and sentenced to nine years and nine months in State prison on April 9, 1885, under the name of Harry Thorn.

His picture is a good one, taken in 1880.

16

FREDERICK ELLIOTT, alias JOE ELLIOTT,
alias JOE REILLY.
FORGER.

DESCRIPTION.

Thirty-one years old in 1886. Born in United States. Married. No trade. Slim build. Height, 5 feet 3 inches. Weight, about 115 pounds. Black hair, black eyes, dark complexion. Generally wears a black mustache, sometimes a full black beard, not very heavy growth.

RECORD.

"JOE ELLIOTT," or JOE REILLY, which is his right name, is well known from his connection with Charley Becker, the notorious forger and counterfeiter. In 1873, when Reilly was a boy, he was taken to Europe by Becker, who, in company with Joe

Chapman and Ivan Siscovitch, alias Adams, a Russian, and others, flooded Turkey with forged sight drafts. All of them were arrested and sentenced to three years and six months each in prison at Smyrna, in Turkey. Becker, Elliott and the Russian made their escape, went to Europe, and lived with Joe Chapman's wife in London. One day Mrs. Chapman was found dead, and all her money and jewelry were missing. The escaped forgers were suspected of the murder, and left for America shortly after. Siscovitch opened a drinking saloon under Booth's Theatre, New York City, which place was headquarters for all the noted forgers in America.

The following interesting account of Elliott, which was published, has been corrected, and is here given :

"Little Joe" Elliott, forger and bank robber! Who would ever imagine that such an inoffensive-looking little man as he could ever be guilty of crime? And yet "Little Joe's" face is one of the best known in the Rogues' Gallery. He started in at shoplifting when he was only a boy; advanced from a position of sneak thief to the rank of bank robber, and finally was graduated as an expert forger. He has committed crimes all over this continent and in half the countries of the other, and has seen the inside of at least a score of prisons.

There is nothing wicked in the appearance of "Little Joe." He has proved himself a desperate man when actively engaged in professional work, but away from it he was polite and gentlemanly. He dressed well, was quick-witted, a ready conversationalist and withal quite a dashing young fellow. He kept company with many of the most aristocratic young bloods about town and could set up as much champagne in a night as any of them. He always had money. Very few knew him to be a thief, most of them looking on him as a well-to-do sporting man.

This was "Little Joe" as he was when he first met Kate Castleton, the actress, and won her affections. It was about ten years ago, and she was playing at the time with the San Francisco Minstrels in this city. "Little Joe" was a regular patron of the theatres, and in one of his nightly tours he heard Kate sing. She was then a fresh, rosy-cheeked girl, a trifle younger than she is to-day, and the bad little man was charmed with her. He was introduced to her by a young blood, courted her three days, and then was married to her at the Little Church Around the Corner. It was one night after her customary performance had taken place. She wore her stage clothing, and every member of her company went with her. There were a number of young men about town present also, and after the wedding there was a great dinner at Delmonico's. The couple made a wedding tour, which lasted a month, and then settled down in elegantly furnished quarters in Twenty-first Street.

Miss Castleton was aware of her husband's true character when she married him, but he promised to give up his unlawful profession and lead an honest life, assuring her that he had enough money to support them both for a while, and that when that had gone he could earn more. He insisted on her leaving the stage and for a while they lived happily. Then Kate went back to the stage once more against her husband's will, and a cloud darkened the domestic horizon. It arose and increased in blackness until "Little Joe" became tired of his quiet life and went back to his old tricks. In the early part of April, 1877, he was arrested for forging a draft for $64,000 on the

New York Life Insurance Company. While on the way to the Tombs, on June 9, 1877, he made his escape. He was re-arrested on February 21, 1878, and identified as having been concerned in an $8,000 robbery from a Boston jeweler. He pleaded guilty and was sentenced to four years in State prison, on November 13, 1878, for the $64,000 forgery. Becker turned State's evidence and secured immunity for himself.

Kate's affection for him was renewed with his trouble, and she visited him as often as prison regulations would permit. Indeed, it is said that she won the hearts of his keepers in the course of time, and was permitted to visit him more frequently. She also tried in many ways to have him pardoned, and went so far as to pay the governor a personal visit and intercede in his behalf. All her efforts, however, were futile, and " Little Joe" was obliged to serve out his time, less a generous commutation for good behavior.

After his release from prison, on November 12, 1881, the brilliant young swindler made a second vow to reform and became his wife's manager. He became jealous, however, because of her many admirers, and secured a divorce, only to re-marry her again within a year. He was her manager for a time three years ago, while she was starring in " Pop" at the Bijou. Jealousy made trouble for them once more and they parted forever. The last straw which broke the back of their domestic happiness was a young man of wealth and position who became infatuated with Kate. " Little Joe" thought that his wife returned the young man's affection, and decided to end matters. He found that his rival was in the habit of seeing Kate home when he failed to call for her, and one night he " laid in wait for them." He met them, arm in arm, at the junction of Broadway and Sixth Avenue, just as the crowds from the theatres were going home. His rival was at least three sizes larger than he, but he hit him under the ear which dropped him, after which " Little Joe" proceeded to walk on him. He left him fearfully bruised and mangled, and quietly slipped away just in time to escape the police. Thereafter he refused to recognize his wife and deserted her. Kate has since married Harry Phillips, the manager of "Crazy Patch," in which she is now playing. " Little Joe" had been abroad a short time previous to his first marriage to Miss Castleton, and he was suspected of having a guilty knowledge of the murder of Mary Chapman, in London, which occurred about ten years ago. Mary Chapman was the wife of Joseph B. Chapman, the famous American forger and counterfeiter. " Little Joe" had a short time previously been convicted of forgery in Constantinople, Turkey, and was sentenced to imprisonment. (See record of No. 18.) Chapman and Carlo Siscovitch, alias " The Dago," were sentenced with him. Mrs. Chapman learned of her husband's imprisonment while she was in London, and went at once to Constantinople to see what could be done. She visited the prison, and found that her husband was confined in a dark cell for breach of discipline, and could not be seen. She had an interview, however, with " Little Joe" and " The Dago," and furnished them with tools to break jail, with the understanding that they should bring her husband out with them. The men promised, and were supplied with saws and files which the woman took to them concealed in her clothing. As a matter of precaution she started back to London before they broke out. A few months later the two men made their escape, leaving Chapman behind, and returned to London.

Mrs. Chapman was very angry when she learned of their treachery, and threatened to expose them to the police. A few weeks later her body was found in bed, having died suddenly, and was not murdered, as has been heretofore reported. "Little Joe" and Siscovitch shortly after sailed for America, arriving in July, 1876.

Joe Reilly, alias Elliott, Gus Raymond and George Wilkes were arrested in New York City on March 16, 1886, for forgeries committed in Rochester, N. Y. Raymond was discharged, and Elliott and Wilkes were delivered to the police authorities of Rochester, N. Y., and taken there. The following is a newspaper account of their transactions in that city:

ROCHESTER, March 18, 1886.—Much interest is felt here over the arrest in New York of Wilkes and Elliott, the forgers. They came to Rochester during the races last August (1885). Wilkes remained a night at the new Osborne House, under the name of Gordon. He is believed to have prepared the draft with three signatures, which was very carefully drawn, and purporting to have been issued by the Bank of Montreal on the Bank of the Republic at New York. Elliott, under the name of Edwards, worked with a confederate who went under the name of James W. Conklin. These two rented offices near each other, and each hired a clerk. Conklin opened an account at the Commercial National Bank, and Elliott, alias Edwards, opened one at the Flour City National Bank. Edwards deposited the draft, and on August 10, 1885, sent his clerk, a young man named Blum, to get $2,500 on a check, which was paid. Conklin tried the same tactics at the Commercial Bank, but his clerk was told to have him call, which he failed to do. Two weeks later they turned up in Dayton, O., and tried to work the same game, after changing names. President Hathaway, of the Flour City Bank, says that Elliott can positively be identified as the man who left at that bank the forged $2,500 draft.

Elliott was tried and convicted, on May 11, 1886, and was sentenced to fifteen years in State prison, for forgery on the Flour City Bank of Rochester, N. Y., on May 14, 1886, by Judge Morgan, County Judge of Monroe County, N. Y.

One David Lynch, alias George Edwards, was arrested in New York City on April 30, 1886, in connection with these forgeries. He was taken to Rochester, pleaded guilty, and was used as a witness to convict Elliott. He was sentenced on the same day with Elliott to five years in State prison, by Judge Morgan.

See records of Nos. 18, 26, and George Wilkes.

Elliott's picture is an excellent one, taken in April, 1877.

17

LESTER BEACH.

FORGER.

DESCRIPTION.

Fifty-nine years old in 1886. Born in United States. Married. Painter. Stout build. Height, 5 feet 9 inches. Weight, 166 pounds. Gray hair, brown eyes, light complexion. Heavy nose lines and wrinkles under the eyes. Hair thin on top of head. Generally wears a brown and gray mustache.

RECORD.

LESTER BEACH is a well known forger, having been arrested several times. He is an associate of Charles R. Titus, alias Doctor Thompson (44), another professional forger, who attempted to pass a forged check for $100,000, drawn on J. B. Colgate & Co., brokers, of No. 47 Wall Street, New York City, in 1869.

Beach was arrested in New York City on November 26, 1878, in company of Titus, charged with having obtained $70 from Morris Steinhart, of No. 67 Hudson Street, New York City, on a bogus certified check on the Bank of New York. He stated when arrested that he was furnished the check by a man named Browning, who was to meet him and receive the proceeds. This man proved to be Dr. Titus. Additional complaints were made against Beach by R. J. Clay, of No. 176 Broadway, and G. F. Morse, of No. 174 South Fifth Avenue, New York City. Mr. Clay stated that Beach obtained $30 from him on a certified check on the Newark City, N. J., National Bank, which proved to be a forgery. Mr. Morse stated that he had given Beach $99 on a certified check for $100 on the Merchants' Bank of Brooklyn, N. Y., which also proved worthless.

Beach was tried and convicted of forgery in the Steinhart case, and sentenced to three years and six months in State prison at Sing Sing, N. Y., on December 18, 1879, by Judge Gildersleeve, in the Court of General Sessions, in New York City.

See record of No. 40.

Beach's picture is an excellent one, taken in November, 1876.

18

CHARLES BECKER, alias CHARLEY BECKER.

FORGER AND COUNTERFEITER.

DESCRIPTION.

Thirty-eight years old in 1886. Born in Germany. Trade, engraver. Stout build. Height, 5 feet 6 inches. Weight, 170 pounds. Iron-gray hair, hazel eyes, light complexion. Generally wears a brown mustache.

RECORD.

CHARLEY BECKER is a native of Wurtemberg, Germany, but came to America when a mere lad, and learned the engraver's trade. His expertness as an engraver led him to associate with George Engles, George Wilkes, and other celebrated forgers and counterfeiters, and he soon became their most valuable ally. He first came into notoriety through his connection with the robbery of the Third National Bank of Baltimore, Md., in August, 1872. He fled to Europe with Joe Elliott, alias Little Joe, where they met Joe Chapman, Ivan Siscovitch, a Russian, and others, and at once started in to flood Turkey with forged sight drafts. All hands were arrested, convicted, and sentenced to three years and six months each in prison at Smyrna, in Turkey. Becker, Elliott, and Siscovitch made their escape, went to Europe, and lived a while with Joe Chapman's wife in London. One day Mrs. Chapman, who knew their secrets, was found dead. All her money and jewelry was missing. Siscovitch was suspected for the murder, and left at once for America. Becker and Elliott also arrived in America in July, 1876. Siscovitch opened a saloon under Booth's Theatre, New York, which was the headquarters of nearly all the forgers in this country at that time. Becker, Joe Elliott, alias Little Joe, and Clement Herring, Becker's father-in-law, were arrested in New York City on April 10, 1877, for the $64,000 forgery on the Union Trust Company of New York. Elliot was convicted on Becker's testimony, who turned State's evidence to save himself.

Becker and George Engles were arrested again on January 1, 1881, on suspicion of being engaged in a scheme with George Wilkes and others, then under arrest in Florence, Italy, to issue large quantities of forged mercantile paper in Europe. They were turned over to the United States authorities upon an application of the Vice-Consul of Italy, and were confined in Ludlow Street jail to await an application for their extradition, which was not granted. They were both discharged by Commissioner Osborn in the United States Court on January 5, 1881.

Becker and one Nathan Marks were arrested in Brooklyn, N. Y., on September 16, 1881, charged with counterfeiting a 1,000-franc note of the Bank of France. They lay in Raymond Street jail until October 3, 1881, when they were bailed by Justice Pratt, of Brooklyn, in the sum of $20,000. Becker was finally convicted and sentenced to six years and six months in the Kings County Penitentiary, December 14, 1881, for the 1,000-franc note forgery, by Judge Moore.

Becker, Elliott, and Chapman, after many professional exploits in America, England, and on the Continent, either tired of Europe, or else, having worked the European field to a perilous extent, sallied into Turkey. They did not counterfeit Turkish money, because it isn't worth counterfeiting. Money that takes a hatful to pay for a drink is too debased for imitative genius to trifle with. Instead, the trio posed as travelers and victimized local banks with letters of credit, indorsed by somebody with a solid financial standing, and made encouraging progress until brought up with a round turn in Smyrna. Here they were locked up and convicted, getting three and a half years apiece.

The following is a detailed account of Becker's escape from the Constantinople concierge, in company of Joe Elliott and Siscovitch, obtained from Becker while confined in Kings County, N. Y., Penitentiary, on March 19, 1886, by a reporter, in presence of the warden:

Becker said, "The jail at Smyrna hadn't anything but mud walls, and we'd have left it quick enough if we'd cared to. It was the country, not the jail, that held us. We couldn't get out of the country.

"The authorities, lacking confidence in the jail, shipped us to Constantinople, where we were put into a prison of the old-fashioned sort, with walls four feet in thickness, solid cell doors and caststeel grate-bars an inch and a half square, and of this seclusion we soon tired. It chanced on the day we were convicted in Smyrna that Carlo Siscovitch was gathered in at Constantinople for working the very same game. Funny, wasn't it, that there should have been another American in the same line? If he'd read the papers he'd have known that the art had ceased to be popular in Turkey, but he didn't. The result was that we fell into each other's company. When we got tired we began planning to get out. And let me say here that the story about Chapman's wife coming to our aid and we going off leaving her husband inside was all wrong, as well as the yarn that Elliott had murdered her because she made him trouble later in London ; all wrong, the whole." Here Mr. Becker paused to chuckle intensely, and proceeded : " It wasn't Chapman's wife at all that came to our help, but it was the wife of Siscovitch. The 'Dago?' well, I never heard him called that. They call all Italians and Portuguese that, though, and he, in my opinion, was born in Trieste, or some Austro-Italian town. I knew him then as Howard Adams, or Charles Adams, something of the sort with an Adams in it, and as an American. His wife came and helped us out. It took a month, almost, before we could fix things. Did we leave Chapman inside? We did. There was good reason for it. He gave us away three times, and as we wanted to get out we didn't include him in the fourth attempt. The cell doors locked with top and bottom bolts, and though each had its key, there was a general key that fitted all of them. A key like that was useful, and it was by a mere accident that we got one. It happened one day that the prison marshal—they don't have wardens there—came rushing in to have a prisoner sign some papers, and rushed out again, leaving his key sticking in the keyhole. It wasn't very long before we had an impression of it, and it was back in the lock again."

Here Mr. Becker's emotions quite mastered him, and the innocent reporter's query as to where he got his wax, added to his merriment until he was forced to extract a handkerchief from the basement of his zebra trousers and mildly smother himself. Then he explained kindly that wax wasn't at all necessary, for soap or bread or anything soft that could hold together would answer just as well. Casually remarking that the prison was stronger than the Flatbush article, Mr. Becker continued :

"After getting the shape of the key we had Mrs. Siscovitch bring us two blank keys, some little files, Turkish caps and three lanterns. She smuggled them in. You see you've got to carry a lantern if you're going to travel in Constantinople. The streets are dark. Chapman, Elliott and I were in one cell. Siscovitch was in with some sailors around the corner of the corridor. . I was the last man to be shut up at night. So when we were all ready, and had put enough rope where it was wanted, I slipped around and unlocked the door of Siscovitch's apartment and then went back to be locked up. About midnight when the guards were snoring, he gets out and in turn unlocks our door. Chapman was asleep. Did we wake him ? Not much. He'd have hollered murder if we had. We went out and steered at once for the store-room where our clothes were piled away—put there you know when we went in. We broke open the store-room, got our things, and then found our way into the yard and sized up the prison wall. It was forty-two feet high, but fortunately there was a grating over the arching of the gate and our rope was ready. We boosted little Elliott up on the arch way, and as luck would have it he stepped on the wire of the prison bell leading into the room where the keeper's head clerk slept, and set it to jingling in a way that froze us stiff. The jig looked up if ever it did. We'd had lots of fun with that bell. The wire ran under the cell window on its way, and we used to hitch a bent pin to a string and fooled him many times by setting her to going."

Here Mr. Becker's emotions again brought salt water to his eyes, as his memory bore him back to the clanging bell and the deceived and wrathful Ottoman officeholder. When he overcame them he went on :

" It was lucky we had fooled him in that way so often. If the bell woke him up he concluded it was another joke and went to sleep again. We waited fifteen minutes for somebody to come and catch us, and then went at it again. The rope was weighted with a piece of wood, and we threw it over the wall to catch it at the grating, and by fastening it there were able to climb to the top. There was enough rope beside the loop to reach to the ground, and down it we scrambled to-run into more trouble. We woke up right away about sixty Mohammedan dogs, who had been snoozing peacefully in the shadow of the wall. I never heard curs bark louder ; but they brought no one. Sliding down the rope Elliott dropped the matches and we couldn't light the lanterns. All three of us got down on the ground and hunted. By-and-by we found one brimstone splinter, and lighted up. The dogs stopped howling then. They do not howl at people who are properly illuminated, and we traveled on to find the apartments which Mrs. Siscovitch had engaged. While hunting around we heard the rapping of watchmen's night sticks and dropped into an all night café filled with Greeks, where a band was playing, had some coffee, and stayed until morning. Half-a-dozen of the watch came in, but they did not know us. We were pretty well disguised and topped off with fezzes. Finally we got settled with Mrs. Siscovitch, but one day she glanced out of the window and saw the cavasse or interpreter from the American consulate, and the porter who had brought her baggage to the place, staring straight at the house ; then we knew they were after us, and didn't wait five minutes. We went out and hired a cab, not knowing which way to go, but telling the man to take us toward the English Cemetery. There we stopped at a café, and were sitting about our wine wondering what had better next be done, when a man came up who had seen Siscovitch tried. He knew us !"

Here Mr. Becker looked grateful, and professing not to know the obliging gentleman's name continued :

" He took us to his home and took care of us for two months. I sent Elliott to England after some money I had there, and when it came we went to London also. We made our friend a good present and he saw us safe over the border."

The warden asked what inducement this man, presumably a Greek, had for his extraordinary benevolence. Mr. Becker said he didn't know, but guessed he did it out of natural sympathy. They promised him a good present, though, and gave it to him. That was all. With a confidence in humanity shaken by five years of prison care, the warden shook his head, but Becker only smiled and began to wind up his story :

" Mrs. Siscovitch was arrested and held a while, but got off and rejoined her husband in London. I gave them funds to get to America and supposed they had gone ; hoped so, for I did not like the fellow. Both Elliott and I went to board with

Mrs. Chapman. I'd known her for years, and Elliott had left his things with her before going into the Orient. Didn't she feel mad at our leaving her husband in the crib? Not at all. She knew what he was; he'd no courage. His giving us away was to earn commutation time. Now about the story of her murder: I hadn't been there long before who should turn up but Siscovitch and his wife, seeking lodgings, with a letter of introduction to Mrs. Chapman from an American friend. I left them. I didn't trust him. Elliott had left before. He was somewhere in Germany and I in Paris, two months afterward, when we heard she was killed, and both came right back to London to testify if need be. When the jury found that she might have died of heart disease, and that if poisoned there was no sign of it, we came back to America, and I guess my story from that time on is pretty well known."

Again Mr. Becker chuckled softly to say:

"Do I think she was murdered? I hardly know. Where was Siscovitch? Well, he left her house either the day before or ten minutes before she died. I shall always think he took her jewels and perhaps more. She had plenty of money in the house and some in the Post-office Bank. I know this, for I paid her eighty pounds, Elliott as much more, and she had two other gentlemen boarders. She often offered to help me out if I needed it. What makes me think he took her jewelry is that a friend of mine met him a year or so later in the Bowery, New York, loaded down with rings and pins. I doubt if she was murdered, though. She'd suffered from heart disease for years, and if she was murdered, the doctors said at the inquest, she couldn't have lived twenty-four hours longer, any way."

Since Becker's confinement in the Kings County (N. Y.) Penitentiary he has made a bold but unsuccessful attempt to escape.

See records of No. 16 and George Wilkes.

Becker's picture is a good one, taken in 1877.

19

JOHN HOPE, alias WATSON.

MANHATTAN BANK BURGLAR.

DESCRIPTION.

Thirty years old in 1886. Born in United States. Single. Stout build. Height, 5 feet 9 inches. Weight, 160 pounds. Brown hair, blue eyes, round face, light complexion. Scar about one inch long over left eyebrow.

RECORD.

JOHNNY HOPE is the son of old Jimmy Hope (20), the celebrated bank burglar, now in State prison at San Quintan, Cal., for burglary. He branched out as a pickpocket, and was arrested for that offense in New York City in 1877. He is known in several large cities in the United States, and is considered a clever burglar.

Hope was arrested in New York City on February 18, 1879, for the robbery of the Manhattan Savings Institution, corner Broadway and Bleecker Street, New York, which occurred on October 27, 1878. He was placed on trial in the Court of General Sessions on June 12, 1879. He was convicted, and sentenced to twenty years in State prison, for robbery in the first degree, on July 18, 1879. His case was appealed up to the highest court, and confirmed. He was taken from the Tombs prison in New York to Sing Sing prison on February 3, 1881. The other parties implicated in this robbery were Patrick Shevelin, the watchman of the bank; William Kelly, old Jimmy Hope, Abe Coakley, Pete Emerson, alias Banjo Pete; John Nugent, and Eddie Gearing, alias Eddie Goodie. The following is a complete list of securities, etc., taken from the bank.

THE MANHATTAN SAVINGS INSTITUTION was, on the morning of Sunday, October 27, 1878, robbed of securities to the amount of $2,747,700, of which $2,506,700 are registered in the name of the Institution, and are not negotiable, and $168,000 are made payable to it, and $73,000 are in coupon bonds and $11,000 in cash.

CHARLES F. ALVORD, Secretary.　　　　　　　　　　　　　EDWARD SCHELL, President.
NEW YORK, October 27, 1878.

THE STOLEN SECURITIES.

The following is the statement prepared by the officials of their lost securities :

United States 5's of 1881, registered—8 of $50,000 each, Nos. 165, 166, 643 to 646, 737 and 738 ; 10 of $10,000, Nos. 13,486 to 13,495, inclusive...................................$500,000

United States 6's of 1881, registered—20 of $10,000 each, Nos. 9,276 to 9,295, inclusive.. 200,000

United States 10-40 bonds, registered—60 of $10,000 each, Nos. 8,744 to 8,763 and 18,903 to 18,942, inclusive.. 600,000

United States 4 per cents, registered—30 of $10,000 each, Nos. 1,971 to 2,000, inclusive.. 300,000

United States 5-20's of July, 1865; 26 of $500 each, Nos. 82,006, 82,144, 82,145, 84,903, 85,046, 85,107, 86,080, 86,943, 87,475, 89,707, 89,728, 90,319, 90,419, 93,043, 93,170, 94,577, 97,928, 97,933, 99,570, 99,876, 101,110, 102,792, 102,908, 103,421, 105,099, 106,636 ; 35 of $1,000 each, Nos. 152,410, 152,411, 153,986, 154,410, 157,844, 161,662, 163,159, 165,120, 165,167, 166,794, 166,821, 169,044, 169,747, 171,959, 172,543, 172,544, 173,052, 173,784, 173,785, 175,642, 178,050, 184,791, 187,141, 194,439, 194,597, 194,742, 199,678, 201,292, 202,897, 207,085, 208,069, 208,746, 208,828, 209,419, 209,686.. 48,000

New York State sinking fund gold 6's, registered, No. 32........................... 32,000

New York City Central Park fund stock, certificate No. 724, registered................ 22,700

New York County Court House stock, No. 2, six per cent. registered—-

Certificate, No. 4... $10,000
Certificate, No. 23... 35,000
Certificate, No. 24... 5,000
Certificate, No. 32... 10,000
Certificate, No. 33... 47,000
Certificate, No. 39... 95,000
　　　　　　　　　　　　　　　　　　　　　　　　　　　　　　　　　　————— 202,000

New York City accumulated debt, seven per cent. bonds, registered—

Two of $100,000 each, Nos. 1 and 2, due 1886........................$200,000
One of $50,000, due 1887, No. 1 50,000
　　　　　　　　　　　　　　　　　　　　　　　　　　　　　　　　　　————— 250,000

New York City Improvement stock, seven per cent. registered ; ten certificates of $20,000 each, Nos. 1 to 10 inclusive.. 200,000

New York City Revenue Bond, registered... 200,000

Yonkers City seven per cent. coupon bonds, 118 of $1,000 each, Nos. 233 to 242, 251 to
　　278, 281 to 310, 311 to 340, 531 to 550, all inclusive.............................$118,000
Brooklyn City Water Loan coupon bonds, 25 of $1,000 each, Nos. 2,167 to 2,191, inclusive.　25,000
East Chester Town coupon bonds, 50 of $1,000 each, Nos. 27 to 76, inclusive...........　50,000

All of the above bonds and securities are registered in the name of the Manhattan Savings Institution, payable to it, except the $48,000 five-twenty bonds of July, 1865, the $118,000 Yonkers bonds, $50,000 East Chester bonds, and the $25,000 Brooklyn City Water Loan coupon bonds. The bank officers notify all persons not to purchase or negotiate the bonds or securities, or any of them, "as the same are the property of the said The Manhattan Savings Institution."

☞ If any of the above bonds are offered you will please notify the police of New York City.

This was no doubt the largest bank robbery that ever occurred in this country. Fortunately nearly all of the bonds and securities were registered in the name of the bank. The United States Government and the Legislature of the State of New York came to their rescue, and ordered new bonds and securities to be issued, thereby reducing the loss from nearly $3,000,000 to less than $20,000, the larger part of which was in money.

Hope's picture is an excellent one, taken in February, 1878.

20
JAMES HOPE, alias OLD MAN HOPE.
BANK BURGLAR.

DESCRIPTION.

Fifty years old in 1886. Born in Philadelphia. Married. Machinist. Short; stout build. Height, 5 feet 6 inches. Weight, 170 pounds. Round, full face; light complexion. Is inclined to be round-shouldered; generally wears a full, reddish-brown beard. Light brown hair, blue eyes. Has a long scar at right angle of mouth.

RECORD.

OLD HOPE is a daring and skillful bank burglar, and hails from Philadelphia, Pa. He has been concerned in some of the most important bank robberies committed in this country for the past twenty-five years. He is renowned not only for his successful burglaries, but for his success in escaping from jails and prisons. He first came into prominent notice in 1870, in connection with the robbery of the paymaster's safe in the Philadelphia Navy Yard. Although never arrested for this job, it was pretty well known that himself, Ned Lyons (70), who was arrested and jumped his bail, and two others were concerned in the robbery. His next exploit was the robbery of "Smith's Bank," at Perry, Wyoming Co., N. Y. He was arrested and sentenced to five years in State prison at Auburn, N. Y., for this robbery, on November 28, 1870, under the name of James J. Watson. He escaped from there with Big Jim Brady, Dan Noble and Charles McCann, on January 3, 1873, leaving two years and six months of unexpired time behind him.

Hope and four other desperate burglars rented a house next door to the First National Bank of Wilmington, Del., and on November 7, 1873, succeeded in capturing the cashier of the bank and his whole family. The servant escaped, gave the alarm, and the gang, consisting of Hope, Big Frank McCoy (89), Tom McCormack, Big Jim Brady and George Bliss, were captured, tried, and sentenced to forty lashes and ten years each in prison, on November 25, 1873. They all succeeded in making their escape from jail in Delaware a short time afterwards. In February, 1878, Hope and Abe Coakley were arrested for an attempt to rob the Deep River Bank, at Deep River, Conn.; both were sent to jail, and while there the murder of Cashier Barron, of the Dexter Bank of Maine, occurred. The authorities tried to ascertain from Hope who committed this double crime, as they were sure he knew. In this, however, they failed. Hope was taken from Deep River to Dexter, and from there to Lime Rock, Maine, and placed on trial for the Lime Rock Bank robbery, which took place in May, 1870. After a week's trial Hope was acquitted. Hope is said to have been engaged in the Wellsboro, Pa., Bank robberies, which took place in September, 1874, and again in 1875. His most conspicuous and successful robbery was that of the Manhattan Savings Institution, situated on the corner of Broadway and Bleecker Street, New York City, on Sunday, October 27, 1878, where himself and confederates succeeded in carrying away just $2,747,700, the larger part of which was in registered securities. The plans for the robbery were laid nearly three years before it took place. It is said that Hope had once before entered the bank vault and attacked the safes. His son, John Hope (19), is now serving a twenty years' sentence in Sing Sing prison for this robbery. For a list of the securities stolen, and the names of the other parties implicated in the robbery, see record of No. 19.

Old Jimmy Hope went West, and was arrested in San Francisco, California, on June 27, 1881, for an attempt to rob the safe in the banking house of Sauther & Co. of that city. The safe contained on that day about $600,000 in money and securities. He was committed for trial in default of $10,000 bail by Judge Rix, tried, convicted, and sentenced to seven years and six months in "San Quintan" prison, California, on November 1, 1881. Big Tom Biglow and Dave Cummings, alias Little Dave (50), who was with Hope in this job, succeeded in making their escape.

Hope's time will expire in California on November 16, 1886, allowing him full benefit of the commutation law. Upon his discharge he will be re-arrested and returned to Auburn prison, to serve out his unexpired time.

Hope's picture is the only good one of him in existence, taken in June, 1881.

21
JOHN CLARE, alias GILMORE.
BANK BURGLAR.

DESCRIPTION.

Thirty-six years old in 1886. Born in United States. Photographer by trade. Single. Height, 5 feet 7½ inches. Weight, 150 pounds. Black hair, dark hazel eyes, dark complexion.   Wears black side whiskers and mustache.   Has a slight scar on left arm near elbow.

RECORD.

CLARE is a clever and desperate bank burglar, and was at one time an associate of Ike Marsh's and his brother, and was with them in several bank robberies.   He is credited with being able to make a good set of tools.

He was arrested in Baltimore, Md., on November 4, 1865, charged with the murder of Henry B. Grove on October 17, 1865.   On January 29, 1866, his trial commenced in Baltimore City, but was changed upon application of his counsel to Townstown, Baltimore County, on January 30, 1866.   His trial occupied from December 13 to 20, 1866, when the jury rendered a verdict of murder in the first degree.   A motion for a new trial was denied, and on January 14, 1867, he was sentenced to be hanged.   The Court of Appeals granted him a new trial, and he was tried again on March 29, 1870, and acquitted.

On June 27, 1874, an attempt was made to rob the safe of the New York County Bank, corner Fourteenth Street and Eighth Avenue, New York City.   Clare, under the name of Gilmore, hired a basement next door to the bank, and had a steam engine at work boring out the back of the safe, which they reached by removing the brick walls of both houses.   At the time of the raid by the police, William Morgan, alias Bunker, James Simpson, and Charles Sanborn were arrested, convicted, and sent to State prison.   Clare, or Gilmore, made his escape, but was captured on March 27, 1876, twenty-one months afterward, in New York City, tried, convicted, and sentenced to four years and six months in State prison by Judge Sutherland, in the Court of General Sessions, New York City.

Clare's picture is an excellent one, taken in 1876.

22

LANGDON W. MOORE, alias CHARLEY ADAMS.

BANK BURGLAR.

DESCRIPTION.

Fifty-six years old in 1886.   Born in New Hampshire.   Light complexion. Height, 5 feet 9 inches.   Weight, 180 pounds.   Stout build.   Always dresses neatly. Generally wears a full beard, which is now quite gray.   He has a very good appearance, and looks like a sharp business man, with the exception of his eyes, which have an expression peculiarly their own.   When off his guard he is quite nervous.

RECORD.

LANGDON W. MOORE, his right name, was born in the town of East Washington, N. H., in 1830.   His parents, very respectable people, were in moderate circumstances.   His father was a farmer.   From East Washington, N. H., the family moved to Newburyport, Mass., and remained there until Langdon was twelve years old, when the family moved to Lisbon, N. H. Langdon's mother died when he was fifteen. The father and children then moved to East Boston, where Langdon, when about twenty years of age, went to work in a currying establishment; from there to a boot and shoe store on Pearl Street. Along in 1854 Moore went into the grocery business, in South Boston, for about three years; he then sold out this place and opened another on Eutaw Street. His second venture was not a profitable one; and after paying all his creditors dollar for dollar, he gave up the grocery business and went into the express business. He afterwards sold out the express business and opened a liquor saloon on Broome Street, New York, where he remained for three years. He moved from Broome Street to Mercer, near Canal, where he remained for two years more. In 1857 he purchased a farm at Natick, Mass., of ninety-four acres, and increased it later on to one hundred and seventy acres; this place he sold in 1866. In 1861 Moore bought an eating-house and saloon at No. 16 East Houston Street, New York City, which he managed until 1863, when he bought a house corner Houston and Crosby streets. He soon after left New York and went to the farm at Natick, Mass., which he carried on until October 10, 1865—which is a very interesting fact to note— as the Concord National Bank was robbed on September 25, just fifteen days before Moore left the farm. From Natick he went to Paulsboro, N. J., where he remained six months, living as a man of means. He next appeared in Jersey City, where in May, 1866, he bought a house corner of Grand and Warren streets. He then began to speculate in horses, carriages, and about everything else that offered him a chance to turn a dollar. He lived at Jersey City and Bayonne, N. J., until the fall of 1877, when he moved to Eighty-first Street, New York City. In 1866, while engaged in speculating, he was married at Bayonne, N. J., to Mrs. Rebecca Cunningham, the widow of Dad Cunningham and a daughter of old Bill Sturges, an old English sneak thief and pickpocket. Moore's wife was familiarly known as Becky Moore. In June, 1877, Moore and his wife went to Toronto, Canada, where they remained until September; from there to Hamilton, Ont.; then to Niagara Falls, where they remained a month or two, and returned to New York in December, 1868. He bought out a livery stable and saloon on 125th Street, between Third and Fourth Avenues, New York City. This place he kept until May, 1870, the time of the robbery of the Lime Rock National Bank of Rockland, Maine. This bank was entered on the night of May 3, 1870. The parties engaged in this robbery were Charles B. Hight, Alden Litchfield, ex-policeman Kieser, John Black, John Graves, Joshua Daniels, Jack Rand and Langdon W. Moore. Kieser's part in the robbery was to get the policeman out of the way and get the men out of town after the robbery. He induced the policeman, whose suspicions had been aroused, to go to another part of the village, which gave the burglars a clear coast. The safe was blown and they secured about $23,000. Kieser took the men out of town with his team and concealed them in the woods, where he was to call for them on the following night. In the meantime he was under suspicion, and finally weakened and took the authorities to their hiding-place, where all hands were arrested (except Jack Rand, who escaped and went to Canada). Kieser, Black and Graves took the stand for the government, and Daniels and Hight managed to get the burden of responsibility thrown upon Moore. Moore and Hight subsequently pleaded guilty and took their sentences. Litchfield stood a trial, was convicted, and sentenced to four years. Daniels died in jail of consumption, not, as has been reported, from injuries received from the explosion of the bank safe. He was an outside man and was not in the bank at all, and the story that he was frightfully injured by the explosion is untrue. Moore was sentenced to the State prison at Thomaston, Maine, for six years in this case, but was pardoned for good behavior before he had served his full time. Becky Moore, his wife, managed his place in 125th Street, New York, until the lease expired in 1873, when she went to the corner of Eighth Avenue and Forty-sixth Street, and kept a place called the "Woodbine" until Moore's release from prison in 1876. Upon his discharge he went to the "Woodbine," and remained there until April, 1877, when he sold out and removed to Twelfth Street, where he kept a saloon until September, 1877, when he moved to No. 123 East Twenty-ninth Street.

Moore was arrested again in New York City on October 24, 1877, with Kid Leary, charged with being concerned in the Cambridgeport, Mass., Bank robbery in September, 1877. He was discharged in this case, as he could not be identified as one of the men in the robbery. The police of New York as well as Boston were at that time looking for the men that had robbed Mr. Garry of the latter city of $8,000 in United States bonds. This was one of the coolest transactions ever perpetrated in any city. Two men walked into the store of Mr. Garry, who was absent, and while one of them engaged the young lady attendant in conversation, the other one quietly removed the bonds from Mr. Garry's overcoat pocket almost under her eyes. Moore was arrested on October 25, 1877, in New York City, and held until the young lady came on and identified him, and he was taken to Boston, tried and acquitted, on November 24, 1877. Moore returned at once to New York, but was unable to find his wife and children, whom he ascertained had been living with a man named Thompson, who was a witness for old Jimmy Hope in the Dexter Bank robbery. After searching in vain for them some time he learned that they frequented a saloon corner of Eighth Street and Sixth Avenue. Moore went there, laid in wait until half-past twelve o'clock at night, when he saw Thompson and Becky enter. Moore walked in, and Thompson attempted to draw a revolver, but was prevented from using it. Moore could not be pacified, and attacked Thompson with a knife, slashing his cheek and leaving an ugly scar. Moore was arrested in this case and held in $2,000 bail. The Grand Jury failed to indict him, and he was discharged in April, 1878. Moore's wife returned to him, and he went to Chicago, Ill., where he remained until December, 1878, when he returned to New York and went to live at No. 105 East Twenty-sixth Street, where he was arrested for the robbery of the Charlestown, Mass., Post-office in March, 1880.

In the spring of 1865 Moore gave his attention to the Concord National Bank and the Middlesex Institution for Savings, both of which were located in the same building, in Concord, Mass. After considerable labor and visits to Concord, he succeeded in getting a key fitted to a heavy outside door. Moore had for an assistant Harry Howard, better known as "English Harry," a notorious cracksman, well known in London and New York. Harry soon obtained all the knowledge he required of the people in and around the bank, and on one occasion Moore and Harry went into the bank while the cashier was at dinner. They found that the cashier kept the combination of the safe marked in lead-pencil on the side of the safe. The next day was set to commit the robbery. Taking a fast horse, they drove from Framingham to Concord, shortly before noon. Moore went to a store almost opposite the bank and bought four pounds of nails, and then visited a saloon close by. It seems that he had his attention all the while directed to the bank, for as soon as the cashier closed the door of the bank to go to dinner he gave Harry the prearranged signal. Harry, with the aid of the duplicate key, soon had the door open, but while proceeding to enter was accosted by a little girl, who wanted to see the cashier. Harry told her the cashier had gone to dinner and would not be back until two o'clock, and then went coolly up stairs, shutting the door behind him. He soon opened the safe with the aid of the combination left behind by the cashier, and then ransacked the vault, which he locked when he got through. The property stolen consisted of $40,000 registered government bonds, $10,000 in Marlboro, Mass., registered bonds, $180,000 United States coupon bonds, and other securities—in all, amounting to $306,000. Harry placed his plunder in an old bag, and then coolly left the bank, locking the door after him. He was shortly after picked up by Moore in the wagon, and the pair started at breakneck pace for Framingham. Harry went to England and Moore to Canada. Moore was afterwards arrested at his home in Paulsboro, N. J. The officers started away with him. On the road Moore asked them on what conditions the bank would compromise the matter. He was told that he must give up all the proceeds of the robbery in his possession and disclose the hiding-place of "English Harry," who was known to have received $100,000 in money which had been realized from some of the bonds sold. As a result Moore went back with the detectives to his place at Paulsboro, and, going to his stable, ripped up the floor of one of the horse stalls, and handed over a glass jar covered with pitch and rubber, which was found to contain $79,000 in government bonds. He then proceeded down the bank of the Delaware River, and with a spade unearthed a square tin box which had been soldered tightly, in which was found $100,000 more in bonds. Other sums were afterwards surrendered by him which made the total amount returned $202,331. The day this property was surrendered by Moore it was the intention of a woman named Hattie Adams, whom Moore was then living with, to have taken it and fled. Moore then tried to place "English Harry" in the hands of the authorities, and for that purpose had a "personal" placed in a New York paper. Harry never noticed it, although it was the method agreed upon to bring them together. Moore soon after broke up house on the Delaware. Hattie went to live with a man in Brooklyn, and soon after died, having been drowned in a hack, the horses of which had run away and jumped into the East River. It was after this that he (Moore) married Dad Cunningham's widow, who was afterwards known as Becky Moore.

Moore, Ike Marsh, Charley Bullard, and another well known man, who has since reformed, were charged with robbing the messenger of the American Union Express Company on the Hudson River Railroad. They were all arrested in Canada, but finally discharged.

The Cambridgeport Bank robbery was laid to Moore, but there never was evidence enough against him to warrant his arrest. He was assisted in this robbery by Johnny

O'Brien, alias the "Kid," and a third party. The third party went into the bank and drew the cashier's attention away from the safe, when the "Kid" sneaked in and robbed it. It is also claimed that Moore was the prime mover in the Lechmere Bank robbery, in Cambridge, Mass., in March, 1878. It is a curious fact in connection with this robbery that two gangs—one from Chicago, and the other from New York—were each awaiting an opportunity to commit this robbery, unknown to the other. The New Yorkers succeeded, but the Chicago parties were so close on them that they all stood in on the division of the spoils. Louise Jourdan, alias Little Louise, who was married to Tom Biglow at the time, was a leading spirit in this burglary. All the plunder, with the exception of about $12,000, was recovered and returned to the bank. Shortly before Moore's arrest for the Charlestown Post-office robbery it appears that he had formed a plan to rob the bank at Quincy, Mass. Both he and his partner, George Mason, alias Gardner, visited that institution, and got a look at the safe. Moore had received information that there was only one night-watchman in the town, and that he was employed in a factory some distance from the bank; and furthermore, that there were no telegraph wires attached to the bank to give an alarm. The bank was pronounced a "soft job" by Moore, whose plans were frustrated by the arrest of Mason for the Charlestown (Mass.) Post-office robbery. Mason, after spending some time in jail, and finding that Moore, who had escaped, had done nothing for his family nor anything in the way of providing a lawyer for him, informed upon him, and he was arrested in New York City and charged with breaking and entering the Warren Institution for Savings—a bank in the Bunker Hill district of Boston, Mass., on December 4, 1879. He was convicted in the Superior Criminal Court, before Judge Bacon, on March 18, 1880, and sentenced to ten years in State prison, for breaking and entering. On March 30 he was tried again, on another indictment, for having burglars' tools in his possession, and sentenced to six years—making sixteen years in all. He is now in Concord (Mass.) State prison.

His picture is a good one, taken in 1880.

23

DANIEL WATSON, alias DUTCH DAN.

BURGLAR, TOOL MAKER, AND KEY FITTER.

DESCRIPTION.

Fifty-one years old in 1886. Stout build. Height, 5 feet 9 inches. Weight, 186 pounds. Machinist by trade. Single. Born in Germany or Prussia. Quite wrinkled forehead, dark hair, blue eyes, light complexion. Generally wears a goatee and mustache tinged with gray. Heavy lines on each side of nose to corner of mouth (nose lines). A cross-looking man. Has a sort of a suspicious look about him when he meets a stranger.

RECORD.

"DUTCH.DAN," the name he is best known by, is considered one of the best key fitters in America. He is also an excellent toolmaker, and his many exploits would fill an ordinary sized book.

Dan was arrested in Philadelphia, Pa., on April 11, 1881, in company of George Hall, alias Porter, a burglar and confidence man, Charles Lilly, alias Redman, and Bill Morris, alias Gilmore, burglars, charged with a silk burglary. Wax was found on Dan, with a key impression on it. Watson and Hall were each sentenced to two years in the Eastern Penitentiary on a charge of conspiracy on July 8, 1881; Lilly and Morris to one year. Watson makes a specialty of entering buildings and obtaining impressions of keys (which are sometimes hung up in a convenient place by the janitor or occupant of the premises). In this manner he collects a large number of impressions from which he makes duplicate keys. He then selects a number of expert burglars and furnishes them with a set of keys and a diagram of the place to be robbed. If the burglars are successful, he receives about twenty per cent. of the robbery for his share. He is known to have had as many as six parties of men to work at one time.

Dan has spent fifteen years of his eventful life in Sing Sing, N. Y., Cherry Hill, Philadelphia, and other Pennsylvania prisons.

His picture is an excellent one, taken in 1878.

24

GEORGE MASON, alias GORDON,
alias GARDINER.

BANK BURGLAR.

DESCRIPTION.

Forty-five years old in 1886. Slim build. Height, 6 feet. Weight, 155 pounds. Born in Boston, Mass. Married. Black curly hair mixed with gray, dark blue eyes, sallow complexion. Wears a full black beard. Has a long scar on his left cheek, which is well covered by his beard. Has an anchor in India ink on his right fore-arm, and a heart on his left arm.

RECORD.

MASON, or GEORGE B. GORDON (his right name), was arrested on December 4, 1879, in an attempt to rob the Warren Institution for Savings and the Charlestown, Mass., Post-office. The robbery was planned by Langdon W. Moore, alias Charley Adams, Mason, who gave the name of Gardiner when arrested, and a New York burglar named John Love, alias Wells, and took place on December 4, 1879. The police became suspicious, and began an investigation. Love, the outside man, took fright and ran away, followed by Moore, who was in the building, but somehow or other managed to get out. Mason, who was also in the building, did not hear Moore when he left, and consequently was captured by the police. He was locked up, and while in jail made disclosures which led to the arrest of Moore in New York City. At the trial of Moore, Mason took the stand for the government and testified that this robbery was committed upon information obtained privately by Moore, who also had an eye on several other places in that city and vicinity. Mason, when arrested, gave the name of George B. Gardiner, but on the stand said his right name was Gordon. He has borne the names of Mason, Gardiner, Bennett, Graham, and about twenty others. He admitted that he was arrested in 1874 at Wellsboro, Pa., for a bank robbery there, and that he had been convicted for assault, burglary, and larceny. Mason is now, 1886, about forty-five years of age. He was born in the east end of Boston, and left there when young and went to New York, where shortly afterwards he was left an orphan. He began his checkered career in a small way, but soon adopted bank burglary, and in this line he has certainly figured to a considerable extent for the past twenty years. Before he was twenty years old he was convicted of robbing a bank in New York, and for this offense he served four years in Sing Sing prison. After the expiration of his term there in 1863, he was concerned in the robbery of the First National Bank of Wilmington, Del., where himself and partners, Jim Williamson and old Jimmy Hope, got $63,000. In 1865, Gordon, Ned Lyons, Jimmy Hope, and another man, one of the most dangerous combinations of cracksmen that was ever made in this country, broke into and robbed a savings bank in Baltimore, Md., of $25,000, and succeeded in eluding arrest. In 1860, Gordon, Johnny Hughes, another man, and Ned Lyons broke into the Oldtown National Bank at Oldtown, Maine, and blew the vault open. The noise of the explosion, however, very fortunately alarmed the people of the town, and the burglars were forced to flee for their lives, and succeeded in reaching Bangor in safety. Just before this attempt the same party made an unsuccessful attempt to blow open the vault of a bank at Framingham Centre, Mass., but as at Oldtown, the explosion alarmed the town and they had to run for their lives. In 1869 Gordon, Hope, Lyons, Big Haggerty (now dead), and another man attempted to rob the National Bank at Rochester, N. H. They loaded the safe with a heavy charge of gunpowder and touched off the fuse. The force of the explosion was so great that the safe door was blown entirely off, and the building was so badly shaken that it partly fell down. The burglars had overdone their work, and the townspeople, hearing the report in the dead of the night, ran out to ascertain the cause; their footsteps alarmed the burglars, who again had to make themselves scarce. They soon after tried their luck again on the Townsend National Bank of Massachusetts, but the result was a failure, and they only succeeded in giving the town a scare and the newspapers a sensation. Gordon, Lyons, Hope, and Johnny Hughes then tried their skill on the vault of the Fairhaven National Bank of Massachusetts. Hope and Hughes were arrested and convicted, but Lyons and Gordon escaped, and with Mose Vogle, alias "Jew Mose," who has just (1886) finished serving a term of thirteen years for a bank robbery in New Jersey, and another man, made an attempt upon the vault of the Great Barrington Bank, and blew the vault down. The explosion alarmed the people; they gave chase to the burglars, who made good their escape. They were more successful, however, a little later, when they succeeded in abstracting $200,000 from the safe of the Milford National Bank, at Milford, N. H. This was a masked burglary, and was well planned and carried out. Somewhat encouraged by the result of the Milford Bank, they next tried their hand on the Quincy National Bank of Quincy, Ill., in 1874. A room over this bank was quietly hired by them, the flooring timbers were torn up, and they worked down into the vault by cutting through the top. Then they let Gordon down by a rope, and he reported that none of the securities could be reached until the safe was blown. He loaded the safe with gunpowder, using an air-pump. He then touched the fuse with a lighted match, and gave his partners the signal to draw him up. They did so, and when he was about half-way between the floor and the ceiling the charge was prematurely ignited. Gordon was pulled out nearly suffocated, and as black as a coal; the party, however, got the safe open, and carried off about $200,000. Gordon, with another party, was concerned in the robbery of $160,000 from the Planters' Bank in Virginia, and it is well known that he was the prime mover in the Covington (Ky.) bank robbery. This bank had a large burglar and fire proof safe of the Hall pattern, which was loaded with four pounds of powder; the explosion which followed was heard all over the city, and the vault was nothing but a mass of débris when the people reached the bank soon after. The back of the safe was forced out, and the money and securities were untouched, as the burglars were compelled to fly, leaving their anticipated booty, which they had no time to move. After this robbery Gordon was in prison several times. He was also concerned with old Jimmy Hope in the first but unsuccessful attempt on the Manhattan Bank in New York; and after his failure at Great Barrington, Vt., he returned there and robbed a jewelry store of goods valued at $9,000, to make expenses. He was also implicated in the Wellsboro, Pa., Bank robbery in September, 1874, when $90,000 was stolen.

He was arrested on December 4, 1880, at Charlestown, Mass., as previously stated, turned State's evidence against Langdon W. Moore (22), who was sentenced to sixteen years, and Gordon to three years, on March 30, 1880, for assault and battery. The charge of burglary not being pressed, he was discharged from prison on November 18, 1882.

According to his own testimony he has been a thief and burglar for twenty-five years.

Mason was arrested again in Philadelphia, with John Williams, on March 1, 1883, charged with having burglars' tools in their possession. They were convicted on March 15, 1883. They applied for a new trial, which was granted, and they were arraigned for trial again on October 30, 1883. By advice of counsel they pleaded guilty, and were sentenced to seven months in the penitentiary, to date from their former conviction (March 15, 1883), which made the State of Pennsylvania indebted to them fifteen days.

Mason was arrested again in Hoboken, N. J., on September 2, 1885, for breaking and entering a house in Hudson County, N. J., and was sentenced to five years in Trenton prison on September 11, 1885, under the name of George Smith.

Mason's picture is not a very good one, as it was taken under difficulties in December, 1880.

25

HORACE HOVAN, alias LITTLE HORACE.

BANK SNEAK.

DESCRIPTION.

Thirty-seven years old in 1886. Medium build. Born in Richmond, Va. Very genteel appearance. Height, 5 feet 8 inches. Weight, 150 pounds. Dresses well. Married to Charlotte Dougherty. Fair complexion. A fine, elegant-looking man. Generally wears a full brown beard.

RECORD.

HORACE HOVAN, alias LITTLE HORACE, has associated with all the best bank sneaks in the country. In 1870 Horace, in company of a man that has reformed and is living honestly, and Big Ed. Rice (12), stole $20,000 from a vault in a Halifax (N. S.) bank. Hovan and this party were arrested, but Rice escaped with the money. The prisoners were afterwards released, as the money was returned to the bank.

Horace was convicted under the name of W. W. Fisher, alias Morgan, for a bank sneak job in Pittsburg, Pa., and sentenced to two years and eleven months in the Western Penitentiary, at Alleghany City, on November 22, 1878.

He was arrested on March 23, 1878, at Petersburgh, Va., with Rufe Minor, George Carson, and Charlotte Dougherty (Hovan's wife). See remarks of picture No. 1.

Arrested again March 31, 1879, at Charleston, S. C., for the larceny of $20,000 in bonds from a safe in the First National Bank in that city. He dropped them on the floor of the bank when detected and feigned sickness, and was sent to the hospital, from which place he made his escape.

Arrested again October 16, 1880, in New York City, for the Middletown (Conn.) Bank robbery. See records of pictures Nos. 1 and 3. In this case he was discharged, as the property stolen was returned.

Arrested again in June, 1881, at Philadelphia, Pa., with Frank Buck, alias Bucky Taylor (27), for the larceny of $10,950 in securities from a broker's safe in that city. He was convicted of burglary, and sentenced to three years in the Eastern Penitentiary, at Philadelphia, Pa., on July 2, 1881, his time to date back to June 6, 1881. He was pardoned out October 30, 1883, on condition that he would go to Washington, D. C., and testify against some officials who were on trial. He agreed to do so if the Washington authorities would have the case against him in Charleston, S. C., settled, which they did. He then gave his testimony, which was not credited by the jury. He remained in jail in Washington until May 10, 1884, when he was discharged.

Hovan and Buck Taylor were arrested again on June 18, 1884, in Boston, Mass., their pictures taken, and then escorted to a train and shipped out of town.

Hovan is a very clever and tricky sneak thief. One of his tricks was to prove an alibi when arrested. He has a brother, Robert Hovan (see picture No. 179), now (1886) serving a five years' sentence in Sing Sing prison, who is a good counterpart. The voices and the manners of the two men are so nearly alike, that when they are dressed in the same manner it is hard to distinguish one from the other. Horace has often relied on this. He would register with his wife at a prominent hotel, and make the acquaintance of the guests. About an hour before visiting a bank or an office Horace would have his brother show up at the hotel, order a carriage, drive out with his (Horace's) wife in the park, and return several hours later. Horace, in the interval, would slip off and do his work. If he was arrested any time afterwards, he would show that he was out riding at the time of the robbery.

Horace Hovan is without doubt one of the smartest bank sneaks in the world.

Latest accounts, the fall of 1885, say that he was arrested in Europe and sentenced to three years in prison for the larceny of a package of bank notes from a safe.

His partner, Frank Buck, made his escape and returned to America.

His picture is an excellent one, taken in 1884.

26

AUGUSTUS RAYMOND, alias GUS RAYMOND,
alias Arthur L. Barry.
SNEAK.

DESCRIPTION.

Thirty-three years old in 1886. Medium build. Born in United States. Single. Height, 5 feet 3½ inches. Weight, 155 pounds. Black hair, turning gray; dark brown eyes, dark complexion, round full face. Dresses well, and is a very gentlemanly person.

RECORD.

Raymond is a clever bank sneak, and a good general thief. He has plenty of nerve and works with the best people only. He is known in several of the large cities of the United States and in Canada.

Arrested April 2, 1878, in New York City, for larceny of a trunk of jewelry. The facts are, that on May 12, 1877, the firm of Alling Brothers & Co., of Worcester, Mass., shipped by rail a trunk containing $9,000 worth of jewelry from Worcester to Hartford, Conn., to their agent. On the road Raymond slipped into the baggage car and changed the checks on the trunk. On the arrival of the train at Hartford it was discovered that the trunk had been stolen. It was traced from Hartford, Conn., to a New York hotel, and from there to Baltimore, Md., where it was found empty. Thomas Leary, alias Kid Leary (6), was with Raymond and was the party that received the trunk at the hotel in New York, for which he was sentenced to five years in State prison, in New York City. Raymond was taken to Worcester, Mass., on April 18, 1878, and sentenced to five years in State prison there, on October 2, 1878, by Judge Aldrich.

He has been arrested in several cities in the United States since his release—the last time was on February 16, 1886, in New York City, with Joe Elliott, alias Reilly (16), and George Wilkes, charged with forgery in Rochester, N. Y. Raymond was discharged and Elliott and Wilkes were taken to Rochester for trial.

Raymond was arrested again in Philadelphia, Pa., on May 8, 1886, on suspicion of forging a check on the Third National Bank of Philadelphia, which he gave to a boy, who attempted to get the money at the bank. Raymond was not arrested until two days after, when the boy could not be found and he was discharged.

Raymond's picture is an excellent one, taken in 1878.

27

FRANK BUCK, alias "BUCK" TAYLOR,

alias Buck Wilson, alias George Biddle.

BANK SNEAK.

DESCRIPTION.

Forty-four years old in 1886. Born in Philadelphia, Pa. Married. Engineer. Stout build. Height, 5 feet 5 inches. Weight, 150 pounds. Light hair, gray eyes, light complexion. Three India ink dots on left hand, one on right hand. Bald on front of head. Generally wears a light-colored mustache.

RECORD.

"Buck" is a very clever bank sneak. He has been working with Horace Hovan, alias Little Horace (25), since 1881. He has also worked with Langdon W. Moore, alias Charley Adams (22), Johnny Price and other notorious bank sneaks.

"Buck" was arrested in June, 1881, at Philadelphia, Pa., with Horace Hovan (25), for the larceny of $10,950 in securities from a broker's office in that city. He was convicted of burglary and sentenced to three years in the Eastern Penitentiary at Philadelphia with Hovan, on July 2, 1881. His time dated back to June 6, 1881. Hovan was pardoned. Buck served his time, and afterwards joined Hovan in Washington, D. C., in May, 1884.

They both traveled around the country and were arrested coming out of a bank in Boston on June 18, 1884, and their pictures taken for the Rogues' Gallery. Buck and Hovan went to Europe in the spring of 1885, and Buck returned alone the same fall, Horace having been arrested there and sentenced to three years' imprisonment for the larceny of a package of money from a bank safe.

Buck's picture is an excellent one, taken in 1884.

28

JOHN TRACY, alias BIG TRACY,
alias REILLY.
PICKPOCKET, BURGLAR, AND SECOND–STORY MAN.

DESCRIPTION.

Thirty-seven years old in 1886.   Born in United States.   Plumber by trade. Single.   Stout build.   Height, 6 feet 1½ inches.   Weight, 180 pounds.   Dark brown hair, light complexion.   Has a cross in India ink on right fore-arm.   Generally wears a dark brown beard and mustache.   Scar on back of hand.

RECORD.

" BIG " TRACY does considerable " second-story " or house work, and is well known in New York, Chicago, and all the large cities.   He has served considerable time in Eastern prisons—one term of five years from Troy, N. Y., for highway robbery, in 1878. (See Addenda.)

He was arrested again in the spring of 1884, in company of Billy Ogle (13), for robbing a residence on Jersey City Heights, N. J., of diamonds and jewelry valued at $1,500.   They were both tried and convicted on June 26, 1884 ; their counsel obtained a new trial for them, and they were discharged in July, 1884.

Tracy and Ogle went West, and in the fall of 1885 Ogle was arrested in Tennessee for " house work," and sentenced to the penitentiary for ten years.   He shortly after escaped from a gang while working on the railroad.

Tracy escaped arrest, and is now at large in the West.

His picture is a good one, taken in 1877.   (See records of Nos. 13 and 110.)

29

CHARLES WILSON, alias LITTLE PAUL,
alias CHARLES WILLIS.
SNEAK AND SHOPLIFTER.

DESCRIPTION.

Thirty-three years old in 1886.   Stout build.   Born in England.   Not married. Height, 5 feet 2½ inches.   Weight, 140 pounds.   Brown hair, gray eyes, round full face, light complexion.   Whiskers, when grown, are a little sandy.

RECORD.

" LITTLE PAUL " is quite a clever sneak and shoplifter.   He was sent to State prison in New York City in January, 1878, and again on June 18, 1883, for four years, for larceny in the second degree, by Recorder Smyth.   On November 14, 1883, in company of Frank Harrison, alias Frank Reilly (79), he escaped from the mess-room at

Sing Sing prison early in the morning, by sawing off the iron bars of a window and crawling into the yard ; they then went to the west end of the prison wall, which projects over the Hudson River docks, and there, by means of a convenient float, reached the shore outside the prison wall, where they left their prison clothes and put on civilian's attire, that had been "planted" there for them some time before. Paul was re-arrested in New Orleans, La., on January 26, 1884, and returned to Sing Sing prison in February of that year. His full time will expire on June 17, 1887.

His picture is a good one, taken in 1878.

30
DAVID GOLDSTEIN, alias SHEENY DAVE,
alias Lewis.
SNEAK AND SHOPLIFTER.

DESCRIPTION.

Forty-two years old in 1886. A Jew, born in Poland. Married. No trade. Stout build. Height, 5 feet 7¼ inches. Weight, 180 pounds. Dark complexion, black hair, dark eyes, cast in left eye. Black beard, when worn. Dresses well. Is very quick in his movements.

RECORD.

"SHEENY DAVE," whose right name is David Levitt, is an old New York thief, and is pretty well known in all the principal cities of the United States. He has served time in State prison in a number of States.

He was arrested in Buffalo, N. Y., on January 26, 1878, in company of a man who reformed about six years ago, for shoplifting (working jewelry stores), and both sentenced to one year's imprisonment in Auburn (N. Y.) prison. When his time expired he was taken to Baltimore, Md., for a crime committed there, but was not convicted. He was arrested again in New York City, under the name of James Lewis, on January 15, 1881, for the larceny of two pieces of blue silk from the store of Edward Freitman & Co., No. 473 Spring Street, valued at $140. For this offense, upon his plea of guilty, he was sentenced to two years and six months in State prison at Sing Sing, on April 12, 1881, by Judge Cowing.

He was arrested again in New York City on December 21, 1883, under the name of Samuel Newman, for the larceny of a diamond bracelet, valued at $500, from Kirkpatrick, the jeweler, on Broadway, New York. He was indicted by the Grand Jury on January 10, 1884, and forfeited his bail on January 15, 1884. He was arrested again on September 30, 1884, in York County, Maine, for picking pockets, and sentenced to three years in prison at Alfred, Maine, under the name of Herman Lewis.

For expiration of sentence, see commutation law of Maine.

He is still a fugitive from justice, and is wanted in New York City.

His picture is an excellent one, taken in January, 1878.

25

HORACE HOVAN,
ALIAS LITTLE HORACE,
BANK SNEAK.

26

AUGUSTUS RAYMOND,
ALIAS GUS. RAYMOND,
SNEAK AND FORGER.

27

FRANK BUCK,
ALIAS BUCKY TAYLOR,
BANK SNEAK.

28

JOHN TRACY,
ALIAS BIG TRACY, ALIAS REILLY,
PICKPOCKET,
BURGLAR & SECOND STORY MAN.

29

CHARLES WILSON,
ALIAS LITTLE PAUL,
SNEAK AND SHOP LIFTER.

30

DAVID GOLDSTEIN,
ALIAS SHEENY DAVE,
SNEAK AND SHOP LIFTER.

31

LOUIS R MARTIN,
FORGER.

32

WILLIAM E BROCKWAY,
FORGER AND COUNTERFEITER.

33

TIMOTHY J. GILMORE,
FORGER.

34

RICHARD O. DAVIS,
CHECK FORGER.

35

ROBERT S. BALLARD,
ALIAS BULLARD,
FORGER.

36

EDWARD DARLINGTON,
CHECK FORGER.

37

ALBERT WILSON,
FORGER.

38

CHARLES J. EVERHARDT,
ALIAS MASH MARKET JAKE,
SNEAK AND FORGER.

39

ROBERT BOWMAN,
ALIAS HOGAN,
FORGER.

40

CHARLES R. TITUS,
ALIAS DR. THOMPSON,
FORGER.

41

CHARLES FISHER,
ALIAS PURDY,
SNEAK AND FORGER.

42

EDWARD A. CONDIT,
BOGUS CHECKS.

43

WILLIAM FALE,
ALIAS BROOKS,
HOTEL THIEF.

44

CHARLES HYLEBURT,
ALIAS RED HYLE,
HOTEL THIEF.

45

EDWARD STURGESS,
ALIAS HYATT,
HOTEL THIEF.

46

FRANK AUBURN,
BOARDING HOUSE THIEF.

47

EMILE VOEGTLIN,
HOTEL AND BOARDING HOUSE THIEF

48

EDWARD FAIRBROTHER,
ALIAS DOCTOR WEST,
HOTEL THIEF.

31
LOUIS R. MARTIN, alias MARTIN LUTHER.
BOND FORGER AND COUNTERFEITER.

DESCRIPTION.

Sixty-three years old in 1886. Born in United States. Horse dealer. Medium build. Height, 5 feet 10¾ inches. Weight, 164 pounds. Gray hair, eyes dark gray and weak, complexion light. Is a fine, gentlemanly-looking man.

RECORD.

MARTIN was believed to be the capitalist of the Brockway gang of forgers and counterfeiters. He was well known by all the reputable horse and sporting men in this country, as a man of means engaged in the transportation of cattle between the United States, Engiand and Australia.

He was indicted in the United States Court of the Western District of Pennsylvania in 1875, with an accomplice named Henry Moxie, alias Sweet, for passing counterfeit $500 notes. He was never tried. Previous to that time he had been known as an expert engraver and printer of counterfeits, under the name of Martin Luther. He made and owned the plate with which the $500 notes for which himself and Moxie were indicted were printed. He has been connected in several large counterfeiting schemes with William E. Brockway (32), J. B. Doyle, Nathan B. Foster, English Moore, and others. He is well known by the United States officers as a counterfeiter.

Martin was arrested in New York City, on November 10, 1883, with Brockway (32) and Nathan B. Foster, charged with having in his possession forged $1,000 bonds of the Morris & Essex Railroad of New Jersey. At the time of his arrest, in the St. James Hotel, New York City, there was found in two valises in his room fifty-four $1,000 bonds of the above road, thirty-three of which had been numbered and signed ready for use. For this offense Martin was convicted, and sentenced to ten years in State prison, on August 6, 1884, by Judge Cowing, in the Court of General Sessions in New York City. His counsel obtained a stay of proceedings, and he was granted a new trial, and admitted to bail; while confined in the Tombs prison from some cause he became totally blind.

His picture is an excellent one, taken in November, 1883.

32
WILLIAM E. BROCKWAY
BOND FORGER AND COUNTERFEITER.

DESCRIPTION.

Sixty-four years old in 1886. Born in Connecticut. Engraver by trade. Married. Tall, thin man. Height, 6 feet 1½ inches. Weight, 162 pounds. Gray hair, blue eyes, light complexion.   Long, thin neck.   A remarkable looking man on account of his height and thinness.   He has been a counterfeiter and forger since 1850.   An account of all his transactions would fill this book.   He is well known in all the principal cities in the United States, especially by the United States authorities.   Wears a gray beard and mustache.   He studied chemistry at Yale College, and later on became a printer and electrotyper.

RECORD.

BROCKWAY and Charles Smythe were arrested in Brooklyn, N. Y., by the United States authorities on October 22, 1880, charged (in connection with one James B. Doyle, who was arrested in Chicago, Ill., and sentenced to ten years on June 24, 1881) with forging and uttering $204,000 of United States government 6 per cent. coupon bonds of the denomination of $1,000, and a number of forged United States Treasury notes.   The bonds and notes were found in Doyle's possession when arrested in Chicago, Ill.   Brockway was convicted by the evidence of Smythe, and sentenced to thirty years' imprisonment by the United States Court in New York City.   Sentence was suspended in this case by the Judge, on Brockway undertaking to surrender all the plates for forging bonds and notes which he had in his possession or the whereabouts of which he knew, also to give up other counterfeit apparatus and give the authorities information about other schemes then on foot to defraud the government, all of which he did, and he was discharged from custody on November 27, 1880, by Judge Benedict, of the United States Court, with the understanding that if he ever was arrested again for forging or counterfeiting anything the property of the United States government, his suspended sentence would go into effect.

Brockway was arrested again in New York City on November 10, 1883, pleaded guilty, and was sentenced to five years in State prison on March 5, 1884, by Recorder Smyth, for forging a number of Morris & Essex Railroad bonds.   Nathan B. Foster and Louis R. Martin (31) were also arrested with Brockway in this transaction.

Brockway's sentence will expire, allowing him full good time, on August 4, 1887.

His picture is an excellent one, taken in 1884.

———

33

TIMOTHY J. GILMORE.

FORGER.

———

DESCRIPTION.

Forty-eight years old in 1886.   Born in United States.   Widower.   Clerk.   Stout build.   Height, 5 feet 7½ inches.   Weight, 175 pounds.   Dark brown hair, brown eyes, ruddy complexion, high forehead.   Generally wears brown mustache, cut short. Gilmore has three young sons who are now in an orphan asylum.

RECORD.

GILMORE is a professional forger, well known in New York and several of the Eastern cities. He is said to have formerly lived in St. Louis, Mo., and has served time in prison there.

He was arrested in New York City on June 24, 1878, and sentenced to four years and six months in State prison for forgery. He was arrested again in New York City on February 7, 1884. Mr. Goodwin, a baker, of No. 228 Front Street, New York, identified Gilmore as the man to whom on July 30, 1883, he had sold ten barrels of bread for $25.22, and who gave him a check for $70 in payment. The check was worthless. Thomas A. O'Brien, bookkeeper for Fitzpatrick & Case, spice dealers, of No. 7 James Slip, New York, said that on December 11, 1883, Gilmore paid him a check for $80, signed " R. H. Macy & Co.," for $45 worth of tea. In this case he obtained $35 change. Gilmore pleaded guilty to both complaints, and was sentenced to eight years in State prison on March 5, 1884, in the Court of General Sessions, New York.

Gilmore's picture is a good one, taken in 1878.

34

RICHARD O. DAVIS.

CHECK FORGER.

DESCRIPTION.

Twenty-eight years old in 1886. Married. Born in United States. Cloth cutter by trade. Medium build. Fair complexion. Height, 5 feet 9½ inches. Weight, 161 pounds. Brown hair, brown eyes. Dresses well. Davis and his partner, No. 36, are considered clever people. They are well known in New York, Boston, and in several other cities in the United States.

RECORD.

DAVIS was arrested in New York City on November 22, 1883, in connection with Edward Darlington (36) and Charles Preston, alias Fisher (41), charged with forging a check for $400, drawn on Harris & Co. The complaint was made by Howes & Co., bankers, No. 11 Wall Street, New York City. He was committed in $2,000 bail by Justice Duffy. Davis pleaded guilty in the Court of General Sessions in New York City, and was sentenced to six years in State prison on December 27, 1883. His sentence will expire, allowing him his full commutation time, on February 26, 1888.

This man and his partner, Darlington, had been traveling around the country for some time, before their arrest in New York City, passing forged checks.

His picture is a good one, taken in 1883.

35
ROBERT S. BALLARD, alias BULLARD,
alias MALTBY, alias RIGGS.
FORGER.

DESCRIPTION.

Forty-nine years old in 1886. Born in Ireland. Married. Physician. Medium build. Height, 5 feet 6¼ inches. Weight, 137 pounds. Dark hair mixed with gray, blue eyes, dark complexion. Has a wart on left side of his nose.

RECORD.

BALLARD, alias HARVEY C. BULLARD, alias W. C. RUSSELL, alias HENRY C. MALTBY, was arrested in New York City on March 31, 1883, for swindling Ferdinand P. Earle, of Earle's Hotel, out of $150 by means of a worthless check. . He was also charged with bigamy and swindling. He was at one time a practicing physician, and connected with one of the New York hospitals. He was also wanted at the time of his arrest for swindling by the use of bogus checks and other devices, in New York City, Poughkeepsie, N. Y., Providence, R. I., Baltimore, Md., Atlantic City, N. J., Brooklyn, N. Y., and Philadelphia, Pa. In 1881 he married a Miss Amelia Black, at Poughkeepsie, and deserted her a few days afterward. In November, 1882, he married Miss Annie Van Houten in Baltimore, and brought her to New York, where he deserted her at Earle's Hotel, after swindling the proprietor. At the time of his arrest, in his valise was found hundreds of bogus checks and drafts, signed R. S. Ballard, Riggs & Co., R. S. Riggs, W. C. Riggs & Co., for sums ranging from $500 to $6,000, all bearing recent dates ; and also a large number of check and bank books. One of the latter showed an alleged deposit of $15,900 in the Fifth Avenue Bank of New York. Another exhibited a credit of $10,600 on a Tarrytown, N. Y., bank, and the third represented a deposit of $14,594 in the Western International Bank of Baltimore, Md. He had checks of banks in nearly every prominent city in America. The Bankers' and Brokers' Association offered a reward of $1,000 for his arrest under the name of W. C. Russell.

Ballard pleaded guilty on May 2, 1883, in the Court of General Sessions, New York City, and was sentenced to five years in State prison by Recorder Smyth. His sentence expires, allowing him full commutation, on December 1, 1886.

His picture is an excellent one, taken in 1883.

36
EDWARD DARLINGTON.
CHECK FORGER.

DESCRIPTION.

Thirty-three years old in 1886. Born in England. Medium build. Not married. Height, 5 feet 8½ inches. Weight, 138 pounds. Sandy hair, blue eyes, sallow complexion. Genteel appearance. Known in New York, Philadelphia, Boston, and several other cities in the United States.

RECORD.

DARLINGTON was arrested in New York City on November 21, 1883, in connection with Richard O. Davis (34) and Charles Preston, alias Fisher (41), charged with forging the name of J. J. Smith to a check for $700 on the Continental Bank, No. 6 Nassau Street, New York City. He was committed in $2,000 bail by Justice Duffy.

Darlington pleaded guilty in the Court of General Sessions, New York City, and was sentenced to nine years in State prison on December 27, 1883. His sentence will expire, allowing him full commutation time, on November 26, 1889.

This man, who no doubt is the cleverest of the three, and his partner (34), had been traveling through the country for some time, victimizing people with forged checks. At the time of his arrest in New York he was wanted in Boston, Mass., for a similar transaction.

His picture is a good one, taken in 1883.

37

ALBERT WILSON, alias AL. WILSON, alias E. R. MARSHALL.

FORGER.

DESCRIPTION.

Forty-four years old in 1886. Stout build. Height, 5 feet 6¾ inches. Weight, 170 pounds. Brown hair, slightly bald on top of head; wears light brown mustache and whiskers, generally cut short. Prominent nose, which is inclined to be hooked. Has a gunshot wound on back of left fore-arm; also a small scar half an inch long on lower lip, which runs down from corner of mouth, left side. Speaks in a calm, easy tone. Born in State of Louisiana.

RECORD.

Al. Wilson is well known in many of the Eastern cities as an expert burglar and shoplifter, and has served two terms of imprisonment for the above offenses. He afterwards became an expert negotiator of forged paper of every description, and was known to the authorities of several cities as a member of "Brockway's Gang of Forgers." He also was identified with George Wilkes, George Engles (deceased), and Charley Becker, with whom he left for Europe in the spring of 1880, for the purpose of negotiating forged circular notes. This scheme failed, and he returned to America about August 15, 1880.

Wilson was arrested in New York City on October 18, 1880, and delivered to the police authorities of Baltimore, Md., charged, in connection with Henry Cleary, George Bell (193), and Charles O. Brockway (14), with forging and uttering checks amounting to $10,051 on the Merchants' National Bank and the Third National Bank of Baltimore, Md., on July 16 and 17, 1880. One check for $2,160, another $3,901, and another of $1,300, were drawn to the order of J. Hunter and others, and, with the forged signature of J. H. Fisher, were presented at the Merchants' National Bank; and a check for $1,394, and another for $1,296, drawn to the order of J. W. Kimball, and bearing the forged signature of Middleton & Co., of Baltimore, were presented at the Third National Bank. All five of these checks were paid on presentation.

Wilson pleaded guilty to two cases of forgery, and he was sentenced to two years on each indictment (making four years in all), on November 3, 1880, by Judge Pinkney, at Baltimore, Md. Shortly after his release from prison in Maryland he was arrested in Milwaukee, Wis. (June 26, 1884), under the name of Edward R. Marshall, charged with attempting to pass forged fifty-pound Bank of England notes. As he had failed to get rid of any of them there, he was delivered over to the Chicago (Ill.) authorities, who wanted him for disposing of some of the same notes. He was taken to Chicago, and escaped from a police station there on July 5, 1884, and went to England, where a gang was organized consisting of George Wilkes, George Engles, Charley Becker, Shell Hamilton, William Bartlett, Edward Burns, Edward Cleary, George Bell, and himself; and, as above referred to, they entered into a gigantic scheme to flood France, Germany and Italy with forged circular notes, full particulars of which appear in the record of George Wilkes. A reward of one hundred dollars was offered for his arrest by the chief of police.

Al. Wilson, alias W. H. Hall, registered at St. Lawrence Hall in Montreal, Canada, on May 18, 1885, and on May 19 he went to the Bank of British North America and asked the manager of the bank to cash him a letter of credit for fifty pounds on the Union Bank of Scotland. He said that "he had fifteen hundred pounds more which he would like to have cashed in a few days." The manager became suspicious and detained him, and sent for an officer, who arrested him when leaving the bank. One Robert Fox, a Scotchman, was arrested with him. He is about fifty-five years old. Height, 5 feet 7½ inches. Weight, about 190 pounds. Stout build. Gray hair. Side whiskers and mustache, generally dyed black. Very bald. Sharp features. Round shoulders, and slightly stooped. Fox did not attempt to pass any of the letters of credit, but when arrested a large package of the letters was found on his person. He tried to destroy them, but was prevented by the officers. Wilson claimed that all the letters belonged to him, and that Fox had nothing to do with them. Wilson pleaded guilty on June 6, 1885. Fox was tried and found guilty on June 9, 1885. On June 13, 1885, Wilson was sentenced to twelve years in St. Vincent de Paul Penitentiary, and Fox was sentenced to six years.

Wilson's picture is an excellent one, taken in 1880.

38

CHAS. J. EVERHARDT, alias MARSH MARKET JAKE,

alias HARTMAN, alias PETERS, alias McGLOIN, alias COOK, alias HILLBURN.

SNEAK AND FORGER.

DESCRIPTION.

Forty-five years old in 1886. Single. Slim build. Born in Baltimore, Md. High forehead. Height, 6 feet. Weight, 159 pounds. Brown hair, bluish gray eyes, sallow complexion. Wears mustache and beard of sandy color. Has a bright eye. Has an anchor in India ink, a letter "J" and dot on left fore-arm. He is known in Canada as Charles Webb and Charles Young.

RECORD.

MARSH MARKET JAKE, the sobriquet he is best known by, has followed as a business all professions in the thieving line, beginning with till-tapping when a boy, and going up through the various grades of pickpocket, shoplifter, burglar, sneak and forger. During his lifetime he has served about fifteen years in prison, five years of which was spent in the Kingston, Canada, Penitentiary. When out of prison he works with the most expert thieves in the country, and it is only since his last release from Kingston prison that he has entered into the profession of forgery. Jake is well known in all the principal cities in the United States, especially in New York, Boston, Baltimore, Cincinnati and Chicago, Ill., where he formerly lived with Mary Ann Taylor, an old and accomplished thief. For the past twenty-five years, Everhardt, which is his right name, has been one of the most notorious and industrious sneak thieves in America. He originally came from Baltimore, where he was born in the immediate neighborhood of the "Marsh Market," in that city, and it is from this fact that he derives the name that he is best known by.

On April 16, 1880, Jake, under the name of Wm. Hillburn, was arrested in Philadelphia, Pa., in company of three noted sneak thieves, Billy Morgan (72), Little Al Wilson and George Williams, alias Woodward (194)—they gave the names of Roberts, Carroll and Moran—for the larceny of $2,200 in bank bills, the property of Henry Ruddy of that city. They tried to obtain their release by a writ on April 19, 1880, but failed. The whole party was convicted and sentenced to eighteen months in the Eastern Penitentiary on April 26, 1880. Jake served another term of three months in the penitentiary at Philadelphia, having been arrested there as a professional thief, and convicted on a charge of vagrancy.

Everhardt finished a three years' sentence in the spring of 1885, in Kingston, Canada, Penitentiary, under the name of Charles Webb, for robbing a Toronto jeweler.

He had previously been convicted in Toronto for shoplifting, in company of four notorious shoplifters named Eddie Miller (7), Sheeny Sam, Tilly Miller and Black Lena. This time he gave the name of Yost, and served five years.

Jake was arrested again in New York City on October 22, 1885, in company of Charles Fisher, alias Fountain (41), Walter Pierce, alias Porter, and Charles Denken (the man who did the forging), charged with forging a check for $460 on the Bank of New York, purported to have been signed by Leaycraft & Co., of Pearl Street, New York City. Denken confessed that he received a check for $25 from the firm, from which he forged the $460 check, and gave it to Fisher, who gave it to Pierce, who had it cashed. In this case all the others were convicted except Jake, who was discharged, but was re-arrested at once on an indictment which the Corn Exchange Bank and the Bank of America, of New York City, caused to be found against him (on the evidence of Nelson J. Gaylor and two boys named Philip Dreiger and Leonard Nickerson, who were accomplices) for forging a check of $500, drawn on the German American Bank and purported to have been signed by Baltzer & Lichtenstein, a private banking firm in New York City. On this particular charge Jake was tried, found guilty, and sentenced to ten years in State prison on January 7, 1886, by Judge Gildersleeve, in the Court of General Sessions in New York City. There were other complaints from the Bank of America and Corn Exchange Bank, which were not tried. His counsel appealed the case, and Everhardt has remained in the Tombs prison since his conviction. Efforts were made to have him admitted to bail, without success.

His picture is an excellent one, taken in 1885.

39

ROBERT BOWMAN, alias J. C. HOGAN,
alias George Munroe.

FORGER.

DESCRIPTION.

Forty-six years old in 1886. Height, 5 feet 9¼ inches. Gray eyes, gray whiskers and mustache. Complexion medium. Stooped shoulders. Looks hump-backed. High forehead. Bald on front of head. Scars on bridge of nose, back of neck, and between the shoulder-blades. Born in New York. Weight, 140 pounds.

RECORD.

Bowman was an associate of Wm. H. Lyman, a notorious forger, who died in prison in 1883. Both of them were sent to Clinton prison, New York State, for four years and six months in August, 1878, for forgeries committed in Catskill, N. Y.

Bowman and Lyman were again arrested at Hudson, N. Y., on September 16, 1881, and taken to Fitchburg, Mass., where they were sentenced to prison for three years for forging drafts on the American Express Company, at that place. They were also charged with raising drafts that were drawn by the National Bank of St. Albans, Vt., on the Park Bank of New York City. Also with forging a draft, on September 5, 1881, on Clipperly, Cole & Haslehurst, Troy bankers. When arrested $1,200 in money was found on them.

Bowman was arrested again in Chicago, Ill., on January 14, 1886. About January 6, 1886, a man giving the name of J. F. Hall, presented to the Floyd County Savings Bank, of Charles City, Iowa, a draft payable to himself, purporting to have been drawn by the First National Bank of Joliet, Ill. Hall also had a letter of introduction from the Joliet bank ; the draft was deposited to his credit, and on January 9, 1886, he wrote to the Floyd County Bank from Chicago, enclosing his receipt for the draft, and asking that the money be sent to him by the United States Express. It was sent, and when Hall called for it he was arrested and recognized as Bowman. One of the detectives went to Fort Wayne, Ind., where Hall had lived, and captured the latter's valise, in which was found a large number of counterfeit checks and certificates. It was estimated that Bowman and his gang had defrauded the banks in the western country out of $50,000.

Bowman's case in Chicago, Ill., was nolle prosequi, by Judge Rogers, on June 1, 1886, because the State's attorney was unable to obtain sufficient evidence to convict him of the forgeries committed there.

He was discharged, and immediately re-arrested and taken to Vermont, where he was committed for trial, charged with having committed forgeries on the First National Bank of Brandon, Vt., the Vermont National Bank, the Rutland County National Bank, of Rutland, Vt., and the Farmers and Mechanics' Bank of Burlington, Vt. These forgeries were committed in 1881, by Bowman and Ned Lyman, and amounted in the aggregate to $30,000.

Bowman's picture is a good one, taken in 1886.

40

CHARLES R. TITUS, alias DOCTOR THOMPSON.

FORGER.

DESCRIPTION.

Forty-three years old in 1886. Born in United States. Slim build. Dark complexion. Height, 5 feet 7¾ inches. Weight, 133 pounds. Black hair, brown eyes. Wears a full black beard. Married. A fine, genteel appearing man. Well known in most of the Eastern cities and in Canada.

RECORD.

"Doc" Titus was arrested in New York City on November 26, 1878, in connection with one Lester Beach (17), for having obtained $70 from Morris Steinhart, No. 65 Hudson Street, New York City, on a bogus certified check on the Bank of New York.

Beach when arrested stated that he obtained the check from Titus. Titus is a very clever forger, and has been mixed up in several transactions in paper. He is a warm friend of Charles B. Orvis, of Buffalo, New York and Erie bond fame.

Titus was arrested again in New York City on September 11, 1879, with one Samuel J. Hoyt, a real estate and insurance broker, charged with having in their possession a forged check on the Bank of America for $100,000, with intent to utter the same. It was drawn to the order of John B. Baker, trustee, dated September 11, 1879, and purported to have been signed by J. B. Colgate & Co., a banking firm on Wall Street. It appears that one J. B. Baker was introduced to the accused by Charles B. Orvis. He, as alleged, was informed that the check was genuine, and that some of the employes of Colgate & Co. were implicated in its procurement. Titus, it was claimed, handed the check to Hoyt, who handed it to Baker, and requested him to buy four per cent. United States bonds for it. Baker, who it appears was in the employ of Colgate & Co., took the check to them, and they pronounced it a forgery. The arrest followed, and Titus and Hoyt were committed in $10,000 bail for trial.

Hoyt pleaded guilty to the charge on January 30, 1880, and was used by the authorities as a witness against Titus, who was tried, convicted, and sentenced to two years in State prison on January 31, 1880, by Recorder Smyth, in the Court of General Sessions at New York City.

Titus' picture is an excellent one, taken in 1880.

41

CHARLES FISHER, alias PURDY,

alias Fountain, alias Palmer.

BANK SNEAK AND FORGER.

DESCRIPTION.

Twenty-seven years old in 1886. Medium build. Hatter by trade. Dark complexion. Height, 5 feet 7½ inches. Weight, 140 pounds. Black hair, blue eyes ; dot of India ink on right hand ; mole on right elbow. High forehead. Very quick in his movements. Born in Germany.

RECORD.

Charles Fisher has been a thief since he was twelve years old. This worthy's life is best told by a letter which he wrote while confined in the Tombs prison, New York, in December, 1878, for breaking a window.

Here is the communication he penned to Judge Otterbourg on December 18, 1878:

"I was requested by a gentleman to give a brief history of my life. I was born in March, 1859, in Germany. When five years of age I was sent to a public school, and remained there for three years. When I was seven years of age my father gave me lessons in Latin. When I left the public school my father put me in a Latin school. I was there four years, and while I was there I was boarding in a Franciscan convent, with about sixty others. At four o'clock every day we used to get a pint of ale, and I was not there six months before I was able to drink two quarts in as many hours. I only remarked this to let you understand better afterward that I knew how to spend money like a man three times my age. I made my examination for a higher class in 1870, but I failed, being intoxicated the night before I made it. My father would not allow me to repeat the class, but sent me to a commercial school. Wealthy men from several parts of the world sent their sons to this institution. My father allowed me a certain amount of pocket money, which ought to have been enough for me, but I wanted to live as fast as those foreigners. Two miles from the school my grandfather practised as county doctor, and there I went every Sunday and stole $5 or $6 from him every time. I was not found out for a year and a half, when I was detected at last (the term at school was just ended) and sent home to my father, who gave me a sound thrashing and locked me up for some weeks in my room. When I stole from my grandfather I stole for the first time. My father then sent me to a friend of his, a wholesale druggist. There I met some friends who had been my former companions. I wanted to keep up my reputation as a fast boy, and I could not do it with my allowance of pocket money. I had no grandfather to steal from now, but had to find out another way to get it. A part of my work was to deliver and receive the mail. I cashed different money orders, the amount always being between $20 and $50. I was detected after two months' stealing and sent home to my father. When I arrived at home I was astonished to see my father's face calm, but icy. Next day he told me that I was going to the United States, although my mother and the rest of my relatives were against it. As soon as everything was ready for departure he took me to Bremen and put me on board of a ship. He gave me $250. It did not take me long to find out those free and easy places along the Bowery and Chatham street. There I made the acquaintance of thieves—males and females. I very seldom stole with them, but stole all alone until my arrest and conviction to the House of Refuge stopped it rather suddenly. After serving one and a half years I was discharged. Having behaved myself very badly I had quite a reputation among the young thieves of New York. I was out only a month and I commenced the old career over again. I stole steadily from October, 1875, till October, 1876, and got along first rate. On the 9th of October, 1876, I was arrested for grand larceny, pleaded guilty and was sentenced to State prison for two and a half years. I took it as easy as any man could take it. The first few months I behaved myself badly, being punished no less than five times in three months. When I received letters from home and heard that my mother was dying I was watching for opportunities to escape, but the keeper had his eye on me continually on account of my bad behavior. My mother begged me to lead an honest life. I promised her to do so, and I meant it at the time I made it, and I mean it yet. My mother begged my father to take me home after I had served my term. When I was discharged from Sing Sing prison my father had not sent me the money as he promised to do, but I was full of courage and hope, because I thought a man must get work if he would try hard. Even an errand boy is expected to have references, and it would never do to show them my prison discharge. I was discharged on the 11th of October, 1878, and I have lived on bread and a cup of coffee once in a while, until I came here. My object of getting arrested was to get a place to stay until I could get relief from home. My father accused my mother after her death that she spoiled me, and I want to show him that my dead mother has sufficient influence over me by keeping my promise to her; and I mean to keep it, so help me God."

Fisher obtained employment through the intercession of Judge Otterbourg—how well he kept his promise, and how strong his desire was to reform, will be seen by what follows.

Not long after he returned into the old channels, and shortly after obtained considerable notoriety as a middle man, between the maker and utterer of forged checks, etc. Next heard from him was in Chicago, Ill., in 1879, where he was arrested with four other forgers. It was discovered that the "gang" had passed forged checks on nearly all the banks in Chicago. Fisher pleaded guilty and took the stand against his associates, who were all convicted and sentenced to long terms of imprisonment. Fisher was discharged on promise to leave the State, which he did, and he came to New

York City. He was shortly after arrested on a charge of larceny, and sentenced to Blackwell's Island for six months. On his liberation he went back to his old associates in the forgery business, and was shortly after arrested in New York City for being concerned with three others in a scheme to defraud the banks of that city by means of forged checks. In this instance, as before, he saved himself by turning State's evidence and convicting his associates. The next that was heard of him was his arrest in Boston, Mass., on August 19, 1885, with Jake Everhardt, alias Marsh Market Jake (38), coming out of one of the banks there. No case being made out against them they were discharged. He was arrested again in New York City on October 23, 1885, with Everhardt, Charles Denken and Walter Pierce, alias Porter, charged by Leaycraft & Co., of Pearl Street, New York, with forging a check of the firm for $460 on the Bank of New York. In this case Fisher, Denken and Pierce were convicted and sentenced to ten years in State prison each on November 18, 1885, by Recorder Smyth, in the Court of General Sessions, New York City. Everhardt was discharged, re-arrested, and convicted in another case. See his record, No. 38.

Fisher's picture is a very good one, taken in 1885.

42

EDWARD A. CONDIT.

SWINDLER BY BOGUS CHECKS.

DESCRIPTION.

Forty-one years old in 1886. Medium build. Height, 5 feet 11 inches. Weight, 167 pounds. Dark brown hair, hazel eyes, long pointed nose, sallow complexion. Has a scar on right side of neck. Small dark mole on left cheek. Prominent eyebrows.

RECORD.

EDWARD A. CONDIT, a swindler who had a peculiar method of dealing in worthless checks, was arrested in New York City on March 2, 1883. Condit's manner of doing business was to inquire by letter the terms upon which a broker would deal in a stock, and then ordering him to buy or sell, giving as margin a check on the Orange (N. J.) Savings Bank. Condit had only a small amount on deposit in that bank, but owing to the time required for the passage of the check through the Clearing-house, and other delaying causes, several days elapsed before its worthless character was exposed, and he was enabled to reap the benefit of the fluctuations in the price of the stock within the time required to collect the check. If the stock moved to his advantage, he contrived to meet or intercept the check, and take the benefit. If the transaction went against him, he allowed the check to go to protest, so that the broker was the loser.

Condit has a pleasing address, and is apparently a man of some education. He gave a short history of his life after confessing his operations. He said that he inherited a small fortune in 1869, which in the course of the next two years he increased to

$100,000. He began to speculate in Wall Street in 1872. At first he was successful, but after the "panic" he began to lose, and by 1876 he was a beggar. Then it was that he attempted to retrieve his losses by the mode described above.

When arrested on March 2, 1883, he was committed for trial by Judge Cowing, but was turned over to the Jersey City police authorities in October, 1884. On December 1, 1884, he made a nearly successful attempt to escape from the Hudson County Jail, on Jersey City Heights, where he was confined awaiting trial for swindling several storekeepers in Jersey City by worthless checks. He was convicted on December 24, 1884, and sentenced, January 23, 1885, to four years in State prison at Trenton, N. J., where he was taken on June 28, 1885.

Condit's picture is an excellent one, taken in 1884.

43

WILLIAM FALE, alias BROOKS..

HOTEL THIEF AND SLEEPING-CAR WORKER.

DESCRIPTION.

Fifty-five years old in 1886. Medium build. Height, 5 feet 7¼ inches. Weight, 150 pounds. Dark brown hair, gray eyes, dark complexion. Wears a brown mustache. A German. Baker by trade.

RECORD.

FALE, or BROOKS, is an old hotel and sleeping-car worker, and is pretty well known in the principal Eastern and Southern cities, where he has been arrested and convicted for similar offenses.

He was arrested at the Grand Central Railroad depot, in New York City, on December 23, 1874, for the larceny of a gold watch and chain from a sleeping-car. He was tried, convicted, and sentenced, in the Court of General Sessions, to four years in State prison on January 18, 1875. His manner of working was to meet the in-coming trains in the morning by walking up the railroad yard, jump on them, and rob the berths, while the persons who occupied them were washing and getting ready to leave.

Fale's picture is a fair one, taken in 1874.

44

CHARLES HYLEBERT, alias CINCINNATI RED, alias RED HYLE.

HOTEL THIEF.

DESCRIPTION.

Thirty-six years old in 1886. Stout build. Height, 5 feet 7 inches. Weight, 153 pounds. Red hair and whiskers, when grown; florid complexion. Butcher by trade.

He is a great hand for disguising himself. His red beard grows very rapidly, and he could appear from time to time in cockney style, with long flowing side-whiskers, or with simple mustache, or with smooth face, as he might choose. He is quite genteel-looking.

RECORD

RED HYLE, or CINCINNATI RED, is one of the most celebrated hotel thieves in this country. He was born and raised in Cincinnati, and when a boy learned the butcher's trade. He was called Red Hyle, on account of his red hair and florid face. He has been a professional thief for fifteen years. For many years this clever thief has robbed hotels all over the United States. He made Cincinnati his home, and his wife and children reside there now.

Hyle seldom works with a partner, preferring to work alone since he and William Carter, alias Three-Fingered Jack, were arrested and sentenced to the Georgia penitentiary for five years, in 1880, for a hotel robbery in Atlanta. Joe Parish (84) was implicated in this robbery, but returned the property and was discharged. Parish was subsequently sent to an Illinois penitentiary for robbing a bank. Hyle was released from the Georgia prison, and was next heard from in Washington, D. C., on March 6, 1885, where he was arrested on suspicion of committing several hotel robberies there during the inauguration week. He was charged with stealing a watch and chain, value $65, from the room of one S. M. Briggs, in the St. James Hotel, and was committed in default of $3,000 bail for a further hearing. This case was not tried, as Hyle was arrested on the cars at Indianapolis, Ind., for grand larceny, stealing a valuable watch and chain from A. P. Miller, of New York, at the Circle House, in Indianapolis, on June 17, 1885. He was found guilty after a strongly contested trial, and sentenced to four years in the Northern State prison at Michigan City, on July 18, 1885.

Red Hyle generally managed to keep on the right side of the detectives while in Cincinnati, on the ground that he was not stealing anything in that city. He gave the officers considerable information about other thieves. There is no doubt that many a professional thief in this country will be glad to hear that Red Hyle, after dodging the Northern penitentiaries for so many years, has at last been sent to State prison.

Hyle's picture is an excellent one, taken in 1885.

45

EDWARD STURGESS, alias HYATT,

alias HOYT.

HOTEL THIEF.

DESCRIPTION.

Thirty-six years old in 1886. Slim build. Claims to have been born in Havana, Cuba. Married. No trade. Height, 5 feet 9¼ inches. Weight, 137 pounds. Brown hair, blue eyes, light complexion. Full, light-colored whiskers and mustache. Two dots of India ink on left fore-arm.

RECORD.

STURGESS is a very clever hotel worker, well known in most of the large cities in the United States. He was at one time a pickpocket, but now confines himself to hotel work.

He was sentenced to three years and six months in State prison in New York City, on February 20, 1871, for larceny from the person, under the name of Edward Hoyt. He was was again sentenced in New York City on June 2, 1873, to three years in State prison, under the name of Edward Sturgess, for a hotel robbery. While confined in prison in 1873, Sturgess escaped in a swill barrel, but was recaptured the same day and taken back. Nothing has been heard of him lately, having gone West in October, 1877, when he escaped from an officer in New York City, who was arresting him for forfeiting his bail in an old case.

His picture is an excellent one, taken in 1877.

46

FRANK AUBURN, alias JOHN F. AUSTIN.

BOARDING-HOUSE SNEAK.

DESCRIPTION.

Twenty-six years old in 1886. Born in United States. Medium build. Single. Height, 5 feet 5 inches. Weight, 120 pounds. Brown hair, gray eyes, dark complexion. No trade. Has busts of boy and girl, and two hearts with words "You and me" on them, in India ink, on right fore-arm.

RECORD.

AUBURN is quite a clever boarding-house thief, but does not confine himself to that work entirely. He is well known in New York and Boston. He was arrested in New York City on November 1, 1883, for petty larceny from a boarding-house, and convicted and sentenced to five days in the Tombs prison on November 28, 1883, by Judge Gildersleeve, in the Court of General Sessions. His light sentence was the result of the intercession of some good people, and on account of its being his first appearance in court. He was arrested again in Boston, Mass., on April 28, 1884, in company of Joseph W. Harris, alias Wm. J. Johnson, for picking pockets in the churches of that city. He was tried, convicted, and sentenced to four years in Concord prison on May 16, 1884. His time will expire in November, 1887.

Auburn's picture is a good one, taken in 1884.

47

EMILE VOEGTLIN.

HOTEL AND BOARDING-HOUSE THIEF.

DESCRIPTION.

Twenty-six years old in 1886. Born in United States. Single. Scenic artist by trade. Medium build. Height, 5 feet 10½ inches. Weight, 155 pounds. Brown hair, hazel eyes, dark complexion. Wears black mustache and side-whiskers. Has a very genteel appearance.

RECORD.

VOEGTLIN, who branched out lately as a boarding-house and hotel thief, is the son of very respectable people in New York City. That he is a professional there is no doubt. He is a clever man, and his picture is well worth having, as he is not very well known outside of New York.

He was arrested in New York City on April 23, 1882, for stealing jewelry at No. 7 Fifth Avenue, where he was boarding. On account of his family judgment was suspended, after he had pleaded guilty and promised to reform.

He was arrested again in New York City on December 12, 1883, charged by a Mrs. Josephine G. Valentine, a guest of the Irving House, corner Twelfth Street and Broadway, with stealing from her room there a diamond-studded locket and other jewelry. The scoundrel almost implicated an innocent girl, whom he was keeping company with, by giving her some of the stolen jewelry.

Voegtlin was convicted of grand larceny in Part I. of the Court of General Sessions, and sentenced to five years in State prison on January 8, 1884. Immediately after his sentence he was taken to Part II. of the same court, and sentenced to one year on the old suspended sentence, making six years in all. His imprisonment will expire, if he earns his commutation, on March 7, 1888.

Voegtlin's picture is an excellent one, taken in 1884.

48

EDW'D FAIRBROTHER, alias DR. EDW'D S. WEST, alias DOCTOR ST. CLAIR.

HOTEL AND BOARDING-HOUSE THIEF.

DESCRIPTION.

Fifty-five years old in 1886. Born in England. Physician. A small, nervous man. Speaks very rapidly. Has long, thin, white hair. Hollow cheeks; high, sharp cheek bones. No upper teeth. Large, long nose. Has a fine education, and speaks five languages.

RECORD.

Dr. West, the name he is best known by, was arrested in New York City on July 7, 1873, for grand larceny from a boarding-house in 128th Street. The complaint was made by Charles E. Pierce. The Doctor was convicted, and sentenced to two years in State prison on July 14, 1873, by Judge Sutherland, in the Court of General Sessions, New York. West was arrested again in New York in January, 1880, charged with committing twenty-two robberies inside of seven months. He freely admitted his guilt, and confessed to all of them. The best piece of work he had done, he said, was the robbery of Major Morton's residence on Fifth Avenue, New York City, where he secured $6,000 worth of diamonds and jewelry, with which he got safely away and pawned for $450. When taken to Major Morton's residence, however, the people in the house failed to identify him, and went so far as to say that he was not the man who had called there. West told the officers how he robbed Morton's house and several others. At the time of his arrest he had $20 in his possession. Out of this he gave $13 to a poor man named Kane, from whom he had stolen a coat. A poor servant-girl also came to court. West recognized her, and offered her the last of his money, $7; but she would only take five of it. West, in speaking of himself at that time, said, "I have not always been a criminal; I have seen better days, far better days than many can boast of, and bright opportunities, too. I had no disposition for crime—in fact, no inclination that way. But time's whirligig turned me up a criminal; and I fought hard against it, too. I came to this country from England in 1855. I had just then graduated from Corpus Christi College, founded by Bishop Fox, of Winchester. I am an alumnus of Oxford. I took my degree of M. D., and came to this country, and became a practicing physician in New York City. I lived then in Clinton Place. In 1863 I was arrested for malpractice, and was sent to Sing Sing State prison for five years. While in the prison I associated with all kinds of people, and there I learned the art of robbery. After my time was up I returned to New York City, and tried to lead an honest life; but I had learned too much, and was again arrested for larceny, and sent to prison. I got out, and went back again for another term, which ended in June, 1879." West was arraigned in the Court of General Sessions in New York City on four indictments for grand larceny, and the District Attorney accepted a plea of guilty on one of them, and Judge Cowing sentenced him to five years in State prison on January 29, 1880. His sentence expired, allowing him full commutation, on August 28, 1883.

West's picture was taken since 1873. He looks much older now.

49
GEORGE W. GAMPHOR, alias JAMES F. ROGERS.
HOTEL THIEF.

DESCRIPTION.

Thirty-eight years old in 1886. Born in Philadelphia. Medium build. Clerk. Not married. Height, 5 feet 7 inches. Weight, about 148 pounds. Blonde hair, dark gray eyes, sandy complexion and mustache.

RECORD.

GAMPHOR was arrested in New York City on February 1, 1876, for the larceny of a gold watch and chain, valued at $100, from one E. W. Worth, of Bennington, Vt., at one of the hotels on Cortlandt Street. He was convicted, and sentenced to two years and six months in State prison in the Court of General Sessions, on December 20, 1880, by Recorder Smyth.

He is a clever hotel thief, and has traveled all over this country, robbing hotels and boarding-houses, and is regarded as a first-class operator. He is well known in a number of large cities.

Gamphor's picture was taken in 1876.

50

DAVID CUMMINGS, alias HOGAN,

alias LITTLE DAVE.

HOTEL THIEF AND BURGLAR.

DESCRIPTION.

Thirty-eight years old in 1886. Born in Chicago, Ill. Slim build. Married. Height, 5 feet 6½ inches. Weight, 130 pounds. Black hair, blue eyes, light complexion. Has small cross and dots of India ink on right hand. Dark brown beard.

RECORD.

DAVE CUMMINGS, whose right name is David Cronin, was arrested at Oshkosh, Wis., under the name of J. H. Smith, for robbing a Chicago salesman of his watch, diamond pin, and $200 in money, at the Tremont Hotel in that town. Dave pleaded guilty and was sentenced to three years in State prison there on September 14, 1881. A complete history of this celebrated criminal would fill this book. I will, therefore, describe only a few of his many exploits. "Dave Cummings" started in life as a waiter in a Chicago hotel, afterwards filling a similar position on the boats of the Upper Mississippi. About this time a singular series of robberies occurred, and it was ascertained that every boat that young Cummings had worked on had been plundered. After a time he was betrayed by another boat-thief named Johnny O'Brien. Dave was arrested, and a large amount of stolen property was found in his possession. This was in 1865, at St. Louis, Mo., and was the first time he became known to the police.

The first robbery of importance with which he was connected was in New Orleans, La., in 1868, when, in the company of Billy Forrester (76), and Frank Dean, alias Daigo Frank, they robbed the safe of Schooler's jewelry store on Canal Street in that city. The safe stood in front of a glass door, where the watchman could see it in passing. Cummings rigged up a dummy safe and dragged the other one into the rear room, opened it, and secured diamonds and jewelry valued at $100,000, none of which was ever recovered. They next robbed the bank in the French district of New Orleans of money and bonds valued at $65,000, and with this sum they fled to Memphis, where they were joined by Jess Allen (deceased). In that city the police tried to arrest them, but they escaped. In a short time after this the party robbed Barney Spiers, a diamond broker and pawnbroker in St. Louis. Next to the store was a saloon which was frequented by the thieves. Tunneling through the wall, they entered and pulled the back out of the safe, securing about $12,000 worth of diamonds. Shortly after the great fire Cummings went to Chicago and operated very successfully as a hotel thief. In the fall of 1872, in company with Daigo Frank, he entered a room in the house of the notorious Jenny Jenks, in Chicago, and took from under her mattress diamonds and jewelry to the value of about $7,000, with which they fled to New York. In the winter of 1872 the gang was changed by Cummings, and consisted of Mose Vogel, a New Yorker; Ed. Johnson, a Chicagoean, and Daigo Frank. They rented rooms directly over the First National Bank of Jersey City, and ostensibly carried on the business of stucco work. In the meantime they had taken up the floor, were removing the bricks over the vault, piling them up at the side of the room, where they were covered with a screen, and replaced the floor every night. They had worked through to about the last layer of brick, when an old woman who lived in the building became suspicious, and one evening notified the police. A squad of them surrounded the bank, and captured the men at their work. But the usual good luck of Cummings stood by him. It was his duty that night to keep an outside watch. Becoming careless, he had gone into a billiard room, and thus, without being able to alarm his companions, escaped himself and fled to New York. The prisoners, Mose Vogel, Ed. Johnson and Daigo Frank were sentenced to fifteen years each.

Dave went back to the hotel business and continued at it until the spring of 1873, when, in connection with George Leslie (deceased) and Pete Emmerson, alias Banjo Pete, he robbed a bank in Macon, Ga., of about $50,000. They were all arrested in Washington, D. C., for this robbery, and a compromise effected by the return of the money. In the fall of 1873 Dave visited the fairs at Quincy, Ill., and Kansas City, and found in the former place that rooms could be had over the vault of the First National Bank there, which was located similarly to that of the bank at Jersey City. He rented the rooms, giving at the time the name of a noted Chicago thief, in order to divert suspicion if anything should occur, and started at once for New York, where he organized another party, consisting of James Dunlap, formerly of Chicago; Robert S. Scott, also of Chicago; Jack Burke, George Mason, and a man since reformed. They rented a house at Quincy, Ill., and one of their wives acted as housekeeper, staying there during the day and working, as they did in Jersey City, at night. In Quincy they were successful, securing $89,000 in currency, $100,000 in government bonds, and $350,000 in railroad and other securities, leaving one safe untouched, probably for lack of time. This is the first bank in which the "air-pump" was used with success. It forces or draws the powder into the crevices of the safe. The device was invented by a man who was at one time in the employ of Herring, the great safe manufacturer. In this case the owner got $10,000 for the use of it.

The following is a circular issued by the bank immediately after the robbery:

FORTY THOUSAND DOLLARS ($40,000) REWARD!

The First National Bank of Quincy, Illinois, offer and will pay THIRTY THOUSAND DOLLARS for the recovery and return of the Eighty-Four Thousand Dollars ($84,000) which were stolen from its Bank at the time the same was burglariously entered and robbed on the morning of the 13th day of February, 1874; and said Bank will also pay *pro rata* for the return of any part of said $84,000.

Of this amount there was in new notes of this Bank $2,600, of the denomination of ones and twos; about $1,000 in mutilated notes of this Bank; one $1,000 U. S. Treasury note; $1,800 in new fractional currency; $4,000 in notes of $50 and $100, and the balance in Legal Tender and National Bank Notes.

There were also taken from the safe two U. S. 7-30 Bonds, viz.: No. 160,114, June series, $1,000 No. 181,116, June series, $1,000.

And also the following MUNICIPAL BONDS, on deposit for safe keeping, viz.: One hundred and forty-nine Bonds of the Quincy, Missouri and Pacific Railroad Company, each for $1,000, dated July 1, 1871, and payable to bearer on the first day of July, 1901, in gold, with interest at 7 per cent., payable semi-annually, on the first days of January and July; signed by Charles A. Savage, President, and Chas. H. Bull, Treasurer, under the corporate seal of the Company, and with the name, Chas. H. Bull, Treasurer, engraved upon the interest coupons. As near as can be ascertained, said Bonds are numbered as follows: No. 1002 to 1005 inclusive; No. 1092 to 1100 inclusive; No. 1127 to 1130 inclusive; No. 1151 to 1200 inclusive; No. 1251 to 1300 inclusive; Nos. 1009, 1010, 1023, 1024, 1102, 1105, 1106, 1115, 1148, 1149, 1207, 1208, 1214, 1215, 1219, 1225, 1226, 1227, and fourteen others, the numbers of which are unknown.

Also, 180 Bonds of the County of Adams, in the State of Illinois, issued to the Quincy, Alton and St. Louis Railway Company, or bearer, dated January 1, 1870, each for $1,000, payable twenty years from date, bearing interest at six per cent. per annum, with coupons attached representing the interest; signed by Baptist Hardy, Chairman, and C. H. Morton, Clerk, with the seal of the County Court of said County. Said Bonds are numbered as follows: No. 221 to 400 inclusive.

Also, $100,000 of Bonds of the City of LaGrange, in the State of Missouri, consisting of eighty Bonds of $1,000 each, and forty Bonds of $500 each, dated Dec. 1871, or Jan. 1872, and signed by J. A. Hay, Mayor, and R. McChesney, Clerk, under the corporate seal of the City. Said $1,000 Bonds are believed to be numbered from No. 96 to 175, inclusive, and said $500 Bonds from No. 186 to 225 inclusive.

The above is believed to be a substantially correct description of Bonds stolen.

All persons are cautioned against purchasing or becoming interested in said Bonds, as the same cannot be enforced, and will be worthless in the hands of any purchaser.

And all persons are earnestly requested, in case of any knowledge of the existence or whereabouts of any of said Bonds, to communicate with the officers of this Bank, and to aid in tracing and recovering the same.

From the appearance of the inside of the safe, and the condition of some of the papers left by the thieves, it is believed that nearly all of the money and Bonds taken are more or less scorched and blackened by the gunpowder explosion.

Said Bank will also pay TWENTY-FIVE HUNDRED DOLLARS for the arrest and delivery at the County Jail, in Quincy, Illinois, of each or either of the persons engaged in committing said burglary and robbery, upon his conviction for the same.

By order of the Board of Directors of said Bank.

C. M. POMROY, *President,*
U. S. PENFIELD, *Cashier.*

QUINCY, ILL., March 10, 1874.

Direct all communications to J. C. McGRAW, Dep'y Sheriff, in care of the First National Bank, Quincy, Adams County, Ill.

The following is the description of the persons suspected of being concerned in the robbery as near as can be ascertained :

No. 1.—J. R. BIGELOW.—Thirty to thirty-one years old; five feet ten inches in height, trim, well built, well proportioned, walks erect but with downcast look. Dark hair, brown or hazel eyes and very red cheeks.

No. 2.—A. D. HARPER.—Age thirty to thirty-five years; height six feet, slim build, and rather long face with high forehead. Brown hair cut short; close cut brown or dark sandy Burnside whiskers; blue or gray eyes; dressed in dark clothes, with plug hat; wore heavy gold watch in vest pocket and large gold chain with long links.

No. 3.—C. G. GREEN.—Age about thirty; height five feet eight to ten inches, rather heavy build, dark complexion, Roman nose, hair black and cut short; black mustache, and side whiskers not connected with mustache. Dressed dark, with plug hat.

No. 4.—NAME UNKNOWN.—Thirty-five years old; height five feet seven to eight inches, slim build, coarse features, very prominent Roman nose, very large mouth; cheeks a little sunken, upper teeth seemed remarkably short; black hair cut very short, and dark eyes. Wore plain gold ring on right little finger, and gold ring—flat, square on top—on left middle finger. Dressed in dark clothes, with plug hat.

For a while Cummings led a riotous life, as usual. Wine, women, and faro soon made havoc with his portion of the Quincy plunder and his wits were again brought into play. He brought his organized talent to his aid, and started to Montreal, Canada, for the purpose of robbing Marshalla's Bank, but an overcharge of dynamite blew out the entire front of the building, and the robbers narrowly escaped with their lives. Again they fled, and their next field of operations was on the Falls City Bank of Louisville, Ky., which they operated upon as they did at Quincy, Ill., with the difference that their base of operations was under the altar of a Masonic temple. They removed the carpet and the floor, replacing them at the close of each night's work. During the time they were operating several lodge meetings were held, when the burglars stopped work and went for a walk and refreshments. For their trouble there they obtained $400,000. As usual, "broke" again in a few months, Dave started, in the summer of 1875, with a "kit" of tools, and in company with Billy Flynn and Jimmy Blake, was arrested for robbing rooms at the Capitol Hotel in Harrisburg, Pa. They were all sentenced to seven years each in the Eastern Penitentiary at Philadelphia. This was Cummings' first conviction. He was discharged from there on July 4, 1880.

After a short rest he went to New York and fell in with old friends. He then took a tour of New York State, robbing safes in the country post-offices and at railroad stations; but this did not suit him, and he went back to his old business, and in January, 1881, he was arrested at the Sinclair House, New York City, a porter having caught him coming out of the room of a son of United States Senator Pinchback's, with a full outfit of tools and some valuables of the guests. He was committed, obtained bail, and again went into hiding. His next appearance was at Philadelphia, where he formed a partnership with Walter Sheridan, Joe McClusky, and other noted bank sneaks. Their first robbery was that of a diamond broker on Chestnut Street, near Twelfth, where Cummings and Sheridan engaged the attention of the clerk, and McCluskey secured about $6,000 worth of diamonds. In May, 1881, Sheridan, Dave, and Jack Duffy made a trip to Baltimore, where they ran across a traveling salesman of the jewelry house of Enos, Richardson & Co., of Maiden Lane, New York. They followed him to the Clarendon Hotel, where they watched till he went to dinner, entered his room and stole his entire stock, valued at $15,000. The chase becoming hot for Cummings, he finally returned the proceeds of the robbery, and received $2,500 for it.

He then started for the Pacific slope with Old Jimmy Hope and Big Tom Bigelow, and after looking about, these enterprising burglars concluded to rob Sauthers &

Co.'s Bank, a Hebrew institution, where there was $600,000. They again put into operation their favorite tactics of securing a vacant room over the vault. They had tunneled through four layers of brick and several tiers of railroad iron, when the chief of detectives learned they were in the city. He took possession of several offices in the vicinity of the bank with his men, and about 10:30 P. M., on the night of June 27, 1881, he made a raid on them. He found Jimmy Hope at work. Cummings heard them coming and ran to the roof, crawled through the scuttle, and running over the tops of several buildings, finally descended through a vacant store, and was once more at large. Bigelow, who was supposed to have been working inside with Hope, in some manner escaped also.

Cummings left his trail at every hotel where he stopped, in Southern California, New Mexico, Denver, Col.; and at a small town, twenty miles from Denver, he robbed a well known Chicago liquor dealer, named Al. Arundel, of $1,400 in money, a $500 watch, and a $400 diamond stud. He then paid a flying visit to Chicago, then to Saint Joseph, Mo., from there to St. Paul, then to Oshkosh, Wis., where, as above stated, he was sentenced on September 14, 1881, for three years. Since his release he is remaining very quiet, no doubt locating something rich. Look out for him, as he is liable to turn up when least expected. Cummings, while admired by his comrades for his skill and daring, has always been regarded by them as willing to sacrifice everybody to save himself.

The fate of a number of persons mentioned in connection with Cummings, is as follows: Scott died in Concord prison recently, and Dunlap is serving twenty years there for robbing the Northampton Bank, Mass.; Jim Brady is serving runaway time and a sentence for felonious assault, in Auburn prison, in all about seven years; Ike Marsh is working out a seventeen years' sentence in the Eastern Penitentiary at Philadelphia, for a bank robbery; Jesse Allen is dead; Sam Perris is a fugitive from justice, being accused of the murder of the cashier of the Dexter Savings Bank, in Maine; George Leslie's body was found in the woods near Yonkers, N. Y., shot by his associates; Frank Dean, alias Daigo Frank, Ed Johnson, and Mose Vogel, have just finished serving a term of fifteen years in Trenton (N. J.) State prison; Jimmy Hope is serving a sentence of seven years and six months in San Quintan prison in California; Walter Sheridan is serving time in St. Louis for counterfeiting, and Pete Emmerson, alias Banjo Pete, was sentenced to ten years in Trenton State prison for attempt to rob a bank cashier in New Jersey.

Cummings' picture is a fair one, taken in January, 1881.

51

WILLIAM CONNELLY, alias OLD BILL,
alias Watson.

HOTEL THIEF.

DESCRIPTION.

Seventy years old in 1886. Born in Ireland. Stout build. Married. Height, 5 feet 9½ inches. Weight, about 200 pounds. Hair gray, head bald, eyes gray, complexion light. Stout, full face. Has a double chin. Mustache gray, when worn.

RECORD.

OLD BILL CONNELLY, or WESTON, as he is sometimes called, is considered one of the cleverest hotel workers in America. Of late years he has worked generally in the small cities, on account of being so well known in the larger ones. He has served two terms in prison in New York State, one in Philadelphia, and several other places.

He was arrested in the Astor House, New York City, on November 24, 1876, coming out of one of the rooms with a watch and chain (one that was left for him as a decoy). He pleaded guilty, and was sentenced to four years in State prison on December 5, 1876, by Judge Gildersleeve, in the Court of General Sessions. His time expired on October 20, 1880.

Connelly was arrested again in the Continental Hotel, Philadelphia, Pa., for robbing some French naval officers, who were about visiting the Yorktown celebration. He was tried, convicted, and sentenced to three years in the county prison on October 28, 1881. He is now at large, and is liable to make his appearance anywhere.

Connelly's picture is an excellent one, although taken since 1876.

52
WILLIAM PEASE, alias BILLY PEASE,
alias STEWART.
HOTEL AND BOARDING-HOUSE THIEF.

DESCRIPTION.

Forty-five years old in 1886. Born in United States. Slim build. A painter and sailmaker by trade. Married. Dark complexion, dark blue eyes. Height, 5 feet 5 inches. Weight, about 135 pounds. Dark brown hair, sharp face; has a scar near the crown of head. Has a cross and the letters "C. I." in India ink on right arm; also dots on left arm and near left thumb.

RECORD.

BILLY PEASE is an old and very expert burglar and boarding-house thief, and is well known in the principal Eastern cities. He was arrested in New York City on June 8, 1876, for having burglars' tools in his possession, and sentenced to one year in the penitentiary on Blackwell's Island. He was shortly after discharged, and robbed a boarding-house at No. 22 Irving Place, with one George Harrison. He was arrested again on September 16, 1877, by the same officer, in New York City, for an attempt at burglary at No. 12 Avenne A, for which he pleaded guilty, and was sentenced to two years and six months in State prison on September 27, 1877, by Judge Gildersleeve, in the Court of General Sessions, New York City. Nothing further that is authentic appears upon the record to date.

Pease's picture is a very good one, taken in 1877.

53

WILLIAM MILLER, alias BILLY MILLER.

HOTEL THIEF AND SHOPLIFTER.

DESCRIPTION.

Forty years old in 1886. Born in United States. Married. No trade. Stout build. Height, 5 feet 6½ inches. Weight, 140 pounds Brown hair, brown eyes, sallow complexion. Generally wears a brown mustache.

RECORD.

MILLER is a professional hotel and boarding-house sneak. He has served ten years in Sing Sing prison, independently of the sentence below, for robbing a boarding-house in Clinton Place, in New York City. He escaped from Sing Sing prison with Big Jim Brady the burglar, in 1873, by bribing a keeper with $1,000. The keeper was afterwards sent to prison himself for letting them escape. Miller was recaptured, and returned to Sing Sing, where he served his time out. This is a very clever man, and well worth knowing.

He was arrested again in New York City on October 28, 1879, on suspicion of robbing the room of one M. Vanderkeep, a Spanish cotton merchant, who was stopping at the New York Hotel. The room was entered on October 26, 1879, and diamonds and jewelry valued at $2,500 were carried away. In this case he could not be identified. At the time of his arrest there was found upon his person a watch and some Canada money, which, it was ascertained, were stolen from a gentleman's room in the Cosmopolitan Hotel, corner of Chambers Street and West Broadway, New York City, a few nights previous to his arrest.

For this last offense he was held for trial, and finally pleaded guilty, and was sentenced to ten years in State prison again on November 7, 1879.

His sentence expired May 6, 1886.

Miller's picture is an excellent one, taken in October, 1879.

54

ALBERT CROPSEY, alias WILLIAMS.

HOTEL THIEF.

DESCRIPTION.

Thirty-three years old in 1886. Medium build. Born in United States. Light complexion. Not married. Height, 5 feet 8 inches. Weight, 135 pounds. Light hair and mustache when worn. Has letters "A. C." in India ink on right fore-arm ; also letters "A. C." and "A.," bracelet, anchor and dots on left hand.

RECORD.

CROPSEY is a very clever hotel and boarding-house thief, and is a man well worth knowing.

He was arrested in New York City on May 10, 1878, for robbing a safe in Stanwix Hall, a hotel in Albany, N. Y., and delivered to the Albany police authorities. He was convicted there and sentenced to five years in the Albany, N. Y., Penitentiary on June 29, 1878, by Judge Van Alstyne. He was arrested again in New York City on November 4, 1883, and sent to Passaic, N. J., where he was charged with stealing $300 worth of silverware from a Mr. Lara Smith. In this case he was tried, but the jury failed to convict him and he was discharged. He is known in Philadelphia, New York, Boston, and several other cities in the United States.

Cropsey's picture was taken in 1878.

55

STEPHEN RAYMOND, alias STEVE MARSHAL.

FORGER AND GENERAL THIEF.

DESCRIPTION.

Fifty-four years old in 1886. Born in England. Stout build. Married. Height, 5 feet 8 inches. Weight, 180 pounds. Has considerable English accent when talking. Gray mixed hair, blue eyes, dark complexion. Mole on the upper lip, right side. The right eye is glass.

RECORD.

STEVE RAYMOND has a remarkable history as a forger and negotiator of forged bonds and securities. He had only left Sing Sing prison, where he had been confined for forgery, a few months, when he was arrested in London, England, on January 8, 1874, charged with being implicated in the great Buffalo, Erie and New York Railroad bond forgeries. Over $400,000 of fraudulent bonds of these railroads were sold in New York City, and an equal amount in other places, before their genuineness was doubted. They were so cleverly executed that one of the railroad companies accepted $40,000 of them without suspicion. These forgeries were the largest that were ever committed and successfully carried out in this or any other country. The capital to carry this scheme was said to have been furnished by Andrew L. Roberts and Valentine Gleason. Raymond's share was $40,000 cash, the larger part of which was stolen from him before he left for Europe in July, 1873.

Raymond was taken before Justice Henry, a London magistrate, and remanded for extradition on January 16, 1874, and was shortly after brought back to America.

While awaiting trial in the Tombs prison in New York, with his confederates, Walter Sheridan, alias Ralston (8), Charles Williamson, alias Perrine (202), Andy Roberts and Valentine Gleason, Raymond was taken to Elmira, N. Y., on habeas corpus proceedings, to be examined as a witness in some case, and while there he succeeded in making his escape from the Sheriff. He was arrested some time afterwards and committed to the Eastern Penitentiary on Cherry Hill, Philadelphia, for fifteen months, under the name of Frank Stewart, for a petty pocketbook swindle, which he carried on through the newspapers, and remained there without recognition until a short time before his release, when the fact became known to the New York authorities, who arrested him at the prison on January 27, 1877 (just two years after he had left the Tombs for Elmira), and brought him back to New York.

Raymond was convicted of forgery in the third degree and sentenced to State prison for five years on March 20, 1877, and was discharged from there in October, 1880. The list of the forgeries he was implicated in is as follows : New York Central Railroad bonds, $250,000 ; Buffalo, New York and Erie bonds, $200,000 ; Western Union Telegraph Company bonds, $200,000 ; New Jersey Central Railroad bonds, $150,000. A total of $800,000.

Raymond was arrested again in New York City on July 3, 1882, charged with the larceny of a watch on a street car. He could not be identified as the party who stole it, but a bunch of keys was found upon his person and the magistrate construed these keys as being equivalent to burglars' tools and committed him in $1,500 bail for trial. This was reduced to $500 by Judge Haight, of the Supreme Court, and Raymond was shortly after discharged.

Raymond was arrested again in New York City on September 1, 1883, charged with altering the numbers and cashing coupons of the Union Pacific Railroad Company, which had been stolen from the Northampton Bank in Massachusetts, in 1876. He presented at the office of the Union Pacific Railroad Company on September 1, 1883, twelve coupons and received a check for $480 in payment. When placed on the stand at the time of his trial, he said : " I met a man named George Clark, with whom I had been acquainted for years, in a liquor store on Eighth Avenue, about two years ago ; during the conversation he asked me if I would cash some coupons ; I was promised a percentage of $50 on $480, the amount of interest ; Clark said to me, ' You can't expect the coupons to be straight ; they are cut from stolen bonds.' I cashed several lots of coupons ; I never suspected that the numbers of the coupons had been altered or I would not have had anything to do with them ; I saw three detectives near the bank when I entered it, but they were looking in another direction. In my extensive experience with crooked bonds I never before heard of the numbers of the coupons being altered. If I had had plenty of money I would not have touched the coupons, but as my wife was sick I wanted money. When I came out of prison in 1880 I sold directories and afterwards gambled."

Raymond was convicted of forgery (second offense) and sentenced to State prison for life on October 22, 1883. The law under which he was sentenced reads as follows : " If the subsequent crime is such that upon a first conviction the offender might be punished, in the discretion of the court, by imprisonment for life, he must be imprisoned for life." The Court of Appeals of New York State confirmed Raymond's sentence on April 29, 1884.

Raymond's picture is a good one, taken in 1882.

56

GEORGE F. AFFLECK, alias ADAMS,
alias KID AFFLECK, alias DAVIS.

THIEF AND CONFIDENCE MAN.

DESCRIPTION.

Thirty-eight years old in 1886. Stout build. Height, 5 feet 7¼ inches. Weight, about 150 pounds. Born in United States. Married. Says he is a shoemaker. Dark hair, light blue eyes. Dark, sallow complexion. Wears light-colored mustache. Has a scar on his left cheek.

RECORD.

KID AFFLECK is a noted confidence man, having been arrested in several Eastern cities. His favorite hunting-ground was along the docks in New York City, where he was arrested several times, plying his vocation. He is also well known in Boston, Mass., and Providence, R. I., where he has worked around the railroad depots and steamboat landings with Plinn White (now dead), Dave Swain, and his old partner, Allen. He has served time in prison in Boston, Philadelphia, and New York, other than what is mentioned below. He cannot be called a first-class man, still he manages to obtain considerable money. His victims are usually old men. He works generally with Old Man Allen (alias Pop White).

Affleck was arrested in New York City on March 7, 1883, with Old Man Allen, who gave the name of James Adams, charged with robbing an old man named Jesse Williams, at the Broad Street Railroad depot in Philadelphia, of a satchel containing $7,000, on March 5, 1883. Shortly after this robbery Affleck's wife, Carrie, deposited $1,000 in two New York Savings banks—$500 in each. This was part of the stolen money. He was delivered to the Philadelphia officers, and taken there, where, by an extraordinary turn of luck, he got off with a sentence of eight months in the Eastern Penitentiary on March 30, 1883. Williams, who was robbed by Affleck, recovered about $1,000 of his $7,000, and made his way to South Bend, Ind., his old home, where he died of grief on October 29, 1883, having lost all he had saved for the last twenty years.

Affleck was arrested again in Central Park, New York City, on Sunday, March 21, 1886, and gave the name of George E. Wilson. He was in company of James Morgan, alias Harris, another notorious confidence man. They were charged with swindling Christopher Lieh, of Brush Station, Weld County, Col., out of sixty dollars, by the confidence game. They both pleaded guilty, and were sentenced to two years and six months each in State prison on March 24, 1886, by Judge Gildersleeve, in the Court of General Sessions, New York City.

This clever rogue has been traveling around the country for some time, swindling people, and the community is well rid of him.

His picture is a good one, taken in 1883.

57

DANIEL S. WARD, alias CAPTAIN WARD,
alias Morgan, alias Pape, alias Miller.

SWINDLER BY WORTHLESS CHECKS.

DESCRIPTION.

Forty-nine years old in 1886. Slim build. Born in Indiana. Planter. Height, 6 feet 2 inches. Weight, 136 pounds. A very tall, slim man. Single. Dark brown hair, gray eyes, sallow complexion. Has several front teeth out.

RECORD.

Col. Daniel S. Ward was one of the six men arrested in New York City on November 28, 1864, for being concerned in a plot to burn the hotels. He was confined at police headquarters for four months by order of Gen. Dix. The plan was to burn Lovejoy's, French's, the Astor House, the Albemarle, the Fifth Avenue, and the La Farge House, now the Grand Central Hotel. Captain Kennedy, one of the conspirators, was hung in Fort Lafayette, and Captain Bedle, another, was hung on Bedloe's Island, in New York Harbor. Ward was sent to Fort Lafayette, and after being confined there several months was sent South and permitted to go. It was also suspected that he was concerned in the burning of Barnum's Museum, in July, 1865.

In 1875 Ward went to Woodville, Miss., and represented himself as N. W. Page, of Baton Rouge, La., and obtained on a forged check $1,100. For this he was arrested, and after remaining in jail a year was discharged. He then came to New York as H. W. Keller, of Woodville, Miss., and secured from W. C. Browning & Co., of Broome Street, a suit of clothes and $100 in cash, change for a worthless check. In August of 1884, he was in New York City, representing himself as Wm. H. Morgan, of Woodville, Miss., and handed in a letter of introduction to Bates, Reed & Cooley, merchants on Broadway, who in turn gave him a letter to Naumberg, Krauss & Co., of Broadway, who sold him a long list of goods. They were asked to send one outfit down to the Cosmopolitan Hotel, where Ward, alias Morgan, was in waiting, and received them. In one day he secured goods from half a dozen firms.

On October 9, 1884, Ward went to James M. Shaw, the china dealer, on Duane Street, New York City, and said he was the captain of the steamer Eclipse, running between New Orleans and New York. He ordered $462 worth of goods, displayed a draft for $3,000 on the Park Bank of New York, and when he drew up a check of $500, the difference, $38, was handed him and he departed. He visited Collender's billiard sales-rooms on Broadway, New York, saying that he was about fitting up a large place in New Orleans, talked about prices, was invited out to dinner by the cashier, who introduced him to Pettus & Curtis, tailors, corner Seventeenth Street and Broadway. The last named was promptly swindled out of a suit of clothes and $150 in cash. At the

Meriden Britannia Co.'s, on Fourteenth Street, New York, he ordered $965 worth of goods, drew a check for $150 more, and walked off with the difference. On October 11, 1884, he went to Chickering & Sons and selected two pianos, took a fancy "by the way" to the manager, took him to lunch, and from the restaurateur, to whom he was introduced, borrowed $20 for change, as he had accidentally run short. F. F. Kramer, a piano cover maker on East Fourteenth Street, New York, was sent for, came, and sold a piano cover for $150, which Ward took with him in a coupé, together with $100 cash, the change of a $250 worthless check. He drove down to Lord & Taylor's, on Broadway, displayed the receipted bills of Shaw, Kramer, and the Meriden Britannia Company, and selected $875 worth of linen for the steamer Eclipse. He drew a check for $1,000, and having received $125, told Lord & Taylor not to send the goods until his check was certified. The goods of course never went. As he was passing out of the store his eye caught a lot of silk underwear, and $100 worth of this was placed in his coupé, as he "thought his wife might want to look at it." Boston, Providence, Chicago, Cleveland, Cincinnati, Louisville, St. Louis, and Philadelphia were all visited and victimized in the same manner, under the careless and guileless fashion of undue trusting common among business men.

Ward was arrested in New York City in connection with these swindling transactions on July 20, 1885, and tried on two complaints, one made by the Meriden Britannia Company, and another by Pettus & Curtis. He was convicted and sentenced to three years in State prison, in the Court of General Sessions, on July 20, 1885. His sentence will expire on February 19, 1888.

Ward was also known as A. C. Wood, and as Col. Sellers. His right name is Albert C. Ward, and he was born and brought up in Indianapolis, Ind., where his relations are highly respected.

Ward's picture is a good one, taken in 1885.

58

HUGH L. COURTENAY, alias LORD COURTNEY,

alias LORD BERESFORD, alias "SIR HARRY VANE OF HER MAJESTY'S LIGHTS."

SWINDLER—A BOGUS LORD.

DESCRIPTION.

Thirty-four years old in 1886. Born in England. Claimed to be married when arrested, which is not a fact. Slim build. Height, 6 feet 2 inches. Weight, 175 pounds. Dark hair, heavy eyes, bronzed complexion. Has a small, light-colored mustache. Tall, gentlemanly-looking man. Looks and assumes the air of an Englishman. Has a poor education, and is a poor writer. A bogus lord, with "R. N." on his baggage. This party's right name is supposed to be Clinton, and he is the clever son of a former lodge-keeper of the Earl of Devon, in Devonshire, England.

RECORD.

LORD COURTENAY, the bogus British nobleman, is well known in New York City since 1874, and, in fact, all over the United States and Canada. There are several people to-day in England, Utah Territory, Montreal (Canada), Richmond (Va.), Baltimore, Newport (R. I.), and, in fact, in all the principal cities in the United States, that would like to have the pleasure of meeting him again, and handing him over to the police authorities.

He was arrested in New York City on December 3, 1880, and delivered over to the Salt Lake (Utah) police authorities, for forgery on the London Bank of Utah. He was tried there, and acquitted; again arrested in Salt Lake, by the New York police authorities, and brought to New York, charged with forging an acceptance of a bill of exchange for the sum of seventy-two pounds sterling by Herbert S. Sanguinetti, of No. 13 Pall Mall, London, England. He was delivered to the captain of the steamship Spain, of the National Line, that sailed from New York for England on May 14, 1881, and was delivered by him to the police authorities of Liverpool, England, and taken to London, where he was credited with a five-years sentence. The fact is, he was sentenced to three months at hard labor in Clerkenwell prison, London, England, on October 17, 1881, under the name of Marcus Beresford, alias Walter Constable Maxwell. He was afterwards shipped to one of the West India Islands, but turned up again in Boston, Mass., the same fall.

Charles Pelham Clinton, another of his aliases, is wanted in Montreal, Canada, for a little confidence game he played on a merchant there. He represented himself as C. C. Bertie, adjustor for some estate in England. So well acquainted was he with English law, and so well did he describe the accession of the estate and the history of the family, that he completely deluded his victim, got into his confidence, and then cleared out. There was a reward of $1,000 offered for him in Montreal. In 1876 he made his début as a society swindler in Baltimore, Md., under the name of "Sir Hugh Leslie Courtenay," of the "British Royal Navy." Here he managed, by letters from confederates, to establish his identity in the eyes of the public. He was at once received in the best society, and by his distinguished appearance and manners completely captivated the female portion of the community. He spent money on cheap trash which he generously presented to his friends. A young Baltimore belle describes him as a most fascinating personage, and says that he was the first who ever "fired her soul with love." The elegant uniform of the British Royal Navy, which he always wore at the fashionable balls, delighted and infatuated the young ladies, who cut the buttons off for souvenirs. The lady alluded to above still has in her possession one of the gold (?) buttons, with the monogram of the Royal Navy, cut from Sir Hugh's uniform. He was wined and lionized, and ran on his credit there for months, wondering "what could be the matter with his stupid banker in England." His male friends grew suspicious, and made excuses for not being able to accommodate him with loans. Then he changed his tactics, and by different devices managed to extract from his female friends small amounts from their allowance for pocket-money. It is said that the daughter of a prominent citizen of Norfolk, Va., gave Courtenay $500. Notwithstanding these loans, his extravagant tastes involved him heavily in debt, and he was obliged to decamp, and did so just in time, as the evening before he took his leave he was recognized as a fugitive by one of his former victims. Before his departure from England he undoubtedly studied up thoroughly the pedigrees of many English families of noble title for the sole purpose of swindling unsuspecting Americans or marrying some silly American heiress.

His picture is a good one, although a copy.

59

CHARLES McLAUGHLIN, alias McLAIN,
alias LAMBERT, alias SEAMAN, alias JOHNSON.
HOTEL THIEF.

DESCRIPTION.

Fifty years old in 1886. Stands his age well. Born in Troy, N. Y. Is a saddler by trade. Well built. Height, 5 feet 7½ inches Weight, 160 pounds. Brown hair. Wears full, dark, sandy whiskers and mustache, turning gray. He has quite a respectable appearance, and is a good talker.

RECORD.

McLaughlin is one of the cleverest hotel workers in the country, and is said to be the son of a planter in Louisiana. He was a book-keeper, but lost everything during our civil war and became a hotel thief. On April 3, 1875, he robbed a room in the Westminster Hotel in New York City of a watch and chain and some diamonds and money. As he was leaving the hotel with his booty, his victim came downstairs and reported his loss to the clerk, who followed McLaughlin and had him arrested, and found the property upon his person. McLaughlin was tried, convicted, and sentenced to three years in Sing Sing prison for this robbery. It is said that the day he was sentenced his father was shot and killed by negroes in Grant Parish, La.

He was convicted and sent to prison in Quebec, Canada, for a hotel robbery in January, 1881. He was arrested again in New York City on June 10, 1884, for entering three rooms in the Rossmore Hotel. A full set of hotel-workers' tools was found on his person at the time of his arrest. He had robbed two rooms in this house some time before and secured $400 in money and two watches. In this case McLaughlin pleaded guilty to burglary, and was sentenced, under the name of Chas. J. Lambert, to two years in the penitentiary on Blackwell's Island, in the Court of General Sessions in New York City, on June 25, 1884, by Judge Gildersleeve. His sentence expired February 24, 1886.

McLaughlin's picture is a fair one, taken in 1875. He looks much older now.

60

JOHN O'NEIL, alias HUGHES,

alias Smith.

CONFIDENCE MAN, SELLS PAWN TICKETS.

DESCRIPTION.

Forty-five years old in 1886. Born in Ireland. Slim build. Painter by trade. Height, 5 feet 8 inches. Weight, about 140 pounds. Dark hair, turning gray; light eyes, dark complexion, cast in one eye. His hand is drawn up from a gunshot wound, and he is paralyzed on one side of his body, drawing one leg somewhat after him.

RECORD.

John O'Neil, alias Hughes, alias Jason Smith, has a method of working which is entirely his own. Whenever a robbery or burglary has been committed, the victim receives a poorly spelled and written note from O'Neil, stating that "although he is a thief, so help his God he had nothing to do with the burglary" of your residence, or whatever it may be—he has, however, pawn tickets representing the property stolen, which he will sell you. An interview is arranged, and during the conversation he remembers a few descriptions that you give of your property, and says that he has pawn tickets representing so-and-so. "Why did you not bring them with you?" is the question naturally asked. "Oh, no; I did not know whether I could trust you or not." Being assured that he can, another meeting is arranged for the purpose of going and redeeming the property, which is done in the following manner: a cab is hired, "as he is a thief, and it would not be safe for you to be seen walking with him," and both are driven to the pawnbroker's shop, which always has two entrances. Before the cab arrives at the place, he will say, "It will cost so much to redeem the goods," showing you the tickets and counting the amounts up, "give me the money, you remain in the cab at the door, and I will go in and redeem them, and bring them to you, when you can pay me for my tickets." He enters the pawnshop and passes out the other door, and you, after waiting some time in the cab, realize that you have been swindled, enter the place, but fail to find your man.

O'Neil was arrested at Staten Island, N. Y., by the police and brought to New York City on April 4, 1879, under the name of John Hughes, charged with swindling one Zophar D. Mills out of $172, as above described. O'Neil represented that he had pawn tickets for seven pieces of silk stolen from Mr. Mills on November 30, 1878. O'Neil, alias Hughes, pleaded guilty and was sentenced to three years in State prison in this case on April 23, 1879, by Judge Cowing, in the Court of General Sessions, New York City.

He was arrested again in New York City, under the name of John O'Neil, on September 12, 1885, for swindling several people in the same way. This time he also

49

GEORGE W. GAMPHER,
HOTEL THIEF.

50

DAVE CUMMINGS,
ALIAS HOGAN,
HOTEL THIEF.

51

WILLIAM CONNELLY,
ALIAS OLD BILL,
HOTEL THIEF.

52

BILLY PEASE,
ALIAS STEWART,
HOTEL AND BOARDING HOUSE SNEAK.

53

WM. MILLER,
SNEAK AND HOTEL THIEF.

54

ALBERT CROPSEY,
ALIAS WILLIAMS,
HOTEL THIEF.

55

STEPHEN RAYMOND,
ALIAS MARSHAL,
SNEAK AND FORGER.

56

GEORGE ADAMS,
ALIAS KID AFLECK,
CONFIDENCE MAN AND GENERAL THIEF.

57

DANIEL S. WARD,
ALIAS CAPT. WARD,
WORTHLESS CHECKS.

58

HUGH L. COURTENAY,
ALIAS LORD COURTENEY,
SWINDLER.

59

CHARLES McLAUGHLIN,
ALIAS McCLAIN,
HOTEL THIEF.

60

JOHN O'NEIL,
ALIAS HUGHES,
SWINDLER.

61

THOMAS O. CONNOR,
ALIAS TOMMY CONNORS,
SNEAK AND BURGLAR.

62

JOHN MAHANEY,
ALIAS JACK SHEPPARD,
BURGLAR AND SNEAK.

63

AUGUST PALMER,
BURGLAR.

64

MICHAEL KERRIGAN,
ALIAS JOHNNY DOBBS,
BURGLAR.

65

JOSEPH WHALEN,
ALIAS JOE WILSON,
BURGLAR AND SNEAK.

66

THOMAS KELLY,
ALIAS BLINK KELLY,
BURGLAR.

67

JOSEPH STEIN,
ALIAS PIGGIE REAL,
BURGLAR AND HOUSE SNEAK.

68

JOHN LOVE,
ALIAS LOWREY,
BURGLAR.

69

JOSEPH OTTERBERG,
ALIAS STEARN,
BURGLAR AND HOUSE SNEAK.

70

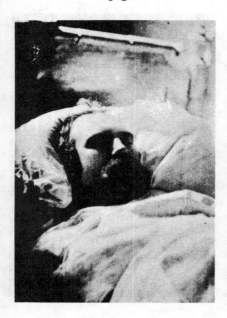

EDWARD LYONS,
ALIAS NED LYONS,
BURGLAR, SNEAK AND PICKPOCKET

71

DANIEL HUNT,
ALIAS CARTER,
BURGLAR AND SNEAK.

72

WILLIAM MORGAN,
ALIAS BILLY MORGAN,
BURGLAR AND SNEAK.

pleaded guilty, and was sentenced to one year in State prison on September 17, 1885, by Judge Cowing, in the same court.

Several of O'Neil's victims refused to prosecute him on account of his infirmities, and the fact that he had served twelve years of the last fifteen of his life in prison.

O'Neil's picture is an excellent one, taken in 1870.

61
THOMAS O'CONNOR, alias TOMMY CONNORS.
BURGLAR.

DESCRIPTION.

Twenty-six years old in 1886. Born in New York. Single. Teamster. Stout build. Height, 5 feet 7½ inches. Weight, 170 pounds. Dark hair, hazel eyes, dark complexion, freckled face. Has a star in India ink on right hand, and letters "T. O. C." in a circle on left arm.

RECORD.

"TOMMY CONNORS," the name he is best known by, is a desperate west side, New York, burglar. He is well known in the Eastern States as the former partner of Clark Carpenter, alias Clarkey (deceased), and James McDonald, alias Milky McDonald, two other notorious west side burglars. He has served a term in Sing Sing prison and in the penitentiary on Blackwell's Island, New York. He first came into prominent notice when arrested in New York City on December 2, 1884, in company of John McKeon, alias Kid McKeon, alias Whitey, and William Pettibone, for robbing a safe in the Bay State shoe-shop, in the Kings County Penitentiary of New York. Pettibone was at the time in the employ of the company. McKeon had served a term in the penitentiary, and worked in the shop. These two, in company of Connors, tore the safe open, and secured $3,104 in money in November, 1884. Pettibone was arrested and used by the people as a witness to convict McKeon, who was sentenced to six years and six months in State prison. Connors escaped conviction in this case.

He was arrested again in New York City on January 14, 1886, in company of Clark Carpenter, alias Clarkey, and James McDonald, alias Milky McDonald, and delivered to the police authorities of Boston, and taken there to answer for a series of burglaries. One of the burglaries occurred on October 1, 1885, at No. 470 Harrison Avenue; another on Thanksgiving morning, 1885, at No. 428 Tremont Street; another on December 26, 1885, at No. 390 West Broadway, South Boston, and several others in the city of Boston and vicinity.

Connors, McDonald, and Clark were tried in Boston on February 11, 12, and 13, 1886, and the jury disagreed; they were remanded to Charles Street jail to await another trial. This case was finally brought to a close on April 15, 1886, when Thomas O'Connor pleaded guilty and was sentenced to five years in State prison. Milky McDonald was discharged on April 15, 1886. Clarkey was also discharged on the same day, but, being very sick, died in Charles Street jail on the following day, April 16, 1886.

O'Connor's picture is an excellent one, taken in 1886.

62

JOHN MAHANEY, alias MAHONEY,
alias JACK SHEPPERD, alias JOHN H. MATTHEWS.

BURGLAR, SNEAK, WAGON THIEF.

DESCRIPTION.

Forty-three years old in 1886. Born in United States. Married. Medium build. Height, 5 feet 7 inches. Weight, 140 pounds. Dark curly hair, dark eyes, dark complexion. A sharp, quick-moving fellow. Makes a specialty of driving away trucks loaded with merchandise.

RECORD.

"JACK SHEPPERD," the name he is best known by, is an old offender. This sobriquet he deservedly bears, for few thieves in America have such a record as a successful thief and jail breaker. His notoriety dates back fully twenty years. First he was a petty thief, whose exploits were only fitful and trifling, but he improved his opportunities, so to speak, and quickly ripened into a full-fledged burglar. While plying the "jimmy" he one night fell into the hands of the New York police, and was taken to police headquarters. He was inside the building, in the very heart of the thief-takers' hive, but Jack was not a bit appalled by official terrors, and he opened his custodians' eyes, on April 9, 1870, when they saw him break away, dash through the door, clear the stoop at a jump, and go around the corner like a streak. There was a hue and cry and much hunting done, but Jack had escaped. He next turned up in the West, and played the mischief with lock-ups and vigilance committees. He was in a tight strait many a time, but his eye was always open to chances, and he somehow managed to get out of trouble. He has not indulged much in burglary of late years, but has a process of operating which he himself might be said to have patented, to wit, driving away trucks and their valuable contents.

Mahaney was arrested in Yonkers, N. Y., in 1866, by a Boston officer, and taken to Boston, where he was wanted for the larceny of a wagon loaded with broadcloth, etc., valued at $5,000. He was convicted for this offense on March 12, 1866, and sentenced to five years in State prison, this time under the name of John Wood. He was discharged from prison there on January 19, 1871.

He was arrested again in New York City on May 5, 1875, charged by Henry Dobson (colored), a driver for Overton & Co., No. 34½ Pine Street, with driving away a truck loaded with goods valued at $3,000. He was tried for this on June 30, 1875, in New York City, and the jury failed to agree. He was tried again on August 9, 1875, with the same result. He was then turned over to the police authorities of Philadelphia, Pa., and taken there by requisition on August 14, 1875, charged with burglary in entering the store of Matther, Reese & Son, No. 325 Chestnut Street, Philadelphia. He was also indicted for grand larceny on April 22, 1875, in Philadelphia, on complaint of Frank Stewart, of Bank Street, that city. He was convicted and sentenced to three years in the Eastern Penitentiary in one of the above cases, at Philadelphia, on September 15, 1875, by Judge Briggs.

Jack was arrested again in New York City on December 26, 1878, under the name of John H. Matthews, for the larceny of a truck from James Lynch, of No. 35 City Hall Place, New York, on July 9, 1878. On this date Jack engaged Lynch to carry off three bales of wool from the corner of Reade Street and West Broadway. A number of bales of wool had been left outside the establishment there, and Jack, on the truck's arrival, superintended the work of removing them with quite an assumption of ownership; then he took a seat on the truck beside Lynch, who drove off. He induced Lynch to leave the truck for a minute and go on a message to the top floor of a house they were passing; he was only a short time out of sight when Jack caught up the reins, lashed the horses into a quick run, and was soon out of sight with truck and wool. The wool was unloaded and the truck turned adrift. Jack then hailed another truckman who was returning to New Jersey, the wool was taken to New Jersey, where it was afterwards found. Jack was finally discharged on December 28, 1878, as the authorities could not get the Jersey truckman to come to New York and identify him.

Mahaney was arrested again in Boston, Mass., in April, 1879, for driving away a truck load of goods. He was tried, convicted, and sentenced for this offense to five years in State prison, on April 25, 1879. This sentence expired on August 24, 1883. He was arrested again in Philadelphia, Pa., on July 19, 1884, for the larceny of a truck and three bales of Irish linen from G. B. Haines & Co., of Market Street. For this he was sentenced to three years in the Eastern Penitentiary on August 11, 1884. This time he gave the name of James Robinson. His time expires April 11, 1887.

Shepperd has also served time in Joliet prison, Illinois, from 1871 to 1875.

His picture, although taken some time ago, is a fair one.

63

AUGUST PALMER.

BURGLAR.

DESCRIPTION.

Twenty-nine years old in 1886. Stout build. German, born in United States. Married. Cigar-maker. Height, 5 feet 10 inches. Weight, 180 pounds. Light hair, gray eyes, round full face, fair complexion.

RECORD.

AUGUST PALMER is a brother of Herman Palmer (189), both desperate New York burglars. They, in connection with Robert Clifford, Peter Wilson (deceased), and John Anderson, alias Little Andy, all expert burglars, succeeded in doing considerable work in and around New York before their capture. The Palmer brothers are expert safe burglars.

August Palmer and Peter Wilson (who was shot and killed at Chester, Pa., while committing a burglary on May 2, 1884) were arrested in New York City on June 8, 1880, for an attempt to rob the safe at the pawnbroker establishment of Patrick Ganley, in Division Street, in which there was at the time $15,000 worth of jewelry, etc. Wilson was bailed out, and escaped conviction for lack of evidence. Palmer, at the time of his arrest, lived with his wife, Mary Steele, in Seventy-sixth Street, near Third Avenue, New York. The detectives searched his rooms, and concealed behind a mirror they found three pawn-tickets, which represented an amethyst ring, a gold watch and chain, and a pair of opera glasses, which, when redeemed, were at once identified as part of the property stolen from Meyer's pawn-shop, No. 528 Second Avenue, which was burglarized on the night of April 30, 1880. The safe was torn open, and its contents of jewelry, etc., valued at $6,000, carried away by August Palmer and associates. August was tried in the Court of General Sessions for the Meyer burglary, convicted, and sentenced to five years in State prison on June 28, 1880.

At the time that August's home was searched and the pawn-tickets found, there was also found two pieces of silk dress goods, that were stolen from Mannassa L. Goldman's dry-goods store on Canal Street, New York. The store was entered by burglars on Christmas-day, 1879. August's wife claimed the silk, and she was sent to the penitentiary for having stolen goods in her possession.

Palmer was arrested again in New York City for assaulting a party who gave evidence against his brother Herman, and sentenced to three years for assault in the second degree, on September 19, 1884. His sentence will expire, if well behaved, on January 14, 1887.

Palmer's picture is a good one, taken in 1880.

64

MICHAEL KERRIGAN, alias JOHNNY DOBBS.

BANK BURGLAR.

DESCRIPTION.

Fifty-one years old in 1886. Born in England. Married. Machinist. Stout build. Height, 5 feet 5½ inches. Weight, 150 pounds. Gray hair, blue eyes, dark complexion, smooth round face, large mouth. Has some English accent. Stands his age well.

RECORD.

Kerrigan, or Johnny Dobbs, was born and brought up in the slums of the Fourth Ward of New York City. He started out as a pickpocket, and was afterwards connected with Patsey Conroy (deceased), Larry Griffin, Denny Brady, Pugsey Hurley, and other notorious river thieves. Later on he became one of the most expert bank burglars in America. He is well known in almost every large city in America, and is considered a first-class workman. His associates were Charles Adams, alias Langdon W. Moore (22); George Mason, alias Gordon (24); Big Frank McCoy (89), Old Bill Meagher, Abe Coakley, Fairy McGuire (78), Sam Perris, alias Worcester Sam (199); Johnny Hope (19), Jimmy Hope (20), and, in fact, all the best men in the profession. He has been engaged in almost all the important bank robberies that have occurred in this country during the past twenty-five years. Dobbs, Worcester Sam, and old man Hope, were implicated in the robbery of the Dexter Bank of Maine, and the murder of the cashier. Worcester Sam, it is claimed, threw Cashier Barron into the bank vault and shut the door on him, because he refused to give them the combination of the safe in the vault, and next morning he was found dead. Sam is wanted now for this murder.

Dobbs, alias Rice, escaped from State prison at Wethersfield, Conn., in company of another convict, on May 3, 1875. He was serving a sentence of four years for a burglary committed in Collinsville, Conn. When in jail at Hartford, Conn., before his transfer to Wethersfield, he made an attempt to escape, but was detected when he had almost dug himself out.

Dobbs was arrested again in Philadelphia, Pa., on May 7, 1879, while attempting to sell some of the bonds stolen from the Manhattan Savings Institution in New York on October 27, 1878. He was brought to New York City, and confined in the Tombs prison until February 6, 1880, when he was delivered to the authorities of Connecticut, and taken back to Wethersfield prison, to serve out his unexpired time.

The following is an account of the last arrest of Dobbs and his gang in Lawrence, Mass., as published in the police news of Boston at the time. With a few corrections, it is given in full.

The value of strict police surveillance of strangers was never better illustrated in this country than at Lawrence, Mass., on Monday night, March 3, 1884. Officer Carey of the day patrol had reported to the city marshal two days before the presence at the Franklin House of four persons, whom the officer thought were worth watching. A description of the men was placed on the blotter at police headquarters for the information of all members of the force. When these men alighted in Lawrence at 4 P. M., March 3, and carried their gripsacks to a different hotel from that they had patronized on their visit two days before, the eye of the "countryman copper" was wide open and kept them within view. They registered at the hotel, and, later, "connected" with two other members of the gang who had hired teams at different stables in Lowell, Mass., and driven over the road ten miles. Four of the gang took supper at Arthur Dodge's restaurant and left their gripsacks there and took a stroll around the city. About 7:30 P. M. one of them bought a pair of rubbers at a shoe store, and then the gang sought out a billiard saloon to put in the time till the night was ripe for business. City Marshal James T. O'Sullivan, Assistant Marshal John Sheehan, Police Inspector Hiram R. Neal, Night Watch Captain James T. Brady and officers O'Connor, Mahoney and John J. Sullivan, in citizens' clothes, watched the billiard saloon, and had but a brief time to wait, when three of the desperados were heard coming down the stairs. They were on the street conversing in a low tone of voice, when Inspector Neal jumped in upon them and grabbed George Day, alias Moore, alias McCarty (87), by the neck, and speedily pinioned him.. The other two ducked their heads and eluded his grasp, one running towards Hampshire Street, pursued by Captain Brady, and the other toward Franklin, both firing as they ran. The captain, as his man who was William Thompson, alias Dennis Carroll, alias Big Slim (147), turned down towards the canal, ordered him to stop, and when he failed to comply, fired one shot. Thompson continued on the run, firing three shots at the captain as he ran, and now the shooting began in earnest.

The noise of the shots, none of which took effect, attracted officers O'Connor and J. J. Sullivan from Amesbury Street, and they, too, joined in the pursuit. Thompson threw his revolver away, and ran into the alley between the Atlantic blocks, where again Capt. Brady levelled at him and fired, and Thompson fell, crying: "I'm hit! I'm hit!" The captain, with the other officers came upon him, and when told to throw up his hands, he did so, and was taken to the station, where it was found that he was uninjured.

The marshal paid his attention to the other rascal, who fled through the alley, firing after him as he went, and the burglar returning the fire, shooting over his shoulder. He managed to escape, however. This man was John Love (68).

The report of revolvers awakened the two burglars who remained in the billiard room, and they made a bolt for the street. They broke from the billiard room, but did not reach the street before they were pinioned by the marshal, officers Carey and Dennis Sullivan, and Matthew McDonald. These men were James Rodgers and Frederick P. Gray (73).

Rodgers was the leader of the gang. He has been identified as Johnny Dobbs. One detective called him Johnny Irving, which, of course, was a mistake.

In the gripsacks were found a complete set of tools for safe-blowing—bellows, steel bits, dark lanterns, fuse, cartridge caps, sectional jimmies, tubes through which to blow explosives, and other implements of the craft. All had self-cocking revolvers of 32 calibre, and a quantity of cartridges to match, and among the party there was over $500, and each had a gold watch. In Dobbs' sack was found a box of Reading, Pa., powder, and a box of troches, labelled Edward S. Kelley, Boylston, corner Berkeley Street, Boston.

A formidable set of burglars' tools were those which the gang had, some of them, such as the pusher, for opening combination locks, extremely rare and expensive. The jimmies included a sectional one, five feet long, in three joints, and a smaller one sixteen inches long. There was a bellows worked by the feet, a lot of half-inch rubber hose and seven tin tubes for powder to be forced through in blowing open safes. This powder, contained in two flasks and a bottle, was very fine and well adapted to the work. Besides this explosive were several pounds of nitro-glycerine and atlas powder, in cartridges, so arranged as to be exploded by electricity if desired.

There were three coils of waterproof fuse, a fur muff, intended to deaden sound, and a gossamer to hide rays of light, two pocket dark lanterns, a thin spatula to work window fastenings, an adjustable wrench, a bit-stock, fifty-eight drills of silver-steel, and thirty-four steel wedges, ranging from three-quarters of an inch to four inches in length. For coercion and defense there were four new pattern revolvers and two pair of Bean's improved handcuffs. A map of New England and one of Essex county, two bottles of whiskey, with the paper labels scratched off, and a machine for cutting out door locks, made up the interesting collection.

At the examination in the Lawrence police court, March 6, 1884, each member of the gang was held in $15,000 for having burglars' tools in their possession, and Thompson was held in $10,000 additional for shooting at the officer.

Dobbs and Thompson pleaded guilty to having burglars' tools in their possession, and were sentenced to ten years each in Concord prison on June 9, 1884.

Day, alias McCarty, and Gray were tried some time after, and convicted. They carried their case up to the Supreme Court, which confirmed the verdict of the lower court, and they were finally sentenced to ten years each on February 11, 1885.

See records of Nos. 68, 80, 86, 88, 90, and 199.

Dobbs' picture is an excellent one, taken in 1884.

65

JOSEPH WHALEN, alias JOE WILSON.

BURGLAR AND SHOPLIFTER.

DESCRIPTION.

Twenty-five years old in 1886. Born in United States. Medium build. Married. Height, 5 feet 6¾ inches. Weight, 143 pounds. Brown hair, blue eyes, sallow complexion. Wears black mustache. Has a scar on right temple, another on corner of left eye.

RECORD.

JOE WHALEN, alias WILSON, is a clever shoplifter, and is well known in all the principal Eastern and Western cities, having formerly lived in Chicago. He was arrested in New York City on November 21, 1883, for shoplifting.

He was arrested again in New York City on August 25, 1885, in company of George Elwood, alias Gentleman George (114), a desperate Colorado burglar, with a complete set of burglars' tools in their possession. When the detectives searched their rooms in Forsyth Street, New York, they found considerable jewelry, etc. Among it was a Masonic ring engraved "Edson W. Baumgarten, June 25, 1884." This ring was traced to Toledo, O. In answer to inquiries about the same, Chief of Police Pittman of that city sent the following telegram: "Hold Elwood and Wilson; charge, grand larceny, burglary, and shooting an officer." The circumstances were as follows: On August 13, 1885, masked burglars broke into Mr. Baumgarten's house in Toledo, O., and being discovered in the act of plundering the place fired several shots at the servants and escaped. An alarm was raised and the police started in pursuit. Coming up on Elwood, the officer demanded to know what was in a bag he was carrying. He said, "Nothing of much value—take it and see." The officer took the bag to a lamp near by, and when in the act of examining it, Elwood shot him in the back and escaped.

Whalen and Elwood were taken to Toledo on August 29, 1885, to answer for this and a series of other masked burglaries in that vicinity, in almost all of which there was violence used.

They were both tried there on December 12, 1885. Elwood was found guilty, and sentenced to ten years in the penitentiary at Toledo on December 19, 1885. Wilson was remanded for a new trial, as the jury failed to convict him.

Elwood hails from Denver, Col., and is a desperate man. Whalen was formerly from Chicago, but is well known in New York and other Eastern cities. These two men committed several masked burglaries, generally at the point of the pistol, in Cleveland, Detroit, St. Paul, Milwaukee, and St. Louis.

Whalen, or Wilson, was tried again in Toledo, and found guilty of grand larceny on May 5, 1886, and sentenced to five years in State prison at Columbus, O., on May 15, 1886, by Judge Pike, Judge of the Court of Common Pleas of Lucas County, Ohio. See record of No. 114.

Whalen's picture is an excellent one, taken in 1883.

66
THOMAS KELLY, alias BLINK.
BURGLAR.

DESCRIPTION.

Twenty-eight years old in 1886. Born in New York. Waiter. Single. Slim build. Height, 5 feet 7½ inches. Weight, 134 pounds. Brown hair, brown eyes, dark complexion. Right eye out.

RECORD.

KELLY is a young New York burglar, and is credited with being able to handle a safe with some of the older ones. He was born and brought up in the Seventh Ward of New York City, and is a member of Patsey Carroll's gang. He was sentenced to two years in State prison on April 13, 1879, for grand larceny in New York City ; again, on December 23, 1880, for two years and six months for grand larceny under the name of Thos. Jourdan, just ten days after his release on the first sentence.

He was arrested again in New York City on August 21, 1883, in company of Patsey Carroll, John Talbot, alias the Hatter, Clarkey Carpenter (now dead), and Wm. Landendorf, "Dutch Harmon's" brother, at Martin Reeve's saloon, No. 38 Forsyth Street, New York City, a resort for thieves, charged with burglarizing the premises of Geo. Tarler & Co., manufacturing jewelers, at No. 7 Burling Slip. The premises were entered on the night of August 20, 1883, and jewelry, plated ware, etc., carried away valued at $1,379. Patsey Carroll and John Talbot pleaded guilty to burglary in the third degree in this case and were sentenced to four years in State prison on October 22, 1883, in the Court of General Sessions, New York City. Kelly was discharged.

Kelly's picture is a good one, taken in 1883.

67
JOSEPH REAL, alias JOE STEIN,
alias HOGGIE REAL.
HOUSE SNEAK AND BURGLAR.

DESCRIPTION.

Twenty-six years old in 1886. Born in New York City. Bricklayer by trade. Single. Medium build. Height, 5 feet 7 inches. Weight, 143 pounds. Black hair, hazel eyes, dark complexion. Left-handed.

RECORD.

HOGGIE REAL is a very smart and nervy house-thief. He generally works with Joe Otterburg (69), both of whom are well known in New York and Philadelphia.

Real was arrested in New York City, and sentenced to four years in Sing Sing prison by Judge Gildersleeve, on April 24, 1883, on conviction of burglary in the third degree, but escaped from there on June 22, 1883. He was returned to Sing Sing prison, under the name of John Williams, on another charge from New York City, on January 22, 1884, for four years, which, together with his runaway time, makes his sentence nearly eight years. Watch this man when you arrest him, as he carries a pistol in his outside coat-pocket, left hand side, and will use it.

His picture is an excellent one, taken in 1883.

68

JOHN LOVE, alias JAMES D. WELLS.

SNEAK AND BANK BURGLAR.

DESCRIPTION.

Forty-two years old in 1886. Born in United States. Medium build. Plane-maker by trade. Married. Height, 5 feet 8¼ inches. Weight, 140 pounds. Sandy-brown hair, gray eyes, florid complexion. Generally wears reddish-brown mustache. Has figures "33" in India ink on left leg, also letters "J. L." on each arm.

RECORD.

LOVE, alias JAMES D. WELLS, is a clever store and bank burglar. He has had considerable luck in escaping punishment considering his long career of crime. He is a desperate man and will shoot on the first opportunity, and is well known in most of the Eastern States as a leader of a desperate gang of burglars.

He was implicated with Langdon W. Moore, alias Charley Adams (22), and George Mason, alias Gordon (24), for the robbery of the Warren Savings Bank and the Post-office in Charlestown, Mass., on December 4, 1879. Mason, on whose testimony Adams was convicted, refused to testify in any manner against Love, and he was not indicted. Mason was afterwards sentenced to three years in the House of Correction, and Moore, or Adams, received sixteen years. Love was traveling around the country with Johnny Dobbs and his gang, and was the fifth man that escaped from an officer at Lawrence, Mass., on March 3, 1884, when the rest of them were arrested. He and others were concerned in the robbery of the post-office in Gloucester, Mass., in March, 1884, also the post-office in Concord, N. H., and several other robberies in New England.

Love was formerly the partner of "Jack" Welsh, alias "John the Mick," who killed "Jack" Irving, and who in turn was killed by Wm. O'Brien, alias "Billy Porter" (74), Irving's partner, in a saloon on Sixth Avenue, New York City, on October 20, 1883. John Love, alias "James D. Wells;" Charles Lowery, alias "William Harris," alias "Hill," of Canada; George Havill, alias "Harry Thorn," alias "Joseph Cook (15), of Chicago, Ill.; Frank McCrann, alias "Wm. McPhearson," alias "Big Frank," and Mike Blake, alias "Mike Kerwin," alias "Barney Oats," alias "Little Mickey," of

Pittsburg, Pa., were arrested near Elmira, N. Y., on February 14, 1885, for the robbery of the Osceola, Pa., Bank on the night of February 13, 1885.

The bank vault was built of solid masonry two feet thick, but the concussion of the dynamite cartridge used was so great that the neighbors heard the explosion and notified the proprietors of the bank, who in turn notified a constable. The latter gathered a posse and pursued the burglars, who had escaped in a sleigh. They drove at such a furious rate that their team soon gave out. At that moment, a farmer came from his stable with a fresh horse and sleigh, which the robbers appropriated without ceremony and continued their flight. When within four miles of Elmira, N. Y., the gang was cornered, having been traced by their tracks in the snow. Lowery, a most desperate fellow, fired two shots at Constable Blanchard, one of them slightly wounding him in the arm. The marshal, joined by others, gave chase to the burglars across Mount Zoar, and a running fire was kept up. The pursuers were joined by other officers from Elmira, and when near that city two of the desperadoes were captured. One of them, Mike Blake, alias Kerwin, was shot through the wrist; John Love, alias Wells, Frank McCrann, alias McPhearson, and George Havill, alias Harry Thorn, alias Cook, the other members of the gang, were chased until evening, when they were captured and placed in jail at Elmira, N. Y. The robbery was small, amounting to about $1,500, of which $500 was in silver and was nearly all dropped by the burglars in their flight.

Charles Lowery, alias Wm. Harris, alias Hill, is without doubt one of the most desperate criminals in America. After his arrest, he was also charged with the murder of the town marshal of Shelby, Ohio; and a $6,000 burglary at Galt, Ont.; also a $10,000 jewelry robbery in Montreal, Canada. While Lowery and another burglar named Andrews were in a bank cashier's house at Belleville, Ont., they were surprised and captured. Lowery, a short time before that, had killed a hackman. In this case he escaped his just deserts through numerous appeals and the diplomacy of his wife, who lived in Toronto, Canada. He was convicted in the Osceola Bank case, and sentenced to ten years in State prison on April 9, 1885.

Love was sentenced to nine years and eleven months, Havill to nine years and nine months, Frank McCrann to nine years and seven months, and Mike Blake to nine years and six months, in the same case and on the same day (April 9, 1885).

Love's picture resembles him very much, taken in July, 1882.

69
JOSEPH OTTERBURG, alias JOE STEARN,
alias OATSEY.
HOUSE SNEAK AND BURGLAR.

DESCRIPTION.

Twenty-eight years old in 1886. Born in New York City. Single. No trade. Medium build. Height, 5 feet 5½ inches. Weight, 125 pounds. Brown hair, blue eyes, light complexion. Generally wears a light-brown mustache.

RECORD.

JOE OTTERBURG is a very clever house sneak, that being his principal business. He will stand watching when you go to arrest him, as he generally uses a pistol. He is an associate of Hoggie Real (67), and is well known in several Eastern States. He was arrested in New York City and sentenced to four years in State prison on October 6, 1870, under the name of James Oats, by Recorder Hackett, for a sneak robbery.

Otterburg was convicted for having burglars' tools in his possession at White Plains, N. Y., on September 19, 1875, and was discharged from the penitentiary at Albany on July 15, 1877, after serving two years there, under the name of Joseph Osborne.

He was arraigned for trial in the Kings County Court of Brooklyn, N. Y., on May 11, 1878, for robbing the residence of Mrs. Adolphus Nathan, of No. 117 Adelphi Street, that city, on January 25, 1875, of $450 worth of property. In this case he was tried and acquitted on May 31, 1878.

Christopher Spencer, who was in this robbery with Otterburg, was afterwards sentenced to the Albany (N. Y.) Penitentiary for five years for breaking jail and assaulting his keeper at White Plains jail, Westchester County, N. Y.

Otterburg was arrested again in New York City, and sentenced to four years in State prison by Judge Gildersleeve, on April 24, 1883, for robbing a house in Harlem in company of Joseph Real (67). His time expired on April 23, 1886.

His picture is a good one, notwithstanding his eyes are closed, taken in April, 1883.

70

EDWARD LYONS, alias NED LYONS.

BURGLAR AND SNEAK.

DESCRIPTION.

Forty-seven years old in 1886. Born in England. Married. Stout build. Height, about 5 feet 8 inches. Weight, about 180 pounds. Hair inclined to be sandy. Wears it long, covering the ears, one of which (the left one) has the top off. Wears a very heavy reddish mustache. Bald on front of head, forming a high forehead.

RECORD.

NED LYONS was born in Manchester, England, in 1839; came to America in 1850. His father had hard work to make both ends meet and look after his children, and in consequence young Ned had things pretty much his own way. They lived in West Nineteenth Street, New York City, a neighborhood calculated to develop whatever latent powers Ned possessed. The civil war, with its attractions in the shape of bounties, etc., proved a bonanza while it lasted, and after that Ned loomed up more prominently under the tuition of Jimmy Hope (20). He was afterwards a partner of Hope's, and was arrested several times, but never convicted. In 1869 Lyons, Hope

Bliss, Shinborn, and others, robbed the Ocean Bank, of New York, of money and bonds amounting to over a million of dollars. The bank was situated on the corner of Fulton and Greenwich streets. A basement directly underneath was hired, ostensibly as an exchange. To this office tools were carried, and a partition erected, between which the burglars worked day and night, when opportunity served, cutting up through the stone floor of the bank, and gaining an entrance on Saturday night, after the janitor had left. To tear open the vaults was a task requiring time; but they operated so well, that on Monday morning the iron front door of the bank was found unlocked, the vault literally torn to pieces, and the floor strown with the débris of tools, mortar, stone, bricks, bonds, and gold coin—the bonds being left behind as worthless, and the gold coin as too heavy.

A few years before this robbery Lyons married a young Jewess, named Sophie Elkins, alias Levy (128), a *protégee* of Mrs. Mandlebaum. Her mania for stealing was so strong that when in Ned's company in public she plied her vocation unknown to him, and would surprise him with watches, etc., which she had stolen. Ned expostulated, pleaded with, and threatened her, but without avail; and after the birth of her first child, George (who, by the way, has just finished his second term for burglary in the State Reformatory at Elmira, N. Y.), Ned purchased a farm on Long Island, and furnished a house with everything a woman could wish for, thinking her maternal instinct would restrain her monomania; yet within six months she returned to New York, placed her child out to nurse, and began her operations again, finally being detected and sentenced to Blackwell's Island.

Early in the winter of 1870 Lyons, in connection with Jimmy Hope, George Bliss, Ira Kingsland, and a well known Trojan, rifled the safe of the Waterford (N. Y.) Bank, securing $150,000. Lyons, Kingsland and Bliss were arrested, and sentenced to Sing Sing prison. Hope was shortly after arrested for a bank robbery in Wyoming County, and sentenced to five years in State prison at Auburn, N. Y., on November 28, 1870. He escaped from there in January, 1873. Lyons escaped from Sing Sing in a wagon on December 4, 1872. About two weeks after Ned's escape (December 19, 1872), he, in company of another person, drove up in the night-time to the female prison that was then on the hill at Sing Sing. One of them, under pretense of bringing a basket of fruit to a sick prisoner, rang the bell; whereupon, by a preconcerted arrangement, Sophie, his wife, who had been sent there on October 9, 1871, for five years, rushed out, jumped into the carriage, and was driven away. They both went to Canada, where Ned robbed the safe of a pawnbroker, securing $20,000 in money and diamonds, and returned to New York, where their four children had been left—the eldest at school, the younger ones in an orphanage. About this time (September, 1874) the bank at Wellsboro, Pa., was robbed. Lyons was strongly suspected of complicity, with George Mason and others, in this robbery. Although Sophie and Ned were escaped convicts, they succeeded in evading arrest for a long time. Both of them were finally arrested at the Suffolk County (L. I.) Fair, at Riverhead, in the first week in October, 1876, detected in the act of picking pockets. Two weeks later he was tried in the Court of Sessions of Suffolk County, L. I., found guilty, and sentenced to three years and seven months in State prison, by Judge Barnard. Sophie was discharged, re-arrested on October 29, 1876, by a detective, and returned to Sing Sing prison to finish out her time. Lyons had on his person when arrested at Riverhead $13,000 of good railroad bonds. In 1869 Lyons had a street fight with the notorious Jimmy Haggerty, of Philadelphia (who was afterwards killed by Reddy the Blacksmith, in Eagan's saloon, corner Houston Street and Broadway). During the mélee Haggerty succeeded in biting off the greater portion of Lyons' left ear. On October 24, 1880, shortly after Ned's release from prison, in a drunken altercation, he was shot at the Star and Garter saloon on Sixth Avenue, New York City, by Hamilton Brock, better known as "Ham Brock," a Boston sporting man. Brock fired two shots, one striking Lyons in the jaw and the other in the body.

Lyons was arrested again on July 31, 1881, in the act of breaking into the store of J. B. Johnson, at South Windham, Conn. He pleaded guilty in the Windam County Superior Court, on September 14, 1881, and was sentenced to three years in State prison at Wethersfield, Conn. At the time of his arrest in this case he was badly shot. That he is now alive, after having a hole put through his body, besides a ball in the back, imbedded nine inches, seems almost a miracle.

Upon the expiration of Ned's sentence in Connecticut, in April, 1884, he was re-arrested, and taken to Springfield, Mass., to answer to an indictment charging him with a burglary at Palmer, Mass., on the night of July 27, 1881. Four days before he was shot at South Windham, Lyons, with two companions, entered the post-office and drug store of G. L. Hitchcock, and carried away the contents of the money-drawer and a quantity of gold pens, etc. They also took a safe out of the store, carried it a short distance out of the village, broke it open, and took some things valued at $350 from it.

In this case Lyons was sentenced to three years in State prison on May 29, 1884.

His picture was taken while he was asleep at the hospital in Connecticut, in 1881.

71

DANIEL HUNT, alias CARTER,
alias Martin, alias Mason.

SNEAK, HIGHWAYMAN, PICKPOCKET, SHOPLIFTER AND WAGON THIEF.

DESCRIPTION.

Thirty-eight years old in 1886. Medium build. Ship-joiner by trade. Born in United States. Single. Dark brown mustache. Height, 5 feet 8 or 9 inches. Weight, about 160 pounds. Brown hair, hazel eyes, dark complexion.

RECORD.

DAN HUNT is a very nervy and clever pickpocket, sneak and shoplifter. He will also drive away a loaded truck. He is pretty well known in New York and most Eastern cities, and works with the best people. He was arrested in New York City on

March 25, 1878, and delivered to the police authorities of Brooklyn, N. Y., in company of William Bartlett, charged with robbing the cashier of the Planet Mills, in South Brooklyn. The cashier was knocked down and robbed of $3,500 on March 25, 1878, while within a block of the mills, by three men, who, after the robbery, which was committed in broad daylight, jumped into a wagon and escaped. He had drawn the money from a New York bank, and was returning with it to the mills for the purpose of paying off the hands. He was accompanied by a watchman, but the attack was so sudden that both men were knocked down before either could offer any resistance.

Hunt and Bartlett were arrested on suspicion, brought to trial in Brooklyn, and both found guilty on June 29, 1878. The testimony was so contradictory that Judge Moore, who presided at the trial, had strong doubts as to the guilt of the prisoners. He therefore did not sentence them, but remanded them back to Raymond Street jail, pending a motion for a new trial made by their lawyer. A new trial was granted, and as the District Attorney had no additional evidence to offer, they were discharged by Judge Moore on June 28, 1879, over a year after their arrest.

Hunt was arrested again in New York City under the name of Mason, and sentenced to two years and six months in State prison on January 22, 1880, by Judge Cowing, for grand larceny.

Hunt's picture is an excellent one, taken in 1871.

72

WILLIAM MORGAN, alias BILLY MORGAN, alias WILLIAMS.

BURGLAR, SNEAK AND TILL-TAPPER.

DESCRIPTION.

Thirty-three years old in 1886. Born in New York. Medium build. Single. No trade. Height, 5 feet 8 inches. Weight, about 142 pounds. Brown hair, blue eyes, florid complexion. Has "W. B. Morgan" in India ink on his right arm; one dot of ink on left hand.

RECORD.

BILLY MORGAN is considered one of the smartest till-tappers and shoplifters in the business. He has confined himself to till-tapping and work of that description of late years, and has been arrested in several of the principal cities in America, and is well known in New York, Boston, and Philadelphia. He has worked with the best people in this line, and thoroughly understands his business.

He was arrested in Philadelphia, Pa., on April 16, 1880, with "Marsh Market Jake" (38), Little Al. Wilson, and George Williams (194), for the larceny of $2,200 in bank bills from one Henry Ruddy of that city. The whole party were convicted and sentenced to eighteen months in the Eastern Penitentiary at Philadelphia on April

26, 1880. Since his release he has been traveling through the country working almost every kind of schemes to get money. He has been arrested in New York several times. An account of all his arrests would fill many pages.

His picture is a very good one, taken while under arrest, in August, 1882.

73

FREDERICK P. GREY.

BURGLAR.

DESCRIPTION.

Thirty-two years old in 1886. Born in United States. Medium build. Single. No trade. Height, 5 feet 10 inches. Weight, 165 pounds. Brown hair, blue eyes, light complexion, brown mustache, and a thin growth of brown beard. Large ears.

RECORD.

GREY, or GRAY, is no doubt a clever burglar, from the fact that he was one of the "Johnny Dobbs" gang, that gave the authorities all over New England so much trouble in 1884. He is from the West, and is not very well known in the Eastern cities.

He was arrested in Lawrence, Mass., on March 3, 1884, in company of Johnny Dobbs (64), Denny Carroll, alias Wm. Thompson, alias "Big Slim" (147), and Tommy McCarty, alias Day, alias Tommy Moore, alias "Bridgeport Tommy" (87). See record of No. 64 for full particulars.

Kerrigan, alias Dobbs, and Carroll pleaded guilty. McCarty and Grey stood trial, were convicted, appealed their case without avail, and were finally sentenced to ten years each in State prison, at Concord, Mass., on February 11, 1885. See record of No. 87.

His picture is an excellent one, taken in March, 1884.

74

WILLIAM O'BRIEN, alias BILLY PORTER,

alias MORTON.

SAFE BURGLAR.

DESCRIPTION.

Thirty-six years old in 1886. Medium build. Born in Boston. Married. Printer. Height, 5 feet 5½ inches. Weight, about 145 pounds. Black curly hair, dark eyes, dark complexion. Has fine set of teeth. Has the following India ink marks: Sailor, with American flag and star, in red and blue ink, on right arm; star and cross on outside of same arm ; crucifixion of Christ, woman kneeling and man standing up, on left arm.   He is a bright, sharp-looking fellow.   Dresses well, and has plenty of nerve. Generally wears a black mustache.

RECORD.

This celebrated criminal is well known all over America as the partner of Johnny Irving, who was shot and killed by John Walsh, alias "John the Mick," during a fracas in Shang Draper's saloon, on Sixth Avenue, New York City, on the morning of October 16, 1883.   Walsh was killed at the same time, and Porter was tried for killing him, but was acquitted by a jury on November 20, 1883.

Porter, or O'Brien, the last being his right name, began his criminal career early in life, and has been arrested in almost every city in the Union, and is considered second to no one in his business.   The following are a few of the cases in which Porter has figured :

He was arrested in New York City on October 11, 1877, for the burglary of E. Tilges' warehouse, No. 487 Broome Street, on September 1, 1877.   Joe Dollard, Johnny Irving, and George Howard, alias Leslie (the last mentioned two are now dead), were with him.   They succeeded in carrying away about $2,000 worth of silk hat linings. Porter was committed in default of $4,000 bail by Justice Morgan, but was subsequently released.

Porter and Irving were arrested in New York City, June 5, 1878, and delivered to the police authorities of Brooklyn, N. Y., where they were wanted for the robbery of Mr. Betterman's dry goods store, in Williamsburg, of $5,000 worth of silk and $1,400 in money.   They were not fully identified in this case, and were discharged.

Billy Porter, Johnny Irving, and Gilbert Yost (the latter a notorious burglar, was sentenced to fourteen years in the Northern Indiana State prison at Michigan City on April 25, 1883, for robbing a jewelry store at La Porte, Indiana), were arrested in Brooklyn, N. Y., on August 11, 1878, at Porter's residence, No. 152 Patchen Avenue, for the burglary of Martin Ibert's Sons' flour and grain store, at No. 148 Graham Avenue, on August 10, 1878.   Porter was tried twice for this burglary, and each time the jury failed to agree.   He finally escaped with Irving from Raymond Street jail, in Brooklyn, on June 1, 1879.

They both went to Boston, and from there to Providence, R. I., where they were joined by Joe Dollard, and on June 27, 1879, the party burglarized the safe of C. R. Linke, a large jeweler, at No. 77 Westminster Street, securing watches and silverware of the value of $15,000.   On the night of June 30, three nights after this robbery, an attempt was made to arrest them in New York City by some private detectives, but it failed.

On July 23 following, Porter and Irving were chased by the police authorities in Passaic, N. J., and again escaped.   Porter was finally captured in New York City on September 28, 1879, and delivered to Sheriff Reilly, of Brooklyn.   He was again tried, convicted, and sentenced to five years in the Kings County Penitentiary by Judge Moore, of Brooklyn, on October 23, 1879.   It is said that Porter's mother died in Massachusetts during his confinement at "Crow Hill," and left him $12,000.   After

73

FREDERICK P. GRAY,
BURGLAR.

74

WILLIAM O'BRIEN,
ALIAS BILLY PORTER.
BURGLAR.

75

GEORGE LOCKWOOD,
ALIAS CULLY,
BURGLAR.

76

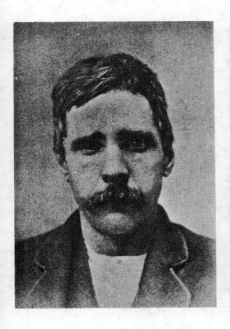

BILLY FORRESTER,
ALIAS CONRAD FOLTZ,
BURGLAR AND SNEAK.

77

GUSTAVE KINDT,
ALIAS FRENCH GUS,
BURGLAR AND TOOL MAKER.

78

ANDREW CRAIG,
ALIAS FAIRY McGUIRE,
BURGLAR.

79

FRANK REILLY,
BURGLAR AND SNEAK.

80

MICHAEL KURTZ,
ALIAS SHEENY MIKE,
BURGLAR.

81

FREDERICK BENNETT,
ALIAS DUTCH FRED,
BURGLAR.

82

MICHAEL QUINN,
ALIAS SHANG QUINN,
BURGLAR.

83

JOHN JOURDAN,
ALIAS JAMISON,
BURGLAR AND BANK SNEAK.

84

JOSEPH PARISH,
BURGLAR AND SNEAK.

85

WILLIAM BEATTY,
ALIAS BILLY BURKE,
BURGLAR.

86

JOHN IRVING,
ALIAS OLD JACK.
BURGLAR.

87

THOS. McCARTY,
ALIAS MOORE,
BURGLAR AND SNEAK.

88

MICHAEL HURLEY,
ALIAS PUGSEY HURLEY,
MASKED BURGLAR.

89

FRANK McCOY,
ALIAS BIG FRANK,
BANK BURGLAR.

90

PETER EMERSON,
ALIAS BANJO PETE,
BANK BURGLAR.

91

JAMES CASEY,
ALIAS BIG JIM CASEY
BANCO AND PICKPOCKET.

92

CHARLES MASON,
ALIAS BOSTON CHARLEY,
PICKPOCKET AND BANCO.

93

PETER LAKE,
ALIAS GRAND CENTRAL PETE,
BANCO.

94

JAMES ALLEN,
ALIAS POP WHITE and DR. LONG,
HOTEL AND CONFIDENCE MAN.

95

JOSEPH LEWIS,
ALIAS HUNGRY JOE,
BANCO.

96

WILLIAM JOHNSON,
PICKPOCKET.

Porter's release he remained quiet, and finally sailed for Europe in February, 1884, in company of Michael Kurtz, alias "Sheeny Mike" (80), where they had considerable luck. They returned to America in January, 1885, with $25,000 each, realized from many burglaries in England, France, and Germany.

Porter was arrested in New York City on Tuesday, January 19, 1885, charged with robbing the jewelry store of Emanuel Marks & Son, at Troy, N. Y. The robbery occurred on February 24, 1884, and the burglars carried away some $14,000 worth of jewelry. He was taken to Troy and committed for trial. If not convicted in this case, he will probably be taken to Brooklyn, N. Y., where he is wanted for robbing Haydn's jewelry store in 1884. Michael Kurtz was also arrested for this robbery in Jacksonville, Fla., on January 19, 1885, returned to Troy, tried and convicted. See No. 80.

Billy Porter also obtained a great deal of notoriety as being one of the men suspected of the murder of the noted burglar, George Leonidas Leslie, alias George Howard, whose remains were found on June 4, 1884, near Tramp Rock, Westchester County, N. Y., with a bullet through his head. He was shot on the night of May 29, and carried to where he was found in a wagon.

Porter's picture is a good one, taken in September, 1875.

75

GEORGE LOCKWOOD, alias CULLY LOCKWOOD.

BURGLAR AND SNEAK.

DESCRIPTION.

Forty-four years old in 1886. Born in New York. Medium build. Married. Plumber. Height, 5 feet 7½ inches. Weight, 153 pounds. Reddish brown hair, brown eyes, sandy complexion; generally wears a sandy mustache. Has pistol-shot wound on his arm.

RECORD.

GEORGE LOCKWOOD, or "CULLY," the alias he is best known by, is a professional safe-burglar, and a son of respectable parents who reside in New York City. His father, a boss plumber, learned Cully his trade. When but a boy he became entangled with a gang of thieves who frequented Mrs. Brunker's basement, on the corner of Wooster and Houston Streets, New York City, and was arrested for robbing a pawn-broker in Amity Street, and again in the Eighth Ward, in November, 1873, for having a set of burglars' tools in his possession, one hundred and eight pieces in all. Later on he was arrested on suspicion of robbing the premises of Brougham & McGee, gold pen and pencil manufacturers, Nos. 79 and 81 William Street.

He was also arrested for attempting to assassinate Charles Brockway (14), the forger, in West Houston Street. Lockwood, as Brockway was passing by, jumped out of the hallway of his wife's (Mrs. Brunker's) residence, and shot Brockway in the back. Brockway turned and shot him through the arm. He was not prosecuted, as Brockway refused to make a complaint.

He was arrested in New York City in January, 1871, in company of Pete Burns, alias McLaughlin, for an attempt at burglary and carrying burglars' tools. Judgment was suspended in this case.

He was arrested again in January, 1874, with Pete Burns, in a thieves' resort that had been raided by the police. They were both arraigned on the old suspended indictment on January 14, 1874, and Burns pleaded guilty and was sentenced to two years and six months in State prison. Lockwood was remanded until January 21, when he also pleaded guilty to burglary in the third degree, and was sentenced to two years and six months in State prison at Sing Sing, under the name of George Jackson.

He was arrested in the Eighth Ward, New York City, on December 1, 1878, on suspicion of a burglary, but was discharged.

Next he was arrested in New York City on January 8, 1880, with Charley Woods, alias Fowler, on suspicion of robbing Station F, New York Post-office, but was discharged by Justice Bixby for lack of evidence.

Arrested again in New York City on January 1, 1880, and tried in the Court of Special Sessions, on June 15, 1880, for assaulting a man named James Casey, of New Jersey, whom he mistook for an officer who had arrested him some time before for burglary. He succeeded in keeping Casey out of court on the day of his trial, and the court, being in ignorance of his character, discharged him.

He was afterwards arrested in New York City with Jim Elliott, the prize-fighter (now dead), on June 24, 1880, secreted in the cellar of Cornelius Clark's saloon, at No. 86 Henry Street. They had bored through the floor with the view of robbing a safe containing about $500 in money, and some jewelry that was in the store. A full set of burglars' tools was found with them. In this case they pleaded guilty, and were sentenced to two years each in State prison, on June 30, 1880, by Judge Cowing.

Lockwood was arrested again in New York City on October 14, 1884, in company of Frank Russell, alias Little Frank, another sneak and burglar, for the larceny of three watches from the store of Conrad Baumgarth, No. 16 Sixth Avenue, in July, 1884. "Cully" was committed for trial in $1,000 bail, by Judge Patterson, but discharged in the Court of General Sessions, by Judge Cowing, on November 7, 1884. He was arrested again in Albany, N. Y., in company of Andrew McAllier, for attempt at burglary. They were sentenced to eighteen months in the Albany Penitentiary, on June 26, 1885, by John C. Nott, County Judge, and his sentence will expire on September 25, 1886. Lockwood ten years ago was considered a very skillful and nervy burglar. It is claimed that he is a first-class mechanic and manufactured all his tools. He and Johnny Coady generally use the wood screw for forcing in an outside door. A hole is bored with an auger in the jamb of the door, exactly behind the nosing of the lock, after which a wood screw is inserted into the hole, and with the aid of a good bit-stock or brace, the nosing of the lock is easily and quietly forced off. Of late he has become somewhat dissipated, and is not rated now as a first-class criminal.

His picture is a good one, taken in November, 1877.

76

BILLY FORRESTER, alias CONRAD FOLTZ,

alias MATTHEWS, MARSHALL, FRANK CAMPBELL, LIVINGSTON, HOWARD, MATTHEW RILEY, BROWN, FRANK HARDING, and LEW KERNS.

BURGLAR AND SNEAK, AND SO-CALLED NATHAN MURDERER, OF NEW YORK.

DESCRIPTION.

Forty-five years old in 1886. Height, 5 feet 6 inches. Dark complexion, dark hair, dark hazel eyes, that are very piercing. Wears dark mustache. He is a broad-shouldered, well-built man. Weighs 150 pounds, and although in prison so long is a good man yet. Has a goddess of liberty in India ink on his right arm; an eagle, flag and dim anchor on left hand, between thumb and forefinger; Indian queen sitting on the back of an eagle on the left leg; full-rigged ship on his breast; United States coat-of-arms on left arm; red and blue ink bracelets on each wrist. Small but prominent scar one inch below the right eye. Both ears pierced for earrings; high, square forehead; small, narrow foot; tooth out of upper jaw, left side. Born in Lafourche County, La., and has served time in Sing Sing, N. Y.; Jackson, Miss.; Baton Rouge, La.; Chicago, Ill.; Memphis, Tenn.; Detroit, Mich.; and Philadelphia, Pa.

RECORD.

BILLY FORRESTER, as an expert, outranks many of the leading criminals in America. The first robbery of any importance that he committed was that of a United States paymaster, from whom he got $1,200, on a steamboat, near Vicksburg.

He was next arrested for the murder of a man named Neely, in Detroit, Michigan, after robbing him of $3,500 at cards. Of this charge he was acquitted on the ground of self-defense. He went to Canada, then to Baltimore, Md., where it is said he married a wealthy woman; shortly after which he paid Chicago, Ill., a visit, and was arrested there for highway robbery, and sentenced to thirteen years in Joliet (Ill.) Penitentiary on June 13, 1868. He soon made his escape, was recaptured, and escaped again in 1869. On June 12, 1870, Forrester was arrested in New Orleans, La.; he was discharged on a writ on June 16, and was re-arrested, and again discharged, and remained around New Orleans.

On January 1, 1871, Schoeler & Co.'s jewelry store on Canal Street, New Orleans, was robbed of diamonds, watches and jewelry valued at $83,000. Daigo Frank and Dave Cummings (50) were arrested for this robbery, but Forrester escaped, and shortly after assisted in releasing three burglars from jail in Mobile, Ala., in a most daring manner. His next appearance was at the time of his arrest, in New York City, for the murder of Benjamin Nathan, on Twenty-third Street, near Fifth Avenue. The only witness in the case identified him, but he was discharged after proving an alibi. He offered during his confinement in the Tombs prison to name the Nathan murderer if his unexpired sentence at Joliet prison should be commuted. His offer was declined, and he was returned to Joliet. His sentence expired there January 12, 1880.

On May 23, 1881, one Conrad Foltz was arrested in Philadelphia, Pa., for the Ashton burglary. A strong effort was made to bail him, when he was recognized as Billy Forrester, and he was tried, convicted, and sentenced to five years in Cherry Hill prison. His sentence expired in November, 1885. He is now at large, and is liable to turn up at any minute.

Forrester's picture is an excellent one, taken in 1881.

77
GUSTAVE KINDT, alias FRANK LAVOY,
alias FRENCH GUS, alias ISADORE MARSHALL, alias "FRENCHY," alias GUS MARECHAL.
BURGLAR AND TOOLMAKER.

DESCRIPTION.

Fifty years old in 1886. Stout build. Born in Belgium. Widower. Height, 5 feet 6½ inches. Weight, 180 pounds. Brown hair, keen gray eyes, fresh rosy face, dark complexion. High forehead. Generally wears a gray silky mustache and imperial. He is a square, muscular man. Speaks English fluently. Dresses like a well-to-do mechanic. Has a scar on his left jaw.

RECORD.

KINDT, or "FRENCHY," is a celebrated criminal. He came to this country when very young. He is a skillful mechanic, and is credited with being able to fit a key as well, if not better, than any man in America. He also manufactures tools and hires them out to professional burglars on a percentage.

In January, 1869, he was sent to Sing Sing prison for ten years for robbing the watch-case manufactory of Wheeler & Parsons, in Brooklyn, N. Y., where he was employed. On February 5, 1871, he escaped from Sing Sing by cutting through the bars of his cell with saws, which friends had managed to convey to him.

On October 17, 1872, he was arrested for robbing a jewelry store in Hackensack, N. J., and sent back to Sing Sing prison. He devoted his time to the invention of a lever lock, by which a single key could unlock all or part of the cell doors at once, and offered the lock, which he completed in 1874, to the prison authorities on condition that he should receive his freedom. The proposition was laid before Governor Tilden, who rejected it. "Frenchy" escaped again in 1875, and went to Canada, where he was sentenced to three years' imprisonment for robbing a pawnbroker in Montreal. Thirty-seven diamonds, which he had shipped to his daughter in New York, were recovered. After serving out his time in Montreal, where he introduced his lock, he went to

St. Albans, Vt., where he was arrested as an escaped convict on February 3, 1880. While on his way back to Sing Sing prison, in custody of an officer of Sing Sing prison, when near Troy, N. Y., on February 4, he made a dash for liberty. He leaped out of the car and ran across the fields. The officer followed and fired one shot. French Gus staggered, put his left hand to his cheek, but kept on. He fired again, and the burglar, flinging his arms in the air, fell headlong to the earth. He had been hit in the cheek and the back of the head. He was carried back to the train, and reached Sing Sing in a dying condition. He recovered, however, and on February 21, 1884, he was discharged, having finally expiated the crime of 1869.

Immediately upon his discharge he was arrested and taken to Hackensack, N. J., to be tried for robbing a jewelry store there in 1872, an indictment having been found during his confinement in Sing Sing. There was not evidence enough to convict him, and he was released, after two months' confinement.

Kindt was next arrested in New York City, on May 23, 1885, charged with burglarizing the safe of Smith & Co., No. 45 Park Place, on April 27, 1885, where he obtained one $5,000 and one $1,750 bond, two watches, and $80 in money. He was also charged with robbing the store of G. B. Horton & Co., No. 59 Frankfort Street, of $234 in money and some postage stamps. The detectives searched the rooms of his daughter, Rose Kindt, in East Eleventh Street, New York City, and there found a complete and beautifully made set of burglars' tools. In a sofa which they tore apart were sectional jimmies of the most improved pattern; under the carpet were saws and small tools of every variety; concealed elsewhere in the rooms were drags, drills, wrenches, crucibles for melting gold and silver, fuses, skeleton keys, wax, impressions of keys, etc. They also found what had been stolen from Smith & Co., and Horton & Co., with the exception of the money. When Kindt was confronted with his daughter, who had been arrested but was subsequently released, he confessed to all, and also charged Frank McCoy, alias "Big Frank" (89), with trying to obtain his services to rob the Butchers and Drovers' Bank of New York City.

Kindt pleaded guilty to two charges of burglary, and was sentenced to six years in State prison on June 4, 1885, by Judge Barrett, in the Court of Oyer and Terminer, New York City.

Kindt's picture is an excellent one, taken in May, 1885.

78

ANDREW McGUIRE, alias "FAIRY" McGUIRE, alias ANDREW CRAIG.

BURGLAR.

DESCRIPTION.

Forty-six years old in 1886. Born in United States. Slim build. Married. Cigar-maker. Height, 5 feet 7½ inches. Weight, 120 pounds. Brown hair, blue eyes, fair complexion, bald head. Generally wears a full reddish-brown beard and mustache.

RECORD.

"FAIRY" McGUIRE is probably one of the most daring and desperate thieves in America, and is well known in almost all the large cities. He served a fifteen years' sentence in Bangor, Maine, for highway robbery; also a term in Clinton prison, New York State, for burglary.

He was arrested in New York City on March 6, 1881, in front of No. 53 Nassau Street, occupied by L. Durr & Bro., assayers and refiners of gold and silver. An officer discovered the burglars at work in the store, and while looking in the window was approached by McGuire, who commenced talking loudly, thereby giving the men on the inside a chance to escape. McGuire was arrested, and upon the premises being examined it was found that three safes were partly torn open; they also found a full set of burglars' tools. As no connection could be made with McGuire and the people on the inside, he had to be discharged.

He was arrested again in New York City on March 17, 1881, and delivered to the Brooklyn police authorities, charged with robbing Miss Elizabeth Roberts, of Second Place, in that city. Four men entered the basement door of the house, bound the servant and tied her to a chair; then went upstairs, bound and gagged Miss Roberts, and took $3,000 in Cairo City Water bonds, numbered respectively 52, 71 and 72, also about $500 worth of jewelry. Although there was no doubt that McGuire was one of the four men engaged in this robbery, he was discharged, as the parties could not identify him, on account of being disguised on the day of the robbery.

He was arrested again in Newark, N. J., on July 5, 1881, charged with "blowing" open the safe in James Traphagen's jewelry store on Broad Street, that city. When the officers pursued McGuire, he turned and fired several shots at them. A party giving the name of George Williams, alias Dempsey, was arrested also. McGuire was tried and convicted on three indictments on October 18, 1881, one for burglary and two for felonious assault. He was sentenced to ten years in Trenton prison on each indictment, making thirty years in all, on October 19, 1881.

Williams was sentenced to two years for burglary the same day.

McGuire's picture is an excellent one, taken in March, 1881.

79
FRANK REILLY, alias HARRISON,
alias DONOVAN, alias STUART.
PICKPOCKET AND BURGLAR.

DESCRIPTION.

Thirty-three years old in 1886. Born in New York. Medium build. No trade. Married. Height, 5 feet 6 inches. Weight, 132 pounds. Light-brown hair, brown eyes, thin face, ruddy complexion. Small, light-colored mustache.

RECORD.

REILLY has been known under a great many names. He is now thirty-three years old, and was only seventeen when he made the acquaintance of the police. That was in 1870, when he was arrested in Morrisania, N. Y., for a burglary at White Plains. While in the jail at White Plains awaiting trial, he noticed that the inner door of the prison was open at dinner-time and the outer door was shut, while at other times the outer door was open and the inner door closed. By the simple expedient of hiding himself between the two doors at dinner-time he found himself a free man. The following year he was recaptured, and sentenced to Sing Sing prison for five years. Two constables started to drive with him to the prison, and when about half-way Reilly suddenly slipped the handcuffs off, darted out of the coach, and disappeared. For two days the woods were searched in the vicinity by the constables and country folk, and then Reilly was found hidden in a swamp, half starved. After serving two years at Sing Sing he was transferred to Clinton prison, from which he almost succeeded in escaping, having got out of his cell and was in the act of breaking open the door to the roof when discovered. He had torn his bedclothes into strips and braided them into a rope, with which to let himself down.

In the latter part of 1874 his term expired, he having been granted commutation for good behavior, and he returned to New York, where he speedily became embroiled with the police. In that same year (1874) he was arrested for trying to rescue two burglars from the police, and was sent to Blackwell's Island penitentiary for one year for disorderly conduct. He stayed there exactly two hours, walking calmly out past the keepers without being questioned by any one, and coming back to the city on the same boat which took him to the Island.

The next year (1875) he broke out of the Yorkville prison, New York City, where he was confined for stabbing a United States deputy marshal, by spreading the bars of his cell with a lever made out of a joist. He went to Philadelphia, where, in February, 1876, he and some of his companions were caught breaking into a warehouse. One of the burglars fired at a policeman, wounding him. The other policemen returned the fire, and Reilly received four bullets in his body.

After spending five months in a hospital he spent two years in the Eastern Penitentiary, at Philadelphia. On his release he returned to New York, and between 1878 and 1882 he served two terms for burglary in Sing Sing prison. It was after being released from Sing Sing the second time that he made a desperate attempt to break out of the Tombs prison, in New York, where he was awaiting trial for assault. His cell was on the eastern side of the second tier. He had a common pocket-knife, and a broken glazier's knife, which served as a chisel. With these tools he dug through the wall, under a drain-pipe in his cell, and one night was discovered by a keeper in the prison yard. He was taken to a new cell, and when he was sentenced to Blackwell's Island the warden breathed a sigh of relief.

After his release from the penitentiary he was arrested again in New York City, and sentenced to Sing Sing State prison on September 25, 1883, for five years, for robbing a man in Bleecker Street of $140. He escaped from the mess-room there on November 14, 1883, with Charles Wilson, alias "Little Paul" (29), by sawing the bars of a window opening into the yard, and after getting out of prison they walked to New York.

Scarcely three weeks had elapsed when Reilly again got into trouble in New York City. He and some companions resisted an officer who tried to arrest them for disorderly conduct. In the row Reilly got clubbed, and was sent as a prisoner to the Presbyterian Hospital, where an officer was sent to watch him. The officer fell asleep, and Reilly, whose wounds had been bandaged, got up, stole the orderly's clothes from under his pillow, and made his way to a second-story window, from which he dropped to the ground. He could find no shoes in the hospital, and had to walk three miles in his bare feet before reaching the house of a friend.

He was arrested again in New York City for beating a woman named Clara Devine, on New-year's day (1884), and committed for ten days, for disorderly conduct, by Justice White, in Jefferson Market Police Court. Shortly after his committal he was identified by a detective sergeant, and taken back to Sing Sing prison on January 5, 1884, to serve out his runaway time. His sentence will expire, if he does not receive any commutation, on September 24, 1888. Should he receive his commutation, it will expire on April 24, 1887.

Reilly's picture is a very good one. It was taken in November, 1878.

80

MICHAEL KURTZ, alias MICHAEL SHEEHAN, alias SHEENY MIKE.

BURGLAR.

DESCRIPTION.

Thirty-six years old in 1886. Born in United States. A Jew. Married. Slim build. Carpenter. Height, 5 feet 9 inches. Weight, 115 pounds. Black hair, hazel eyes, dark complexion, heavy eyebrows, Roman nose. Has a small wreath in India ink and number "44" on right arm; left arm spotted with ink; ink ring on the third finger of left hand.

RECORD.

"SHEENY MIKE." This celebrated criminal's history is a most eventful one. He was for years associated with a gang of skillful burglars, of which George Howard, alias Leslie (now dead), was the leader. Kurtz, which is his right name, made the acquaintance of Howard in Philadelphia, Pa., and was associated with him in several burglaries in that city.

When Howard took up his quarters in Brooklyn, N. Y., he gathered about him one of the strongest bands of burglars and thieves that ever existed. Among them was " Eddie" Goodey (110), "Johnny" Dobbs (64), "Billy" Porter (74), " Jim" Brady, Johnny Irving (now dead), John Green, John Wilson, alias " Dutch Chris," Jimmy Wilmont, alias " Mysterious Jimmy," Frank McCoy, alias "Big Frank" (89), Pete Emmerson, alias Banjo Pete (90), George Mason, alias Gordon (24), Joe Dollard, and Kurtz. Howard won his place as chief by his knowledge of safes and mechanism of combination locks, which he made a special study. Sheeny Mike was esteemed as a valuable member of the combination by reason of his quickness to observe the peculiar construction of buildings which it was determined to rob, and to demonstrate their weak points. He was never a bank burglar, but he is very clever at secreting himself in buildings and cutting through floors and partitions. He is also an expert safe-blower, and has a particular affection for jewelry and silk goods, and has been arrested so many times that it would be almost impossible to enumerate them. I will mention a few of them, which may be of service to you, should he fall into your hands.

Mike and John Wilson, alias "Dutch Chris," were arrested in New York City on February 15, 1877, charged with robbing the cloak house of Hahn, Benjamin & Co., Nos. 313 and 315 Broadway, on the night of February 4, 1877, of silk cloaks, etc., valued at $6,000. Mike was discharged on account of witnesses failing to fully identify him. Dutch Chris pleaded guilty, and was sentenced to three years in State prison by Judge Sutherland, in the Court of General Sessions, on February 19, 1877.

On March 4, 1877, Mike was arrested in Baltimore, Md., and taken to Boston, Mass., charged with robbing the silk house of Scott & Co. of that city. He was convicted on March 29, 1877, and sentenced to twelve years in State prison. While in prison there he made himself very sick and thin by drinking soap-water, and with the aid of a preparation, and by making an incision, he caused a pus to flow from his side. The prison physicians in examining him, gave it as their opinion that he would not live a month, as he was wasting away on account of prison confinement. On their report he was pardoned by Governor Butler, on October 19, 1880. Before his pardon was granted, he told Mr. Scott that all the stolen silk was sold to Mrs. Mandelbaum in New York. The firm commenced suit against her and obtained a judgment for the full amount stolen.

He was arrested again in New York City on January 30, 1881, and delivered to the police authorities of Washington, D. C., charged with robbing a dry goods store there on December 23, 1880, of silks, etc., valued at $5,000. In this case he was discharged.

Mike was arrested again in Pittsburg, Pa., on May 17, 1882, for having burglars' tools in his possession. In this case he was also discharged.

He was arrested again in New York City on July 19, 1882, with John Love (68), for complicity in the robbery of $5,000 from the Italian-American Bank of New York. They were both discharged, as the parties who had previously given a good description of them to the police failed to identify them when confronted with them.

Arrested again in New York City, on August 27, 1883, on a warrant issued by United States Commissioner Osborn, dated June 5, 1883, charging him with the larceny of diamonds and jewelry, valued at $658, from one Charles F. Wood, of Washington

City. He was delivered to United States Marshal Bernhard, and admitted to bail by Judge Brown, in the United States Court, on September 9, 1883.

In February, 1884, the jewelry store of Marks & Son, of Troy, N. Y., was robbed of diamonds and jewelry valued at $14,000. Suspicion pointed towards Sheeny Mike and Billy Porter, both of whom left for England shortly after. In April, 1885, they returned to America and remained only a short time, going back. Mike made a second visit to America in November, 1885, leaving Porter behind him in France. He remained in New York for a short time and went into the cigar business with his brother on Eighth Avenue, but the store was sold out, and they, in company of Mike's wife, went to Jacksonville, Florida, and started in the tobacco business. He also purchased an orange grove. In the early part of January, 1886, the tobacco factory burned down and Mike went to live on his grove. On January 19, 1886, he was arrested there charged with the Troy robbery. He obtained a writ of habeas corpus and fought the officers. The writ was dismissed by the Circuit Court at Jacksonville, Florida, on February 11, 1886, but his lawyer appealed from their decision, and the case was argued in the Supreme Court at Tallahassee, Florida, and decided against him. He was delivered to the officers and lodged in the jail at Troy, N. Y., on March 21, 1886. He was tried at Troy, N. Y., for the Marks burglary, on March 26, 27, and 28, found guilty, and sentenced to eighteen years and six months in State prison at Dannemora, N. Y., on March 30, 1886. After his sentence he made a statement, or "squealed," and implicated several people in this robbery. He, however, subsequently refused to substantiate it.

Billy Porter was arrested in this case. See record of No. 74.

Joe Dubuque was also arrested in this case, but finally admitted to bail.

Kurtz's picture is a splendid one, although avoided. It was taken in February, 1877.

81
FREDERICK BENNER, alias DUTCH FRED,
alias FRANK BELMONT, alias FREDERICK BENNETT.
PICKPOCKET AND BURGLAR.

DESCRIPTION.

Thirty-three years old in 1886. German. Born in United States. Barkeeper. Married. Well built. Height, 5 feet 6½ inches. Weight, 148 pounds. Light hair, blue eyes, light complexion. Wears a light-colored mustache. Has letters "F. E." in India ink on his left fore-arm.

RECORD.

BENNER, alias "DUTCH FRED," is a New York burglar and pickpocket, having served time in Philadelphia and New York penitentiaries for both offenses. He is very well known in both cities and is considered a clever man.

He was arrested on May 31, 1879, in the Lutheran Cemetery, on Long Island, N. Y., in company of Johnny Gantz, another New York pickpocket, charged with picking a woman's pocket. He was sentenced to five years in Sing Sing prison, in the Queens County, Long Island, Court, in June, 1879. He made his escape from the jail in Long Island City, in company of three other prisoners, on June 28, 1879, by sawing through the iron bars of the jail windows. He was arrested again in New York City on July 24, 1879, and delivered to the Sheriff of Queens County, who at once delivered him to the prison authorities at Sing Sing.

Benner was arrested again in New York City, and sentenced to three years and six months in State prison at Sing Sing, on August 20, 1883, for burglary, under the name of Frederick Bennett. His time expired on April 20, 1886.

"Dutch Fred's" picture is a good one, taken in October, 1877.

82

MICHAEL QUINN, alias SHANG QUINN, alias IRVING.

BURGLAR.

DESCRIPTION.

Forty-five years old in 1886. Medium build. Born in Ireland. Single. Blacksmith. Height, 6 feet 1 inch. Weight, about 180 pounds. Black hair, gray eyes, dark complexion. Wears black mustache and side-whiskers. Has a star in India ink on left arm.

RECORD.

"SHANG" QUINN is an old and expert burglar and pickpocket, and is known in most all the principal cities of the United States, and has served considerable time in State prisons. He is considered to be a very clever safe burglar.

He pleaded guilty in the Court of General Sessions, New York City, on August 23, 1880, to larceny of $85 from one Edward Stroyck, of No. 21 Tenth Avenue, and was remanded to August 28, 1880, when he was sentenced to two years and six months in Sing Sing prison, under the name of William Parker, by Judge Cowing. He had previously served two years in the same institution for a larceny.

Quinn's picture is a good one, taken in November, 1875.

83

JOHN JOURDAN, alias JONATHAN JAMISON, alias DUPONT.

BURGLAR AND BANK SNEAK.

DESCRIPTION.

Thirty-six years old in 1886. Born in United States. Married. No trade. Medium build. Height, 5 feet 8¾ inches. Weight, 150 pounds. Light brown hair, dark eyes, dark complexion, long slim nose, pock-marked. Cross in India ink on left fore-arm; number "6" on back of one arm; wreath, with the word "Love" in it, on left arm.

RECORD

JOHNNY JOURDAN is a professional safe-blower and sneak thief, and has worked with the best safemen and sneaks in America, and has quite a reputation for getting out of toils when arrested.

He was arrested in Philadelphia, Pa., and sentenced to four years in the Eastern Penitentiary in August, 1874, under the name of Jonathan Jamison. He was again arrested in New York City in November, 1880, and confined in the Tombs prison, charged with robbing the Middletown Bank, of Connecticut, in July, 1880, where the gang, Rufe Minor, George Carson and Horace Hovan, obtained some $48,000 in money and bonds. Jourdan played sick, and was transferred from the prison to Bellevue Hospital, from which place he escaped on Thursday, April 14, 1881.

In the fall of 1884 Jourdan made up a party consisting of Philly Phearson (5), Johnny Carroll, "The Kid" (192), and Old Bill Vosburg (4). They traveled around the country, and did considerable bank sneaking. They tried to rob a man in a bank at Rochester, N. Y., but failed. They followed him from the bank to a hotel, and while he was in the water-closet they took a pocket-book from him, but not the one with the money in it. Phearson and Carroll escaped. Jourdan and Vosburg were arrested and sentenced to two years and six months for assault in the second degree, by Judge John S. Morgan, on June 15, 1885. Jourdan gave the name of Henry Osgood.

He is well known in all the principal cities in America, and is considered one of the cleverest men in America in his line.

His picture is a very good one, taken in 1877.

84

JOSEPH PARISH.

PICKPOCKET, PENNYWEIGHT, SLEEPING-CAR WORKER, BANK SNEAK AND BURGLAR.

DESCRIPTION.

Forty-six years old in 1886. Born in Michigan. An artist by trade. Married. Stout build. Height, 5 feet 7 inches. Weight, 164 pounds. Hair black, mixed with gray; bluish-gray eyes; large and prominent features; dark complexion. Generally wears a full, dark-brown beard, cut short. High, retreating forehead. High cheek bones and narrow chin.

RECORD.

JOE PARISH is a Western pickpocket and general thief, and is one of the most celebrated criminals in America. He has been actively engaged in crooked work for the last twenty-five years, and if all his exploits were written up they would astonish the reader. In his time he is said to have had permission to work in many of the large cities in the West. He attempted to ply his vocation in New York City a few years ago, but was ordered to leave the city. Several Southern cities have suffered from his depredations. He is said to have been with General Greenthal and his gang, who were arrested at Syracuse, N. Y., on March 11, 1877, for robbing a man at the railroad depot there out of $1,190, on March 1, 1877. Parish is well known in Chicago, Ill., where he has property and a wife and family of three girls and one boy. He at one time kept a large billiard parlor in Davenport, Iowa, but, being crooked, he was driven out of the town.

He was finally arrested in Chicago, Ill., on February 13, 1883, and delivered to the chief of police of Syracuse, N. Y. He was taken there, and sentenced to eight years in Auburn prison, N. Y., on April 29, 1883, for robbing one Delos S. Johnson, of Fabius, N. Y., on the Binghamton road.

Parish's picture is an excellent one, taken in May, 1883.

85

WILLIAM BEATTY, alias BILLY BURKE, alias BAKER.

BURGLAR AND SNEAK.

DESCRIPTION.

Forty-six years old in 1886. Born in United States. Medium build. Married. Barkeeper. Height, 5 feet 8½ inches. Weight, 148 pounds. Black hair, gray eyes, dark complexion. Has letters " W. S." and coat of arms in India ink on left fore-arm. Generally wears a brown mustache.

RECORD.

BEATTY was arrested in New York City and sentenced to three years and six months in Sing Sing prison, on April 8, 1875, for burglary, under the name of William Brown. He was arrested in company of Andy Hess, another New York burglar, who gave the name of Alfred Brown, for a silk burglary in the Eighth Ward, New York City.

He was arrested again in New York City on May 18, 1878, for the larceny of $57 from a poor woman named Brady, who lived at No. 214 East Thirty-eighth Street, New York. He was committed for trial by Judge Wandell, but discharged by the District Attorney on a promise to return some stolen property to one Mr. St. John, which he never did.   He is a mean thief, and is called by other thieves a "squealer." He is well known in New York, Boston and Albany, and other Eastern cities.

His picture is a good one, taken in February, 1878.

86

JOHN T. IRVING, alias OLD JACK.

BURGLAR.

DESCRIPTION.

Forty-eight years old in 1886.   Born in New York.   Married.   Medium build. Height, 5 feet 4 inches.   Weight, about 130 pounds.   Gray hair; generally wears a gray mustache.   He shows his age on account of his long prison life, but is still capable of doing a good job.

RECORD.

"OLD JACK," as he is called, is one of the most celebrated criminals in America. He was born and brought up in the Fourth Ward of New York City, and has, for some offense or other, served time in State prisons from Maine to California.

He created considerable excitement in the early part of 1873, while under arrest for burglary in San Francisco, Cal., by declaring himself the murderer of Benjamin Nathan, who was killed at his residence in Twenty-third Street, New York City, on Friday morning, July 29, 1870.   He was brought from California on an indictment charging him with burglarizing the jewelry store of Henry A. Casperfeldt, at No. 206 Chatham Street, on June 1, 1873, and stealing therefrom eighty-seven silver watches, four gold watches, and a number of gold and precious stone rings.   Irving and another man rented a room at No. 3 Doyer Street, and forced an entrance into the store from the rear.

After his return from California he was confined in the Tombs prison, and while there, on November 22, 1873, he made another statement in which he alleged that he was one of the burglars who robbed Nathan's house, and offered to tell who it was that killed the banker.   The matter was thoroughly investigated by the authorities, who concluded that Irving was only trying to avoid the consequences of the two burglaries he was indicted for.   He was therefore placed on trial in the Court of General Sessions, in New York City, on December 8, 1873, and found guilty of the Casperfeldt burglary, and also for another one, committed in the Fifth Ward.   He was sentenced to five years on the first charge and two years and six months on the second one, making seven years and six months in all.

Irving, some years ago, was shot while escaping from a bonded warehouse in Brooklyn, N. Y., and believing himself about to die, betrayed his comrades.   He recovered from his wounds, and was discharged from custody.

After that, in company with others, he attempted to rob Simpson's pawnshop, in the Bowery, New York City. The burglars hired a suite of rooms in the adjoining house, and drilled through the walls into the vault. The plot was discovered by the police, who, however, were unable to capture them, as the cracksmen were frightened away by a party living in the house.

He was arrested again in New York City on April 26, 1881, under the name of George Mason, in company of another notorious thief named John Jennings, alias Connors, alias "Liverpool Jack," in the act of robbing the tea store of Gerhard Overhaus, No. 219 Grand Street. They were both committed in $3,000 bail for trial by Justice Wandell. Both pleaded guilty to burglary in the third degree, in the Court of General Sessions, and were sentenced to two years and six months in the penitentiary, on May 10, 1881, by Judge Gildersleeve.

Irving was arrested again in New York City on suspicion of burglary, on April 22, 1886. The complainant failed to identify him, and he was discharged. He is now at large.

Irving's picture resembles him to-day, although taken some fifteen years ago.

87

THOMAS McCARTY, alias TOMMY MOORE,
alias GEORGE DAY, alias BRIDGEPORT TOMMY.

BURGLAR.

DESCRIPTION.

Thirty-six years old in 1886. Born in Ireland. Stout build. Sandy complexion. Height, 5 feet 7 inches. Weight, 160 pounds. Light brown hair, brown eyes, high cheek bones. Has an India ink ring on second finger of left hand. Generally wears a sandy mustache.

RECORD.

"TOMMY MOORE," or McCARTY, the latter being his right name, is a well known New York sneak, pickpocket and burglar. He was formerly an associate of Joe Parish. He went to Europe, and on his return fell in with Johnny Dobbs, and worked with him all over the United States until the gang was arrested in Massachusetts. He is known East and West, and is considered a first-class outside man. He formerly lived in Bridgeport, Conn., where he was known as "Bridgeport Tommy."

He was arrested in Lawrence, Mass., on March 3, 1884, under the name of George Day, in company of Mike Kerrigan, alias Johnny Dobbs, Dennis Carroll, alias Wm. Thompson (147), Frederick P. Gray (73) and John Love (68), with burglars' tools in their possession. They had just left their rooms to commit a burglary, when the marshal and his officers made a dash for them and succeeded in holding four of them. The fifth man, Johnny Love, escaped from the officer. After their arrest, their rooms at the Franklin House were searched, and one of the most complete set of burglars' tools ever made was found there.

On March 6, 1884, Dobbs, Day and Gray were committed for trial in $10,000 bail each. Thompson, who had fired several shots at the officers, was committed in $20,000 bail.

Kerrigan, alias Dobbs, and Thompson pleaded guilty, in the Superior Court of Lawrence, Mass., to having burglars' tools in their possession, and were sentenced to ten years each in Concord prison, on July 9, 1884.

McCarty, or Day, and Gray stood trial, were convicted, and sentenced in the same court, on February 11, 1885, to ten years each.

McCarty's picture is an excellent one, taken in March, 1884.

88

MICHAEL HURLEY, alias PUGSEY HURLEY, alias REILLY, alias HANLEY.

MASKED BURGLAR.

DESCRIPTION.

Forty years old in 1886. Born in England. Medium build. Machinist by trade. Height, 5 feet 7 inches. Weight, 135 pounds. Brown hair, hazel eyes, fair complexion, pug nose. Has an eagle, with star underneath, in India ink, on inside of right arm.

RECORD.

"PUGSEY" HURLEY is an old Seventh Ward, New York, thief. He was one of the New Rochelle, N. Y., masked burglars. The gang consisted of "Dan" Kelly, Larry Griffin, Patsey Conroy (now dead), Big John Garvey (now dead), Frank Kayton, Frank Woods, "Shang" Campbell, Mike Kerrigan, alias Johnny Dobbs, John O'Donnell, John Orr (now dead), Dennis Brady, George Maillard and Hurley, and their headquarters was at Maillard's saloon, corner Washington and Canal streets, New York City.

The principal offense of which Hurley was convicted and for which he was sentenced to twenty years' imprisonment, was committed at the country residence of Mr. J. P. Emmet, known as "The Cottage," at Pelham, near New Rochelle, N. Y., on December 23, 1873. On that night Hurley, in company with others of the gang of well organized and desperate masked burglars, of which "Patsey" Conroy was said to be the leader, broke into Mr. Emmet's residence, and after surprising the occupant, his nephew and servants, bound and gagged them, and afterwards ransacked the house, getting altogether about $750 worth of plunder, with which they escaped. The same gang, on the night of October 17, 1873, broke into the house of Abram Post, a wealthy farmer, living three miles from Catskill village, on the Hudson River, tied up the occupants and plundered the house, collecting bonds, jewelry and other property worth $3,000, with which they decamped.

On December 20, 1873, three days prior to the Emmet robbery, the same band of masked marauders surprised the watchman at the East New York depot of the Jamaica, Woodhaven and Brooklyn Railroad, and, after binding and gagging him, blew open the safe, which contained $4,000 in cash. In less than a week after the plundering of the Emmet cottage, Mr. Wm. K. Souter, his family and servants, at his house at Sailors' Snug Harbor, at West Brighton, Staten Island, were awakened in the dead hour of the night to find that they were the prisoners of a masked gang of burglars who terrified them with threats of instant death. The thieves were all heavily armed and had no trouble in frightening the occupants into submission.

These depredations created considerable excitement among the residents of the suburbs of New York at the time, and nearly all the small villages were banded together and vigilance committees formed to look out for the band of masked marauders. All the gang were arrested by the police, and with the exception of two or three who established alibis, were sentenced to twenty years in State prison. Shang Campbell and Kerrigan, alias Dobbs, escaped to Key West, Florida, and were subsequently apprehended there. Campbell was brought back and sent to prison, but Kerrigan, who had plenty of money, succeeded in gaining his liberty, through the technicalities of the law. Orr (now dead) was next arrested ; then Hurley was made a prisoner on August 15, 1874. He was tried, found guilty, and sentenced to twenty years in State prison on October 1, 1874, by Judge Tappan, at White Plains, Westchester County, N. Y.

While in Auburn prison in the spring of 1876, and also of 1877, he was foiled by the guards in two desperate efforts at escape. He then feigned insanity, and was transferred to the asylum attached to Clinton prison. He had not been there long before he made another break for liberty, but being detected he was re-examined, pronounced cured, and drafted back to Auburn prison. He made several attempts to escape after that, and finally, with assistance from the outside, in April, 1882, he cut through the prison roof and bid his prison chums and guards a hasty good-by. He was re-arrested in New York City on August 1, 1882, on the corner of Liberty and Washington streets, delivered to the prison authorities on August 2, 1882, and taken back to serve his unexpired term of twelve years.

Hurley's picture is an excellent one, notwithstanding his eyes are closed. It was taken in July, 1882.

89
FRANK McCOY, alias BIG FRANK.
BANK BURGLAR.

DESCRIPTION.

Forty-seven years old in 1886. Born in Troy, N. Y. Medium build. Cabinet-maker by trade. Married. Height, 5 feet 11¾ inches. Weight, 176 pounds. Dark-red hair, light-gray eyes, full face, sandy complexion, bald on front of head, dimple in point of chin. Has letters "F. M. C." in India ink on right fore-arm, a cross and heart on left fore-arm. Generally wears long, heavy red whiskers and mustache.

RECORD.

FRANK McCOY, alias BIG FRANK, is a famous bank burglar, and a desperate criminal. He is one of the men who originated the "butcher-cart business," robbing bank messengers and others in the street, and quickly making off with the plunder by jumping into a butcher cart or wagon. He was arrested with Jimmy Hope, Ike Marsh, Jim Brady, George Bliss, and Tom McCormack, in Wilmington, Del., for an attempt to rob the National Bank of Delaware, on November 7, 1873. They were convicted on November 25, 1873, and sentenced to ten years' imprisonment, one hour in the pillory, and forty lashes. McCoy and McCormack made their escape from New Castle jail, with tools furnished by Bill Robinson, alias Gopher Bill. McCoy was associated with Jimmy Hope in the robbery of the Beneficial Savings Fund and other savings banks in Philadelphia, and several other robberies. He is said to have stolen over two million dollars during his criminal career. He is well known all over the United States, and is a treacherous criminal, as several officers can attest. He owes his nickname, "Big Frank," to his stature. He was arrested in June, 1876, near Suffolk, Va., a small town between Norfolk and Petersburg, in company of Tom McCormack and Gus Fisher, alias Sandford. A lot of burglars' tools was found concealed near the railroad depot there, and suspicion pointed to them as the owners. The citizens armed themselves and tracked the burglars with bloodhounds to their tent, which they had pitched in a dismal swamp near the village. They were arrested, taken to the Suffolk jail, and chained to the floor. McCoy was shortly after returned to Delaware prison, from where he afterwards escaped. Fisher, alias Sandford, was sent to Oxford, N. J., and was tried for a burglary. McCormack managed to regain his liberty through his lawyer, in October, 1876.

McCoy was arrested again in New York City on August 12, 1878, charged with robbing C. H. Stone, the cashier of Hale's piano-forte manufactory. The cashier was knocked down and robbed at the corner of Thirty-fourth Street and Ninth Avenue, New York City, on his return from the West Side Bank, on August 3, 1878. In this case McCoy was discharged, as Mr. Stone was unable to identify him.

McCoy was arrested again in New York City on April 12, 1881, charged with robbing Heaney's pawnbroker's establishment, on Atlantic Avenue, Brooklyn, on March 8, 1875, of $2,000 worth of jewelry, etc. He was arrested for this robbery in 1879, and upon an examination before Judge Terry, of Brooklyn, he was discharged. The grand jury afterwards indicted him, and he was arrested again as above, and committed to Raymond Street jail. He afterwards gave bail, and was released. He was finally arrested again in New York City on May 26, 1885, on suspicion of being implicated in a conspiracy to rob the Butchers and Drovers' Bank of New York City, in connection with one Gustave Kindt, alias French Gus (77), a notorious burglar and toolmaker. No case being made out against him, he was delivered to the Sheriff of Wilmington,

Del., on November 6, 1885, and taken back to the jail that he had twice escaped from, to serve out the remainder of his ten years' sentence.

McCoy has killed two men during his criminal career, one on the Bowery, New York, and another in a saloon in Philadelphia, Pa., some years ago.

Frank's picture was taken in August, 1878.

90

PETER ELLIS, alias BANJO PETE,

alias LUTHER, alias BIG PETE, alias PETER EMMERSON.

BANK BURGLAR, SNEAK AND HIGHWAYMAN.

DESCRIPTION.

Forty-one years old in 1886. Born in New York City. Slim build. Height, 5 feet 11 inches. Weight, 160 pounds. Light complexion, brown hair, stooped shoulders, thin face, high cheek bones, dark eyes. Generally wears a brown mustache.

RECORD.

BANJO PETE, the name he is best known by (Peter Ellis being his right name), was formerly a minstrel, but drifted into crooked channels about eighteen years ago. He was considered a good man, and was generally sought for when a job of any magnitude was to be done. He was an intimate associate of all the great bank burglars in America.

He was arrested with Abe Coakley in Philadelphia, Pa., on April 28, 1880, charged with robbing the Manhattan Bank in New York City, on October 27, 1878. It was claimed that Emmerson was the man who carried out the tin boxes from the vault, and sorted the bonds, etc.; that Coakley was the man who wore the whiskers, and dusted off the shelves in the bank while Johnny Hope and his father were in the vault with Nugent; that Billy Kelly stood guard over the old janitor; and Johnny Dobbs, or Kerrigan, and Big John Tracy, who was a friend of Shevelin, the watchman of the bank, were supposed to be the men who planned the robbery; while Old Man Hope was the man who did the work. Johnny Hope (19) was convicted, and sentenced to twenty years in State prison for this robbery. Kerrigan, alias Johnny Dobbs, was arrested while negotiating one of the stolen bonds in Philadelphia, and was turned over to the Sheriff of Wethersfield, Conn., who took him back to Wethersfield prison, to serve out an unfinished term of seven years. John Nugent was tried and acquitted. Patrick Shevlin, the night-watchman, was used to convict the others, and was finally discharged. Jack Cannon was also arrested in Philadelphia trying to dispose of some of the stolen bonds, and was sentenced to fifteen years there. Old Man Hope (20) went to California, and was sentenced to seven years and six months for a burglary there. Pete Emmerson was discharged from the Tombs, in the Manhattan Bank case, on October 4, 1880.

He traveled through the country with John Nugent and Ned Farrell, a notorious butcher-cart thief, and was finally arrested in the Hoboken, N. J., Railroad depot, on Saturday, July 28, 1883, for an attempt to rob Thos. J. Smith, the cashier of the Orange, N. J., National Bank, of a package containing $10,000 in money. Nugent and Farrell were arrested also. They pleaded guilty and were sentenced to ten years in Trenton State prison, on July 30, 1883. Emmerson stood trial, was convicted, and sentenced to ten years also, on October 30, 1883.

Emmerson's picture is not a very good one, although recognizable. It was taken in 1880.

91

JAMES CASEY, alias BIG JIM CASEY.

BANCO AND PICKPOCKET.

DESCRIPTION.

Forty-eight years old in 1886. Born in United States. Single. No trade. Stout build. Height, 5 feet 8 inches. Weight, 200 pounds. Black hair, dark eyes, dark complexion ; generally wears a full black beard, turning gray.

RECORD.

Big Jim Casey is a well known Bowery (New York) pickpocket and "stall" for pickpockets. He was formerly an associate of Poodle Murphy (134), Pretty Jimmie (143), Big Dick Morris (141), and all the first-class men. Of late years he cannot be relied on, and the clever ones give him the go-by, as he is fond of drink. Lately he has turned his hand to banco business, and generally handles the bag of cloth samples. He is now working with Pete Lake (93) and Ed Parmelee, two notorious banco steerers. Casey was arrested at Clifton, Canada, with a gang of American pick-pockets, during the Marquis of Lorne's celebration, and sentenced to three years' imprisonment. He has served time in Sing Sing prison, and in the penitentiary on Blackwell's Island, and is well known in all the Eastern cities as Big Jim Casey. He was arrested again in New York City on January 26, 1884, in company of Poodle Murphy (134), Tom Burns, alias Combo (148), Joe Gorman (146), and Nigger Baker (195), charged with sneaking a package of Elevated Railroad tickets, valued at $75, from a safe in the station at Houston Street and the Bowery, New York. For this offense he was sentenced to six months in the penitentiary on Blackwell's Island, on February 26, 1884. (See record of No. 134.)

His picture is a fair one.

92
CHARLES MASON, alias BOSTON CHARLEY.
PICKPOCKET, BANCO AND STALL.

DESCRIPTION.

Forty-five years old in 1886. Heavy build. Height, 5 feet 11 inches. Weight, 200 pounds. Dark-brown hair, turning gray; brown eyes, fair complexion. Generally wears a heavy, reddish-brown mustache; rather fine features. A very active man for his size.

RECORD.

"Boston" Charley's principal occupation is "banco." He has been in several jails in the East and West, and has traveled from Maine to California working various schemes. In New York he worked with Jimmie Wilson (143) and Shang Campbell (107), picking pockets; also, with Jack Strauss, on the sneak. He worked in the winter of 1876 in Boston, Mass., with Charlie Love, alias Graves, alias Scanlon, and was in the scheme to rob a man named Miller out of $1,200 by the banco game. Charley fell into the hands of the police, and Love escaped. He was afterwards implicated in a robbery in the Adams House, where Mrs. Warner, of St. Paul, Minn., lost considerable property. He then left Boston, and remained away until 1881. During the interval he is credited with having served five years in Joliet prison.

Mason was arrested again in New York City, and sentenced to four years in Sing Sing prison on December 20, 1881, by Recorder Smyth, for robbing one John H. Lambkin, of Cork, Ireland, out of $1,139, at banco. His time expired, allowing full commutation, on May 19, 1885.

Mason's picture is a good one, taken in 1881.

93
PETER LAKE, alias GRAND CENTRAL PETE,
alias Lane.

BANCO STEERER.

DESCRIPTION.

Forty-five years old in 1886. Born in United States. Stout build. Married. No trade. Height, 5 feet 7 inches. Weight, 165 pounds. Hair black, turning gray; dark hazel eyes, ruddy complexion, smooth face generally; sometimes wears a brown mustache.

RECORD.

"Grand Central Pete" is one of the most celebrated and persistent banco steerers there is in America, "Hungry" Joe possibly excepted. Like all others of his class, he has been arrested in almost every city in the Union, but seldom convicted, for the reason that as soon as he falls into the hands of the police, his confederates give the victim back his money, and he is only too glad to make himself scarce.

He was arrested on March 9, 1877, in New York City, in company of another confidence man named Charles Johnson, better known as " Tip " Farrell, of Chicago, for swindling one John Slawson, the superintendent of the Star Silver Mining Company, of Idaho Territory, out of $100, at the banco game. Slawson was stopping at the St. Nicholas Hotel, and was met by Pete, who had a "sure thing" for him. Lake and Farrell pleaded guilty in the Court of General Sessions, and were sentenced to six months in the penitentiary on Blackwell's Island, and fined $100 each, on March 15, 1877, by Judge Gildersleeve.

Pete Lake has been arrested at least fifty times since, but never convicted, for reasons above stated. He obtained his nickname through prowling around the Grand Central Railroad depot, in New York City.

Pete's picture is a good one, taken in March, 1877.

94
JAMES WHITE, alias POP WHITE,
alias ALLEN, alias DOCTOR LONG.
HOTEL THIEF AND CONFIDENCE MAN.

DESCRIPTION.

Seventy years old in 1886. Born in Delaware. Painter by trade. Very slim. Single. Height, 5 feet 8½ inches. Weight, about 135 pounds. Gray hair, dark-blue eyes, sallow complexion, very wrinkled face. Looks like a well-to-do farmer.

RECORD.

OLD POP WHITE, or "DOC" LONG, is the oldest criminal in his line in America. Over one-third of his life has been spent in State prisons and penitentiaries. He has turned his hand to almost everything, from stealing a pair of shoes to fifty thousand dollars. He was well known when younger as a clever bank sneak, hotel man and confidence worker. He is an old man now, and most of his early companions are dead. He worked along the river fronts of New York and Boston for years, with George, alias " Kid " Affleck (56), and old " Hod " Bacon, and was arrested time and time again. One of their victims, whom they robbed in the Pennsylvania Railroad depot at Philadelphia in 1883 of $7,000, died of grief shortly after.

Old White was discharged from Trenton, N. J., State prison on December 19, 1885, after serving a term for grand larceny. He was arrested again in New York City the day after for stealing a pair of shoes from a store. He pleaded guilty, and was sentenced to five months in the penitentiary on Blackwell's Island, in the Court of Special Sessions, on December 22, 1885.

Pop White's picture is a good one, taken in July, 1875.

95

JOSEPH LEWIS, alias HUNGRY JOE,

alias FRANCIS J. ALVANY, alias HENRY F. POST.

BANCO STEERER.

DESCRIPTION.

Thirty-six years old in 1886. Born in United States. Married. Speculator. Medium build. Height, 5 feet 9 inches. Weight, 163 pounds. Brown hair, brown eyes, light complexion. Dresses well. Has a beardless face generally. Large nose, and heavy scar on his chin.

RECORD.

"HUNGRY JOE," the name he is best known by, is a very persistent and impudent banco steerer. He is a terrible talker—too much so for his own good—and he is well known in every city in the United States. Although arrested several times, he has never served more than five or ten days in prison at one time. This man has victimized more people by the banco game than any other five men in the profession.

During Oscar Wilde's visit to this country he and "Hungry Joe" were chums for about a week. They lunched and dined together in the café at the Hotel Brunswick, in New York. After a while Joe played the confidence game on Oscar, in which the latter, it is said, was fleeced out of $5,000. Joe was not given the money, but a check drawn on the Second National Bank of New York City. Oscar, realizing that he had been swindled, stopped the payment of the check at the bank.

Joe was arrested in Detroit, Mich., in 1880, for shooting Billy Flynn, a notorious character, but was discharged on the ground of self-defense. He was finally arrested in New York City on May 27, 1885, when he pleaded guilty, and was sentenced to four years in State prison by Recorder Smyth, for robbing at banco one Joseph Ramsden, an English tourist, who was stopping at the Metropolitan Hotel, in New York City, out of five ten-pound notes, valued at about $250. The following is a very interesting account, clipped from one of the New York papers of May 22, 1885, of the manner in which Joe victimized Mr. Ramsden:

Among the passengers on board the steamship *Gallia*, which arrived from Liverpool on Monday last, (May 25, 1885,) was an elderly English gentleman of fine appearance but somewhat in ill-health. His name is Joseph Ramsden, a merchant of Manchester. He came to this country with a view to recuperating his health. Mr. Ramsden stopped at one of the first-class hotels uptown, and commenced to admire the beauties and attractions of the metropolis. Tuesday afternoon he strolled downtown on Broadway. Reaching the Metropolitan Hotel, Mr. Ramsden was sauntering leisurely along when he was surprised by a well-dressed stranger familiarly addressing him with:

"Why, how do you do, Mr. Ramsden?"

The latter expressed his inability to recognize the stranger, but the affable young man soon put the old gentleman at ease by adding:

"Oh, you don't know me; I forgot. But I know you from hearsay. My name is Post—Henry F. Post. You came over in my uncle's steamer yesterday. Capt. Murphy, of the *Gallia*, is my uncle, and since his return has been stopping at my father's residence. He has spoken of you to us. Indeed, he has said so much about you and of your shattered health that it seemed to me I knew you a long time. I could not help recognizing you in a thousand from my uncle's description of you."

Mr. Ramsden had had a very pleasant voyage on the *Gallia*, during which Capt. Murphy and he had become very friendly, and thus he was not surprised that the gallant skipper should speak of him. "Mr. Post" walked arm-in-arm with his uncle's English friend, chatting pleasantly and pointing out prominent business houses, until they reached Grand Street.

"I am in business in Baltimore—in ladies' underwear and white goods," said Mr. Post, "and have been home laying in a stock of goods. I should much like to remain a day or two longer and show you around, but I am sorry that I must return to Baltimore this evening. In fact, I am on my way now to get my ticket and my valise is already in the ticket office."

It needed but a few words to induce the elderly gentleman to accompany Post to "the office," in Grand Street, and the two soon entered a room on that street, west of Broadway. There the young man bought a railroad ticket of a man behind a counter.

"And now my valise," added Post.

Throwing the bag on the counter, the young man opened it, saying, "Here are some muslins that can't be duplicated in England," and exhibited to the old gentleman some samples of that fabric. Near the bottom of the bag he accidentally came upon a pack of playing cards, seizing which, he exclaimed:

"Ah, this reminds me. Don't you know that last night some fellows got me into a place on the Bowery and skinned me out of $400 by a card-trick in which they used only three cards? But I've got on to the game and know how it is done. They can't do me any more."

At that moment a man, showily dressed, emerged from a back room and said: "I'll bet you $10 you can't do it."

"All right, put up your money," responded Joe.

The cards were shuffled by the deft hand of the stranger, and Joe was told to pick up the ace. He picked up a Jack and lost. He lost a second time, and offered to repeat it, but the stranger said, "I don't believe you've got any more money."

"Well, but my friend here (pointing to Mr. Ramsden) has."

"I don't believe he has," sneeringly retorted the stranger.

"Oh, yes I have," interrupted the venerable Englishman, at the same time pulling a roll of ten crisp five-pound notes from his inside vest pocket and holding them to the gaze of the others.

The temptation was too great for Hungry Joe. He so far forgot himself and his uncle's friendship for the Manchester merchant that he grabbed the roll from Ramsden's hand. The latter tightened his grasp on the notes, but Joe violently thrust the old man backwards, and, getting possession of the money, ran out of the place, followed by his confederates.

Mr. Ramsden notified Inspector Byrnes that evening, giving an accurate description of "Capt. Murphy's nephew," which resulted in Hungry Joe's arrest. Joe was sitting in the basement of the house quietly smoking a cigar and resting his slippered feet on a chair. He was in his shirt sleeves. He tried to bluff off the Inspector, as is his custom, but finding it useless he donned his coat and boots and accompanied the Inspector to headquarters.

Last night Mr. Ramsden was summoned to headquarters, where he was confronted in the Inspector's room by Hungry Joe and eight other men.

"There is the man," quickly said Mr. Ramsden.

"I never saw you before, sir," replied Joe.

"You scoundrel," excitedly exclaimed Mr. Ramsden, "you are the fellow that robbed me of my money."

Joe's picture, though somewhat drawn up, is recognizable. It was taken in December, 1878.

96

WILLIAM J. JOHNSON, alias JOSEPH W. HARRIS.
PICKPOCKET AND BOARDING-HOUSE THIEF.

DESCRIPTION.

Twenty-nine years old in 1886. Born in United States. Single. Printer. Well built. Height, 5 feet 10 inches. Weight, 180 pounds. Brown hair, brown eyes, dark complexion; generally wears a brown mustache. Has scar over left eye; dot of India ink on left hand. Claims to have been born in Philadelphia.

RECORD.

JOHNSON, or HARRIS, is a clever pickpocket and boarding-house thief. He is well known in New York and Boston, Mass., and other cities, and is an associate of Frank Auburn, alias Austin (46), with whom he has been working in several of the Eastern cities.

He was arrested in Boston, Mass., on April 28, 1884, in company of Auburn, charged with picking pockets in the churches in that city, tried, convicted, and sentenced to three years in State prison at Concord, Mass., on May 16, 1884.

His sentence will expire on December 23, 1886.

His picture is an excellent one, taken in April, 1884.

97

COL. ALEXANDER C. BRANSCOM.
FORGER AND SWINDLER.

DESCRIPTION.

Forty-four years old in 1886. Born in Virginia. Medium build. Single. Claims to be a book publisher. Height, 6 feet. Weight, 178 pounds. Medium brown hair, dark gray eyes, ruddy complexion. Good education; converses well. Right arm off at the elbow.

RECORD.

COL. BRANSCOM is an expert forger and swindler. He was sentenced to three years and six months in State prison in August, 1880, in New York City, for forging Florida bonds. His expertness with the pen is a marvel, in view of his being obliged to write with his left hand, his right arm having been cut off at the elbow. His correspondence while conducting his swindling operations, large as it has been, was entirely written by himself, and does equal credit to his powers of invention and to his skillful penmanship. Not a detail calculated to convey confidence was lacking in any of his transactions.

He was arrested again in New York City on November 2, 1884. During August of that year he made several contracts with business men in New York to publish and advertise in an official guide to the New Orleans Exposition; and a highly decorated pamphlet, "The Diversified Industries of the South." He contracted with Conroy Brothers, paper dealers, of No. 33 Beekman Street, New York City, on August 14, 1884, for $7,000 worth of white paper for his publications, and gave them a note for $7,000, purported to be indorsed by Colonel Edward Richardson, the millionaire president of the Mississippi Mills, at Wesson, Miss., and at that time president of the World's Exposition at New Orleans.

Branscom uttered about $40,000 worth of similar notes in New York, and when arrested he confessed that he had forged endorsements to $52,000 more, and had intended to issue about $110,000 worth in all. If he had succeeded, he said, he would have carried his publications through and cleared $50,000. In addition to the money collected by the notes, Branscom also got orders for $6,000 worth of advertisements in the blank space of his two books, and he planned to collect $30,000 more from the same source. His cash collected from all sources in this transaction enabled him to deposit $14,000 in the Shoe and Leather Bank of New York, but two-thirds of this amount he subsequently drew out.

Branscom was convicted of the forgery of one note for $7,000, and was sentenced to ten years in State prison in the Court of General Sessions, New York, on March 14, 1885, by Recorder Smyth.

Branscom's picture is a good one, taken in November, 1884.

98

FRANKLIN J. MOSES, alias EX-GOV. MOSES.

SWINDLER BY BOGUS CHECKS.

DESCRIPTION.

Forty-four years old in 1886. Born in South Carolina. Lawyer. Married. Slim build. Height, 5 feet 8¾ inches. Weight, 130 pounds. Dark hair, turning gray; blue eyes, sallow complexion, large Roman nose; generally wears a heavy mustache, quite gray. Dresses fairly. Good talker.

RECORD.

Ex-Governor Moses, of South Carolina, graduated from Columbia College, and served as private secretary to the Governor of South Carolina for two years. At the close of the war of the Rebellion he was one of the first of any that were conspicuous in the State to submit to the Reconstruction Act; and he was, after serving as Speaker of the House two years, made Governor, holding that office for two years. His father, an estimable man, was at one time Chief Justice of the Supreme Court of South Carolina. Shortly after his term of office expired, Moses started in victimizing friend and foe alike. An account of all his swindling transactions would fill many pages. Below will be found a few of his many exploits.

He was first arrested in New York City, and delivered to the South Carolina authorities on September 17, 1878, for making and uttering a forged note in South Carolina for $316. When he arrived there he was placed on parole, and allowed to escape. He was arrested again in New York City on October 3, 1881, for defrauding Major William L. Hall out of $25. For this he was sentenced to six months in the penitentiary on Blackwell's Island. He was arrested again in Chicago, Ill., on July 27, 1884, for false pretenses, but the case was settled up. He was arrested again in Detroit, Mich., on October 12, 1884, for swindling the Rev. Dr. Rexford, under the name of Thomas May, and sent to jail for three months. He was again arrested in Detroit, upon the expiration of his three months' sentence, on January 27, 1885, by Boston officers, for swindling Colonel T. W. Higginson, of Cambridge, out of $34, under false pretenses. He was brought to East Cambridge, Mass., and pleaded guilty in the Superior Criminal Court there on February 11, 1885, and was sentenced to six months in the House of Correction. He was brought from the House of Correction on May 29, 1885, on a writ, and arraigned before Judge Aldrich, of the Superior Criminal Court, and committed for trial for swindling, in February, 1884, Mr. Fred. Ames out of $40; ex-Mayor Cobb, $40; Dr. Bowditch, $20; Dr. Henry O. Marcy, $20; and Mr. Williams, a bookseller, $20. Moses pleaded guilty again to these complaints on September 25, 1885. He was finally sentenced to three years in the House of Correction on October 1, 1885, by Judge Aldrich. His sentence will expire, allowing him full commutation time, on May 10, 1888. When the ex-governor was arraigned for sentence in Boston, his counsel, John B. Goodrich, Esq., said that he wished to state to the court the remarkable circumstances of the case, not for the purpose of extenuation, but because of the qualities of the man, and consider if something could not be done to restore him to his former place in the community. Judge Aldrich said:

"If I were sitting in another place than upon the bench, I should think, after listening to the remarks of the counsel for the defense, that I was listening to a eulogy of some great and good man." The judge, continuing, said he would rather see a member of the bar starve before he would commit a State prison offense. He himself would suffer cold all day, sweep the streets, before he would go into a gentleman's house and commit such offenses as those charged. The defense made for the prisoner the judge characterized as trivial, and said it was time such frauds were stopped. He did not see what good it would do to send him to any of the reformatory institutions. He felt that a severe sentence ought to be imposed upon the prisoner, and therefore sentenced him to be imprisoned in the State prison for three years.

Moses' picture is an excellent one, taken in March, 1882.

99

DAVID SWAIN, alias OLD DAVE.

CONFIDENCE MAN.

DESCRIPTION.

Forty-two years old in 1886. Born in New York City. Stout build. Height, 5 feet 9 inches. Weight, 180 pounds. Light brown hair, blue eyes. Ruddy complexion. Wears full sandy beard and mustache. Married. Scar on forehead over left eye. Part of an anchor in India ink on right fore-arm.

RECORD.

SWAIN is one of the sharpest, meanest, and most dangerous confidence men in the business. He has no favorites, and would rob a friend or a poor emigrant as soon as a party with means. He may be found around railroad depots or steamboat landings, and is well known in all the Eastern cities, especially Boston, Mass., where, it is said, he has a mortgage on the Eastern Railroad depot.

Swain was arrested in New York City on July 17, 1873, for grand larceny from **one** Edward Steinhofer, of Brooklyn. He was committed to the Tombs prison on July 18, 1873, but was shortly afterwards delivered over to the Albany, N. Y., police authorities, and taken there upon an old charge. He was convicted and sentenced to three years in the Albany Penitentiary, at the Court of Quarter Sessions, in Albany, on September 20, 1873. His time expired in March, 1876.

Swain passed considerable of his time in and around Boston, Mass., when out of prison, and has fleeced many a poor victim there. In August, 1883, he robbed two poor Nova Scotians, man and wife, out of $150 in gold, all the money they had saved for years.

He was finally arrested in Boston, Mass., on December 12, 1884, for robbing the Nova Scotians, whose name was Taylor. He lay in jail there until May 23, 1885, when he was brought to court, where he pleaded guilty to the charge, and was sentenced to two years in the House of Correction.

Swain has been working these last few years with George Gifford, who was arrested in Brooklyn, N. Y., on March 15, 1886, for swindling one John Reilly by the confidence game, and sentenced to four years in the Kings County Penitentiary on April 30, 1886. He has also served a term in Boston, Mass., for the same offense. Young Gifford is the son of Harry Gifford, a very clever old confidence man, who died a short time ago.

Swain's picture is a good one, taken in 1881.

100

EDWARD LILLIE, alias HENRY A. WATSON.

CONFIDENCE MAN, FORGER, AND BOARDING-HOUSE THIEF.

DESCRIPTION.

Sixty-five years old in 1886. Born in United States. Sailmaker. Married. Slim build. Height, 6 feet 1 inch. Weight, 166 pounds. Black hair, turning quite gray; gray eyes. Wears a gray chin whisker. Has a sloop and owl in India ink on right arm; spots of ink on left arm.

RECORD.

ED. LILLIE is one of the most notorious confidence operators in America. He does not confine himself to that particular branch of the business, as he has done service for forgery and robbing boarding-houses. He is known in a number of the large cities of the United States and Canada, and is considered a very clever man.

He was arrested in New York City on November 25, 1876, under the name of James H. Potter, charged with purchasing from George C. Flint, of West Fourteenth Street, New York City, $600 worth of furniture, and giving him in payment therefor a worthless check for $750 on the National Bank of Newburg, N. Y. The bank's certification on the check was forged, and he received $150 in change. In this case Lillie pleaded guilty, and was sentenced to two years and six months in State prison, on February 2, 1877, by Judge Gildersleeve. He was arrested again in New York City on July 28, 1879, in company of one John Hill, alias Dave Mooney (173), charged by Mrs. Lydell, who kept a boarding-house at No. 46 South Washington Square, with entering the room of one of her boarders and stealing $575 in money, three watches, two chains, and a locket, altogether valued at $1,000. In this case he was discharged for lack of evidence.

Lillie was arrested again on board of a Galveston steamer, lying at the dock in New York City, on January 9, 1881, charged with obtaining $50 from Miguel S. Thimon, a Texan, by the confidence game. In this case Lillie was sentenced to two years and six months in State prison, on January 12, 1881, by Judge Cowing. He was again arrested plying his vocation along the river front in New York, in June, 1884, and sentenced to six months in the penitentiary, charged with vagrancy. He obtained a writ, and was discharged by Judge Lawrence, of the Supreme Court, on June 13, 1884.

He fell into the hands of the police again in New York City, on February 27, 1885, charged by Benjamin Freer, of Gardiner, Ulster County, N. Y., with swindling him out of $250 in money. One David Johnson, of Catasauqua, Pa., also charged him with swindling him out of 102 English sovereigns on January 2, 1885, on board of an Anchor Line steamer, while lying at the dock in New York City. Johnson was on his way to Europe. Lillie was tried for swindling Johnson, and sentenced to five years in State prison on March 9, 1885, by Recorder Smyth, in the Court of General Sessions.

Lillie's picture is an excellent one, taken in November, 1876.

101

JOHN CANNON, alias JACK CANNON,
alias Davis, alias Stewart, alias Bartlett.
HOTEL THIEF AND SAFE BURGLAR.

DESCRIPTION.

Forty-seven years old in 1886.   A Pennsylvania Dutchman.   Married.   No trade. Height, 5 feet 5½ inches.   Weight, 150 pounds.   Dark brown hair, inclined to curl in front of his ears ; large, light gray eyes, left eye watery ; large nose ; very heavy brown beard and mustache.   Small scar near end of nose.   Claims to be an American-born Irishman.   Can fix himself up to look like a " Sheeny."

RECORD.

JACK CANNON is one of the most widely-known and dangerous thieves in America. He was arrested in New Orleans, La., on March 10, 1886, in company of Thomas White, alias Montreal Tom, and George Wilson, alias " The Peoria Kid," charged with robbing one Effie Hankins, of Chicago, of $8,000 worth of diamonds at the house of May Banker, on Union Street that city the night previous.

The following is a very interesting account published in one of the papers of the arrest of Cannon and his associates in New Orleans :

A full and complete history of this man's adventures would fill a volume with thrilling escapes, desperate undertakings, and successful burglaries and robberies.

If Cannon was not born in the city of New Orleans he was raised here, and up to a few years ago had a brother engaged in mercantile pursuits here.   His real name is said to be Hannon, and he formerly resided on Dryades, between Girod and Julia streets.   He attended the St. Joseph's School, on Common Street, and his first step in crime was made in this city.

Of his earlier exploits but little is known to the detectives, as they were comparatively trifling robberies or larcenies, and either escaped the memory of one of the oldest detectives in the city, or were of no import, and hence never came to his knowledge.

Detectives Gaster and Cain had been looking for Cannon for some time past and had been warned to move cautiously when arresting him as he would shoot " at the drop of a hat."   On the morning of the arrest, March 11, 1886, when they espied Cannon in front of the St. Charles Hotel with Roberts, alias Tommy White, and Wilson, they accosted him and requested his presence at the office of the Chief of Police.   Cannon was at first disinclined to go quietly and made several suspicious movements with his hand to his hip pocket.   Cain was watching him closely while Gaster was eloquently arguing and pleading with Cannon and his two friends as to the propriety of going along quietly.   Cannon hesitated a while, and turning to Gaster informed him that he had doubtless made a mistake, as he was a gentleman and was stopping at the Hotel Royal. Gaster did not dispute this, especially as Cannon exhibited the key of his room, but Cannon could not be convinced that he ought to go to the Chief's office.

Fearing doubtless that his refusal would excite still more suspicion, Cannon asked who was Chief of Police. Gaster replied that the Chief was sick and that his secretary was acting in his stead. This satisfied Cannon, who became assured that the secretary would not know him, and the three prisoners and the two detectives arrived safely at the Chief's office.

The first man they met in the office was Captain Malone, and Cannon was visibly agitated and sought to turn his head. The Captain eyed him keenly a few moments and said: "I know your face, but can't place you just now." He sat looking at Cannon a few moments and then recognized him, and called him by name.

Cannon denied his name, said that he was named Collins, and had never been known as Cannon. The Captain then entered into conversation with him, and recalled many names of thieves and suspicious characters, now dead, but who had been known to Cannon some fifteen or twenty years ago. Cannon became interested, and commenced asking questions of others.

Captain Malone informed Cannon that his picture was in the "gallery," but this Cannon would not believe. He said that no picture of himself was extant. The Captain told him that some nineteen or twenty years ago, whilst Cannon was rooming on Toulouse, between Dauphine and Burgundy streets, his room had been searched for burglars' tools and plunder, and the officers had then found a full length photograph of him in the room and had carried it away with them. This picture had been placed in a conspicuous position in the gallery, and all during the political troubles and changes had remained there and was there then. This was a disagreeable surprise to Cannon, and he desired to see the picture, but this request was not granted and the trio were locked up.

Roberts was conducted to Clarke's gallery, where his picture was taken, and when the three prisoners were brought to the First Recorder's Court, the detectives concluded to have a picture of Cannon taken. When they entered the dock they informed Cannon of what they intended to do. Cannon became greatly excited, and, pulling off his coat, declared that he would die before they should take his "mug." His picture was not in any collection in the United States, he said, and it shouldn't be taken in New Orleans.

"Who ordered this?" asked Cannon.

"The Chief of Police," said the detectives.

Cannon thereupon directed his wrath against Captain Malone and hurled invectives on his head. "I am sorry I didn't kill him years ago," said the burglar. "I had the chance then and was laying for him. Oh, I know well where he lives—down on Dauphine Street, near Esplanade. I piped him off one night, and was hid near his house. I had a gun drawn on him, and was about to shoot, but at the last moment I relented, and Malone entered his house in safety, and unconscious of the peril he had been in. I'm very sorry now I didn't finish the job I started out to do."

After having vented his spleen in words, Cannon was again informed that his picture was to be taken.

"There is no law for it," he said; "you will have to take my picture after I'm dead, if you want it."

The detective tried coaxing, but Cannon was obdurate, and turning to Roberts, asked his advice.

Roberts replied, "I haven't anything to do with it; it's your 'mug,' not mine."

Finding Cannon very stubborn, the officers informed Recorder Davey of what they wanted, and when the prisoners were arraigned, Judge Davey told Cannon that the police were very anxious to secure his photograph, and that he had better submit quietly.

After being remanded the detective entered the dock and proceeded to place handcuffs on Cannon's wrists. He resisted, and again becoming excited, cursed everybody connected with the police. He said that he could have escaped from the parish prison that morning had he been able to run, and regretted not having made the attempt anyhow.

Cannon was securely handcuffed, and was then marched down to Clarke's Gallery, on Canal Street. Four detectives escorted him, and in due time he arrived there, and was placed in a chair in front of the camera. The operator had been informed that he would encounter considerable difficulty in catching Cannon, and he therefore moved with great caution. Before Cannon knew that he was ready the operator quickly removed the cover, and as quickly replaced it, securing a good likeness by the instantaneous process. He then said to Cannon:

"Are you ready now?"

"Yes," replied the latter, and screwing up one corner of his mouth, shutting one eye, and distorting his features, he said, "Go ahead."

The appearance of the man's face was most ludicrous, and the operator and detectives burst into a laugh. They enjoyed it the more as they had already obtained what they were after, and the result of it all was an excellent likeness of Cannon, the noted burglar and desperado—the only one in existence, as far as known. (See No. 101.)

Cannon appeared to be very despondent when he ascertained that he had been beaten at every point, and remarked, "Well, I guess you'll do me up this time."

He became communicative later, and spoke of old times in this city, and of himself.

"I never robbed a poor man in my life," he said, "and haven't turned a trick in New Orleans this winter." He had no money, but said he had plenty of friends to help him in case money could save him. He did not appear to be at all worried about going to Baton Rouge, as he believed he could make his escape either here or there. He spoke of the late detective Bobbie Harris, who was killed by the late chief of aids, Thomas Devereux. He told Gaster and Cain that he was with Harris when he broke his back. He said that Harris fell into a well near Vicksburg, Miss., while seeking to escape with him, and thus injured his spinal column, making him a cripple for life.

Cannon has been the companion and pal of the most noted safe-blowers, bank-robbers and cracksmen in this country, and is himself classed as one of the most expert hotel thieves on this continent. New Orleans, it would appear, has been the home

97

ALEXANDER C. BRANSCOM,
FORGER AND CONFIDENCE MAN.

98

FRANKLIN J. MOSES,
ALIAS EX. GOV. MOSES,
SWINDLER.

99

DAVID SWAIN,
ALIAS DAVE SWAIN,
CONFIDENCE.

100

EDWARD LILLIE,
ALIAS WATSON,
CONFIDENCE.

101

JOHN CANNON,
ALIAS OLD JACK,
HOTEL THIEF.

102

EDWARD LYMAN,
ALIAS NED LYMAN,
PICKPOCKET AND CONFIDENCE MAN.

103

FRANK WOODS,
ALIAS McKENNA,
BURGLAR, PICKPOCKET AND
SECOND STORY MAN.

104

CHARLES WARD,
ALIAS HALL,
CONFIDENCE.

105

SOLOMON STERN,
FORGED ORDERS.

106

WILLIAM B. TOWLE,
DOCTORS' OFFICE SNEAK.

107

JAMES CAMPBELL,
ALIAS SHANG CAMPBELL,
BURGLAR AND PICKPOCKET

108

JAMES LEE,
BOGUS CUSTOM HOUSE COLLECTOR.

109

WILLIAM E. FARRELL,
BUTCHER CART THIEF.

110

EDWARD GEARING,
ALIAS EDDIE GODDIE.
BUTCHER CART THIEF.

111

JAMES TITTERINGTON,
ALIAS TITTER,
BUTCHER CART THIEF.

112

CHARLES SMYTH,
ALIAS DOC. SMITH,
SAW DUST GAME.

113

JAMES FITZGERALD,
ALIAS THE KID,
BANCO.

114

GEORGE ELLWOOD,
ALIAS GENTLEMAN GEORGE,
MASKED BURGLAR.

115

ELLEN CLEGG,
ALIAS ELLEN LEE,
SHOP LIFTER AND PICKPOCKET.

116

MARY HOEY,
ALIAS MOLLY HOLLBROOK,
PICKPOCKET.

117

MARGRET BROWN,
ALIAS OLD MOTHER HUBBARD,
PICKPOCKET AND SATCHEL WORKER.

118

CHRISTENE MAYER,
ALIAS KID GLOVE ROSEY,
SHOP LIFTER.

119

LENA KLEINSCHMIDT,
ALIAS RICE and BLACK LENA,
SHOP LIFTER.

120

MARY CONNELLY,
ALIAS IRVING,
PICKPOCKET AND SHOP LIFTER.

and the scene of the début of some of the most skillful and notorious burglars. First on the list of these is Billy Forrester (see No. 76), who is now in Massachusetts. He is a native of Lafourche, La., and was the leader of the gang who broke into Scooler's jewelry store, on Canal, near Camp Street, at the time being associated with Daigo Frank and Dave Cummings. (See No. 50.)

Cannon, as has already been stated in the *Picayune*, jumped his bonds in New Orleans in the Lilienthal robbery, which was committed on April, 11, 1876. His bondsman then was George Foster, proprietor of a restaurant and keeper of a fence on Toulouse Street, who has since died. Foster was a well known character and harborer of thieves in his day, and when the Lilienthal robbery was committed Cannon was lodging there. When Cannon left the city and his bondsman in the lurch descriptions of him were sent far and wide around the country, and he was compelled to remain very quiet. Captain Malone's untiring efforts are what aroused Cannon's animosity, and considering him as a relentless enemy, he determined to rid himself of him.

One day the Captain received a letter telling him that if he would meet the writer at the corner of Broad and Canal streets after dark on an appointed night, he would receive valuable information in regard to a gang of thieves. The Captain suspected something wrong, as the place appointed was in a very quiet and isolated part of the city, but he exhibited the letter to the then Chief of Police, Gen. A. S. Badger, who coincided with him in his suspicions. Determined, however, to see the matter through, the Captain took two detectives with him, and proceeded to the appointed place at the appointed time. No one was in sight except a policeman in uniform, who was on the sidewalk, and on the approach of the detectives he moved leisurely away. The detectives concealed themselves, and Malone waited patiently, but no one came except one of the mounted policemen, who had been ordered to proceed to the place and remain in the vicinity until ordered away by Captain Malone. After remaining long after the time specified the officers returned to headquarters, and then the Captain sought to ascertain the name of the officer who was on foot at the place. To his surprise he found that no policeman was on duty in that neighborhood except mounted men, hence the man they saw was a bogus policeman, and doubtless a pal of the pretended informer, or the writer of the letter himself. the Captain kept this letter, and still has it in his possession, and when Cannon's remark was repeated to him he at once came to the conclusion that Cannon was either the author of it or had caused it to be written, and that it was part of a plot the object of which was to put him out of the way.

Cannon's pal on the occasion of the Lilienthal robbery was John Watson, who escaped from the First Precinct Station by making a skeleton key out of the handle of a waterpail. He opened the lock of his cell door by means of this, and then opened a door in the rear wall of the station opening into the alleyway on the east side of what was then the barroom known as the Marble Hall. The police station and headquarters were then located where Soule's Commercial College now is, and Watson, after opening the rear door, walked out to Lafayette, near Carondelet Street, where he broke into a run. He was recaptured out on Claiborne Street, having run into the arms of the Maria driver, George Bernard, who was subsequently killed by his head striking the arch over the gateway through which the Maria entered and came out of the workhouse.

Bernard was just going to answer roll-call when Watson ran into his arms, and he held him fast and brought him back to the Central Station. Watson subsequently again escaped, and made his way North, and from thence to England.

About a year ago a very large amount of diamonds and jewelry were stolen in England, and cuts and descriptions of the gems were sent to all parts of the world. The robbery became known as the Hatton Garden robbery, and the Scotland Yard detectives were sent all over the civilized world to recover the diamonds and capture the thieves. In Paris Watson and his wife were captured and convicted of the robbery, and sentenced to long terms of imprisonment.

Cannon, some time after the Lilienthal robbery, left New Orleans, and kept away for a number of years. He established his headquarters in Philadelphia, where he was known as John Bartlett. He visited the South every winter, but up to two or three years ago, as far as known, kept away from New Orleans.

When arrested for the Lilienthal robbery he presented a rough and uncouth appearance, more like that of a laboring man than of a "flash cove," and when Captain Malone first laid eyes on him after his capture in the gutter under the street-crossing at the corner of Chartres and Bienville streets, he was surprised that such a looking man should be capable of so skillful a piece of work as opening the combination of Lilienthal's safe, and it was not until some days afterward that Cannon's ability to do such work became apparent. He was then a young, strapping fellow; now he is a middle-aged, comparatively respectable-looking man, with a full chin beard and mustache.

A few among the many robberies attributed to Cannon, or in which he was implicated, are the following :

Hotel robbery at Jacksonville, Fla., in which a quantity of diamonds, watches and jewelry were stolen.

Robbery of a store at Brownsville, Texas.

Robbery of Schmidt's store in Houston, Texas.

Safe blowing at J. F. Meyer's store at Houston, Texas.

Safe blowing at Macatus' store, in the same place.

Jewelry robbery at Galveston, Texas.

Hotel robbery at Hotel Royal in New Orleans, also the robbery at the Gregg House in April, 1885 ; and many others.

Efforts were made to hold Cannon for the Lilienthal robbery. Of the officers who made the arrest at the time only two are living. Sergeant—afterwards Captain—James Gibney, promoted for this very arrest, died of consumption in 1873. Corporal—afterwards Sergeant—Kennedy was killed on September 14, 1874. Officer Coffee was killed by the notorious negro garroter and robber, Al Gossett, April 19, 1883.

Officer Diehl is the proprietor of a grocery store at the corner of Miro and Dumaine streets, and with Officer Duvigneaud, who is at present engaged in the fruit business on Canal Street, is still alive. Cannon was captured with his portion of the booty on his person, and the last two mentioned officers were present at the time.

Cannon now claims Detroit, Mich., as his home, and when he registered his name in the Gregg House, in New Orleans, in April last, he booked himself as J. H. Stewart, Detroit, Mich.

Roberts denied that he was the Tommy White who escaped from the penitentiary at Clarksville, Tenn., and stated his willingness to return there without the formality of a requisition if the authorities would take him there and then release him if it was proven that he was not the man.

The picture of Roberts was identified, and that at once by the proprietress of the boarding-house, No. 6 St. Peter Street, New Orleans, adjoining the store of Mr. Piccaluga. She stated that during the month of December, 1885, the original of the picture rented the room on the first floor front for himself and a companion. On or about Christmas the store of Mr. Piccaluga was entered by burglars, who broke open the windows on the gallery on the same story occupied by her lodger. The safe was blown open and $60 in money stolen. Fortunately there was no more money than that amount in the safe that night, but several nights previously there had been large amounts in the safe. The burglars on this occasion were doubtless Roberts and Cannon. As regards Roberts' identity as Tommy White, alias "Curly Tommy," the Chief of Police of Chicago said he was wanted in Clarksville, and was only too anxious to return thither in order to escape prosecution and punishment in New Orleans.

Cannon appeared to rely greatly on the judgment and advice of Roberts, and the detectives infer from this that Roberts was the brain of the firm and Cannon the skill and muscle to carry out plans conceived by Roberts.

Wilson, the younger of the three, was not known at that time to the police, although they claim for him the alias of the "Peoria Kid," and give him the reputation of being a first-class pickpocket. Cannon said to Roberts one day: "If we hadn't been with the 'Kid' we would have been all right."

A telegram was received in New Orleans on March 22, 1886, from Peoria, Ill., identifying the picture of Wilson sent thither as that of George Stacey, alias H. B. Wilson, a former pupil of Joe Parish's, and a most expert pickpocket and "pennyweight man." The latter is the name applied to thieves who enter jewelry stores, and, whilst pretending to make purchases, unobservedly secrete diamonds and other valuables about their persons.

The three accused were brought before Recorder Davey to be arraigned for the Hankins diamond robbery, which was committed on Wednesday morning, March 10, 1886.

Cannon appeared to be greatly worried, and his sinister light blue eyes roamed unceasingly around the room. He was very nervous and appeared to dread recognition from every person whom he detected eyeing him closely. His brown beard and mustache gave his face quite a respectable appearance, and had it not been for his restlessness a casual observer would most likely have taken him to be a lawyer employed to defend the other two.

The first and only witness introduced was Mr. Charles Bush. The accused were asked to stand up, and the witness was asked if he could identify any of them. He replied that he had seen Cannon before, but did not recollect ever having seen the other two—Roberts and Wilson. As regards the recovery of the Hankins diamonds, and the alleged payment of a reward or a compromise to recover the jewels, he knew nothing.

Wilson, alias the Peoria Kid, and Tom White were discharged in this case on March 23, 1886. They immediately left town, but were arrested again in April, in Montgomery, Ala., while attempting to pawn some stolen property.

The last arrest of White and Wilson was made by the Chief of Police of Montgomery, Ala., and when searched a package of burglars' tools and a pawn ticket for a gold watch were found in their possession. Subsequently it was ascertained that the watch was the property of Mr. H. Jackson, of Selma, Ala., who, while on a visit to New Orleans and a guest at the Hotel Royal, had been robbed of his gold watch and about seventy-five dollars in money. This was the night prior to the arrest of John Cannon and the two above mentioned parties, March 9, 1886.

It was subsequently ascertained that Cannon, who had a room in the Hotel Royal, had invited White, alias Roberts, to share his bed with him, and that night the rooms of several of the boarders, among them Mr. Jackson's, were entered and robbed.

Cannon was an inmate of the parish prison, New Orleans, being held to answer a charge of assault and battery, until May 15, 1886, when he was convicted and sentenced to two years at hard labor. He was taken to Baton Rouge prison on June 17, 1886. On their arrival at Montgomery White and Wilson disposed of their stolen property, and were arrested.

The following is some of Miss Hankins's evidence relative to the loss of her diamonds. She said :

"I am from Chicago. I reside in this city at the Hotel Victor. On the night of the 9th or morning of the 10th March, 1886, I was at No. 68 Union Street. I am the person who was robbed. It was about 4 o'clock in the morning when the three men entered my room. A portion of the jewelry was on my arms and the balance on my dresser. My door was locked. The door was opened by a party in the room for the purpose of getting a glass of water. As the door opened a man put a revolver to his head and three men rushed in. I had retired. I retired that night about 1 o'clock. It was the front room on the first floor. It was not my first night in the room. I had occupied it several nights. I was May Banker's guest. I saw May Banker that night. She was in my room. She left me about 12 o'clock. I had not disrobed. She occupied a room at the head of the stairs on the floor above.

"I had a diamond pin, a pair of earrings, four bracelets, watch and finger rings. Three of the bracelets were worth about $1,000 each, the fourth one about $7,000. They were on my wrists. The pin and earrings were under my pillow. The earrings were worth about $8,000, the pin about $5,000. My other jewelry was in my trunk.

"When the men entered they said: 'We won't harm you, but keep quiet.' One of them took me by the throat and placed a revolver at my head. They then took the jewelry. I had a revolver under my pillow. I always have it there. They broke open a desk in the room. My door was open during all this. I did not go to the ball. Nobody persuaded me not to go. It would be hard to identify the thieves, as they wore handkerchiefs over their faces.

"The prisoners do not look like the men. They are not stout enough." [Pointing to Cannon witness said:] "He is about the height of one of the men. Could not say if they had beards. I have gotten the property back—three or four days after it was stolen. On the advice of my attorney I shipped it away.

"The thieves were in my room twenty or twenty-five minutes. When they left they locked the door on the outside. I don't know how they got out. I did not hear their footsteps, as they made no noise. I saw Miss Banker about an hour after the robbery; she expressed sympathy for the loss. Miss Banker told me she was awake in her room between 3 and 4 o'clock, and was smoking. Yes, she knew I had the jewelry; she has seen me wear it."

On the return of Effie Hankins to Chicago she talked freely to the reporters, and implicated May Banker in the robbery of her diamonds—in so far as knowledge of the thieves and disposition of the plunder was concerned—and likewise hinted that May Banker's paramour knew more about the affair than had been made apparent on the trial of the case.

May Banker was discharged on preliminary examination before Recorder Davey, but her house had gained so bad a reputation that none dared to venture into it for fear of being robbed, and she sold out all her furniture and effects, except her wardrobe and jewelry, and left the city for parts unknown. Detective Kerwin went to Montgomery, and on April 12, 1886, returned to New Orleans, having Tommy White, alias Roberts, alias J. C. Smith, in his custody. The charge against him is robbing Mr. Jackson, of Selma, Ala., a guest at the Hotel Royal, in New Orleans. Kerwin had a requisition for Wilson, the "Peoria Kid," but it does not appear that Wilson was returned. White was convicted for this offense, and sentenced to eighteen months in State prison at Baton Rouge, La., on May 28, 1886. He was taken there on June 17, 1886. This latter fact is mentioned as, under the laws of Louisiana, a convict's sentence does not commence until he enters the prison.

The following is a description of Cannon's companions :

Tom White, alias Roberts, alias Montreal Tom, hotel thief and bank sneak, was forty-two years old in 1886. Height, 5 feet 10 inches. Weight, 150 pounds. Black hair and mustache, gray eyes, dark complexion. Born in Canada. Is a consumptive.

George Stacy, alias Wilson, alias The Peoria Kid, was twenty-three years old in 1886. Height, 5 feet 8 inches. Weight, 150 pounds. Gray eyes, auburn hair, freckled face, fresh complexion. Very smiling address. Is well educated. He was discharged at Montgomery, Ala., on April 5, 1886, and arrested again at Cairo, Ill., and sent to jail, in May, 1886, in company of George Jelt, of Jeff, another desperate thief.

Cannon's picture is a very good one, taken in New Orleans, La., in 1886.

102

EDWARD LYMAN, alias NED LYMAN, alias Ackerson.

PICKPOCKET, SNEAK AND CONFIDENCE MAN.

DESCRIPTION.

Forty-two years old in 1886. Born in Boston, Mass. Stout build. Height, 5 feet 8½ inches. Weight, 180 pounds. Light hair, blue eyes, light complexion, full face. Married. Painter by trade. Has " E. L." in India ink on his arm ; scars on three fingers of right hand and on under lip.

RECORD.

NED LYMAN is probably one of the cleverest general thieves in America, and is well known in all the principal cities East and West, especially in Boston, where he makes his home.

Lyman, under the name of George Ackerson, was convicted in the Superior Court of Boston, Mass., on January 17, 1863, for larceny from the person, and sentenced to the House of Correction for four months. Discharged May 15, 1863.

He was convicted again in the same court on May 19, 1864, for larceny from the person, and sentenced to the House of Correction for six months. He was discharged September 14, 1864.

Again convicted in the same court on May 25, 1868, for assault and battery with a knife, and sentenced for two years in the House of Correction. Discharged December 23, 1870. There is evidently some mistake in the date of Lyman's discharge from the House of Correction in Boston, as the record shows that he was arrested in New York City on July 22, 1870, for till-tapping, and committed in $1,500 bail by Judge Cox.

The records also show that he was arrested and convicted of larceny from the person in Philadelphia, Pa., and sentenced to four years in the Eastern Penitentiary on March 27, 1880.

Again, in the Superior Court of Boston, Mass, April 17, 1884, he was convicted of an attempt to commit larceny from the person, and sentenced to the House of Correction for twelve months. Discharged March 12, 1885. This last time he gave the name of George Ackerson.

Lyman was arrested in Boston again in June, 1885, for larceny from the person, and gave bail, which was defaulted.

In August, 1885, he was arrested in Providence, R. I., for larceny from the person, and was sentenced to one year in prison there. When his time expires, he will be taken back to Boston and tried on the complaint he ran away from.

Lyman's picture is an excellent one, taken in Boston in 1884.

103

FRANK WOODS, alias McKENNA.

PICKPOCKET, BURGLAR AND SECOND-STORY MAN.

DESCRIPTION.

Thirty-five years old in 1886. Born in New York City. Single. No trade. Medium build. Height, 5 feet 6 inches. Weight, 135 pounds. Black hair, gray eyes, fair complexion. Has scar on left hand, near thumb joint. Has figures "25" in India ink on outside of left fore-arm.

RECORD.

Woods is perhaps one of the smartest house thieves there is in this country. He confines himself to second-story work generally, and usually works wealthy manufacturing towns and summer resorts. He was arrested in New York City on July 15, 1874, under the name of Frank McKenna, in company of William Johnson, charged with entering the house of J. A. Terhune, No. 416 West Twenty-eighth Street, by removing a panel of the basement door. The noise awakened the occupants of the house, who pursued them, and caused their arrest. Woods and Johnson both pleaded guilty to burglary in the third degree, and were each sentenced to State prison at Sing Sing for five years on August 4, 1874, by Recorder Hackett.

Woods escaped from Sing Sing on June 2, 1876, but was recaptured and returned to prison the same month.

He was arrested again in New York City on March 5, 1885, and delivered to the authorities of Pawtucket, R. I., charged with robbing the house of William Sayles, a wealthy manufacturer of that place. This robbery was what is called a second-story job. He was tried on July 3, 1885, and the jury disagreed. He was afterwards admitted to bail, an official becoming his bondsman, so as to insure his return in case any further evidence could be obtained against him. This was a lucky escape for him.

Woods is well known in all the large Eastern cities. He has served time in State prisons in New York, Massachusetts, and Pennsylvania, and is a very clever thief.

Woods' picture is a good one, taken in December, 1877.

104

CHARLES WARD, alias WM. H. HALL.
CONFIDENCE MAN AND SWINDLER.

DESCRIPTION.

Fifty-two years old in 1886. Born in United States. Book-keeper. Married. Medium build. Height, 5 feet 9 inches. Weight, 159 pounds. Brown hair, mixed with gray, wears it long; blue eyes, light complexion. Generally wears a full, heavy gray beard and mustache. Dresses well, and has an extraordinary gift of the gab.

RECORD.

Charley Ward, whose right name is Charles Vallum, is one of the most noted confidence operators in America. He enjoys the distinction of being the only man in his line who can play the confidence game successfully on women. His principal forte, though, is collecting subscriptions for homes and asylums.

He was arrested in New York City on April 6, 1877, for collecting money for the Presbyterian Hospital of New York City without authority. For this he was sentenced to five years in State prison, on April 12, 1877, by Judge Sutherland. He was pardoned by Governor Cornell in 1880.

He was arrested again in New York City on August 4, 1881, for collecting considerable money, without authority, in aid of the "Society for the Relief of the Destitute Blind," of New York City, and appropriating it to his own use. In this case, owing to the efforts of a loving wife, he escaped with eighteen months' imprisonment in State prison, on September 7, 1881, being sentenced by Judge Cowing.

Ward's picture is an excellent one, taken in April, 1877.

105

SOLOMON STERN.

BOGUS CHECKS AND CONFIDENCE OPERATOR.

DESCRIPTION.

Thirty-two years old in 1886. Jew. Born in United States. Single. Bookkeeper. Slim build. Height, 5 feet 3½ inches. Weight, 115 pounds. Black hair, gray eyes, sallow complexion.

RECORD.

SOLOMON STERN is the son of very respectable parents. He was arrested in New York City on June 29, 1883, charged with obtaining large quantities of jewelry, etc., from merchants by means of bogus checks.

The story of Stern's downfall is interesting. In the spring of 1882 he became attached to a woman in an up-town resort in New York City. He was then a salesman in his father's store, and resided at home. His salary was small, his father being a strict disciplinarian and an unbeliever in the fashionable follies of young men. Young Stern had little spending money, and in order to gratify his inamorata began stealing from his father. He purchased diamonds for her and paid her board at a seaside hotel. Her tastes were very expensive, and her demands on Stern for money very frequent. He began going every Sunday morning to his father's store, and always went away with a roll of costly woolen cloth. An inventory of stock was taken, and the father discovered that he was being systematically robbed. More than $5,000 worth of woolens had been stolen. Mr. Stern soon found that his son was the thief, and discharged him. He also turned him out of his home. When this occurred the young man had become a confirmed drinker.

Stern was still infatuated with the woman, and was determined to get money to supply her demands. He endeavored to borrow from his acquaintances, but without avail. Then he went to his mother, but she discarded him, and his paternal uncle also gave him the cold shoulder. It was then he resolved upon a career of crime.

He wrote his mother's name to a check of $650 which he gave in payment for some diamonds to C. W. Schumann, of No. 24 John Street, New York City, on September 24, 1882. The check was on the Germania Bank. He sold the diamonds, and with his companion went to Baltimore, where he stayed until all his money was spent. When the woman wanted more he returned.

On December 16, 1882, he obtained a sealskin sacque with a $250 worthless check from Henry Propach, a furrier, at No. 819 Broadway, New York, and three days later a precious stone worth $525 from A. R. Picare, a jeweler, of Fifteenth Street, New York, whom he paid in similar fashion.

When the police got on his track he went out of town again. He didn't return to New York until January 6, 1883, when he swindled Joseph Michal, of No. 150 Ewen Street, Brooklyn, out of $800 by giving a worthless check in payment for jewelry.

There were four complaints against Stern. He pleaded guilty to one of them, and was sentenced to five years in State prison by Judge Gildersleeve, on August 3, 1883, in the Court of General Sessions, New York City.

His sentence will expire on March 3, 1887.

His picture is a good one, taken in June, 1883.

106

WILLIAM B. TOWLE.

DOCTOR'S OFFICE SNEAK.

DESCRIPTION.

Twenty-eight years old in 1886. Born in Australia. Very slim build. Married. Height, 6 feet 1¼ inches. Weight, 160 pounds. Sandy hair, blue eyes, sandy complexion. Has scars on the left arm, near the wrist; freckled hands.

RECORD.

WILLIAM B. TOWLE makes a specialty of robbing doctors' offices. Twenty-seven physicians, all Towle's victims, were present in court in New York City on July 19, 1884, to testify that he had entered their offices and stolen medical instruments, etc.

His method of operating was the same at nearly all the places which he visited. Sometimes he would dash up to a doctor's door in a cab, and after hastily inditing a note, be left alone in the office and suddenly leave the premises with whatever he could lay his hands on. At one time he was a clerk in a drug store, there becoming familiar with the value of different articles used by physicians and surgeons. He was convicted and sentenced to two years in State prison on August 6, 1884, by Judge Cowing.

Towle was recognized in court as a man who in January, 1884, was arrested for assaulting a man named Oliver, in Abingdon Square, New York. It was said at the time that Oliver had found his wife and Towle under suspicious circumstances. For this assault Towle was sent to Blackwell's Island, and was only a short time from there when arrested for robbing doctors' offices and sentenced as above.

His picture is an excellent one, taken in July, 1884.

107

JAMES CAMPBELL, alias SHANG CAMPBELL,
alias TRAINOR.
BURGLAR AND PICKPOCKET.

DESCRIPTION.

Forty-two years old in 1886. Born in New York. Single. No trade. Stout build. Height, 5 feet 7½ inches. Weight, 160 pounds. Irish descent. Sandy hair, bluish-gray eyes, sandy complexion. Straight nose. Generally wears a sandy mustache.

RECORD.

"SHANG" CAMPBELL is a well known New York burglar and pickpocket. He is an associate of Poodle Murphy (134), Charley Allen, Joe Gorman (146), Dick Morris (141), Curly Charley, and other first-class men. He is also well known in all the principal cities in the United States and Canada. He is a big rough fellow, well calculated for a "stall."

His first offense was burglary on a bonded warehouse in the lower part of New York, for which he was arrested and sentenced to five years in Sing Sing prison, under the name of Thomas Burns.

Campbell was one of the gang of masked burglars that operated so extensively in Westchester County, N. Y., and in other places in the vicinity of New York City, in 1873. (See record of No. 138.) The entire gang, consisting of Dan Kelly, Patsey Conroy (now dead), Denny Brady, John, alias Brittley Burns, Larry Griffin, George Milliard (138), and others, were arrested in New York City, and sent to State prison for terms ranging from two and a half to twenty years. Campbell and Johnny Dobbs escaped through the side door of Milliard's saloon when the police entered and arrested the gang.

After their narrow escape Campbell and Dobbs turned up in Florida as gentlemen of leisure, traveling for their health. They had plenty of money, and drank to excess. Campbell let out their real character while on a spree. A drunken brawl furnished a pretext for their arrest, and Campbell's baggage was found to consist only of a complete set of burglars' tools. They sufficed to hold Campbell, but Dobbs was discharged, and lost no time in quitting Florida for New York, where he barely escaped arrest for shooting at a person in Cherry Street whom he had accused of furnishing the information upon which his old associates were arrested.

While the identification of Campbell was yet in doubt, the Sheriff of Key West was very much surprised by a letter from a well known man in New York, vouching for Campbell as a reputable resident of that city. The letter urged upon the Sheriff the unconditional release of the prisoner. Some difficulty was experienced in obtaining a warrant of extradition from the Governor of the State of New York (Dix), but one was granted at the urgent solicitation of District-Attorney Briggs, of Westchester County. While the necessary papers were in preparation Campbell escaped. He was shut up in a rickety old jail with a negro held for murdering a United States marine, and one Edward Baker, a local offender. Baker stood on Campbell's shoulders, and with an old case-knife cut a hole in the ceiling large enough for them to squeeze through. The Key West Aldermen offered a reward of $200 for the arrest of the negro, and $100 for Campbell. Baker's brother earned the reward by guiding a party of soldiers to the island on which they were hidden. Campbell was returned to jail and securely anchored with three hundred pounds of iron riveted to his legs, where he remained until the arrival of the New York officers, who brought him back and took him to White Plains, where he was sentenced to two years and six months in State prison on April 22, 1874, by Judge Gifford.

He was arrested again in Montreal, Canada, in January, 1882, in company of Billy Dewey (now dead), and Charles Douglas, alias Curly Charley, for sneaking from a train a valise containing $14,000 in money, the property of one McNamee. They were all arrested, the money was returned, and the complainant was sentenced to ten days in jail for refusing to make a charge against them. In this case they were discharged. Since then "Shang" has been traveling around the country with a clever "mob" of pickpockets, and at last accounts was in Canada.

Campbell's picture is a good one, taken in November, 1877.

108

JAMES LEE, alias HARTMAN,
alias COLEMAN.

BOGUS CUSTOM-HOUSE COLLECTOR.

DESCRIPTION.

Forty-five years old in 1886. Born in United States. No trade. Single. Stout build. Height, 5 feet 9¼ inches. Weight, 175 pounds. Hair sandy, eyes gray, sandy complexion, reddish-brown mustache. Has a naval coat-of-arms, anchor and eagle, in India ink, on right arm.

RECORD.

JAMES LEE was evidently in the government employ, so well is he posted in custom-house matters.

He was arrested in New York City on April 23, 1882, charged by Mrs. C. F. Chillas, of Livingston Place, with defrauding her and thirty others out of $9.98. Lee claimed to be a custom-house collector, and would collect this amount and give the parties an order on the custom-house stores for a package which he claimed was consigned to them from Europe.   In this case Lee was sentenced to two years and six months in State prison on May 5, 1882, by Judge Gildersleeve.   His sentence expired on May 5, 1884.

He was arrested again in Baltimore, Md., on September 17, 1884, charged with swindling eight persons in that city under similar circumstances.   In several instances Lee sat at the piano and played " Nearer, my God, to Thee," while the ladies left the parlor to procure the money for him.   He was again sentenced to three years in State prison on October 15, 1884.   His sentence will expire April 14, 1887.

Lee's picture is an excellent one, taken in April, 1882.

109
WILLIAM E. FARRELL, alias SHERIDAN,
alias FRANK ALEXANDER.
BURGLAR AND BUTCHER–CART THIEF.

DESCRIPTION.

Thirty-one years old in 1886.   Medium build.   Born in New York City.   Single. No trade.   Height, 5 feet 10¾ inches.   Weight, 167 pounds.   Black hair, dark eyes, dark complexion.   Has a scar over the left eye, another on right side of chin.   Left arm has been broken at elbow.

RECORD.

FARRELL is a desperate and daring thief.   He is a burglar, but of late years has done considerable butcher-cart work.   He is the man that makes the assault, generally using about eighteen inches of lead water-pipe as a weapon.   He has served two terms in Sing Sing prison, one in the penitentiary on Blackwell's Island, and one in Boston, Mass., for burglary and larceny.

He was arrested in Philadelphia, Pa., on January 15, 1884, by the New York detectives, assisted by Philadelphia officers, with one James Titterington, alias Titter (111), charged with assaulting with a piece of lead pipe and robbing Luther Church, the superintendent of John E. Dwight's Harlem Soda Works, of $2,300, as he was descending the steps of the 111th Street station of the Second Avenue Elevated Railroad in New York City, on December 31, 1883.   Farrell pleaded guilty to robbery in the first degree, and was sentenced to fifteen years in State prison on January 25, 1884, by Judge Cowing, in the Court of General Sessions, New York.

Eddie Gearing, alias Goodie (110), the celebrated butcher-cart thief, was also arrested in connection with this robbery, and sentenced to twenty years in State prison. Titterington (111) turned State's evidence and was used to convict Goodie.   He was finally sentenced to seven years and six months in State prison on March 14, 1884.

Farrell's picture is a good one, taken in December, 1877.

110

EDWARD GEARING, alias EDDIE GOODIE,
alias GOODRICH, alias MILLER.
BUTCHER–CART THIEF.

DESCRIPTION.

Thirty-eight years old in 1886. Born in New York. Married. Medium build. Height, 5 feet 6¼ inches. Weight, 145 pounds. Brown hair, gray eyes, fair complexion. Has a goddess of liberty in India ink on left fore-arm, anchor and clasped hands on right fore-arm, and a heart on right hand. Bald in front of head. Generally wears a red mustache and whiskers, which he dyes black occasionally.

RECORD.

EDDIE GOODIE, or GEARING, which is his right name, was the originator of butcher-cart work, in company of Steve Boyle and Big Frank McCoy (89), several years ago. He has been connected with nearly every robbery of that character which has taken place in New York City and vicinity for the last twenty years. He is one of the smartest thieves in America, a man of wonderful audacity and resources. He is so cunning and clever that he has always managed to slip out of the meshes of the law, while others not so crafty or culpable have slipped in.

He was arrested in New York City on February 13, 1870, in company of a man who has since reformed, for stealing a case of silk valued at $17,000 from a Custom-house truck. The party arrested with Goodie was sent to prison for five years, he assuming all the blame and swearing that Goodie had nothing to do with the robbery.

In 1874 Goodie and Mike Hurley, alias Pugsie Hurley (88), robbed a butter merchant in Brooklyn, N. Y. They were let out on bail, which ended it.

In 1875 Goodie, Billy Williams, Big John Tracy, and John McKewan robbed William B. Golden, a book-keeper, of $5,000, while he was on his way to pay off the hands of the Badger Iron Works Company, in New York City. The book-keeper left the Dry Dock Bank, then in East Tenth Street, New York, taking a horse-car. Two men entered after him, and seated themselves by his side. Another man, who was on horseback, followed the car. At Fourteenth Street and Avenue D the two men grabbed the money bag and threw it to the man on horseback, who was Goodie, and they all escaped.

In 1876 the book-keeper of the Standard Oil Works left their main office, in Pearl Street, New York City, with $8,000 in money, to pay off the hands in Greenpoint. He was followed from New York by Goodie and two other men, who assaulted and robbed him. He was also implicated in robbing the cashier of the Planet Flour Mills, in Brooklyn, N. Y., of $3,500, in March, 1878.

Goodie was the driver of the wagon used in the Northampton, Mass., bank robbery in January, 1876, and was an associate of Red Leary, George Bliss, Bob Dunlap, and several other expert bank robbers. He was also connected with the Manhattan Bank robbery in New York City, in October, 1878.

In the latter part of 1880, Goodie and Willie Farrell (109) robbed a man of $2,200 near the Bank of the Metropolis, New York. They escaped by driving away in a butcher-cart.

It was Goodie who drove the butcher-cart when Ruppert's collector was robbed of $9,600 in money, in East Forty-second Street, New York, in July, 1881.

Goodie was the man that was described as wearing a big brown mustache, who jumped over the fence in Jersey City, N. J., on July 18, 1883, when Cashier Smith, of the National Bank of Orange, N. J., was assaulted and an attempt made to rob him of $10,000 in money. Pete Emmerson, alias Banjo Pete (90), Ned Farrell, and John Nugent, the other parties in this robbery, were arrested at the time, and are now in State prison.

Goodie was arrested in New York City on February 7, 1884, charged, in connection with William Farrell (109) and James Titterington (111), with assaulting with a piece of lead pipe and robbing one Luther Church of $2,300, on December 31, 1883. He was tried, found guilty, and sentenced to twenty years in State prison on February 21, 1884, by Recorder Smyth, in the Court of General Sessions, New York City.

Goodie's picture is a good one, taken in February, 1884.

111

JAMES TITTERINGTON, alias TITTER,

alias HENDERSON.

BURGLAR AND BUTCHER–CART THIEF.

DESCRIPTION.

Thirty years old in 1886. Born in New York. A driver. Single. Medium build. Height, 5 feet 10¼ inches. Weight, 155 pounds. Black hair, gray eyes, sallow complexion. Has letters "J. T." in India ink on right arm. Stutters when talking.

RECORD.

"TITTER," the name he is best known by, was born in New York City. He branched out as a sneak thief, from that to a burglar, and then a highwayman. He has served time in Sing Sing prison, and in the penitentiary on Blackwell's Island, New York, for larceny and burglary.

He was arrested in Philadelphia on January 15, 1884, and brought to New York City in connection with Willie Farrell (109) and Eddie Goodie (110), for robbing one Luther Church of $2,300, on December 31, 1883, as Mr. Church was descending the steps of the Elevated Railroad station at 111th Street and Second Avenue, New York.

Titterington and Farrell were on the stairway, and as soon as he passed down by them they followed, and Farrell hit him with a piece of lead pipe about eighteen inches long and knocked him down. Titter snatched the bundle of money and both jumped into a butcher-cart and were driven away by Goodie. Titter made a confession after his arrest, and was made the principal witness against Goodie, who was convicted. Farrell pleaded guilty, and was sentenced to fifteen years' imprisonment. Titterington also pleaded guilty, and was sentenced to seven years and six months in State prison on March 14, 1884.

His picture is an excellent one, taken in December, 1876.

112

CHARLES SMYTH, alias DOCTOR SMYTH, alias HARRISON.

CONFIDENCE AND SAWDUST GAME.

DESCRIPTION.

Forty-three years old in 1886. Born in Germany. Single. Medium build. Height, 5 feet 8½ inches. Weight, 155 pounds. Light hair, blue eyes, fair complexion. Wears glasses, and a light-colored mustache.

RECORD.

"Doc" Smyth is a well-known Bowery, New York, confidence and sawdust man. He generally works with Charley Johnson and Freddie Reeves, and is an old offender. He is also well known in a number of other cities, having been arrested several times, and is considered a clever man at his business.

He was arrested in New York City on December 1, 1885, charged with using the United States mails in flooding the Western States with circulars offering "Green goods, in samples of $1, $2, $5 and $10," to farmers and others, assuring them of a safe and rapid fortune by dealing in the stuff, which was understood to be counterfeit money.

The "Doctor" pleaded guilty, and was sentenced to twelve months' imprisonment by Judge Benedict, of the United States Court, in New York City, on December 17, 1885.

Smyth's picture is a very good one, taken in March, 1878.

113

JAMES FITZGERALD, alias RED FITZ, alias THE KID.

BANCO STEERER.

DESCRIPTION.

Twenty-nine years old in 1886. Born in Washington, D. C. Slim build. Single. Height, 5 feet 7 inches. Weight, 130 pounds. Red hair, dark auburn eyes, sandy complexion, straight nose, beard red (when worn), hair very thick and coarse.

RECORD.

"THE KID," as he is called, is well known in New York, Boston and several other large cities, and is considered one of the cleverest men in the banco business. He generally worked with Johnny Norton (now dead).

He and Norton were the two men that succeeded in obtaining $7,000 from Charles Francis Adams, in Boston, in 1882, by the banco game. "The Kid" was arrested, tried, convicted, and sentenced to five years in the Charlestown, Mass., State prison on June 23, 1882. His sentence will expire August 27, 1886.

Norton escaped at the time and never was captured. He died in New York City in March, 1885.

Fitzgerald's picture is a good one, taken in October, 1881.

114

GEORGE N. ELWOOD, alias GENTLEMAN GEORGE.

MASKED BURGLAR.

DESCRIPTION.

Twenty-eight years old in 1886. Born in Chicago, Ill. Single. No trade. Stout build. Height, 5 feet 9½ inches. Weight, 163 pounds. Hair dyed black, eyes dark-blue, complexion sallow. Has small scar on back of head, left side.

RECORD.

ELWOOD WILSON is a daring and murderous Western thief. Nothing much is known of him in the Eastern country.

He was arrested in New York City on August 24, 1885, in company of Joe Wilson, alias Whalen (65), charged with a series of masked burglaries in several of the Western States.

When Elwood's and Wilson's rooms, at No. 220 Forsyth Street, New York City, were searched, after the capture of the cracksmen, among the articles seized was a Masonic ring, marked "Edison W. Baumgarten, June 25, 1884." The ring was traced to Ohio, and on August 25, 1885, in response to some inquiries made by telegraph, the Chief of Police of New York City received the following reply from the Chief of Police of Toledo:

"Hold Elwood and Wilson. Charge, grand larceny and burglary and shooting officer with intent to kill. Will send requisition papers immediately."

Subsequent correspondence on the same subject stated that the men were also wanted for a robbery which they had committed at Detroit. The crime for which the Toledo authorities requested the detention of the prisoners was committed on August 13, 1885. On that night, it was alleged, they broke into a house, and being discovered in the act of plundering the place, fired several shots at the servants. An alarm was raised, and a policeman who started in pursuit of the fugitives was shot in the breast and dangerously wounded. The men then came on to New York. They had been there only a few days before they were under surveillance, and while they were being watched the detectives became aware of the plans they were hatching for a series of burglaries which they contemplated committing in Saratoga. When they were about to start on that trip the detectives arrested them. All through the West, Elwood is known as a daring and desperate burglar, and it is said that some two years ago he murdered two of his associates.

Elwood and Wilson were on August 25 arraigned at the Jefferson Market Court in New York City, and at the request of their captors they were committed until the arrival of the Toledo authorities with the requisition papers. They were both delivered to the police authorities of Toledo, Ohio, on August 29, 1885, and taken there for trial.

Elwood and Wilson were the parties who robbed the residences of Messrs. Oakes and Merriam in St. Paul, Minn., in August, 1885. Merriam's diamond scarf-pin was found in their possession, and a pawn ticket taken at Detroit for his diamond collar-button was also found upon them. A requisition was taken out at St. Paul to intercept the prisoners at Toledo, where they were being taken for the robbery of Mr. Baumgarten's residence and the murder of a policeman. The intention was to take them to St. Paul in case they could not be held for the Toledo crimes.

The trial of George A. Elwood, one of the notorious burglars, closed at Toledo, Ohio, on December 12, 1885, with a verdict of guilty. The defense offered no evidence, but argued that Elwood had not been sufficiently identified. A motion for a new trial was made, which was overruled. Elwood said he believed he would get the full extent of the law. He and his partner, Joseph Wilson, are the original gentlemanly burglars who emptied the houses and filled the newspapers of Cleveland, Detroit, St. Paul, Milwaukee and St. Louis, until their doings in Toledo led to their apprehension in New York. These men are well known thieves, and considerable excitement was caused among the fraternity at the time they were arrested and were about to be taken back to the West. Their methods employed to transfer the possessions of others to their pockets were so peculiarly bold that the whole West was startled by their exploits. Detroit in particular suffered from them, mainly because the police were nonplused by the audacity of their performances. They invariably awakened the parties they intended to rob, and compelled them to comply with their wishes at the points of their revolvers. Oftentimes they would repair to the dining-room with the owner of the premises and indulge in a feast before their departure. Besides doing this, at a residence in Cleveland, they compelled the victim to sign a check for $100 and made him promise not to dishonor it. While leaving a Detroit residence early one morning they met the gentleman of the house returning from out of the city, and not at all taken aback by the encounter, they robbed him on the porch, and then sent him into the house to see what they had left. These eccentricities caused their fame to spread far and wide, and the "gentlemanly burglar" was patterned after in many localities. But there were few equals, and none superior. For coolness and daring Elwood and Wilson stood in the front rank of masked burglars.

Elwood was found guilty on December 19, 1885, and was sentenced to ten years in the Ohio penitentiary. In the case of Wilson there was a disagreement of the jury. A second trial resulted in his conviction. (See record of No. 65.)

Before Wilson associated with the desperado Elwood he operated for months alone in Brooklyn, N. Y. House robbery was his line of business, and silverware his plunder. He committed a series of mysterious robberies, and although an active search was made for the "silver king," he succeeded in avoiding arrest. His repeated successes stimulated other thieves, who began operating in Brooklyn. One of the latter was caught, and it was then believed that the cunning "silver king" had been at last trapped. Such was not the case, for Wilson had set out for the Western country.

Elwood's picture was taken in August, 1885.

115

ELLEN CLEGG, alias MARY WILSON,
alias Mary Gray, alias Mary Lane, etc.
SHOPLIFTER, PICKPOCKET, AND HAND–BAG OPENER.

DESCRIPTION.

Forty-five years old in 1886. Born in United States. Lives in New York. Married. Stout build. Height, 5 feet 5 inches. Weight, 145 pounds. Brown hair, brown eyes, light complexion, big ears.

RECORD.

ELLEN CLEGG is an old and expert pickpocket, shoplifter, and hand-bag opener. She was one of Mrs. Mandelbaum's women, and is well known throughout the country. Her picture is in the Rogues' Gallery in several of the large cities. She is a clever woman, and the wife of Old Jimmy Clegg, alias Bailey, alias Lee, alias Thomas, who was convicted and sentenced in Portsmouth, N. H., in April, 1882, for four years, for picking pockets. This team has traveled through the country for years, and been arrested time and time again.

Ellen was arrested in Boston, Mass., on December 6, 1876, in company of Tilly Miller, Black Lena, and four other notorious shoplifters, and her picture taken for the Rogues' Gallery.

She was arrested again in Boston in 1878 for picking pockets, and sent to the House of Correction.

Again arrested in New York City on November 24, 1879, in company of Walter Price (197), under the name of Mary Gray, charged with shoplifting. (See record of No. 197.) She pleaded guilty, and was sentenced to three years in the penitentiary on Blackwell's Island, N. Y., by Judge Gildersleeve, on December 16, 1879. Price went to State prison. Ellen's time expired in this case on April 16, 1882.

She was arrested again in Boston on May 21, 1883, for shoplifting, and sentenced to one year in the House of Correction.

Arrested again in Boston on December 22, 1885, and again sent to the House of Correction for one year. In this case Ellen was detected in the act of opening a lady's hand-bag and attempting to remove a pocket-book.

Her picture is a pretty good one, taken in 1876.

116
MARY HOLBROOK, alias MOLLIE HOEY,
alias Harvey.
PICKPOCKET, SNEAK AND SHOPLIFTER.

DESCRIPTION.

Forty-eight years old in 1886. Born in Ireland. Married. Housekeeper. Medium build. Height, 5 feet 2 inches. Weight, about 135 pounds. Light hair, blue eyes, light complexion. Shows her age.

RECORD.

Mollie Holbrook was in early life a resident of the West End, in Boston, Mass. She is well known in Chicago and in all the principal cities of the United States. She has served terms in prison in Boston, Chicago, and New York, and is without doubt the most notorious and successful female thief in America. She is well known of late years as the wife of Jimmy Hoey, alias Orr, a negotiator of stolen property. Mollie was formerly married to one George Holbrook, alias Buck Holbrook, a well known Chicago gambler and thief. He kept a sporting house in Chicago, also a road house on Randolph Street, over which Mollie presided.

"Buck" was arrested for a bank robbery in Illinois in 1871, and sent to State prison. He was shot and killed while attempting to escape from there. He had dug up the floor of his cell and tunneled under the prison yard, and was in the act of crawling out of the hole outside the prison wall, when he was riddled with buckshot by a prison guard.

In January, 1872, Mollie was arrested in Chicago, on complaint of her landlady, who charged her with stealing forty dollars from her. Mollie deposited $1,200 in money as bail, and after her discharge she came to New York City, fell in with Jimmy Hoey, and married him.

She was arrested in New York City for robbing a Western man in her house in Chicago of $25,000, on March 3, 1874, on a requisition from Illinois, and delivered to a detective of the Chicago police force. While at Hamilton, Canada, on their way back to Chicago, Mollie threw herself into the arms of a Canadian policeman and demanded protection. She had the officer arrested for attempting to kidnap her. They were taken before a magistrate and Mollie was discharged. The officer returned to Chicago, and lost his position for his bad judgment. Mollie was arrested again in New York City on the same complaint on July 16, 1874, and returned safely to Chicago, where she was sent to prison.

She was arrested in Boston, Mass., on April 17, 1878, for picking pockets, and gave the name of Mary Williams (which is supposed to be her maiden name). She was released on $1,000 bail, and forfeited it.

She was arrested again in Boston on March 19, 1883, for picking pockets at Jordan & Marsh's dry goods store. This time she gave the name of Mary Harvey, pleaded guilty, and was sentenced to one year in State prison, in April, 1883.

After her sentence expired in Boston she was arrested coming out of the prison by New York officers, taken to that city, and sentenced to five years in the penitentiary on Blackwell's Island, on March 3, 1884, for the larceny of a pocket-book from Catharine Curtis, some years before. This time Mollie gave the name of Lizzie Ellen Wiggins. After her conviction she gave the District Attorney of New York some information that led to the finding of a number of indictments against Mrs. Mandelbaum, who fled to Canada. For this she was pardoned by Governor Cleveland on January 5, 1885.

Mollie was arrested again in Chicago, Ill., on September 25, 1885, charged with attempting to pick a lady's pocket in Marshal Field's store. She gave bail, and is now a fugitive from justice, in Windsor, Canada. She occasionally pays Detroit a visit, where Jimmy Hoey is located. Mollie Holbrook is looked upon by her associates in crime as a woman that would sacrifice any one to save herself from prison. It is well known that this woman has been in the employ of the police in a number of large cities, and has furnished them with considerable information. Her husband, Jimmy Hoey, is an unprincipled scamp, and lives entirely upon the proceeds of his wife's stealings, often selling the plunder and acting as a go-between for Mollie and receivers of stolen goods, he of late years not having sufficient courage to steal.

Mollie's picture is an excellent one, taken in March, 1883.

117

MARGARET BROWN, alias YOUNG,
alias HASKINS, alias OLD MOTHER HUBBARD.
PICKPOCKET AND SHOPLIFTER.

DESCRIPTION.

Fifty-eight years old in 1886. Born in Ireland. Married. Housekeeper. Slim build. Height, 5 feet 3 inches. Weight, 120 pounds. Gray hair, gray eyes, light complexion. Generally wears a long cloak when stealing.

RECORD.

MARGARET BROWN, which is her right name, has been a thief for fifty years. She makes a specialty of opening hand-bags, removing the pocket-book, and closing them again. She was arrested in Chicago, Ill., and sentenced to three years in Joliet prison, where, in an attempt to escape, she fell, and was nearly killed. She was discharged from Joliet in 1878, and after that operated in St. Louis, New York, Philadelphia, Boston, and other cities.

She was arrested in Boston, Mass., on March 24, 1883, in R. H. White's dry goods store, for stealing a hand-bag, which was found on her person; for this offense she served six months in the House of Correction there.

She was arrested in New York City on March 26, 1884, for stealing a pocket-book from a Mrs. H. S. Dennison, of Brooklyn, N. Y., in Macy's store on Fourteenth Street; for this she was sentenced to three months in the penitentiary on Blackwell's Island on April 2, 1884.

On the expiration of this sentence on July 2, 1884, she was arrested again on a requisition from Boston, Mass., charged with the larceny of a satchel containing $260 in money from a store there. She was taken to Boston, and sentenced to two years in the House of Correction in the latter part of July. She was subsequently transferred to Deer Island, on account of her old age and infirmities.

Her picture is an excellent one, taken in March, 1883.

118

CHRISTENE MAYER, alias KID GLOVE ROSEY,
alias MARY SCANLON, alias ROSEY RODER.
SHOPLIFTER.

DESCRIPTION.

Thirty-nine years old in 1886. Born in Germany. Married. Housekeeper. Slim build. Height, 4 feet 11 inches. Weight, about 125 pounds. Dark brown hair, dark blue eyes, dark complexion.

RECORD.

KID GLOVE ROSEY is a well known New York shoplifter. She is also well known in several other Eastern cities.

She was arrested in New York City, in company of Lena Kleinschmidt, alias Louisa Rice, alias Black Lena (119), on April 9, 1880, charged with stealing from the store of McCreery & Co., corner of Eleventh Street and Broadway, two pieces of silk containing 108 yards, valued at $250. The property was found in their possession, together with some other property which had been stolen from Le Boutillier Brothers on West Fourteenth Street, New York City.

Mayer was tried, convicted, and sentenced to five years in the penitentiary on Blackwell's Island on April 30, 1880. Kleinschmidt, who had been bailed, left the city, but was re-arrested, pleaded guilty, and was sentenced to four years and nine months on the same day by Recorder Smyth.

Mayer's sentence expired on November 30, 1883, and Kleinschmidt's on September 30, 1883.

"Rosey's" picture is a good one, taken in April, 1880.

119

LENA KLEINSCHMIDT, alias BLACK LENA,
alias RICE, alias SMITH.
SHOPLIFTER.

DESCRIPTION.

Fifty-one years old in 1886. Born in Germany. Married. Housekeeper. Stout build. Height, about 5 feet 5 inches. Weight, about 150 pounds. Dark hair, dark eyes, dark complexion. Wrinkled face.

RECORD.

LENA KLEINSCHMIDT, or "BLACK LENA," is a notorious shoplifter. She is well known from Maine to Chicago, and has been arrested and sent to prison several times, three times in New York City alone.

She was arrested in New York City, in company of Christene Mayer, alias Mary Scanlon, alias Kid Glove Rosey (118), on April 9, 1880, for the larceny of 108 yards of silk dressings, valued at $250, from the store of McCreery & Co., Broadway and Eleventh Street. The property was found on Lena; and other property, stolen from Le Boutillier Brothers, on Fourteenth Street, New York, was found on Rosey. Kleinschmidt gave $500 bail, and left the city, but was re-arrested and brought back, pleaded guilty, and was sentenced to four years and nine months in the penitentiary on Blackwell's Island on April 30, 1880, by Recorder Smyth.

Rosey was tried, convicted, and sentenced to five years, the same day.

Lena's picture is a good one, taken in April, 1880.

120

MARY ANN CONNELLY, alias ELIZABETH IRVING,

alias HALEY, alias TAYLOR.

PICKPOCKET, SHOPLIFTER, AND BLUDGEON WORKER.

DESCRIPTION.

Fifty years old in 1886. Born in Ireland. Single. Very fleshy, coarse woman. Height, about 5 feet 4 or 5 inches. Weight, 240 pounds. Black hair, black eyes, ruddy complexion. Talks with somewhat of an Irish brogue.

RECORD.

MARY ANN CONNELLY is a well known New York pickpocket, shoplifter and prostitute, and a coarse, vulgar woman, that would stop at nothing to carry her point.

She was arrested in New York City, and sentenced to six months in the penitentiary, on January 12, 1875, for shoplifting in New York City.

She was arrested again in New York City, for picking pockets, and sentenced to one year in State prison, by Judge Sutherland, on December 11, 1875.

Arrested again in New York, for picking a woman's pocket, and sentenced to six months on Blackwell's Island, on April 1, 1878, by Judge Gildersleeve.

She was arrested again in New York City, in company of Joseph Volkmer and his wife Mary on November 27, 1879, for drugging and attempting to rob one Charles Blair, a countryman, whom the trio met on a Boston boat.

She turned State's evidence, and was used against the Volkmers, who were tried, found guilty, and sentenced to twelve years each in State prison, on December 15, 1879, by Judge Cowing, in the Court of General Sessions. She was discharged in this case.

Her picture is an excellent one, taken in 1875.

121

MARY ANN WATTS, alias MARY WILSON,

alias MARY WALKER.

PICKPOCKET AND SHOPLIFTER.

DESCRIPTION.

Thirty-eight years old in 1886. Born in United States. Dressmaker. Medium build. Height, 5 feet 3½ inches. Weight, about 145 pounds. Dark brown hair, hazel eyes, ruddy complexion. Coarse features.

RECORD.

MARY ANN WATTS is a well known New York female thief. She is considered a very clever woman, and is known in all the principal cities East and West. She is credited with having served one term in the House of Correction in Boston (Mass.), one in Chicago and Philadelphia, besides two terms in New York State prison and two in the penitentiary.

She was arrested in New York City under the name of Mary Wilson, pleaded guilty to an attempt at grand larceny, and was sentenced to two years and six months in State prison, by Recorder Hackett, on December 19, 1873.

She escaped shortly after, and was at large until her arrest in New York City again for shoplifting. In this case she was tried, found guilty, and sentenced to three years in State prison, by Judge Sutherland, on April 6, 1876.

After this last sentence expired she had to serve out about two years she owed on the previous sentence, making about five years in all.

This is a clever woman, and well worth knowing.

Her picture is a good one, although taken ten years ago.

122

BERTHA HEYMAN, alias BIG BERTHA.

CONFIDENCE QUEEN.

DESCRIPTION.

Thirty-five years old in 1886. Born in Germany. Married. Very stout woman. Height, 5 feet 4½ inches. Weight, 245 pounds. Hair brown, eyes brown, fair complexion. German face. An excellent talker. Has four moles on her right cheek.

RECORD.

BERTHA HEYMAN's maiden name was Bertha Schlesinger. She is a native of Koblyn, near Posen, Prussia. Her father served five years in prison there for forging a check. She was married twice, first to one Fritz Karko, when she first came to this country in 1878. After living in New York a short time they went to Milwaukee, where she was afterwards married to a Mr. Heyman, although her first husband was still living. She has been concerned in a number of swindling transactions, and has the reputation of being one of the smartest confidence women in America.

In September, 1880, she was sued in the Superior Court of New York City for obtaining by false pretenses $1,035 from E. T. Perrin, a conductor on a palace car, whom she met in traveling from Chicago.

She was arrested in London, Ontario, on February 8, 1881, in company of one Dr. J. E. Cooms, charged with defrauding a Montreal commercial man out of several hundred dollars by the confidence game.

She was tried in Richmond County, Staten Island, N. Y., in June, 1881, for obtaining $250 in money and two gold watches from a Mrs. Pauline Schlarbaum, an old lady of Southfield, S. I.   She was acquitted in this case.

She was arrested on leaving the court and brought to New York City on June 29, 1881, charged with obtaining, under false pretences, $960 from Mr. Charles Brandt, a liquor merchant, at No. 19 Bowery, New York City; also $500 from Mr. Theodore W. Morris, a glass importer, of No. 27 Chambers Street, New York.   She was tried and found guilty on the Morris indictment on October 26, and on Friday, October 29, 1881, she was sentenced to two years in the penitentiary by Judge Cowing.

While in prison on Blackwell's Island she made the acquaintance of a trustful German named Charles Karpe.   She was employed as a servant in the Warden's house.   Karpe visited her during her confinement there, and she finally, while a prisoner, victimized the poor man out of $900, all the money he had in the world.

After her discharge from the Island, she went to live at the Hoffman House in New York.   On June 28, 1883, she visited Edward Saunders, of the firm of Saunders & Hoffman, brokers, at Broadway and Fulton Street, New York, and induced him to advance $40 on the representation that a check for $7,000 belonging to her was in the Hoffman House safe.   She obtained $215 more and a valuable diamond from him, and $200 from his partner, by placing in their hands a sealed package of worthless papers which she pretended were securities worth $87,000.   In the course of these negotiations she professed to be worth $8,000,000.   Even this stupendous statement was received with respectful attention until the worthlessness of the so-called securities in their safe was discovered.   In this case she was tried and convicted in the Court of General Sessions, on August 22, 1883.   An application for a new trial was denied, and she was finally sentenced to five years in the penitentiary on August 30, 1883.   Her sentence will expire, allowing full commutation, on March 30, 1887.

This remarkable woman used to lodge at the leading hotels, and was always attended by a maid or man servant.   At the Windsor and Brunswick Hotels in New York City she had elegant quarters.   When plotting her schemes she would glibly talk about her dear friends, always men well known for their wealth and social position.   She possesses a wonderful knowledge of human nature, and can deceive those who consider themselves particularly shrewd in business matters.

Bertha's picture is a good one, taken in June, 1881.

123

ELLEN DARRIGAN, alias ELLEN MATTHEWS.
SHOPLIFTER.

DESCRIPTION.

Thirty-three years old in 1886.   Born in England.   Married.   Housekeeper. Medium build.   Height, 5 feet 4½ inches.   Weight, about 135 pounds.   Red hair, hazel eyes, light complexion.   Her nose has been broken.

RECORD.

ELLEN DARRIGAN is a well known New York shoplifter. It is claimed that she has been married three times, first to Jerry Dunn, next to John Mahaney, alias Jack Shepperd (62). He is a thief who gained considerable notoriety on account of escaping from a number of State prisons and penitentiaries. Billy Darrigan (180), the lady's third spouse, is an old New York thief, whose picture is in several Rogues' Galleries throughout the United States. Mrs. Darrigan was considered a pretty woman until Billy broke her nose in December, 1875. She is well known as Ellen Matthews.

Ellen was arrested in New York City on December 13, 1875, for shoplifting, and was sentenced to four years in State prison. She has served terms in several other cities since.

She finally fell into the hands of the police again on April 1, 1885, with Margaret Bell, another notorious shoplifter. They were arrested after leaving Altman's dry goods store, on Sixth Avenue, New York City, taken to police headquarters, and searched. Nothing was found on Mrs. Bell, but a large pocket ("kick") in Mrs. Darrigan's skirt contained a piece of beaded cloth, valued at $50, the property of James A. Hearn & Son, No. 30 West Fourteenth Street, New York. In this case they were both tried in the Court of Special Sessions, in the Tombs prison, New York, on April 9, 1885. Mrs. Bell was discharged, and Mrs. Darrigan was convicted and sentenced to five months in the penitentiary on Blackwell's Island, by Justice Kilbreth, the presiding magistrate.

Her picture is an excellent one, taken in 1875.

124

ELIZABETH DILLON, alias BRIDGET COLE.

PICKPOCKET.

DESCRIPTION.

Forty-two years old in 1886. Born in Ireland. Married. Housekeeper. Slim build. Height, 5 feet 8 inches. Weight, about 145 pounds. Brown hair, dark brown eyes, swarthy complexion, high cheek bones. A remarkably tall, thin woman ; big lips.

RECORD.

ELIZABETH DILLON, or COLE, is a well known female pickpocket. She has been arrested in almost every city in the Union, and has done considerable service in State prisons and penitentiaries throughout the country. She is well known in Baltimore, Philadelphia, New York, Boston, Providence, R. I., and several other Eastern cities. She is very quick in her actions and difficult to follow.

She was arrested in Providence, R. I., on February 1, 1879, charged with picking pockets, and sentenced to two years in State prison on March 11, 1879. Since then she has served two terms in the penitentiary on Blackwell's Island, New York.

Her picture is a very good one, taken in March, 1879.

125

TILLIE PHEIFFER, alias MARTIN,
alias KATE COLLINS.
HOTEL AND HOUSE SNEAK.

DESCRIPTION.

Thirty-six years old in 1886. Born in France. Servant. Married. Slim build. Height, 5 feet 3 inches. Weight, 128 pounds. Dark brown hair, hazel eyes, dark complexion. Mole on the right side of the nose under the eye.

RECORD.

TILLIE PHEIFFER, or MARTIN, is a notorious house and hotel sneak thief. She sometimes hires out as a servant and robs her employers; but her specialty is to enter a hotel or flat, and wander up through the house until she finds a room door open, when she enters and secures whatever is handy and decamps. She is known in New York City, Brooklyn, Paterson, N. J., and Baltimore, Md., where she also served a term in prison. She is said to have kept a road-house near Paterson, N. J., some years ago.

Tillie was arrested in New York City a few years ago, endeavoring to rob the Berkeley Flats, on the corner of Ninth Street and Fifth Avenue, and sentenced to one year in the penitentiary, but subsequently released on habeas corpus proceedings in 1879.

She was arrested in Brooklyn, N. Y., disposing of a stolen watch in a pawnbroker's shop. When arrested, she drew a revolver and attempted to shoot the officer. For this she was sentenced to one year in the penitentiary there.

She was arrested again in New York City on June 15, 1881, taken to police headquarters and searched. There was found upon her person four pocket-books, which contained money and jewelry. In one of them there was $10 in money, a gold hairpin and earrings, and the address of Miss Jennie Yeamans, of East Ninth Street, New York City, who testified that her rooms had been entered by a sneak thief during her absence, and the property stolen. Two other parties appeared against her and testified that she had robbed them also. Tillie pleaded guilty in this case, and was sentenced to one year in the penitentiary on Blackwell's Island, on June 23, 1881, by Judge Cowing.

She was arrested again in New York City on June 19, 1882, for entering the apartments of Annie E. Tool, No. 151 Avenue B, and stealing a gold watch and chain and a pair of diamond earrings valued at $300. For this she was sentenced to eighteen months in the penitentiary on June 26, 1882, by Judge Gildersleeve.

Her picture is a fair one, taken in June, 1882.

126
MARY BUSBY, alias JOHNSON,
alias MITCHELL.
PICKPOCKET AND SHOPLIFTER.

DESCRIPTION.

Forty-eight years old in 1886. Born in England. Married. Stout build. Height, 5 feet. Weight, 221 pounds. Dark brown hair, gray eyes, dark complexion.

RECORD.

MARY BUSBY is a clever pickpocket and shoplifter, and is well known in all the large cities. Harry Busby, alias Broken-nose Busby (135), her husband, is an old New York pickpocket and "stall."

She was arrested in New York City for shoplifting on October 25, 1882, under the name of Mary Johnson, and sentenced to six months in the penitentiary on October 30, 1882, by Judge Ford.

Arrested again in Boston, Mass., on May 3, 1883, for larceny of $40 worth of silk garments from Jourdan & Marsh's dry goods store. For this she was sentenced to one year in the House of Correction on May 18, 1883. After her discharge in Boston, she went to New York City, and was arrested for the larceny of a bonnet from Rothschild's millinery establishment on West Fourteenth Street. For this she was sentenced to five months in the penitentiary on Blackwell's Island on May 20, 1884. This time she gave the name of Mary Mitchell.

Mary Busby had previously served two years on Blackwell's Island, and two years in the House of Correction in Boston, Mass.

She was again sentenced to fourteen months in the Eastern Penitentiary on September 14, 1885, for picking pockets in Wannemaker's store in Philadelphia, Pa.

Her picture is an excellent one, taken in October, 1882.

127
ANNIE REILLY, alias LITTLE ANNIE,
alias KATIE COOLEY, alias KATE CONNELLY, alias KATE MANNING.
DISHONEST SERVANT.

DESCRIPTION.

Forty-two years old in 1886; looks younger. Born in Ireland. Married. Medium build. Servant and child's nurse. Height, 5 feet 1 inch. Weight, 113 pounds. Brown hair, gray eyes, fair complexion. Round, full face. Speaks two or three languages.

RECORD.

"LITTLE ANNIE REILLY" is considered the cleverest woman in her line in America. She generally engages herself as a child's nurse, makes a great fuss over the children, and gains the good-will of the lady of the house. She seldom remains in one place more than one or two days before she robs it, generally taking jewelry, amounting at times to four and five thousand dollars. She is well known in all the principal Eastern cities, especially in New York, Brooklyn, and Philadelphia, Pa.

Annie was arrested in New York City, for grand larceny, on complaint of Mrs. A. G. Dunn, No. 149 East Eighty-fourth Street, and others, and committed for trial, in default of $6,500 bail, by Judge Ledwith. She was convicted, and sentenced to four years and six months in State prison, by Judge Sutherland, in the Court of General Sessions in New York, on April 23, 1873, under the name of Kate Connelly.

She was arrested again in New York City, on August 3, 1880, for robbing the house of Mrs. Evangeline Swartz, on Second Avenue, New York. She was convicted of this robbery, and sentenced to three years in the penitentiary on Blackwell's Island, on September 8, 1880, by Judge Gildersleeve, under the name of Kate Cooley. After her release, in January, 1883, she did considerable work in and around New York.. She robbed the guests of the New York Hotel of $3,500 worth of jewelry, etc., while employed there as a servant. She then went to Brooklyn, N. Y., and was arrested there, under the name of Kate Manning, on June 5, 1884, for the larceny of a watch and chain from Charles A. Jennings, of Macon Street, that city. At the time of her arrest a bronze statuette was found in her possession, which was stolen by her from a Mr. Buckman, of Columbia Street, New York City.

Annie pleaded guilty in Brooklyn, N. Y., on Saturday, June 27, 1884, and was sentenced to four years and six months in the Kings County Penitentiary. Her sentence will expire June 27, 1887, allowing full commutation.

This woman is well worth knowing. She has stolen more property the last fifteen years than any other four women in America. She has served terms in prison in Pennsylvania and on Blackwell's Island independently of the above.

Her picture is an excellent one, taken in August, 1880.

128

SOPHIE LEVY, alias LYONS.

PICKPOCKET AND BLACKMAILER.

DESCRIPTION.

Thirty-six years old in 1886. Jew. Born in United States. Married. Medium build. Height, 5 feet 2 inches. Weight, 115 pounds. Brown hair, gray eyes, light complexion. Has four children, two boys (thieves) and two girls, who were brought up in a convent in Canada, and are an exception to the rest of the family.

RECORD.

SOPHIE LYONS, or LEVY, is a notorious shoplifter, pickpocket and blackmailer. She has appeared before the public of late years as an adventuress, and has blackmailed scores of business men throughout the country. She is the wife of Edward Lyons, better known as Ned Lyons, the bank burglar (see No. 70), and is well known all over the United States.

Sophie was arrested in New York City, and sentenced to five years in State prison, on October 9, 1871, for grand larceny. She escaped from Sing Sing prison, with the assistance of her husband and others, on December 19, 1872.

She was re-arrested at the Suffolk County, Long Island, N. Y., fair, with her husband, caught in the act of picking pockets, and returned to Sing Sing on October 26, 1876. After serving out her time she went to Boston, Mass., where she made her début as a blackmailer, accompanied by Kate Leary, alias "Red Kate," wife of the notorious Red Leary. She went to one of the principal hotels, where she attracted the notice of a wealthy merchant, and lured him to her room. She secured his clothing and threatened him with exposure if he did not comply with her demands. He surrendered, filled out a check for $10,000, which was handed to her confederate, Kate, who went straightway to the bank. It happened that his account fell short of the amount required, and Kate being questioned, grew alarmed and made known the whereabouts of the merchant, when a policeman being sent to the hotel, the plot was exposed. Sophie and Kate were arrested, but their intended victim refused to appear against them, and they were discharged. His money was saved, but his character was ruined, and the result was the breaking up of a happy home. She continued blackmailing people until February 6, 1883, when she was convicted at Ann Harbor, Mich., and sentenced to three years in the Detroit House of Correction for larceny, in connection with one of her schemes. Some months before that she made a daily practice of sitting on a horse-block in front of the residence of one of her Grand Rapids, Mich., victims, who was a very prominent man. He got rid of Mrs. Lyons by turning the hose on her, and pounding an unfortunate theatrical agent who espoused her quarrel.

Sophie Levy was arrested again in New York City on June 2, 1886, charged by Koch & Sons, dry-goods dealers on Sixth Avenue, with the larceny of a piece of silk. She gave the name of Kate Wilson, and her identity was not established until the day of her trial (June 10, 1886), when she was convicted, and sentenced to six months in the penitentiary on Blackwell's Island. Of late she has become addicted to the opium habit.

Sophie Elkins, an old-time shoplifter, is Sophie Levy's mother. She was sentenced to four years in State prison, in New York City on November 22, 1876, by Recorder Hackett, under the name of Julia Keller, for shoplifting.

Sophie Levy's picture is a good one. It was taken in 1886.

129
KATE RYAN.
PICKPOCKET.

DESCRIPTION.

Fifty years old in 1886. Born in Ireland. Seamstress. Married. Stout build. Height, 5 feet 3½ inches. Weight, 150 pounds. Dark brown hair, light hazel eyes, dark complexion.

RECORD.

KATE RYAN is an old New York pickpocket and shoplifter. She works parades and stores, and is known in Philadelphia and New York, and some of the Western cities.

She was arrested in New York City on St. Patrick's day, March 17, 1876, charged with picking pockets during the parade. She was convicted and sentenced to four years in the penitentiary on March 28, 1876, by Recorder Hackett, in the Court of General Sessions.

Kate has served time in State prison and in the penitentiary since the above.

Her picture is a good one, taken in March, 1876.

130
MARY MACK, alias BOND,
alias BROCKEY ANNIE.
SNEAK AND SHOPLIFTER.

DESCRIPTION.

Twenty-five years old in 1886. Born in United States. Married. No trade. Stout build. Height, 5 feet 2 inches. Weight, 150 pounds. Brown hair, hazel eyes, fair complexion. Very heavily pock-marked. Part of first joint of thumb off of right hand.

RECORD.

MARY MACK is one of a new gang of women shoplifters and pennyweight workers. She works with Nellie Barns, alias Bond, and Big Grace Daly. They have been traveling all over the Eastern States the last two years, and many a jeweler and dry goods merchant have cause to remember their visits.

Mary was arrested in New York City on August 24, 1885, in company of Nellie Barns and Grace Daly, coming out of O'Neill's dry goods store on Sixth Avenue. A ring was found upon her person, which was identified as having been stolen from the store. For this she was sentenced to six months in the penitentiary on Blackwell's Island on September 4, 1885. This woman, although young, is considered very clever, and is well worth knowing. Barns and Daly were discharged in this case.

Her picture is an excellent one, taken in August, 1885.

131

LOUISE JOURDAN, alias BIGLOW,

alias DARRIGAN, alias LITTLE LOUISA.

PICKPOCKET AND SHOPLIFTER.

DESCRIPTION.

Forty-two years old in 1886. Born in England. Married. Medium build. Height, 5 feet 3 inches. Weight, about 135 pounds. Brown hair, blue eyes, dark complexion, round face. Is lady-like in manner and appearance. Wears good clothes.

RECORD.

LOUISE JOURDAN, alias LITTLE LOUISE, is an expert female thief, well known in New York, Chicago, and all the principal cities in the United States as the wife of Big Tom Biglow, the burglar. She was born in England. Her father once kept a public-house in Manchester, England. She served a term in an English prison for larceny. Upon her release she went to Brazil as a companion of a wealthy Spanish lady. While in that country she stole all her mistress's diamonds, was arrested, convicted, and sentenced to receive forty lashes at the whipping-post, and was condemned to have the lower part of her right ear cut off. She wears her hair over her ears to cover this deformity.

Louise afterwards appeared in New York City as the mistress of Billy Darrigan, a New York pickpocket. She was arrested for shoplifting at A. T. Stewart's dry goods store, and sent to Blackwell's Island. After her release she operated in Boston, Philadelphia, and other cities.

She was married several times after leaving Darrigan; first to Tom McCormack, the bank burglar, who killed Jim Casey in New York, some years ago, while disputing over the proceeds of a robbery. After him, she took up with Aleck Purple, an Eighth Ward, New York, pickpocket; then with Dan Kelly, who was convicted and sentenced to twenty years in State prison for a masked burglary, with Patsey Conroy and others. After that she lived with a well-known New York sporting man, and finally married Big Tom Biglow, and has been working the country with him since. She has been in several State prisons and penitentiaries in America, and is considered one of the smartest female pickpockets in this country.

Louise Jourdan was arrested again in Cincinnati, Ohio, under the name of Mary Johnson, on May 19, 1886, in company of Sarah Johnson, a tall, blonde woman, charged

121

MARY ANN WATTS,
PICKPOCKET AND SHOP LIFTER.

122

BERTHA HEYMAN,
CONFIDENCE.

123

ELLEN DARRIGAN,
ALIAS ELLEN MATTHEWS,
PICKPOCKET.

124

ELIZABETH DILLON,
ALIAS BRIDGET COLE,
PICKPOCKET.

125

TILLY MARTIN,
ALIAS PHIEFER,
SNEAK.

126

MARY BUSBY,
ALIAS JOHNSON,
PICKPOCKET AND SHOP LIFTER.

127

ANNIE REILLY,
ALIAS LITTLE ANNIE
DISHONEST SERVANT.

128

SOPHIE LYONS,
ALIAS LEVY,
PICKPOCKET AND BLACKMAILER.

129

KATE RYAN,
PICKPOCKET.

130

MARY MACK,
ALIAS BOND,
SNEAK AND SHOP LIFTER.

131

LOUISA JOURDAN,
ALIAS LITTLE LOUISE.
PICKPOCKET AND SHOP LIFTER.

132

CATHARINE ARMSTRONG,
ALIAS MARY ANN DOWD, ALIAS DILLON,
PICKPOCKET.

133

PADDY MARTIN,
ALIAS ENGLISH PADDY,
PICKPOCKET.

134

TERRANCE MURPHY,
ALIAS POODLE MURPHY,
PICKPOCKET.

135

HARRY BUSBY,
ALIAS MITCHELL,
PICKPOCKET AND SHOP LIFTER.

136

TIMOTHY OATS,
ALIAS CLARK,
PICKPOCKET.

137

JAMES LAWSON,
ALIAS NIBBS
PICKPOCKET

138

GEORGE MILLIARD,
ALIAS MILLER.
PICKPOCKET.

139

THOMAS FITZGERALD,
ALIAS TOM PHAIR.
PICKPOCKET.

140

EDWARD TULLY,
ALIAS BROKEN NOSE TULLY.
PICKPOCKET.

141

RICHARD MORRIS,
ALIAS BIG DICK,
PICKPOCKET.

142

JAMES ANDERSON,
ALIAS JIMMY THE KID.
PICKPOCKET.

143

JAMES WILSON,
ALIAS PRETTY JIMMY,
PICKPOCKET.

144

GEORGE HARRISON,
ALIAS BOSTON and FRIDAY,
PICKPOCKET.

with picking the pocket of a woman named Kate Thompson of $90, in one of the horse-cars. They both gave bail in $1,000, and at last accounts the case had not been disposed of.

Her picture is an excellent one.

132

KATE ARMSTRONG, alias MARY ANN DOWD,
alias DILLON, alias SANDERS.
PICKPOCKET AND SHOPLIFTER.

DESCRIPTION.

Forty-five years old in 1886. Born in England. Married. Cook. Stout build. Height, 5 feet 2½ inches. Weight, 200 pounds. Dark brown hair, hazel eyes, florid complexion. Wears gold eye-glasses. Has a large space between upper front teeth. Vaccination mark on left arm.

RECORD.

MARY ANN DOWD (right name Catharine Armstrong) is a very clever woman. She was arrested in the spring of 1876, during Moody and Sankey's revivals, in Madison Square Garden, in New York City, for picking a lady's pocket, and sent to Sing Sing for two years.

She was arrested again in Providence, R. I., on May 14, 1878, and sentenced to two years in State prison in June of the same year, for picking a woman's pocket on the street.

After her time expired in Providence she went West, and visited Chicago (Ill.) and St. Louis. Mrs. Dowd generally works alone, and confines herself principally to opening hand-bags, or stealing them. Her operations have been greatly aided by her respectable appearance and her perfect self-control.

She was arrested in New York City on October 20, 1884, charged with the larceny of a diamond, sapphire and pearl bar-pin, valued at $250, from the jewelry store of Tiffany & Co., New York, on July 7, 1884. The pin was found on her person, with the diamond removed and a ruby set in its place. For this she was tried by a jury, convicted, and sentenced to five years in State prison. She obtained a new trial in this case, which resulted in her discharge by Judge Cowing, on December 18, 1884.

She was arrested again in Philadelphia, Pa., at Wannemaker's grand depot, in company of Harry Busby (135), on November 3, 1885, for picking pockets. Busby was discharged and Mary Ann was convicted, and sentenced to two years and six months in the Eastern Penitentiary on November 11, 1885.

Her sentence will expire on September 11, 1887.

Mrs. Armstrong's, or Dowd's, picture is a good one, taken in November, 1885.

133

PATRICK MARTIN, alias ENGLISH PADDY,
alias FRANK HILTON.

PICKPOCKET.

DESCRIPTION.

Twenty-nine years old in 1886. Born in Ireland. Single. Laborer. Medium build. Height, 5 feet 6 inches. Weight, 148 pounds. Light hair, blue eyes, sandy complexion.

RECORD.

PADDY MARTIN, or ENGLISH PADDY, is an English thief. He has been traveling through the country with a gang of Bowery (New York) pickpockets, and is considered a pretty clever man.

He was arrested in New York City on June 19, 1885, in company of another pickpocket, named Frank Mitchell, for an attempt to pick a man's pocket on Bowling Green, near the Battery, New York. Both of them were sentenced to one month in the penitentiary on Blackwell's Island, by Justice Duffy, on June 20, 1885.

Paddy was arrested again in Jersey City, N. J., on December 12, 1885, in the act of robbing a Mrs. Margaret Peters, of Montgomery Street, Jersey City, on a Pennsylvania ferry-boat. He tried to make her believe that he mistook her for his wife, and offered her ten dollars to release him. She rejected his overtures, and held on to him until a policeman arrived. He was tried, found guilty, and sentenced to three years and six months in Trenton State prison on December 14, 1885, under the name of Frank Hilton.

His picture is an excellent one, taken in June, 1885.

134

TERRENCE MURPHY, alias POODLE MURPHY,
alias ROBINSON.

PICKPOCKET.

DESCRIPTION.

Thirty-seven years old in 1886. Born in Albany, N. Y. Married. Slim build. Height, five feet 7 inches. Weight, 135 pounds. Hair, auburn, slightly mixed with gray ; blue eyes, light complexion. Can grow a full red beard quickly.

RECORD.

"POODLE MURPHY" is the most notorious and successful pickpocket in America. He is well known in every city in the United States as the leader of a Bowery (New York) gang of pickpockets. He is an associate of James Wilson, alias Pretty Jimmie (143), Dick Morris, alias Big Dick (141), Charley Allen, Aleck Evans, alias Aleck the Milkman (160), Johnny Williams (149), Joe Gorman (146), Jim Casey (91), Nigger Baker (195), Tom Burns (148), and others.

Murphy and Charley Woods were arrested in New York City on July 20, 1881, and delivered to the police authorities of Philadelphia, charged with robbing ex-Secretary of the Navy Robeson of a watch, on a railroad car in that city. After several days had been set for the trial, and as many adjournments obtained, the Secretary became tired and abandoned the case, and the thieves were once more given their liberty on September 30, 1881.

Murphy is without doubt the smartest pickpocket in America. He is the man who does the work, while his confederates annoy the victim and attract his attention. This is what is called "stalling." He has been arrested in every large city in the Union, but never sent to a State prison before.

He was arrested in Philadelphia on January 16, 1885, in company of James Wilson, alias Pretty Jimmie (143), another notorious pickpocket, charged with robbing one Shadrach Raleigh, of Delaware, of $526 in money and $3,300 in notes, etc., on a Columbia Avenue car in that city, on December 24, 1884. For this he was sentenced to three years in the Eastern Penitentiary, on March 16, 1885. There were four other charges against him at the time, but they were not tried.

Pretty Jimmie, his partner, was also sent to the penitentiary for two years and six months the same day.

Poodle's picture is an excellent one, although somewhat drawn. It was taken in January, 1885.

135

HARRY BUSBY, alias WILLIAMS,
alias MITCHELL.

PICKPOCKET AND SHOPLIFTER.

DESCRIPTION.

Forty-two years old in 1886. Born in London, England. Married. House-painter. Stout build. Height, 5 feet 6 inches. Weight, 170 pounds. Hair black, mixed with gray; brown eyes, round face, ruddy complexion. Marks on face and neck from skin disease. Short, pug nose. Has quite an English accent.

RECORD.

Busby is a well known Eastern pickpocket, and husband of Mary Busby (126), one of the cleverest women in America in her line. He is known in all the principal cities in the United States and in Montreal, Canada.

He was arrested in New York City and sentenced to two years and six months in Sing Sing prison, under the name of Henry Williams, on May 19, 1873, for an attempt at grand larceny, by Judge Sutherland.

He was arrested again in New York, on January 26, 1877, in company of John Anderson, another pickpocket, charged with robbing one Wm. Smyth of a pocket-book on a Fourth Avenue car, on January 22. They were discharged, as the complainant failed to identify them.

Harry was arrested in Washington Market, New York, with Mary Kelly, as suspicious characters, on March 27, 1886, and discharged by a Police Justice.

Busby's picture is an excellent one, taken in Philadelphia, Pa., where he has also served a term in the penitentiary.

136

TIMOTHY OATS, alias TIM OATS,
alias Clark.
PICKPOCKET AND SNEAK.

DESCRIPTION.

Thirty-six years old in 1886. Born in United States. Married. Speculator. Stout build. Height, 5 feet 8½ inches. Weight, 198 pounds. Sandy hair, blue eyes, sandy complexion. Generally wears a light-colored mustache.

RECORD.

Tim Oats is an old New York panel thief and pickpocket. He was arrested in New York City in 1874, with his wife Addie Clark, charged with robbing a man by the panel game. They escaped conviction on account of the complainant's departure from the city.

He was arrested again in New York City, under the name of Timothy Ryan, charged with robbing William Vogel, on July 30, 1875, of a diamond stud valued at $200, while riding on an East Broadway railroad car. He was tried, convicted and sentenced to four years in Sing Sing prison, on September 17, 1875, by Recorder Hackett.

Tim was arrested again in New York City, under the name of Timothy Clark, on January 11, 1879, in company of James Moran, whose name is Tommy Matthews (156), charged with robbing a man named Michael Jobin, of Mount Vernon, N. Y., of $200, on a Third Avenue horse-car. Both were committed in default of $5,000 bail for trial, by Judge Murray. They pleaded guilty to larceny from the person and were sentenced to two years in the penitentiary on February 6, 1879, by Judge Gildersleeve.

Tim Oats, Theodore Wiley (171) and William Brown, alias Wm. H. Russell, alias "The Student," were arrested at Syracuse, N. Y., on January 4, 1883, charged with grand larceny. They stole a tin cash-box from behind a saloon bar, containing $250, the property of Seiter Brothers, No. 99 North Salina Street, Syracuse. Two other people were with the above party but escaped. Oats played the "fit act" in the back room, kicking over chairs and tables. The proprietor and all the parties in the store ran into the back room to help the "poor fellow," when one of the party sneaked behind the bar and stole the cash-box.

Tim Oats gave the name of Charles Oats, pleaded guilty, and was sentenced to two years' imprisonment in Auburn State prison, on March 1, 1883. His sentence expired November 1, 1885.

"The." Wiley gave the name of George Davis, alias George Marsh, and was tried and convicted also. (See No. 171.)

Brown, alias Russell, alias "The Student," pleaded guilty in this case and was sentenced to five years in Auburn prison, on March 1, 1883.

Oats's picture is a very good one, taken in January, 1879.

137
JAMES LAWSON, alias "NIBBS,"
alias "NIBSEY."
PICKPOCKET.

DESCRIPTION.

Forty-three years old in 1886. Born in Ireland. Single. No trade. Stout build. Height, 5 feet 7 inches. Weight, about 160 pounds. Black hair, gray eyes, dark complexion; generally wears a full black beard. Has a vaccination mark on his right arm.

RECORD.

"NIBBS" is an old-time Bowery, New York, pickpocket; he is as well known in Philadelphia, Chicago and Boston as he is in New York. He has been arrested in almost every large city in the Union, and is considered a clever thief. He travels all over the country, and can generally be seen with some of the local thieves. He is an impudent fellow, and wants to be taken in hand at once.

He was arrested in New York City for attempting to pick pockets, and was sentenced to one year in the penitentiary on Blackwell's Island, on March 18, 1875.

He was arrested in Philadelphia, Pa., on April 24, 1876, charged with picking a man's pocket; his picture was taken, and he was discharged.

He was arrested again in Jersey City, N. J., on December 20, 1876, charged with robbing a German farmer of his pocket-book and money in the Pennsylvania Railroad depot. When searched at Police Headquarters, a kid glove was found in his pocket; in the finger of the glove was a large and beautiful diamond, valued at $1,000. In his vest pocket was found the setting of the stone, a stud for a shirt front. It was advertised, and turned out to be the property of Captain Wilgus, of Lexington, Ky., who had been robbed of the stone by a mob of pickpockets while getting on a train in Louisville, Ky.

"Nibbs" was convicted of robbing the German in the depot, and sentenced to five years in Trenton, N. J., State prison, on January 27, 1877.

He was arrested again in New York City on February 11, 1882, for robbing a man on a Grand Street horse-car of his pocket-book. For this he was sentenced to three years and six months in Sing Sing prison, on March 8, 1882.

Lawson is now at large.

"Nibbs's" picture is an excellent one, taken in 1876.

138

GEORGE MILLIARD, alias MILLER.

BURGLAR AND PICKPOCKET.

DESCRIPTION.

Forty-four years old in 1886. Born in United States. Married. Saloon keeper. Slim build. Height, 5 feet 7 inches. Weight, 118 pounds. Brown hair, blue eyes, light complexion, bald on front of head. Generally wears a full black beard. Has an anchor in India ink on right fore-arm.

RECORD.

MILLIARD is an old New York pickpocket, burglar, and receiver of stolen goods. He formerly kept a liquor saloon on the corner of Washington and Canal streets, New York, which was the resort of the most desperate gang of river thieves and masked burglars in America.

Milliard was arrested in New York City on January 5, 1874, in company of John Burns, Big John Garvey (now dead), Dan Kelly, Matthew McGeary, Francis P. Dayton, Lawrence Griffin, and Patsey Conroy (now dead), charged with being implicated in several masked burglaries. One in New Rochelle, N. Y., on December 23, 1873; another at Catskill, on the Hudson River, on October 17, 1873, and one on Staten Island, N. Y., in December, 1873, about a week after the New Rochelle robbery. The particular charge against Milliard was receiving stolen goods, part of the proceeds of these burglaries. He was tried in New York City, convicted, and sentenced to five years in Sing Sing prison on February 13, 1874. The other parties arrested with him at the time were disposed of as follows :

Dan Kelly, Larry Griffin, and Patsey Conroy were each sentenced to twenty years in State prison for the New Rochelle burglary on February 20, 1874.

Burns was sentenced to sixteen years in State prison for the Catskill burglary on October 23, 1874.

Big John Garvey (now dead) was sentenced to ten years in State prison in New York City on June 22, 1874.

McGeary was discharged on January 13, 1874.

Dayton was put under $1,000 bail for good behavior on January 13, 1874.

Shang Campbell, John O'Donnell, John Orr (now dead), and Pugsey Hurley (88), were also arrested in connection with these burglaries, and sent to State prison.

Since Milliard's discharge he has been traveling through the country picking pockets with Jimmie Lawson, alias " Nibbs " (137), and a Chicago thief named Williard. He is considered a first-class man, and is known in all the principal cities in the United States. He has been arrested several times, but manages to escape conviction.

His picture is a good one, taken in August, 1885.

139

THOMAS FITZGERALD, alias TOM PHAIR.

PICKPOCKET.

DESCRIPTION.

Forty-nine years old in 1886. Born in Ireland. Married. Carpenter. Stout build. Height, 5 feet 11 inches. Weight, about 200 pounds. Brown hair, blue eyes, light complexion. Generally wears a sandy chin whisker and mustache.

RECORD.

"Big Tom Phair," the name he is best known by, is a clever thief, and generally works with his wife, Bridget Fitzgerald, an old Irish pickpocket, or some other woman, and can be found in the vicinity of funerals, ferry-boats, or churches. They are mean thieves, generally robbing poor women.

Fitzgerald and his wife, and Mary Connors, were arrested in New York City on May 1, 1873, charged with robbing a woman named Sophie Smith, on Broadway, of a pocket-book containing a quantity of checks and her husband's pension papers from the United States Government. Tom pleaded guilty and was sentenced to two years and six months in State prison, on May 26, 1873.

Bridget, his wife, was discharged.

Mary Connors also pleaded guilty to an attempt at grand larceny, and was sentenced to one year and nine months in State prison, the same day, by Judge Sutherland.

Fitzgerald and his wife were arrested again under the names of Tom and Sarah Thayer, on a Staten Island ferry-boat, at the Battery, New York, which was conveying the friends of the Garner family to Staten Island to attend the funeral of Wm. F. Garner. Mrs. Fitzgerald was again discharged. Tom was held under the Habitual Criminal Act, and sentenced to ninety days in the penitentiary on Blackwell's Island, on July 27, 1876. He was afterwards discharged on habeas corpus proceedings.

He has been very lucky of late years. Although arrested several times, he manages to keep out of jail.

His picture is a very good one, taken in November, 1875.

140

EDWARD TULLY, alias BROKEN-NOSE TULLY.

PICKPOCKET.

DESCRIPTION

Forty-one years old in 1886. Born in Ireland. Single. No trade. Stout build. Height, 5 feet 6½ inches. Weight, 155 pounds. Dark hair, gray eyes, dark complexion, broken nose. Rather large, long head. Wears a brown mustache. Easily recognized by his picture. Has an Irish brogue and face.

RECORD.

"Broken-Nose Tully" is an old and expert New York pickpocket, and is well known in every large city in the Union. He travels with the best people in the business, and is considered a clever pickpocket. He has a remarkable nose, which he claims always "gives him away."

Tully was arrested in Philadelphia and sentenced to fourteen months in the Eastern Penitentiary, on June 29, 1880, for picking the pocket of a small boy of $83.

He was arrested again in Boston, Mass., with Shinny McGuire (155), on July 16, 1881, awaiting an opportunity to do a "turn trick" in the Naverick National Bank, After getting a good showing up they were escorted out of town.

He was arrested again in Lancaster, Pa., for picking pockets, and sentenced to eighteen months in the Eastern Penitentiary at Philadelphia, on November 18, 1884. He is now at large.

Tully's picture is an excellent one, taken in Buffalo, N. Y.

141

RICHARD MORRIS, alias BIG DICK.

PICKPOCKET.

DESCRIPTION.

Forty-two years old in 1886. Born in United States. Married. Carpenter. Medium build. Height, 5 feet 10½ inches. Weight, 155 pounds. Brown hair, blue eyes, fair complexion. Generally wears a light-colored beard and mustache, inclined to be sandy.

RECORD.

"BIG DICK" is a well known New York pickpocket. He works with Charles Douglas, alias Curly Charley; Poodle Murphy (134), Shang Campbell (107), James Wilson, alias Pretty Jimmie (143), and all the other good New York men. He has traveled all over the United States, and is well known in all the principal cities. Morris formerly kept a drinking saloon in New York that was a resort for nearly all the pickpockets in America, but business fell off and he went back to his old business again.

He was arrested in New York City, and sentenced to five years in Sing Sing prison, January 7, 1872, for larceny from the person, under the name of Richard Morris.

He was arrested again in Albany, N. Y., by New York officers, and brought to New York City, where he pleaded guilty to grand larceny, and was sentenced to one year in the penitentiary on August 10, 1885, for stealing a coat from Rogers, Peet & Co., some months previously. He gave bail in this case, which he forfeited, and was subsequently re-arrested as above.

Morris's picture is a good one, taken in October, 1877.

142

JAMES ANDERSON, alias JIMMIE THE KID, alias EVANS.

PICKPOCKET.

DESCRIPTION.

Forty-three years old in 1886. Born in Ireland. Married. Tailor. Medium build. Height, 6 feet. Weight, about 180 pounds. Hair black, turning gray; gray eyes, light complexion. Generally wears a sandy mustache.

RECORD.

"JIMMIE THE KID" is a clever old New York thief. He has been traveling through the country for a number of years, and is well known in all the principal cities East and West. He is a great big rough fellow, and will get the money at any cost.

He was arrested several times in New York, but never with a clear case against him until April 10, 1876, when he was arrested for robbing George W. Mantel, on one of the horse-cars, for which he was convicted, and sentenced to ten years in Sing Sing prison, on June 16, 1876, by Recorder Hackett, in the Court of General Sessions, New York. His time expired on December 16, 1882.

His picture is an excellent one, taken in January, 1876.

143
JAMES WILSON, alias PRETTY JIMMIE.
PICKPOCKET.

DESCRIPTION.

Forty-two years old in 1886. Born in United States. Married. No trade. Medium build. Height, 5 feet 6 inches. Weight, 155 pounds. Brown hair, hazel eyes, florid complexion. Has the following India ink marks on his person : a woman, in short dress, in red and blue ink, with bow and staff in hand, on right arm ; another woman, in short dress, holding in her left hand a flag, on which is a skull and cross-bones, on left arm ; anchor on back of left hand ; a shield between thumb and forefinger of left hand.

RECORD.

"Pretty Jimmie" is an old New York pickpocket, and partner of Terrence, alias Poodle Murphy (134).

He was arrested in Montreal, Canada, during the Marquis of Lorne celebration, with a gang of American pickpockets, from whom a box of stolen watches was taken. He was sentenced to two years' imprisonment there.

He was arrested again in New York City, and pleaded guilty to an attempt at larceny from the person of Stephen B. Brague, and sentenced to one year in State prison, on July 12, 1875, by Judge Sutherland, under the name of James Anderson.

Since 1876 Wilson and Murphy have robbed more people than any other four men in America.

He was finally arrested in Philadelphia, Pa., on January 16, 1885, with Poodle Murphy (134), charged with robbing one Shadrach Raleigh, of Delaware, of $526 in money and $3,300 in notes, etc., on a Columbia Avenue horse-car, on December 24, 1884. He was tried, convicted, and sentenced to two years and six months in the Eastern Penitentiary, on March 16, 1885.

Murphy, his partner, who did the work, was sentenced to three years.

There were four other charges against this team, which were not tried.

His picture is a good one, taken in January, 1885.

144
GEORGE HARRISON, alias "BOSTON,"
alias "FRIDAY."
PICKPOCKET.

DESCRIPTION.

Forty-five years old in 1886. Born in Scotland. Single. Machinist. Medium build. Height, 5 feet 9 inches. Weight, about 160 pounds. Black curly hair, gray eyes, light complexion.   Generally wears a brown mustache.   Had weak eyes.   Has scar under right eye.

RECORD.

"Boston," the name he is best known by, is a well known New York pickpocket. He has been arrested in almost every large city in the Union.   He is said to have served terms in prison in Philadelphia and Boston.   When he first appeared in New York City he came from Boston, Mass., and the fraternity christened him after that city. He is not able to do much alone, but is considered an excellent "stall."   He works sometimes with Jersey Jimmie (145), Charley Allen, and other New York pick-pockets.

He was arrested in New York City, and sentenced to four years and six months in Sing Sing prison on November 8, 1882, under the name of George Wilson, for grand larceny from the person.   His time expired, allowing him full commutation, on March 8, 1886.

"Boston's" picture is a good one, taken in 1876.

145

JAMES JOHNSON, alias JERSEY JIMMIE.

PICKPOCKET.

DESCRIPTION.

Forty-two years old in 1886.   Born in New York.   Married.   No trade.   Stout build.   Height, 5 feet 4½ inches.   Weight, 170 pounds.   Dark brown hair, gray eyes, florid complexion.   Whiskers, when worn, are light brown.

RECORD.

"Jersey Jimmie" is one of the luckiest thieves in America.   He is known from Maine to California, and has had the good fortune to escape State prison many a time. He works with Joe Gorman (146), Boston (144), Curly Charley, Big Dick (141), and nearly all the Bowery "mob" of New York, where he makes his home.

He was arrested in New York City, and sentenced to six months in the penitentiary on Blackwell's Island, under the name of James Johnson, on April 22, 1869, for an attempt to pick pockets.

He was sentenced again to one year in the penitentiary on Blackwell's Island, on February 7, 1878, for picking pockets, and pardoned by Governor Robinson on May 8, 1878.

Since then he has been arrested in almost every city in the Union, but his usual good luck stands to him, and he succeeds in obtaining his discharge.

Johnson's picture is an excellent one, taken in August, 1885.

146

JOSEPH GORMAN, alias CLIFFORD,
alias Brown.
PICKPOCKET.

DESCRIPTION.

Thirty-seven years old in 1886. Born in New York. Married. Carpenter. Medium build. Height, 5 feet 8 inches. Weight, about 130 pounds. Sandy hair, blue eyes, small nose, thin face, light complexion. Has letter " J." in India ink on left fore-arm ; dot of ink on left hand.

RECORD.

Joe Gorman is a very clever pickpocket. He generally does the work. He is well known in all the large cities of the Union, and is as likely to be found, with two or three other clever men, in Maine or California, as he is in New York, working the cars, fairs, conventions, or any crowded place. He comes of a family that is criminally inclined, as he has two brothers, Tom, a sneak and till-tapper, and John, a clever general thief. Joe was born in New York, and makes it his home. Although arrested several times of late years he has escaped State prison. He is one of the smartest pickpockets in America, and a man well worth knowing.

He was sentenced to twenty years' imprisonment in Auburn prison, from New York City, several years ago, for highway robbery, and was pardoned after serving six years.

Gorman's picture is a very good one, taken in September, 1885.

147

DENNIS CARROLL, alias WILLIAM THOMPSON,
alias Big Slim.
BURGLAR AND PICKPOCKET.

DESCRIPTION.

Twenty-eight years old in 1886. Born in United States. Single. No trade. Slim build. Height, 5 feet 11 inches. Weight, about 150 pounds. Dark hair, dark eyes, quite weak; dark complexion. Generally wears a light, thin mustache. Slightly pitted with pock-marks.

RECORD.

" Big Slim," the name he is best known by, is a Chicago thief, and was formerly a partner of Joe Parish (84). He is a bold, desperate thief, having shot an officer out

West who was trying to arrest him and Parish for picking pockets in one of the towns that ex-President Garfield's body passed through.

He came East four or five years ago, and has been working the country with Johnny Dobbs and his gang.

He was arrested in Lawrence, Mass., on March 3, 1884, in company of Johnny Dobbs (64), Thos. McCarty, alias Day (87), and Frederick P. Grey (73). Carroll, or Thompson, is the man that did the shooting. (See record of No. 64.)

Carroll and Dobbs pleaded guilty and were sentenced to ten years each, on June 9, 1884. Carroll was pardoned on September 23, 1885, by Governor Robinson, of Massachusetts. It was claimed that he was suffering from an incurable disease. His health returned, however, upon his release. When last seen he was in New York City, apparently as well as ever. (See record of No. 87.)

His picture is an excellent one, taken in March, 1884.

148

THOMAS BURNS, alias COMBO,

alias HAMILTON.

PICKPOCKET.

DESCRIPTION

Forty-nine years of age in 1886. Born in United States. Married. No trade. Medium build. Height, 5 feet 10½ inches. Weight, 165 pounds. Black hair, brown eyes, dark complexion. Has scar on forehead ; mole on right cheek. Generally wears a black beard, turning gray.

RECORD.

"Combo" is a well known New York pickpocket. He works with "Jersey Jimmie" (145), "Nigger" Baker (195), "Curly Charley," Dick Morris (141), "Aleck the Milkman" (160), and the best people in the cities he visits. He was considered second to none in the business ; but of late years he has fallen back, and does only "stalling," on account of his love for liquor. He is pretty well known in Baltimore, Philadelphia, New York, Boston and Chicago, and, in fact, in almost all the large cities in the States.

He was arrested in New York City, for the larceny of a watch from one Lawson Valentine, on a Sixth Avenue horse-car, on February 8, 1875. He was tried, found guilty, and sentenced to four years in State prison, on March 9, 1875, under the name of Thomas Hamilton, by Judge Sutherland.

Combo was again arrested, at the Grand Central Railroad depot in New York City, on November 24, 1885, in an attempt to ply his vocation. He was sentenced to one year in the penitentiary on December 1, 1885, in the Court of Special Sessions, New York.

Burns's picture is an excellent one, taken in November, 1885.

149
JOHN WILLIAMS.
PICKPOCKET AND SHOPLIFTER.

DESCRIPTION.

Thirty-five years old in 1886. Born in New York. Single. Jeweler. Slim build. Height, 5 feet 7 inches. Weight, about 140 pounds. Black hair, gray eyes, light complexion. Generally wears a light brown mustache.

RECORD.

Johnny Williams is a very clever New York pickpocket and shoplifter. He is also well known in every important city in the United States. He is an associate of Poodle Murphy (134), Tim Oats (136), Nibbs (137), Big Dick Morris (141), Pretty Jimmie (143), Boston (144), Jersey Jimmie (145), Joe Gorman (146), and all the clever people. He is credited with purchasing almost everything that the New York thieves steal. Since his return from State prison he has been traveling around the country with a gang of pickpockets, and although arrested several times, he manages to keep out of State prison. He is now keeping a jewelry store on Sixth Avenue, New York City.

He was arrested in New York City on April 1, 1876, in company of John Meyers, charged with stealing a roll of cloth from the store of Albert Schichts, No. 88 Greenwich Street, New York City.

Meyers and Williams both pleaded guilty, and were sentenced to five years each in State prison, by Judge Gildersleeve, on June 5, 1876. There were three other cases against these people, at this time, which were not prosecuted.

Williams's picture is an excellent one, taken in 1876.

150
JAMES WELLS, alias "FUNERAL WELLS."
PICKPOCKET.

DESCRIPTION.

Forty-four years old in 1886. Born in United States. Married. No trade. Slim build. Height, 5 feet 9½ inches. Weight, 145 pounds. Gray hair, gray eyes, light complexion. Generally wears a full beard, light color. His eyes are small, weak and sunken.

RECORD.

"Funeral Wells" is an old and expert New York pickpocket. His particular line is picking pockets at a funeral, with a woman. The woman generally does the work and passes what she gets to Wells, who makes away with it, the woman remaining behind a little time to give him a chance to escape.

Wells has served a term in Sing Sing prison and in the penitentiary on Blackwell's Island, New York, and is known in all the principal cities. He has been traveling through the country lately (1886) with Billy Peck (157), and Jimmy Murphy, two other New York pickpockets, working the fairs, churches, etc.

He was arrested in New York City on April 3, 1880, charged with having attempted to rob one Ambrose P. Beekman, a merchant, residing in Jersey City, N. J., while the latter was riding on a cross-town horse-car. The complainant was unable to identify him, and he was discharged.

Wells was arrested again in New York City, on June 19, 1885, under the name of James Hayden, in company of James McKitterick, alias "Oyster Jim," and sentenced to three months each in the penitentiary, on June 30, 1885, in the Court of Special Sessions, for an assault with intent to steal as pickpockets.

McKitterick is a hotel and sleeping-car thief, pickpocket, and banco man. His home is in Hudson, N. Y. He is a great fancier of dogs and fighting cocks. Sometimes he has a full beard, and again a smooth face; at other times, chin whiskers. He was arrested in Schenectady in 1883, tried in Albany for picking pockets, and settled the matter by paying a fine of $800. He has been the counsel and adviser of thieves for years, and has been what is termed a "steerer." For a partner he has had James, alias "Shang" Campbell, Thomas Hammill, Funeral Wells, Peck, alias Peck's Bad Boy, and others of note. He was arrested some years ago in Brooklyn, N. Y., for picking a man's pocket. A Brooklyn judge who met him on the steamer for Florida identified him as his gentleman companion, and he was discharged. Soon after the close of the war, on the Mississippi he robbed a woman of $1,700. She demanded a search of all on the steamer. Jim had been so kind and attentive to her that he was not searched. A short time ago he was stakeholder for a dog fight in Boston to the amount of $300, and made off with the funds.

He took $1,000 worth of bonds from a gentleman in Philadelphia in 1868. His first experience in the East was when the Ball robbery was committed in Holyoke, Mass. He was in it, and was the principal.

He, with another, about two years ago, followed a well known lady of Springfield from New Haven to her home for the purpose of stealing her sealskin cloak. The theft was left to his partner, who failed for want of heart to do his work. This noted thief has been known in New York and all the principal cities of the United States under fifty different names. About two years ago, at Bridgeport, Conn., he was on a wharf to see an excursion party land from a steamboat. A man fell in the dock. A policeman standing on the edge of the wharf helped to get the man up. Jim, for fear he might fall into the dock again, kindly put his arms around him to hold him, and robbed him of his watch and eight dollars in money.

In 1880, when the Armstrong walk occurred on the Manhattan Athletic grounds, New York City, Jimmy was stakeholder for $480 wagered on the event. Jimmy "welshed," and the winners never saw the color of their money.

Wells's picture is an excellent one, taken in December, 1885.

151

OSCAR BURNS, alias JOHN L. HARLEY.

PICKPOCKET AND BURGLAR.

DESCRIPTION.

Thirty-six years old in 1886. Born in United States. Married. Cigar maker. Stout build. Height, 5 feet 7 inches. Weight, 162 pounds. Dark brown hair, brown eyes, dark complexion, heavy nose-lines. Generally wears a heavy brown mustache. Looks like a man that dissipates. Has a pearl in his right eye.

RECORD.

OSCAR BURNS is well known all over the United States. He is known out West as a "stall" and "hoister"—a Western term for a shoplifter. He works with Jim Barton, who is well known in Boston and Medford, Mass. They were both arrested in Springfield, Mass., for burglary. Burns gave bail, which was forfeited, and Barton was discharged from custody in February, 1881.

Burns was arrested again in New York City, on December 23, 1881, for a burglary committed in Grand Rapids, Michigan. He was delivered to the Michigan officers, taken there, and pleaded guilty to the crime, and was sentenced to ten years in State prison on December 29, 1881, by Judge Parrish, of Grand Rapids, Michigan. See Michigan Commutation Law for expiration of sentence.

Burns's picture is an excellent one, taken in Buffalo, N. Y.

152

ABRAHAM GREENTHAL, alias GENERAL GREENTHAL,

alias MEYERS.

PICKPOCKET.

DESCRIPTION.

Sixty years old in 1886. Jew, born in Poland. Calls himself a German. Widower. No trade. Stout build. Height, 5 feet 8½ inches. Weight, about 185 pounds. Dark hair, turning quite gray. Prominent nose-lines ; mole near one of them. Beard when grown, is a sandy gray. Generally has a smooth face.

RECORD.

"GENERAL" GREENTHAL is known all over the United States as the leader of the "Sheeny mob." He is acknowledged to be one of the most expert pickpockets in

145

JAMES JOHNSON,
ALIAS JERSEY JIMMY,
PICKPOCKET.

146

JOSEPH GORMAN,
ALIAS CLIFFORD,
PICKPOCKET.

147

DENNIS CARROLL,
ALIAS THOMPSON, ALIAS BIG SLIM,
BURGLAR.

148

THOMAS BURNS,
ALIAS COMBO and HAMILTON,
PICKPOCKET.

149

JOHN WILLIAMS,
PICKPOCKET AND SHOP LIFTER.

150

JAMES WELLS,
ALIAS FUNERAL WELLS,
PICKPOCKET.

151

OSCAR BURNS,
ALIAS JOHN L. HARLEY,
PICKPOCKET AND BURGLAR.

152

ABRAHAM GREENTHAL
ALIAS GENERAL GREENTHAL
PICKPOCKET.

153

HERMAN GREENTHAL,
ALIAS HARRIS GREENTHAL,
PICKPOCKET.

154

JAMES PRICE,
PICKPOCKET.

155

JOHN F. McGUIRE,
ALIAS SHINNY McGUIRE,
PICKPOCKET.

156

TOMMY MATTHEWS,
PICKPOCKET.

157

WILLIAM PECK,
ALIAS BILLY PECK,
PICKPOCKET.

158

THOMAS PRICE,
ALIAS DEAFY PRICE,
PICKPOCKET.

159

AUGUSTUS GREGORY,
HOTEL THIEF.

160

ALEXANDER EVANS,
ALIAS ELECK THE MILKMAN,
PICKPOCKET.

161

FREDERICK LAUTHER,
ALIAS WILSON,
PICKPOCKET.

162

WILLIAM BURKE,
ALIAS BILLY THE KID,
BANK SNEAK.

163

BENJAMIN B. BAGLEY,
GENERAL THIEF.

164

WESLY ALLEN,
ALIAS WES ALLEN,
PICKPOCKET AND BURGLAR.

165

JAMES BURNS,
ALIAS BIG JIM,
BANK SNEAK AND BURGLAR.

166

JOHN RILEY,
ALIAS MURPHY,
SNEAK AND PICKPOCKET.

167

EDWARD McGEE,
ALIAS EDDIE McGEE,
BURGLAR AND SNEAK.

168

THOMAS SHORTELL,
GENERAL THIEF.

America. His home is in the Tenth Ward in New York City, and he has been a thief and receiver of stolen goods for the last thirty years. He has served time in several prisons and penitentiaries, but has generally obtained his release before his sentence expired. He is a clever thief, and will fight when forced to.

The "General" was arrested in Rochester, N. Y., on March 1, 1877, in company of his brother, Harris, and Samuel Casper, his son-in-law, for robbing a man (see record of No. 153), and sentenced on April 19, 1877, to twenty years in Auburn, N. Y., State prison. He was pardoned in the spring of 1884 by Governor Cleveland.

He was arrested again in Brooklyn, N. Y., on December 30, 1885, in company of Bendick Gaetz, alias "The Cockroach," for robbing Robert B. Dibble, of Williamsburg, N. Y., of a pocket-book containing $795 in money, on a cross-town horse-car in that city. The "General" pleaded guilty to grand larceny in the second degree, on March 23, 1886, and was sentenced to five years in Crow Hill prison by Judge Moore, in the Brooklyn Court of Sessions.

The "General" is an old friend of Mrs. Mandelbaum, who is now in Canada. Greenthal's picture is a splendid one, taken in March, 1877.

153

HARRIS GREENTHAL, alias HERMAN GREENTHAL,
alias BROWN.
PICKPOCKET.

DESCRIPTION.

Fifty-eight years old in 1886. Jew, born in Poland. Married. No trade. Medium build. Height, 5 feet 5 inches. Weight, about 150 pounds. Brown curly hair, turning quite gray; brown and gray whiskers, high forehead.

RECORD.

HARRIS GREENTHAL, a brother of the "General's" (152), is also an old New York thief and member of the "Sheeny gang" of pickpockets, who have been traveling through the country robbing people for a number of years. He resides in New York City, and is well known in all the principal cities in the United States and Canada.

Harris Greenthal, alias Brown, the "General," alias Meyers, and Samuel Casper, the "General's" son-in-law, were arrested in Rochester, N. Y., on March 1, 1877, charged with robbing William Jinkson of $1,190 in money, at the Central Railroad depot. Jinkson was a farmer who sold his farm in Massachusetts, and with the proceeds had started West. The "Sheeny gang" had seen him showing his money in Albany, N. Y., and had followed him from that city. At the Central depot in Rochester they told him he would have to change cars. One of the trio took his valise, and the entire party entered another car. In jostling through the crowd the "General" relieved Jinkson of his pocket-book containing the money, which was in bills. They escaped, but were arrested about an hour afterwards. They were indicted, tried, and convicted.

The "General," alias Meyers, was sentenced on April 19, 1877, to twenty years at hard labor in Auburn, N. Y., State prison. Harris Greenthal, alias Brown, received a sentence of eighteen years, and Casper fifteen years.

Harris and Casper were pardoned by Governor Cleveland in December, 1884, the "General" having been pardoned some months before. (See record of No. 84.)

Harris's picture is an excellent one, taken in March, 1877.

154
JAMES PRICE, alias JIMMY PRICE.
PICKPOCKET.

DESCRIPTION.

Forty-five years old in 1886. Born in New York. Married. No trade. Stout build. Height, 5 feet 7½ inches. Weight, 170 pounds. Brown hair, dark eyes, thick nose, dark complexion.

RECORD.

Jimmy Price is an old New York pickpocket. He has been a "Moll Buzzer" (one who picks a woman's pocket) ever since he was a boy, and confines himself generally to that particular branch of the business. This big, lazy thief has sent many a poor woman home minus her few hard-earned dollars, after her visit to a crowded market, fair, or railroad car. He is a brother of Tommy Price, alias "Deafy" Price, the pickpocket (158), and Johnny Price, the bank sneak. (See record of No. 9.) He is well known in all the principal cities in the United States and Canada. He has served terms in Sing Sing prison and on Blackwell's Island.

He was arrested in New York City, and sentenced to one year in Sing Sing prison, on October 20, 1876, under the name of William A. Hoyt, for grand larceny from the person. Since then he has done service for several States, and is now at large.

Price's picture is not so good as it might have been, on account of some difficulty he had with the officer, at the time of his arrest, in 1877.

155
JOHN McGUIRE, alias SHINNY McGUIRE.
SNEAK AND PICKPOCKET.

DESCRIPTION.

Thirty-four years old in 1886. Born in New York. Married. No trade. Medium build. Height, 5 feet 6 inches. Weight, about 145 pounds. Black hair, gray eyes, ruddy complexion. Has letter "F" in India ink on left arm. Generally wears a dark brown beard.

RECORD.

"SHINNY" MCGUIRE is considered one of the cleverest pickpockets in America. Tom Davis, the sawdust swindler, who was shot and killed in New York on August 31, 1885, by T. J. Holland, of Abilena, Texas, married two of McGuire's sisters. He is an associate of Joe Gorman (146), Jersey Jimmie (145), Charley Allen, and several other New York pickpockets, and is well known in all the principal cities.

He was arrested in New York City on October 11, 1878, charged with the larceny of a pocket-book from a man who had just left the Seaman's Savings Bank, corner of Pearl and Wall streets, and was sentenced to two years in the penitentiary on Blackwell's Island, on July 2, 1879, by Recorder Hackett.

He escaped from the penitentiary library, where he was engaged as librarian, on July 1, 1879. He gave New York a wide berth, working the other cities, until September 21, 1885, when he was arrested in Philadelphia, Pa., and returned to Blackwell's Island to finish his unexpired time.

He will be discharged on December 20, 1886.

McGuire's picture is an excellent one, taken in 1876.

156

THOS. MATTHEWS, alias TOMMY MATTHEWS.

PICKPOCKET.

DESCRIPTION.

Forty-seven years old in 1886. Born in United States. Married. Cooper by trade. Medium build. Height, 5 feet 5 inches. Weight, 133 pounds. Hair gray, eyes gray, nose a little flat, ruddy complexion. Generally wears a full, dark beard and mustache, turning very gray.

RECORD.

TOMMY MATTHEWS is an old and expert thief. He has been on the road for at least twenty years, and has served terms in a dozen prisons throughout the United States. He is known in all the large cities from Maine to Colorado, and although getting old, is quite clever yet. He generally associates with the best local talent, and is a very careful worker of late, preferring to lose a "trick" than to take any chances of going to State prison.

Matthews was arrested in New York City, on January 11, 1879, in company of Tim Oats (136), charged with robbing a man named Michael Jobin of $200, on a Third Avenue horse-car. Both were committed in $5,000 bail for trial. They pleaded guilty, and were sentenced to two years each in the penitentiary on February 6, 1879, by Judge Gildersleeve, in the Court of General Sessions. In this case he gave the name of James Moran.

Matthews was arrested again in New York City, under the name of Morgan, for picking pockets. He pleaded guilty, and was sentenced to two years and six months in State prison at Sing Sing, on October 29, 1885, by Recorder Smyth. (See records of Nos. 136, 161.)

Matthews' picture is a pretty good one, taken in January, 1879.

157
WILLIAM PECK, alias PECK'S BAD BOY, alias PARKS.

PICKPOCKET.

DESCRIPTION.

Twenty-six years old in 1886. Born in New York. Single. No trade. Slim build. Height, 5 feet 9 inches. Weight, 140 pounds. Dark brown hair, hazel eyes, light complexion. Has two moles, and two scars from burns, on his right arm. Generally wears a small brown mustache and side-whiskers.

RECORD.

BILLY PECK is one of a new gang of pickpockets which are continually springing up in New York City. He is an associate of all the Bowery (New York) "mob" of pickpockets, and is considered a promising youth. He is known in Philadelphia, New York, Albany, Boston, and several other Eastern cities. With the exception of a short term in the penitentiary on Blackwell's Island, nothing is known about him, except that he is a professional thief.

He was arrested in New York City on January 3, 1885, in company of another pickpocket, named William Davis, for attempting to pick pockets on one of the horse-cars. No complaint was obtained against him, and he was discharged, after his picture was taken for the Rogues' Gallery.

He was arrested again in Albany, N. Y., in August, 1885, during Grant's obsequies, in company of a gang of New York pickpockets, locked up until after the funeral, and then discharged.

He was arrested again in Boston, Mass., on December 21, 1885, in company of James Wells, alias Funeral Wells (150), and Jimmie Murphy, two other New York pickpockets, attempting to ply their vocation in Mechanics' Hall, during one of Dr. W. W. Downs's sensational lectures. He was in luck again, for, after having their pictures taken, they were escorted to the train and ordered to leave town.

This is a very clever thief, and may be looked for at any moment in any part of the country.

He was arrested again in Hoboken, N. J., under the name of William Parker, on February 16, 1886, charged with attempting to pick a lady's hand-satchel, and sentenced to three months in jail there.

His picture is an excellent one, taken in December, 1885.

158

THOMAS PRICE, alias "DEAFY PRICE."

PICKPOCKET.

DESCRIPTION.

About forty-four years old in 1886. Born in New York. Single. No trade. Medium build. Height, 5 feet 7 inches. Weight, about 150 pounds. Brown hair, dark eyes, sallow complexion, high forehead, an Irish expression, and is very deaf.

RECORD.

"DEAFY PRICE" ought to be well known all over America, as he has been a thief for at least twenty-five years. He is one of the old Bowery gang of pickpockets, and an associate of Old Jim Casey, "Jimmy the Kid" (142), "Big Dick" Morris (141), "Pretty Jimmy" (143), "Jersey Jimmy" (145), "Combo" (148), "Nibbs" (137), "Funeral" Wells (150), and, in fact, all the old timers. He is a brother of Jimmy Price, the "Moll Buzzer" (154), and Johnny Price, the bank sneak. (See record of No. 9.) He is a saucy, impudent thief, and wants to be taken in hand at once.

He was arrested in New York City and sent to the work-house on Blackwell's Island, N. Y., on July 3, 1866.

He was arrested again in New York City, in company of another man who has since reformed, for an attempt to pick pockets, and sentenced to four months in the penitentiary, on October 17, 1866, by Judge Dodge.

He was arrested in New York City again on July 21, 1875, charged with violently assaulting Samuel F. Clauser, of No. 38 East Fourth Street, New York, while that gentleman was walking down Broadway. He was placed on trial on July 27, 1875, in the Court of Special Sessions, in the Tombs prison building, on a charge of assault with intent to steal, as a pickpocket. The evidence of the complainant was not strong enough to convict him of the intent to steal, and he was discharged.

He was arrested again on September 8, 1876, in company of George Williams, alias "Western George" (now dead), at the Reading Railroad depot, near the Centennial Exhibition Grounds, in Philadelphia, Pa. They were taken inside the grounds, and sentenced to ninety days in the penitentiary on September 9, 1876, under a special law passed to protect visitors to the Exposition from professional thieves.

He was arrested again in New York City on December 25, 1879, charged with attempting to rob one Marco Sala, an Italian gentleman, while riding on a horse-car. He was committed for trial by the police magistrate, and afterwards discharged by Judge Cowing, in the Court of General Sessions, on January 30, 1880.

Price's picture is a good one, although taken fifteen years ago, in New York City.

159

AUGUSTUS GREGORY, alias GEO. SCHWENECKE.

HOTEL THIEF.

DESCRIPTION.

Twenty years old in 1886. Born in United States, of German parents. Lived in New York. Single. No trade. Slim build. Height, 5 feet 9 inches. Weight, 126 pounds. Light-colored hair, light eyes, long nose, thin face, light complexion.

RECORD.

GREGORY is a very clever boy. He was in prison in Colorado, and after he was liberated he worked all the hotels in all the principal cities from there to New York.

The following is an interesting account of his doings in New York, clipped from one of the papers at the time :

No Will-o'-the-wisp was ever more ubiquitous than a clever hotel sneak thief who for the past month has led the detective force such a dance that they were almost despairing of catching their game, when, by one of those mistakes which even the most experienced criminal sometimes makes, he gave the detectives the clue for which they were seeking, that led to his capture.

The first intimation of the fellow's operations came on the 25th of September, 1884, through the proprietor of the Hoffman House, New York, one of whose guests had been robbed of $350 worth of jewelry, which had been taken from his room. The thief had entered and departed through the transom, but no one in the hotel had any idea who he could be. Three days later another robbery occurred at the hotel. A week afterward a similar robbery was committed at the St. Denis Hotel, where a guest lost $300 worth of jewelry from his room.

When Detective-Sergeants Lanthier, Mulvey and Wade went to the hotel, they learned that the only person whom they could suspect was a slim young man, dressed in rather dudish attire, who had been seen loitering about the hotel. Another complaint came on the 7th of October from the Murray Hill Hotel, where two guests had been robbed of $1,200 worth of jewelry by a sneak thief who had climbed through the transom. Again the detectives were puzzled ; but in the course of their inquiries they learned that a slim young man, who had registered under the name of Edward Sussey, had arrived the day before the robbery and left two days afterward.

The next sufferer from the adroit thief's operations was the Park Avenue Hotel, where five rooms were ransacked one evening, and $1,500 worth of jewelry taken. Following this robbery came a complaint from the Rossmore Hotel, where a guest lost a small sum of money and a few articles of jewelry from his room, and on the 31st of October a guest at the Coleman House discovered that during his absence from his apartment a thief had entered and stolen two watches, one gold and the other platinum, worth $800.

Brooklyn next enlisted the thief's attention, and the Pierrepont House and Mansion House guests found occasion to regret his visits.

The Chief of Detectives, who had been visited by the irate hotel keepers bristling with indignation at the apparent inability of the detectives to catch the thief, tried vainly for a time to gain some clue to his identity. The slim young man who had been seen around nearly all the hotels robbed was, he thought, the culprit, as no one but a slight and muscular man could squeeze through some of the narrow transom windows which furnished the thief with the means of ingress and egress.

There was no doubt of his cleverness, as well as the fact that he was an expert who would not readily fall into the ordinary traps of the thief catchers. Chance, the great ally of the detectives, threw them on the right scent. The platinum watch which he had stolen from the Coleman House was of so peculiar a character that a few days ago, when Detective-Sergeant Lanthier heard that one had been pledged, he at once went to the pawnbroker, and from a description in his possession he found that it was the identical watch for which he and his associates had been on the lookout.

The pawnshop was watched, and on Saturday, November 1, 1884, when a waiter in a Bowery saloon presented a ticket for the watch, he was interviewed by the officer. The man was frightened, and willingly pointed out a notorious Fourth Ward cyprian as the person from whom he had obtained the ticket. A close surveillance was kept upon the woman, who, it was found, was frequently in the company of a slim young man who passed by the name of White.

Under the name of August Gregory the young man lived with his mother at No. 171 East Eighty-seventh Street. On Monday night, November 3, 1884, Detective-Sergeants Lanthier, Mulvey and Wade took the young man into custody and locked him up at police headquarters.

When the detectives began to look up Gregory's antecedents they found that he was the son of a keeper of a Cherry Street, New York, sailor boarding-house, and, as a youth, had displayed pilfering pro-clivities. Four years before, when 17 years old, he went with his mother, who had left her husband, to Denver, Col. There he robbed his mother of $4,500, but was arrested before he had spent but a few hundred dollars of the money. He was not punished for the crime, and, emboldened by this, he began his career as a hotel sneak thief. He was lithe and muscular, and managed, by a course of gymnastic training, to be able to perform feats which an ordinary thief would hesitate at.

Twice he was arrested, but for lack of evidence escaped free. The third time, however, he was convicted and sentenced to two years' imprisonment in Colorado. What he did not know about criminal ways he was not long in learning in jail, where he received his finishing lessons in thievery.

In August, 1884, he was discharged from the Colorado prison, an accomplished thief, and came with his mother to New York City, where she hired apartments at No. 171 East Eighty-seventh Street. Not long after his arrival here he resumed his old ways, and found in the hotels a splendid field for his peculiar talent. His address and manner were prepossessing, and he had gathered a fund of knowledge about hotels that served him in good stead. As he freely confessed on his trial, he found the meal hours the best time for his operations, and while the guests were in the dining-room he would scale the transom and make his way into the vacant room. He was clever enough not to dispose of his booty in the shape in which he had stolen it, but would generally take out the stones in the jewels and sell them separately, and melt up the gold.

Some articles, however, which he did not care to destroy thus, he sold in Philadelphia. He confessed everything to Inspector Byrnes, and gave information as to the whereabouts of a considerable amount of his booty.

"Gus" Gregory, the swell hotel thief, was sentenced on November 17, 1884, in General Sessions, to ten years' hard labor at Sing Sing. Recorder Smyth made a few remarks on the occasion. Looking severely at the prisoner as he stood at the bar carelessly twirling his fashionable Derby hat, the Judge said :

"You have a mother, young man, and I sympathize very deeply with her in having such a son. You are an unmitigated scoundrel, and employ yourself in cleaning out the various hotels of everything of value that you can lay your hands on. You have already served a term of imprisonment for stealing in the State of Colorado. You are wanted also in Wyoming Territory for burglary. Inside of seven or eight weeks you have robbed about ten hotels in New York and Brooklyn of considerable property, and you have made no effort toward restitution. You have the nature of a thief without a redeeming quality. I shall make an example of you in sending you to prison for ten years—the full term allowed by law."

The prisoner is twenty years of age, slim in build and of gentlemanly appearance. He made no sign when he was sentenced, and took no notice of the burst of approval which came from the spectators. There were three indictments against him, two for burglary, on which he pleaded guilty, and one for grand larceny, which is still held over him. William A. Boyce, deputy warden of the Colorado State Penitentiary at Canyon City, wrote to Inspector Byrnes, and stated that "Gregory is one of the slickest sneak thieves that ever struck this country." His real name is George Schwenecke, and his aliases are many. Gregory had robbed guests at the Hoffman House, St. Denis, Park Avenue, Rossmore, and Murray Hill hotels in New York, and also at the Mansion House, Brooklyn. He secured in one haul from the Pierrepont House, Brooklyn, over $4,500 in diamonds. Altogether Gregory has stolen about $15,000 worth of jewelry from various hotels during his Eastern trip.

The two complainants on the present indictments are Samuel B. Wellington, a broker, of Room No. 234 Coleman House, from whom the prisoner stole $800 worth of jewelry, and Claudia Guernsey, of Room No. 553 Park Avenue Hotel, from whom he stole about $400 worth. In both cases he entered the rooms of the guests with false keys. He is described on the record as a student. He is well educated, and has a most polite manner. On leaving the bar he bowed respectfully to the Court, and whispered, "Thank you." The police speak of him as an adroit, cunning rascal, who lives by his wits. When Gregory left the court he was handcuffed to a dirty, ferocious looking prisoner, who regarded his dainty, elegantly dressed companion with contempt.

Gregory's picture is an excellent one, taken in November, 1884.

160

ALEX'R EVANS, alias ALECK THE MILKMAN,

alias CHARLES WATSON.

PICKPOCKET.

DESCRIPTION.

Thirty-eight years old in 1886. Born in United States. Married. Peddler. Stout build. Height, 5 feet 5½ inches. Weight, 207 pounds. Brown hair, hazel eyes, florid complexion. Bald on front of head.

RECORD.

"ALECK THE MILKMAN" is a professional thief, and one of the Bowery, New York, gang of pickpockets. He is known from Maine to California. He "stalls" generally, but is credited with being a clever "wire" (a term for one who actually picks the pocket).

He has served terms in Sing Sing prison and Blackwell's Island, N. Y.

His last arrest was in New York City, for an attempt at grand larceny, for which he was convicted and sentenced to two years and six months in State prison at Sing Sing, N. Y., on June 23, 1885, under the name of Charles H. Williamson. Evans' sentence will expire, allowing him full commutation, on April 23, 1887.

Evans's oldest son, Geo. W. Evans, who, unlike his father, is not a thief, was sentenced to fifteen years in State prison on January 22, 1886, for shooting and killing a negro named Thos. Currie in an altercation as to the janitorship of a flat house in West Twenty-first Street, on the night of January 30, 1885.

His picture resembles him, although his eyes are closed. It was taken in April, 1881.

161

FREDERICK LAUTHER, alias FREDDIE LOUTHER,

alias F. R. Wilson,

SNEAK AND PICKPOCKET.

DESCRIPTION.

Forty-five years old in 1886. Born in United States. Married. No trade. Medium build. Height, 5 feet 8 inches. Weight, 145 pounds. Dark hair, dark gray eyes, dark complexion. Generally wears a heavy sandy beard; sometimes dyes it. Has numbers "33" in India ink on his left fore-arm.

RECORD.

LAUTHER is an old New York sneak thief and pickpocket. He formerly kept a drinking saloon in the Tenth Ward, New York City, which was the resort of a large number of the professional thieves in America. He is the husband of Big Mag Shaffer, a very clever old-time shoplifter and pickpocket.

Lauther was arrested in New York City, and sentenced to Sing Sing prison for two years and six months on April 20, 1874, for grand larceny under the name of Robert Campbell.

He was arrested again in Philadelphia, Pa., on February 21, 1878, under the name of Shaw, his picture taken, and discharged.

Arrested again with George Milliard (138), and Tommy Matthews (156), in New York City, on the arrival of the Fall River steamer Newport, on April 12, 1879, for the larceny of a watch and $12 in money from Daniel Stein, during the passage from Boston to New York. So cleverly was the robbery committed that Judge Otterbourg was forced to discharge them.

He was arrested and convicted in Harrisburg, Pa., in June, 1879. Again, on April 3, 1880, in Philadelphia, in company of Will Kennedy, for larceny from the person, and sentenced to eighteen months' solitary confinement in the Eastern Penitentiary.

He has been arrested from time to time in almost every city in the Union. He has served terms in Sing Sing prison and the penitentiary on Blackwell's Island, N. Y., and is a man well worth knowing.

His picture is an excellent one, taken in June, 1885.

162

WILLIAM BURKE, alias BILLY THE KID,
alias MURPHY, alias PETRIE, etc.

BANK SNEAK.

DESCRIPTION.

Twenty-eight years old in 1886. Born in United States. Married. Printer. Stout build. Height, 5 feet 6¼ inches. Weight, 140 pounds. Dark brown hair, dark gray eyes, straight nose, round face, florid complexion. Small ears. Upper lip turns up a little. Cross in India ink on his left hand, near thumb. Dot of ink on right hand, between thumb and forefinger.

RECORD.

"BILLY THE KID" is one of the most adroit bank sneaks in America. He is now about twenty-eight years old, of pleasing address, and claims Chicago, Ill., as his home. He is known in all the principal cities in America and in Canada. This young man is credited with being the nerviest bank sneak in the profession. He is an associate of Rufe Minor (1), Minnie Marks (187), Big Ed Rice (12), Georgie Carson (3), Johnny Jourdan (83), and several other clever men. He has been arrested one hundred times, at least, in as many different cities, and although young, has served terms in three prisons.

At 12.30 P. M. on August 1, 1881, a carriage containing two men drove rapidly up to the Manufacturers' Bank at Cohoes, N. Y. At the same moment a man walked briskly into the bank, and toward the directors' room, in the rear. One of the men in the carriage jumped out, and entering the building, asked the cashier, N. J. Seymour, to change a $20 bill. While the change was being made the man at the rear of the bank forced the door of the directors' room and obtained entrance to the space behind the desk. He rushed up to the safe, the door of which stood open, and snatched a large pile of bills, done up in packages of $100 and $500 each, and amounting in all to over $10,000. James I. Clute, the discount clerk, who sat at the desk at the time, not more than ten feet from the safe, sprang from his seat, grasped a revolver, and followed the thief. The burglar was so quickly pursued that he dropped the packages of money in the directors' room. Clute kept after him, and tried to bar the way at the door, when the thief pushed him aside and ran quickly down two or three streets, crossed the canal, and fled toward the woods. The thief who remained in the carriage drove furiously down the street, and the man who asked for the change meanwhile had left the bank. He met the carriage a short distance from the scene, jumped in, and was driven out of the city. The thief who fled toward the woods succeeded in eluding his pursuers, and shortly after entered the house of a Mrs. Algiers and took off his clothes and crawled under the bed. A man who was at work in a mill opposite the house saw the man's proceedings, and notified the police. The house was surrounded, and the intruder captured. A search of his clothing revealed a false mustache, a watch, $45 cash, two pocket-books, some strong cord, and other things. He was afterwards identified as Billy Burke. After remaining in jail some little time he was released on $10,000 bail.

On September 9, 1881, an attempt was made to rob the vault of the Baltimore Savings Bank, in Baltimore, Md. Four men (no doubt Burke, Jourdan, Marks, and Big Rice) entered the treasurer's room, where were several customers of the bank, and one of them engaged the attention of the treasurer by asking him about investments, holding in his hands several United States bonds. Another then walked back toward the vault, in a rear apartment, but his movements were observed by one of the clerks, who followed and arrested him in front of the vault. The other three retreated hastily and escaped.

The party arrested gave the name of Thomas Smith, but was recognized by the police as Billy Burke, alias "Billy the Kid." In this case, as at Cohoes, N. Y., he was bailed, went West, and was arrested in Cleveland on December 12, 1881, and delivered to the police authorities of Albany, N. Y., taken there, and placed in the Albany County jail, from where he escaped on January 7, 1882. A reward of $1,000 was offered at the time for his arrest.

He was finally re-arrested at Minneapolis, Minn., on March 13, 1882, in an attempt to rob a bank there, but afterwards turned over to the Sheriff of Albany County, N. Y., taken there, tried, convicted, and sentenced to five years' imprisonment in the Albany Penitentiary by Judge Van Alstyne (for the Cohoes bank robbery), on March 31, 1882.

He was tried again the same day for breaking jail, convicted, and sentenced to one year more, making six years in all. Burke was sentenced in this case under the name of John Petrie.

His sentence expired on June 2, 1886. Warrants were lodged against him at the penitentiary some time previous from Lockport, N. Y., Detroit, and Baltimore. He was re-arrested, as soon as discharged, on the Lockport warrant, which, it is said, was obtained by his brother-in-law, for an alleged assault. The scheme was to prevent him from being taken to either Detroit or Baltimore, where there are clear cases against him.

His picture is an excellent one, taken in March, 1880.

163

BENJAMIN B. BAGLEY, alias BENTON BAGLEY.

SNEAK THIEF.

DESCRIPTION.

Thirty-five years old in 1886. Born in the United States. Married. No trade. Medium build. Height, 5 feet 9¼ inches. Weight, 153 pounds. Brown hair, gray eyes, dark complexion. Has scar on chin. Has a peculiar expression in one eye; it is hardly a cast.

RECORD.

BAGLEY is a very clever sneak thief. He works houses, churches, receptions and weddings, and is pretty well known in New York, Philadelphia, Boston, and in the Eastern States generally. He starts out occasionally and travels South and West, and is liable to turn up anywhere.

He was arrested in New York City, and sentenced to five years in Sing Sing prison, on February 21, 1872, under the name of Benton B. Bagley, for grand larceny. He has done service since.

He was arrested again in New York City on January 22, 1883, in company of Frank Shortell (168), and John T. Sullivan, two other expert sneaks, for the larceny of a sealskin dolman, valued at $350, from the Church of the Incarnation, Thirty-fifth Street and Madison Avenue, during a wedding, on December 27, 1882. Bagley and Sullivan were discharged on January 30, 1883, and Shortell was sent to the Elmira reformatory, by Judge Cowing, on February 5, 1883.

Bagley's picture is a good one, taken in January, 1883.

164

WESTLEY ALLEN, alias WESS. ALLEN.

PICKPOCKET, SNEAK AND BURGLAR.

DESCRIPTION.

Forty-six years old in 1886. Born in New York. Widower. No trade. Slim build. Height, 5 feet 10 inches. Weight, 155 pounds. Right eye gray, left eye out, and replaced at times by a glass one. He sometimes wears green goggles, or only a green patch over the left eye. Dark hair, mixed with gray ; sallow complexion. Generally wears a black mustache. Scar on left side of face. Has letters " W. A.," an anchor, and dots of India ink on left fore-arm.

RECORD.

" WESS." ALLEN is probably the most notorious criminal in America, and is well known all over the United States. He is a saucy, treacherous fellow, and requires to be watched closely, as he will use a pistol if an opportunity presents itself.

Wess.'s brothers are Theodore Allen, well known as " The. Allen," a saloon keeper in New York, John Allen, a jeweler in New York, Martin Allen, a burglar, now in Sing Sing State prison, sentenced to ten years on November 1, 1883, for burglary in New York City (a house robbery, second offense), and Jesse Allen, a burglar (now dead).

Wess. has been a thief for many years, but has not served much time in prison.

He was arrested in New York City for an attempt to break into a silk house, and sentenced to five years in Sing Sing prison, on July 7, 1873, under the name of Charles W. Allen.

Since his release, in 1877, he has been arrested in almost every city in America, but always manages to escape conviction. The following are a few of his arrests since 1880:

He was arrested in New Haven, Conn., on January 29, 1880, in company of Wm. Brown, alias Burton, and James H. Johnson, at the Elliott House, whither they had followed Parnell and Dillon, the agitators. After a few days' detention he was discharged.

He was discharged from custody at Reading, Pa., on April 14, 1880, where he was detained on five indictments for picking pockets at a fair there in the fall of 1879.

He proved an alibi, and was acquitted by a jury in the Kings County Court of Sessions in Brooklyn, N. Y., on December 23, 1880. He was charged with picking the pocket of Thomas Rochford of his watch, on the night of October 29, 1880, near the City Hall in Brooklyn.

He was arrested in New Haven, Conn., on August 30, 1883, for an attempt to pick the pocket of John McDermott on a railroad train. As usual, he was discharged.

He was discharged from arrest in the Jefferson Market Police Court, New York City, on July 30, 1884. The complainant, Edward P. Shields, a barkeeper for Theodore Allen, Wess.'s brother, charged him with " jabbing two of his fingers in his left eye."

He was arrested again in New York City, after a severe tussle, on September 13, 1885, while attending the funeral of his wife, Amelia, on a warrant issued by Justice Mulholland, of Syracuse, N. Y., charging him with grand larceny. He was delivered to a detective officer, who took him back to Syracuse, where he again escaped his just deserts.

In November, 1885, two men of gentlemanly appearance called upon an Alleghany City, Pa., tailor named Rice, and were measured for some suits of clothing. " Send them C. O. D. to West Jefferson, Ohio, when they are finished," they said, and bowed themselves out, after giving their names as Fisher and Grimes. The clothes, valued at $146, were shipped by Adams Express a week later, and the night they arrived in West Jefferson the express office was broken into and the clothing stolen. Fisher proved to be Wess. Allen. He had assumed his father-in-law's name, Martin Fisher, whose house in New York City was searched by the police, and they found three of the missing suits there and also some silk. Fisher and his wife were taken into custody as receivers of stolen goods, and subsequently discharged. The former is over seventy years old, and the latter only a few years younger.

Allen could not be found, as from the latest accounts he had gone to England to try his fortune there.

His picture is an excellent one, the best in existence, taken in March, 1880.

165

JAMES BURNS, alias BIG JIM,

alias BOSTON JIM, alias BAKER, alias JAMES BOYLE, alias JOHN BOWEN, alias HAWKINS, etc.

SNEAK AND BURGLAR.

DESCRIPTION.

Forty-six years old in 1886. Born in Boston, Mass. Single. No trade. A large, well-built man. Height, 5 feet 8½ inches. Weight, about 200 pounds. Brown hair, dark hazel eyes, dark complexion. Has fine spots of India ink between thumb and forefinger of left hand. Generally wears a sandy-brown mustache and whiskers.

RECORD.

JIM BURNS, alias BIG JIM, is a celebrated bank sneak, burglar and forger. He is a native of Boston, Mass., and is called by the fraternity "The Prince of Thieves," on account of his great liberality with his money, and the many charitable acts performed by him. It is a well known fact that he has always contributed to the support of the wives and families of his associates whenever they were in trouble.

Some years ago, after a large and successful bank sneak robbery, Burns, and the others who were with him, returned to New York and went to their usual rendezvous, a saloon corner of Fourth Street and Broadway, New York, kept by one Dick Platt. The entire party imbibed quite freely and Burns fell asleep. When he awoke he found that he had been robbed of his portion of the plunder. On being informed by one of his companions who had done it, Burns said, "It was hard, that after doing a lot of work, and getting a good lump of money, to have an associate rob me. He can't be much good, and will die in the gutter." The fact is, that about one week after the occurrence the party referred to was walking down Broadway and was stricken with paralysis, fell into the gutter, and died before any assistance could be rendered him.

Burns was connected with all of the most celebrated criminals in this country, and took part in a large number of the most prominent bank robberies.

Owing to his genial good-nature he never was able to save a dollar. He has served terms in prison in Sing Sing, New York, and Boston, Mass., and is well known all over America and Europe.

He was arrested in New York City on March 11, 1878, for the larceny of a carriage clock, valued at $52, from Howard, Sanger & Co., Broadway and Grand Street. He was released on $500 bail, and when his case was called for trial he failed to appear.

He was arrested again in New York City on December 17, 1878, for attempting to rescue "Red" Leary from a private detective. He was indicted, and again admitted to bail. While at large, he was arrested with George Carson (3) for the larceny of

$12,000 in money from the Government Printing Office, in Washington, D. C. No case being made out against them, they were discharged on July 1, 1879, by Commissioner Deuel, at Washington.

Burns was arrested upon his discharge on a bench warrant in the old clock case, brought to New York City, tried, convicted of grand larceny, and sentenced to three years and six months in Sing Sing prison, on July 11, 1879, by Judge Cowing.

He made his escape from Raymond Street jail in Brooklyn, N. Y., on Friday night, July 31, 1883, where he was confined for the larceny of a package containing $3,000 in money from the desk of the postmaster of Brooklyn, N. Y.

After his escape he went to London, England, and from there to Paris, where he devoted his talents to picking pockets, and had to leave there to keep out of the clutches of the police. When next heard from he was in Stockholm, Sweden, with Billy Flynn, alias Connolly, and Bill Baker, alias Langford, where the party obtained about eighteen hundred kroners from a bank in that city. They were arrested for the robbery, but having no evidence against them a charge of vagrancy was preferred, and they were imprisoned for six months as vagrants. A few months after their time expired they went to Hamburg, Germany, where, on June 22, 1885, they succeeded in robbing the Vereins Bank of 200,000 marks, about $44,000. On July 15, 1885, the bank offered a reward of 10,000 marks, about $2,200, for them. They were all arrested in London, England, in the latter part of July, 1885, and returned to Paris, France, they having been tried, convicted and sentenced to one year's imprisonment each for an offense committed in that city. According to French law, any person may be tried convicted, and sentenced for an offense during his absence. After their sentence expires they will be taken to Hamburg for trial for the larceny of the 200,000 marks.

Burns's picture is an excellent one, taken in 1882.

166
JOHN RILEY, alias JOHN MURPHY.
SNEAK, PICKPOCKET AND SHOPLIFTER.

DESCRIPTION.

Fifty-one years old in 1886. Born in Ireland. Married. Printer. Medium build. Height, 5 feet 8¼ inches. Weight, 142 pounds. Light hair, blue eyes, sandy complexion; whiskers, when worn, are sandy. Has letters "J. R." in India ink on his left arm.

RECORD.

JOHNNY RILEY is an old New York pickpocket, sneak and shoplifter. He generally works with his wife, Annie Riley, and pays considerable attention to funerals and markets. His wife is a very clever pickpocket, John generally doing the "stalling" for her. He has served terms in prison in Philadelphia, Sing Sing, and on Blackwell's Island, New York. He lives in New York, but is well known in several of the Eastern cities.

Riley, Annie his wife, Fred. Benner, alias Dutch Fred (81), and Mag. Sweeny, alias Bell, were arrested in New York City on August 1, 1885, for picking the pocket of a woman named Eliza J. North, in Washington Square Park. Riley and Benner were sentenced to one year in the penitentiary on Blackwell's Island on August 12, 1885. Mrs. Riley and Sweeny were sentenced to six months in the penitentiary the same day by Judge Gildersleeve.

Riley's picture is a good one, taken in May, 1877.

167

EDWARD McGEE, alias EDDIE McGEE.

SNEAK AND BURGLAR.

DESCRIPTION.

Thirty-nine years old in 1886. Southerner by birth. A baker by trade. Height, 5 feet 10½ inches. Weight, 130 pounds. Tall, slim man. Brown hair, dark eyes, dark, sallow complexion. Has a coat-of-arms and sunburst in India ink on his right fore-arm. Dark mustache and chin whiskers; grows thin.

RECORD.

EDDIE McGEE is one of the cleverest burglars, sneak thieves and pennyweight workers there is in the country. He is a partner of Johnny Curtin, alias Cunningham, alias Roberts (169), another daring and desperate thief. McGee is well known in all the principal cities of the United States, especially Chicago, Philadelphia (Pa.), New York and Boston, in all of which he is said to have been sent to prison.

McGee and Curtin were arrested in Philadelphia, Pa., for shoplifting, and sentenced to eighteen months each in the Eastern Penitentiary. When their time expired, on August 14, 1883, they were both arrested by New York officers, at the penitentiary gate, and brought to New York City, to answer an indictment charging them with the larceny of $1,200 worth of jewelry from Theodore Starr, a Fifth Avenue jeweler, in January, 1882. In this case there was no conviction.

Shortly after their release they went to England. Curtin was arrested there and sent to prison. McGee returned to America, and was arrested in Brooklyn, N. Y., on February 12, 1884, for burglary, and sentenced to five years and six months in the Kings County Penitentiary on April 16, 1884, under the name of B. C. Earl.

McGee's picture is an excellent one, taken in August, 1883.

168

THOMAS SHORTELL, alias FRANK SHORTELL.

SNEAK THIEF AND DEALER IN COUNTERFEIT MONEY.

DESCRIPTION.

Twenty-seven years old in 1886. Born in New York. Single. Conductor. Medium build. Height, 5 feet 7 inches. Weight, 148 pounds. Brown hair, gray eyes, dark complexion. Eyebrows meet; high cheek bones. Has an anchor in India ink on back of right hand.

RECORD.

SHORTELL, although young in the business, is a very clever sneak thief. He was formerly a conductor on one of the New York railroad cars, and first made the acquaintance of the police in New York City on November 20, 1880, when he was arrested for perjury in a seduction case—Murry *vs.* Cronin—which was being investigated in one of the police courts. In this case he was not convicted.

He was arrested again in New York City on January 22, 1883, in company of Benton B. Bagley (163) and John T. Sullivan, two other expert sneak thieves, for the larceny of a sealskin dolman, valued at $350, from the Church of the Incarnation, on Madison Avenue, New York City, during a wedding, on December 27, 1882.

Bagley and Sullivan were discharged on January 30, 1883, and Shortell was sent to the Reformatory at Elmira, New York, by Judge Cowing, on February 5, 1883.

Shortell was arrested again, under the name of Frank Wilson, in company of Tommy Connors, another New York thief, who gave the name of Thomas Wilson, at Nashville, Tenn., for picking pockets during the race week, in May, 1885. On searching their baggage in their rooms it was found to contain $1,000 in counterfeit $10 United States Treasury notes. They were indicted in the Federal Court, and the charge of picking pockets withdrawn. They were delivered to the United States authorities, tried, and both sentenced to a fine of $100 and five years' imprisonment in Chester (Ill.) prison on May 26, 1885.

Shortell's picture is a very good one, taken in January, 1883.

169

JOHN CURTIN, alias REYNOLDS.

SNEAK AND BURGLAR.

DESCRIPTION.

Thirty-six years old in 1886. Born in the United States. Single. Carver by trade. Stout build. Height, 5 feet 5½ inches. Weight, 182 pounds. Brown hair.

gray eyes, dark complexion, dark brown whiskers, bald head. Bracelets in India ink on each wrist ; stars and eagle in ink on left fore-arm.

RECORD.

JOHNNY CURTIN is one of the most notorious shoplifters and burglars in America. He is known all over America and in several European cities. He is credited with escaping from court-rooms and jails in California, Ohio, Indiana, New Jersey, Philadelphia, Pa., and Chicago, Ill. He is a desperate man, and requires watching. He is a partner of Eddie McGee (167).

On September 11, 1878, Curtin went into the jewelry establishment of Taylor Brothers, No. 676 Broadway, New York City, and asked to be shown a gold watch and chain. After looking at several watches he left, promising to return at three o'clock in the afternoon and purchase a watch and chain from a clerk named Heiser. He was on hand at three o'clock, when the clerk left him in the store while he went out to get some money changed. Heiser returned in a few minutes, and found Curtin standing in front of the store. He asked him to go inside, but he refused to do so, saying that he had an engagement and could not wait. Shortly after his departure it was discovered that fifteen diamond rings, valued at $747, and $15 worth of razors had been stolen from a table near which Curtin had stood.

Curtin left New York, and was arrested in Chicago, Ill., on October 14, 1878, thirty-three days after, under the name of Cunningham, for the larceny of a diamond ring from one of the jewelry stores. He had on his person when arrested $50 in money and nineteen loose diamonds—four more than were stolen from Taylor Brothers, in New York.

Curtin made his escape from the Chicago jail on October 26, 1878, twelve days after his arrest, and returned to New York, where he was again arrested on October 29, 1878, for the Taylor Brothers robbery. He pleaded guilty and was sentenced to four years and six months in State prison at Sing Sing, on November 17, 1878, under the name of James Roberts, by Judge Gildersleeve.

Curtin and Eddie McGee (167) were arrested in Philadelphia, Pa., in June, 1882, and sentenced to eighteen months each in the Eastern Penitentiary for shoplifting. Upon their release from prison on August 14, 1883, they were both arrested at the penitentiary gate and brought to New York City, to answer an indictment charging them with the larceny of $1,200 worth of jewelry from Theodore Starr, a Fifth Avenue, New York, jeweler, in January, 1882. In this case there was no conviction.

Shortly after their discharge Curtin and McGee went to Europe, where Curtin fell into the hands of the police, and was sentenced to four years in prison in Paris, France, in March, 1884. He, however, succeeded in having his sentence reduced to two years, and obtained his release about April 15, 1886.

McGee returned to America when Curtin was arrested, and is now (September, 1886) in Crow Hill prison, Brooklyn, N. Y. (See his record, No. 167.)

After Curtin's release in Paris he came to America, and visited his home in Cohoes, N. Y., where he was arrested on suspicion. He was released from Cohoes, and while returning from the Troy jail, where he had been paying his friend Billy Porter a visit, he had some difficulty with a policeman on the streets of Troy, N. Y., and was arrested and heavily fined for assault.

After getting out of this trouble in Troy he returned to Europe, sailing from Boston. He stated to associates in Troy, before sailing, that Porter would be bailed and would join him in Europe, and together with Frank Buck, alias Bucky Taylor (27), who is also in Europe, they would make a tour of the Continent, as they had considerable work laid out for them by Adam Worth, a noted receiver of stolen goods in London, who formerly resided in the United States, and to whom all the American thieves go, on their arrival in London, for points. Worth was formerly a bank burglar in the United States, but has lived in London for a number of years, and is very rich. Curtin said this would enable Porter to make up for losses he had met with in connection with his arrest for the Marks burglary, at Troy, N. Y. Porter, however, found some trouble in giving the large amount of bail asked by the Court for his appearance for trial in October, 1886. He was therefore delayed in leaving this country. Curtin concluded to make expenses while waiting for Porter's arrival, and on June 7, 1886, he sauntered into the establishment of the association of diamond merchants, No. 6 Grand Hotel Building, Charing Cross, London, and was arrested under the name of John Colton, charged with the larceny of a small package of diamonds, valued at sixty pounds sterling.

Mr. George W. Bullard, the manager of the store, testified that Curtin, or Colton, as he called himself, entered the store on Monday afternoon, June 7, 1886, and asked to be shown some diamonds. He opened a parcel containing six thousand pounds' worth of loose diamonds. Mr. Bullard's attention was attracted to the window, and in the meantime Curtin secreted a small package of diamonds, valued at sixty pounds, upon his person. His action was witnessed by one of Mr. Bullard's assistants, who immediately gave him information. Curtin attempted to leave the store, but was prevented. He was then observed to slip a parcel on the counter, which upon being examined was found to be the one missing. The door of the store was secured, and a constable was sent for. Curtin was taken to the police station in a cab at his own request. On the way he was seen to tear up some papers. He put one piece in his mouth and swallowed it, and threw the remainder out of the cab window into the roadway, which was picked up, and after being placed-together, was found to be a letter dated from New York, addressed to John W. Curtin, Box 126, Cohoes, N. Y. The letter requested the return of a check drawn on a Paris house for 16,000 francs. Curtin was committed for trial, and shortly after he was sentenced to eighteen months' imprisonment at hard labor from the Middlesex Sessions.

Curtin's picture is a good one, taken in August, 1883.

170
JAMES McMAHON.
BURGLAR AND RIVER THIEF.

DESCRIPTION.

Thirty-six years old in 1886. Born in New York. Single. No trade. Stout build. Height, 5 feet 6 inches. Weight, 163 pounds. Light hair, blue eyes, light complexion, big nose, thick lips.

RECORD.

McMahon is a well known New York burglar and river thief. He has served a term on Blackwell's Island, and is a desperate man. He is also well known in Philadelphia and other cities.

He was arrested in New York City on May 16, 1880, charged with robbing the schooner Victor, of Prince Edward's Island, while lying at one of the wharves. McMahon was detected in the act of robbing the vessel by the mate, John Williams, who, while in an attempt to arrest McMahon, was terribly beaten by him.

McMahon was committed for trial in default of $3,000 bail, by Justice Morgan, on May 15, 1880, indicted on May 18, pleaded guilty, and was sentenced to ten years in State prison on May 18, by Recorder Smyth, in the Court of General Sessions, New York City. His sentence expires on September 18, 1886.

His picture is a good one, taken in May, 1880.

171
THEODORE WILDEY, alias THE. WILEY,
alias George Davis, alias George Brewster.
SNEAK AND GENERAL THIEF.

DESCRIPTION.

Forty-four years old in 1886. Born in United States. Married. Printer. Medium build. Height, 5 feet 11 inches. Weight, 166 pounds. Brown hair, brown eyes, dark complexion, dark brown mustache, high forehead. Two joints off fingers of right hand. "Josephine," and numbers "1858," in India ink on left fore-arm.

RECORD.

"The." Wiley is a clever sneak thief, burglar and pickpocket. He is what might be called a good general thief, as he can turn his hand to almost anything. He is well known in New York and nearly all the principal cities in the United States. He is an old criminal, and has served terms in Sing Sing and other prisons.

He was arrested in New York City on August 14, 1875, and delivered to the Brooklyn (N. Y.) police authorities, for robbing a safe in Calvin Cline's jewelry store on Fourth Street, that city, of $5,000 worth of diamonds, on August 12, 1875. He was tried in the Kings County Court of Sessions in Brooklyn, on October 6, 1875, convicted, and sentenced to ten years in the penitentiary by Judge Moore, for burglary in the second degree, under the name of George Marsh. He cut off the fingers of his right hand, while confined in the Kings County Penitentiary, so he would not have to work. His sentence expired on April 5, 1882.

He was arrested again in Syracuse, N. Y., on January 4, 1883, in company of Timothy Oats (136) and William A. Brown, alias "The Student," charged with stealing a tin box containing $250 in money from a saloon there. (See record of No. 136.) Wiley gave the name of George Davis, alias George Marsh, and was tried, convicted, and sentenced to five years in Auburn (N. Y.) State prison, on March 1, 1883. His sentence expires October 1, 1886. Oats pleaded guilty and was sentenced to two years on the same day in this case. Russell also pleaded guilty, and was sentenced to five years in Auburn prison at the same time.

Wiley's picture is an excellent one, taken in September, 1882.

172

WM. H. LITTLE, alias "TIP LITTLE,"
alias AUSTIN.
SNEAK, CONFIDENCE AND FORGER.

DESCRIPTION.

Forty-five years old in 1886. Born in New York. Married. No trade. Slim build. Height, 5 feet 6 inches. Weight, 140 pounds. Dark curly hair, gray eyes, dark complexion. Generally wears a black curly beard. Has a peculiar expression about the eyes.

RECORD.

"TIP" LITTLE is an old New York "panel thief," confidence man, sneak thief and forger. He is well known as the husband of Bell Little, alias Lena Swartz, alias Eliza Austin, a notorious pennyweight worker, shoplifter and "bludgeon thief." This team is well known all over the United States. They worked the "panel game" in New York and other cities for years, and their pictures adorn several Rogues' Galleries. Of late they have been working the "bludgeon game" or "injured husband racket" with considerable success, as their victims are generally married men and will stand blackmailing before publicity.

"Tip" and "Bell" have been arrested in New York City several times, but with the exception of a few short terms in the penitentiary, they have both escaped their just deserts (State prison) many a time.

Little was arrested in New York City on November 28, 1885, in company of a negro accomplice named Isaac Hooper, for attempting to negotiate a check that had been raised from $4 to $896. About one week before the arrest Hooper obtained a check for $4, on the Nassau Bank of New York, from Henry Carson, a grocer, of Fulton Street, Brooklyn, N. Y., by pretending that he wanted to send money to a relative, and that he had only silver dollars. He raised the check himself from $4 to $896, and also made a spurious check for $1,200, on the Nassau Bank of New York, and signed Carson's name to it. With the $1,200 check, Tip Little, on November 25, 1885, went to Wm. Wise & Son's jewelry store on Fulton Street, Brooklyn, and selecting articles worth $400, tendered the check in payment. He was so indignant when it was suggested that it would be nothing more than a common business transaction to ask Mr. Carson if the check was all right, that he snatched it up and left the store.

Then he planned to swindle Daniel Higgins, a furniture dealer on Eighth Avenue, New York City, with the raised check of $896, which had been certified by the cashier of the Nassau Bank. He visited Mr. Higgins on November 27, 1885, and selected furniture worth $300. Higgins went to the West Side Bank, which was close by his store, and its cashier ascertained by telephone that Mr. Carson repudiated the check. When Mr. Higgins returned to the store, "Tip" had left without his change.

Hooper (the negro) was tried, convicted, and sentenced to seven years in State prison on January 15, 1886, by Recorder Smyth, in the Court of General Sessions, Part I. He had been previously convicted and sentenced to State prison for forgery in Providence, R. I.

"Tip" Little pleaded guilty on January 15, 1886 (the same day), and was sentenced to five years in Sing Sing prison, by Judge Gildersleeve, in the Court of General Sessions, Part II.

"Little's" picture is a very good one, taken in April, 1879.

173

DAVID MOONEY, alias LITTLE DAVE,
alias Hill, alias Farrell.

SNEAK AND BURGLAR.

DESCRIPTION.

Thirty-eight years old in 1886. Born in New York. Single. Shoemaker. Medium build. Height, 5 feet 4 inches. Weight, 147 pounds. Dark wavy hair, dark eyes, dark complexion; dark brown beard, when grown. The lower lip is quite thick and projecting; high and expansive forehead. A noticeable feature is his eyes, which seem to twinkle behind eyelids almost closed, thus giving him a sharp expression. Has letters "N. E. S.," and figures "13," and two dots of India ink on left wrist.

RECORD.

" LITTLE DAVE " MOONEY is a well known New York thief. His specialty is private house work, entering generally by the second story window while the people are down stairs at their meals. He is well known in all the principal cities in the United States, and is considered a very clever " second-story man."

He was arrested in New York City on August 19, 1874, and delivered to the police authorities of Hunter's Point, Long Island, N. Y., where he was wanted for burglary. He was convicted and sentenced to two years in State prison at Sing Sing, in the Queens County Court of Sessions at Hunter's Point, on October 19, 1874, by Judge Pratt, under the name of John H. Smith.

He was arrested again in Albany, N. Y., on December 30, 1880, and taken to Boston, Mass., for the murder of his partner in crime, Edmond Lavoiye, alias Frenchy Lavoiye, and Charles E. Marshall, at No. 22 Florence Street, Boston, where they were rooming, on the night of February 12, 1880. He was also charged with breaking and entering the house of George Norman, in Boston, on the night of February 11, 1880, and stealing therefrom bonds and jewelry valued at $1,500. He was tried in the Supreme Judicial Court of Boston on September 16, 1881, and found guilty of murder in the second degree, and sentenced to Concord prison for life on September 19, 1881.

The following article clipped from the Boston *Herald*, of January 1, 1880, gives a detailed account of his arrest and statement concerning the murder :

MANACLED MOONEY.—PARTICULARS OF HIS ARREST IN GREENBUSH, N. Y.—HIS WHEREABOUTS SINCE HIS FLIGHT FROM BOSTON.—HE DENIES COMMITTING THE LAVOIYE MURDER.

David Mooney, alias John H. Hill, alias James P. Brady, who was arrested in Greenbush, N. Y., Thursday night, December 30, 1880, on the charge of murdering his pal, Edmund A. Lavoiye, at the house No. 22 (now No. 20) Florence Street, this city, reached here last evening in custody of Inspectors Gerraughty and Mahoney. The murder was committed on the evening of February 12, but was not discovered until several days after, when the body of the victim was found in an advanced state of decomposition by Mr. Orpen, the landlord of the house.

It appears, according to the Albany authorities, that Mooney has been residing in Greenbush, a suburb of Albany, for some time, being known to his neighbors as " David Farrell." For about four weeks Detective Riley, of Albany, has suspected him to be the fugitive, but it was not till within a few days that he became confident that Farrell was really Mooney. The detective Thursday evening went to Greenbush about nine o'clock, and, after waiting quietly in a beer saloon on Broadway, smoking a cigar, he soon had the satisfaction of seeing the man he was in search of come in with a tin pail, for the purpose of getting beer. He had no sooner set the pail on the counter than Riley approached him, and stated that he was wanted in Albany to give some information about a diamond pin that had been stolen. Detective Brennan was in company with Riley, and together they brought Mooney across the river and took him to the chief's office, where it was found that he corresponded in every particular to the description contained in the circular, thus leaving no doubt of his being the right party. He was then committed to jail by Chief Malloy.

In answer to questions put to him, Mooney stated that he had been living in Greenbush for the past three months, and had also stopped at Newburg, Hudson, and other river towns, and admitted having been in Boston quite frequently in his lifetime. On going up to the jail he said to Riley, who had previously told him what he was arrested for : " Young fellow, the parties that gave you the 'tip' gave it to you straight." The chief telegraphed to Supt. Adams, informing him of the arrest, and soon afterwards officers went to Albany. During the night Mooney maintained a sullen disposition, but early yesterday morning exhibited an inclination to be defiant. He told one detective (Dewire) that he would not be taken to Boston alive, and said it in such a way that the detective became suspicious that he might attempt to make good his threat. The officer searched him, and found, carefully concealed in his clothing, it is claimed, a piece of steel wire, some four inches long, filed down to a sharp point at one end. Mooney felt quite chagrined, but repeated his threat. He was carefully looked over, and all the marks contained in the description given of him in the Boston *Herald* at the time of the murder were found on him.

At one o'clock P. M., Detectives Gerraughty and Mahoney, of Boston, with Mr. Henry Orpen, at whose house the murder was committed, on Florence Street, arrived here. They presented their papers to Chief Malloy, who pronounced them in proper form and all right. Detectives Riley and Brennan at once proceeded to the jail, and soon after brought Mooney to police headquarters. The prisoner's appearance was in sad contrast to that which marked him while in the "Hub." He was dressed in rough and ill-fitting garments, in place of the broadcloth in which he was wont to appear while mingling in society in Boston. He wore a plush jockey cap, and, with his short and newly-grown bushy whiskers, looked more like a recently-arrived Canadian than the American he has been described. On being introduced to the Boston officers his face changed to an ashy hue, but he said nothing until placed directly before Mr. Orpen, who, without hesitation, said : "That is the man who was at my house with the murdered Lavoiye." Mr. Orpen, continuing, said : "Well, Hill, you look somewhat changed since I saw you last. Don't you know me?"

MOONEY—"Oh, yes ; I know you. I don't deny that I was there. It's kind of hard. Well, I am somewhat changed, but not altogether so good-looking."

MR. ORPEN—"Well, it's many a dollar your doings at my house has cost me."

MOONEY—"Well, I am sorry for it ; but I suppose you will, or ought to, get your share of the reward."

Mooney soon after was questioned by Detective Gerraughty as to his threat that he would not be taken to Boston alive, whereupon the prisoner remarked he would give his word of honor that he would go to Boston peaceably and without trouble. The officers, with their man, left for Boston on the 2:30 train, and arrived here at 9:45 last evening.

During the evening a *Herald* reporter had an extended interview with Mooney. At first he declined positively to say anything bearing on the subject of the murder of Lavoiye or the robbery of Mr. George H. Norman's house, until he could have an opportunity of consulting counsel, but he finally yielded to persuasive pressure, and said :

"Why, one would think from the manner I was arrested at Greenbush that I was some sort of a wild animal. Those officers of Albany are a hard lot. After I left Boston I visited several places, but most of the time I spent at Greenbush, where I boarded and roomed nearly the whole time. It is an easy thing to try a man on circumstantial evidence, especially before he is brought before a proper jury, and I feel certain that at the proper time my claim of innocence of the crime with which I am now charged will be satisfactorily established. I can conscientiously say that I am not guilty of the murder of Lavoiye ; neither do I know anything about the robbery of Mr. Norman's house. I do not, however, claim to have a fair or unblemished character, and, more than that, I do not claim to have always been honest. To make such claims would be foolish under the circumstances in which I am now placed.

"It is hardly necessary for me to go into the details of what my professional calling has been. It is enough to say that it is not altogether complimentary to myself ; but yet I can truthfully say that I have never committed murder, neither have I garroted a person or broken into a house. I am now thirty years of age, and I am sorry to say that my education has been sadly neglected. I was born in New York City. and during the war my father kept a hotel on the Hudson River. He died ten years ago. My mother, a brother and sister are of good character and above reproach. I am grieved at the sorrow I have caused them. I suppose I may attribute my misfortunes to the company I kept in my youth. I have for a long time been well acquainted with Boston, and was here off and on several months before the murder of Lavoiye. I never knew him by that name, however, but was always under the impression his name was Charles E. Marshall, and I called him Charley. I met him during a visit here, and went to lodge with him, but not with any desire to be connected with him in the business he followed. He was a quiet and very peaceable man, and always kept his business to himself, as I did mine. While at the house I never had any trouble with any one, and always paid my bills and treated everybody decently. I sometimes drank a glass of lager and occasionally a glass of whiskey, but never indulged in strong liquors to excess. I was seldom with my companion when he was out of the house, and never saw anything about him or the room that would indicate his calling. I did not know that he carried a revolver, and did not know anything about the robbery of Mr. Norman's house, on Beacon Street, until the day after it is said to have been committed, when I read it in the Boston *Herald*. Marshall, I suppose, also saw a report of the robbery—although he did not tell me of it—as he was in the habit of reading the daily papers.

"I remember something I read about calling on Mr. Orpen relative to the key of my room. It happened that Marshall was out, and had the key of the room with him, on the day it was said I left. Mr. Orpen said he would get a key, and I finally said, 'No matter,' and later on met Marshall and got his key. I did not leave Mr. Orpen's house on the day after the Norman robbery, but went away some days afterwards, and when I last saw Marshall he was alive and well. The day I left him I told him I was going away to be absent some time, but would return. I went to New York. While there I saw in a paper an account of Marshall's murder. I was astounded, and could hardly believe it, and read the report over and over again. I soon realized my position, felt almost bewildered, and went to get the opinion of some of my intimate friends, to see what was best for me to do. My first impulse was to surrender myself to the authorities of Boston. My friends urged me to wait, as they said a certain cop or other party was going to Boston to see if he could identify Marshall. I concluded to wait, and after the identification was established again proposed to give myself up and stand trial. On second reflection I concluded that on account of the excited state of the community, it would be best for me to wait until the heat of the people had time to cool off. I argued that if I went among strangers without money I would stand a poor chance of getting justice; so I concluded to keep out of the way, with the intention of waiting until I got together sufficient money to employ able counsel; but this wish I have never been able to realize, although I have managed to live comfortably. I soon left New York, and came up in the vicinity of Greenbush, a very retired place. I secured board and lodging in a very respectable family, which never until now suspected my calling. One night, shortly after my arrival at my new abode, I was in a saloon on South Pearl Street, Albany, when two men, representing themselves as Boston detectives, came into the place. One of these men was quite drunk, and loudly proclaimed he had come to Albany to get Mooney and the reward offered for his arrest. I stood facing him, and as he spoke he exhibited before my astonished gaze a copy of my photograph, which has been spread broadcast throughout the country. Although startled I tried to keep cool, and left the place without any delay, without exciting any suspicion. I went to several places from time to time, but continued to hold my residence in Greenbush. In the latter place, soon after my arrival, I learned that a woman had been attracted by a certain resemblance between me and a cut of myself in the *Police Gazette*. She made allusion to it, but hearing nothing further from her, I came to the conclusion that she had forgotten all about the matter. During last summer I went once or twice to Springfield, where I had friends interested in horses, and was not discovered, or 'given away.' I felt at times that I would not be discovered, because my brother, since Marshall's death, has twice been mistaken for me by officers. I felt, however, that at some time or another I must surely stand my trial. For weeks I have anticipated arrest. Several times I again thought of surrendering myself, but the old fear—lack of money to supply desirable counsel—would always come up, and I would give up the idea. I am now glad, however, that I am arrested, and that I will be tried, as the agony I have suffered has been terrible; not because of any crime I have committed, but simply because the charge of murder was constantly hanging over my head. All I ask now is a fair trial, and I am willing to abide by whatever may be the result. I understand one suspicious circumstance counted against me is the fact that I stood with the door of my room ajar while the little girl of Mr. Orpen came up to deliver towels on the day the murder was committed. The inference I draw is that I was supposed to have kept the little girl out so that she could not see anything that had occurred within. This is a very funny circumstance if it is to be considered as evidence, considering that both Marshall and myself commonly stood in the doorway in the same way when either of us was lying on the bed and did not want to be seen. Then it is hinted that I wrote the slip which was found in the room with the body, and signed 'Charles E. Marshall.' I can hardly read, let alone writing. The letter which was sent to Miss Annie Sullivan, the young girl who worked in a restaurant on Harrison Avenue, and who resided in South Boston, was written by Marshall for me. He signed the name 'John H. Hill,' and the letter was purely in fun. That is how, I suppose, I have got the alias of 'Hill.' I never heard myself called James H. Brady until the police of Boston sent out their circulars for the purpose of effecting my arrest. I suppose I will find myself possessed of other aliases before I get through with Boston. Now, in relation to the Sullivan girl, I always considered her a good young lady. I never courted her, or proposed marriage to her. My relations to her were like those of a person charitably inclined. I have never been troubled about women, and I never have intrusted any of my secrets with them. I do suspect, however, that the woman who thought she saw a similarity between my face and the police photograph was the woman who finally caused my arrest by apprising Detective Riley of her suspicions. When the detectives appeared in the beer saloon in Greenbush I supposed they were a crowd of railroad men who had dropped in to pass away a few hours. The first I knew, I was pounced upon by five of them, and although I called for an explanation, they hustled me off in a hurry towards Albany. They carried me to the ferry, and then only did they condescend to tell me a falsehood when they said I was wanted in the city for the larceny of a diamond pin. When I reached headquarters I was shown my photograph, and of course at once surmised the real object of my arrest. In regard to my friend Marshall, I wish to say that while I was with him in Boston he frequently had other men call at the house, 22 Florence Street, to see him. I knew them by sight, and probably could recall some of the places they were in the habit of visiting. I knew them by their given names simply; they came frequently, at all hours, and it is possible that some one of them might have murdered Marshall. I know of one instance, when I came home from the 'road' one morning, that I found a man asleep with Marshall. Another circumstance which has been held up to sustain the supposition that I committed murder is that the gold watch owned by the murdered man was missing when the body was found. Now I know that in January, prior to the murder, Marshall pawned his watch in Providence, because he told me he did. I asked him why he did not borrow from me, but he said he had rather pawn the watch. I had plenty of ready money at the time. I also know that Marshall had a large account in some bank in one of the Eastern cities, but he never told me which city. I am willing to bet that bank account is still standing, but I suppose it will be hard to find it, as it cannot be ascertained under what name he made the deposits. I think Marshall had considerable money, but cannot say how much. While living on Florence Street he frequently made trips to New York, but for what purpose I cannot say. I was acquainted with a man named Glover in New York, and I suppose Marshall also knew him. I never had any dealings with the man. I never saw anything about Marshall to indicate that he was mixed up with the Norman robbery, and I do not know anything about the bonds said to have been stolen at the time. I never saw any crucibles about the room for melting jewelry; neither did I, to my recollection, hire a hack on Kneeland Street, in which I was said to have dropped a diamond ring which was claimed to have been stolen from the house of Mr. Norman. I did not get shaved on the day I left Boston; I had nothing I wished to shave off. It is very funny how stories get started. Time will show my innocence of the charges against me, and all I ask is that the press and the people will give me a fair chance."

After arriving at the central office in Boston, Mooney was, after a short delay, placed in a cell in the basement of the City Hall, in charge of an officer. He appeared quite fatigued, and soon after reaching his cell fell into a sound slumber. He will be committed to jail to-day, to await trial.

The following article also appeared in one of the New York papers :

A MURDERER'S CONFESSION.—WHY ONE BURGLAR KILLED ANOTHER.—A WOMAN AND DIAMONDS THE CAUSE.

(*Special Dispatch to the New York Evening Telegram.*)

BOSTON, September 27, 1881.—Mooney, the New York burglar, recently sentenced to imprisonment for life for killing his confederate, Lavoiye, has confessed his guilt. A quarrel arose, it appears, about a pair of diamond earrings. Mooney discovered that Lavoiye had given them to a woman, and Lavoiye denied the fact. Mooney, who had obtained them from the woman, then drew them from his pocket. Lavoiye became angered, and attempted to draw his pistol, when Mooney shot him. The earrings were stolen property, and Mooney feared they might serve as a clew.

Mooney's picture is an excellent one, taken in January, 1881.

174
WILLIAM WRIGHT, alias ROARING BILL.
GENERAL THIEF.

DESCRIPTION.

Fifty-three years old in 1886.   Born in United States.   Single.   No trade.   Slim build.   Height, 5 feet 4½ inches.   Weight, 130 pounds.   Brown hair, turning gray; gray eyes, sallow complexion.   Generally wears a mustache, which is quite gray.   Scars on right eyebrow, under lower lip, and on chin.

RECORD.

"Roaring Bill" is an old New York thief.   He has spent the best portion of his life in State prisons and penitentiaries, and is well known in all the principal cities in America.   He is a general thief, can turn his hand to almost anything, and is considered a very clever man.   He is credited with having served four years for an express-train robbery in Colorado; also, with robbing an Adams Express Co. money-car, out West, of $15,000.

Bill was arrested in Providence, R. I., and sentenced to four years in the Rhode Island State prison on March 21, 1881, for the larceny of a valise containing a sealskin sack and several other things from a railroad train between New York and Providence. His sentence expired on October 25, 1884.

He was arrested again in New York City on August 10, 1885, and committed to Blackwell's Island for three months, in default of $500 bail, as a suspicious person, by Justice Murray.

Wright's picture is a good one, taken in August, 1885.

175
WILLIAM PERRY, alias BILLY PERRY,
alias WILSON, alias GRAHAM.
PICKPOCKET, SNEAK AND SHOPLIFTER.

DESCRIPTION.

Thirty-seven years old in 1886.   Born in Virginia.   Married.   No trade.   Slim build.   Height, 5 feet 4½ inches.   Weight, 115 pounds.   Light hair, gray eyes, light complexion.   Generally has a clean-shaven face.

RECORD.

Billy Perry is one of the most expert and successful professional thieves in America.   He has been traveling around the country for years, generally working with a woman.   He is well known in all the large cities, and is considered a first-class man.

Perry was arrested, and sentenced to three years in State prison, in Richmond, Va., in 1871, for picking pockets.   He served two years in Sing Sing prison since.

On June 1, 1882, Eldridge G. Rideout, a publisher on Barclay Street, New York, was robbed of his gold watch at the South Ferry, New York.   Perry was arrested, and recognized as the thief.

Soon after his release on bail in this case he was arrested again, for robbing a man of a gold watch on one of the Coney Island boats.   When Perry was brought to court in New York City he was discharged, because the crime with which he was charged had been committed out of the jurisdiction of the court.

When Perry's case, for stealing of Mr. Rideout's watch, was set down for trial in the Court of General Sessions he had disappeared, and his bail was forfeited.   He was re-arrested, bailed again, and when the case was set down again for trial the pickpocket could not be found.

Nothing was heard of him until the arrival of the survivors of the Greely Arctic expedition at Newburyport, Mass., on August 13, 1884, when he was arrested there, with a number of other professional thieves.   Before the New York officers could reach Newburyport, Perry had been handed over to the Portsmouth (N. H.) authorities for a theft which he had committed there a few weeks before.   On that charge he was sentenced to one year's imprisonment in the Portsmouth jail on August 27, 1884. Perry's sentence expired on August 27, 1885, when he was arrested, at the jail door, brought to New York City, committed to the Tombs prison on August 30, 1885, and subsequently discharged again on bail.

Perry's picture is an excellent one, taken in August, 1884.

176
MARK SHINBURN.
BANK BURGLAR.

DESCRIPTION.

Forty-eight years old in 1886.   Born in Germany.   Height, 5 feet 8 or 9 inches. Weight, about 170 pounds.   Very erect, broad shoulders, thick neck, broad full face ; small, sharp, light blue eyes ; a very deep dimple in a small chin ; dark hair, parted behind.   Generally wears a black mustache and side whiskers, now quite gray.   Has India ink rings on the first and third fingers of left hand.   Speaks at times with just a perceptible German accent. Dresses well. Quite gentlemanly in manner.   Always stops at first-class hotels.

RECORD.

MARK SHINBURN.   This celebrated criminal is a German by birth.   He arrived in New York in 1861, and boarded at the Metropolitan and other first-class hotels for several years.   He was the associate of sporting men and gamblers, in consequence of which he was under the surveillance of the police.

On April 21, 1865, the Walpole Savings Bank of Walpole, New Hampshire, was robbed by Shinburn, George Bliss, alias White, and Dave Cummings (50).

Shinburn was arrested in Saratoga, N. Y., on July 26, 1865, and seven one-thousand dollar bonds were found upon his person, all of which were identified as a portion of the proceeds of that robbery. He had also in his possession a number of clipped coupons from off other government bonds, which were also part of the proceeds of that robbery. For this offense he was convicted at Keene, N. H., and sentenced to ten years at hard labor in the Concord, N. H., State prison, by Judge Porter.

On the night after the day of his conviction (November 2, 1865), he, by the aid of confederates, effected his escape, and was not heard of again until May, 1866, when he, with others, attempted to rob the St. Albans Bank, at St. Albans, Franklin County, Vt. They were surprised by the watchman of the bank, who fired upon them. They all escaped, Shinburn taking refuge in a car of a slowly passing train of the Vermont Central Railroad, in which he pretended to fall asleep.

One of the passengers who had been a juryman on his trial at Keene, N. H., recognized him, and suspecting something wrong called an officer, on stopping at the first station, and he was arrested. He was subsequently returned to the New Hampshire State prison to serve out his ten-year sentence.

After serving about nine months he again escaped, with the aid of his friends, and was not heard from again until 1867, when he was arrested at Wilkesbarre, Pa, for the robbery of the Delaware, Lackawanna and Hudson Canal Company's safe of $33,000. An officer arrested him for this last offense, and was obliged to remain in Wilkesbarre that night owing to the trains not running. A room was engaged at the Valley Hotel, Wilkesbarre, and on their retiring to bed the prisoner was handcuffed to the officer, who, on awakening in the morning, discovered his prisoner had escaped by picking the lock of the cuffs with a small piece of steel which it is supposed he had concealed in his mouth. He also carried away with him the officer's watch and money.

The next heard from Shinburn was after the robbery of the Ocean National Bank of New York City, in 1868, when he and his confederates secured over one million of dollars, since which time he has been a fugitive from justice, and, I understand, has been living in France and Switzerland, where he bought himself a title and castle.

Shinburn, if cleanly shaven, has a deep dimple in his chin. He speaks English fluently, and is a most polished conversationalist. He might be called a good-looking man.

When arrested at Saratoga, N. Y., for the Walpole Savings Bank robbery, his house was searched, and on the top floor was found a complete workshop for the manufacture of burglars' tools. A number of wax impressions of keys were found, which, upon investigation, proved to be of keys fitting the Cheshire County Bank at Keene, N. H., and also fitting its vaults and steel money chests, which contained at that time $232,000 in money.

Mark Shinburn's specialty was the taking of wax impressions of bank and safe keys, which he obtained by ascertaining that the bank officials carried them, and then effecting an entrance to their sleeping-room at night, and abstracting them from their pockets.

George White, alias Bliss, was associated with Shinburn in all the above transactions. He was convicted in September, 1875, and sentenced to fourteen years in State prison for robbing the Barre Bank of Vermont.

White, while arranging to rob the Walpole Bank, to give color to his appearance in Walpole, and also to assist the robbery, got up a grand gift enterprise there, and while doing this he ascertained the habits of the bank people, and gave Shinburn an opportunity to get impressions. The jury disagreed on this trial for this robbery, and with the aid of confederates he escaped from the county jail.

Dave Cummings (50), who was with Shinburn and White in this robbery, was discharged for want of jurisdiction, as it could not be proved that he sold any of the bonds in the State of New Hampshire. He did sell some in New York and Pennsylvania.

Shinburn was next heard from in attempting to dispose of the proceeds of a bank robbery at Baltimore, Md., in the office of a prominent lawyer in New York City. The go-between in this transaction was a noted receiver of stolen goods in New York City, who negotiated with this lawyer to purchase the bonds; the lawyer made an appointment, and then notified the police.

Shinburn not willing to trust the receiver with the bonds, accompanied him to the lawyer's office, where the police arrested them both and secured the recovery of $137,000 in bonds. The prisoners were wanted in Baltimore, and being willing to go there without a requisition, were handed over to the Baltimore detectives. When they arrived in Jersey City their counsel demanded the authority on which they took them through the State of New Jersey, and they not having any, the prisoners were discharged.

During the month of November, 1863, a number of $500 bills of the Haverhill Bank were circulated in the city of Boston, Mass., for which Charley Bullard was arrested in New York City, and by requisition he was conveyed to Boston, where, upon an examination, he was held in $5,000 bail to answer, and on being liberated fled from justice and concealed himself in some of our Western cities.

In 1866 or 1867, a baggage car of the New Haven Railroad Company was entered and a safe thrown off at a point between New York and Bridgeport, Conn., which contained a large amount of money, the property of Adams Express Company of New York City. For this offense Bullard was arrested in Canada, brought to this country, and lodged in jail at White Plains, N. Y., from which, in a few months, he escaped, and left for Europe, landing at Liverpool, England, where he married a pretty "bar-maid," with whom he went to Paris, and was next heard of as the proprietor of the American café in Paris, a place much frequented by Americans abroad.

Here he became dissipated and impoverished, and again returned to this country, where he was arrested charged with robbing the Boylston Bank of Boston, Mass., to which he pleaded guilty, and was sentenced to twenty years' imprisonment.

He remained in Concord, Mass., State prison about one year, when he again made his escape to Canada, and while at Toronto, Canada, was arrested for burglary, and upon conviction sentenced to five years' hard labor, which sentence he served. On his being released he left for Europe, fell in with Shinburn, and was arrested with him leaving the yard of a small bank in Viveres, in Belgium, in September, 1883.

The arrest of Shinburn and Bullard in Belgium is very interesting. It appears that Shinburn became straitened in circumstances and was very short of money. He therefore took a look around for a good place to get some, and finally decided that the Provincial Bank at Viveres, in Belgium, was an easy one to rob. The next thing to do was to get a good man to help him. He finally hunted up Charley Bullard, who was then in Europe, and told him he had a chance to get some money, and if he (Bullard) would help him, he would give him $6,000 if the job was successful, Shinburn firmly believing that if he was successful in robbing the bank he would obtain at least $100,000. So hungry was Shinburn for the money, that he would not take Bullard in the robbery and share it with him. After all their arrangements were made, they both visited the bank one night, "to look it over." They approached it from the rear, entering the yard by fitting a key to the gate, after which their progress was barred by an old-fashioned oak and iron door, which had an immense lock on it on the inside. Shinburn proceeded to remove a large keyhole plate that was upon the outside of the door, by unscrewing a number of small screws that were in it; these he placed in his vest pocket, so he could find them again when wanted. After the plate was removed there was not much difficulty in picking the old-fashioned lock. Before entering the bank they both removed their shoes and placed them in the corner of the yard, then entered and made a general survey of the premises, after which they decided to return the next night and proceed to force the safe.

While they were engaged inside the bank, an officer appeared whose custom it was to come down the back way and try the gate, which, in their hurry, they had neglected to fasten. Finding it open, he flashed his bull's-eye light around the yard and discovered the shoes. He picked them up, and after examining them, became suspicious, and started at once for the police station with them. During the time that the officer had taken to go to the police station and return with a posse of men, who stationed themselves outside the bank, front and rear, to await developments, Shinburn and Bullard had left the bank and were in the act of replacing the keyhole plate, previous to their departure, when it was discovered that one of the small screws was missing. After searching in vain for it, Shinburn finally took a small piece of wax from a larger piece that he had in his pocket, and filled the hole with it, forming a head on it by drawing his finger-nail through it. They then proceeded to leave the yard, first going to where they had left their shoes, which were missing. This aroused their suspicions, and thinking that they were detected, approached the gate cautiously. Shinburn tried it and found it open, and it was not until Bullard had assured him that he had forgotten to fasten it, that they decided to leave the yard.

Immediately after leaving the yard they were arrested. Bullard broke away, and while the officers were pursuing him he fired several shots at them from a revolver. He was finally run down, and lodged in jail with Shinburn. They were both searched, but nothing of importance was found upon them, except the piece of wax that Shinburn had in his vest pocket. This, however, they paid no particular attention to, as it was evident that they did not know its use.

The authorities then proceeded to make a thorough examination of the bank, and found everything as usual. They were about discharging the prisoners, who had satisfactorily explained their presence in the bank yard, when they decided to call in some experts and re-examine the bank and its surroundings. One of the experts, a chemist, took the piece of wax for the purpose of examining and analyzing it, and while so doing he found deeply imbedded in it a small screw. They then proceeded to the bank, in company of the other expert, a locksmith, who examined the door in the yard, and found one of the screw holes filled up with wax and the screw missing. The wax that was taken from the hole was saved, analyzed, and found to contain the same ingredients as the piece found in Shinburn's pocket. The screw was a fac-simile of the others in the plate, all of which showed recent marks upon them. It was this series of circumstantial evidence, and their previous record, sent to Viveres, Belgium, by the police authorities of New York City, that convicted them.

Shinburn and Bullard were tried for the attempt upon this bank and found guilty. Shinburn received a sentence of seventeen years and six months, and Bullard sixteen years and six months.

For further particulars of Shinburn, see also record of No. 70. For George White, or Bliss, see also records of Nos. 20, 70, 80, 89 and 110. For Dave Cummings, see No. 50.

177

HENRY CLINE, alias WESTON,
alias KLEIN.
BURGLAR, SNEAK AND COUNTERFEITER.

DESCRIPTION.

Thirty-one years old in 1886. German, born in the United States. Married. Machinist. Medium build. Height, 5 feet 9 inches. Weight, 148 pounds. Black hair, brown eyes, dark complexion. Has a scar on his forehead ; mole under the right eye.

RECORD.

CLINE is one of the most expert house and office sneaks there is in this country. He generally works with another man, who enters the room or office under pretense of selling something, thereby occupying the attention of whoever may be there, while Cline sneaks in and gets what he can. He is an expert machinist. One of the finest set of "house-workers'" tools that was ever captured was taken from him at the time of his arrest on April 24, 1885. He claimed to have made them while confined in prison.

Cline has served several terms in the penitentiary of New York City. He was sentenced to three months on January 11, 1876, for petty larceny, in New York City, and again in May, 1879, for six months.

169

JOHN CURTIN,
ALIAS REYNOLDS,
BURGLAR AND SNEAK.

170

JAMES McMAHON,
BURGLAR AND RIVER THIEF.

171

THEODORE WILDEY,
ALIAS THEE WILEY,
SNEAK.

172

GEORGE LITTLE,
ALIAS TIP LITTLE,
SNEAK AND FORGER.

173

DAVID MOONEY,
ALIAS LITTLE DAVE,
SNEAK AND BURGLAR.

174

WILLIAM WRIGHT,
ALIAS ROARING BILL,
GENERAL THIEF.

175

WILLIAM PERRY,
ALIAS BILLY PERRY,
PICKPOCKET AND SNEAK.

176

MARK SHINBORN,
BANK BURGLAR.

177

HENRY CLINE,
ALIAS WESTON,
SNEAK.

178

JOSEPH COLON,
ALIAS RYAN,
HOUSE BURGLAR AND SNEAK.

179

ROBERT HOVAN,
ALIAS MUNROE and PARKER,
HOUSE SNEAK AND BURGLAR.

180

WILLIAM DARRIGAN,
ALIAS BILLY DERRIGAN,
PICKPOCKET.

181

PETER LAMB,
ALIAS DUTCH PETE,
SHOP LIFTER.

182

FRANK LOENTHAL,
ALIAS SHEENY ERWIN,
SHOP LIFTER.

183

WILLIAM SCOTT,
ALIAS SCOTTY,
PICKPOCKET AND SHOP LIFTER.

184

RUDOLPH LEWIS,
ALIAS YOUNG RUDOLPH,
SHOP LIFTER.

185

GEORGE LEVY,
ALIAS LEE,
SHOP LIFTER.

186

WM. DOUGHERTY,
ALIAS BIG DOCK,
PICKPOCKET AND SNEAK.

187

EMANUEL MARKS,
ALIAS MINNIE MARKS AND THE
RED HEADED JEW,.
BANK SNEAK.

188

CHARLEY BENNETT,
BURGLAR AND WINDOW SMASHER.

189

HERMAN PALMER,
BURGLAR.

190

HENRY HOFFMAN,
ALIAS MEYERS,
RECEIVER.

191

JULIUS KLEIN,
ALIAS YOUNG JULIUS,
SNEAK AND SHOP LIFTER.

192

JOHN CARROLL,
ALIAS KID CARROLL,
BANK SNEAK.

He was arrested again in New York City on July 6, 1885, under the name of Henry Weston, in company of a girl named Kitty Wilson, charged with counterfeiting United States silver coins. The United States officers searched the rooms occupied by them, and found twenty-five sets of plaster moulds, such as are used in making counterfeit coins, batteries, chemical solutions, and a number of spurious coins, among which were two hundred bogus United States standard dollars. They were rather poor imitations of the genuine, and could be readily detected.

Kitty Wilson, who is about twenty-five years of age, is of German descent, and is well known as one of the women who frequent the disreputable resorts in the vicinity of the Bowery, and Bleecker and Great Jones streets, New York. She formerly lived with a man named Wilson, and took his name. She met Cline a short time before their arrest, and went to live with him at No. 44 First Avenue, New York, and began the coining of counterfeit silver pieces in their apartments on the third floor. Weston and Kitty were committed to jail, in default of $5,000 bail, by United States Commissioner Shields, on July 7, 1885. Weston, or Cline, was sentenced to three years in State prison at Buffalo, N. Y., by Judge Benedict, in the United States Court in New York City, on October 28, 1885. Kitty Wilson was discharged.

Cline's picture is an excellent one, taken in May, 1879.

178

JOSEPH COLON, alias JOHNSON,

alias JOSEPH ROGERS.

PICKPOCKET, SNEAK, HOUSE BURGLAR AND SLEEPING–CAR WORKER.

DESCRIPTION.

Thirty-nine years old in 1886. Born in New York. Single. No trade. Slim build. Height, 5 feet 8 inches. Weight, 138 pounds. Brown hair, brown eyes, nose flat and turns up at the end, sandy complexion; sandy mustache or beard, when grown. Has scar on side of head; mole on the left cheek. A woman's head on right fore-arm, and a star on the right hand in India ink.

RECORD.

JOE COLON is a very clever sneak thief and house man. He may be found around boat regattas, fairs, etc., and sometimes works with a woman. Of late he has been doing considerable house work. He travels all over and has been quite successful, as he drops into a town or city, does his work, and takes the next train out of it.

Colon first made the acquaintance of the New York police on October 23, 1877, when he was arrested at the Grand Central Railroad depot, on the arrival of a Boston train, for having in his possession a vest, watch and chain belonging to Elliot Sanford, a broker, in New York, which he had stolen from a sleeping-car. Mr. Sanford, after getting his property back, refused to go to court, and Colon was discharged, after his picture was taken for the Rogues' Gallery.

Colon was arrested at Troy, N. Y., on August 20, 1884, under the name of Joseph Rogers, for the larceny of a gold watch and chain, the property of George L. French, from a locker in the Laureate Club boat-house during a regatta. He was convicted under Section 508 of the New York Penal Code, and sentenced to one year in the Albany, N. Y., penitentiary, and fined $500, on Saturday, August 30, 1884. He was, however, discharged before his time expired.

He was arrested again in Boston, Mass., on November 11, 1885. Tools for doing house work, consisting of a palet-knife for opening windows, a screwdriver, soft black hat, rubber shoes, and a one-inch wood-chisel for opening drawers, etc., were found in a satchel he was carrying. His picture was taken, and he was discharged, as no complaint could be obtained against him.

Colon's picture is a good one, taken on November 11, 1885.

179

ROBERT HOVAN, alias ROBERT MUNROE, alias Henry Parker, alias Paul Harrington, alias Charles H. Adams.

BURGLAR AND HOUSE SNEAK.

DESCRIPTION.

Thirty-four years old in 1886. Born in the United States. Married. Produce dealer. Medium build. Height, 5 feet 9½ inches. Weight, 160 pounds. Hair, light brown. Hazel eyes, fair complexion. Generally wears a full, sandy beard. Has an anchor on the right fore-arm, a star on the left fore-arm, and five dots of India ink on right hand. Inclined to be feminine in his actions.

RECORD.

Bob Hovan is a very clever house sneak and burglar. He is a brother of Horace Hovan, alias Little Horace (25), the bank sneak; also, a brother-in-law of Bill Vosburg (4), another notorious bank sneak. Hovan is pretty well known in all the principal cities in America.

He was arrested in New York City, on June 18, 1880, for a house robbery, and sentenced to one year in the penitentiary on Blackwell's Island, by Judge Cowing, on June 28, 1880, under the name of Charles H. Adams.

In December, 1882, Hovan, or Harrington, as he then called himself, was arrested by the police in Brooklyn, N. Y. He had no difficulty in securing his release upon bail, which, when the case was called for trial and Harrington did not appear, proved valueless. A warrant was issued, and detectives Corr and Looney, of Brooklyn, came to New York, and located Harrington at No. 1225 First Avenue, where he was living with a Mrs. Adams, or Charlotte Dougherty, Horace Hovan's wife. The detectives, soon after dark, on the night of February 17, 1883, stationed themselves in an opposite door-way, and patiently watched. They had not long to wait, and in the twilight they could see a man entering the house who in build and general appearance resembled Harrington. He, however, did not wear a full beard like that usually worn by the burglar, but had his chin cleanly shaven, and had a mustache and small side-whiskers. They waited for him to come out, and after half an hour's watch the man they suspected came out of the house. Corr and Looney came to the conclusion that it was Harrington. They followed him to the corner of Sixty-fifth Street, where he caught sight of them, and apparently it flashed across him who his pursuers were. He quickened his pace, and the two detectives did likewise. Near the corner of Second Avenue, Corr said to Looney, "That's our man ; let us close in on him." They moved forward rapidly, and as they did so Harrington made a feint as if to ascend the stairs leading to the Elevated Railroad station. The detectives and the fugitive at that time were the only people in sight. Looney was about six feet in advance of his companion, and when he came within two or three paces of the fugitive there was a flash and a report from a weapon which Harrington held in his outstretched hand. With the report Looney fell prostrate into the gutter, shot in the neck. With the flash Corr whipped out his weapon, and as he brought it to bear on the burglar the fellow fired a second shot, which missed the officer. Corr returned the fire, and discharged two shots from his revolver. As he was about to fire a third shot he received a bullet from another chamber of the burglar's pistol, which passed through his cheek and buried itself in his neck. Before the officers could recover from the shock of their wounds Harrington had made good his escape.

Hovan was arrested again on March 18, 1883—a little over a month after he shot Looney and Corr—in the east end of Allegheny City, Pa., for robbing a safe in a feed store. He was shortly after sentenced to three years in the Western Penitentiary, at Allegheny City, under the name of Henry Parker. His time expired on November 28, 1885, when he was re-arrested on a requisition by New York officers and returned to New York City, to answer an indictment for assault in the first degree. His case went to trial in the Court of General Sessions, but Judge Cowing allowed Hovan, during the progress of the trial, to plead guilty to one of the indictments. He was remanded until December 10, 1885, and in the time intervening several church people interceded for him, and Judge Cowing sentenced him to five years' imprisonment in Sing Sing prison —this being his fourth term served in that prison.

Hovan's sentence will expire on July 10, 1889, allowing him commutation.

His picture is a good one, taken in June, 1880.

180

WILLIAM DARRIGAN, alias BILLY DERRIGAN,

alias Wilson, alias Drake.

PICKPOCKET.

DESCRIPTION.

Thirty-eight years old in 1886. Born in New York. Married. No trade. Stout build. Height, 5 feet 6 inches. Weight, 150 pounds. Dark hair, brown eyes, dark complexion. A short, thick-set, saucy fellow.

RECORD.

Billy, or Hugh, Darrigan is a well known New York pickpocket. He was an associate of Jersey Jimmie (145), Combo (148), Shinny McGuire (155), Freddie Louther (161), and Johnny Price (150). He has spent the best portion of his life in State prisons and penitentiaries all over the United States. Some years ago he was considered a very clever man, but he cannot be relied upon now on account of his love for liquor. The "clever" ones shun him, as he is what is termed a "marker"—one known by everybody. He is very well known in all the large cities, also in Canada.

He was arrested in New York City on February 21, 1872, for picking pockets, and sentenced to four years in Sing Sing prison, under the name of Hugh Derrigan, by Recorder Hackett, on March 4, 1872.

He was arrested again in New York City on the night of October 20, 1880, for the larceny of a gold watch and chain from John H. Ford, in Tammany Hall. He pleaded guilty, and was sentenced to one year and six months in Sing Sing prison, under the name of William Davis, by Judge Cowing, in the Court of General Sessions, on November 10, 1880.

His picture is a good one.

181

PETER LAMB, alias DUTCH PETE,

alias Hall, alias Peter Hart, alias John Willett, alias Henry Minor, alias Miller.

SHOPLIFTER AND BURGLAR.

DESCRIPTION.

Forty-six years old in 1886. German, born in United States. Married. An auctioneer. Stout build. Height, 5 feet 10¼ inches. Weight, 210 pounds. Brown hair, brown eyes, light complexion. Generally wears a light brown mustache.

RECORD.

"DUTCH PETE," or PETER RINEHART, which is his right name, is a very clever shoplifter and burglar. He is well known in New York, Boston, Chicago, and several of the other large cities. He has served three terms in Sing Sing prison, N. Y.

Pete was arrested in New York City on December 4, 1879, in company of John Cass, alias Big Cass, another notorious burglar, charged with committing a burglary at No. 329 Canal Street, New York, a Russia leather establishment. He was also charged with another burglary, committed at No. 73 Grand Street, New York City, where the burglars carried away $2,000 worth of silks. For the latter offense he was sentenced to three years in Sing Sing prison, on December 18, 1879, by Judge Cowing, in the Court of General Sessions.

Lamb was arrested again in New York City, in December, 1882, for the larceny of some penknives (a sneak job) from a safe in a store on Broadway, near Duane Street, New York. For this he was sentenced to four years in Sing Sing prison (his third term), for grand larceny in the second degree, on January 3, 1883, by Judge Gildersleeve, under the name of John Willet. His sentence expired on January 3, 1886.

Lamb's picture is a good one, taken in April, 1879.

182

FRANK LOWENTHAL, alias SHEENY IRVING, alias AUGUST W. ERWIN.

SHOPLIFTER AND RECEIVER.

DESCRIPTION.

Forty-two years old in 1886. Jew, born in United States. Married. Telegraph operator and jewelry dealer. Slim build. Height, 5 feet 3 inches. Weight, 121 pounds. Brown hair, hazel eyes, dark complexion. Jewish appearance.

RECORD.

FRANK LOWENTHAL, alias "SHEENY IRVING," is a noted shoplifter and receiver of stolen goods. He shot his wife, Delia, and then himself, in the Allman House, in East Tenth Street, New York City, on July 15, 1885.

He was arrested in New York City on September 28, 1882, for the larceny of some opera glasses from a jewelry store in Maiden Lane, New York. Julius Klein, alias "Sheeny" Julius (191), another notorious young thief, was arrested with him for the same offense, but was not held. Erwin, however, was committed in $500 bail for trial, which he furnished. His case had not come to trial up to the time of his arrest for assaulting his wife.

Erwin is a man of good education, and speaks German fluently. He says that he was born in Cincinnati of wealthy parents, who sent him to Germany to be educated.

After spending two years at the high school at Magdeburg, he entered the University of Heidelberg as a student of the natural sciences, and graduated with the degree of B. A. After his return to the United States he was connected with a St. Louis newspaper; he afterwards came to New York, and commenced his criminal career. Erwin was prompted to shoot his wife by rum and unhappy domestic experience. She was going to Europe with her father, who was anxious to separate them when he found out that Erwin was a thief. Mrs. Erwin recovered from her wounds, and Erwin pleaded guilty to assault in the second degree, and was sentenced to five years in State prison and fined $1,000, by Recorder Smyth, in the Court of General Sessions, New York City, on September 21, 1885.

His picture is a good one, taken in September, 1882.

183

WILLIAM SCOTT, alias SCOTTY,
alias Wm. Clark, alias Kirby.
SHOPLIFTER AND PICKPOCKET.

DESCRIPTION.

Forty-six years old in 1886. Born in United States. Married. Marble-cutter. Stout build. Height, 5 feet 6½ inches. Weight, 183 pounds. Black hair, brown eyes, light complexion. Generally wears a dark brown mustache. Short nose, with scar on it.

RECORD.

"Scotty" is an old professional pickpocket and shoplifter. He is well known in New York and all the principal cities in the United States. His picture adorns several Rogues' Galleries. He has served two terms in State prison in New York State, and three in the penitentiary on Blackwell's Island, N. Y. He pays considerable attention to funerals and fairs, and sometimes works with a very clever woman.

He was arrested in New York City for shoplifting, and sentenced to two years and six months in Sing Sing prison, on April 17, 1879, by Judge Cowing, in the Court of General Sessions, New York City.

He was arrested again in New York City for picking pockets, pleaded guilty to grand larceny, and was sentenced to four years in State prison at Sing Sing, N. Y., on July 12, 1882.

His sentence expired on July 12, 1885.

Scott's picture is an excellent one, taken in May, 1878.

184

RUDOLPH LEWIS, alias YOUNG RUDOLPH,
alias RUDOLPH MILLER.
SHOPLIFTER.

DESCRIPTION.

Twenty-one years old in 1886. German, born in the United States. Single. No trade. Slim build. Height, 5 feet 8 inches. Weight, 130 pounds. Brown hair, hazel eyes, sallow complexion. Three dots of India ink on inside of left fore-arm. Large ears.

RECORD.

YOUNG RUDOLPH is, perhaps, one of the smartest young thieves in America. He has just started out, and from his career so far he is calculated to develop into a first-class man. He is pretty well known in all the Eastern cities, especially in New York and Boston, where his picture is in the Rogues' Gallery. He is an associate of Frank Watson, alias Big Patsey, Little Eddie Kelly, Jack McCormack, alias Big Mack, and Charles Lewis, all notorious east side, New York, thieves.

Lewis was arrested in New York City on September 22, 1883, charged with stealing a piece of silk, valued at $100, from the store of Lewis Brothers, No. 86 Worth Street, New York. He forfeited his bail and went to Boston, Mass., where he was arrested for shoplifting, and sentenced to eighteen months in the House of Correction, on November 19, 1883, under the name of Rudolph Miller. His time expired in Boston on April 25, 1885, when he was re-arrested on a requisition, and brought back to New York, to answer for the larceny of the piece of silk.

Lewis pleaded guilty in the silk case, and was sentenced to two years in Sing Sing prison, on April 3, 1885, by Judge Cowing. His sentence will expire on December 30, 1886.

Young Rudolph's picture is a good one, taken in September, 1883.

185

GEORGE LEVY, alias LEE.
SHOPLIFTER.

DESCRIPTION.

Forty-six years old in 1886. Jew, born in Poland. Single. No legitimate trade. Slim build. Height, 5 feet 10½ inches. Weight, 135 pounds. Brown hair, hazel eyes, dark complexion, mole on right cheek. Three India ink marks on left arm. Generally wears brown mustache and chin whisker.

RECORD.

Levy is a smart sheeny shoplifter and sneak thief, who has been traveling through the Eastern cities for years. He is as liable to sneak into a bank as into a store. He is considered quite clever, and is pretty well known in all the Eastern cities, especially in New York, where he has served time in State prison at Sing Sing, and in the penitentiary on Blackwell's Island.

He was arrested in New York City on June 7, 1882, for the larceny of $24 worth of Japanese articles from the store of Charles W. Fuller, No. 15 East Nineteenth Street. He was tried in the Court of Special Sessions, in the Tombs building, on June 12, 1882, and discharged by Justice Murray, who was ignorant of his character.

He was arrested in New York City again on September 9, 1885, in the fur store of Solomon Kutner, No. 492 Broome Street. Mrs. Kutner noticed that a light overcoat that he carried over his arm was much larger than when he entered. She shut the door, and stood before it. Finding himself locked in, he threw the bundle to the floor, seized the woman, and pushed her to one side. He found that he had been foiled again, as she had taken the key out of the door after locking it. Mrs. Kutner shouted, and her son and husband held Levy until an officer arrived and arrested him. The property he attempted to steal consisted of a sealskin sacque, valued at $170; two pairs of beaver gloves, and a roll of satin lining. Levy pleaded guilty in this case, and was sentenced to three years in State prison at Sing Sing, on September 21, 1885, by Judge Cowing, in the Court of General Sessions, New York.

Levy's picture is a good one, although he tried to avoid it. It was taken in June, 1882.

186

WILLIAM DOUGHERTY, alias BIG DOCK,

alias William Gleason.

SNEAK AND PICKPOCKET.

DESCRIPTION.

Forty years old in 1886. Born in New York. Married. No trade. Stout build. Height, 5 feet 11 inches. Weight, about 180 pounds. Dark brown hair, dark eyes, dark complexion. Generally wears a brown mustache. Hair worn long and inclined to curl. He is a tall, fine-looking man. Dresses well.

RECORD.

"Big Dock" is an old Eighth Ward New York pickpocket and sneak thief. He is well known in a number of the principal cities in the United States and Canada, and is an escaped prisoner from Sing Sing prison, New York. There is a standing reward of fifty dollars for any officer in the United States who arrests and holds him until the prison authorities can come for him. He is a big, desperate fellow, and requires watching before and after arrest.

Dougherty has served terms in Sing Sing prison (New York), and in the penitentiary on Blackwell's Island; also, in Canada. He is an associate of "Curly" Charley, "Big Dick" Morris (141), "Jimmy the Kid" (143), Freddie Louther (161), "Aleck the Milkman" (160), and several other first-class pickpockets.

He was arrested in New York City on October 7, 1875, for grand larceny and felonious assault. Mr. Joseph Wolf and his wife got on board of a Third Avenue car in Park Row, intending to go up-town. Before the car had proceeded far, his watch was torn from his pocket by Dougherty, who then jumped off the platform and ran away. Mr. Wolf gave chase to the fugitive, and overtook him in Nassau Street. The thief struck him a blow in the face, and continued his flight, still pursued by Mr. Wolf. The latter again overtook the runaway, in Theatre Alley, when Dougherty turned upon him, knocked him down, and while he was lying upon the ground fired a shot at him from a revolver. When Mr. Wolf came to his senses the thief was out of sight. An officer who was in the vicinity heard the shot, and arrived on the scene in time to pursue the culprit, whom he captured.

Dougherty was tried, found guilty, and sentenced, on November 11, 1875, to ten years in State prison for the larceny, and five years for the assault, making fifteen years in all, by Recorder Hackett. He gave the name of William Gleason. "Big Dock" escaped from Sing Sing prison on January 30, 1876, and is now wanted by the prison authorities. The white affair on his breast is a pocket-handkerchief which he placed there to hide a bloody shirt when his picture was taken.

Dougherty's picture is a good one, although taken fifteen years ago.

187

EMANUEL MARKS, alias MINNIE MARKS,
alias THE RED-HEADED JEW.
BANK SNEAK, CONFIDENCE MAN AND SKIN GAMBLER.

DESCRIPTION.

Forty-four years old in 1886. Jew, born in Illinois. Married. No trade. Medium build. Height, 5 feet 10 inches. Weight, about 160 pounds. Florid complexion, bushy brown hair, almost sandy. He is a little stooped shouldered. Blue eyes that have a bold, searching look. Walks with a very slouchy gait. He is a good talker, and rattles away at a furious rate. Speaks good English, German and Hebrew. Used to dress well, but getting careless of late.

RECORD.

MINNIE MARKS, alias THE RED-HEADED JEW, is a Chicago thief, and is well known in Cincinnati, Cleveland, Detroit, Baltimore, and New York. He received considerable notoriety when arrested in New York City, on October 21, 1881, and was delivered to the police authorities of Detroit, Mich., charged with robbing the First National Bank of that city of $2,080. It was a sneak robbery, which was done by four men, with a light wagon, on June 22, 1881.

In Chicago, where Marks is well known, he is not considered a very smart thief, although other people who know him say he is a good man. He works with men like Rufe Minor (1), Mollie Matches (11), Johnny Jourdan (83), Georgie Carson (3), Big Rice (12), Billy Burke (162), Paddy Guerin, and other celebrated thieves.

Marks's picture is in the Rogues' Gallery at New York, Chicago and Detroit. He is said to have been with Jourdan, Minor, Carson and Horace Hovan in the Middletown Bank robbery in July, 1880. He is also said to have been one of the men who, in April, 1881, attempted to rob the bank at Cohoes, N. Y.

Marks succeeded in making his escape from the jail in Detroit, Mich., on March 12, 1882, with twelve other prisoners, and has never been recaptured. Since that time he has served two years in St. Vincent De Paul prison in Montreal, Canada. The latest accounts say that he is now employed as a porter in a first-class hotel in Montreal, Canada.

Marks's picture is a very good one, taken in Detroit, Mich.

188

CHARLES BENNET, alias CHARLEY BENNETT, alias AGNELL, alias BENTLEY.

SNEAK, BURGLAR AND WINDOW SMASHER.

DESCRIPTION.

Thirty-seven years old in 1886. Height, 5 feet 7 inches. Weight, 145 pounds. Dark complexion. Had cast in one eye, which was operated upon, and is hardly noticeable now. Very genteel-looking. Good-talker and writer. Dark brown hair. Generally wears a full dark beard, or mustache and whiskers, as in picture.

RECORD.

BENNETT is a very daring thief. He was an old partner of Fairy McGuire (78) and Sleepy Gus, and traveled through the country with them smashing in windows and robbing them. He is an expert burglar, and is well known in all the large cities, especially Philadelphia and New York.

Bennett was arrested in Middletown, Conn., on December 5, 1878, with a lot of burglars' tools in his possession. He was tried and sentenced to two years in State prison, by Judge Morton, on the same day of his arrest. He has served terms in Sing Sing and the Eastern Penitentiary in Philadelphia since. This man, of late years, is not relied upon much by the fraternity, on account of his fondness for liquor.

Bennett's picture is an excellent one, taken in December, 1878.

189
HERMAN PALMER, alias DUTCH HERMAN.
BURGLAR.

DESCRIPTION.

Twenty-nine years old in 1886. German, born in New York. Single. Shoemaker and carpenter. Stout build. Height, 5 feet 8 inches. Weight, 167 pounds. Light hair, small gray eyes, light complexion, thick lips. German appearance. Hair inclined to be curly. A good, stout lump of a man. Has plenty of nerve.

RECORD.

HERMAN PALMER is a brother of August Palmer (63), both of whom are well known in all the Eastern cities, especially in Philadelphia and New York, where they made a specialty of blowing open pawnbrokers' safes. They are both expert safe burglars, and have a quick and noiseless method of opening a safe in a very short time. Herman has served terms previously in Sing Sing prison and on Blackwell's Island, N. Y.

He was arrested in New York City on February 17, 1881, charged with robbing a safe in Meyer's pawnshop, at No. 528 Second Avenue, on the night of April 30, 1880, of $6,000 worth of watches and jewelry. His brother August was arrested in this case, tried, convicted, and sentenced to five years in State prison at Sing Sing, N. Y., on June 28, 1880. Herman was discharged in this case, as there was no evidence against him.

He was arrested again in New York City on July 19, 1884, charged with burglarizing a hardware store at No. 1011 Third Avenue, on July 17, where he obtained $800 worth of silverware. For this he was convicted of receiving stolen goods, and was sentenced to four years in Sing Sing prison on August 12, 1884.

Ferdinand H. Hoefner, who had bought $200 worth of the stolen property from Herman, and who was used as a witness against him on the trial, was assaulted and terribly beaten by August Palmer, Herman's brother. For this August was sentenced to three years in State prison, for assault in the third degree, on September 19, 1884.

Herman's sentence will expire on August 12, 1887.

His picture is an excellent one, taken in February, 1881.

190
HENRY HOFFMAN, alias MEYERS,
alias JAMES, alias MAY, alias TANNER, alias FRANCIS.
GENERAL THIEF AND RECEIVER OF STOLEN GOODS.

DESCRIPTION.

Thirty-two years old in 1886. Jew, born in United States. Married. No trade. Medium build. Height, 5 feet 8½ inches. Weight, 154 pounds. Black hair, dark eyes, dark complexion. Generally wears a black mustache. Big nose. Parts his hair in the middle. Has a Jewish appearance. Has "H. H." near wrist on right arm. Scar on left cheek.

RECORD.

HOFFMAN, which is his right name, is a well known New York thief and receiver, and has been arrested from time to time in almost every city in the United States. He has served two terms in State prison for burglary, and is a man well worth knowing.

He was arrested in New York City on October 14, 1882, in company of Frank Watson, alias Big Patsey, and Julius Klein (191), and delivered to the police authorities of Boston, Mass. Hoffman, Watson and Klein were arraigned in court in Boston, Mass., on November 24, 1882, and pleaded guilty to breaking and entering the store of Mr. Thomas, No. 35 Avon Street, that city, and carrying away velvet and cloth valued at $1,000.

Hoffman and Watson were sentenced to three years each in Concord prison. Their sentence expired on July 3, 1885. Klein was sentenced to two years in the House of Correction at South Boston. His sentence expired on October 2, 1884.

During the months of October and November, 1885, two express wagons and their contents were stolen in Boston, Mass. The wagons were recovered, but their contents, valued at $4,000, were only partly recovered. Shortly after the robbery two notorious wagon thieves, named Stephen Dowd and William W. Alesbury, were arrested in Boston for the offenses. In Dowd's pocket was found the directions of Hoffman's house in New York City. Hoffman was arrested in New York, and part of the stolen property found in his possession. He was taken to Boston on December 15, 1885, and used as a witness against Dowd and Alesbury, who were convicted and sentenced to four years each in the Charlestown State prison. Alesbury has previously served a three years' sentence in the same prison for a similar offense.

Hoffman was arrested again in Baltimore on May 7, 1886, under the name of Henry Stiner, charged with burglary. He pleaded guilty on June 3, 1886, and was sentenced to five years in State prison.

His picture is an excellent one, taken in May, 1886.

191

JULIUS KLEIN, alias YOUNG JULIUS,
alias SAMUEL FRANK.
SNEAK, SHOPLIFTER AND PICKPOCKET.

DESCRIPTION.

Twenty-four years old in 1886. Born in Germany. Single. Furrier by trade. Slim build. Height, 5 feet 7¼ inches. Weight, 122 pounds. Brown hair, hazel eyes, light complexion. Strong bushy hair. Has a mole on his left arm.

RECORD.

"Young' Julius is a very smart young sneak thief and shoplifter. He is well known in a number of the Eastern cities, especially in New York and Boston, where he has served terms in State prison. He is a sneak thief well worth knowing.

He was arrested in New York City in June, 1882, for the larceny of a gold watch from a passenger on a Long Branch boat. He obtained $1,000 bail and was released.

He was arrested again in New York City in October, 1882, for the larceny of $100 from a lady while she was admiring the bonnets displayed in a Sixth Avenue window. Although morally convinced that Klein was the party who robbed her, the lady refused to make a complaint against him and he was discharged.

He was arrested again in New York City on October 14, 1882, in company of Henry Hoffman (190) and Frank Watson, alias Big Patsey, two other notorious New York sneaks and shoplifters, charged with robbing the store of W. A. Thomas & Co., dealers in tailors' trimmings, No. 35 Avon Street, Boston, Mass., of property valued at $3,500. All three of them were delivered to the Boston police authorities, taken there, tried and convicted. Hoffman and Watson were sentenced to three years in Concord prison, on November 24, 1882, and Klein to two years in the House of Correction.

Julius was arrested again in New York City on November 27, 1885, in company of Frank Watson, alias Big Patsey, charged with (shoplifting) the larceny of some velvet and braid, valued at $60, from the store of A. C. Cammant, No. 173 William Street. Both pleaded guilty and were sentenced to one year in the penitentiary on Blackwell's Island, New York, on December 17, 1885, in the Court of General Sessions.

Klein's sentence will expire on December 16, 1886.

His picture is a good one, taken in April, 1882.

192

JOHN CARROLL, alias THE KID,
alias Barnes.

BANK SNEAK.

DESCRIPTION.

Twenty-three years old in 1886. Born in New York. Single. No trade. Medium build. Height, 5 feet 3½ inches. Weight, 115 pounds. Brown hair, blue eyes, straight nose, slim face, light complexion. Has India ink spot on left arm.

RECORD.

Young Carroll is a first-class bank sneak. He traveled through the country with Charles J. Everhardt, alias Marsh Market Jake (30), working the banks. Carroll was known as "Marsh Market Jake's Kid." A number of people claim that this is the boy that used to work with Rufe Minor, alias Pine (1). Such is not the case, as Jake brought this boy out and left him behind him in Baltimore. He is not the first man that Jake left behind.

Jake and "The Kid" entered the Citizens' Bank in Baltimore, Md., on October 22, 1885, and did what is called a ' turn trick." A citizen, named Jeremiah Townsend, had drawn some money and was in the act of counting it, when Carroll, who gave the name of James F. Barnes, called his attention to some bills on the floor. While Mr. Townsend was in the act of picking up the money from the floor, Carroll snatched $525 of the money from the desk. He was not quick enough, however, as Mr. Townsend caught him and held him until he was arrested. Jake, as usual, made good his escape.

Carroll, alias Barnes, pleaded guilty and was sentenced to five years and six months in the Maryland penitentiary, at Baltimore, on October 24, 1885.

See Commutation Laws of Maryland for expiration of sentence.

Carroll's picture is an excellent one, taken in October, 1885.

193

GEORGE BELL, alias WILLIAMS.
PICKPOCKET, SNEAK AND FORGER.

DESCRIPTION.

Forty years old in 1886. Born in United States. Single. No trade. A well-built man. Height, 5 feet 11½ inches. Weight, 180 pounds. Brown hair, hazel eyes, light complexion. Vaccination mark on right arm. Small scar on right arm, above the wrist. Scar on right temple, over the eye. He is generally clean-shaven, and affects a staid and religious air during his operations.

RECORD.

GEORGE BELL is as good a general thief as there is in this country. He is well known in most of the principal cities in the United States and Europe, having operated with Charles O. Brockway, alias Vanderpool (14), the celebrated forger, on both sides of the water, and was considered one of Brockway's cleverest men. Bell has traveled considerably, but claims New York City as his home. He has been a professional thief, forger and manipulator of forged paper for years.

He was arrested in Philadelphia, Pa., on March 25, 1876, and sentenced to one year in Cherry Hill prison. Shortly after his discharge he was arrested again, in Philadelphia for a "pennyweight" robbery, and sentenced to eighteen months in the Philadelphia County prison. Early in 1880 Bell went to Europe with Al. Wilson, Cleary and others, for the purpose of flooding the Continent with forged circular notes. The scheme, which was managed by George Wilkes, Engle and Becker, proved a failure, and they returned to America.

Bell, Charles Farren, alias the "Big Duke," and Henry Cleary, were arrested in New York City on July 27, 1880, charged with having defrauded the Merchants' National Bank and the Third National Bank of Baltimore, Md., to the amount of $12,000, by forged checks, on July 16 and 17, 1880.

Farren was discharged for want of evidence.

Cleary was claimed by the Albany (N. Y.) police authorities, and delivered to them, to answer a charge of forgery (a check for $490), for which he was tried, convicted, and sentenced to two years and six months in Dannemora prison, New York State, in November, 1880.

Bell was delayed in New York City, by habeas corpus proceedings, until August 1880, when he was delivered to Deputy Marshal Frey, of Baltimore, Md., and taken to that city by him. He was tried in Baltimore on November 30, 1880. The trial lasted until December 1, when the jury disagreed. He was tried again on December 16 and 17, 1880, with the same result. The venue was changed, and he was again tried, in an adjoining county. This trial resulted in a conviction, and he was sentenced to ten years in State prison on July 9, 1881.

Bell's sentence will expire on October 9, 1889. (See records of No. 37 and George Wilkes.)

When Henry Cleary's sentence expired in the Albany (N. Y.) case he was arrested at Clinton prison, Dannemora, N. Y., and taken to Baltimore, Md., where he pleaded guilty to forgery, and was sentenced to the Maryland penitentiary for five years on January 17, 1883, by Judge Phelps, of Baltimore, Md.

His picture is a good one, taken in 1876.

194

CHARLES WOODWARD, alias WILLIAMS,

alias The Diamond Swallower, alias Hoyt, alias C. B. Anderson, alias Henderson.

SNEAK AND PENNYWEIGHT.

DESCRIPTION.

Forty-five years old in 1886. Jew, born in America. Married. No trade. Medium build. Height, 5 feet 8½ inches. Weight, about 150 pounds. Dark hair, turning gray; dark eyes, dark complexion. Generally wears a black mustache.

RECORD.

Woodward, alias Williams, is one of the most notorious sneak thieves and shoplifters there is in America. He is known all over the United States and Canada as the "Palmer House Robber." This thief was arrested in New York some years ago for the larceny of a diamond from a jewelry store. When detected he had the stone in his mouth, and swallowed it. He has served terms in State prison in New York, Pennsylvania, Illinois and Canada, and is considered a very smart thief.

He was arrested in Chicago, Ill., and sentenced to one year in Joliet prison on January 31, 1879, for the larceny of a trunk containing $15,000 worth of jewelry samples from a salesman in the Palmer House. The jewelry was recovered.

Another well known sneak thief was also arrested in this case, and sentenced to five years in Joliet prison on February 1, 1879. Since then, it is claimed, he has reformed, and I therefore omit his name.

Woodward, alias Williams, was arrested again in Philadelphia, on April 16, 1880, in company of William Hillburn, alias Marsh Market Jake (38), and Billy Morgan (72), for the larceny of $2,200 in bank bills from a man named Henry Ruddy. The trio were tried, convicted and sentenced to eighteen months in the Eastern Penitentiary on April 26, 1880.

Woodward was arrested again at Rochester, N. Y., under the name of Charles B. Anderson, alias Charles B. Henderson, and sentenced on September 18, 1883, to two years in the Monroe County (N. Y.) Penitentiary, for grand larceny in the second degree; tried again the same day, convicted, and sentenced on another complaint of grand larceny in the second degree to two years more, making four years in all, by Judge Rouley, Judge of Monroe County, N. Y.

His sentence will expire, allowing him full commutation, on September 18, 1886.

His picture is a fair one, taken in April, 1880.

195

JOE RICKERMAN, alias NIGGER BAKER.

PICKPOCKET AND BURGLAR.

DESCRIPTION.

Thirty-nine years old in 1886. Born in New York. Single. No trade. Medium build. Height, 5 feet 6¾ inches. Weight, 145 pounds. Black hair, hazel eyes, dark complexion. Generally wears a black mustache. Two vaccination marks on right arm.

RECORD.

JOE RICKERMAN, alias "Nigger" Baker, so called on account of his very dark complexion, is a well known New York burglar and pickpocket. He is an associate of Will Kennedy, Joe Gorman (146), Big Jim Casey (91), "Poodle" Murphy (134), "Pretty" Jimmie (143), Jimmy Scraggins, and other well known New York thieves and pickpockets. He is pretty well known in all the Eastern cities, especially in Philadelphia and New York, where his picture is in the Rogues' Gallery. He has served terms in prison in Philadelphia (Pa.), Sing Sing (N. Y.), and in the penitentiary on Blackwell's

Island, and is considered a very handy man with a set of tools. Of late years Joe has been traveling through the country, "stalling" for a gang of pickpockets.

He was arrested in New York City and sentenced to three years and six months in Sing Sing prison for burglary, on September 15, 1881.

His sentence expired on July 15, 1884.

Rickerman's picture is a good one, taken in November, 1878.

196

WILLIAM HAGUE, alias CURLY HARRIS,
alias JAMES MARTIN.

BURGLAR, HOTEL SNEAK AND MURDERER.

DESCRIPTION.

Forty-three years old in 1886. Jew, born in United States. Married. No trade. Medium build. Height, 5 feet 5¾ inches. Weight, about 140 pounds. Looks like, and is, a Jew. Dark eyes, black curly hair, dark complexion. Generally wears a black mustache. Four dots of India ink on left arm. Has a vaccination mark and mole on right arm above the elbow.

RECORD.

"CURLY" HARRIS is one of the most desperate thieves and ruffians in America. He is well known in all the large cities in the United States, especially in Philadelphia, where he makes his home.

Harris, with "Brummagen Bill" and James Elliott, two other notorious Philadelphia thieves, robbed Hughy Dougherty, the minstrel performer, in a saloon on Ninth Street, above Jayne, in Philadelphia, some years ago. The thieves subsequently, in passing the corner of Sixth and Market streets, were accosted by Officer Murphy, whereupon Harris deliberately drew his revolver and fired. The ball, fortunately for the officer, struck the buckle of his belt, which saved his life. "Brummagen Bill" and Elliott were arrested and convicted, and sentenced respectively to eleven and sixteen years' imprisonment in the Eastern Penitentiary. Harris escaped, but was afterwards arrested in Pittsburg, Pa. The authorities of Philadelphia chartered a special car, and traveled westward after the fugitive criminal. While returning, Harris, with his hands still manacled, escaped from his captors, and although the train was traveling at the rate of forty miles an hour, he jumped from the rear platform of a car, and a diligent search failed to reveal his whereabouts.

Nothing was heard of "Curly" for some years, and this was owing to the fact that he had been arrested and convicted in the northern part of the State of New York for a hotel robbery, and sentenced to six years in State prison.

After his release he boldly went back to Philadelphia, and was arrested there for robbing the American Hotel. He was acquitted, however, and when the old charge against him for the Dougherty affair was spoken of, it was found that the minstrel performer and the officer could not be found to prosecute him.

Harris was arrested again in New York City on May 6, 1880, and delivered to the police authorities of Philadelphia, charged with the murder of James Reilly, alias John Davis, another hotel thief. The murder was committed on August 25, 1879. Reilly resided with his wife on Orange Street, Philadelphia. Upon the day mentioned he was picked up bleeding in front of a saloon at Eighth and Sansom streets. On September 13, 1879, the wounded man died from a fracture of the skull. From facts subsequently gathered it appears that Harris met Reilly and asked him for some money, and the latter replied that he had none. He was then told to go to his wife and obtain some, which he abruptly declined to do. Harris, in his usual cowardly manner, drew a revolver, aimed it directly at his partner in crime and pulled the trigger. The cartridge did not explode, and the desperado then pushed the barrel of his pistol with so much force into one of Reilly's eyes as to fracture his skull and cause his death. Harris was tried and convicted in June, 1880, and sentenced to ten years in State prison on July 3, 1880, by Judge Yerkers, in Philadelphia. His sentence will expire on June 3, 1888.

His picture is a good one, taken in 1876.

197

WALTER PRICE, alias HENRY,
alias Lewis, alias Gregory.

PICKPOCKET AND SHOPLIFTER.

DESCRIPTION.

Forty-seven years old in 1886. Born in United States. Married. No trade. Stout build. Height, 5 feet 8½ inches. Weight, 180 pounds. Sandy hair, gray eyes, light complexion. Sometimes wears a light beard; generally shaved clean. Quite a clerical-looking old fellow.

RECORD.

Price is no doubt one of the most expert old pickpockets and shoplifters in America. He is known from Maine to California, and has served terms in prison in almost every State in the Union. This man generally works with a smart woman, doing the "stalling" for her; he, however, is quite handy himself, and does considerable work alone.

He was arrested in New York City, in company of one George Williams, for shoplifting. He was charged with the larceny of a silver watch from a jewelry store. In this case Price and Williams, on a plea of guilty, were sentenced to six months in the penitentiary on February 18, 1875, in the Court of General Sessions. Price gave the name of Louis Lewis.

After this he is credited with serving another term in Sing Sing prison.

He was arrested again in New York City, on November 24, 1879, under the name of George W. Henry, in company of Mary Grey, alias Ellen Clegg (115), another notorious female pickpocket and shoplifter. The complainant testified that Price and Ellen visited his establishment on November 24, and while Price engaged the attention of one of the salesmen by exhibiting a sample piece of silk, stating he wanted a large quantity of the pattern, Ellen, who carried a large bag or "kick," quietly slipped into its recesses $120 worth of silk which lay on the counter. As they were leaving the store, which was at No. 454 Broome Street, New York City, one of the salesmen missed the goods and caused their arrest. On the way to the police station, Ellen tried to drop the bag which was under her dress, but she was detected in the act. Both pleaded guilty in the Court of General Sessions, before Judge Gildersleeve, on December 16, 1879, when Price was sentenced to three years in State Prison at Sing Sing, and Clegg to three years in the penitentiary on Blackwell's Island, New York City.

Price's picture is a very good one, although taken ten years ago.

198

JOHN, alias "JOE," PETTENGILL.
BURGLAR, FORGER AND COUNTERFEITER.

DESCRIPTION.

Fifty-one years old in 1886. Born in the United States. Single. No trade. Stout build. Height, 5 feet 6 inches. Weight, about 150 pounds. Blue eyes, very weak; light hair, light complexion. Thick lower lip, broad, high forehead. Has India ink marks on left arm and back of left hand. Small scar on back of neck from a boil.

RECORD.

PETTENGILL is an old New York thief. He is what may be called a general thief, as he can turn his hand to almost anything—burglary, boarding-house work, handling forged paper or bonds, counterfeiting, etc. He has been arrested in almost every State from Maine to California, and has spent considerable of his life in State prison. He is well known in all the cities, and is considered more of a tool than a principal.

He was arrested in Philadelphia, Pa., on June 24, 1875, and sentenced to two years in Cherry Hill prison. Since then he has served terms in Sing Sing prison, New York, and other places.

He was finally arrested in the ferry house in Hoboken, N. J., on April 18, 1885, in company of Theodore Krewolf, charged with passing a number of counterfeit ten-dollar bills, of the series of 1875, on several shopkeepers in Hoboken. He was sentenced to six years in Trenton State prison for this offense, on July 22, 1885.

His picture is a good one, taken in June, 1875.

199
SAM PERRIS, alias WORCESTER SAM.
BANK BURGLAR.

DESCRIPTION.

Forty-six years old in 1886. Born in Canada. A French Canadian. Single. No trade. Height, 5 feet 8 inches. Weight, about 180 pounds. Looks something like a Swede or German. Brown hair, blue eyes, light complexion. Face rather short. Has a prominent dimple in his chin. Is thick set and very muscular. Has a quick, careless gait. Speaks English without French accent; also, French fluently. He changes the style of his beard continually, and is "smooth-faced" a part of the time. Generally wears some beard on account of his pictures having been taken with smooth face. He drinks freely and spends money rapidly. He has a scar from a pistol-shot on his right eyebrow.

RECORD.

"WORCESTER" SAM is one of the most notorious criminals in America. He has figured in the annals of crime in the Eastern and New England States for years. He is an associate of Old Jimmie Hope (20), Mike Kerrigan, alias Johnny Dobbs (64), and all the most expert men in the country. He has no doubt participated in every bank robbery of any magnitude that has taken place in the United States for the past twenty years. He is a man of undoubted nerve, and has a first-class reputation among the fraternity. His specialty is banks and railroad office safes.

Sam is wanted now by the Worcester (Mass.) police; also, for the robbery and alleged murder of Cashier Barron, of the Dexter Bank of Maine. He was in custody at Worcester, Mass., but escaped from jail there on April 5, 1872. He has never been recaptured, although there is a standing reward of $3,000 offered for him by the county commissioners. (See records of George Wilkes and No. 50.)

Perris's picture is the best in existence. It was copied from one taken with a companion, and resembles him very much.

200
JOSEPH BOND, alias PAPER COLLAR JOE.
BANCO STEERER.

DESCRIPTION.

Thirty-six years old in 1886. Born in United States. Married. No trade. Medium build. Height, 5 feet 7½ inches. Weight, about 148 pounds. Dark hair, hazel eyes, light complexion. Generally wears sandy side-whiskers and mustache. High forehead. Looks somewhat like a Jew.

RECORD.

"PAPER COLLAR" JOE is a well known banco man. He formerly hailed from Philadelphia, but is well known in New York and other large cities. He is considered one of the smartest men in the banco business.

Bond was arrested in Philadelphia during the Centennial, and sentenced to one year in Cherry Hill prison on August 1, 1876, for plying his vocation on a stranger. He has been arrested time and time again, but like all the men in that line of business, is seldom punished. He is credited with fleecing a man in Pennsylvania out of five thousand dollars in October, 1885, and at last accounts he had taken a trip to Europe.

Joe's picture was taken in August, 1876.

201

THOMAS McCORMACK, alias TOM McCORMACK.

BANK BURGLAR.

DESCRIPTION.

Forty-three years old in 1883. Born in United States. Married. Machinist. Medium build. Height, 5 feet 8¼ inches. Weight, 150 pounds. Hair black, turning gray; dark gray eyes, very dark complexion. Looks like a Spaniard. Generally wears a full black whisker and mustache. Dresses well, and is a great wine drinker.

RECORD.

THOMAS McCORMACK has had a checkered career and is a desperate man. He was associated from time to time with all the first-class bank burglars, and was implicated in many important bank robberies. Several years ago he shot and killed Big John Casey, another burglar, over a quarrel on the division of the moneys stolen from the Kensington Savings Bank in Philadelphia, which they and others had robbed on February 4, 1871, of a large amount of money.

The bank referred to was robbed by McCormack, Casey, Dobbs, Brady, Burns, alias Combo, and three others. One of them during the day went to the president and represented having been sent by the Chief of Police to tell him that information had been received that either that night or the one following the bank was to be robbed. That he must not impart this information to any one, but that the Chief would send three or four policemen in uniform that afternoon, who were to be locked in the bank, and that the president could leave a porter with them. This programme was followed out, and two watchmen were left. When night set in they sent one of the watchmen out for beer, and during his absence bound and gagged the other, and tied him up in a back room. On the return of the other they served him the same way, and then proceeded to rob the bank. They secured between $80,000 and $100,000.

McCormack was arrested in New Haven, Conn., by Marshal Hamilton, on Sunday evening, December 9, 1882, for breaking open and robbing a safe in Walpole, N. H., on the night of December 8, 1882. When arrested in New Haven he gave the name James Crandell. He was taken to Keene, N. H., on December 21, 1882, and upon an examination he was committed to await the action of the Grand Jury. He was indicted on April 1, 1883. He pleaded guilty and was sentenced to eight years in State prison on April 12, 1883.

Sam Perris, alias Worcester Sam, was with McCormack in this robbery, but escaped after a desperate fight with the officers, who only succeeded in holding McCormack.

For further particulars see records of Nos. 89 and 131.

His picture is a fair one, taken on June 27, 1877.

202

CHARLES WILLIAMSON, alias PERRINE.

BANK OF ENGLAND FORGER.

DESCRIPTION.

Forty-three years old in 1886. Born in Malone, New York State. Single. Professional forger. Stout, portly built man. Height, 5 feet 9½ inches. Weight, 220 pounds. Brown hair, hazel eyes, dark complexion. Generally wears a full black beard. Dresses well, and converses in an easy tone.

RECORD.

WILLIAMSON, alias PERRINE (the latter is his right name), is one of the most extraordinary criminals this country has ever produced—a man of great ability, imposing appearance, and iron nerve. Himself and William E. Grey are credited with being the two smartest people in their line in the world.

A man who gave the name of George A. Vincent, was arrested by the St. Louis police on February 29, 1884. The charge against him was attempting to pass forged drafts on New York City. Vincent had evidently set out on an elaborate scheme of robbery. He had opened accounts in several of the St. Louis banks, and at once began the deposit of a large number of drafts, and appeared, from the accounts, to be doing a very brisk business. He was a portly man, and would be described in brief as a "solid business man." The Chief of Police, who had carefully worked the case up, was convinced that his prisoner was a criminal of no ordinary type, and that he belonged to the upper circles of professional forgers. The police of St. Louis were detailed to look at the alleged Vincent, but not a man on the force had ever seen him before. A photograph was taken, and with a description annexed was sent to the police of several cities. At once came back a series of responses, and the man was shown to be none other than Charles Perrine, alias Charles J. Williamson, alias Charles

Sherwood, alias Charles Cherwood, alias Stevens, well known in this city as a burglar and forger, and particularly valuable to the gangs of forgers as a "layer down" or presenter at the banks and banking offices of the forged paper prepared by other hands. His appearance was very much in his favor for his part of the business, and few of the extensive forgeries of a dozen years past were carried on without the assistance of Perrine, under some alias. He came of a family in the northern part of New York State, and has a brother-in-law now doing business in Wall Street, New York. His family, which is of the highest respectability, have long since cut off this member and utterly ignore him.

He first came into the hands of the police about fifteen years ago, when, under the name of Stevens, he was convicted on a charge of burglary, a quantity of silk and fine cutlery having been removed by him from the bonded warehouse in Howard Street, New York City. He served four years for this (his time expired on March 1, 1873), and upon his release was not heard of again until August, 1873, when a wholesale scheme of plunder was started, and bonds to the amount of more than a million dollars were placed on the market. Among the bonds cleverly counterfeited were those of the Buffalo, New York and Erie Road, the New York Central and the Chicago and Northwestern. They were counterfeited so well that they readily passed muster before bank clerks and cashiers. The gang that was interested in the gigantic steal included Roberts and Gleason, Walter Stewart, alias Sheridan ; Steve Raymond, Spence Pettis (now dead), and Dr. Blaisell (now dead).

Three different banking houses on Wall Street, New York, were forced into bankruptcy because of the number of the forged bonds which had found their way into the strong boxes of the firms. Among the houses victimized were the New York Guarantee and Indemnity Company and the National Trust Company. Perrine as Charles D. Williamson acted as the banker for the forgers, and all the bogus bonds passed through his hands and were by him put on the street. His share of the proceeds of the transactions, it is said, amounted to about $100,000. He was among the first of the gang to disappear when the exposure came. He went abroad, and for a time was lost in Great Britain.

In 1875 a man sold, or attempted to sell, to Rollins Brothers, of Broad and Wall streets, New York, a number of seven per cent. gold bonds of the Central Pacific road, California and Oregon branch. These were detected as counterfeits, and as the seller was to call on the following day with an additional number of the bonds, the Captain of the New Street police station was notified and took the man into custody. He had given the name of Howard, but he turned out to be the Charles J. Williamson who was "wanted" for the big forgeries of three years previous. He was taken to the District Attorney's Office, where from the pigeon-holes were drawn out a number of indictments against him in connection with the previous forgeries on the Buffalo, New York and Erie, and other roads named. The District Attorney insisted upon bail for the entire batch, and this making up a great aggregate, Williamson was unable to command it, and remained in the Tombs until his trial. This occupied several days, and a hard fight was made to save the now celebrated criminal, but he was convicted, and sentenced on October 31, 1876, to the limit of ten years in the State prison. Upon motion of an Assistant District Attorney, who had conducted the case, an additional five years was added to the sentence—making fifteen years in all—because it was the second offense of the prisoner.   He was sent to Sing Sing, and at once began plotting for an escape.   He, with several other convicts, entered into a conspiracy.   The bake-house was fired, and in the confusion which followed a number escaped.   The majority were retaken, but Williamson got away.   This was on June 26, 1877, about eight months after his arrival at the prison.

He went to London, and there, under the name of Charles Cherwood, alias Sherwood, was arrested in March, 1878, for some forgeries directed against the Union Bank of London, by which that institution was to be swindled by means of false drafts and bills of exchange on the Continent.   The Scotland Yard force had made the arrest, and knowing that they had an American professional, they sent a photograph and description to New York City, and word was sent back telling who the man was, and giving his entire unsavory American record.   He was tried, and received, after conviction, a ten years' sentence.   He at once turned State's evidence, and by his information an extended conspiracy on the part of American forgers to operate in England and on the Continent of Europe was laid bare.   Dan Noble, Joe Chapman and Clutch Donohue were arrested, and, on the evidence of Williamson, convicted.   In return his sentence was shortened, and in October, 1883, he was released.

Fearing to come direct to New York City, he took ship for Canada, and thence crossed the line, and about January 15, 1884, he was seen in New York, and then went West, to begin business at St. Louis.

He was held without bail to answer the charges of the bank officials in St. Louis, but steps were taken to bring him back to Sing Sing, to serve the fourteen years and four months still charged against him on the books of the prison.

Williamson was convicted in St. Louis, Mo., for attempting to swindle the St. Louis National Bank out of $6,500, by means of a forged letter of credit, and was sentenced to ten years in the penitentiary on February 11, 1885.

See records of Nos. 16, 18, and George Wilkes.

Williamson's picture, which was taken in England, is an excellent one.   The Slate shows his handwriting.

203
ALBERT WISE, alias JAKE SONDHEIM,
alias AL. WILSON, alias JEW AL, alias JAMES T. WATSON, alias CHAS. H. WHITTEMORE.
PICKPOCKET, SNEAK, CONFIDENCE MAN AND FORGER.

DESCRIPTION.

Forty-three years old in 1886.   A Jew, born in Germany.   Married.   No trade. Slim build.   Height, 5 feet 6½ inches.   Weight, 120 pounds.   Light brown hair, light brown whiskers and mustache, light complexion, blue eyes. Has a small India ink spot on the left hand between the thumb and forefinger, and a small dark mole on the back of the left hand. Two vaccination marks on each arm. Wears a No. 7 shoe.

RECORD.

WISE, or SONDHEIM (the latter is supposed to be his right name), is a very clever professional pickpocket, bank sneak, confidence man, forger and swindler. He is well known all over the United States, and has been arrested in almost every city in the Union, several of which have his picture in the Rogues' Gallery.

He was arrested in Philadelphia, Pa., on April 7, 1877, for a sneak robbery.

He was arrested again in Boston, Mass., on July 10, 1880, charged with obtaining $1,000 in money from one H. P. Line, in July, 1875, by falsely representing to him that he had a large amount of jewelry in Adams Express Company's office, and showed him a bill of the goods marked C. O. D. This case was nolle prosequi, on account of some valuable information given by him to the police authorities in relation to some bank robberies.

He was next arrested in Buffalo, N. Y., under the name of James T. Watson, tried, found guilty in the Superior Court, of forgery and swindling, and sentenced to five years in Auburn prison, New York, on February 7, 1883.

The history of Watson's operations reveals a series of swindles such as none but a professional could have worked. About the middle of November, 1882, a stranger called at the Merchants' Bank of Buffalo, New York, and stating that he was in the lumber business, and wished to open an account, deposited $600 in currency. A similar statement was made to the cashier of the Manufacturers and Traders' Bank of that city, and $1,000 was deposited there. Subsequently Watson deposited in the Merchants' Bank a draft for $1,700, made by the Second National Bank, of Wilkesbarre, Pa., upon the Fourth National Bank of New York.

A draft for $3,400, made by the Cleveland National Bank of Commerce upon the Manhattan Bank of New York, was also deposited in the Manufacturers and Traders' Bank. Within two days Watson checked against these amounts, leaving but a small balance to his credit. Shortly afterward the Merchants' Bank discovered that the $1,700 draft had been raised from $17. The other draft was also shown to have been raised from $34. Search was made for Watson, but he had flown, leaving no trace. Descriptions of the swindler and his operations were immediately scattered through the country. A New York detective, seeing the description, immediately associated the criminal with the well known professional " Al " Wilson. Wilson was arrested and held until some of the bank officers from Buffalo arrived to identify him. They were accompanied by Joseph Short, a boy whom Watson employed in his office. The latter immediately identified the swindler. Notwithstanding Wilson's protestations that he was not the man and had not been out of New York in six months, he was taken to Buffalo, indicted and held for trial.

The trial took place on February 6, 1883, and the court room was crowded. The prisoner, who is a bright, good-looking fellow, appeared sanguine of acquittal, which feeling was shared by his counsel. The bank officials were positive that Wilson was the man, but their testimony was exceedingly conflicting. The office boy swore positively that Wilson and Watson were identical. The Maverick National Bank of Boston, learning of the arrest, sent a clerk, Henry A. Lowell, to ascertain whether the accused was the individual who swindled its institution of nearly $5,000 under like circumstances a short time before. Lowell identified the prisoner, and swore that he operated in Boston under the name of Whittemore. The defense produced a number of witnesses from New York, who swore that Wilson was in the metropolis when the crime was committed. Detectives from New York testified that Wilson was a professional thief, and had been so for years. Certain witnesses swore that the prisoner had worn a beard during November, and others swore that he wore only a mustache.

The testimony being so conflicting, public interest was excited as to the result. The judge's charge was against the prisoner, and the jury retired at noon, returning at 3:30 P. M., on February 7, 1883, with a verdict of guilty. Watson, who had looked for an acquittal, was surprised, but maintained his composure. Before the sentence was passed he made an eloquent appeal for leniency on the part of the court. He said that he had a wife and mother, who were left penniless. Rising to his full height, he denied that he was a professional thief and said that his innocence would be proved some day. He requested that he might be sent to Sing Sing instead of Auburn, which request was denied. The spectators in court were unanimously of the opinion that Watson is the coolest rascal ever seen.

Sondheim's Boston operations were as follows: Some time in August, 1882, under the name of Whittemore, he went into the Maverick National Bank and deposited the sum of $2,000, announcing his determination to carry on business at the bank. The following day he entered the bank, bringing with him a boy whom he introduced as a messenger, and who, so he said, would transact his business for him. He then began to draw against the deposit until it was almost gone, when he reappeared and deposited a check for $5,000.

The next day the boy also reappeared and drew one-half of the $5,000 deposited, and finished on the following day with drawing the entire deposit, minus about $17. Whittemore, after making a similar attempt upon another banking house in Boston, took his departure for Portland, Me., where he also tried to victimize a banking institution. He then went to Buffalo, where he carried on the operations for which he was found guilty, as above stated.

His sentence will expire September 7, 1886.

Wise's picture is a pretty good one, taken in April, 1877.

204
LOUIS BROWN, alias FRENCH LOUIE.
BURGLAR, TOOL–MAKER AND KEY–FITTER.

DESCRIPTION.

Fifty-nine years old in 1886. Born in France. Married. Machinist. Slim build. Height, 5 feet 10 inches. Weight, about 145 pounds. Gray hair, very thin; hazel eyes, fair complexion. Large nose. Thin face. Small mole near right eye. Wife's name, Annie L. Wolf.

RECORD.

BROWN, or FRENCH LOUIE, the name he is best known by, is one of the most expert burglars in America. His particular line is the manufacture of burglars' tools and making false keys from impressions in wax. He seldom takes a hand in a burglary, unless it is a large one. He generally paves the way for the operations of confederates, and works from 6 A. M. to 8 A. M. in the morning, when his operations can generally be carried on with impunity, as any person seeing him at that hour would fancy that he was simply opening the store for the day's business. French Louie has spent at least twenty years in State prison in America, two-thirds of it in Sing Sing prison, New York.

Louie was arrested in New York City on July 15, 1877, in the act of committing a burglary at Nos. 27 and 29 White Street. He was convicted and sentenced to three years and three months in State prison at Sing Sing, N. Y., on August 16, 1877. He escaped from Sing Sing on July 16, 1878, and was re-arrested in Philadelphia, Pa., on February 18, 1879, and returned to Sing Sing prison to serve out his unexpired time.

He was arrested again in New York City, on August 27, 1881, for tampering with the padlock on the store of E. H. Gato & Co., No. 52 Beaver Street. There was $50,000 worth of imported cigars in the store at the time. Louie pleaded guilty of an attempt at burglary, and was sentenced to two years and six months in State prison, on September 12, 1881, by Recorder Smyth, in the Court of General Sessions, New York City. His time expired on October 12, 1883.

French Louie was arrested again, under the name of John Yole, in Hoboken, N. J., on March 18, 1886, and sentenced to ninety days under the Disorderly Act. He had some tools and keys in his possession when arrested. His case was referred to the Grand Jury, which body failed to indict him.

Brown's picture is an excellent one, taken in Philadelphia, Pa.

193

GEORGE BELL,
PICKPOCKET, SNEAK AND FORGER.

194

CHARLES WOODWARD,
ALIAS THE DIAMOND SWALLOWER,
SNEAK AND PENNY WEIGHT.

195

JOSEPH RICKERMAN,
ALIAS NIGGER BAKER,
PICKPOCKET AND BURGLAR.

196

WILLIAM HAGUE,
ALIAS CURLEY HARRIS,
BURGLAR AND SNEAK.

197

WALTER PRICE,
ALIAS HENRY LEWIS,
PICKPOCKET AND SHOP LIFTER.

198

JOHN PETTINGILL,
BURGLAR AND FORGER.

SEVERAL NOTABLE FORGERS.

WHILE the records given in the preceding pages are those of the professional forgers of to-day, a few of the men who figured prominently in criminal proceedings in the past cannot be left unnoticed. Several of these have been lost sight of for years, and some are perhaps dead, but as their exploits shed light upon crimes of the past and point to a moral, their careers are certainly worthy of mention here.

WALTER G. PATTERSON was a quarter of a century ago classed as an expert forger. His first crime of note was on June 1, 1861, when he succeeded in cashing at the Pacific National Bank of New York a check for $1,075. It was made payable to the Hon. Simeon Draper, Commissioner of Charities and Corrections, and bore the forged signature of Henry Carr. The forger was run down, but he was afterwards released on bail, which he forfeited and fled from the city. He was recaptured in June, 1865, and when called for trial pleaded guilty. Recorder Hoffman, before whom Patterson was arraigned, after the prisoner's confession of guilt, and upon a promise to reform, suspended sentence. In the August following the forger was again arrested upon the old charge, and the Recorder then sentenced him to five years in Sing Sing prison. Previous to his being brought up for the Pacific Bank forgery, Patterson was living with a woman named Ryan at Collins's Hotel, at the foot of Canal Street. The pair occupied costly apartments at the hotel, were spending money freely, and it was suspected that the self-confessed forger was concerned in the passing of several other checks, although it was impossible to fasten the crimes legally upon him.

Vermillyea & Co., bankers of this city, in February, 1870, gave a certified check for $156, payable at the Bank of Commerce, to a stranger who had had a small business transaction with them. The draft was afterwards "raised" to $16,000, and deposited with the Mechanics' Banking Association for collection. The Bank of Commerce paid the check on their own certification. This led to a long litigation, which resulted in a verdict for the Bank of Commerce, the courts holding that it was only responsible for the original amount of the certification of the check. It was well known that Walter G. Patterson and Spence Pettis were the men who secured the large sum of money upon the raised paper. Pettis was an expert in the use of chemicals, and it was claimed that he altered the figures upon the check.

When the forgery was discovered Patterson had disappeared. Pettis was arrested, however, but was afterwards released for want of evidence. When the case fell through the prisoner was sent to Boston, Mass., to answer for a forgery which he had committed there. Pettis was convicted of the latter offense, and while serving his sentence in the Charlestown State prison the convict hanged himself to the grating of his cell door. Thus ended the career of a most notorious criminal.

JOHN ROSS, while plotting several gigantic schemes in 1866, lived in princely style at the Metropolitan Hotel. He ran an office in Exchange Place for two months, and during that period had large transactions with brokers, buying and selling gold. In that way he secured their confidence. This obtained, he bought gold to the amount of $1,000,000, and gave his own certified checks in payment. The checks were worthless. A few days previous to the stupendous transaction in gold, Ross employed Garten & Co., of Broad Street, to buy for him a number of Western railroad bonds, for which he paid in good money. On the day of his disappearance Ross hypothecated for a loan of $17,000 from the bankers a bundle of bonds supposed to be the identical ones they had purchased for him. When, however, his forgeries became known, Garten & Co. discovered that the bonds on which they had advanced money to Ross were counterfeits.

After plundering right and left, Ross boarded a steamer for South America, leaving the vessel at Pernambuco, Brazil. He was tracked to Bahia and Rio Janeiro, and at the latter place all trace of the fugitive was lost.

JOHN HENRY LIVINGSTON, alias Lewis, alias Matthews, alias De Peyster, on December 3, 1867, in the garb of an express messenger, with the words "American Express Co." upon a plate on the front of his cap, appeared at the National City Bank. From a large leather wallet the spurious messenger took a check drawn to the order of Henry Keep, President of the New York Central and Hudson River Railroad, and signed "C. Vanderbilt." The check also bore the endorsement, "American Express— collect and deliver at Albany—Henry Keep." Livingston presented the forged draft to Mr. Work, the paying teller, and requested that bills of a certain denomination be used in making up the package, saying that he would return in a few minutes, having another errand close by. On his return to the bank Livingston was handed the package, containing $75,000, the amount called for by the fraudulent check.

With the money he fled to the West, where he purchased a farm and engaged in stock raising. He was captured there a year or so afterwards. There was a peculiar and interesting incident in connection with the search for the forger. The features and manners of Livingston were so impressed upon Mr. Work's mind, and his recollection of the entire transaction was so clear that it enabled him to draw a pen and ink sketch of the "layer down." The portrait revealed Livingston's identity and led to his arrest.

The prisoner, when brought to trial, pleaded guilty, and was sentenced to four years and nine months' imprisonment. His farm and stock were confiscated, and the proceeds of the sale given to the bank he had duped.

CHARLES B. ORVIS was in 1873 the proprietor of the City Hotel, and the place was then the rendezvous of the gang of forgers of which Roberts and Gleason were the leading spirits. The hotel keeper had long been a shady character. He was originally a "coniacker" (dealer in counterfeit money), and was first arrested at Cleveland, Ohio, with a confederate named Webster for passing forged bank-bills.   They were convicted and sentenced to three and a half years each in the Columbus Penitentiary, and they served their full terms.

Orvis, in June, 1873, while we was still running the hotel, had several financial transactions with the banking firm of George B. Ripley, at No. 66 Broadway.   He was simply paving the way for the successful culmination of a well planned scheme.   When he had at last established confidence and made his credit good, Orvis one day succeeded in borrowing from the firm $20,000 upon some forged bonds.   Since then he has been arrested several times for defrauding various banking firms, and at present there are indictments against him on file in the District Attorney's office.

The forger's audacity was most surprising.   The New York *Sun* and *Times*, several years ago, exposed his character, and Orvis afterwards began suits against the newspapers for showing him up.   The suits, of course, collapsed when it was proven that Orvis was really a dangerous criminal.

GEORGE B. WATSON was discharged from State prison in 1873, having completed a term of five years' imprisonment for burglary.   Upon his return to the city the ex-convict married a very respectable young woman, and with his innocent bride went to live in a fashionable apartment house on Fifty-fourth Street, near Broadway.   He had not been out of prison long before he entered into co-partnership with a forger, who took him in training.   After the necessary education Watson started out as a full-fledged "scratcher."   At the banking office of Samuel White & Co., on Wall Street, several years since, he disposed of some Government bond coupons, for which he received a due-bill calling for the payment of $125.   Instead of presenting the latter to the cashier immediately, Watson waited until lunch-time, and then presented the claim.   In the meantime he had raised the amount which the due-bill called for to $12,000, and just as the money was being handed to him the forgery was detected.   Watson, who had been on the alert, fled from the office and escaped.

When the gigantic fraudulent scheme to flood the market with forged New York, Buffalo and Erie Railroad bonds became known, Watson, who was concerned in the great conspiracy, fled to Europe.   Upon his return, several years later, he was arrested. He was then a complete wreck from dissipation, and had to be assisted into the court room.   His condition was so pitiful that the complainant asked for the discharge of the prisoner on his own recognizance.   Watson was thereupon released, but he rallied, and a few months later on he was again arrested and brought up for a small forgery. Upon his conviction he was sentenced to the penitentiary, where he died before his term expired.

CHARLES R. BECKWITH was arrested January 1, 1876, for robbing his employer, B. T. Babbitt, the soap manufacturer, out of $205,645 by means of forged receipts. Beckwith had been stealing for years before it was suspected that the funds of the firm were being made away with.   He was sentenced to ten years' imprisonment.   Beckwith is at present living in Canada.

THOMAS R. LEWIS, the accomplice of Beckwith, who also realized about $200,000 by making false entries in Mr. Babbitt's books, fled to Europe when the fraud was discovered. He was captured in London, England, and brought back. Upon his return to this city Lewis made restitution as far as he was able, returning altogether property worth $58,000. He was convicted and sentenced to two and a half years imprisonment. Lewis died a few years since in Switzerland.

J. LLOYD HAIGH for many years held an exalted position in society, but like other good men he wandered from the path of rectitude, thereby destroying his good name and casting a dark shadow over that of his family. In 1879 he was arrested and accused of hypothecating forged paper. He was indicted and convicted of forgery in the third degree, and on August 8, 1880, was sentenced to five years' imprisonment.

LEWIS M. VAN ETEN, on March 1, 1871, was paid $19,000 by the Park National Bank on a check purporting to have been drawn by Hall, Garten & Co., brokers, of No. 30 Broad Street, and certified by the Continental Bank. Upon the discovery of the forgery the Continental Bank refunded the Park Bank the amount they had paid on the check. After the forgery Van Eten disappeared, and remained away for some time. On his return to New York he was arrested, and upon conviction was sentenced to a term of ten years' imprisonment in Sing Sing. He had not been long in prison before he was pardoned, but upon his release he was re-arrested for a forgery committed at San Francisco, Cal. While on the way to that place for trial, Van Eten committed suicide by swallowing a dose of laudanum, which he had kept concealed upon his person.

LEVI COLE, a man with innumerable aliases, figured as a burglar, forger and dealer in counterfeit money for many years. His first start in crime was handling spurious bank-notes. When the State banks went out of existence Cole turned burglar, and made a specialty of robbing the safes of country banks. His jimmies and other tools he expressed from place to place in a sole-leather gun-case. He was in the habit of calling at the express office with a game-bag over his shoulder and a cartridge belt around his waist. Cole would pass the day in the woods, and in the night the country bank would be robbed. He served two terms for burglary, and at the expiration of the second sentence went direct from prison to a Western city, where his brother kept a hotel. Cole demanded assistance, but it was refused, because, under promises of reformation, he had before deceived his brother. Upon the request being refused, the burglar and forger went to one of the rooms up-stairs and blew his brains out with a revolver.

GEORGE ENGLES, the two Bidwells, and McDonald, with the intention of carrying out gigantic forgeries on an elaborate scale, went to England, and in 1871 commenced operations in Liverpool, where they obtained about £6,000. With this capital they proceeded to London, and opened a banking and commission house for the discounting and shaving of commercial paper. McDonald organized the firm under the name of "Warner & Co." He opened an account with one of the leading London banks, and bona fide transactions were conducted for some time. After gaining the confidence of the bank's officers, they commenced to discount the paper of Warner & Co., which had been presented for discount by their customers, some of the leading merchants of London.

Previous to the consummation of the scheme, George McDonald and one of the Bidwells became infatuated with two women with whom they lived. Engles objected to this, fearing that his companions would reveal his secrets to their mistresses. McDonald and Bidwell were then residing at St. John's Wood, Kensington, London. The men refused to give up the women, and laughed at Engles, who threatened to cut off business relations with them. After the gang had realized about a quarter of a million pounds sterling Engles became frightened when informed that the women knew all about the scheme, and with his share of the plunder disappeared. When McDonald and Bidwell undertook to continue the business they were discovered, and the sequel shows that had it not been for the women in whom they had so much confidence, they would have escaped.

In their recklessness the men presented one of the forged notes which had not been dated. The clerk discovered the error, and forwarded it to the firm by whom it was supposed to have been issued. They pronounced it a forgery. One of the Bidwells fled to Scotland, and was there arrested, and his brother was apprehended in Havana, Cuba. McDonald endeavored to get clear of his mistress, but could not. He induced her, however, to accept a passage ticket from Liverpool to New York, telling her that he would join her at the Northern Hotel before the steamer sailed. He did not attempt to meet her, but took a train from London to Folkstone, crossed to France, and took passage at Havre for this city. McDonald's mistress, becoming enraged at her disappointment, and suspecting the route her lover had taken to get away, betrayed him to the police. A cablegram was sent to this city, and upon the arrival of the steamer the fugitive forger was arrested on board the vessel in the lower bay. After months of litigation McDonald was returned to England, where he was convicted and sentenced to life imprisonment. The Bidwell brothers received like sentences.

McDonald had just finished a sentence of five years' imprisonment for a forgery which he had committed upon Ball, Black & Co., the jewelers, when he set out with Engles and the Bidwells for Europe to execute the scheme of flooding the financial world with spurious Bank of England notes.

George Engles is dead, and for other mention of him see records of George Wilkes and No. 18.

BUCHANAN CROSS was called "Colonel," on account of his frequent appearance in a sort of military-cut suit, which aided him many times in the laying down of forged paper. For this class of crime he was sentenced to Sing Sing prison, and while there he forged his own pardon and was liberated. Afterwards he was arrested and tried for forging the Governor's signature. Cross proved by the warden of the prison that it was impossible for him to have committed the forgery, on account of his not being able to get pen and ink. He was acquitted of the charge, but was detained to serve out his unexpired term.

After his release Cross forged the name of Robert Bonner to a check for $3,156, on the Nassau Bank, New York City, being assisted in the crime by Charley Bishop. The latter went to the *Ledger* office and subscribed for the paper, and gave his address as at East Orange, N. J. Bishop gave a twenty dollar gold piece in payment for his subscription, and asked that a check for the change be given him, as he wished to send it to Orange. The request was complied with, and thus the forgers obtained Mr. Bonner's signature. The check was given to David Beech, alias Leach, who took it to Henry Siebert, engraver, at No. 93 Fulton Street, and ordered a book of blank checks, similar to the sample, to be printed for him.

The blanks were taken to "Colonel" Cross, and he made out the check in the name of Robert Bonner. The money was obtained from the bank, and on the following day the forgery was discovered. Beech's girl was first arrested. She said that her lover had started for Boston the night before, intending to sail for Europe that day. He was arrested by the Boston police on the steamer just as the vessel was leaving the dock. Beech was sentenced to five years' hard labor and Bishop to three and a half years, on October 29, 1860.

Cross was arrested in Canada, but for want of sufficient evidence he was discharged.

CHARLES FREDERICK ULRICH, a Prussian by birth, is one of the few engravers able to cut a United States Treasury plate without any assistance. He is the son of a jeweler and engraver of Dantzig, Germany. Ulrich learned the first part of his trade at his father's shop, and then finished at a regular establishment at Berlin, Prussia. He came to this country in 1853, being then about twenty years old. His career since has been a checkered one. Ulrich had been here but a few years before he embarked freely in the counterfeiting business, he doing all the engraving, which was a marvel of exactness. Among the plates which he engraved prior to his first conviction in 1868, were a $100 counterfeit on the Central National Bank of New York, a $100 counterfeit of the First National Bank of Boston, Mass., and a $100 counterfeit on the Ohio National Bank of Cincinnati. He printed and disposed of, without a glimmer of detection, all of these, and became quite wealthy, and then, in the early part of 1867, settled himself in Cincinnati for a final effort. He engaged a small house, and there began to engrave a counterfeit of the $500 United States Treasury note. He was engaged upon the plate when he was arrested, and sentenced to the Columbus, Ohio, penitentiary for twelve years.

Ulrich served eight years of his time in the Ohio penitentiary, and in 1879, when arrested with Old Harry Cole and Jacob Ott, he made a confession in which he revealed some interesting information concerning counterfeiting. During the course of his statement he said:

"Counterfeits are usually of small denominations, because there is more money in them for the wholesale dealer. A large bill will soon be stamped as a counterfeit, while the small ones can be changed from bank to bank, and people are not so shy of them. After I came out of the Columbus, Ohio, penitentiary, I started in the lithographing and engraving business in Cincinnati, but failed. Then I went to Philadelphia and took a house at the corner of Sixth and Cumberland streets. There I started to engrave two $50 plates. They were counterfeits of the Central National Bank of New York and the Third of Buffalo. Before they were finished I moved to a place called Oak Lane, six miles from Philadelphia. When these plates had been completed, I started on a $5 plate. In October, 1877, I moved out to Sharon Hill, where another lot of fives and fifties were printed. The latter were on the Tradesmen's Bank of New York, and were sent to Europe. There were 2,000 fifties and 8,000 fives printed at Oak Lane, and 2,000 fifties and between 16,000 and 20,000 fives at Sharon Hill, in all nearly $350,000. There was always a man with capital back of me. I know one of my counterfeits just as well as a man would know his own handwriting."

The first time Ulrich was arrested was in this city. He was caught at work upon a vignette for a counterfeit bank-bill, and upon conviction was sentenced to five years' imprisonment in Sing Sing. The counterfeiter only served three years of his term, when he was pardoned by Governor Morgan. He had been out of prison but a short time when he engraved the plate from which the Bank of England notes were printed. So well were they executed that the " water mark " was perfect. All these bills were received as genuine by the Bank of England, and an unlimited number of the counterfeits are believed to be still in circulation.

Ulrich, before he became known to the police, served for eighteen months in the British army. That was during the Crimean war. He was, he claimed, enlisted in New York by an English agent, sent to Boston, and from thence by schooner to Halifax, Nova Scotia. As soon as his time was up he returned to the United States and became a full-fledged counterfeiter. He is now in Switzerland.

For further mention of Ulrich see record of George W. Wilkes.

THOMAS BALLARD, for years known all over the Union as the King of Counterfeiters, died while serving out a thirty years' sentence in the penitentiary at Albany, N. Y. He was a superior engraver, and the fine work on some of his bills was so cleverly and artistically executed as to deceive even the banks and the government. He was classed as a professional in 1865, and his work was then exceedingly fine. Previous to his arrest in October, 1871, Ballard carried on his operations near Buffalo, N. Y., being located in a lonely house on the outskirts of Beach Rock. He was dogged about for months before he was finally traced to his lair. One dark night his secret retreat was surrounded. As soon as Ballard became aware of the trap that had been sprung on him he tried hard to escape, but without avail. At his rendezvous a number of dies and other untensils of the counterfeiter's art were captured, including an admirably executed plate upon a Buffalo bank. Bailard was duly tried, convicted, and sentenced to the long term in the Albany penitentiary. While the counterfeiter was in prison he made use of his spare time to plan and perfect a valuable invention for registering the actual number of papers printed by any printing press. He made several strenuous but fruitless efforts to invoke the clemency of the law for a pardon or a partial remittance of his sentence.

WILLIAM C. GILMAN was not a professional criminal, still his forgeries, when they were discovered in the fall of 1877, created the greatest excitement in Wall Street. He was an insurance scrip broker, at No. 46 Pine Street, and as his connections were very good indeed, his fall was thereby all the more deplorable. Gilman raised scrip of the Atlantic Mutual and Commercial Mutual Insurance Companies amounting to nearly $300,000, and his forgeries existed for years without discovery. He speculated on false capital, and each year his prospects of redeeming himself became more and more hopeless. His distress became daily more and more terrible, and these symptoms of trouble were obvious to his intimate friends, while the causes were unknown. Gilman was indicted for forgery in the third degree, the specific charge being for the forgery of a $10,000 insurance scrip on the Atlantic and Mutual Insurance Company, bearing date April 27, 1877, and the number 2,100. When the prisoner was arraigned before Recorder Hackett, in the Court of General Sessions, on October 12, 1877, one of the most affecting scenes ever witnessed in a court room took place. Gilman pleaded guilty to the charge, and, at the request of his counsel, the Court afterwards permitted the prisoner to read a confession he had made explaining the manner in which his crime had been committed. The insurance broker's confession was as follows:

OCTOBER 3, 1877.

To REV. DR. HOUGHTON AND MY DEAR WIFE, BROTHERS AND SISTERS:

It is proper to state certain facts in explanation, not extenuation, of my conduct. From the time I began business I had placed in my hands, by friends trusting me implicitly, sums of money ranging from $100 to $20,000. These sums would often remain undisturbed for weeks and months, and as I paid for the privilege, it was proper and was understood that I employed them in business; I never speculated in stocks on margin, nor lost nor won money by any wager or game. I did make investments in enterprises which promised well from time to time, in good faith, and which turned out utterly bad. For this my judgment is to be blamed. The possession of so much money and the control of it gradually made me feel and act as if it were my own, and encroachments upon it, whether from losses or expenses, which began many years ago, came so gradually that I was scarcely sensible of them, and, while I knew that I was running behind, I could not bear to look the deficiency squarely in the face, but hoped for better times. Times grew worse instead of better. The failure of the Sun Insurance Company and the vicissitudes of the other companies impaired the confidence of buyers in everything but Atlantic, and competition for that the last few years has carried prices so high as to leave no margin for profit, and has made the commissions utterly inadequate to meet the scale of expenses on which I was doing business and living. Consequently my business was greatly restricted. The worse my affairs grew the more unwilling I became to investigate them. My books and accounts, which had been my pride, were neglected. I drifted hopelessly in a sea of trouble, seizing every straw which seemed to give a little present help, and in some cases I allowed my reputation to suffer by long delay in making up accounts which were called for. This moral weakness was quite inexcusable. How easy to say so now, but how hard it seemed to do what I should years ago have done in reducing expenses at home and in the office, and in resolutely closing accounts which were a temptation to me, and which, if honestly treated, must at that rate of interest have proved unprofitable.

Prior to the panic of 1873 I had made improper use of trust funds in my hands under the pressure of declining business, and the troubles of that year involved me in additional losses. After that time the accounts in my hands began to be drawn on by the depositors more freely than before, and not unfrequently I found myself sorely pushed, but always managed to extricate myself without doing anything criminal, though I must confess the moral baseness of my proceedings these many years.

As nearly as I can remember I must have put forth the first "raised" certificate not quite two years ago. It was so easy to do it! Yet what a struggle it cost me!

I have suffered more all these months in thinking of my baseness in abusing the confidence of my friends in No. 39 Pine Street, in the two insurance companies and in the bank, every one of whom has always treated me with the greatest kindness, than at the absolute wickedness of these crimes.

Blindly hoping that the next step would extricate me, I plunged in deeper and deeper. I hope I make it plain that my endeavor was to cover the deficiencies of a term of years.

It is impossible for me to state without reference to memoranda, which I have not by me, what amounts are afloat, but I am confident that there is nothing but what will be found at the American Exchange Bank, Union Insurance Company, Commercial Insurance Company, Henry Talmadge & Co.'s, and my friends will find the whole truth there. I have not sold any fraudulent securities, but borrowed on them.

It is proper for me to say that I am alone responsible for every wrong act. No human being would have had a suspicion of it, and I alone am to blame for the false pride which has made me incur expenses at home and in my business which could not lawfully be met. My wife never persuaded me to any extravagance, and she would have accepted any restraint I might have put upon her.

In addition to these fraudulent transactions other persons than those named must suffer to a considerable degree—chiefly my brothers and sisters—probably to the extent of $75,000, and several other persons who have had accounts with me for years. I cannot now state amounts of these latter accounts approximately.

To sum up briefly, I would say that a declining business, bad investments, heavy expenses, both business and domestic, and personal extravagance, have betrayed me. No, I must be just with myself, and confess that I have deliberately walked, in the clearest light and knowledge, in the face of the best instruction, into this pit. Some may call it madness ; I call it sin. Those who knew me in business relations alone may not be aware of it, but every one who knows me personally will bear witness that my intimate friends and associates are all with some of the best and purest who ever lived. They know that I loved better to give away money than to spend it for myself ; they know that my thoughts and my interests were more with the various charitable works with which it was my happiness to be connected than on money getting, by right means or wrong. They will mourn with me that I should have valued the good opinion of good men more than a good conscience and my own self-respect. They will wonder how it was possible for a man to so far deceive himself as to believe that he really cared for and valued things that were true, honest, pure, just, lovely and of good repute, while, beneath a smooth surface, his heart was rotten and dishonest to the core.

I suppose no one will be much surprised that suicide has been much in my thoughts for many years, and while I hoped that some change of fortune might avert the impending disclosure, I have feared for some weeks that it might be near at hand. I deliberated before this whether I should add sin to sin, but had resolved to meet the crisis as soon as it should come meekly and frankly. I have now but one desire, and that is to throw all possible light on every dark corner of these transactions, regardless of consequences personal to myself, and to aid in distributing everything that remains to those who are entitled to it. Then commending my wife and worse than fatherless children to God, how gladly, if it be his will, will I do penance for my crime in prison and pray for death whenever He pleases to send it—or, hardest lot of all, if life be possible to one who has forfeited the respect of every human being, I will try to live and to add not another stain to the name of

WILLIAM C. GILMAN.

Nearly every eye in the court room was moistened when the reading of the foregoing touching appeal had ended. Tears coursed down the cheeks of the stern Recorder as he proceeded to pass sentence. It was a moment of painful suspense for all in the court. He said :

"After the representations which have been made and the statements which have just been read in court, statements made by the accused to those whom he loved dearest in life, I cannot be guided by my own feelings in this matter. I cannot depend upon them, and I have one of the greatest duties to perform that belong to any age. In view of the enormity of the crime the prisoner has committed, while feelings of the utmost sympathy were extended to his wife and family, I feel it my duty to pronounce the sentence of the Court, that the prisoner be confined in the State prison for the term of five years at hard labor."

Sad as was the scene in the court room, there was another sadder still on December 3, 1879. It occurred in the Yantic cemetery, near Norwichtown, Conn., when Gilman, who had been pardoned by Governor Robinson, fresh from Auburn prison, stood by the open grave of his wife. While in prison his daughter had died, and he was released in time to attend the funeral of his wife, whose heart had been broken with sorrow over her husband's sin. Gilman's false step will stand forever as a warning to others.

INTERNATIONAL FORGERS.

SECRET HISTORY OF THE WILKES, HAMILTON, BECKER AND ENGLES GANG OF
FORGERS.—THEIR CHIEF'S CONFESSION.

THERE was a lively sensation during the Christmas holiday week, 1880, when brief cablegrams were received in New York City announcing that a skillful and desperate gang of American counterfeiters and forgers, with their wives, had been arrested in Milan and Florence, Italy. The names of Willis and Burns and Hamilton were given as those of the ringleaders, and it was said that they had swindled, or tried to swindle, a large number of bankers in Europe.

While in prison one of the culprits, the leader and arch conspirator, Henry W. Wilkes, alias Willis, was led to make a full confession. It was reduced to writing before the United States Consular representative, Colonel J. Schuyler Crosby, and filed among the police archives, only a brief reference to it being permitted to go to the press.

The story, which is here given in full, is one of the most extraordinary chapters of crime ever printed.

HENRY WADE WILKES, alias George Wilkes, alias Willis, the chief of the only international band of bond forgers and counterfeiters ever organized, with his boon companion, the notorious "Pete" Burns, alias James Joy Julius, fell into the hands of the Italian criminal authorities at Florence on Christmas Day, 1880, just after "Shell" Hamilton, alias Colbert, had been apprehended at Milan. Wilkes was, after several months, quietly released, and he returned to New York. Burns while in prison became aware for the first time of Wilkes's duplicity in making a confession, and knowing that he had been betrayed, choked himself to death with a prayer-book. His three widows are at present engaged in a litigation over his estate, which is said to be worth about $400,000. This money was Burns's share of the profits of the operations of the gang of which he was one of the leading spirits and Wilkes was the acknowledged chief. The band was composed of none but professional forgers, counterfeiters, and first-class "check raisers," and they operated with wonderful success in almost every city of North America and Europe. They were not concerned in any paltry schemes, but only took part in well planned and gigantic plots. They realized altogether by their forgeries perhaps millions, and the lion's share of their plunder was afterwards squandered at the gaming table. The members of the international gang made New York, London and Paris in turn their headquarters, and flooded the two continents with their worthless bonds and securities.

Wilkes's standing among criminals may be imagined when it is known that "Andy" Roberts and Valentine Gleason sought his advice before they attempted to dispose of any of the Buffalo and Erie Railroad bonds. George Engles (now dead) and Charles Becker, astute forgers as they were, were really only Wilkes's tools. In fact, during the past fifteen years forgers and counterfeiters of all grades sought his advice in all dangerous transactions. He was the power behind the throne in all stupendous swindling schemes.

It was under his advice that Becker succeeded in carrying out the $64,000 check forgery on the Union Trust Company which bore the unauthorized indorsement of the New York Life Insurance Company. It was through influence that Wilkes succeeded in getting out of prison in Italy, and since his return here he has been shunned by his old associates in crime.

The capture of Wilkes and the consequent breaking up of his gang, was owing to information furnished by the authorities of New York City to the various police officials in Europe, that Wilkes and his gang had sailed from America for the purpose of flooding the Continent with counterfeit circular notes, checks, etc.

The confession alluded to was made at Florino, and is as follows :

"I, Henry W. Wilkes, alias George Wilkes, was born in Highland Mills, Orange County, N. Y., on May 25, 1837. From the age of twenty to twenty-seven years I was employed in different occupations by the Erie Railroad Company. I left the employ of that corporation for the purpose of becoming a professional gambler, and I followed that profession for many years. My first gambling house was situated at the corner of Broadway and Fourth Street, New York. I was in partnership with John Sollmon and Charles Schaeffer, and for two years and a half I devoted all my time to playing cards.

"It was in the latter part of 1869 or the beginning of 1870 that I was first arrested by the New York police for forgery. A man named Sudlass was arrested with me. We were arrested for forging a check upon the Board of Education, and were also accused of other forgeries of minor importance. After being kept in prison for three days we were brought before Judge Gunning S. Bedford and discharged. My next deed was to induce several merchants and makers of brandies of New York and the West into a scheme by which they could introduce their liquors into New York at fifty cents a gallon. We succeeded in doing so by the aid of the Office of Appraisement of the Thirty-second District. That was at the time that the duty upon brandy was $2 per gallon. James Black, John Sudlass and I were the principals in the 'brandy ring,' as we used to call it. James Pike, of Cincinnati, came to see us, and he had a talk with John Sudlass at the Fifth Avenue Hotel, but we declined to do business with him. We told the merchants to give us the names of the brandies that they wanted to introduce, and we would pledge ourselves to fulfil the bargain. By means of that swindling scheme we each made about $40,000.

"Afterwards, in company with Joseph Chapman, of Fourth Street and Washington Square (who is now in prison in Munich for passing and forging a greenback bill of $50 of the Tradesmen's National Bank of New York), and one Deneran, an Englishman, then temporarily living in New York, I went to Chicago, where I remained one day, and then we started for St. Joseph, Mo., where we stopped three days, trying to pass a forged draft for $6,000. We had the books of drafts made in New York by order of Chapman and regularly stamped. These drafts were upon a bank of Louisville, Ky., and others on a bank of Galveston, Texas. I do not remember the names of the banks. We were not lucky at St. Joseph. From there we went to Council Bluffs, and thence to Cheyenne. The Union Pacific Railroad then only ran to Green River. N. V. Clinton, a native of Indiana, was also with us, and was engaged in the same operations.

"At Cheyenne Chapman cashed a draft for $3,000 by means of letters of introduction he had secured from small banks in that locality. We proceeded to San Francisco, and upon arriving there I stopped at a hotel in the 'Bend' of Bush Street. The others took residences in different hotels. On account of a telegram alluding to the exposure of the other forged drafts business with us was poor in San Francisco. We only disposed of a draft for $2,300.

"Clinton obtained in San Francisco a letter of credit from the British Bank of North America on the same bank of New York City. I did not know the amount of the draft because Clinton refused to show it to me. He set out for Acapulco, where we joined him in a week, and then we all went to Panama. At Acapulco Clinton cheated several bankers, but I never knew how much he realized. On the steamer between Acapulco and Panama Clinton robbed a cabin mate of a letter of credit, upon which he got $600 at Panama. This letter was addressed to Duncan, Sherman & Co., and their agent paid the amount, but had Clinton arrested before the steamer could leave. He was arrested while I was *en route* to New York, having left Chapman, Denevan and Clinton behind. I reached New York in October, 1871, where I remained one day, starting on the next to Boston to visit my wife, who was living with the family of a coffin maker. Returning to New York, I stopped for two weeks at the house of Mrs. Sartorio, in West Twenty-first Street, near Sixth Avenue.

"Next I proceeded to New Orleans with my wife and thence to Havana, for the purpose of meeting Chapman, according to an agreement we made in Panama. He was anxious to get rid of the others. While we were in San Francisco Chapman had obtained a draft for a small sum from the British Bank of North America. This draft was raised and altered by me to $5,000, and was negotiated by Chapman by means of a false letter of introduction from Panama.

"Upon rejoining Chapman he came with us back to Boston, where we took up a residence at the St. James Hotel. Then we went to Norwich, Conn., where I left my wife with the Peakes family. Chapman and I then set out for Philadelphia, where we were joined by George Barlow, and then we set out for Chicago. We supplied ourselves with money by altering and raising a small draft to the sum of $1,600, which Chapman collected. Barlow also bought a small draft in Chicago, which I raised to $5,000. From Chicago we went to Louisville, Ky., and there Chapman disposed of the latter draft to the Trades Bank of that city. We paid another visit to Boston, where I passed a month with the Peakes family.

"From Boston Chapman, Barlow and I went to Montreal, Canada, where we took rooms at a hotel. We tried to effect some business, but could not. From Canada we hastened to New York, where Barlow and wife, I and mine, hired a small house at Thirty-seventh Street and Seventh Avenue.

"Chapman followed us a week later. Knowing that the police were looking for us, we remained idle. Meanwhile Clinton succeeded in escaping from the prison at Panama by corrupting his keepers. He joined us in New York. During the five months that we were idle we were preparing for new operations.

"We succeeded in securing several certificates of deposit from Duncan, Sherman & Co., and we had note paper printed with the same heading as theirs, also envelopes. This work was done by order of Chapman or Clinton. We obtained other certificates from other bankers in New York—one on Alexander Bronson & Son, which certificate we tried to use in Richmond, Va. I altered that certificate from $15 or $16 to $1,500 or $1,600. I set out for Mobile, Ala., to await the arrival of my associates there. Chapman presented his certificate of deposit in Richmond, got the money, but was arrested before he could leave the city. When captured he had all the money on him, which was confiscated. Clinton left before Chapman was arrested, with several certificates of deposit, and he was arrested in Virginia while attempting to dispose of some of them. Barlow was the only one who joined me in Mobile. This was in the winter of 1874, and during that time I again became a professional gambler.

"Barlow went back to Philadelphia, and thence to Indiana, where his wife was living on an estate. On his way he stopped at Richmond to leave money collected for Chapman, who was still in prison awaiting trial. Within eight months Clinton returned to New York, and during all that period I was living at the house of Mrs. Sartorio, on Twenty-first Street. Barlow, upon coming back, joined Clinton and myself, and we went to Cincinnati, where Barlow lived with me in a small hotel. There we became acquainted with Eph Holland, Pat Riley, and one Hogan. We easily obtained there drafts of small denominations from several bankers, which we altered and raised to large sums. Barlow 'laid down' one of these raised drafts. He bought a horse and collected the balance of $1,300 or $1,400. We went to Cedar Falls, but being unable to pass any drafts returned to Cincinnati. Barlow and Clinton proceeded to Kentucky. I remained in Cincinnati.

"Barlow presented a draft for $6,000 in Kentucky, received the money, and was arrested. I heard of the arrest from Clinton, and set out at once for New York, where I remained all winter. Clinton remained behind. My next transactions were with Webb, an Englishman, with whom I forged several small checks on banks, using the name of Hunt & Co., Broad Street. It was 'Tall' Barlow, the brother of George, who obtained the small checks. He used to live opposite the Greenwich Bank, on Hudson Street. By these checks we made between $8,000 and $10,000. In the winter of 1876 we went to Chicago with Phil Hargraves, an old time forger, of Charlton Street, between Hudson and Greenwich Streets.

"In Chicago we stopped at the St. James Hotel. We intended doing business with Milwaukee from Chicago. Our plan of operation was: We would go to some banker in Chicago and buy drafts payable in New York, and would request them to send our signatures to their correspondents in Milwaukee, or to such places as we intended working. We thus gained their confidence. After two or three genuine transactions we would send out a false draft. Webb bought a small draft, which I raised to $3,000, which was paid in Milwaukee.

"After an absence of six weeks Hargraves, Webb and myself returned to New York, where we met Chapman. Then the four of us made a trip to New Orleans. We bought paper there and worked in the same manner. Webb, after several attempts, did defraud a banker of Galveston out of $4,000. Chapman worked Vicksburg, where he got $2,000. Then we all went back to New York and thence directly to Sacramento, Cal., with Hargraves and wife and I with mine. At the latter place I engaged a furnished house on I or K Street, and Hargraves proceeded to San Francisco to await us. We began operations in Sacramento by buying genuine drafts from D. O. Mills & Co. from Sacramento to New York, making the same demand to forward our signatures to Portland, Oregon.

"Chapman made two journeys there, but did not succeed in making anything. I then changed our plans. Chapman went to St. Louis and Hargraves and Webb remained in San Francisco. We took all the money that we could control (about $10,000) to St. Louis, and there bought a draft for that amount from the Planters' Bank, and we sent the same by express to Webb in San Francisco. He deposited the draft in the Bank of California and obtained blank checks, thus gaining an introduction.

"He then sent us a draft bought of Hiscock, or Hitchcock & Co., of San Francisco, and Chapman presented it to their correspondent in St. Louis. We sent the money again by draft to Webb, and he collected it through the Bank of California. Webb also sent us a second draft while there was one in existence on the firm of Hiscock & Co. One was for a small amount and the second for a large one. Chapman collected the latter, and subsequently took a small draft from the Planters' Bank of St. Louis. The two small drafts were raised to $8,500, the other for $7,500 or thereabouts. These were sent to Webb, in San Francisco, and he obtained the money. The draft to Chapman by Webb was presented to a correspondent of Hiscock & Co., but he being unable to answer some few questions satisfactorily it was not cashed. Our operations finished, we all met by arrangement in Springfield, Mass. Chapman preceded us. From there we went to New York. Hargraves started business with 'Jem' Mace, the pugilist, in West Twenty-third Street, near the Masonic Temple. Webb returned to his home in England, Chapman and myself remained and worked together in Boston.

"My next transaction was in Central Pacific bonds that Chapman received from some of his friends in Williamsburg, N. Y., one of them being Charles Becker. We went to Chicago, where we readily disposed of $10,000 worth of the bonds. Chapman gave fifty per cent. to the forgers, and the rest was divided equally between him and me. These bonds were of the value of $1,000 each, and I wanted to take some of them to Europe in company with a certain Joseph Spencer. We sailed to Liverpool, England, having in our possession seventeen bonds of $1,000 each. We stopped at the Adelphia Hotel, and we cautioned Chapman to cable us in case the scheme should be discovered before we reached England. We offered one of the bonds to a broker in Liverpool, but as he seemed to think that there was something wrong I left it with him, and on my arrival at the hotel I found a cable message from Chapman, stating that everything had been discovered. We had only time to jump into a coach and drive out of the city, where I destroyed the remainder of the bonds and threw the fragments into the River Mersey.

"From Liverpool we went to London, but discovering that the police were on the lookout for us we sailed back to America by the steamer City of London, having first spent a week in the Inns of Court Hotel. Upon our return to the United States Spencer and I went to Baltimore. Separating from Spencer I joined Chapman, Joseph Reilly, alias 'Little Joe,' and Oscar Decker, a professional bank burglar, who at the time were in Baltimore.

"We started business in Philadelphia in this manner. We would write to some bank in Philadelphia, receiving an answer on their form of printed envelope and note paper, also their handwriting, which we familiarized ourselves with, also obtaining a list of their correspondents in Chicago and Cincinnati. Then we would buy drafts for small sums, raise them to larger amounts, and send them to the correspondents with a forged letter of introduction to the correspondents, and they would cash them. Chapman and Decker presented drafts in Chicago and Cincinnati, obtaining $13,500. I disagreed with Chapman and Reilly as to their mode of doing business, and left them for New York. I there became acquainted with John Phillips, who had just been liberated from Moyamensing prison after serving a term for burglary.

"Decker, Phillips and wife, and myself and wife took passage on the steamer Adriatic for England. We had with us several bonds that had been stolen from the Bank of Trenton, N. J. They consisted of thirteen bonds of the Northern New Jersey Railroad of $1,000 each, one of the Oregon Central Railroad, one of the Central Pacific Railroad, three of Iowa City and other bonds which we sold to our friends.

"On reaching England Decker and I lived with the family of John Carr, at Pimlico. Phillips took up quarters at the East End of London, and there Phillips disposed of the bonds to his friends for £900. Before starting for England we had decided with some of our confederates to make a letter of credit on Bosrole Brothers. One of the confederates was the notorious 'Andy' Roberts. I returned with my wife to New York. Phillips and Decker followed me. They immediately returned to England and Roberts and I sailed after them on the steamer City of London. As soon as we got there we went to work lively, but during our stay of a month we were unable to do any business, although we had a genuine letter of credit for £500 on Bosrole Brothers. On the next trip of the City of London we returned to New York, and went to live on Third Avenue, four doors above Twenty-fifth Street.

"We remained a little while in New York and then made up the combination of Decker, Phillips, Roberts and myself to take to England forged bonds of the Buffalo and Erie Railroad, which, if properly filed and collected, would amount to the value of $200,000. We obtained them from Roberts in an unfinished state.

"I went with Roberts to London by the steamer City of Brooklyn, Phillips and Decker following. I first resided with Decker and his wife at Chelsea. There we were joined by others—Joseph Reilly, alias 'Little Joe," Joseph Chapman, Samuel Perry, alias 'Worcester Sam,' and Walter Sheridan. They came for the same business, having with them forged bonds of the Chicago, Western and Southern Railroad to the amount of about $150,000. We had a consultation and decided to join issue with each other. 'Andy' Roberts prepared the Buffalo and Erie bonds, and Walter Sheridan the Chicago, Western and Southern Railroad bonds.

"Amsterdam was the place selected for the starting of operations. Sam Perry made an attempt there to sell $50,000 worth of the forged Chicago, Western and Southern Railroad bonds by means of frauds on the United States Consulate. The entire scheme failed, as there were no bonds of that sort yet on the foreign market. While we were traveling from place to place endeavoring to dispose of these bonds, Phillips' brother-in-law, who lived in Gravesend, hearing that the police were about to search his house, destroyed all the models and blanks of the Buffalo and Erie bonds.

"I then cut off all business relationship with them and returned to New York alone. I had saved a large sum of money and for two years did nothing, during which time my wife died. It was during my first voyage to California that I first became acquainted with my present wife.

"I next conspired with John Donohue, Charles King, James Green and Philip Hargraves to buy $50,000 worth of counterfeit greenbacks and take them to Europe. Hargraves bought them from Charles E. Ulrich aud William E. Gray, paying twelve and one-half per cent. of their nominal value. (Ulrich and Gray were afterward arrested and convicted.) I sailed for Europe on the steamer Donan with Green, stopping in England in a house on Tottenham Court Road. King went to the house of some friends, and Donohue took up quarters in a small hotel on the Strand. Our first meeting took place, according to agreement, at St. John's Wood Station, Marlborough Road. We met there every day. Our plan was to send out two gangs, one to start from Naples and the other from Vienna, and try to dispose of the counterfeit green-backs along the road. Green and King, who were to start from Naples, took with them $20,000 worth of that money. Not knowing the language and customs of the country they became scared and did no business. They returned to Paris, where I met them at the Hôtel du Louvre.

"Chapman and Donohue started business in Vienna and there sold $5,000 worth of forged bank-notes of the Tradesmen's National Bank and of the Broadway National Bank of New York, of the denomination of $50. They were on their way from Vienna to Munich when Chapman was arrested. Donohue telegraphed me at the Hôtel du Louvre that 'the family was ill.'

"I informed my associates Green and King, and we immediately went to London. I met Green and Donohue several times after. The latter took passage for Canada, where he sold $15,000 worth of forged bank-notes at fifteen per cent. of their face value. During the first week of the Paris Exposition we disposed of a large quantity of the forged bank-notes. I returned to New York by the steamer Adriatic and joined my wife, who was stopping at the Maison Cortoni.

"My next speculation was the putting in circulation of forged letters of credit of the London County Bank. The genuine letter was bought by me from Frank or Valentine Gleason in London. It was a certificate and letter of identification for £10. I gave him £20 for it. I gave it to John Quinn, who was then living in Twenty-seventh Street, near Lexington Avenue. He gave it to one of his confederates, who raised it to £600 in bank-notes and 100 letters of identification.

"Quinn, Hargraves, John Conn and an Englishman named William Griffis, alias 'Lord Ashburton,' alias 'Saville,' then went to work. Quinn, Hargraves and Griffis proceeded to Canada. There Griffis presented a bank-note for £1,200, and received the money from the Bank of Montreal. He gave Hargraves and Quinn £900 in these notes, keeping £1,000 of them, with which he went to Quebec. There he said that the fraud had been discovered, and we all left for New York by different routes. This statement was afterwards found to be untrue, and we later on learned that he sold a portion of the bank-notes and purchased jewelry with the balance at Kirkpatrick's, Nineteenth Street and Broadway.

"Griffis, upon ascertaining that we had unearthed his duplicity, suddenly left for San Francisco, where he was arrested. Jack Cannon (now dead), who was in the habit of only handling stolen bonds, and William Bartlett, alias 'Big Bill,' of Brooklyn. were afterwards sent out with the bank-notes. They were given £1,000 in counterfeit money of the Bank of England, which was disposed of in Philadelphia, Baltimore and Cincinnati. I remained all this time in New York, superintending the forged bank-note business.

"I next entered into partnership with George Engles and Peter Burns. They proposed that we should go to Europe and study the way Seligman & Co., of New York, did business with their agents in London. Engles had a genuine draft of Seligman & Co., and he was to counterfeit the blanks during our absence. Peter Burns and wife and myself and wife left New York in February, 1879, for England on the steamer Germanic. Arriving in London we took rooms in the Inns of Court Hotel. Before leaving New York we bought a draft for not less than £1,000 from Seligman & Co. on their agents in London, and one of £10. Burns collected the big draft and I the small one.

"When presented to Seligman's agent the drafts were certified and stamped with the signature of the firm and the stamp on the back. I took a copy of the certificate and a drawing of the stamp, with which Burns and I returned to New York. Burns left his wife in London, on Oxford Street, near Hyde Park. We gave George Engles the drawing of the stamp and the copy of the signature. He made a good cut of the stamp on wood and also of the signature. We then sailed back to London on the steamer Wieland. I took my wife. In London we took quarters in a house on George Street. Burns went to his wife on Oxford Street. The rest of the party consisted of Decker, Edward Howard, 'Al' Wilson, who was known as 'the Jew,' and a man named Connor.

"Before commencing operations I presented a draft of Seligman & Co., in London. for £2,000, to see if they would make any difference between drafts representing big sums or small ones. The forged drafts were all prepared in New York by Engles before we left America, with the exception of the number that was to be added by me upon the back. Two days after this draft was presented and collected three forged drafts were presented in succession payable by Smith, Payne & Smith, of Lombard Street, for a total of £8,000.

"I had perhaps better explain more fully how these operations were conducted. We bought also, in New York, three small drafts at the same time that we bought the one for £2,000, with the intent to present them to Seligman & Co., to obtain the number to put upon the backs of the forged drafts. The forged drafts were presented by Howard, Cannon and Wilson, and were all paid by Smith, Payne & Smith. Edward Howard was once in prison for forgery, in which Barlow had a hand. His residence is New York, where he was once a policeman. Cannon and Wilson both live in New York.

"All of these people were found by Engles, and I was unknown to them. Decker acted as middle-man between them and me. Howard, Cannon and Wilson, after collecting their share, left the same evening for the Continent, thence to New York.

"One week later Burns and I left for Paris, and after five or six weeks I returned with my wife to New York by the steamer Pereire, via Havre. That was in June, 1879. Burns lived in Paris and Decker in London. Upon my return to New York I boarded at the Belvedere House for two months and then went to board in a private house opposite Washington Square.

"During this time I was conspiring with Burns and Decker, who were in London. One day I received a cable message from Burns saying that he wanted to see me. In a letter which preceded it he told me that he had something good on hand, and I was to share it with him. I sailed with my wife and a friend on the steamer City of Berlin. In London we took rooms on Southampton Street, and on arriving we communicated with Burns and Decker. This was in the latter part of 1879. They explained that they had found two Frenchmen, one named Picou or Pick and the other a Dr. Hammel. The latter had received a druggist's diploma. They said that they could forge and alter three per cent. French certificates. The work was done entirely by Picou and Dr. Hammel.

"It took them three weeks, during which Burns, Decker, myself and our wives went to Paris. I stopped at the Hôtel de Russie and Burns at the Hôtel du Louvre. Decker and Burns took a flying trip to Brussels for the purpose of passing a few notes of the Bank of England, obtained from the forgeries made against Seligman & Co. Decker was arrested and is now serving his sentence in the prison of Grand Belgium under the name of John Mills. Burns rejoined me. While in Paris in the early part of that year Oscar Decker came to me and said that he had a stolen letter of credit which was issued by Brown Brothers, of New York. He then made a voyage to Madrid to dispose of the remaining forgeries on Seligman & Co. He stopped at Biarritz and another adjoining city, and collected in all 6,000f. The letter he spoke of had been altered by him while in New York.

"The French certificates were now ready, having been made in John Phillip's house, at No. 3 St. James Place, Forrest Lane.

"I put the signature on them. We then decided to send Picou and Hammel to Naples to meet there a certain Baron —— (a Frenchman who had a bank account). We also decided that the Baron should dispose of the certificates in Naples, or wherever he could. I think he sold one in Rome and nine or ten in different other localities. In this journey they went as far as Vienna. They told Phillips, who was with them, that the police were after him. He fled to London, leaving them all the valuables—about twenty certificates. Those that could not be disposed of were sent by express to

Dr. Hammel, who made his headquarters at Munich. About nine were sent back and eighteen or nineteen, of the value of 10,000f., were kept. There were twenty-nine documents forged, of the nominal value of 240,000f. In 1880 Dr. Hammel and his wife disappeared, and it is supposed that the pair joined Picou and the Baron.

"I next became associated with George Engles, Charles Becker, Shell Hamilton, William Bartlett, Edward Burns, Edward Cleary, 'Al' Wilson, 'the Jew,' George Bell, and an old man known only to me as 'Andy.' They all came from America, and were under the management of Engles. Decker and Engles brought with them a letter of credit on the Société Générale of Brussels. It was their intention to take five different directions on the Continent and to defraud all the bankers that they met in their way. Before they proceeded they decided to try places with genuine letters of credit, which they were unable to get, and abandoned for the time being. During this time Engles and wife went to Paris to see some relatives, and to procure rooms where we could safely talk business. He changed his mind and returned to London.

"Our next move was to send Bartlett, Cleary and Wilson to Toulon, Brussels, Rotterdam, Amsterdam, Berlin, Hamburg and Bremen, with instructions to procure drafts from bankers on their correspondents in London. They had to make several trips before they could study the way and means of doing business of the bankers. The last voyage was made to Cologne and Aix-la-Chapelle, when we heard that Inspector Byrnes, the chief of detectives, had cabled to the London police all the names of the individuals that had left New York. Fearing arrest, we abandoned the scheme and paid the passage of the men back to America. Hamilton, Engles and Becker remained to do other business. We had previously engaged rooms at No. 5 Fincheley Road, where Hamilton, alias Neilson, resided with us. I went to Brussels with a Mr. Coswell, whom I made believe that I could buy gutta percha, for the purpose of getting a letter of credit and to learn a figure which was in a letter of credit of the Société Générale of Brussels. I got the letter from Mr. Coswell and collected in Rotterdam 13,000f., returning directly to London, where the balance of the letter of credit was drawn. My voyage in other respects was fruitless. I did not learn the figure, and abandoned the project. In my absence Becker and Engles had been working upon Italian bonds, at No. 7 Leamington Road.

"Small certificates of Italian incomes were bought from Baronoff in Milan and Turin. They consisted of twenty-five bonds bearing an income of 5f. These Engles and Becker worked upon. They erased by instruments and acids the indication of their value and restored their original color. The process was only known to Becker. All I knew was the printed denomination. The figures were substituted by a woodcut made by Becker. In the second voyage there were thirty-five certificates of income of the value of 500f. each, paying five per cent. They were taken to Engles and Becker, who made the alterations advancing their value to 30,000f. income, or equal to a capital of 600,000f. Several of these certificates were of 500f. income. The first lot used by Baronoff was for 1,000f. income. He disposed of them with the Crédit Lyonnais and with the Caisse Générale of Paris. They were the certificates tied up under the name of H. G. or G. H. Hendel, who received seventy-five per cent. by advancement. Another lot was disposed of in the same way to the Parisian Bank, the interest collected amounting to 10,000f. A third lot of 11,000f. income was sold at the principal office of the Société Générale at the Stock Exchange and at the Crédit Lyonnais.

"Those who took part in that line of work were Peter Burns, alias Colbert, John Carr, James Pasvell, George Engles, alias Hilgor, Charles Becker and myself. Charles Baronoff received twenty-five per cent. and the rest of the money, 400,000f., was divided among ourselves in equal shares. Hendel, or Baronoff, ordered the sale of the bonds. He sent a man called 'Cranky Jimmy,' with a check to the Société Générale.

"He obtained 4,000f. by means of a hotel messenger, and upon discovering that there was no trouble to dispose of the certificates he went himself and presented a check for more than 40,000f. He had to wait a long time. and, getting scared, ran away from the bank.

"Some time afterward he wrote a letter to the Société Générale or the Crédlt Lyonnais, either from Belgium or Holland, saying he had sent his clerk to Paris with a check for the purpose of paying notes, and that he had not received any news either from the clerk or of the check, and that he would go himself to Paris as soon as possible to find out what had become of them. This was to explain his hasty departure from the bank after presenting the check for 40,000f. Baronoff lived in Paris, Boulevard Malesherbes, under the name of Hendel.

"My first introduction to that gang traveling in Italy was on the occasion of the sending out of the letters of credit of the Société Générale of Brussels. 'Al' Wilson was introduced to me by John Phillips. The men who operated extensively in Italy were Phillips, Wilson and Shell Hamilton.

"They started by Geneva, Switzerland, where they were rejoined by Charles Silvio Bixio, who had been living in that city during the summer. They went to Torino, where they separated, Bixio and Hamilton going together to Naples, and Phillips, Wilson and myself going to Venice, where they were to wait for a telegram before beginning operations.

"An attempt was made in Moscow, Russia, by Baronoff and James Pasvell, but the job failed for the reason that the figure and the key kept by the bankers there did not correspond with the forged notes. Learning this I telegraphed for them to come home. This took place when we were working on the Italian certificates of income, altering and filling letters of credit, which were accompanied by forged French passports. All this work was done by Engles and Becker.

"After his return from Italy I was informed that Bixio had the means of disposing of all sorts of forged paper. I sent Hamilton and Wilson, whose alias was 'Lewis,' to Geneva to meet him. They had $3,000 in counterfeit bank-notes on the Tradesmen's and Broadway Banks of New York. The counterfeit money was obtained by Hamilton from a man named Megath. I advanced the money to buy it. They also took a three per cent. French certificate of income (forged), which was not sold on account of some misunderstanding about the price. They came back to London, remaining several weeks, and then took again $2,500 in greenbacks, six or seven three per cent. French certificates of income and $200 in bonds of the Bank of Canada.

"The latter bonds were stolen in Canada about four years before. One bond of

Lombardy came from a robbery on the Calais and Dover steamboat. It was of the value of 100f. With these valuables, assisted by a certain Strogella, of Torino, Bixio sold the American bank-notes, and Wilson, alias Lewis, sold the certificates for $1,000 in all. They also disposed of the bond of Lombardy in Torino and operated in Geneva and Switzerland.

"They borrowed from different Jews, with the aid of a man now in prison with Bixio, some French three per cent. income certificates of the denomination of 300f. The person mentioned as the owner of the bonds was a certain Count Corradino, a notorious thief, well known, who was supposed to live in Torino. He was called count by both Strogella and Bixio. They sold two other forged three per cent. French certificates of income in two different places. These certificates were some of those that Picou and Baron —— sent back from Naples that had remained in Burns' hands. Hamilton made a trip to London, and after his arrival there Bixio telegraphed for more French certificates, and they were sent to him by registered letter. Wilson, alias Lewis, also went back, but kept up a constant correspondence with Strogella, of Torino. Hamilton and Wilson desired very much to have more bonds, either stolen or forged, of the five per cent. Italian income.

"We set out together, and during the crossing of the sea Burns persuaded me to accompany him in a voyage after we should end our business. We were to go to Naples, Rome, Livorno and back to Paris by way of Nizza. Upon our arrival in Torino we met Hamilton, who took us to a café and there told us that he had sold the bonds of Lombardy and the 900f. of Italian income, with the aid of Strogella, to the latter's brother-in-law, who was a broker in Torino. We then gave him more French and Italian certificates of income. Hamilton said that he could not dispose of the French or Russian bonds, but said that the Italian bonds were all right. He brought us next day the money for the 1,000f. Italian certificate and gave us 25,000f. for the bonds sold in Torino.

"We then combined to go to Milan with Strogella and Wilson, alias Lewis, carrying with us two French certificates of 300f. each, and two forged Italian certificates of income of 1,000f. and 500f. each, which had been examined and approved by Strogella and Wilson, alias Lewis. They set out for Milan and were there arrested. We decided not to see any one in Torino except Hamilton.

"Burns and I did not know Strogella. We went to Florence, stopping at the Hôtel di Nuova York. Our plan was to meet Hamilton only. I was to prepare him a letter of credit, and Lewis or Wilson was to come with us, and we would decide where it would be best to try it. The scheme was frustrated by our arrest—that is Burns, alias Julius, and his wife and I and my wife—at Florence.

"I forgot to say that Baronoff was accompanied in his first and second voyages by Carr and Pasvell, but in the third only Carr was with him. They introduced themselves to the Société Générale, Crédit Lyonnais and Banque Parisienne, and sold them different certificates which they bought from other bankers. Megotti, or Megath, sold me the seventeen bonds of Lombardy, Italian and French certificates of income, the Russian bonds and a bond of the Crédit Foncier of France, knowing that it was all stolen property. All the certificates were sold by Strogella to his brother-in-law.

Strogella gave the money to Hamilton and the latter gave it to me. The entire quantity of bonds were bought at forty-five or fifty per cent. of their real value, and were sold by Strogella for their real value.

"The amount of these sales was equally divided among Strogella, Lewis, Hamilton, Burns and myself. James Coswell was introduced to me by James Pasvell, and was deceived by me by telling him that I could buy remnants of gutta percha on the Continent—that is, in Brussells, Colmar, Aix-la-Chapelle and Rotterdam. We made two voyages to Brussels, and there he obtained for me two letters of credit on the Société Générale by means of introductions from his correspondents in London. These letters were for 20,000f. and 25,000f."

Wilkes' confession is the most interesting criminal document in existence to-day. It details nearly all his plots and schemes, and tells just how the men under him succeeded in duping the best financiers of Europe and America, and also gives the names of the men who took part in the several conspiracies with him.

JOE CHAPMAN, one of Wilkes' early companions, is at present in prison in Munich.

IVAN, or CARLO, SISCOVITCH is serving out a term of imprisonment, under the alias of John Smith, in the penitentiary at Cleveland, Ohio.

PHIL HARGRAVES, who still lingers about New York City, has been more fortunate than others of the gang. This is due to the fact that he is a very guarded operator.

WILLIAM GRIFFIS, alias "Lord Ashburton," was released in the spring of 1884, after serving out a term at the prison of San Quentin, Cal., and on his return to New York was arrested for the Kirkpatrick affair. He pleaded guilty, and as he was quite low in health he was released and allowed to go to his home at Dartmouth, Devonshire, England, to die.

ENGLES is dead.

BECKER is now serving a sentence of six years and six months in the Kings County Penitentiary, Brooklyn, N. Y., for counterfeiting a 1,000-franc note of the Bank of France. (See record of No. 18.)

JOHN CARR is a notorious English criminal. After the robbery of the Northampton, Mass., Bank, the proceeds were taken to England, and remained in Carr's house until the negotiations were completed for their return.

BELL is at present serving out a ten years' sentence in Maryland for forgery. (See record of No. 193.)

AL. WILSON finished a term in Baltimore, Md., for forgery, and is now serving a twelve years' sentence in Canada. (See record of No. 37.)

CLEARY, who was also implicated with Bell and Wilson in the Baltimore forgeries, has just completed a five years' sentence there. (See record of No. 193.)

ELLIOTT is serving an eighteen-year sentence at Rochester, N. Y. (See record of No. 16.)

STEVE RAYMOND, another associate of Wilkes, is serving out a life imprisonment for forgery, the first and only man ever sentenced under the new law. (See record of No. 55.)

For further particulars of George Wilkes see records of Nos. 18 and 26.

OTHER NOTED CRIMINALS.

DAN NOBLE, alias Dan Dyson, bond forger, bank burglar and sneak.

This celebrated criminal is now (1886) serving out a twenty years' sentence in the Millbank prison, London, England. For years previous to Noble's departure for England and the Continent, he was an acknowledged leader of the most notable crooked operators in America. He was the master spirit in the Lord bond robbery in New York City in March, 1886, which netted him and his companions, Fred Knapp, James Griffin, and Little Pettingill, nearly $1,700,000. Subsequently (in the spring of 1871) he was sent to Auburn (N. Y.) State prison from Oswego, N. Y., for five years for a burglary. He remained there but a short time, securing his liberty by escaping with two other notorious bank robbers, Jimmy Hope (20) and Big Jim Brady. After remaining in hiding in New York a short time, he started for the old country, arriving in England in 1873. Here he fell in with the big swells in sporting and crooked circles, and, as in America, soon went to the front, on account of his ability to concoct and successfully carry out his schemes. He began his operations with three smart men, Johnny Miller, formerly of New York, Joe Chapman and Jack Phillips. They got rid of a large amount of spurious £5 notes in Bavaria, Brussels and Switzerland, several of which were found upon emigrants after landing in this country. He was sentenced to five years in Paris, France, for a diamond robbery, but escaped shortly after. The crime for which he was sent to prison in London was forgery, his associates being two noted English thieves named Wardley and Garnett, and an American named Charles Lister, who assumed the alias of Edward Hunt. Lister was sentenced to fifteen years' imprisonment, and afterwards gave information to the authorities about Johnny Miller, who was also arrested and sentenced to twenty years. Dan Noble fled to Italy, but was captured and returned, and although Miller swore that Noble was innocent, it was not believed, and Noble was sentenced to twenty years also. They all went to prison together. This will probably wind up Noble's criminal career.

He was known in Paris, Brussels, Geneva, Munich, Bavaria and London as well as in America. Is fifty-two years old in 1886. Born in United States. Married. No trade. Height, 6 feet; weight, 185 pounds. Fair complexion; light hair, inclined to be red; bluish grey eyes, long slim nose. Used to wear an exceedingly long goatee; now wears a long mustache. He is a fine-looking, big, jolly and well-built man. He has a deep scar on his nose caused by a cut from a bottle. Walks straight and erect, dresses well, and is an interesting talker. His description was taken during his trial in London, and is a good one.

Noble, Knapp and Griffin were credited with robbing Leonard W. Jerome, in New York City, on February 6, 1867, of about $100,000; also Bliss & Co., of Pine Street, New York. This last robbery was the cause of one of the firm becoming a raving maniac. The thieves, however, never realized one dollar from the latter robbery, as the bonds that were stolen were given by them to Phil. Furlong and Ned Lyons (70) to dispose of. These worthies never gave an accounting to the thieves, but divided among themselves what was realized on them.

Knapp is a horse sharp, Griffin and Phil. Furlong are dead, and Ned Lyons is serving out a sentence in Connecticut. (See record of No. 70.)

For further particulars of Dan Noble, see records of Nos. 4, 14, 20, 202.

SAMUEL T. PERRY, alias "Bottle Sam," the bank sneak, was convicted and sentenced in Detroit, Mich., on October 31, 1882, to five years' imprisonment at Jackson, Mich., for robbing the office of the County Treasurer in 1870.

Perry is the son of very respectable parents, and was raised in the vicinity of New York, but went to Cincinnati when he was quite young, where he has a sister married to a very respectable gentleman. His first connection with thieves was brought about by Johnny Green, a well known sneak thief, of St. Louis. Perry was caught tapping a till in St. Louis in 1868, and sentenced to the penitentiary for two years. Green succeeded in making his escape with the money. On coming out he returned to New York, where he associated with George Carson, Horace Hovan, alias Little Horace, and Red Tim, well known bank sneak thieves. Through his association with these men he became acquainted with Andy Roberts and Valentine Gleason, the forgers, and was selected by them to aid Walter Sheridan in the disposition of the forged Buffalo, New York and Erie railroad bonds. In this connection he went with Sheridan to England. Shortly after that detectives went there in pursuit of Joe Chapman and Joe Riley, alias Joe Elliott, in connection with the robbery of the Third National Bank of Baltimore, and while tracing them about London, they came across Perry, who was keeping company with them. Through watching Perry they were brought into contact with Walter Sheridan, Ike Marsh, Charley Bullard, alias Piano Charley, and Tom Worth, the Boylston (Boston) Bank robbers. By keeping run of them, the detectives and the London police were also brought in contact with Mark Shinburn, George Wade Wilkes, George McDonald and the two Bidwells, and numerous other American burglars, sneak thieves and forgers then residing in London. All of these men were thoroughly exposed, and it was through this exposure that the London police succeeded in implicating the two Bidwells and McDonald in the great frauds and forgeries on the Bank of England.

In the spring of 1873 Walter Sheridan and Sam Perry (Walter Sheridan under the name of C. Raulston and Sam Perry under the name of William B. Morgan) returned to New York on the steamer Adriatic. On account of Perry's dissipated habits Sheridan separated from him and left Perry none of the money. Sheridan had disposed of $150,000 worth of the Buffalo, New York and Erie bonds without leave of Perry. Perry acquired the habit of excessive wine drinking, and became familiarly known by the name of " Bottle Sam." In one of his drunken bouts he shot Charles H. Dorauss, alias Jack Strauss, the well known burglar, in New York, and was sentenced to State prison for five years on March 11, 1879, but through the influence of his mother obtained a new trial, and did not serve his sentence. After lying around New York and Philadelphia for a couple of years he again went West, and stopped in Chicago with a mob of Eastern thieves. In Chicago he committed several small sneak robberies, and from there went to Detroit, where he was concerned in the robbery of the County Treasurer's office. Perry was arrested the day after the robbery at Windsor, Canada, but succeeded in obtaining his discharge, as the offense against him did not come under the treaty. But he was readily identified as the man who "stalled" the County Treasurer to the rear of the office while the sneak went through the safe. After being liberated he went to Fort Erie, Canada, where he met John, alias "Clutch," Donahue, a well known American thief, who then resided in Canada, and operated with him and Joe Dubuque and Little Joe Harris through the Dominion. Coming to Port Huron, Mich., he was recognized by a Detroit officer, and arrested and taken back to Detroit, tried, and convicted. Perry has been one of the most remarkable thieves in the United States, and had he let liquor alone, was one of the most dangerous men in the country to meet. Dissipation has been his ruin, for in his time he has been associated more or less with the ablest thieves in the country.

Perry is forty years old in 1886. Height, 5 feet 11 inches ; weight, about 150 pounds. Black hair, hazel eyes, nose full in the centre, dark complexion, and generally wears black side-whiskers and mustache.

JOSEPH KILLORAN, alias Joe Howard, was arrested in Philadelphia Sunday, February 8, 1885, for the robbery of the First National Bank at Coldwater, Mich., of $10,000 on August 1, 1883, thus closing for a number of years to come the career of a man who, as a pickpocket, bank sneak thief and bank safe burglar, has operated successfully in one of these three lines of thieving with nearly all of the great professional criminals. Joseph Killoran is a New Yorker by birth, and comes from a good family. At the time of his parents' death, Joe, with his other brothers and sisters, inherited considerable property, but his share was spent in gambling and riotous living. Through gambling he became acquainted with professional thieves, and when his money was gone he joined a party of pickpockets. He was afterwards associated with George Bliss, alias Miles, alias White, the noted bank burglar, now serving sentence at Windsor, Vt., who was the partner of Mark Shinburn, probably the most expert bank safe burglar in the country. Joe was finally convicted for the robbery of the Waterford, N. Y., bank, and was sentenced to Auburn prison. He escaped, in company with Jimmy Hope, who was concerned in the Manhattan Bank robbery, and was next arrested in New York with George Miles, alias Bliss, for the Barre bank burglary of Vermont. The Auburn prison authorities, being informed of his arrest, claimed him as a prisoner who had escaped from them, and he was taken back to Auburn to serve out his term of imprisonment, which expired about three years since. Miles was taken to Vermont and sentenced to fourteen years' imprisonment, where he now is.

Joe Howard was concerned with Jimmy Hope, Worcester Sam, George Bliss and others in the robbery of the Beneficial Savings Fund, and the Kensington Bank burglary at Philadelphia, which occurred on April 6, 1869, and which attracted wide attention because of its magnitude. He was also concerned with Jimmy Hope, George Mason, Ike Marsh, alias "Big Ike," Tom Curley and Mike Welsh, in the successful robbery of the First National Bank at Wellsboro, Pa., on September 17, 1874. Here the family were bound and gagged, and the cashier made to open his own safe, while the contents were taken out. Marsh, Welsh, Curley and Mason were arrested, while the others made their escape. Marsh was sentenced to seventeen years in the Pennsylvania State prison, where he now is. The jury acquitted Welsh and disagreed as to Mason and Curley. With Jimmy Hope and two others he was concerned in the attempted robbery of the First National Bank at Wilmington, Del., November 7, 1873. Four of the party, including Hope and Howard, were arrested and sentenced to ten years' imprisonment each, and were ordered to receive fifty lashes. The sentence was executed, but after a few years' imprisonment all succeeded in making their escape.

Howard has also worked with Scott and Dunlap, of the Northampton (Mass.) bank robbery; also with Sam Perris, alias Worcester Sam, Thomas McCormick, Johnny Love, and in fact with all the leading professional bank burglars in the country. He has always made New York his home. Since coming out after serving his last imprisonment, he quit burglary and set to working almost entirely with bank sneak thieves. He was with Western sneak thieves when he perpetrated the robbery for which he is now serving time. Three parties entered the First National Bank at Coldwater, Mich., about noon, August 1, 1883. Howard engaged the attention of the cashier, while a second party engaged the paying teller. Then Ed. Quinn, the noted professional thief of Chicago, entered the bank, sneaked along the counter, and succeeded in getting into the vault without being observed. He took $10,000 worth of bonds, when, through some act of carelessness on his part, he attracted the attention of the cashier, who, on discovering Quinn in the vault, rushed in to seize him. He was warned off by Quinn, who pulled out a large pistol and threatened to kill the cashier in case he attempted to detain him. In this way he backed out of the bank, where a wagon was in waiting for the whole party. In this they were driven rapidly away. Quinn was arrested about a year ago in Chicago, but was taken to Laporte, Ind., instead of Coldwater, where he was wanted for a jewelry robbery, and was sentenced to ten years' imprisonment. He is now in prison. The other men who committed this robbery, with Howard, have been successful in keeping out of the way.

Killoran pleaded guilty to having assisted in the robbery of $10,000 from the First National Bank of Coldwater, Mich., as above described, and was sentenced to five years in the Michigan State prison on July 26, 1885, at Coldwater, Mich.

For expiration of sentence see commutation laws of Michigan.

WILLIAM E. GRAY was the son of a gentleman who for many years was Chaplain of the United States Senate. This honorable position held by the father gained for the son an *entrée* to the best circles of society, but which he sadly abused by his misconduct. He was extradited from England in July, 1878, for forging certificates to the amount of $30,000, issued by the State of New York for the payment of bounties of volunteers during the late war. Gray was tried and convicted, and sentenced to ten years in Sing Sing on May 29, 1879. During the trial his counsel took a great many exceptions, and carried the case to the Court of Appeals, which took some years, during which time he was locked up in the Tombs. He was finally set free in May, 1881, and is now living in this city. (See records of No. 202 and George Wilkes.)

The following very interesting account of Gray was published in one of the New York papers in May, 1880:

"Gray is a young man of pleasant address and agreeable manners, and while operating in Wall Street many years ago, was regarded as a shrewd speculator and an intelligent observer of financial events. Born of respectable parents, well educated, and given a good start in life, he chose a career of crime in preference to respectability with a more gradual fortune. His father, Rev. E. H. Gray, of Shelburne Falls, Mass., was Chaplain of the United States Senate from 1861 to 1869. After leaving college William E. Gray was appointed to a clerkship in the Fourth Auditor's office of the United States Treasury Department, and served with credit and fidelity until 1866, when he resigned. The following year he came to New York, bringing letters of recommendation from Gen. Butler, Senator Morrill, Acting Vice-President Foster, National Bank Examiner Callander, Senators Pomeroy and Fessenden and others, upon whom he always called when they visited this city. He was then twenty-three years of age, and extremely youthful in appearance. He was abstemious in his habits, refraining from liquors and tobacco, which gained for him the reputation of a model young man.

"His first employment in this city was as clerk for A. W. Dimock & Co., of No. 26 Pine Street, to whom he represented that he desired to learn the secrets of stock brokerage so as to enter the street on his account. In May, 1869, he left Dimock & Co., and began business on his own account in a small way at the office of Mr. J. G. Sands, No. 36 New Street. Among others, Mr. J. G. Eastman gave him power of attorney to act in the Gold Room, and the young Washingtonian was launched on the rough sea of Wall Street speculation under the most favorable auspices. It was here, as far as can be learned, that Gray began the sharp practices which subsequently made him a fugitive from justice, dodging the officers of the law, and finally landed him in the Tombs, awaiting a decision that may consign him to State prison for a long term of years. His first act was to borrow $1,600 on three Government bonds from George H. Lewis, who in turn re-hypothecated them to L. W. Morse for $3,000. Something he had learned awakened Mr. Morse's suspicions, and he called in the loan. Neither Lewis nor Gray responded, and the securities were sold at a loss to Mr. Morse. The purchaser afterwards discovered that the bonds had been stolen from the Common Prayer-Book Society of New York several months previously. Gray refused to make good Mr. Morse's loss, and he was arrested and thrown into Ludlow Street jail. His father intervened, paid the money, and young Gray was released.   He next victimized William H. Chapman, a South Street merchant, and kept up a system of 'kiting' on Mr. Eastman's credit, but his little game was discovered in time to prevent any serious losses.

"In the autumn of the same year, Gray gave out that he expected a legacy of $50,000 from a wealthy aunt, who had accommodatingly died, which, with $10,000 ready cash which he claimed to own, he proposed to enlarge his business operations. He purchased from G. H. Stebbins' Son the lease of the offices No. 44 Broad Street, which were afterward occupied by Victoria Woodhull and Tenny Claflin.   He furnished the rooms in elaborate style, and over the door a sign was hung with the name of W. E. Gray & Co.   Who the company was became a standing conundrum on the street, but it afterwards leaked out that it was composed of T. H. Pratt, William J. Sharkey, William S. Ree, George Larabee, and one or two others.   All the firm afterwards came to grief.   Sharkey is a refugee, having murdered Dunne ; Glover was convicted as an accomplice in the Boylston Bank robbery ; Leighton was arrested in California for being connected with a mining swindle, and Ree and Larrabee have been frequently before the public in connection with heavy forgeries.   While operating in a pool on Quartz Hill mining stock, Gray and his associates came into possession of sixteen New York State Bounty Loan certificates of $1,000 each, which had been stolen a year previous from C. W. Woolsey, a Pine Street broker ; two similar bonds for $15,000 originally issued to Elizabeth F. Taylor, and other stolen Government and miscellaneous securities.   The bounty loan certificates were raised by means of chemicals from $1,000 to $10,000 each, and the registers were changed to W. E. Gray & Co. Pratt was supposed to have done the forging, and that Gray aided in floating the bonds. This worked so well that the system was kept up for a long time.   In December, 1879, the forgeries were discovered, and Gray was sharply catechised by bank officers and detectives.   Gathering together all his available funds, some $50,000, he left his office in a carriage, in company with a veiled woman, and disappeared from view, and for two years all trace of him was lost.   His total debts were $310,000, and the assets he left behind consisted of $20,000, leaving him a net profit of $280,000.

"After Gray's departure a letter was found in his office addressed to a female clerk in the Treasury Department, whom he designated as 'Dear Birdie.'   He told her that he had insured his life for $5,000 in her favor.   The Mining Board expelled Gray, and the Stock Exchange gave Detective Tom Sampson instructions to find where he was and to follow him up and arrest him.   Sampson, after following numerous clues, learned that Gray was luxuriating in London under the name of James Peabody Morgan, a pretended nephew of George Peabody, the great philanthropist.   Being introduced one day to a genuine relative of Mr. Peabody, and being sharply cornered, he laughed the matter off as a joke, and was afterwards known as James Payson Morgan. He dressed like a noble, courted the society of snobs, and rejoiced in the ownership of a finer tandem team than the Prince of Wales drove.   At a dinner given by the niece of Baron Rothschild, when only twenty-eight years of age, he made an after-dinner speech on finances which astonished all his hearers.   He became acquainted with Mr. Chatteris, a London banker, and he placed his son in business with Gray, handing him

£10,000, and accepting as security $50,000 in spurious United States bonds. The venture was not a success, but Gray secured £5,000 more from old Mr. Chatteris by showing him an order, believed to have been forged, stating that $30,000 had been placed to his credit in New York. Young Chatteris quarreled with Gray, and accused him of swindling, when he drew a pistol and was arrested. The bonds deposited with Mr. Chatteris turned out to be stolen and caveated bonds, and Detective Sampson immediately, on learning the facts, had Gray indicted, and, having secured extradition papers, sailed for London on November 18, 1871. Gray, alias Morgan, cunningly made his escape and crossed over to Paris. Captain Sampson chased him all over the Continent, and, failing to catch him, returned to New York.

"Gray next turned up on the Hague as Dr. Georgius Colletso, oculist, and graduate of the Royal College of Surgeons of London, and possessor of diplomas which were never legally issued. Here he attempted to sell to the wealthy capitalists of the Hague a mythical silver mine in Colorado. Gray next appeared in Texas under the name of Colletso, where he inaugurated the Bastrop Coal Mining Company—another mythical concern. Here he formed an alliance with Colonel William Fitzcharles McCarty, and together they returned to England and flooded the market with the stock of the Wichita Copper Company, limited. They raised $20,000 to start the thing, and would have secured more had not the Englishmen learned that the entire thing was an arrant swindle. This led to his identity, and again Captain Sampson started out after him. Upon his arrival he found Gray in custody, and apparently anxious to return to America. Again the persevering veteran detective was doomed to disappointment. Secretary Fish declined to give a promise that Gray should not be tried on any other charge than was contained in the extradition papers, and he was released by the British authorities. This position was subsequently receded from, and George B. Mickle, a son of ex-Mayor Mickle, meeting Gray in Edinburgh, gave Captain Sampson information, and Gray was arrested in London. Captain Sampson was again deputized by the Stock Exchange to go after the long absent prisoner, but being detained here on important Government business, the late Captain Kealy was selected in his stead. Gray was brought back, followed by a niece of Balfe, the great composer, who is his wife. She still resides in this city. As a matter of historic equity, it may be mentioned that Seth Johnson, who was Gray's most intimate friend when in the Treasury Department, was convicted in 1872 of embezzling $50,000."

MARY A. HANSEN, alias Klink, has many wiles in working sharp men for money and her husband helps in her crooked schemes.

On January 15, 1886, Frederick Bohmet, of No. 192 Allen Street, called at Police Headquarters in New York, and informed the authorities that in September, 1885, Julius Klink, a shoemaker, whom he had known for twenty years, called on him and said a wealthy widow named Hansen, on Jersey City Heights, had got infatuated with him and he married her; that he was well fixed and would never work another day at the bench. He said she was left by her uncle, who died at Harrisburg, Pa., $750,000, and the money was on deposit in the United States Treasury, and would be paid in a few days, as the Supreme Court had decided the case in her favor, and they would be obliged to pay the money on July 15, 1886. They had a number of lawyers employed, he said, and they wished to get her money at once. While this conversation was going on Mrs. Klink ran into the house with a telegram, shouting and crying, " You are a nice man. Why didn't you assist me to get our money ? The telegram says if we don't have money and get the Supreme Court seal on our papers we are gone. We will not be able to get our money until July, 1886, and we must have money at once. I must have money too to run on to Washington at once."

Mr. Klink then asked Mr. Bohmet if he would advance the money needed. Mr. Bohmet asked what security he should receive. Mr. and Mrs. Klink said they would give him his money back in a few days, and also as a present a four-story tenement house and lot. Mr. Bohmet went to the bank and gave them $2,316, which money he was to receive on July 15, 1886, also his house and lot. On January 2, Mr. Bohmet called on his lawyer and explained his case to him. He advised him to call on the police, which he did on January 18. While the sergeant was in conversation with Mr. Bohmet a lady named Mary Mesam, of No. 1 First Avenue, called and informed the sergeant that she was robbed by a woman named Hansen, of $2,500. A detective listened to her story and saw by the description that Klink and Hansen was the same woman. Two detective sergeants were detailed on the case, and ordered to bring both complainants before Justice Duffy at Jefferson Market and obtain a warrant, if possible, as the woman resided in Jersey. Justice Duffy issued a warrant for Mr. and Mrs. Klink. Two officers went to No. 72 Hague Street, Jersey City Heights, accompanied by Inspector Lang and Detective Dalton, of Jersey City. As they attempted to enter the house Mrs. Klink's daughter met the officers on the stoop and informed them that her mother was not at home. The officers remained watching the house until evening, when they entered and searched, and found the object of their search on the second floor pretending to be sick. She came to New York and was locked up at the Central Office on January 22, 1886. She was taken before Justice Duffy and held under $8,000 bail.

On January 29, Lawyer James D. McClelland served a writ of habeas corpus on the police authorities, returnable before Judge Van Brunt at the Supreme Court Chambers, and she was discharged on the ground that the money was loaned, and the complainants did not show by witnesses from Philadelphia, Harrisburg or Washington that her representations were false. After she left the court room the detectives arrested her again, and she was taken before Justice Duffy on complaint of Richard C. Perry, of No. 370 Broadway, who charged her with obtaining $300 by representing that the Sheriff of Philadelphia held $11,000 of her money, and she wished to go on to Philadelphia at once and obtain her money. She was held in $4,000 on this charge. She was also charged with obtaining $500 from Annie Mesam of No. 1 First Avenue, New York City, by representing that she owned a number of houses in Philadelphia, and that Mr. Friedenburg, of No. 908 Chestnut Street, Philadelphia, held all her deeds in his safe and had advanced her $700. A detective went to Philadelphia and found her story was false; that she never had any deeds with the above named firms, and they did not know any woman named Mary A. Klink, Mary A. Hansen or Mary A. Gibson, and she was a fraud. She represented to Miss Mesam that her husband,

Julius Klink, was left $490,000 at Harrisburg, and it was in the hands of the Sheriff at Philadelphia, and she expected her money every day, but she had just received a telegram to come on at once and obtain her money. If Miss Mesam was afraid to trust her husband she would pay herself, as Mr. Freidenberg, of No. 908 Chestnut Street, held all her deeds and diamonds in his safe.

She began crying and shouting, clapping her hands and running around the saloon and saying that she was ruined if she did not get the money at once. Miss Mesam gave her $500 to go to Washington to get the money from the United States Treasury. The following are the parties who have been swindled by Mrs. Klink and her husband : Mary Mesam, No. 1 First Avenue, New York City, $2,000 ; Annie Mesam, No. 1 First Avenue, $500 ; Frederick Bohmet, No. 192 Allen Street, New York, $2,316 ; John Lodlobz, Philadelphia, $500 ; William Whiteman, $200 ; Mr. Trost gave on same representations his house and lot, valued at $2,800 ; Daniel Troft, No. 1309 North Front Street, Philadelphia, $1,200 ; Jacob Trost, $2,900 ; Christopher Baure, No. 971 Randolph Street, Philadelphia, $900 ; Caroline Schamer, 23 West Thompson Street, $185 ; Leonard Friedwald, No. 229 East Thompson Street, $610 ; Fred Watters, $110 ; John F. Graff, No. 1337 Greene Street, Philadelphia, $525 ; J. L. Schwartz, $200 ; William Bauer, $90 ; Mr. Henning, No. 59 Warren Street, New York, $195—and a number of others.

Mrs. Klink, alias Hansen, alias Gibson, was arrested by Chief Murphy, of Jersey City, in 1876, for swindling a number of politicians in Jersey City, by representing that she was worth a half million dollars, which was held by Cardinal McCloskey. Cardinal McCloskey took the stand, and swore he never knew the woman or had any money in trust for her.

In the latter part of 1879 Detectives Handy and Fogarty, of New York City, arrested her for obtaining goods from about twenty different firms in the wool business. Among the victims were Bernstrein & Co., Canal Street ; Franklin & Co., Howard Street, New York. She received about $12,000 at this time.

The Jersey City Rogues' Gallery description of the woman is as follows :

" No. 143. Mary Klink, alias Mary A. Hansen, alias Gibson, aged 48, hair brown and gray, eyes hazel, weight about 190 pounds, height 5 feet 1 in., German, but speaks good English."

Mrs. Hansen was committed to Ludlow Street Jail on a judgment obtained in the civil case by Mrs. Mesam. The complaint in this case was withdrawn, and Mrs. Hansen was discharged from the jail on August 30, 1886. She was re-arrested on a warrant issued by a Philadelphia magistrate, charged with swindling a party in that city some years previous. The Grand Jury refused to indict her in this case, as her husband had already served five years in prison for it. She was discharged in New York City on September 10, 1886, and is now at large.

ELLEN E. PECK eight years ago suddenly developed into a dangerous confidence woman. Prior to that she was but an ordinary sharper, and her small exploits were scarcely worthy of notice. When, in 1878, she succeeded in swindling B. T. Babbitt, the soap manufacturer, out of $19,000, she came to be looked upon as an operator of some talent. Mr. Babbitt had been robbed a short time before of over half a million dollars. When the dishonest employés had been arrested, Mrs. Peck visited the soap manufacturer in the rôle of a female detective. She then represented that she was in the possession of valuable information concerning property owned by the clerks which could easily be sued for or seized. Mr. Babbitt was so taken in by his visitor that he advanced the amount demanded, and afterwards discovered that Mrs. Peck's information was false and worthless. Next she swindled Samuel Pingee, a patent medicine man, out of $2,700. She pretended to the latter that she had a friend in the office of Jay Gould, who gave her all the points about financial affairs. The medicine maker was anxious to secure information concerning stocks from Mr. Gould's office, and willingly gave Mrs. Peck the money for "points." Pingee's investments which followed the "tips" were not as fruitful as he had expected. When it was too late he discovered that Jay Gould had been selling the very stocks he had been buying, and that they were on the eve of going down. Later on she secured a large loan from the notorious John D. Grady, the crooked diamond dealer, who was known for years as "Supers and Slangs." Grady, although himself an unusually shrewd sharper, was so completely taken in by Mrs. Peck that he readily handed her over the cash in lieu of a rent receipt for a compartment in a safe deposit vaults where the imaginary diamonds she was borrowing on were supposed to be. The compartment, of course, was empty, and on a small investment the cunning confidence woman realized many thousand dollars. In after years, when Mrs. Peck rose to the front rank among confidence women, she delighted in outwitting professional criminals, and invariably succeeded in her tricks. She roped the notorious Julius Columbani into a transaction over bonds stolen from the residence of the McSorleys, on Staten Island. Mrs. Peck furnished the evidence which led to the recovery of the plunder and the conviction of Columbani. The whole of her exploits, if written, would fill many pages of this book.

Mrs. Peck was indicted for the Babbitt affair, but every time the case came up for trial she was taken very sick, until told that the next time the trial came up she must appear or forfeit her bail. Then she suddenly became insane, and was sent to an asylum in Pennsylvania. Her counsel soon got the complainants to agree to sue her in a civil court, which suit was to take precedence over the criminal charge, and Mrs. Peck's wits, when all was arranged, returned to her and she came back to New York.

The confidence woman was tried and acquitted in the Kings County Court of Sessions, July 18, 1879, on an indictment charging her with obtaining several thousand dollars' worth of diamonds and jewelry, under false pretenses, from Loyance Langer, of this city, and was arraigned four days later in the same court upon the remaining indictments pending against her in the same case. The Assistant District Attorney moved that a nolle prosequi be entered, as the trial had failed to convict her. Judge Moore granted the motion, permitting her to go upon her own recognizance, and remarking at the same time that it was but fair to say that there was an officer in waiting to take Mrs. Peck to New York, where it was understood an indictment had been found against her.

Mrs. Peck was again arrested at her home, No. 307 Putnam Avenue, Brooklyn, on September 16, 1881. She was then accused of having defrauded John H. Johnson, a jeweler, of No. 150 Bowery, New York, of jewelry to the amount of $150. The complainant alleged that when Mrs. Peck selected the jewelry she paid down $25, and represented herself as Mrs. Eliza Knight, giving as a reference a bank in New York. On making inquiries at the bank Mr. Johnson was told that Mrs. Knight had an account there, and he therefore let her have the articles ; but subsequently he discovered that the Mrs. Knight who had the credit at the bank was an entirely different person from the purchaser of the jewelry.

On March 4, 1884, Mrs. Peck obtained an introduction under the name of Mrs. Knight to John Bough, a diamond dealer of No. 22 Liberty Street, New York. She represented herself to be a speculator in precious stones. In the early part of April she called on Mr. Bough and told him she had an order to purchase a diamond cluster ring for a lady friend. She selected a ring valued at $75 and took it away, returning next day and paying for it. Mr. Bough offered her a commission, which she refused, saying that the transaction was only a trifling one, and that she would soon bring him an important order. On April 28 she told Mr. Bough that the wife of a prominent Brooklynite was going to dine with her that night, and she thought that she could sell her some diamonds. She selected a pair of solitaire earrings and two finger rings, valued at $400.

After anxiously waiting the lady's return for several days, Mr. Bough called on the police to work up the case. After an infinite amount of trouble a detective found that the missing jewelry had been pledged at Simpson's, on the Bowery, New York, for $130, and that on the 1st of August Mrs. Peck had called at Simpson's, presented the ticket and demanded the surrender of the property, alleging that the jewels had been stolen from her several months before, and that the ticket had just been returned to her by mail. Simpson refused to comply with her demand, and a replevin suit was instituted by Mrs. Peck's counsel, Champion Bissell, of No. 23 East Fourteenth Street, New York. Simpson got a writ of re-replevin, and the result was a civil suit tried before Judge Clancy on September 12, 1884. Decision was reserved. The day before the trial Mr. Bough called at Simpson's, where he fully identified the jewels by private marks. At the trial Mrs. Peck swore that the jewels had been bought by her last October from one George P. Thomas, of Brooklyn, for $130. Thomas corroborated Mrs. Peck's statement. He was arrested on September 28, 1884, for perjury, and when brought to Police Headquarters he made a full confession in writing. In it he said that he met Mrs. Peck about four years ago, and that on several occasions since then she has befriended him and loaned him various sums of money. Just before the trial he borrowed $20 from her. He felt himself placed under so great an obligation that when he was asked to "do a little swearing" for his benefactress he professed himself to be ready to make oath to anything. As a reward it was arranged that the $20 loan should be cancelled, and that he should receive a bonus of $50 in addition.

In 1884 Richard W. Peck, the husband of the confidence woman, began a suit against Benjamin T. Babbitt to collect from the soap manufacturer $100,000 damages, alleging that he (Peck) had been seriously injured by the defendant's putting a *lis pendens* on his property in connection with proceedings against Mrs. Peck to recover some of the money out of which Babbitt charges that the woman defrauded him.

The Babbitt action was one of fifteen cases in which Mrs. Peck was prepared to act a prominent part. One of these, brought by her husband against Frederick W. Watkins and Daniel C. Mitchell, was to set aside a mortgage for $600 upon the furniture in the Peck residence. In this case the plaintiff alleged that on April 2, 1884, his wife obtained for the defendants in the suit the amount named upon a chattel mortgage upon property which belonged solely to him. Mrs. Peck always came to the assistance of her husband by swearing that the loan was made "on a corrupt and unlawful agreement, namely, that Watkins should receive $150 for a loan of $450 for thirty days."

Mrs. Ellen E. Peck, on December 6, 1884, succeeded in having herself arrested again. A charge of larceny was made against her by Mrs. Ann McConnell, of No. 140 West Forty-ninth Street, who advertised in the newspapers that she had money to loan on good security. On the 20th of September, 1884, she received a visit from a Mrs. Crosby, who said that she had seen the advertisement and wished to borrow $250. Mrs. McConnell was favorably impressed by the appearance of her visitor, who, in addition to her neat and quiet way of dressing and ladylike manner, told in the most plausible way how it happened that she was compelled to make the loan.

"My second son," she said, "is about to engage in business, and the money is needed for that purpose. I own considerable household furniture at No. 307 Putnam Avenue, Brooklyn, N. Y.; I do not owe $10 in the world, and I have a large income, which is paid semi-annually, in May and November."

Mrs. McConnell gave her the $250, and executed a chattel mortgage on the furniture, Mrs. Crosby agreeing in thirty days' time to pay back the $250 and $75 besides as interest. Fifteen days passed and Mrs. McConnell read of the arrest of Mrs. Peck on the charges of perjury and swindling a jeweler, and of her incarceration in the Tombs. It struck her as a curious feature of the case that Mrs. Peck's residence was in Putnam Avenue. The suspicion that Mrs. Peck and Mrs. Crosby might be one and the same person flashed through her mind. She called at the Tombs and saw Mrs. Peck. To Mrs. McConnell's dismay it was no other than Mrs. Crosby. Mrs. McConnell went straightway from the prison to the Tombs Court and asked for a warrant for Mrs. Peck's arrest on a charge of larceny. Justice White advised her to wait until the thirty days agreed upon had expired. Mrs. McConnell did so. The payment was not forthcoming. Worse still, she found that there were half a dozen other mortgages on the same furniture. She again applied for the warrant, which Justice White issued. On it Mrs. Peck was arrested.

Mrs. Peck did not look as jaunty as usual when she was arraigned before Justice Duffy in the Tombs Court. She wore a brown turban and a veil that covered half of her face. She had on a brown polonaise and a gray dress. Her counsel, Henry A. Meyenborg, of Brooklyn, accompanied her. He said that in spite of all the dubious transactions in which she had figured she had never in her life been convicted of any crime or misdemeanor. In this case, he said, she had an excellent defense. Mrs. Peck got $250 and agreed to pay it back with $75 interest in thirty days. She had not paid it. That was all there was to the case. It was a corrupt agreement and could not be constructed into a larceny.

Mrs. Ellen E. Peck was again a prisoner at the Tombs Police Court on January

5, 1885. She was the defendant in twenty-eight civil and criminal cases, and three indictments that had been found against her were pending.

The complainant in the last case was Champion Bissell, a lawyer, of No. 23 East Fourteenth Street, who was once her counsel. On September 1, 1884, she obtained $500 from him on a chattel mortgage on the furniture in her house. She exhibited a letter purporting to be signed by her husband, Richard K. Peck, saying that he would join her in executing the mortgage. The signature was witnessed by George P. Thomas. After lending the money Mr. Bissell discovered that Mrs. Peck, under the name of Mrs. Knight, had, on August 28, obtained $650 on the same furniture from Horatio W. P. Hodson, a lawyer, of No. 132 Nassau Street. Mr. Bissell foreclosed the mortgage on November 4. Then Mr. Peck, who is a member of the iron firm of Peck, Howard & Co., of Nos. 73 and 75 West Street, pronounced the letter a forgery and claimed the furniture as his own.

Mrs. Peck looked pale and anxious when she was arraigned for sentence on June 2, 1885, before Judge Van Brunt for having forged a bond upon a mortgage by which she obtained $3,000 from the Mutual Life Insurance Company of New York City, the Assistant District Attorney, instead of moving for the sentence informed the Judge that it was the opinion of the District Attorney that the ends of justice would be better subserved by granting Mrs. Peck a new trial.

A gleam of joy shot across the face of the prisoner and the color rose to her cheeks when she heard the motion, but paled again when the lawyer continued that the punishment which could be inflicted under the present conviction would not be sufficient for the offense committed.

Mr. Henry Meyenberg, counsel for Mrs. Peck, urged that a second trial of the case be delayed as long as possible, asserting that his client would change the plea on which she had been convicted and would plead insanity at the new trial. "Since the last trial," said the counsel, "I have learned that Mrs. Peck's father committed suicide, and that five years ago she was an inmate of an insane asylum."

After flirting for years with justice, the confidence woman received her first punishment in New York City on October 6, 1885, in the form of a four and a half years' sentence. Mrs. Peck is not a prepossessing looking woman, and as she was brought to the bar of the Court of Oyer and Terminer her masculine-looking face was divested of every vestige of color. Without displaying any outward sign of feeling she clutched the railing before Judge Van Brunt and cast her eyes on the floor. Her counsel asked the court to take into consideration her long imprisonment in the Tombs in passing sentence.

Addressing the prisoner, Judge Van Brunt said that there were a number of indictments against her, but that the District Attorney felt that no good results could be attained by pressing them. In passing sentence he took into consideration her long imprisonment, but felt it was the duty of the court to impose the highest penalty. Her sentence, therefore, would be four and a half years in the penitentiary. Mrs. Peck's head fell lower when she heard the sentence, and she turned from the bar without a word. She had gone only a few feet when she tottered and was about to fall, but a young man, her son, sprang from one of the seats and caught her in his arms.

Supported by him and followed by the Deputy Sheriff, she went sobbing convulsively from the court room.

The crime for which Mrs. Peck was convicted was for forging a bond given with a mortgage on a house owned by her husband in Brooklyn, by which she obtained $3,000 from the Mutual Life Insurance Company of New York. An ex-convict, who was a witness in the case, personated her husband and received the money.

Mrs. Peck, who is about fifty years of age, is now in the penitentiary on Blackwell's Island, New York.

JULIUS COLUMBANI, a forger and negotiator of stolen bonds, was arrested in New York City and sentenced to three years and six months in Sing Sing prison for forgery in the third degree, on October 10, 1878, on complaint of Courtland St. John, of No. 20 Cedar Street, New York City. His time expired there on June 10, 1881. Below will be found full particulars of his last arrest and conviction:

Mrs. E. Peck, whose acquaintance was very costly to Mr. B. T. Babbitt, the soap manufacturer, John D. Grady and others, was once more brought before the public, and in the somewhat unexpected rôle of an aid to the police authorities. On Sunday, September 10, 1882, Edward and Owen McSorley, brothers, who have a homestead at West Brighton, Staten Island, went out driving, leaving their place in the care of Bryan Norton, a credulous old man. An hour later a polite young man went to the house and told Norton that his masters' carriage had broken down a mile away, and that he had been sent by them to tell him to go to their aid with a wrench and some rope. The old man started off as fast as he could, but slackened his speed when the polite young man told him not to hurry. When the McSorleys returned home Norton was absent and their safe had been broken open. Burglars had stolen ten one-thousand-dollar seven per cent. Richmond County bonds, three other bonds, and jewelry and money, amounting in all to $14,000 in value. In January of the following year the store of Higgins & Co., No. 7 Strawberry Street, Philadelphia, was robbed of property worth $7,000, and E. Jacques and his wife were arrested for the crime in Philadelphia, and an accomplice, Tom Gardiner, was caught in this city. In Gardiner's possession was found some of the jewelry stolen from the McSorleys, but he was taken to Philadelphia, and he, with Jacques, sentenced to five years' imprisonment for the Higgins robbery. The bonds stolen from West Brighton were kept out of the market, as honest negotiators had been properly warned. On April 25, 1884, however, Mrs. Peck helped the police to recover some of them.

According to Mrs. Peck's story, a lady who was visiting her advertised on the 13th of April, 1884, for the loan of $5,000 on a large quantity of diamonds. Mrs. Peck's antecedents have caused it to be surmised that she was the advertiser herself, and that the advertisement was to pave the way to one of her peculiar business transactions. Mrs. Peck says that two days later she received a letter, in which were instructions how to recognize at the Astor House a man who might negotiate with her. The letter was written by Julius Columbani, an old criminal, whose specialties are negotiating stolen securities and altering them. He had been in State prison, and was identified at one time with some real estate swindlers. Mrs. Peck did not, until April 25, discover who he was, if her story is to be believed.   She said that as she was a business woman she would not permit her lady friend, who is uninitiated, to carry out the transaction with her correspondent of the Astor House, New York, and so met him herself.   They walked into Vesey Street and talked about the loan.   He said he could not let her have the money, as his capital was tied up, but he would place in her hands ten seven per cent. Richmond County bonds of $1,000 each, to be considered as equivalent to $5,000.   They parted to meet four days later.   Mrs. Peck went to a Broad Street broker immediately to ask about Richmond County bonds.   She was told that they were at par, but cautioned, as some had been stolen, and she received the numbers of those taken from the McSorley homestead.

Meeting Columbani at the Astor House on the 19th of April, 1884, Mrs. Peck walked to Barclay Street with him, and then taxed him with dealing in "crooked" securities.   He evaded a direct answer, but said in effect that she appeared to be keen, and must know that if he offered her bonds at half their value there would be something odd about them.   Mrs. Peck was not dreadfully shocked, and managed matters so well that she appeared to believe Columbani's assertion that with her business talents she could take the bonds at $5,000 and sell them for $10,000.   Columbani, in pursuance of an agreement, met her the next day at the Annex Hotel, in Brooklyn, N. Y., and showed her ten bonds, which were those stolen from the McSorleys.   She demurred as to their value, so as to get another interview with the man, and offered $4,000 worth of diamonds for them.

The next interview was to be at the Astor House at 12:30 P. M. on April 21. When Mrs. Peck left the Annex Hotel she went to the Chief of Detectives and told all she had done, and he detailed two detective sergeants to aid her in capturing the criminal.   A code of signals was agreed upon by which Mrs. Peck could notify the officers if Columbani had the bonds in his possession, so that they should pounce upon him.   On April 21 Mrs. Peck went to the Astor House, and the detectives recognized her companion.   When he left her they followed him to New Jersey, and "located" him in a house where he lived with his wife and daughter.   The next day, at the Barclay Street ferry-house, Columbani gave Mrs. Peck one of the stolen bonds, and she paid him $400 under instructions from one of the detectives.   On receiving the money he said: " I fancy I could let you have two or three more of these at the same price."

"No, Sir.   No more trifling with me," replied Mrs. Peck, simulating indignation. " All or none.   I've run my feet off on this business, and I'm taking all the risk."

Columbani then agreed to bring all the bonds to St. Peter's Church on April 25, and receive $3,600.   Mrs. Peck was there, as were also the officers.   Columbani met her, but evaded her inquiry as to whether he had the bonds, so that she was unable to give the signal for his apprehension.

"Do you think," he asked her in a whisper, "that I would be so 'flat' as to deliver the bonds on the street?   You must come up-town to a place I alone know of."

Mrs. Peck hardly knew what to do when Columbani led her to a Sixth Avenue car, but she decided to trust to luck and go with him.   The detectives dared not let Columbani see them, and they were equally nonplussed, but came to the same decision as the acting Detective Sergeant in petticoats.   Boarding the next car they watched the one ahead, and saw Columbani and Mrs. Peck get off at Sixth Avenue and Fourth Street, and enter Thomas Murphy's groggery, near the corner. After getting on the car Columbani waxed confidential. He began by saying he was transacting a risky business. Mrs. Peck retorted that she was taking a greater risk than he, as she was "playing" her money against his doubtful bonds. Suddenly Columbani turned toward her, looked her full in the face, and said abruptly :

"Do you know Inspector Byrnes?"

Mrs. Peck does not quail or flinch, and she replied quietly that she did not. Then Columbani said, in substance, that he was what is called a "crook," that if he knew that Mrs. Peck—she had masqueraded to him in another name—would "give him away" he would kill her. He had, he said, a pistol and a knife in his possession, and as he had been to State prison he knew its horrors, and would as soon kill himself as go back. If Mrs. Peck got him into trouble he would have her life if he had to wait forty years. He dreaded prison life all the more because he went before an investigating committee and exposed prison treatment, and every keeper was "down" on him.

When the couple reached Murphy's saloon Columbani led the way up-stairs to a room in which were a table and a lounge. Mrs. Peck sat down beside him, and Columbani took a pistol out of his pocket and laid it on the table.

"Well, you've got your pistol out at last," sneered Mrs. Peck. "I'm a woman, but I'm not afraid. You're a man, and my opinion of you is that you are a coward. But look here"—opening the bosom of her dress and displaying a pistol—"I carry one of those things myself."

Columbani was about to reply, when there was a scurrying of feet at the door of the room, and a "psitt, psitt." Snatching his pistol, he went to the door, listened earnestly to some one who whispered for a couple of seconds and darted away. One of the detectives had become very uneasy about Mrs. Peck, and he determined to see if she and Columbani had left the bar-room. He was stalking up to the front door, trying to conceal his gait and his features, when a thief, known to him, darted by and dived into the bar-room. When the officer got inside the door he had disappeared. He then summoned the other detectives, and as he did so he saw a man running across Sixth Avenue. He recognized Columbani, who had escaped by a side door, and pursued him into Jones Street. Then Columbani, who was two hundred feet ahead of the officer, threw away a parcel in which were five of the bonds stolen at West Brighton, and the detective, picking them up, decided that pursuit was useless. He then reported Columbani's escape, and all the detectives that were available guarded the ferries and scoured the city for the fugitive. He was arrested on Saturday, April 26, 1884, at the Park House in Chatham Street, New York, and was remanded by Justice Duffy at the Tombs. Mrs. Peck fully identified him, and the McSorleys identified their bonds. When told who had betrayed him Columbani's anger was intense.

His trial, for having in his possession bonds that were stolen on April 22, 1882, from the residence of Owen McSorley at West Brighton, Staten Island, N. Y., took place at Richmond the county seat of Richmond County, on May 8, 1884, before Judge Pratt.

Miss Mamie O'Neill, who worked for Mrs. Hatch a next-door neighbor of Owen

McSorley, positively identified Columbani as one of the three persons who were about the McSorley premises when the robbery took place. She swore that she saw him across the fence very plainly.

Thomas Ryan, the hired man of the McSorley family, testified to the robbery, and Thomas McSorley identified as his father's property the bond that was bought by Mrs. Peck from Columbani. He also identified the bonds that were found in the alley off Great Jones Street, where Columbani threw them when chased by the detective.

Mrs. Peck related how she negotiated with Columbani, and identified him as the party from whom she purchased the bond and who had the bundle of bonds in his possession, which were wrapped up in a newspaper when recovered by the officer.

The detective identified Columbani as the man he chased and who dodged into an alley where the bonds were found.

Columbani, in his own behalf, said he was a commission broker in general merchandise, particularly drugs and liquors. He positively denied ever having sold Mrs. Peck a bond, or having at any time seen or handled such bond or bonds as she alluded to. On the day that the detective chased a man Columbani swore that he was home with his family on Jersey City Heights, and in this he was corroborated by his wife, who also testified that on the day the McSorley mansion was robbed Columbani was at a dinner party at her aunt's house on Jersey City Heights.

Francis C. Barange, Columbani's father-in-law, and Mrs. Matilda Truatt, the sister of the former, corroborated Mrs. Columbani's testimony.

The jury, after a few minutes' absence, returned a verdict of guilty of larceny in the first degree, as charged in the indictment.

Mrs. Columbani gave a slight cry of anguish as she heard the verdict and turned deadly pale. She was removed from the room with difficulty. Judge Pratt sentenced Columbani to twelve years' imprisonment. The prisoner sobbed convulsively and cried out that they would almost kill him in State prison for his testimony before the Assembly investigating committee.

An attempt was made to have Columbani pardoned on December 27, 1884. Several respectable people became interested in him and made an application to Governor Cleveland, who, after investigating his previous character, refused to grant him a pardon.

Columbani was an associate of Louis Susicovitch, alias Grandi, the notorious Italian forger, lately convicted in San Francisco, Cal.

Louis and Carlos Susicovitch are brothers, and two of the most expert forgers and check-raisers that ever operated in this country.

The trial of Louis Susicovitch, alias Grandi, came to an end in San Francisco, May 6, 1886, with his conviction. Susicovitch belongs to a gang whose specialty has been to get small checks from business men they deal with, remove the figures by chlorine and fill up the check with a larger amount. Susicovitch was counted one of the most expert hands in the country in this business, as he re-sized the paper or check with gelatine, rice or bone dust, so that the forged check could not be distinguished from a genuine one. Susicovitch operated in San Francisco with two associates named Sieger and Garrity. Garrity is a New Orleans man who made Susicovitch's acquaintance as cell-mate in the prison of his native town, where, when quite a lad, he served a few days on conviction of gambling. Sieger is known as a saloon-keeper and waiter at hotels at St. Louis, against whom nothing can be learned previous to his connection with Susicovitch. Susicovitch and Garrity were arrested in St. Louis for check-raising operations last year, Susicovitch being locked up with Italians suspected of murdering a man, whom they threw into a lake, in order to realize the insurance on his life. The authorities had no testimony against them, but the wily forger wormed himself into their confidence and obtained from them a full confession of their connection with the murder. For turning spy, Susicovitch was released, and left his confidant, Garrity, in the lurch, to fight his case alone. Garrity was a man, who, in St. Louis check-raising operations, appeared at the front; while Susicovitch, as usual, performed the secret work. Only his proof of previous good character saved Garrity from conviction. The experience did not benefit him, and after release he joined Susicovitch again, and the three went to San Francisco.

Formerly Louis Susicovitch was not a forger himself, but was a layer down of forged paper. In January, 1886, he was arrested in San Francisco in company with J. J. Garrity and J. Smith, alias Sieger, by J. W. Lees, Captain of Detectives, for raising a check from $10 to $1,500. Garrity was formerly a newsboy in New Orleans, and Smith, who is a Swede, some three or four years ago kept a saloon at No. 1015 North Broadway, St. Louis. Susicovitch, alias Grandi, is supposed to be an Italian or Russian by birth, is forty-two years of age, five feet six inches high, gray hair, blue eyes, dark complexion, dark whiskers mixed with gray, scar on forehead over left eyebrow, scar on left eyebrow, large scar on left fore-arm. Is a sailor by occupation. He has served five years in Sing Sing prison, New York, under the name of Theodore Burnett, and was in the Parish prison in New Orleans in 1872, when he met Garrity.

In this case Louis Susicovitch was sentenced to fourteen years in Folsom prison, California, on May 12, 1886. His associates, John Smith, alias Albert Siegers, and John J. Garrity, were sentenced to seven years each in San Quintin prison, on May 22, 1886, for the same offense. (See also records of Nos. 16 and 18.)

Carlo Susicovitch, alias Charles Grandi, alias Howard Adams, alias John Howe, was arrested in Cincinnati, Ohio, early in March, 1878, in company with a man named Fred. Marker or Maerker, on the charge of forgery. When arrested in Cincinnati the authorities did not know who they had, but his identity was established, and he is now serving a long sentence in the Columbus, Ohio, penitentiary.

Some years ago he kept a saloon under Booth's Theatre in New York, and had as associates Charles Becker, Joe Chapman, Joe Reilly, alias Elliott, George Engle, George Wade Wilkes and others. In 1874 he was arrested in Constantinople for an attempt to defraud the Ottoman Bank on a forged letter of credit, but escaped in September, 1875, with Joe Reilly and Charles Becker and went to London, where he was suspected of the murder of Lydia Chapman. This occurred in Maud Grove, Chelsea, a suburb of London, on April 13, 1876. About the middle of March, 1878, he was arrested at Cincinnati, where he was under the name of Dugan, for trying to defraud the Commercial Bank of that city. He was also concerned in the burglary of the Third National Bank of Baltimore, August 18, 1872, with Chapman, Shell Hamilton, Frank McCoy, an English burglar named "Junco," and little Joe Elliott, alias Reilly. Both the brothers have been barbers.

ADAM WORTH, CHARLES W. BULLARD, alias PIANO CHARLEY, and ISAAC MARSH were for years the associates of Maximillian or Mark Shinburn and Robert Cochran. The first achievement of note in which this daring coalition of thieves took part was the plundering of the vaults of the Ocean Bank in 1869. The bank robbery netted quite a large sum, but the money was soon squandered, and in less than a year the cracksmen were at work again. Their second exploit was the robbery of the messenger of the Merchants' Union Express Company on the New York Central Railroad, between New York City and Buffalo. Bullard, Marsh and a man since reformed broke into the express car, bound and gagged the messenger, and stole $100,000 from the safe. The other members of the combination were aboard the train prepared to cover the escape of the men with the booty. The burglars who took part in the attack on the express messenger fled to Canada, where they were arrested. They were afterwards extradited and lodged in the White Plains jail. Ex-Recorder Smith was engaged to defend the prisoners and was paid a fee of $1,000 by their friends. The thieves were held for trial, and while their lawyer was afterwards on his way to this city the $1,000 was stolen from his pocket in the train. The friends of the prisoners abandoned the idea of fighting the case in the courts and decided to liberate their incarcerated companions. Billy Forrester and a number of other desperate thieves were consulted, and the plan decided upon was to free the imprisoned men by breaking into the jail. The prison was a poor one, and Forrester and his confederates had but little trouble digging through its old and rickety walls. Marsh and Bullard were freed, and before the escape was discovered the jail-breakers had made their way to the city.

Within a few months after breaking out of the White Plains jail, Bullard, under the assumed named of William A. Judson, hired the house next to the Boylston Bank in Boston, Mass. From that day out the institution was doomed, and on November 20, 1869, the vaults of the bank were rifled by Bullard, Adam Worth and brother, Ike Marsh and Bob Cochran. An entrance was effected by cutting through the side wall, and the cash and securities stolen amounted to $450,000. With the plunder the burglars hastened to Europe, and in Paris Bullard, under the name of Charles H. Wells, opened the "American Bar," a café, in the Rue Scribe, near the Grand Hotel, which had been fitted up regardless of expense. In a private parlor in the rear of the saloon "faro" was dealt, and for over a year burglar Bullard did a thriving business.

In the course of time the French authorities closed up the "American Bar," and Bullard was convicted of keeping a gaming-house and sentenced to one year's imprisonment. Upon his release he returned to New York and took up quarters at a house in East Eighteenth Street kept by "Dutch Dan." Bullard was there captured and taken to Boston. He was tried for the Boylston Bank robbery, and on his conviction was sentenced to twenty years in the State prison at Concord, Mass. He escaped from there on September 13, 1878, and fled to Canada, where, in the course of a few months, he attempted to rob a bank and was arrested. He was sentenced to five years' imprisonment at Kingston on January 22, 1879, and upon the expiration of his term he returned to Europe and joined his former associates. He has since been arrested, and is at present serving a term across the water. (See record of Mark Shinburn.)

Bullard is a man of very good education, and speaks English, French and German fluently. He gained his soubriquet from his proficiency as a musician, playing the piano with the skill of a professional.

Adam Worth was long considered the " Prince of Safemen," but several of his pupils are now believed to be far ahead of him in talent. After the Boylston Bank robbery he went abroad and remained there for a long time. He has, however, made several trips to this country, landing quietly in Canada, for the purpose of seeing an old sweetheart of his who is now the wife of a former associate. At the present time a well-known lawyer of this city is trying to compromise the Boylston Bank matter so as to enable Worth to return once more to his native land. He is now living in London, England, and his line of business is the purchasing of stolen goods. About the only time Worth was arrested in New York was for blowing open the safe in Stiner's tea store in Vesey Street several years ago.

Isaac Marsh, alias " Big Ike," after separating from Shinburn, joined partnership with George Mason, and was concerned with him in the Wellsboro, Pa., Bank robbery. He is now serving out a seventeen years' sentence in the Eastern Penitentiary at Philadelphia for a bank robbery.

CHAUNCY JOHNSON is one of the oldest and cleverest bank and general sneaks in America, and has stolen more money collectively than any man in his line. He commenced his career of crime as a burglar. In 1852 he was sentenced to five years' imprisonment for the burglary of a silk warehouse in Reade Street, west of Broadway, New York City. After the expiration of his term he was arrested for the robbery of the Hatters' Bank, at Bethel, Conn., where $36,000 of the proceeds of the robbery was recovered, and Johnson was again sentenced to five years' imprisonment. Being liberated, he went to Philadelphia, Pa., where he first embarked as a bank sneak.

He provided himself with a long, fine steel wire, shaped on the end like a fish-hook, and entered a bank in Philadelphia. Approaching the paying teller's window, he inserted this wire through the window-screen and secured a number of $50 bills. His success made him bold, and he attached this wire to a bundle of $100 bills, the moving of which attracted the attention of the paying teller, who was so surprised to see the money going away by some invisible means that he looked up into the faces of the men in line, and discovered in the countenance of Johnson a flurry of excitement as he was putting the wire into his pocket. The bank porter was standing outside ; he was called to arrest Johnson, which he did, and he was handed over to an officer. When searched his pockets were found to be filled with bank-bills of large denominations. For this offense he pleaded guilty, and was sentenced to three and a half years in State prison. When released he returned to New York City, and entered the banking-house of August Belmont, corner of Wall and William streets, at about a quarter to three, when every clerk was busy settling up the day's work and preparing the bonds for the Safe Deposit Company, and sneaked into Mr. Belmont's private office, where he stole

$25,000 in Government bonds, with which he escaped.   He was arrested, but for want of evidence was released.   Shortly after this he entered the office of the Adams Express Company, 49 Broadway, and waited for the cashier to go to lunch.   At 12 o'clock the cashier took off his office coat and silk cap, throwing them into the chair, and went out.   Johnson sneaked in, put on the coat and cap, and, placing a pen behind his ear, sat down at the desk and proceeded to rob the money drawer of several thousand dollars.   He was arrested some time after, but could not be identified, and was discharged.

In 1870 the vault of the Marine National Bank contained a tin box belonging to one of the directors, who, when he went to cut off the coupons of the bonds it contained, found it missing.   The box held many hundreds of thousands of dollars in securities.   No one in the bank could tell when it was last seen, or when it was likely to have been taken, and from all the searching examination that followed there was not a particle of information obtained concerning the disappearance of the box.

Johnson was known to be a desperate gambler, and at this time it was known that he was losing heavily.   No reports were received from any part of the country of large robberies, and it was concluded that Johnson must have made a large amount of money at some gambling house, which he was now losing.

When this tin box was discovered lost, and reported at police headquarters, Johnson was suspected and arrested ; but he had gambled away what money he had, and as there was no evidence of his having stolen the box he was discharged.   It was never ascertained, but always surmised, that Johnson had stolen these securities.

It was Johnson and Henry Newman, alias Dutch Heindrich, who robbed the president of the Central National Bank of a package of bonds amounting to $125,000, which he had laid down on his desk, and which was stolen while he turned away to remove his overcoat.   The president was followed from Wall Street to his office.

Shortly after this, December 21, 1870, while loitering in the Fifth Avenue Hotel, he saw a clerk place in the safe a package given him by a guest, whom he heard say was very valuable.   Johnson thereupon boldly walked in behind the counter, in among three clerks, and abstracted the package, with several others, from the safe, and was leaving the office, when, near the door, he stumbled over a waste-basket and fell.   The noise attracted the clerk's attention, and Johnson was arrested and sentenced to ten years in State prison.   He was discharged from Sing Sing on December 25, 1878.

After the expiration of this term of imprisonment Johnson returned to New York, to find many of his old acquaintances either gone away, imprisoned or dead.   He was without money, and his long imprisonment had lost for him many friends.   He had become old and broken down, and unfit for the clever work of younger days.   Thus, deserted and hungry, he snatched a pocket-book from a lady's hand at Twenty-second Street and Broadway, and was so weak from want of food that he could not run.   He was arrested, pleaded guilty, and was sentenced to four years in Sing Sing prison by Judge Gildersleeve, on January 19, 1880.

Johnson was arrested once more in Philadelphia, on July 22, 1883, for sneaking a package containing $230 in money from a barber's shop, the property of Mr. W. Warnock, of No. 1610 Masliers Street, Philadelphia.   He was committed in $1,000 bail for trial. He finally pleaded guilty, and was sentenced to three years in Cherry Hill prison on August 16, 1883.

Johnson was arrested again in Philadelphia on June 11, 1886, charged with the larceny of a hand-bag, containing seventeen dollars in money and other articles, from a lady in St. John's Church, that city. He was convicted and sentenced to two years and six months in the Eastern Penitentiary, by Judge Gordon, on June 18, 1886.

He is about sixty-four years old in 1886; weighs 145 pounds, and is 5 feet 8 inches high; sharp, thin face; hair long and generally combed over the ears.

JIM BRADY, or "Albany Jim," as he was sometimes called, was born in Troy, N. Y., and has been the associate of the most expert bank burglars and thieves in this country. He was arrested in New York City in 1865 for highway robbery committed at Cohoes, N. Y. The robbery and assault was of a most desperate character, the victim being badly beaten and left insensible; the property stolen was, however, partly recovered, and the matter was compromised, so that Brady did not have to appear in court to answer the charge.

He was arrested again in 1873 in New York City, charged with burglary and the larceny of $5,000 worth of optical instruments. He was tried, convicted, and sent to Auburn prison, from which, however, he soon made his escape. He was re-arrested on May 27, 1873, in the act of negotiating $40,000 worth of stolen bonds, the proceeds of burglaries in Glenn's Falls and Port Jervis. A detective found him in a second-story room in Carmine Street, between Bleecker and Bedford. Brady jumped out of the window and ran down the street. The officer followed, and shot him in the leg just as he was jumping into a basement window. He was again tried and convicted, and sent to Sing Sing for three and a half years, at the expiration of which time he was to go to Auburn to serve five years, the unexpired time of his former sentence. Hardly a month had elapsed before he again escaped. He was next arrested in Wilmington, Del., for a burglary there, together with Joe Howard, Frank McCoy, alias Big Frank, Jimmie Hope and others. They were sentenced to pay $1,000 fine, receive forty lashes, and spend ten years in Newcastle jail. The lashes were received and the prisoners were sent to jail, but the fine was not paid. While he was in that jail, State Detective Jackson, of Sing Sing, went after him, but the authorities there refused to release him. They had better have done so, as shortly after all four escaped, and Brady was not heard of again until he was arrested on August 1, 1877, in New York City, under the name of Peterson.

Brady's last exploit, when he entered Ward's furnishing store on Broadway, New York, could only have been the act of a madman or a desperate thief. After stealing some goods almost under the eyes of the clerk, when an officer was called upon to arrest him he coolly said: "I will go with you, sir, and you will discover your mistake." In sight of the station house, however, the desperate character of the man was revealed. He turned upon the officer quick as lightning and fired a shot at him, the ball grazing the captor's cheek. Then came the quick pursuit and flight; street after street was traversed; entire neighborhoods were aroused at the sight of an officer following a man who turned at intervals and discharged shots at his pursuer; finally other policemen joined in the chase, and at length the desperate man was hunted down. During the flight a citizen, in endeavoring to arrest the criminal, was wounded by him.   When he was arraigned at the Tombs Police Court this modern Jack Sheppard showed how completely he was master of his art ; his long, flowing beard was cut off and modest, quiet apparel was substituted for the fashionable costume he wore at the time of his arrest.   It would, indeed, almost defy a Cuvier to recognize in the placid features of Jim Brady, the prisoner, the Jim Brady whose facial muscles were swelled, eyes dilated, and mobile mouth working with passion and excitement while the police officers were running him down.

This man is one of a gang of the most dangerous criminals in the country, the more to be feared because possessed of intelligence and address, and having access to channels of communication with wealthy men, bankers and institutions of trust, by which means the most daring schemes of plunder are organized and consummated.

Brady, who gave the name of Oscar D. Peterson, received a cumulative sentence of eleven years on three indictments—two of three years each and one of five years, on September 14, 1877, by Judge Gildersleeve.

Brady was once as expert at prison-breaking as he is at safe-blowing, and therein lies all his present trouble.   Brady sighs for liberty ; but the prison officials blankly refuse to grant him freedom.   The slippery burglar first donned the stripes in Auburn prison early in the spring of 1871.   He remained until January, 1873, when, in company with the notorious Dan Noble, of Lord Bond robbery fame, Dan Kelly and other congenial spirits, he escaped by digging through four feet of solid masonry into an unused water-wheel pit, which adjoined the high stone wall on the outside.   He again turned up in the August following, when he was received at Sing Sing under the name of James H. Morrison, to serve theee years and six months.   In October of the same year he took French leave of Sing Sing, and was gone until September 14, 1877, when he returned to his old quarters as Oscar D. Peterson.   Clinton prison being considered a more secure place for fellows of his ilk, he was transferred to that institution, and after a short sojourn there he was brought to Auburn, where he is now confined.

The prison authorities having the slippery fellow once again in their custody, took a Trinitarian view of his case and determined that the three men, Brady, Morrison and Peterson, were one and the same, and that he should pay his indebtedness of time due the State of New York by serving the allowance he would have earned had he not escaped from Auburn and Sing Sing, about six years all told.   Brady was ignorant of this move on the part of the authorities, and when his term of imprisonment as Peterson had expired he demanded his release.   When told that he had just entered upon his sentence as Peterson and the eight years he had completed would be credited to the old score, his amazement knew no bounds.   He held that he was illegally imprisoned ; that Oscar D. Peterson's sentence had expired, and his custodians had no right to hold Peterson for the offenses of Brady and Morrison.   His next step was to avail himself of the provisions of the law governing the discharge of convicts prior to 1874.   He employed counsel, and when confronted by evidence that the court which convicted him had ordered that Peterson's term of imprisonment should not begin until the expiration of the unfinished sentences of Brady and Morrison, he gave up all hope.

About the middle of December 1885, a mysterious express package was received at the prison from Detroit. Its contents proved to be a bundle of circulars. Accompanying the circular was a letter dated Detroit, December 15, 1885, signed "Geo. Parks, pal of 'O. D. P.'" It was addressed to Major Boyle and advised him to immediately make his peace with Peterson, threatening to publish copies of the circular in all of the Auburn and Syracuse daily and Sunday papers if he failed so to do. It is understood that Governor Hill, Superintendent Baker and the members of the Legislature of 1885 were furnished with a copy.

The boldest part of the whole proceeding lies in the fact that the author of the circular does not attempt to conceal his identity, and that convict "No. 19, or 4" (which translated means 19,004), and convict 19,004 is Jim Brady, will furnish the necessary proof. Its author exhibited a degree of cunning by forwarding the document by express, thereby avoiding the penalty prescribed for sending threatening letters through the United States mail. Major Boyle is a highly respected citizen of Auburn, and the contents of the circular will be read with many grains of salt by his fellow-townsmen, when they consider the source from which it emanated.

There are those who know that Brady is simply playing a game of bluff. Seven more years of prison life for a man so well advanced on life's journey is indeed a long time, and, vexed over his failure to be released, he now proposes to place his custodians on the defensive and has thrown down the gauntlet.

See also records of Nos. 20, 50, 53 and 89.

JOHN, alias CLUTCH DONOHUE, one of the most noted bank sneaks in America, has been a principal or an associate in several large robberies in America and Europe.

The South Kensington National Bank of Philadelphia was on February 2, 1871, robbed by burglars of money and securities worth $100,000. The bank is situated in what is known as the "shipbuilders' quarter" in that city, and the neighborhood is quite lonely at night. The burglars obtained entrance by a very ingenious ruse. Just before the bank closed that day, a man, supposed to have been Clutch Donohue, called at the bank and told William Connell, the cashier, that the lieutenant of the police district had seen suspicious characters lurking around the bank, and was apprehensive that an attempt might be made to rob it. He had been sent to give them information. The intelligence was spread among the bank attachés, and the two watchmen were instructed to let no person into the building after banking hours. At seven o'clock that evening two policemen rapped at the door. They said that the lieutenant had heard from good sources that the bank was to be robbed that night, and had told them to aid in protecting it. The overjoyed watchmen invited them to enter. They seemed to think that it would be better to remain outside, but as the weather was cold, they finally accepted the invitation. Once in the bank, officers and watchmen talked over the situation; one of the policemen said, "I am very dry; I wish I could have a drink." "That you can have," replied one of the watchmen, and went back to get it. The remaining officer told the other watchman that he had better look around outside to see if everything was all right. No sooner was the door closed upon him than the officer joined his comrade, and found him with a bottle of whiskey in his hand. The watchman was drawing water from a cooler. In a trice the officers gagged and bound him hand and foot, laying him out like a mummy. They were no longer officers, but burglars. The absent watchman was admitted, and treated in the same manner. The door was thrown open to their associates, and, by the aid of wedges, muffled hammers and jimmies, the vault was opened and about $100,000 carried away. The robbers worked until three in the morning, and did not succeed in opening the safe containing the most money. They had been gone two hours when one of the watchmen got loose, ran into the street, and sounded the alarm. Nobody was arrested. A well-known ex-detective of Philadelphia had the securities returned to the bank, but the burglars kept the money, about $60,000. Several noted burglars have from time to time been credited with committing this robbery, when in fact they were either in prison or far away from the scene. The following are the names of four of the eight persons who committed the robbery : Mike Kerrigan, alias Johnny Dobbs, Denny Brady, of masked burglary fame, Thomas Burns, alias Combo, John, alias Clutch Donohue, and four others. Dobbs was the only mechanic in the gang.

At Welland, Ont., October 12, 1885, the court room was packed when John, alias Clutch Donohue, was arraigned on the charge of stealing a quantity of meerchaum pipes and tobacco, goods the property of Goldstein Brothers, from their store in the city of Quebec, during the night of February 1, 1882. The prisoner pleaded not guilty.

William Goldstein was the first witness. He testified that he lived in Quebec in 1882, where he carried on the tobacco business. On going to his shop on the morning of February 2, 1882, he discovered that a robbery had occurred, and that a case which had contained eight hundred dollars' worth of goods was empty. He gave information immediately at the police headquarters. His impression was that the shop had been entered by means of a false key. He afterwards found one-fifth of the stolen goods in a store kept by a man named A. J. Rainer as a news depot in Buffalo.

William Hampton, a thief, testified that he was in Quebec, February 2, 1882. The prisoner lived at Fort Erie at that time. On January 31, 1882, he left Toronto with the prisoner for Quebec, each with a satchel. They arrived in Quebec on the morning of February 1, and roomed together at the Albion Hotel. On the morning of February 2 they went to LeMesurier's store. The prisoner represented himself as a merchant of Sherbrooke. Witness occupied the attention of the proprietors while prisoner took an impression in oiled wax of the keys' of the store door and the cash box. Witness got a sheet of copper with which Donohue made the keys. They afterwards went to Goldstein's, where witness occupied the attention of the clerks. Donohue asked for paper to write a note. He had plenty of time to take an impression of the keys. He made the keys at the hotel. Prisoner had keys for other stores in Quebec. They went to Joseph Amyot's with the intention of committing a robbery. Prisoner opened the door while witness went in and filled the two satchels with goods, remaining half an hour. Donohue stood at the door and gave a signal—three raps. They accomplished the robbery at Goldstein's the same way. They procured a trunk, and packing all the goods in it, forwarded it to Brampton, leaving afterwards for home.

The next day they called on Levi Reynardt in Toronto and said they had some goods at Brampton to sell him. Donohue, Reynardt and witness met in Brampton. Reynardt bought a hundred dollars' worth of goods. He got no cigar goods except two holders, which they presented to him. Two days after witness saw the balance of the goods in possession of Donohue at Fort Erie. Then they sent for A. J. Rainer, of Buffalo, to whom they sold the tobacco goods. Donohue got $330 and witness got $165. Witness saw the stolen goods after at Rainer's store.

The jury, after fifteen minutes deliberation, returned with a verdict of guilty. Donohue was sentenced on October 2, 1885, to seven years' imprisonment in the Provincial penitentiary.

Three other indictments were read against Donohue, to which he pleaded not guilty, namely, receiving one thousand dollars' worth of postage stamps, stolen July 24, 1884; stealing pearl and gold buttons, etc., from Joseph Amyot's store in Quebec, February 2, 1882; and having the above goods in his possession. These indictments were not proceeded with.

See also records of George Wilkes and No. 202.

JOSEPH EATON, alias GEORGE C. HAMMOND, a gold brick swindler and card sharp, is forty-nine years old in 1886; medium build; married; born in United States; height, five feet nine inches; weight, 165 pounds; black hair, dark eyes and complexion; generally wears a full black beard. Has had a stroke of paralysis, which is noticeable; long nose. Has a leaf in India ink on his left arm.

He is probably one of the smartest gold brick swindlers in America. He is a partner of Nathan White's, who generally uses the alias of William Johnson. They have been arrested in almost all the principal cities in the United States, but owing to the respectability of their victims, they always escape, through fear of publicity. The following is a very interesting account of the manner in which the scheme is worked. It was clipped from a New York paper of May 4, 1881, when White, alias Johnson, who was with Eaton, was arrested:

"One afternoon in March, 1881, Mr. Smith, the owner of a number of towboats, sat in his office in South Street, when a stranger entered and presented a letter of introduction. The new comer was a tall, gentlemanly person, affable in manner and refined in speech, who, however, bore about him a flavor of the Far West and its blunt, off-hand ways. The letter which Mr. Smith read was over the signature of an old-time friend of his in California, and in it he was requested to show the bearer what courtesy he could, as he was worthy of his esteem, and with the writer would duly appreciate it. The stranger was treated to a cordial reception, and, as Mr. William Johnson, who had come to the metropolis on business, was given the use of the office and what other accommodations he desired. Two weeks later he called again, and in his intercourse with Mr. Smith he increased the good impression he previously had made.

"In the latter part of April he came again. He seemed very thoughtful this time, and a trifle perplexed. Mr. Smith noticed his seeming perturbation, and the other, after a time, revealed its cause, which his confidant remembers much after the following fashion:

"'You are acquainted in New York,' said Mr. Johnson, 'and you are a man of wide

connections.   I am a stranger, and I have come to ask your advice about a matter that
has caused me considerable thought.   Some time ago I was in Leadville.   It was in
the old days when the revolver settled every difficulty and was very often seen in
people's hands.   One night I was in a bar-room when a couple of men quarreled.   One
of them had a pistol in his hand and its muzzle in a line with the other's head.   His
finger was on the trigger too, and the man's life wasn't worth a button, when I threw
up the fellow's arm and the pistol exploded.   The man whose life I saved came to me
a few days ago.   He was a burglar, and it was his partner's bullet I had turned aside.
He told me that after they left Leadville they went to California, where they robbed a
bank of a quantity of gold.   The police were on the scent, though, and fearing apprehension, they buried their booty under ground.   Well, they were arrested for the crime
at last, sent to prison, and not long ago the man I had saved came out alone.   His
partner had died in confinement.   The ex-convict's first work was to recover the stolen
treasure.   But it was composed of bricks of gold, and it would be foolhardy for a man
of his notoriety to attempt to dispose of it.   So he turned his back on the Pacific slope
and came here.   When he learned I was in New York he sought me out, and told me
that he remembered with gratitude the part I had taken in saving his life, and was
willing to do me a service.   The treasure he could not readily dispose of himself, and
he offered me the chance of negotiating for its sale.   He has quite a quantity of it, and
is willing to dispose of it at a great sacrifice.   I thought I would come to you, and see
if you thought well of the scheme.   There would be a big profit in it for us both.   What
would you advise me to do?'

  "The story of the gentleman from California at once aroused Mr. Smith's suspicions as to his real character.   He questioned him further, and believed them confirmed.
Then, to hide his surmises, he determined to parley with the other in the interests of
justice until he could have an opportunity of giving the authorities a clew to the stolen
booty.   He told the latter he wished to consult a friend, and that night he told the
story to an ex-Senator of Brooklyn, who came with him to New York and called on a
police inspector.   When the latter heard the narrative he recognized in it a part of
the programme carried out in a swindling operation which had been plied with success
in the mines, and had shorn not a few unscrupulous men of means in the West.   At
once he directed Mr. Smith how to act.

  "'Meet Mr. Johnson as you agreed,' he said, 'and appear to be unsuspicious, for
men of that class are apt to keep you under surveillance, to see if their plans are
detected.   Go with him to the place of meeting with the supposed ex-convict, and negotiate with him for the purchase of the gold.   They will no doubt show you a brick of
manufactured metal with a tip of gold at one end and a thin wedge of it in the middle.
That's their usual game.   To assure you that it's genuine, they are likely to chip a
piece off the end and a bit off the middle for you to test at the assay office.   Don't
postpone the negotiations for that, though.   Say that Johnson is your friend and you
believe his word.   Buy the booty, and give your check for it.'

  "Mr. Smith looked up in surprise at the proposition.

  "'Give your check for it,' repeated the Inspector.   'You can first have its payment
stopped at the bank.   Then, if they are chary about the check, offer to bring Johnson

to the bank with you to identify him and set things right. We'll be ready for him when you get out of doors.'

"Mr. Smith followed the directions given him by the Inspector, and met Mr. Johnson, and the pair started for the place of rendezvous with detectives in their wake. The Inspector had fancied that some boarding-house or private abode would be selected for the business, as is customary in such cases, and in such a place there would be little difficulty in apprehending the accomplice whom Johnson would leave indoors behind him. The detectives were somewhat taken aback, then, when the gentleman from California escorted Mr. Smith to the Compton House, on the corner of Third Avenue and Twenty-fourth Street, and took him up to one of the seventy or eighty rooms in it. His experience from his entrance savored much of the melodramatic. Johnson preceded him to a room into which he ushered him, carefully closing the door behind. There Smith found himself in front of a rather peculiar figure reclining on the bed. It was that of a man in ordinary attire, whose features, hewever, were completely hidden by a large mask. Johnson explained that in consequence of the ex-convict's deeds in the West, he preferred keeping his identity a secret, but was ready to proceed with business. The masked man then drew from underneath the bolster a bar of gleaming metal about twelve or fifteen inches long and three and a half thick. Mr. Smith looked at it, and it had all the appearance of pure gold. The masked man said that he had eighteen such bars, and was willing to dispose of the lot at a considerable sacrifice. When he turned them into money he proposed giving over his evil ways, and would be heard of no more. The bar he showed, he said, was worth $9,000, but he would part with it for $7,500. As the Inspector had predicted, a piece of the metal was sawed off the end at Johnson's suggestion, and he proposed to Smith to bring it to the assay office to be tested with some grains which were filed off the middle.

"Mr. Smith, according to his instructions, professed to be satisfied ; but a hitch arose here. The masked man did not have all of the gold with him, but only the sample bar. So, after some talk, the negotiations had to be suspended, and Smith and Johnson started away together. The detectives were at their heels in a twinkling, and once they were out of sight of the Compton House, a detective pounced upon Johnson. They had supposed the negotiations completed and the case ready for the courts. Without delay the Compton House was entered. But the accomplice of the gentleman from California had not lingered. He had passed out just as his partner went away with Mr. Smith. The latter's failure to perfect the negotiations had left the case against the prisoner incomplete. Mr. Smith had the piece of gold sawed from the bar, which was afterward shown in the Jefferson Market Court when the prisoner was arraigned, and upon the man was found the following letter, which seemingly had been used by Johnson to ingratiate himself with a friend of another Californian, as he had done in Mr. Smith's case :

NATIONAL BANK OF STOCKTON, February 15, 1881.

D. ALLEN, Esq. :

DEAR SIR,—This will introduce to you Mr. H. S. Walker, of this place, who comes to your city for a short stay. Mr. Walker is a gentleman in every particular, and any courtesy extended him will be appreciated by me as by him.

Yours truly,

R. K. REID.

"According to the paper on which this was written, R. K. Reid is president of the bank, and his name was doubtless forged with the purpose of victimizing a friend in this city."

Eaton was arrested in New York City on June 23, 1881, charged with having swindled Adolph Liebes out of $500, by inducing him to play "faro." He was committed in $2,000 bail for trial, and again his good luck stood to him and he was discharged. He was arrested again in Boston, Mass., on December 28, 1882, with similar results.

NATHANIEL WHITE, alias NAT WHITE, alias WM. JOHNSON, another clever "gold brick" swindler, is forty-four years old in 1886; born in United States; calls himself a speculator; is married; slim build, fair complexion; height, 5 feet 6 inches; weight, 136 pounds; dark brown hair, gray eyes, and wears a full, dark brown beard and mustache; dresses well; talks low and confidingly. He is generally the "outside man"—that is, the man that picks up the party to be swindled. He works with Joe Eaton and a party called Tibbits. He was arrested in New York City and his picture taken on May 3, 1881 (see record of Joe Eaton for account of White's arrest and the manner of working the gold brick swindle), and discharged on May 5, 1881. He was arrested again in Jersey City on October 13, 1881, in company of Tibbits, for an attempt to swindle one John C. Van Horn out of $5,000, the price of two gold bricks. In this case, as in fifty others, White was discharged.

BANK ROBBERIES.

NAME OF BANK.	LOCATION.	DATE OF ROBBERY.	LOSS CLAIMED.	REMARKS.
The Freeman's Bank	Bristol, R. I.	Nov. 24, 1862	$50,000	Money and Bonds.
Sonhegan National Bank	Milford, N. H.	Sept. 27, 1863	25,000	Bonds, Money and Notes.
Malden Savings Bank	Malden, Mass.	Dec. 16, 1863	5,000	
Tioga Bank	Tioga, Pa.	May 25, 1864	29,617.83	Bonds and Money.
Farmers' & Mechanics' Bank	Milford, Del.	Aug. 14, 1864	12,000	Money and Bonds.
Shoe & Leather Dealers' Bank		Sept. 2, 1864	41,805	Money and Bank Notes. A small trunk from counter.
The St. Alban's Bank and the First Nat'l Bank of St. Albans	St. Albans, Vt.	Oct. 19, 1864	96,000	Money, Bonds and Notes.
Willimantic Bank	Willimantic, Conn	Jan. 31, 1865	3,000	Bonds from one safe.
Walpole Bank	Walpole, N. H.	April 25, 1865	86,000	See Record of Mark Shinburn.
Traders' Bank	Providence, R. I.	Feb. 13, 1865	40,000	Cash and Bonds.
Concord National Bank	Concord, N. H.	Sept. 25, 1865	300,000	Money and Bonds. See Record of No. 22.
Liberty Bank	Liberty, Mo.	Feb. 16, 1866	72,000	
Marine Bank	New York City.	Aug. 24, 1866	Unknown	
Hartford National Bank	Hartford, Conn.	Oct. 6, 1866	20,000	
Bowdoinham Bank	Maine	Oct. 21, 1866	75,000	
Tremont Bank	Illinois	Nov. 5, 1867	100,000	
Bank of Republic	New York City.	January, 1868	15,000	
Canal Bank	New Orleans, La.	March, 1868	50,000	
Importers' and Traders' Bank	New York City.	July 20, 1868	80,000	
Bennington National Bank	Vermont	August, 1868	Unknown	
San Francisco Mint	California	August, 1868	12,000	
People's Bank	Baltimore, Md.	August, 1868	17,000	See Record of No. 24
Mechanics' Bank	Brooklyn, N. Y	Nov. 1868	9,000	
Pequonnock National Bank	Bridgeport, Conn.	Dec. 1868	90,000	
Old Town National Bank	Old Town, Me.	Attempt, 1868	Nothing	See Record of No. 24.
Catholic Beneficial Fund Bank	Philadelphia, Pa.	April 6, 1869	1,000,000	See Record of No. 89.
New Windsor Bank	Carroll County, Md.	Jan. 23, 1869	9,000	Money, Bonds, etc.
Ocean National Bank	New York City.	June 28, 1869	1,200,000	See Records of Nos. 70 and 176.
National Bank	Norwalk, Conn.	Sept. 30, 1869	140,500	Money and Bonds.
Boylston Bank	Boston, Mass.	Nov. 20, 1869	500,000	
Citizens' National Bank	Middleton, Del.	Dec. 2, 1869	19,500	Bonds.
Bank of Montreal	Canada	January, 1869	50,000	
Park Savings Bank	Brooklyn, N. Y	February, 1869	Unknown	
Clearfield Bank	Pennsylvania.	May, 1869	30,000	
Williamsburg Savings Bank	Williamsburg, N. Y.	June, 1869	8,000	
Lake Bank	Woolborough, N. H.	Nov. 1869	40,000	
Port Jervis National Bank	Port Jervis, N. Y.	Nov. 1869	50,000	
Glen Falls Bank	Maryland	January, 1870	20,000	

Name of Bank.	Location.	Date of Robbery.	Loss Claimed.	Remarks.
Castleton National Bank	Vermont	January, 1870	$8,000	
Wolcott Savings Bank	Wolcott, N. Y.	March, 1870	Unknown	See Record of No. 8.
Savings and Loan Bank	Cleveland, Ohio	April, 1870	20,000	
Auburn National Bank	New York	April, 1870	31,000	
Lime Rock National Bank	Rockland, Me.	May 3, 1870	23,000	See Records of Nos. 20 and 22.
Mechanics' Bank	Louisville, Ky.	June, 1870	60,000	
Grafton National Bank	Massachusetts	October, 1870	100,000	
North Berwick Bank	New Hampshire	Dec., 1870	8,000	
Kensington Bank	Philadelphia, Pa.	Feb. 4, 1871	80,000	See Record of No. 89.
Fulton County National Bank	Gloversville, N. Y.	June 17, 1871	31,850	
Uxbridge National Bank	Massachusetts	July, 1872	14,000	
Third National Bank	Baltimore, Md.	Aug. 18, 1872	132,200	Bonds and Certificates.
Waterford Bank	Waterford, N. Y.	Oct. 14, 1872	......	See Record of No. 70.
Saratoga Bank	Saratoga, N. Y.	Oct. 15, 1872	500,000	
Lancaster Bank	Lancaster, Pa.	January, 1873	43,000	
Merchants' National Bank	New York City	Nov., 1872	......	Attempted Robbery. See Record of Mark Shinburn.
First National Bank	Wilmington, Del.	Nov. 7, 1873	......	Attempted Robbery. See Records of Nos. 20 and 24.
Falls City Tobacco Bank	Louisville, Ky.	March 8, 1873	Unknown	See Record of No. 50.
Long Island Savings Bank	Long Island, N. Y.	Oct. 13, 1873	47,500	Bonds stolen from a tin box.
First National Bank	Quincy, Ill.	Feb. 13, 1874	431,000	See Records of Nos. 22, 24 and 50.
Conneautville Bank	Pennsylvania	February, 1874	40,000	
New York County Bank	New York City	June 27, 1874	......	Attempted Robbery. See Record of No. 21.
Batavia Bank	Batavia, N. Y.	July, 1874	9,200	
First National Bank	Wellsborough, Pa.	Sept. 17, 1874	50,000	See Records of Nos. 24 and 70.
Milford Bank	New Hampshire	October, 1874	100,000	See Record of No. 24.
Fishomingo Bank	Tennessee	Dec., 1874	9,000	
St. Nicholas Bank	New York City	March 17, 1875	......	Attempted Robbery.
Winthrop Bank	Maine	July 23, 1875	150,000	
First National Bank	Wellsborough, Pa.	Sept. 6, 1875	275,000	
National Bank of Barre	Vermont	Nov. 24, 1875	400,000	
Munroe Bank	Michigan	Jan. 25, 1876	18,000	
Northampton National Bank	Northampton, Mass.	Jan. 25, 1876	720,000	See Record of No. 110.
Dallas Bank	Dallas, Texas	Aug. 19, 1876	2,000	
Sixth National Bank	New York City	April 9, 1877	3,000	
Meridan Bank	Meridan, Conn.	May 18, 1877	100,000	
Courtland Bank	Courtland, N. Y.	Sept. 25, 1877	200,000	
Cambridgeport Bank	Massachusetts	Sept. 26, 1877	12,000	See Records of Nos. 6, 12 and 22.
Deep River National Bank	Deep River, Conn.	Feb. 3, 1878	Nothing	Attempted Robbery. See Record of No. 20.
Lechmere National Bank	East Cambridge, Mass.	March 16, 1868	40,000	See Records of Nos. 12 and 22.
Concordia Bank	Kentucky	Sept. 4, 1878	15,000	
Manhattan Savings Institution	New York City	Oct. 27, 1878	2,747,700	See Records of Nos. 19, 20, 24, 90 and 110.
Rochester National Bank	New Hampshire	......	......	See Record of No. 24.

Name of Bank.	Location.	Date of Robbery.	Loss Claimed.	Remarks.
First National Bank	Charleston, S. C.	March 31, 1879	$20,000	Sneak Robbery. See Record of No. 25. [and 187.
Middleton Savings Bank	Middleton, Conn.	July 27, 1880	64,500	Money and Bonds. See Records of Nos. 1, 3, 25, 83
Townsend National Bank	Massachusetts		......	See Record of No. 24.
Smith's Bank	San Francisco, Cal.		......	See Record of No. 20.
National Bank of Fairhaven	Massachusetts		......	See Record of No. 24.
First National Bank	Jersey City, N. J.		......	See Record of No. 50.
Marshalles Bank	Montreal, Canada		......	See Record of No. 50.
Mechanics' Bank	Scranton, Pa.		37,000	See Record of No. 8.
Farmers' and Mechanics' Bank	Galesburg, Ill.		9,600	See Record of No. 11.
First National Bank	Dexter, Maine.		......	See Records of Nos. 20 and 199.
Sauthers & Co. Bank	San Francisco, Cal.		......	See Records of Nos. 20 and 50.
Manufacturers' Bank	Cohoes, N. Y.	August 1, 1881	......	Attempted Robbery. See Record of No. 162.
First National Bank	Springfield, Ill.		35,000	See Record of No. 8.
Commercial National Bank	Cleveland, Ohio	Fall of 1881	17,000	See Record of No. 1.
Bank of Baltimore	Maryland	Sept. 25, 1881	12,000	See Record of No. 1.
Italian-American Bank	New York City.	July, 1882	5,000	See Record of No. 80. [Howard.
Coldwater National Bank	Michigan	August 1, 1883	19,000	Sneak Robbery. See Record of Joe Killoran, alias
First National Bank	Detroit, Mich.	Feb. 13, 1885	1,500	Sneak Robbery. See Records of Nos. 12 and 187.
National Bank of Augusta	Georgia.	April, 1884	2,700	See Records of Nos. 1 and 9.
Osceola Bank	Osceola, Pa.	February, 1885	......	See Record of No. 68.

MISCELLANEOUS ROBBERIES.

	Location.	Date of Robbery.	Loss Claimed.	Remarks.
Robert Bonner	New York City	October, 1860	$3,156	Forgery. See Record of Col. Buchannan Cross.
Pacific National Bank	" "	June 1, 1861	1,075	Forgery. See Record of G. Patterson.
Bank of Mutual Redemption	Boston, Mass.	Sept. 2, 1864	22,305	Messenger Robbery. Amount stolen in money.
District of Cumberland	Louisville, Ky.	June 10, 1864	49,000	Paymaster Safe Robbery. Amount stolen in money.
North River Insurance Co.	New York City.	July 10, 1865	6,000	Safe Robbery. Amount stolen in Treasury notes and
Adams Express Co.	Georgetown, D. C.	Oct. 13, 1865	4,000	Safe Robbery. Amount stolen in money. [bonds.
Lord Bond Robbery	New York City	March, 1866	1,700,000	
Garten & Co.	" "	1866	17,000	Forged Bonds. See Record of John Ross. [safe.
Royal Insurance Co.	" "	Dec. 10, 1866	208,000	Sneak Robbery of Reg. Stocks and Bonds. Tin box from
John P. Moore	" "	March 23, 1866	65,550	Second Story Robbery. Amount stolen in bonds. Also
Goodwin Safe Robbery	Boston, Mass.	July 9, 1866	9,451	Money. [1,750 shares railroad stock, etc.

	LOCATION.	DATE OF ROBBERY.	LOSS CLAIMED	REMARKS.
Leonard W. Jerome	New York City	Feb. 6, 1867	$100,000	Forgery. See Record of John H. Livingston.
National City Bank	"	Dec. 3, 1867	75,000	
Bennehoff Robbery	"	Jan. 24, 1868	250,000	
Merchants' Union Express Co.	"	April 30, 1868	33,300	Messenger Robbery. Am't stolen in U. S. R.R. Bonds.
United States Sub-Treasury	"	July 1, 1868	43,000	Sneak Robbery. U. S. Bonds.
Star Fire Insurance Co.	"	August, 1868	40,000	U. S. 5-20 Coupon Bonds.
Dutchess Co. Mutual Ins. Co.	"	October, 1869	65,000	
Washington Insurance Co.	"	August, 1869	128,000	
Vermillyea & Co.	"	February, 1870	16,000	Forgery. See Record of Walter G. Patterson.
Maryland Fire Ins. Co.	Baltimore, Md.	June, 1870	50,000	See Record of No. 8.
Hopkins Safe Robbery	New York City	Nov. 4, 1871	300,000	
Park National Bank	"	March 1, 1871	19,000	Forgery. See Record of Lewis M. Van Eten.
Union Trust Co.	"	Nov. 19, 1871	100,000	
Samuel White & Co.	"		12,000	See Record of Geo. B. Watson.
James G. King & Son	"	Feb. 17, 1877	149,000	Sneak Robbery. Bonds, registered bonds and mortgages.
Alling Bros. & Co.	Worcester, Mass.	May 12, 1877	9,000	Jewelry Robbery. See Records of Nos. 6 and 26.
New York National Exchange	New York City	June 5, 1877	2,700	
James H. Young	"	Jan. 2, 1878	98,000	Money and Bonds. See Records of Nos. 1 and 3.
Merritt Trinball's Safe	"	Oct. 15, 1879	28,000	Sneak Robbery. Bonds. See Record of No. 1.
Delaware & Hudson Canal Co.	Wilkesbarre, Pa.		33,000	Safe Robbery. See Record of Mark Shinburn.
Fisher, Preston & Co.	Detroit, Mich.		5,000	Safe Robbery. See Record of No. 12.
Phœnix Bank	New York City		2,400	Forgery. See Records of Nos. 13 and 14.
Philadelphia Navy Yard	Philadelphia, Pa.		.....	Paymaster's Safe Robbery. See Record of No. 20.
Garry Bond Robbery	Boston, Mass.		8,000	See Record of No. 22.
Ganley	New York City		15,000	Pawnshop Robbery. See Record of No. 63.
Meyer	"		6,000	"
Geo. B. Ripley	"		20,000	See Record of Charles B. Orvis. [R. Lewis.
B. T. Babbitt	"		205,645	Forgeries. See Records of Chas. R. Beckwith and Thos.
Bank of England			.....	Forgeries. See Records of Chas. Ulrich, George
Mrs. Elizabeth Roberts	Brooklyn, N. Y.	March 12, 1881	3,500	Bonds and Jewelry. [McDonald and No. 202.
Jewelry Robbery	Baltimore, Md.	April 21, 1881	10,000	Salesman's sample trunk of jewelry.
Bond Robbery	Lexington, Ky.	April 6, 1881	14,000	Bonds.
Bank of Metropolis	New York City	June 23, 1880	2,000	Messenger assaulted and robbed by unknown man.
Marine Bank	"	Dec. 14, 1880	20,000	Messenger James McDowell robbed of checks and notes.
Wm. E. Pratt	"	March 16, 1881	850,000	Sneak Robbery of Stocks and Certificates.
Post Office Robbery	Georgetown, D. C.	May 7, 1881	1,390	Safe broken open by burglars.
Rupert's Brewery	New York City	July 15, 1881	9,600	Messenger Robbery. Amount stolen in money.
Erie County Savings Bank	Buffalo, N. Y.	April 30, 1881	100,000	Sneak Robbery of Bonds.
One Million Dollar Sneak Rob'y	New York City	March 16, 1881	1,200,000	Unsigned Bonds and Jewelry. [Coupon Bonds.
Guarantee Trust & Safe Dep. Co.	Philadelphia, Pa.	March 2, 1883	70,000	Sneak Robbery. People's Passenger Five per Cent.

MYSTERIOUS MURDERS.

THE MURDER OF DORAS DOYEN, ALIAS HELEN JEWETT.

ALTHOUGH fifty years have passed since the notorious and beautiful young woman, Doras Doyen, otherwise known as Helen Jewett, was mysteriously butchered in her bed at No. 41 Thomas Street in this city, the brutal and unavenged crime has not been forgotten. Many old residents still recall with horror the cruel murder of the fair cyprian, which was committed early on the morning of April 12, 1836. Doras Doyen was born in Augusta, Maine, and at the time of her tragic death was but twenty-three years of age. Her many charms were thus described by an able writer, at the time of the murder:

"She was a shade below the middle height, but of a form of exquisite symmetry, which, though voluptuously turned in every perceptible point, was sufficiently dainty in its outline to give her the full advantage of a medium stature to the eye. Her complexion was that of a clear brown, bearing in it all the voluptuous ardor of that shade.

"Her features were not what might be termed regular, but there was a harmony in their expression which was inexpressibly charming; the nose was rather small, which was a fault; the mouth was rather large, but the full richness of its satin lips and the deep files of ivory infantry which crescented within their rosy lines redeemed all its latitudinal excess; while her large, black, steady eyes, streaming now with glances of precocious knowledge, and anon languishing with meditation or snapping with mischievousness, gave the whole picture a peculiar charm which entitled it to the renown of one of the most fascinating faces that ever imperiled a susceptible observer.

"In disposition this lovely creature was equal to her form. She was frank and amiable. Her heart was kind to excess to all who required her assistance, though the ardor of her temperament rendered her amenable to fiercest sentiments of passion."

A young clerk in a Maiden Lane store, named Richard P. Robinson, was among the many admirers of the comely Helen Jewett. He was strikingly handsome, having a frank, boyish face that was well set off by curling hair of golden brown. Robinson, though but eighteen years of age, was an *habitue* of the fast resorts in the city, where he was commonly known as "Frank Rivers." The long Spanish cloak which he wore jauntily about his shapely person became, after the murder of his mistress, the rage among the young men about town, and was known as the "Robinson Cloak."

It was at a theatre that Helen Jewett and Richard P. Robinson met one night by chance. The clerk defended her against the advances of a drunken ruffian and was rewarded with an invitation to call on her at the house of a Mrs. Berry in Duane Street, known to the wild young men of the day as the "Palais de la Duchesse Berri." There Helen received him in an apartment that would have done credit to the palace of Cleopatra. Other visits soon followed, and within a few weeks her passing fancy for the handsome youth ripened into the maddest infatuation.

For a time all went well, but at last rumors began to reach Helen's ears that she was but a sharer in her admirer's affections. Determined to discover the truth she disguised herself as a young man, and posting herself in front of the Maiden Lane store in which Robinson was employed waited till evening, and followed him first to his boarding-house in Dey Street and from there to a house in Broome Street, where she found him in the company of a rival siren.

Mad with jealousy Helen threw herself on the woman and struck her repeatedly in the face, her diamond rings drawing blood at every blow. She repented her violence and wrote to her lover a few days afterwards imploring him to forgive and return to her. A reconciliation followed, but within a few months, Helen, furious at the discovery of some fresh perfidy on the part of Robinson, taunted him with having caused the death of a young girl whom he had wronged and then deserted. Terrified at the consequences of exposure he professed to be ready to do anything that Helen wished, and finally purchased her silence by promising to marry her. Once more all went well until Helen learned that Robinson not only did not intend to keep his promise but was on the eve of being married to a young lady of wealth and position. In a fury she wrote him a letter threatening the most dire consequences if he failed to keep faith with her.

There is little doubt now that that letter sealed the fate of Helen Jewett. Her life only stood between Robinson and fortune. On April 10, 1836, the day preceding the murder, Robinson received a note from Helen begging him to call on her that night and containing a hint of the terrible penalty in case of a refusal to do so. He replied, promising to call the next night.

The house of Mrs. Townsend, No. 41 Thomas Street, an establishment famous for the magnificence of its appointments from one end of the country to the other, was the place where Helen was then living. Robinson, enveloped in his long Spanish cloak, rang the bell of this house between nine and ten o'clock on the night of Saturday, April 11, 1836. At the door the clerk was met by his young mistress, who was heard to exclaim joyously: "Oh, my dear Frank, how glad I am that you have come!"

Helen an hour afterwards from the head of the stairs called for a bottle of champagne. When Mrs. Townsend brought the bottle of wine up-stairs the young woman received it from her at the room door. That was the last time the poor girl was seen alive.

The inmates of the house one by one retired, and at one o'clock on that Sunday morning all was still. Marie Stevens, who occupied a room directly opposite that of Helen's, was aroused an hour later by a noise that sounded like that of a blow or a heavy fall. It was followed by a long and heavy moan. Getting up she listened at the door. All was then as silent as the grave. Presently she heard the door of Helen's apartment open gently and the sound of feet passing along the hall.

Cautiously opening her door she saw a tall figure, wrapped in a long cloak and holding a small lamp, glide down the staircase. Then she returned to her room.

Mrs. Townsend at three o'clock had occasion to go down stairs, and found a glass lamp belonging to Helen still burning on a table in the parlor. Looking around she discovered that the back door was open, and after calling out twice " Who's there ?" fastened it and went up-stairs to Helen's room. The door was ajar, and as she opened it a dense volume of reeking black smoke drove her back and almost overpowered her. Her screams of terror roused the house in an instant, and several of the inmates rushed to the spot and attempted to force their way through the smoke. The draught from the open door at that moment caused the smoldering fire to burst into flames, whose flickering light revealed to the horror-stricken women the form of the ill-fated Helen lying bathed in blood in the centre of the room. Her fair forehead was almost divided by a ghastly axe-stroke. The bed linen in which her form was half enveloped was burning brightly. A sickening odor of scorched flesh pervaded the apartment. The awful discovery redoubled the excitement in the house. The women screamed with terror, and in a few minutes three policemen rushed in. With their assistance the fire was soon extinguished.

Helen Jewett's body, clad in a dainty night-dress, lay with the face towards the bed ; one arm lay across the breast and the other was raised over the head. The left side from the waist up was burned to a crisp. The examination of the remains showed that death had been caused instantly by the stroke of the hatchet on the right temple, and that the burning had taken place after death.

The room in which the tragedy was enacted was a marvel of luxury. It was filled with magnificent furniture, mirrors, splendid paintings and objects of art, and contained many rare and beautiful volumes.

The trail of the assassin was plainly marked. In the yard was picked up a blood-stained hatchet, and close by the rear fence lay the long Spanish cloak which Robinson invariably wore. The murderer after scaling the fence had found himself in the rear of a small frame house inhabited by negroes. He had forced his way into the cellar and from there had made his exit into the street, down which he was seen to run at full speed by a negro woman, who had been awakened by the noise made in forcing open the door.

Robinson was found apparently fast asleep with his room-mate, James Tow. He showed no emotion when told of the murder, and merely remarked, "This is bad business," as he quietly rose and dressed himself. While he was doing so the policeman noticed on the knees and seat of his trousers were marks of whitewash such as might have been received while scaling the fence in Mrs. Townsend's yard. When confronted with the body he retained the most perfect self-possession and turned away repeating, "This is a bad business."

Robinson's trial began on June 2, 1836, and lasted five days. The court room was packed to suffocation every day of the trial. So strongly did sympathy set for the prisoner in some quarters, that the fast young men of the day flocked to the trial in crowds, wearing in his honor glazed caps such as he habitually wore, which were long afterwards known as " Frank Rivers " caps.

District-Attorney Phœnix conducted the prosecution, assisted by Mr. Robert Morris. The prisoner was defended by Mr. Ogden Hoffman, Mr. William M. Price and Mr. Maxwell.

The weight of testimony was overwhelmingly against the accused. Fortunately for him, Marie Stevenson, the woman who saw him leaving Helen Jewett's room, was found dead in her bed before the trial began.

The cloak was proved to be Robinson's, and the hatchet was identified as having been taken from the store where he was employed. The string which was tied round its handle was shown to have formed a part of the cord belonging to his cloak. His trousers, marked with whitewash, were also put in evidence. A drug clerk swore that the prisoner, under the name of Douglas, had attempted to purchase arsenic from him ten days previous to the murder.

Mr. Hoffman made a sentimental but powerful appeal in the prisoner's behalf and undertook to prove by the testimony of Robert Furlong, a grocer at the corner of Cedar and Nassau streets, that the accused had been in his store until a quarter past ten on the night of the murder and therefore could not have entered the Thomas Street house between nine and ten, as was sworn to by Mrs. Townsend.

Furlong committed suicide two weeks after the murder by leaping from the deck of a vessel into the North River.

The rest of the defense consisted of attempts to impeach the veracity of the inmates of the Thomas Street house. The colored woman who saw the prisoner escape from the cellar door was spirited away before the trial began.

On the evening of the fifth day the case was given to the jury, who, in spite of the tremendous array of testimony brought forward by the prosecution and the feeble character of the defense, brought in a verdict of " not guilty" after a very short deliberation.

It was generally believed that some of the jurymen had been corrupted. The verdict was received with a tremendous outbreak of enthusiasm among the glazed-cap sympathizers of the prisoner, and the court adjourned amid a scene of the wildest confusion.

Robinson immediately left for Texas, where he died a few years afterwards.

THE MURDER OF MARY CECILIA ROGERS.

"THE Mystery of Marie Roget," Edgar Allen Poe's famous story, founded on the mysterious murder of Mary Rogers, "the pretty cigar girl," has made that tragedy known wherever the English language is spoken. Mary Cecilia Rogers was the only daughter of a respectable widow who kept a boarding-house for clerks in Nassau Street. She lived under her mother's roof until she was twenty years of age, when John Anderson, the famous tobacco merchant, heard of her marvelous beauty and conceived the idea of making her serve as an attraction in his store on Broadway, near Thomas Street. This was in 1840.

As "the pretty cigar girl," Mary became famous. Custom flocked to the store. The young swells of the time made the shop a lounging-place, and vied with each other in attempts to win the favor of the divinity of the counter. Her conduct, however, appears to have been a model of modest decorum. She was lavish in her smiles, but repelled all undue advances with a decision that checked the boldest of *roués*.

Once only did the breath of suspicion attach to her good name. She disappeared one day from the store, and was absent for a week, when she returned and answered all inquiries with the statement that she had been visiting friends in the country. A widely circulated rumor, however, had it that Mary had been seen several times during her absence with a tall, well-dressed man of dark complexion. Who this man was has never been ascertained, but it was afterwards rumored that on the day on which she was supposed to have been murdered a man answering to that description was seen in company with her.

A week after her return to the store she suddenly resigned her position and went home to assist her mother in household duties. It was soon afterwards announced that she was engaged to be married to Daniel Payne, a young clerk who boarded in her mother's house.

On the beautiful morning of Sunday, July 25, 1841, Mary Rogers was last seen alive. At ten o'clock she knocked at Payne's door, and told him that she was going to spend the day with a Mrs. Downing, in Bleecker Street. Payne replied that he would call for her and bring her home in the evening. A furious thunder-storm, however, broke out in the afternoon, and during the evening the rain fell in torrents. Payne, who was evidently a rather careless lover, failed to keep his engagement, supposing that his betrothed could just as well spend the night at her friend's house. Next morning he went to his work as usual. When afternoon came and Mary did not return, her mother, who took it for granted that the girl had been storm-bound for the night at Mrs. Downing's, became seriously alarmed. When Payne came home to dinner, and learned that Mary was still absent, he started at once for Mrs. Downing's house. To his amazement, he was told that she had not been there on Sunday. The police were notified, and a general search was made. So well known was the girl that the news of her disappearance created a great sensation. No trace was found of her until the following Wednesday, when some fishermen, setting their nets off Castle Point, Hoboken, found the body floating near the shore, not far from a refreshment saloon known as "Sybil's Cave."

The corpse was frightfully disfigured, the face having been entirely destroyed, evidently with repeated blows of some blunt instrument. Round the waist was fastened a stout cord, to the other end of which a heavy stone was attached. Encircling her neck was a piece of lace torn from her dress, tied tightly enough to produce strangulation. Sunk deeply into the flesh of both wrists were the marks of cords. The hands were covered with light kid gloves, and a light bonnet hung by its ribbons around the neck. The clothing was horribly disordered and torn. A further examination disclosed the awful fact that a more fearful crime than murder had been committed.

It was established beyond all doubt that Mary had not gone to the house in Bleecker Street on the Sunday on which she disappeared. No one could be found who had seen her after she had left her home. At the end of a week not the faintest clew to the mystery had been found. The authorities then issued a proclamation calling on any persons who might be possessed of any knowledge of the girl's history or habits that might furnish a possible clew to a motive for her murder to come forward. The next day the Coroner received an anonymous letter from a young man in Hoboken who declared that he had seen Mary in Hoboken on Sunday, but had not come forward before owing to what he termed "motives of perhaps criminal prudence."

The writer stated that while walking in the Elysian Fields, then a famous summer resort on Sunday afternoons, he had seen a boat pull out from the New York side containing six rough-looking men and a well-dressed girl, whom he recognized as Mary Rogers. She and her companions left the boat on the beach and went into the woods. The writer was surprised to see her in the company of such rough-looking characters, and noticed that she evidently went with them willingly, laughing merrily as she walked away from the shore. They had scarcely disappeared in the woods when a second boat put out from New York and was pulled rapidly across the river by three handsomely-dressed gentlemen. One of them leaped ashore, and meeting two other gentlemen who were waiting on the beach, excitedly asked them if they had seen a young woman and six men land from a boat a few minutes before. On being told that they had, and on the direction they had taken being pointed out to him, he asked whether the men had used any violence towards the girl. He was told that she had apparently gone with them willingly, and he then, without making any further remark, returned to his boat, which was at once headed for New York.

The author of this letter was never discovered, but the letter was printed in the newspapers, and the next day the two gentlemen who had been walking on the beach came forward and corroborated the story. They both knew Mary Rogers by sight, and said that the girl who entered the woods with the six roughs resembled her closely, but they were not sufficiently near to be able to positively affirm that it was she. The next important piece of evidence came from a stage-driver named Adams, who, after allowing several weeks to elapse, testified that on the fatal Sunday he had seen Mary arrive in Hoboken, at the Bull's Ferry, accompanied by a tall, well-dressed man of dark complexion, and go with him to a road-house near the Elysian Fields known as "Nick Mullen's." Mrs. Loss, the keeper of the house, remembered that such a man had come to her place with a young woman on the day in question, and had gone into the adjoining woods after partaking of refreshments. Soon after their departure she heard a woman's scream coming from the woods, but as the place was the resort of questionable characters, and such sounds were of frequent occurrence, she gave no further thought to the matter.

The exact spot on which there is no doubt the hapless girl was brutally ill-treated and then butchered was discovered by Mrs. Loss's little children on September 25, exactly two months after the murder. While playing in the woods, they found in a dense thicket a white petticoat, a silk scarf, a parasol, and a linen handkerchief marked with the initials "M. R." The ground all around was torn up and the shrubbery trampled as if the spot had been the scene of a terrific struggle. Leading out of the thicket was a broad track, such as might have been made by dragging a body through the bushes. It led in the direction of the river, but was soon lost in the woods. All the articles were identified as having been worn by Mary on the day of her disappearance.

Every effort was made to trace the "tall, dark-complexioned man," but without success. It was rumored that he was a young naval officer. Mrs. Loss and several witnesses who claimed to have seen him with Mary during the time that she was absent from the cigar store, noticed that he seemed to be a person of a considerably higher social grade than his companion. It was generally believed at the time, that the murdered girl's mother knew more about her daughter's mysterious admirer than she chose to tell.

Daniel Payne never recovered from the shock caused by the awful death of his betrothed. The blow evidently affected his mind, and within a few weeks after the murder he committed suicide.

The crime was ever the subject of more searching and prolonged investigation, but in spite of everything that could be done, the veil of mystery has never been penetrated that shrouded the fate of "the pretty cigar girl."

THE BURDELL MURDER.

A SEVERE storm passed over this city on the night of Friday, January 30, 1857, and as the rain was falling and the wind moaning about ten o'clock a piercing shriek of "Murder!" rang through quiet, aristocratic Bond Street. A gentleman living at No. 36 Bond Street heard the cry, but as he was unable to tell from what direction it came, and as it was not repeated, he closed his door and retired. The city was shocked next morning by the discovery of the mysterious murder of Dr. Harvey Burdell, a wealthy but eccentric dentist who resided at No. 31 Bond Street.

Dr. Burdell owned the house, of which he was in the habit of letting the greater part, reserving for his own use only the reception parlors, operating room and bedroom on the second floor.

In person he was a fine portly man of middle age. . A man of strong passions and ungovernable temper, he had few friends. In spite of his invested wealth, which was considerable, and his large and remunerative practice, his mode of life was so penurious as almost to entitle him to the name of miser. His house was usually let to persons of questionable character, a class among which he had many intimates.

He kept his own servant, an extraordinary girl, who, although in most respects an ignorant creature, possessed a singular facility for acquiring foreign languages. French, German and Spanish she spoke with fluency, having devoted all her spare time to study. She was devotedly attached to the doctor.

On May 1 preceding the murder Mrs. Cunningham, a buxom widow with two daughters, took possession of the house. Like others of the doctor's tenants, her reputation was none of the best. The other inmates of the house were John J. Eckel, who was generally supposed to be paying court to Mrs. Cunningham; Snodgrass, a youth of eighteen, who was very attentive to the two daughters, Helen and Augusta; Daniel Ulman and Hannah Conlan, the cook.

Mrs. Cunningham appears to have divided her affection between Mr. Eckel and the doctor, each of whom did his utmost to supplant the other, with the result of causing frequent uproars in the house.

On October 28, 1856, Mrs. Cunningham was married by the Rev. Dr. Marvine— to whom it has never been clearly proved. The certificate states that it was to Dr. Burdell, but it is by no means certain that he was not personated on the occasion. As his lawful wife, Mrs. Cunningham would, of course, have been entitled to her legal share of his estate in the event of his sudden death.

Whether they were married or not, however, furious outbreaks between the couple continued to be of frequent occurrence, and matters finally came to such a pass that the doctor determined to look out for another tenant.

While Dr. Burdell was out at dinner on the evening preceding the murder Mrs. Cunningham asked Hannah, the cook, what woman it was that she had shown through the house that day. Hannah replied that it was the lady who was about to take the house.

"When does she take possession?" asked Mrs. Cunningham.

"The first of May," replied the servant.

"He better be careful; he may not live to sign the papers," was the reply.

What time the doctor came home that night is unknown, but the exact moment of the murder is fixed at half-past ten o'clock, the time when the cry of murder was heard.

It was eight o'clock in the morning when the boy came, according to custom, to make the fires in the doctor's rooms. He brought a scuttle of coals from the cellar and setting it down opened the doors of the front room on the second floor. It struck against something which seemed heavy and yet yielding. The boy, who was whistling merrily, pushed it back and stepped into the room. The sight which met his gaze struck him rigid with horror. On its back, with arms outstretched and eyes staring blankly at the ceiling, lay the body of the owner of the house, the head resting in a pool of blood. Blood was everywhere—on the walls, carpets, furniture, splashed five feet high on the door and spurted to the very ceiling. The boy's terror found vent in a shriek that was heard by every soul in the house. Mrs. Cunningham, with her family and boarders, were quietly at breakfast in the basement, apparently all unconscious of the awful scene up-stairs.

On learning what had occurred she gave way to a wild outburst of grief. Eckel exhibited little concern.

The room in which the body was found had evidently been the scene of a terrific life and death struggle. The furniture was tossed about in every direction and hardly an article was found to be free from the stain of blood.

No less than fifteen distinct stab wounds, any one of which was sufficient to have caused death, were counted on the corpse, which was fully clothed. They had the appearance of having been inflicted with a long, narrow dagger.

Around the neck, sinking deeply into the flesh, was the mark of a small cord, showing that strangulation had first been attempted. This failing, resort had been had to the dagger.

The gas was burning full. The bed had not been slept in. A complete examination of the house disclosed the startling fact that there were blood marks on the hall, on the stairs, in the lower bed, on the front door, even in the attic room and on the very steps leading to the scuttle in the roof.

The spirit of murder seemed to have staiked through the house, leaving everywhere the gory traces of its fingers.

At the Coroner's inquest, which was held in the house, medical experts testified that the strokes of the dagger had been delivered by a left-handed person. Mrs. Cunningham was left-handed. The verdict charged Mrs. Cunningham and Eckel with the murder, and they were conveyed to the Tombs.

The case against Eckel was dismissed, but Mrs. Cunningham was placed on trial on the 6th of May. She was ably defended by Henry L. Clinton. District-Attorney A. Oakey Hall conducted the prosecution, but was unable to establish anything against the accused except the existence of a motive. The trial lasted three days, and the jury, after deliberating for an hour and a half, returned a verdict of "not guilty."

Mrs. Cunningham, who had assumed the name of Burdell, immediately returned to her home at No. 31 Bond Street. Not satisfied with having escaped the penalty of the crime, which there is little doubt that she committed, and having become entitled by right of dower to a third of the murdered man's wealth, she determined to gain possession of the whole of it, and in furtherance of this object conceived the remarkable idea of palming off on the authorities an infant heir to the estate.

A Dr. Uhl was taken into her confidence, with the understanding that he was to receive $1,000 for his share in the transaction, but the doctor promptly acquainted the District Attorney with the particulars of the widow's ingenious little plan.

Mr. Hall entered eagerly into the spirit of what appeared to him a huge joke and actually undertook to supply the necessary infant. In due time Mrs. Cunningham announced that all was ready for the interesting denouement.

Disguised as a Sister of Charity she went to a house in Elm Street, where the infant, borrowed by Mr. Hall from Bellevue Hospital, was delivered to her by Dr. Uhl, and carried it to Bond Street in a basket. The next day the arrival of the heir was duly announced, and then Mr. Hall and a policeman stepped in and arrested the "mother."

She was soon afterwards, however, set at liberty. The little girl who was used in carrying out this remarkable fraud was named Matilda Anderson. She and her real mother were placed on exhibition at Barnum's Museum.

Mrs. Cunningham soon afterwards went to California. Eckel was imprisoned in the Albany penitentiary for complicity in some whiskey frauds in Brooklyn and died there.

The house in Bond Street, which is but little altered in appearance, is frequently shown to strangers as the scene of the "mysterious Cunningham-Burdell murder."

THE MURDER OF BENJAMIN NATHAN.

THE most celebrated, and certainly the most mysterious, murder that has ever been perpetrated in New York City was committed on the night of July 28, 1870, during the fitting accompaniment of the most terrific thunder-storm that ever visited the city. While the thunder rolled, the lightning lit up the heavens with blinding flashes, and the rain fell in torrents, Mr. Benjamin Nathan, a wealthy stock-broker, was foully murdered in his handsome mansion, No. 12 West Twenty-third Street.

Mr. Nathan's family, with the exception of his two sons, Frederick and Washington, whose business kept them in the city, were at the time absent at his country seat in Morristown, N. J. Mr. Nathan was in the habit of coming into town every day to go to his office in Broad Street. On the evening of Thursday, July 28, he left the house of his brother-in-law, in Nineteenth Street, at seven o'clock, saying that he intended to spend the night with his sons in Twenty-third Street, instead of going out to Morristown. His son Washington was then with him, but parted with his father in the street.

The old gentleman went directly home. A bed had been fitted up for his use in the centre of the front parlor on the second floor. Adjoining this room was the library, which was connected with it by a short passage. In the front room was a writing-desk and a small safe, in addition to the ordinary furniture.

A few minutes after six o'clock next morning, a policeman who was patrolling Twenty-third Street heard screams of murder near the corner of Fifth Avenue, and running in that direction, saw two young men standing in their night-dresses on the stoop of the Nathan mansion.

One of them presented a ghastly appearance, blood covering the front of his white night-dress, and even his bare feet were smeared with blood.

"Come in!" they shouted. "Father's been murdered!"

He hurriedly entered the house, and going up-stairs, was shown by the distracted young men the mangled form of their father stretched on the floor of the front room, close to the door leading into the library.

The corpse presented the most horrifying appearance. It lay on its back, clad only in a white night-dress, with arms and legs outstretched. The head lay in a great pool of blood which flowed from numerous gaping wounds in the skull.

Blood was spattered over the door, door-posts, and adjoining furniture. Close to the body lay an overturned chair, also smeared with blood, which had been placed in front of the writing-desk.

The door of the safe stood wide open. The key was missing. On the bed lay a small drawer taken from the safe. It contained nothing but a few copper coins. On the floor, near the desk, lay a small tin box containing papers, also taken from the safe.

The policeman hastened to summon assistance, and a thorough search of the premises was made. On the desk lay a partially-written check to the order of H. Lapsley & Co., on the Union National Bank. The "stub" in the check-book was marked "July 29—$10,000 subscription for 100 shares German-American Bank."

From the position of the corpse and the chair, it seemed evident that the old gentleman had been stricken down from behind while writing this check. The first blow must have been insufficient, for there were evidences of a struggle in the over-turned furniture and the blood-stains that were distributed in every direction.

In addition to this, it was found that two of the fingers of the left hand had been fractured, evidently in warding off a blow. No less than fifteen wounds were counted on the head, most of them being on top and on the back of the skull. Brain matter, mingled with small splinters of bone, exuded in half a dozen places.

So much did the injuries vary in character, some having evidently been made with a blunt and others with a sharp instrument, that it was at first believed that they must have been inflicted with two weapons, and this led to the theory that more than one person had been concerned in the murder.

This view of the case, however, was disposed of when one of the policemen picked up, between the inner and outer doors of the front hall, an instrument known as a carpenter's " dog," covered with blood and hair. It consisted of a bar of iron about eighteen inches long, turned down and sharpened at each end, somewhat in the shape of a staple.

It was readily seen how with the sharp end of such a weapon the incised wounds could have been inflicted, while the other injuries were caused by blows from the blunt angle.

Simultaneously with the discovery of the weapon a bloody trail of naked footprints was found leading from the chamber of death, down the main staircase, to the front door and out on the stoop.

The discovery made a tremendous sensation among the searchers until Mr. Frederick Nathan explained that on being roused by the cry of his brother Washington, who discovered the body, he had rushed into the room and knelt beside it, thereby smearing his night-dress and feet with the blood. Finding that life was extinct, he had run down stairs to give the alarm, leaving the trail of blood with his naked feet.

The only persons in the house at the time were the two sons, who slept on the floor above their father ; a servant-man, who occupied an adjoining room, and the house-keeper, who slept in the basement. None of these persons heard any noise during the night. Absolutely no trace could be discovered of the manner in which the assassin had gained access to the premises.

The announcement of the murder caused an excitement absolutely unparalleled. For days Twenty-third Street was fairly blocked with dense masses of people, who came to gaze at the windows of the room on the second floor. Stage-drivers either drove slowly past the house or pulled up altogether to give their passengers a chance to stare at the spot. Even private carriages drove slowly through the street all day, forming a long procession, their occupants leaning out of the windows to catch a glimpse of the scene.

Next day the Stock Exchange offered a reward of $10,000 for the arrest of the murderer, and Mayor Hall issued the following circular :

PRIVATE AND CONFIDENTIAL.—$47,000 REWARD.—PROCLAMATION.—THE MURDER OF
MR. BENJAMIN NATHAN.

The widow having determined to increase the rewards heretofore offered by me (in my proclamation of July 29th), and no result having yet been obtained, and suggestions having been made that the rewards were not sufficiently distributive or specific, the offers in the previous proclamation are hereby superseded by the following :

A reward of $30,000 will be paid for the arrest and conviction of the murderer of Benjamin Nathan, who was killed in his house, No. 12 West Twenty-third Street, New York, on the morning of Friday, July 29th.

A reward of $1,000 will be paid for the identification and recovery of each and every one of three diamond shirt studs, which were taken from the clothing of the deceased on the night of the murder. Two of the diamonds weighed, together, 1, 1-2, 1-18, and 1-16 carats, and the other, a flat stone, showing nearly a surface of one carat, weighed 3-4 and 1-32. All three were mounted in skeleton settings, with spiral screws, but the color of the gold setting of the flat diamond was not so dark as the other two.

A reward of $1,500 will be paid for the identification and recovery of one of the watches, being the gold anchor hunting-case stem-winding watch, No. 5657, 19 lines, or about two inches in diameter, made by Ed. Perregaux ; or for the chain and seals thereto attached. The chain is very massive, with square links and carries a pendant chain, with two seals, one of them having the monogram, " B. N.," cut thereon.

A reward of $300 will be given for information leading to the identification and recovery of an old-fashioned open-faced gold watch, with gold dial, showing rays diverging from the centre, and with raised figures believed to have been made by Tobias, and which was taken at the same time as the above articles.

A reward of $300 will be given for the recovery of a gold medal of about the size of a silver dollar, and which bears an inscription of presentation not precisely known, but believed to be either " To Sampson Simpson, President of the Jews' Hospital," or " To Benjamin Nathan, President of the Jews' Hospital."

A reward of $100 will be given for full and complete detailed information descriptive of this medal, which may be useful in securing its recovery.

A reward of $1,000 will be given for information leading to the identification of the instrument used in committing the murder, which is known as a " dog " or clamp, and is a piece of wrought iron about sixteen inches long, turned up for about an inch at each end, and sharp, such as is used by ship-carpenters, or post-trimmers, ladder-makers, pump-makers, sawyers, or by iron-moulders to clamp their flasks.

A reward of $800 will be given to the man who, on the morning of the murder, was seen to ascend the steps and pick up a piece of paper lying there, and then walk away with it, if he will come forward and produce it.

Any information bearing upon the case may be sent to the Mayor, John Jourdan, Superintendent of Police City of New York, or to James J. Kelso, Chief Detective Officer.

The foregoing rewards are offered by the request of, and are guaranteed by me.

(Signed)   EMILY G. NATHAN, Widow of B. Nathan.

The following reward has also been offered by the New York Stock Exchange :

$10,000.—The New York Stock Exchange offers a reward of Ten Thousand Dollars for the arrest and conviction of the murderer or murderers of Benjamin Nathan, late a member of said Exchange, who was killed on the night of July 28, 1870, at his house in Twenty-third Street, New York City.

J. L. BROWNELL, *Vice-Chairman Gov. Com.*
D. C. HAYES, *Treasurer.*
B. O. WHITE, *Secretary.*

A. OAKEY HALL, MAYOR.

MAYOR'S OFFICE, NEW YORK, August 5, 1870.

Great importance was attached to the blood-stained " dog," and every effort was made to discover where it came from, but without success. It was a tool that is often used in building, and might have been left in the house years before by workmen. It certainly was not the kind of weapon that a deliberate assassin or professional burglar would have carried with him, and this suggested the theory that the murder had been committed by one of the inmates of the house.

Of one thing the police were perfectly sure—that the assassin, whoever he was

was thoroughly acquainted with the premises. No one else, they argued, could have so completely covered up his tracks.

Tremendous was the sensation when it began to be whispered that Washington Nathan, then one of the handsomest and most popular young men in the highest New York society, was perhaps not free from the stain of his father's blood. The idea seemed too monstrous for belief, but there were not a few people who clung to it. There was some mystery about the young man's movements during the fatal night that he seemed indisposed to reveal. Then, too, he had been the first to discover the murder and the last one to see his father alive. In addition it was darkly hinted that Washington had much to gain by his father's death. The unhappy young man was closely cross-examined at the Coroner's inquest and fully accounted for every moment of his time from the hour he parted from his father up to a quarter-past twelve o'clock in the morning when he came home. His testimony was corroborated by that of Clara Dale, a young woman in whose company he had passed a portion of the night.

The day after the murder Patrick Devoy, a man employed to take care of the house of Prof. Samuel P. Morse, No. 5 West Twenty-second Street, told the police that at half-past ten o'clock on the night of the murder, a closed carriage had driven up to the entrance of the Nathan stables, which adjoined Professor Morse's house, and had remained there all through the furious storm, until nearly two o'clock in the morning, when it suddenly drove rapidly away.

A gentleman who had come in from Morristown with Mr. Nathan told a story of a rough-looking man who was said to have been seen loitering the evening before about the Nathan country-seat, and who occupied a seat in the same car near Mr. Nathan, and watched him closely until the train reached Hoboken. Nothing ever came of either of these clews.

To enumerate the hundreds of theories propounded would be impossible. While many detectives clung to the belief that the murder had been committed by a member of the household, others insisted that it was the work of a burglar who had secreted himself in the house, and being found by the victim, had slain him to prevent an outcry, while others again held such wild theories as that the deed had been done by some fellow broker who was a rival in business, or that some escaped lunatic had entered the house.

Interest in the murder of the banker was revived by the confession of the notorious burglar, John T. Irving, and the subsequent arrest of Billy Forrester and several other professional cracksmen. Irving in 1873, during a fit of remorse and while in San Francisco, delivered himself up to the authorities for the Nathan murder. He was brought on to this city and made a confession, and promised to produce the necessary corroborative evidence if the District Attorney would consent not to prosecute him for two burglaries—one at Green's pawnshop, No. 181 Bowery, where he had stolen diamonds worth $200,000, and the other at Casperfield's jewelry store. The agreement fell through, and the evidence of the crime was not forthcoming. Irving's confession ran as follows :

"On or about the 15th day of May, 1870, I was passing through Madison Park with Daniel Kelly and Caleb Gunnion, otherwise known as George Abrahams, when our attention was called by Kelly to a man standing in the Park. We advanced towards him, and on reaching him the following conversation ensued, Kelly addressing the man :

"'Well, McNally, what are you doing here? I have not seen you for a long time.'

"'That's so,' responded McNally, 'and you are the last person I expected to meet. You have not been home long, have you?'

"'No—a few months. What are you doing now?'

"'I am at the old business again.'

"McNally took Kelly to one side, about six feet from ourselves. I never knew what transpired at that time; however, a portion of that conversation was overheard by both Gunnion and myself. I give it as follows : Kelly was standing with his back towards Twenty-third Street, McNally facing him. 'Where does your mother live, Mac?' Mac answered, 'Down Twenty-third Street,' pointing with his fingers towards Sixth Avenue. I had almost forgotten to explain how I came to call this man McNally. I and Gunnion were introduced to him by Kelly, at the time when we first came up to where he was sitting. Kelly, turning around toward us, said : 'Come, boys, let us go through Twenty-fourth Street and we will have a drink.' McNally refused, saying at the time that he was going home. We parted and went through Twenty-fourth Street to Eighth Avenue, taking an Eighth Avenue car, and leaving it at the corner of Hudson and Christopher streets. We went into a large hardware store on the same corner that we got out at, which was the northwest corner, and there purchased a bar of steel about four feet long, to be made up into tools. Taking the steel we started through Christopher Street for the Hoboken ferry, and passed over. While on that trip Kelly told me that he had made arrangements with McNally about a job which would turn out well. Nothing further was said until June about the matter, and then, for the first time, I was made aware of this job. I was then told by Kelly that the family was not at home, and that access to the premises could be readily obtained, as we would be let in, and work the safe without any further trouble. Gunnion was also present at this meeting, and it was decided that we work the place. In a very short space of time after this meeting I was arrested at my residence, No. 37 Garden Street, Hoboken, in connection with one Charles Carr, now in Sing Sing, for a robbery in Lispenard Street, where it was alleged that I had broken into and taken laces valued at $5,000; I had no connection with it, so I was discharged, but re-arrested for an attempt at burglary on Wilson & Green's pawnbroking establishment, corner Delancey and Bowery, and held to bail, which was procured, and I was released in the —— part of July, a day or two before the murder of Mr. Nathan. During my stay in the Tombs everything was arranged, so that when I came out all that was to be done was to get our tools and proceed to work. We agreed to meet at eight o'clock, in Madison Park. The evening previous to the morning of the murder we met, according to appointment, and found McNally awaiting us. Kelly took McNally aside, and, after about twenty minutes' conversation with him, he left, going towards Sixth Avenue. Kelly told us that we would have to wait for about ten minutes. He instructed us to follow one after another, a short distance apart, and if everything was right we were to move up close together, by a signal from the man at the gate by wiping his face with a pocket-handkerchief. All was clear, the man was at his post, and we entered the house by the basement door, Gunnion and myself going to the cellar, as we had been previously instructed to do. Kelly went up-stairs, and when all was ready he was to call us. I should judge, from the length of time that elapsed, we must have been in the cellar about four or five hours. It was a very stormy night out, which made the time drag along very slow. At last Kelly made his appearance, telling us to take off our shoes, which we did, and made our way up-stairs (three flights), entering at the side door at the front of the building. I think there was a taper burning. I noticed a person lying on the floor, about three or four feet from the door. In the small room things were scattered about. I stepped on something which at that time appeared to me like a pocket-book, and on picking it up it proved to be a memoranda, or Jewish calendar, with the following names :—Albert Cardozo, Dr. Leo, Samuel Lewis, corner Fourteenth Street ; also papers, or rather —— stock, which had been ——; also Pacific Mail and some —— bonds. I think the Pacific Mail has the name of J. Coke or —— endorsed on them. Am not positive, but that name appears on some of the stock. In the aggregate the amount is $6,000 ; $273 in money was also obtained. The safe had been opened before we went up-stairs. There appeared to be a peculiar kind of odor in the house ; something like kerosene or turpentine. Altogether I don't think we were in the rooms occupied by Mr. Nathan more than fifteen minutes, and about five of the time was spent by Kelly washing his hands off. I think he said he went to the bathroom. We stood waiting inside the room door for him, and I noticed finger-marks on the jam of the door, as if it were blood.

"Our next step was to descend to the lower part of the house, and there await a favorable opportunity to get out, knowing that we had to contend with more on the outside than on the inside. We waited at the foot of the basement stairs until half-past five o'clock in the morning, and then went up to the front door, Kelly looking out of the door to see if all was clear. He passed us once, and we reached the street without being seen, but just as we were about to direct our steps toward Fifth Avenue, a man came along on the opposite side of the street with a dinner-pail in his hand ; this man stooped down and picked up something like an envelope. As yet we had not made a start, and on looking at Kelly I observed blood on his shirt bosom, and told him of it. He went inside of the railing to adjust his vest so as to hide it, when Gunnion saw a young woman coming toward us from Fifth Avenue. Just then we made off toward her. I think I saw a person come toward one of the windows in the Fifth Avenue Hotel, on the third story, and look toward Sixth Avenue. We walked pretty fast, so as to get away as soon as possible, keeping on Twenty-third Street until we reached Third Avenue, knowing that would be our best policy, as the streets running east and west in the morning are never so closely watched at that time as the ones running north and south in that neighborhood. Third Avenue was reached in time for a car, and, without hailing it, we jumped aboard on the front platform, leaving the car at Houston Street. It was now after six o'clock, and people were coming and going in all directions. We went into a house on —— Street, and then and there, in the presence of two women, divided what we had got. Kelly seemed to be somewhat excited, and all at once said : 'You know that dog I got from Nick Jones. Well, I left it behind. Do you think it will cost us any trouble?' I said: 'I don't know. I believe Nick is all right. You had better see him, anyhow, in time.' He asked the elder of the two women to give him a shirt, which was done, and he told her to wash the one he had just taken off as soon as possible, and adding at the same time, 'Here is $20, and I will go see Nick Jones.' I left the house and went to my home in Rivington Street. I returned to wait for Kelly. He came back about ten o'clock the same morning. I believe Nick Jones was very much afraid of Kelly or his friends. I never knew of the exact amount of property taken, as Kelly denied all knowledge of the diamonds, which caused a rupture between us. Have had nothing to do with him since. Have heard since I came to New York that he was in Auburn prison; also heard that Gunnion was in prison. In October of the same year I visited Nick Jones at the Brooklyn Navy Yard by permission of the naval commander, he granting me a permit, as during working hours nobody is allowed to hold any communication with those who are employed therein. On this occasion Jones acted rather green, and when I spoke to him about Kelly he upbraided me for having introduced him to Kelly, saying that I had destroyed his peace of mind. I asked him in what respect. All that he said was by placing his mouth to my ear and whispering 'Nathan,' trembling violently at the same time. I did not make any reply, as I saw it might cause him pain. This ended my visit. I intended when I went over to see if he had received anything from Kelly; but then, when I saw how he became affected, I never mentioned it. The conversation I had with Kelly about the killing of Mr. Nathan occurred in the house in Suffolk Street. He said the return of Mr. Nathan was wholly unexpected, and when he found out that he had come home he thought that he would try and get the key of the safe. He got into the room without disturbing any one, got the key, and was ransacking the safe, when the old man awoke and said, 'Who's there?' On the party coming toward him, as if to lay hold of him, he raised the 'dog' as if to strike him. The old man threw up his hands to protect himself, and received the blow on one of them. He then screamed, and was struck several times on the head. He (Kelly) then ran into the entryway, and in going down stairs he found that no one could have heard the noise, as all was quiet. He waited in the hallway some time, and then got us to return to the room with him to see what we could find."

Irving was afterwards placed on trial for the burglaries, and being convicted of the two charges against him, was sentenced to State prison for seven years and a half. He is at present residing in this city.

THE RYAN MURDERS.

NICHOLAS and Mary Ryan, brother and sister, both unmarried, on November 28, 1873, engaged furnished lodgings from Mrs. Patrick Burke, who rented apartments on the fourth floor of the tenement No. 204 Broome Street. Ryan said that he was a shoemaker, and that his sister, who seemed to be a modest, well-behaved young lady, was a "gaiter-fitter," employed at the establishment of Burt & Co., in Thomas Street.

Mrs. Burke sub-let the front room of her apartments to the Ryans. The place was immediately occupied by the young pair, Nicholas and Mary cooking and sleeping in the single chamber. The room, which was about sixteen feet square, was well carpeted and comfortably furnished with a walnut three-quarter bedstead in the southeast corner and a new black horse-hair sofa at the rear and centre of the apartment, against the wall. The walls were decorated with framed prints representing the "Crucifixion," the "Last Supper," the "Immaculate Conception," and other pictures. The door of this room led out on the front part of the landing of the fourth floor, and had a catch lock or bolt which could be pulled back from within, but could not be opened from the outside excepting by a key made especially to fit the lock.

Although the brother and sister lived in the same apartment, they did not sleep in the same bed. Nicholas Ryan slept regularly on the bed—a very comfortable one— while Mary Ryan slept on a large mattress, which was disposed of nightly in this way : the mattress, or one side of it, was placed on the horse-hair sofa, and the outside part of it was supported by two chairs. The brother and sister appeared to live happily together, working in the daytime and rarely going out of an evening. The young woman always seemed to be in a melancholy mood, and her brother was dark and distant. Nothing unusual transpired to attract attention to the Ryans until Monday morning, December 22, 1873. A policeman who was passing the house between half-past two and three o'clock on that morning heard a window raised with a sudden crash, and, looking upward in the direction of the noise, he saw the head of a man protrude from a window on the fourth story of the six-story brick tenement house No. 204 Broome Street, which gave shelter to twenty-four families. The man was shouting "Murder!" and "Police!" violently. The officer ran into the house, giving an alarm rap at the same moment, to which there was a response in a few moments by three other members of the force. They lit matches and held them above their heads. The policemen found streams of blood pouring down the stairs and banisters, but discovered no human body until they came to the landing of the second story, and on that part of it toward the rooms fronting on the street there was discovered by the officers a most woful and terrible sight. A young man, apparently in the full flush of manhood, wearing nothing but his drawers and undershirt, was stretched, life just extinct and his throat across the jugular vein severed by an awful and deep gash. He had bled, even on this floor, three or four quarts of blood, and the worn and soiled oilcloth presented a smoking, red, ghastly spectacle. The head of the slaughtered man rested against the panels of the door of a German named Charles Miller, whose family occupied rooms on the second floor. On examination long rivulets of blood and pools of the same ghastly fluid were discovered all over the stairs and walls of the third and fourth floors, to which the policemen ascended as rapidly as possible. The face of the man, not long dead, lay downward.

Patrick Burke, who occupied three rooms and let the fourth of his suite to the Ryans, was met on the stairway. He was in his shirt-sleeves and was very much excited. Burke directed the officers to the room in which he said there was another dead body. All entered close after one another, with that expectant gait and bated breath that comes of an unknown terror. And there on the mattress, cleanly covered, and in a dark night-robe, lay a young girl, her head thrown back, her throat cut by a deep gash almost from ear to ear, and her tongue almost lolling out of her mouth and slightly black on the surface. The neck—a fair, white one—was marked with the deadly press of fingers, indicating that the assassin had strangled his victim perhaps into an insensible state before cutting her throat. The improvised couch was in itself very clean, tidy, and not at all disturbed. The fingers of the hand were slightly closed, and the face, bearing marks of considerable intelligence and refinement, had an expression of pain and sudden fright. The mattress was fully soaked with the poor girl's blood, and her skirts and underclothes, of remarkably fine texture, were found placed smoothly and in regular order upon an adjoining chair. A little further on was a small lady's gold open-faced watch, with a black composition chain, a lady's gold lead-pencil, and inside the door was a night-key and a small white-handled penknife, the blades shut and the handle spotted with gouts of blood. The blades, on being opened, had not a stain upon their bright surfaces, but were sharpened in that peculiar way noticeable among shoemakers, the heart of the blade being eaten away by grinding on a whetstone.

The bed which had been occupied by young Ryan was tossed about and looked as if something violent had taken place on it while occupied. The sheets and quilts were thrown in a heap, and on an adjoining chair were discovered a pair of pantaloons belonging to the dead man, a white linen shirt, with two small gold imitation studs in the bosom and having short cuffs. This shirt was spread out in an orderly fashion, as was the trousers. There was besides the shirt a pair of linen cuffs and a pair of gold sleeve-buttons. A razor case, made to hold two razors, was found, and but one razor was in the case ; the other could not be discovered on the premises.

Out on the landing, and all the way up from the fourth to the sixth story were found pools and clots of blood on the oilclothed stairs, and the walls were discovered to be covered with finger-marks and clots of livid red blood. It was a slaughter house, this tenement, which contained over one hundred souls, hived together in such a small breathing place.

But how to explain this horrible slaughter ? Who had done it ? Where was the weapon ? Had young Ryan been followed home and killed for his money, and had his sister been strangled and her throat cut by the assassin ? Was the assassin a resident of the house, full of Poles, Germans, Italians and a curious and mongrel mixture of people whose avocations are uncertain ? The latter theory has its possibility. Or had young Ryan, who was said to be a peaceable and temperate man, in a moment of mad insanity, killed his sister and then cutting his own throat rushed out, not knowing where he was going—anywhere into space and eternity ?

There was a small rosewood lady's box in the room full of trinkets and which contained a bank book on the Bowery Bank, indorsed by the depositor, Miss Winifred Stapleton, while in Mr. Ryan's trunk was discovered two bank books on the Emigrant Savings Bank, Nos. 64,522 and 97,121, indorsed in the name of the deceased Nicholas Ryan. The Miss Stapleton was said to be a niece of the dead brother and sister. The depositors in the three bank books were accredited with a total of over $700. In the bottom drawer of the rosewood case a small revolver, looking quite new, was observed.

Patrick Burke, who rented the room for nine dollars a month, the first month's rent having been paid in advance by Nicholas Ryan, when questioned stated that he had been awakened by some strange noise about half-past two o'clock on that Monday morning. He jumped out of bed instantly and ran out in the hall, but all was dark. Then he listened for a moment and heard a noise which sounded to him something like the wheezing of a cat. As he was hastily clothing himself he heard the cries of his children, who were sleeping in a hall bedroom adjoining the front room occupied by the Ryans, and his daughter, Jennie Burke, aged eleven years, cried to him, "Come here, father; there is something the matter on the landing." Then his wife said, "Go, Pat, and see what's the matter." He did so, and carried a lamp with him through the hallway, when he saw streams of fresh blood on the oilcloth and walls, and this frightened him and he went back and told his wife that murder must have been committed in the house. Then he went to Ryan's room and saw the door open, and on entering he discovered Miss Mary Ryan with her face downward on the mattress and her throat cut. Then he ran to the front window and gave the alarm to the police, whereupon they entered and discovered the body of young Ryan on the second floor and afterwards saw Miss Ryan lying dead in her room.

Patrick Ryan, a married brother of the murdered pair, was sought out in the hope that he might furnish some clew that would lift the bloody veil. He resided in South Brooklyn, and was employed as foreman in the shoemaking establishment of T. Kalliske & Co., No. 34 Warren Street in this city. He said that his brother Nicholas, who had worked under him, was a sober and peaceable young man, and had supported his sister, who was also employed in Burt's shoe factory. Mary was an affectionate girl, and the brother and sister had lived together previous to their removal to Broome Street at No. 3 Canal Street, since the death of their mother. They kept house for the mother; Nicholas loved his sister dearly, and if there was any little disagreement it never amounted to anything more than is usual in any family, and would be forgotten. Nicholas and his sister were brought up too religiously to think of suicide or of any other similar crime. Nicholas had attended St. Mary's Church, in Grand Street, and St. Bridget's Church, in Avenue B. He took tea with a married sister and his own two children at the room of Nicholas and Mary on Sunday evening, and all seemed happy, laughing and joking. All six persons then left the house in Broome Street to go out. His sister Mary and brother Nicholas accompanied as far as the corner of Suffolk and Broome streets and there—it was then seven o'clock Sunday evening—Nicholas left them, and he (Patrick Ryan) said to his brother, "Nicholas, you might tell us where you are going and introduce us to the girl that you are going to see." This was in a joke, and Nicholas left and I did not see him again until I was sent for to see him dead. Mary, my sister, left her married sister's in Lewis Street at or before nine o'clock to go home on Sunday evening, and that is all I know, excepting that my brother had a silver watch valued at $15, and a gold chain attached, valued at $35. Would not know the maker's name or what amount of money he had in his pocket. He always carried money and made good wages.

Several hours after the discovery of the double tragedy a girl named Jenny Burke, the daughter of Patrick Burke, discovered Ryan's vest on the roof-top. There were also bloody footprints on the top of the house and on the stairs leading to the roof. There was no trace, however, of the missing watch, or, most important of all, the weapon with which the deed had been committed.

The deputy coroner carefully examined the bodies, and found on that of the sister a cut on the throat nine and a half inches long, beginning at the back of the neck on the left side and terminating at a straight line from the left jaw. The carotid artery and jugular vein were cut, which must have resulted in almost instant death. Blue marks, as if made by fingers, were on the throat, as if tightly pressed against it, causing the tongue to protrude between the teeth. The medical examiner was of the opinion that the young woman was first strangled until she became nearly unconscious, when a knife or some other sharp instrument was used with the right hand, while the throat was clasped by the left hand of the murderer. The autopsy also revealed something wholly unexpected. It was that Mary Ryan was *enciente* at the time of her death, and that three lives instead of two had perished at the hands of an assassin. An old shoe-knife, upon which there was not the slightest trace of blood, was found in the room of the Ryans several days after the murders, and was said to be the weapon with which the crime had been committed. The accepted theory in the case, outrageous and inconsistent as it was, was that Nicholas Ryan was the father of his sister's unborn child, and to conceal his sin he had murdered the young woman and afterwards committed suicide. There were facts, however, which proved the absolute falsity of this conclusion. The murders were not committed by a robber, but the watch and other articles missing were carried off by the assassin to create such a suspicion. Had he left the weapon he had used behind him the scoundrel well knew that it might prove a tell-tale piece of evidence against him, so he carried it off. All the facts go to show that Nicholas Ryan and his sister Mary were cruelly butchered by a young man who had been keeping company with the latter. Having ruined the young woman he refused to marry her, and when threatened with arrest and exposure he resorted to murder to conceal his sin. He was seen in the vicinity of the Broome Street tenement on the night of the tragedy, and after his brutal work he purchased a drink of whiskey to brace up his shattered nerves at a saloon in the vicinity of the house of blood. The bartender noticed that the customer looked wild, and also that his cuffs were stained with the crimson fluid of his victims. There the trail ended, and although nearly thirteen years have elapsed since the slaying of the brother and sister, the whereabouts of their murderer is yet unknown.

THE MURDER OF ANNIE DOWNEY, ALIAS "CURLY TOM."

AS a flower girl Annie Downey started out in life, and the acquaintances which she formed while peddling bouquets along the Bowery doubtless led to her ruin. Small in stature and possessed of a shapely form and a handsome face, she soon made hosts of friends. In time she became a degraded creature, and was entered upon the books of the filthy dens in which she lived as "Curly Tom" and "Blonde Annie." She was naturally a brunette, but was in the habit of dyeing her hair to a light blonde. All her relatives were respectable people, and to save them from the shame of her disgrace she passed under the name of Annie Martin. She was found dead in the house kept by a woman named Smidt, at No. 111 Prince Street, on January 17, 1880, under circumstances so mysterious as not to give the faintest clue to her murderer.

During the day preceding the night of her murder she remained in the house and received a number of visitors, none of whom were known to the proprietress. The young woman seemed to be in unusually gay spirits. On retiring to her room, the second floor front, at eleven o'clock, she called out over the banisters to Mrs. Smidt, saying that she expected a visit from an old friend before midnight, and asked to be called as soon as he arrived. She was never seen alive again.

Up to half-past twelve o'clock no one entered the house, and at that hour Mrs. Smidt's husband locked the front door and went to bed, taking the keys with him, according to custom. The back door was always left unlocked.

The Smidt bedroom was on the first floor in the rear. Rosa Schneider, the cook, and a colored chambermaid, whose rooms were in the attic, were the only other persons who slept in the house that night.

Bertha Levy, a hair-dresser, called at ten o'clock next morning to dress Annie Downey's hair. She attempted to open the door to the girl's room, but found it locked. Being unable to get any response to her repeated knocks she called Mrs. Smidt, who, becoming alarmed, called a policeman.

There were three doors leading into the room, one from the hall, one from the adjoining hall bedroom, and the third from the rear room. The two former were locked. The bed was placed against the latter.

Going into the rear room the policeman forced open the door, pushing the bed back with it, and entered the room. Lying on the bed, face upward and drenched in blood that had flowed from several ghastly wounds in the head, he found the body of Annie Downey. It was cold and stiff.

Tied so tightly around the neck as to blacken the face and force the eyeballs from their sockets, was a thin pillow-slip taken from the bed. The fingers of the left hand clutched one end of the slip with a death grip. The limbs were extended straight along the bed, and the attitude of the body did not suggest that a struggle for life had taken place. The only other marks were two small cuts over the left eye that looked as if they had been inflicted with a blow of a fist.

Everything about the apartment was in perfect order. The girl's clothing was neatly arranged over a chair by the bedside. In the ears of the corpse were a pair of handsome amethyst earrings and a diamond ring flashed on her finger. Evidently the murderer's motive had not been robbery.

The only thing missing was a watch and chain of little value, but it was soon remembered that the girl had disposed of them a few days before.

Search was made for the key of the door, but it could not be found. All the inmates of the house were strictly interrogated, but no information that could throw a ray of light on the mystery could be elicited. No unusual sounds had been heard during the night.

Smidt was positive that no man was in the house when he locked the door for the night.   Annie's last visitor had gone away long before eleven o'clock, the hour at which she went to her room.   The only theory of the case was that the murderer had entered the house during the evening without attracting attention, and secreted himself in the room until the girl entered, when he surprised and killed her before she could make any outcry.

This view was supported by the condition of the body, which indicated that the murder took place at least ten hours before it was discovered.

By way of the back door the assassin could easily have made his way to an alley running along the eastern side of the house to the street.   The padlock which fastened the door of this alley was found to have been twisted off.

The coroner's examination showed that death had been caused by strangulation, and that the wounds on the head were merely superficial and had been inflicted after the pillow-slip had been knotted round the throat, evidently in an effort to still the girl's struggles for life.

THE ASSASSINATION OF CHING ONG, ALIAS ANTONIO SOLOA.

IN a little underground shop, with the evidences of his careful thrift about him, within hearing of customers in the store overhead and almost in sight of passers by on the walk without, a man was, on November 2, 1885, in broad daylight, hacked to death.

The horrors of murder were in his case intensified by dreadful mutilations, which happily are rare in the domains of civilization, and the extent of ferocity expended in the deed pointed at once to people of semi-barbaric instincts as the authors.   Like most assassinations of this kind it was involved in mystery, and investigation for the truth required to be carried on among people with strange secrets and unfamiliar tongues.

"Antonio Soloa" was printed on the cards of the little eating-house that burrowed under the southeast corner of Wooster and Spring streets, with its single window admitting only such dreary reflections of daylight as straggled down to it through an iron grating.   Antonio Soloa had a Spanish flavor about it, and it rather unsatisfactorily indicated a man with unmistakably Mongolian features, who was often seen bustling about there in the dual capacity of cook and waiter.   Soloa was a Chinaman, and, according to the words of a countryman, had brought from home the more characteristic name of Ching Ong.   But it was not from the West but through the Indies that he had come to New York, and while in Cuba he acquired a Hispano-American name.   His occupation, too, had been learned in the South, and he at first went to work in this city as a cigar-maker.   As such he had been brought into contact with a lot of West Indian coolies, native Cubans and Spanish speaking negroes of the Caribbean Islands.   He went from one quarter of the city to another and finally found engagement in Chio & Soona's factory, in South Fifth Avenue.   There he lived, too, in the heart of the district which has of late years become marked above all others as a foreign quarter.   There Spanish, French and Italian were commonly spoken and were not unfamiliar to the Chinese who herded among the hybrid population of the place, and through Ching Ong's knowledge of them as Antonio Soloa he became a person well known among them.

He had the aptitude of his race for money making, and several years before his tragic death gave up the drudgery of the workroom for a little shop near the Catherine ferry, whence he removed to No. 81 Thompson Street and No. 51 Wooster Street. At these he catered for the cigar-makers, often bringing their lunches to the factories for them. Later on he removed to the basement where he met his death. Stockelberg, Chio & Soona and other tobacconists have factories on South Fifth Avenue, and some of the workmen used to go to Soloa's place. Nearly all were men of his own race or of Cuban extraction, and the dingy little den, with its cleanly linen and dishes attuned to the palates of its patrons, gained favor among them all. About $10 a day was believed to be the extent of the host's receipts, and out of that he was supposed to comfortably run his establishment and save a snug little penny besides.

Soloa's neighbors knew little of him or his guests. John and Peter Waurchus, the German grocers overhead, only occasionally noticed the stream of swarthy visaged men, who, at meal-time, slipped down the stone steps outside and as noiselessly shuffled away. O'Brien & Ryder, the plumbers next door, gave little heed to the Chinaman or his belongings. And probably the children who played about the place only occasionally caught a glimpse through the iron railing of the lamp-lighted snuggery and the dark, strange-speaking people who sat at the tables in it. Soloa himself was a quiet, affable sort of a man. He dressed rather well for a Chinaman, discarding all the native gear, with the exception perhaps of an alabaster bracelet, and he wore his hair like his neighbors', without a suspicion of its ever having been trussed up in a queue. He appeared to be on the best of terms with his guests, too, and seemed altogether a good-natured and hard-working fellow.

At noon on that fatal Monday he was in his kitchen and bustling about the shop as usual when Julius Dichon, a countryman of his, who had known him for ten years, went down to dine. There were the usual set of men dropping in by twos and threes. The long table by the wall was set for eight. The smaller square table was set for four. There were two tables at one side, to accommodate a couple each. Only one was occupied. The diners at it paid their score and went out. The hand of the clock ticking over the mite of a counter little more than a yard long was drawing to one as Dichon arose to go. The pair of canary birds, whose gilded cages were strangely bright as they swung in the dimness of the place, were fluttering about as he went up the steps. Soloa was standing alone with a can in his hand and feeding them.

Almost an hour later John Waurchus went out of his grocery to drive over to Centre Street. He saw the Chinaman coming up the steps at the same moment. Soloa had turned the key in the door, and as he returned the grocer's nod he said:

"I am going over to the Bowery to see about my music box."

As he spoke he went off in that direction and John Waurchus turned to his wagon. He never saw his Chinese neighbor again alive.

It was only a little after that—no more than three-quarters of an hour—when Jim Coughlin, a coal-heaver in the Farrar Company's yard, had a surprise. He was lounging on a box watching a peddler named Daly trundle a handcart of vegetables along and voice their quality for the good of the neighborhood, and he had his eyes on the man when he left his vehicle at the curb-stone and descended the steps of Soloa's restaurant. Dàly was gone only for an instant. When he stumbled out on the walk his eyes were full of horror and his face pale with excitement.

"My God!" he cried to the coal-heaver; "there's a man dead down there."

Coughlin got up and asked, "Where?"

"Down below on the floor," said the peddler.

"Let's go down and see," said Coughlin, and the other, evidently ill-satisfied with his fortune of first discoverer, lagged at his heels as they descended.

The peddler's words were true. A man was lying there dead, but so horribly butchered, so disfigured with gaping wounds, protruding brains and untraceable lineaments as to betray no facial evidence of identity. Blood welled from his heart and head and lay in a pool about him. There were clots upon his hands. There were marks upon the floor, and a dripping knife lay upon it beside him.

The place at first sight seemed undisturbed. The tables were covered with clean linen, and the glasses and bottles on them were polished and ready for use. On the wall two of those grotesque Chinese pictures representing an Oriental procession and a Mongolian horseman in the act of leave-taking, turned a blotch of glaring color with threads of tinsel upon the incomer. Between them was the photograph of a well-dressed Chinaman, who was pronounced to be Antonio Soloa himself. A lot of unpainted boards, reaching from floor to ceiling, divided the eating-room from a kitchen and dark hutch of a place that was found to have been used as a bedroom. From nails along this partition hung strings of garlic; on a shelf in front of it were cans of starch and preserved vegetables, with lemons, cheeses and spices, and along the wall some cheap prints were swinging. A white table-cover, suspended on one side, shut out the dismal glimpse of a black opening, sinking lower, and suggesting a sub-cellar, and it cut off whatever fugitive rays might intrude on that side from a second iron grating on the walk.

So dark it was within that the prostrate figure lying between the kitchen partition and a couple of tables was not clearly discernible. And it was only when a reluctant lamp was lighted and threw its yellow gleams on the floor that the details of the fearful assassination made themselves visible. It was the host of the little restaurant, Antonio Soloa, who had been with the Chinaman, Chong Ong, that lay there, so far as figure and attire indicated. But the red lineaments that were spread upon the floor had every semblance of life crushed out of them. Only a bloody mask was turned to the light divided by a great gash at the chin, slashed deeply on the cheek-bone and temple, with one eye gouged out of its socket and lying at the apex of a mass of bone and muscle which a cut into the forehead had raised out of the skull itself. The head was crushed nearly flat. A portion of the face held in position by the bones seemed unnaturally swollen by contrast with the dreadful mass of features that were driven in alongside it. The nose had shrunk into a red hollow. The head bulged out in places, and through the tangle of hair could be seen great gapes where the brain was oozing out. The sight was horrifying. But that was not all. The red shirt falling back from the breast revealed a cut. It was turned further back, and directly over the heart, repeated again and again, were nine great holes, where a knife had been thrust up to the hilt. It had cut the heart in two, and some of the blows had severed a series of the ribs. The knife must have been wielded with demoniac strength and ferocity. It had almost cut the man to pieces.

The knife itself was there. It lay on the floor—a big kitchen-knife, with a blade eleven inches long, fitted in a handle of dark wood by brass rivets. Through the blood that covered it the inscription, "Lamson & Goodnew Manufacturing Company," appeared on the blade, and this blade, heavy though it seemed, was bent by the force of the blows that had been struck with it. To all appearance it was a kitchen-knife, and there was a suggestion in a cut loaf of bread lying on the table beside the corpse that the knife might have been caught up from the table for the bloody work. It was the only weapon found. How the head had been crushed in, the bones of the face mashed to a jelly, the skull beaten into over threescore fragments, as was later on discovered to be the case, there was nothing about to indicate. A dent was noticed on a stone and a fleck of blood was on the floor beneath it, but the light sheet iron could never have withstood the force of a falling man nor beaten in his skull. The pockets of the dead man were turned out. Beside him, smeared with blood, was a fire insurance policy for $500 in the Phœnix company. An empty pocket-book was on the table.

In his disordered garments, in the blood mark at the stove and in a shivered pane of glass in the door were evidences of a struggle. But where the body lay with all its wounds nothing seemed out of place, as though the man had been beaten down suddenly and without resistance. Beyond the body an opening in the partition led into the kitchen and bedroom. In the former nothing was amiss, but the sleeping apartment had been fairly ransacked. The contents of a trunk were scattered about. An accordeon lay on the bed, a watch ticked beside it, an opium pipe had fallen on the floor. Heaps of clothing were wildly tossed around. Outside in the dining-room the drawer from the counter lay underneath it, the papers and dinner tickets it contained mingled with some small coins. Plunder was certainly hinted by all this as the motive of the crime. The watch was the only valuable left behind, and in the scurry of such a moment and the horror of such a scene the murderer's neglect was natural. That precautions were taken to examine everything was shown in the red smears upon the clothes in the bedroom and the marks of bloody fingers on the counter cards. Nor had need of security been overlooked. The wash-basin on a stand in the dining-room told its tale. It was full of bloody water.

The coroner on his arrival made an autopsy, which revealed that the heart and other organs had been reached by the knife; that the skull had been shattered to pieces, and the brain again and again penetrated. The excessive mutilation could be due only to the body having quivered after the knife thrusts had been delivered, when, to make death a certainty, the skull had been beaten in. It did seem strange that so fearful a death struggle had passed without attracting attention, and the neighbors were closely questioned. No one had heard a cry. Ryder, the plumber next door, had heard a crash of glass, and had sent a boy out to see what was broken. The little fellow did not look into the Chinaman's basement, and so the pane that had been smashed during the fearful work of that half hour escaped attention. In the place nothing was left that could serve as a clue to the murderer. Not a sign that might serve to indicate his identity or even his nationality or station in life had the slayer of Soloa left behind, except the suggestion that lay in the fearful completeness of his work. A weapon left behind might have betrayed something, but the knife with which the stabs were inflicted seemingly belonged to the dead man himself. The wounds were inflicted with a bread-knife, and such a knife was picked up in the kitchen. The heavy instrument with which the head had been crushed in was not discovered. A deep gash on the brow and some wounds on the head, as well as the traces of sprinkled blood upon the walls and ceiling, suggested a hatchet. A search of the basement and cellar failed to reveal any such weapon, and the assassin was wary enough to carry off his murderous implement lest it should afford a clue. The blood spattered on the ceiling seemed to show that he was upright when the blows were struck. The knife was used to complete the work, and was driven again and again into his heart fairly up to the hilt, a few blows falling upon the face and chin. A slash upon the left arm was doubtless received while that member was raised in defense, but it was as probably inflicted by the murderer in the wild fury of his strokes after it was prone and powerless. The crushing of the bones of the head was, like the excessive stabbing, an atrocity to remove all doubt of dissolution.

There had been a witness to the butchery, but that fact did not become known until long after the discovery of the murder. Then William Schimper, a nickel-plater, came forward with his office boy, who was named George Mainz. Mr. Schimper said that the lad could throw some light on the tragedy. Young Mainz was questioned. He said that he had been sent on a message by his employer, and as he was returning through Spring Street, he saw two men quarreling at the top of the basement stairs on the southeast corner of Wooster Street. "One," declared the boy, "was a short, thin man, who looked like a Chinaman. The other was a tall, strong mulatto. The men were very angry with each other, and their loud voices made me stop. I thought there was going to be a fight, so I watched. I saw the tall man draw a knife and plunge it into the little man's breast. He had hard work to draw it out. When he did pull the knife out, the big man ran down stairs out of sight. The little man followed him, but he seemed to fall down, for I heard a crash as he disappeared. I was so frightened that I ran to the office, and did not tell Mr. Schimper till hours after."

"Do you think you would be able to recognize the tall man if you saw him again?"

"Yes, sir, perfectly well."

"How?"

"Because he had a terrible scar on his left cheek."

The description of the assassin furnished by the lad cleared the suspicion that the brutal crime had been committed by a Chinaman believed to be a "highbinder." The murderer had been seen at his bloody work, and the witness said he was a tall negro. That was definite enough, and it was subsequently learned that a man answering the description given by young Mainz had been seen on several occasions in Ching Ong, alias Soloa's restaurant. He was a Cuban negro, and was said to be a member of a

Cuban insurrectionary organization known as "Niazzas." There was a section of that revolutionary society in this city. Its meetings and doings were kept secret, but in a moment of vanity the conspirators, some years before, had had a large photograph of all the leading members taken in a group. A copy of the original picture fell into the hands of the detectives. It was shown to young Mainz.

"There! there!" exclaimed the boy, pointing to a large, dark-complexioned man who stood in the middle of the group, but in the background; "there he is. That is the man I saw stab Soloa."

The photograph was exhibited to many, and at last a man was found who said, "Yes, I know him, (meaning the tall conspirator). His name is Augustus Rebella, but I don't know where he lives or works. He is a cigar-maker." Then for the first time the name of the slayer of the Chinaman was learned. Rebella was sought after, and on November 20, 1885, just eighteen days after the assassination, the tall Cuban negro was traced to the cigar manufactory at No. 161 Pearl Street, and there arrested. Although Rebella had no scar on his cheek, when he was photographed there was the mark of a healed wound on the left side of his face, just as the boy had said, when the suspected man was made prisoner. The scar was very prominent and had been made some eighteen months before by his mistress, whom Rebella had quarreled with at No. 309 Mulberry Street. Rebella said that on the day of the murder of the China-man he had been at work in Los Dos Amigos' cigar factory in Washington Street, Brooklyn. There it was learned that on November 2 the prisoner had only made one hundred cigars, while the usual number he was in the habit of making in a day was two hundred. He admitted that he had known Ching Ong, alias Soloa, and gave his address as at No. 118 West Twenty-seventh Street. Young Mainz positively identified Rebella as the murderer of the Chinese restaurant keeper, and the prisoner was held upon the lad's affidavit of identification. Subsequently it was ascertained that Rebella had made two attempts prior to the murder to kill Ching Ong.

That he was the slayer of Ching Ong, was well known to the Cuban insurrectionists, and also the fact that he was assisted by two others in the completion of the butchery. The weapon with which Ching Ong's skull had been battered in was a slung-shot. Still, Rebella's fellow-conspirators were determined to save him from punishment. Although it was a fact that Rebella had only worked the first half of the day on November 2, and returned to the factory just before closing time, nearly two dozen of the cigar makers made affadavit to the effect that he had not left the shop. The few other workmen in the place, who could not be induced to perjure themselves, were threatened by Rebella's murderous associates with death, if they ventured to testify against the prisoner. The men, aware that their lives were in danger, were therefore afraid to come forward, and vanished before their testimony could be secured. Thus were the hands of Justice tied, and as the preponderance of evidence, such as it was, was in favor of Rebella, it was impossible to legally convict him on the testimony of young Mainz, and the prisoner was consequently released. It is more than probable that the horrible butchery, owing to the machinations of a secret society, will forever remain unavenged.

EXECUTIONS

IN THE TOMBS PRISON, NEW YORK CITY, FROM 1851 TO 1886.

AARON B. STOOKEY, in a fight on April 17, 1851, stabbed and killed Edward Moore. The murderer was placed on trial in the Court of Oyer and Terminer on May 1, 1851. The trial came up before Judge John W. Edmonds and Aldermen Edmund Griffen and Daniel Dodge. The prisoner was found guilty of murder in the first degree. Stookey was executed at the Tombs prison on September 19, 1851.

OTTO GRUNSIG administered to his wife Victorine, who was lying sick on August 8, 1851, at No. 105 Eldridge Street, a quantity of arsenic mixed with sugar. The woman died from the effects of the poison. Grunsig was convicted of murder in the first degree, in the Court of Oyer and Terminer, November 28, 1851. Judge Edmonds, asociated with Aldermen Jedediah Miller and Jonas T. Conklin, presided during the trial. Grunsig was executed February 27, 1852.

WILLIAM SAUL and NICHOLAS HOWLETT shot and killed Charley Baxter, a night watchman, on a ship lying at the foot of Oliver Street, on August 24, 1852. Saul and Howlett, when they committed the crime, were in the act of robbing the vessel. They were convicted in the Court of Oyer and Terminer of murder in the first degree, November 18 and November 25, 1852, respectively. Judge Henry P. Edwards and two Aldermen presided at the trials. They were executed January 28, 1853.

JOSEPH CLARK, a sailor, was arrested on July 10, 1851, for the murder of George T. Gillespie, by striking him in the head with a cart-rung. He was convicted of murder in the first degree, in the Court of Oyer and Terminer, September 16, 1851, before Judge Edmonds and Aldermen Warren Chapman and Patrick Kelly. Clark was executed February 11, 1853.

JOHN D. BROWN, who was jointly indicted with Clark, pleaded guilty to assault and battery, September 16, 1851, and was sentenced to the penitentiary.

PATRICK FITZGERALD, on January 17, 1853, shot and killed Margaret Fitzgerald, his wife. He was convicted of the murder in the Court of Oyer and Terminer, April 19, 1853, before Judge Henry P. Edwards and Aldermen Wm. J. Peck and Oscar W. Sturtevant. Fitzgerald was executed November 15, 1853.

JAMES L. HOARE, on October 5, 1853, stabbed Susan McAnnany in the neck with a dirk, from the effects of which she died three days later. Hoare was convicted of murder in the first degree, in the Court of Oyer and Terminer, November 19, 1853, before Judge Henry P. Edwards. He was executed January 27, 1854.

JOHN DORSEY (negro), a sailor, was executed in the Tombs prison for the murder of Ann McGirr, alias Ann Hopkins. The crime was committed at No. 3 Worth Street on March 10, 1857. The scene of the crime was a five-story tenement inhabited by colored prostitutes. Dorsey and the woman lived together, and on the night of March 10, 1857, he returned home under the influence of liquor. He met his mistress, Ann McGirr, in the alleyway. They had some words, and Dorsey becoming angry drew a razor from his pocket and cut the woman's throat from ear to ear. Dorsey was convicted of murder in the first degree, in the Court of General Sessions, May 21, 1857, before Judge Abraham D. Russell. He was hanged on July 17, 1857.

JAMES ROGERS was hanged November 12, 1858, for the murder of John Swanson. On the night of October 17, 1857, the deceased with his wife was passing along Tenth Avenue in the neighborhood of Twenty-seventh Street. They met the accused with two others passing down the Avenue. One of the three men jostled against Mrs. Swanson in passing. Rogers, when remonstrated with, remarked to Swanson, "What are you talking about?" To which deceased replied, "What is that to you?" A moment intervened when Rogers rushed up and stabbed Swanson with a knife in the heart. Rogers was arrested in Jersey City a few days after. He was convicted of murder in the first degree, in the Court of General Sessions, November 13, 1857, before Judge Abraham D. Russell.

JAMES STEPHENS poisoned his wife, Sophie Stephens, at No. 166 East Twenty-seventh Street. Stephens lived at the above address with his wife and two nieces, Fanny and Sophia Bell. He had manifested a great affection for Sophia Bell. He was in the habit of beating his wife, who was sickly. He administered to her laudanum mixed with lager beer and brandy, on September 22, 1857. She died the next day. Stephens was convicted of murder in the first degree, in the Court of Oyer and Terminer, March 26, 1859, before Judge James J. Roosevelt, and was executed February 3, 1860.

JOHN CRUMMINS stabbed and killed Dennis McHenry with a sword. Crummins and McHenry had some troubles over money matters, and Crummins also charged McHenry with insulting his wife. On the night of October 10, 1857, McHenry and two others went into Crummins's liquor store, at No. 23 Pell Street, to get a drink. When they entered the place they asked for Crummins. They were told he was out. While they were drinking, Crummins entered, and seeing McHenry, ordered him to leave. McHenry in return said, "I'll go, but you dare not follow me." Crummins went into the back room and returned with a sword and pursued McHenry to the street and around some carts in front of the door, and wounded him four times.

Crummins was convicted of murder in the first degree, in the Court of Oyer and Terminer, February 1, 1860, before Judge Daniel P. Ingraham, and was executed March 30, 1860.

BERNARD FRIERY, in company with four or five others, entered the saloon kept by Henry Lazarus, at No. 12 East Houston Street, on the morning of January 3, 1865. Lazarus was standing against the bar when they entered. One of the party, called "California Jack," remarked as he entered : "I'll bet a hundred dollars I've got a man here that can lick any man in the house," and again offered to bet ten dollars that there was a man there who could take Lazarus's pistol away from him. Lazarus declined to bet, saying he had no pistol. Friery then advanced to Lazarus and wanted to shake hands with him. Lazarus shook his head and said, "No, I don't want to shake hands with you." Friery then said, "You are a loafer," and at the same time stabbed Lazarus in the neck with a dirk. Lazarus died instantly. Friery was convicted of murder in the first degree, in the Court of General Sessions, February 17, 1865, before Judge Abraham D. Russell, and was executed August 17, 1866.

FRANK FERRIS killed his wife, Mary Ferris, September 9, 1864, with a blow from an axe, at No. 31 James Street. He was convicted of murder in the first degree, in the Court of General Sessions, on March 1, 1865, before Recorder John T. Hoffman. He was executed October 19, 1866.

GEORGE WAGNER was convicted in the Court of General Sessions, October 20, 1865, before Recorder John T. Hoffman, of the murder of his wife, Mary Wagner. The crime was committed on July 21, 1865, at No. 516 Broome Street. Wagner beat his wife's skull in with a hatchet. He was executed March 1, 1867.

JEREMIAH O'BRIEN was convicted in the Court of General Sessions, November 16, 1866, before Judge Abraham D. Russell, of the murder of his mistress, Lucy A. McLoughlin, alias Kate Smith. He stabbed her to death with a knife, at No. 139 Prince Street, on June 20, 1866. He was executed August 9, 1867.

JOHN REYNOLDS killed William Townsend, a shoemaker, with a knife, at No. 192 Hudson Street, on January 29, 1870. Reynolds was under the influence of liquor at the time of the murder. He was convicted in the Court of Oyer and Terminer, February 22, 1870, before Judge Daniel P. Ingraham, and was executed April 8, 1870. When Reynolds was arrested, he made the remark that "hanging was played out in New York."

JOHN REAL, a car-driver, on July 23, 1868, shot and killed Patrolman John Smedick, of the East Thirty-fifth Street Station, at the corner of Thirty-second Street and First Avenue. Real and Smedick had previously had some difficulty. Real had made an attempt to assassinate Smedick on July 1st, in the same year. He was convicted of murder, in the Court of Oyer and Terminer, February 10, 1869, before Judge George G. Barnard. Real was executed August 5, 1870.

JOHN THOMAS, a negro, had a discussion with Walter Johnson on the night of September 30, 1870, opposite No. 511 Broome Street, concerning their respective fighting abilities. The altercation developed into an affray, during which Thomas shot and killed Johnson. Thomas was convicted of the murder, in the Court of Oyer and Terminer, December 28, 1870, before Judge Albert Cardozo. The murderer was executed March 10, 1871.

WILLIAM FOSTER killed Avery D. Putnam with an iron car-hook, on the night of April 27, 1871, on a Broadway car, on Seventh Avenue, between Forty-sixth and Forty-seventh Streets. Foster was riding on the front platform of the car, and kept the door open. Putnam got up from his seat and closed the door. Foster opened it again. This was repeated five or six times. Finally Putnam went out on the platform and asked Foster "what was the matter with him." Foster made no reply, but followed Putnam inside the car and asked Putnam "what was the matter with him." Foster, who was under the influence of liquor, struck Putnam with the car-hook as he was leaving the car at Forty-sixth Street. Foster was convicted before Judge Albert Cardozo of murder in the first degree, in the Court of Oyer and Terminer, May 25, 1871, and was executed March 21, 1873.

MICHAEL NIXON shot and killed Charles H. Phifer on the night of January 25, 1873, on the corner of Catherine Street and Bowery. Nixon was convicted, in the Court of Oyer and Terminer, of murder in the first degree, April 2, 1873, before Judge John R. Brady. He was executed May 16, 1873.

WILLIAM THOMPSON, WILLIAM ELLIS and CHARLES WERND, alias CHARLES WESTON (negroes), on September 17, 1875, while tramping through the country, attempted to rob Abraham Weisberg, a peddler, at Lydig's Woods, Westchester County, N. Y. They beat Weisberg to death with a club. The three colored men were convicted of murder in the first degree, in the Court of Oyer and Terminer, October 29, 1875, before Judge George C. Barrett. They were executed December 17, 1875.

JOHN DOLAN, on Sunday, August 22, 1875, while committing a burglary at Noe's factory, at No. 275 Greenwich Street, was discovered by the proprietor, James H. Noe. A struggle ensued, during which Dolan beat Noe on the head with a "jimmy," from the effects of which injuries the brush manufacturer died. Dolan was arrested by Detective Joseph M. Dorcey, of the Sixth Precinct, at the corner of Franklin and Centre Streets, October 7, 1875. He was convicted of the murder before Judge George C. Barrett, in the Court of Oyer and Terminer, October 27, 1875. Dolan was executed April 21, 1876.

CHASTINE COX (colored) on the night of June 11, 1879, committed a burglary at the residence of Mrs. Jane L. DeForest Hull, at No. 140 West Forty-second Street. On being discovered in one of the rooms by Mrs. Hull, he gagged and strangled her to death. Cox was convicted of murder in the first degree, in the Court of General

Sessions, on July 17, 1879, before Judge Rufus B. Cowing. He was executed July 16, 1880.

PIETRO BALBO, an Italian, stabbed his wife, Maria Dichaco Balbo, to death on September 13, 1879. Balbo was convicted of murder in the first degree, in the Court of Oyer and Terminer, on December 11, 1879, before Judge Daniels. He was executed August 6, 1880.

WILLIAM SINDRAM, a printer, shot Catharine Craves, at her residence, No. 4 Charlton Street. Sindram had a furnished room at Mrs. Craves's house. He was a troublesome lodger, and Mrs. Craves told him to move. He left the house on the night of January 25, 1881, and came back the following day for his clothes. Mrs. Craves heard him in the hall and asked him what he wanted, and told him he had no business in her house. Sindram replied, " Come down stairs and I'll show you what I want," and at the same time drew a pistol from his pocket and shot Mrs. Craves, who was standing at the head of the stairs. Sindram was convicted of the murder before Judge Brady, in the Court of Oyer and Terminer, December 10, 1881. Sindram was absolutely indifferent as to his fate. He was executed April 21, 1882.

AUGUSTUS D. LEIGHTON (colored) killed his mistress Mary Dean. The crime was committed on June 13, 1880, in front of her residence, No. 138 West Twenty-sixth Street. Leighton had been living with Mary Dean for nearly a year. During a quarrel, Mary ordered him to leave the house. He did so, but returned some time afterwards to get a coat which he had left behind. Mary told him that he could not have it. Leighton said, "By God, I will have it," and rushing toward her, cut her throat from ear to ear with a razor. Leighton was convicted before Judge Brady, in the Court of Oyer and Terminer, December 3, 1880. He was executed May 19, 1882.

PASQUALE MAJONE murdered his mother-in-law, Maria Velindino Selta. The crime was committed on December 9, 1881, at No. 56 Thompson Street. In a fit of jealousy, Majone accused his wife of being intimate with other men. During the quarrel that followed, he drew a pistol from his pocket and shot his wife in the head. His mother-in-law hearing the shot, rushed into the room to ascertain its cause. Majone also shot her. He then shot himself, making a slight wound. On April 25, 1882, he was convicted of the murder, in the Court of General Sessions, before Recorder Frederick Smyth. He was executed on March 9, 1883.

MICHAEL E. McGLOIN and four others, on the night of December 29, 1881, started out on a burglarious expedition, and forcibly broke into the residence of Louis Hanier, a saloon keeper, at No. 144 West Twenty-sixth Street. While ransacking the saloon for money, they aroused Hanier and his family, who slept up-stairs. Hanier hearing the noise, rushed to the head of the stairs and was about to descend when McGloin, who was at the foot of the stairs, shot and killed him. The day following the shooting McGloin remarked to a companion, "A man ain't tough until he has knocked his man out." McGloin was convicted of murder in the first degree, in the Court of General Sessions, March 3, 1882, before Recorder Frederick Smyth. He was executed March 9, 1883.

EDWARD HOVEY was executed October 19, 1883, in the Tombs prison, New York City, for the murder of his sister-in-law, Fannie Vermilyea, whom he shot and killed on April 26, 1882, at No. 273 West Thirty-eighth Street. He was convicted of murder in the first degree, in the Court of General Sessions, September 25, 1882, before Judge Rufus B. Cowing.

MIGUEL CHACON, a Cuban negro, on June 20, 1884, at No. 126 West Twenty-seventh Street, shot and killed his mistress, Maria Williams. The woman had formerly been the mistress of another Cuban negro, but when the latter abandoned her she took up with Chacon. Chacon was infatuated with the woman, and became furious with rage when she ordered him to leave, so that her old lover could return. In the wrangle that ensued, Chacon drew a revolver and shot her dead. He also attempted to assassinate his rival. Then he fled, but was captured several hours afterwards on the roof of a house in Spring Street. One of the leading spirits in the Cuban Revolutionary Society, known as the "Niazza," revealed the hiding-place of the murderer. Chacon was found guilty of the murder of his mistress, in the Court of General Sessions, on October 29, 1884. He was executed on July 9, 1886.

ADVENTURERS AND ADVENTURESSES.

ODD and dubious are the methods of gaining a subsistence which are practiced by the adventurers and adventuresses of the metropolis. There are many lines of money-making in a great city, which, though not exactly "legitimate," are yet not precisely criminal. Still, like the professional criminals, Bohemians, blackmailers, bogus literateurs, agents, models, and the borrowing landlady, make it a business of preying upon society, and an exposé of their operations cannot but serve as a protection for the innocent against these sharpers. The more important of these frauds are well described in the following article, culled from a metropolitan newspaper :

"There is a lady, a little *passé*, but still pretty, who keeps a popular boarding-house, and who has in her time kept several boarding-houses, all of them 'popular' while they lasted, but none of them last very long. That is her little game. She is a woman of very ingratiating nature, and she generally manages to wheedle some favorite boarder—generally some rich old bachelor or widower—out of a large sum of money, in advance for board. Then, suddenly, somehow or other, her affairs become 'entangled,' and she is unexpectedly obliged to 'give up' her house. The house is accordingly given up, and the lady temporarily disappears till the former favorite lodger 'gives up' all hope of ever getting his advanced money back again, or its equivalent. Then she reappears in a new street, occasionally in a new name, and the routine of 'borrowing' from a lodger and then 'giving up' the house again is gone through with once more. She has been known to obtain an advance of $1,000 from a lodger, for more than two-thirds of which sum she has never given and never will give an equivalent. Whenever she 'gives up' a house she generally is more or less in debt to all her lodgers, whom she treats so kindly while they are with her that they generally gladly comply with her request 'for an advance to relieve her from temporary embarrassment.' As a rule lodgers generally victimize their landladies, but this instance shows that sometimes the rule is reversed and the biters are bit.

"A certain smart woman has hit upon a capital way of making money. She is an observing woman, and has noticed that one of the most difficult matters in New York is to procure a reputable yet convenient place at which a lady and gentleman or ladies and gentlemen can be 'private.' There are plenty of 'private supper rooms' in New York, but they are either very nasty or very expensive, and under all circumstances of 'dubious' character. If a lady and gentleman really want to enjoy a little supper or a little chat together without publicity, they will find it almost impossible to accomplish their end without losing caste. To counteract this state of things the lady in question has opened a fine, large house and has furnished it finely. The three upper stories she lets out to gentlemen only as 'furnished rooms,' the parlors on the ground floor and the basement are devoted to the realization of her peculiar design, which is this :—A gentleman and lady or gentlemen and ladies or a party of gentlemen wish to be 'private' for a certain length of time. For a moderate sum they can have the temporary use of the parlors. Important interviews can thus be held privately, card parties and dance parties can be held here ; or, if supper or refreshment is required, the lady is prepared to furnish, at a reasonable tariff, both wine and supper. This sort of thing is really a novelty in New York, and as such attracts attention.

"In a recent interview with the proprietress of this 'new idea,' the lady said that her record for a month back embraced eighteen suppers of ladies and gentlemen, the parties varying from four to twenty persons—three suppers of gentlemen only. Evenings had been devoted to card parties and one evening wholly to dancing. The utmost decorum had been observed and in only one instance had she experienced the slightest trouble.

"Some women are really very industrious and very clever in their peculiar line. One now residing in elegant style up-town, has acquired quite a little fortune by 'trading in her influence.' She has a large circle of acquaintance among moneyed men, and has also a ready perception, a glib tongue and a keen, instinctive knowledge of human nature. These qualities she is constantly turning to the utmost pecuniary account. She is a married woman, though her husband is a nonentity, practically speaking, and keeps house up-town. There in the evenings she receives calls from numerous bankers, brokers and others, whom she elegantly and pleasantly entertains, and meanwhile 'talks them' into, wheedles or coaxes or argues them into favorable notice of any scheme she may have at the time a pecuniary interest in. She does a paying business in this line, as she never undertakes any but a big scheme and a plausible scheme, and when once she undertakes it does her 'level best' to carry it through. Not long ago the lady talked up a mine, got most of the stock subscribed through her own exertions, and took her pay in the shape of an extensive roll of greenbacks, for it is characteristic of this personage that she will never take 'commissions.' She demands so much money down, and generally, having proved that she is worth it, gets it. By her earnings in this line, *sub rosa*, of course, she makes the major part of the family income, and clothes herself and her daughters in excellent style. This lady is widely known by Wall Street and Broad Street magnates, and is held in high esteem with them, as she is considered equally shrewd and 'square.'

"Now and then in New York one comes across a woman, a lady, who, though she could not be properly styled an adventuress, yet has adopted in some respects quite an ingenious and dubious way of adding to her income, or at least of lessening her expenditures. There is, for instance, a young lady in 'society' quite locally famous for obtaining all her gloves and *bijouterie* as 'gifts' from her gentlemen escorts to parties and theatres—gifts which are hinted for if not volunteered. There is another woman who, residing in a furnished suit of rooms and 'taking her meals out,' always manages it that two meals out of her daily three are taken 'at the invitation' of some gentleman, and, of course, at his expense—thus saving the ingenious invitee at least

$10 a week.   A third woman always contrives to fasten herself on some richer woman, making herself a species of 'companion,' living at the expense of the fashionable woman to whom she attaches herself, thus presenting a curious combination of belle and barnacle.   A fourth fair creature has made it for years a practice to become 'engaged' to some rich young man, receive from him as many 'presents' as he will be tempted to present, and finally quarrel with her betrothed, breaking the engagement and retaining the presents.   She has already been engaged four times, and her presents are computed at over $5,000.   Her last lover, however, insisted upon a return of the major portion of his gifts, and as the 'belle's stratagem' is becoming known, her chances for continued success are at a discount.

"Canvassing and book-peddling are growing into favor with females, at least, though their victims are not so enthusiastic in their praise.   While some of those canvassers and book-peddlers are worthy, well-deserving, hard-working women, many of them are merely dead-beats, frauds, bores intolerable.   One of this latter sort will talk to a business man when he is busiest, wring from him in his agony some expression of dubious import, such as, 'Well, well—perhaps I may some time," and then she will go forthwith to the office of some newspaper, state that he has ordered, through her, such and such an advertisement, collect her commission in advance, leaving the collector of the newspaper and her victim to settle the final payment between them.   Others leave books whether or no, or talk a man 'deaf, dumb and blind' into subscribing for them, and so the world wags.

"As for fortune-tellers and clairvoyants, their numbers are large, and are on the increase, but luckily this class of people have been so often and so thoroughly ventilated as to call for nothing but mere mention.   Perhaps the most curious fact lately unearthed about 'the world of women,' is that there are several respectable young women, technically 'ladies' in dress and social surroundings, and really females of good character, who serve in secret the purposes of art as models.   The writer of this sketch is acquainted with an estimable lady—a genuine lady in birth, education and manner—who earns about $10 per week as a model for a 'life class.'   She keeps this fact a profound secret—her own mother is not aware of it—but the fact is as stated, the writer having ascertained it through a visit to an artist's studio, during the sessions of a 'life class' of art students.   Inquiring into this matter further, the writer discovered that the young lady in question had in vain attempted to secure employment in writing, translating or trade pursuits, was on the verge of starvation with her old mother, when a lucky hint suggested the livelihood of a model, which was finally and successfully adopted, though only after severe self-struggles and under conditions of the most profound secrecy.

"A prominent painter, with whom the writer held a conversation recently, stated that the supply of models was at present greater than the demand, and that the majority of models in the city of New York were not only well formed, but well behaved ; 'a really superior class of persons,' forced to exhibit themselves by their necessities.   A model quite in demand is a young German.   Another model has recently been married to a young painter who fell in love with her, from seeing her as a model in a life class which he was then attending, and from all reports the daring and unconventional painter has a worthy wife. Occasionally in our better classes, ay, even in our best society, it is rumored that ladies do not hesitate to serve as partial models for the bust or arms or for classic poses, to please popular artists or to gratify their own vanity; but these are isolated cases and call for but the merest passing allusion.

"Among the most curious phases of ingenious impecuniosity, striving to gain a livelihood without what is called 'working for it,' is the case of a certain young man in New York, who, young, rather handsome and of good family, has for some time past devoted himself almost exclusively to playing the cavalier to a very old and very rich widow, whom he accompanies everywhere. Apropos, it may be remarked that this dancing attendance to dowagers who are rich is growing quite into an 'institution' among the would-be fashionable but not at all wealthy youth of the period. Is it a sign of the times? And perhaps it is another sign of the times that several of our men about town, technically called 'gentlemen,' are really card sharpers, and absolutely live upon the money they make by cheating at cards at their clubs or elsewhere. There are several 'society men,' so-called, who live in luxury, dine well, drink well, dress well, dissipate lavishly, who depend upon their skill in cards for the wherewithal to meet their liberal expenditures. And in the rare cases where their skill does not suffice, these men do not hesitate to cheat. In one case in a hundred they are detected. Then the matter is 'hushed up' for their family's sake, but in the majority of instances their social position saves them even from suspicion, and their victim pays his money without a murmur.

"There are quite a number of Bohemians whose peculiar manner of making a living is certainly very suggestive of the growth of literature as a business in our midst. Translating is becoming quite a necessity in newspaper and business literature nowadays, and it has its tricks, like everything else. There is a man who is now fulfilling several contracts to translate works from the French, the German and the Spanish languages, who really knows no language but his native and imperfect English. He has picked up two or three phrases in the various languages he falsely pretends to understand, and these and his stock of impudence suffice to obtain his orders, for which he charges a good round sum. As soon as he has received his orders, he proceeds to fill them by jobbing out the work among a few half-starved Spanish or German or French hacks, as the case may be, who do his work for him at about one-fifth of the sum he charges for it. It can readily be seen that if there were enough of this trans-lating to be done, this ingenious ignoramus could in time become a Crœsus; but, unfortunately for his poor hacks, the field is limited. Lately one of these hacks—the French one—'struck,' and then struck out for himself, getting orders for translating direct, and the translation jobber is becoming frightened.

"Among the make-shifts of the time is levying literary blackmail. This peculiar species of blackmail is practiced extensively by certain parties in New York, after this fashion: They send proof sheets of certain biographies to the man or woman upon whom they intend to operate. These biographies, they tell the man or woman in a personal note accompanying the proof sheet, are samples of the contents of a forth-coming book which they are preparing to publish, and in which book they design to insert the biography of the 'distinguished' party to whom they are sent. With this note is an accompanying request that the man or woman aforesaid will be kind enough to write his or her biography in a similar style and send it to the publisher's address. Or perhaps the proof sheets of what purports to be one's own biography is sent, with a request to correct the unavoidable mistakes. Not a word is said about money matters, and the party to whom the proof sheets and request are sent feels materially flattered, falls into the trap, and either writes the biographical sketch desired or corrects the proof. So far so good. But lo and behold! in a little while, when the party has probably forgotten all about the matter, the biographical sketch is forwarded in proof sheet, or the proof sheet is returned in a revised form, and is accompanied by a bill for $100, $200 or $300, as the case may be. The victim's eyes are now opened to the game played upon him, but are opened probably too late. He or she has committed himself or herself by complying with the original request, and rather than 'have trouble,' or reveal publicly their own folly, the party pays the bill or compromises for a certain amount, and thus the publisher contrives to make a living, though the book itself is never published, for the very sufficient reason that all 'the illustrious persons' in the world have not yet 'contributed the necessary points' for their biographies—in other words, they have not all been victimized.

"Books descriptive of gentlemen's residences, turfmen's horses, etc., have been started on similar 'principles,' with more or less success.

"It is the fashion of the times to start literary bureaus. Some of them are genuine, most of them are bogus. These literary bureaus propose to do literary work for customers, to afford intellectual facilities and to command literary engagements, whereas, in fact, they do nothing but take the would-be literary man's (or woman's) money. Then there are bogus bureaus of correspondence and professional correspondents and letter writers. Then there are persons, generally women, who deal with 'ladies of neglected education' and proffer to teach them how to correct, or at least how to hide, their deficiencies. Some of these are genuine and useful in their way; others are frauds and shams; but all alike are curious, and really deserve more space and consideration than can be allotted to them in the limits of this article.

"But probably the greatest shams in this line are practiced under the guise of 'dramatic agents,' so called. Now a good dramatic agent is a most desirable and valuable being. None appreciate his services better than those who employ him. He is in his place indispensable. It may safely be said that more 'stars' have succeeded through their 'agents' than through their own merits. But in proportion to the value of a really 'good' and genuine agent is the worthlessness of a poor one, and the poor ones and the shams are greatly in the majority. These bogus agents have nothing but a limited acquaintance with the lower class of newspaper men, who have just enough ability to write a 'puff' and have unlimited 'cheek.' The last quality stands them in the best stead. Supplied with this they call upon the female aspirant for dramatic honors, flatter her and tell her she needs but a proper newspaper man to become famous; tell her that they are 'the proper newspaper men;' speak of their mighty and mysterious 'influence with the press;' guarantee to 'bring her out' (they would guarantee anything else if desired). And being forthwith engaged by the would-be star, they contrive to get in a few paragraphs in the minor papers, take her money, and this is absolutely all—all save waiting till the newspapers come out after the début of their principal (if so be by lavish expenditure of money, and without any real assistance from her agent, she has a début), and then they boldly claim the credit of every favorable criticism which appears, although they have had, and could on the face of things have had no connection with it; and they also do not hesitate to assert, in reference to any unfriendly criticism that may be published, that they did their best to avert it, and that, were it not for their 'influence' the attack would have been infinitely more bitter than it may happen to be.

"One would imagine that the principal would see through such a sham as this; but as a mere matter of fact it may be confidently stated that at least $50,000 are paid out every theatrical season to bogus and worthless agents, some of whom are newspaper Bohemians, some played-out actors, and some without the ability to be either.

"Society in its varied and complex phases affords a field for those who live by their wits, and the field is well cultivated in every direction. Matrimonial advertising is quite a feature in this department of human ingenuity, and although the greater part of the matrimonial advertisements in the papers are inserted either as a joke or for improper purposes, yet quite a percentage of them 'mean business.' There was formerly a regular 'matrimonial bureau' in this city, which did a thriving business. There was another institution of a similar kind far up-town.

"Of a precisely opposite line of business to this are the divorce detectives, male and female, who of late years have become quite numerous, and whose numbers and pecuniary prosperity afford a suggestive commentary on the ills and mistakes incidental to modern marriage. Many of these people do all they can to upset marriages already made, doing so in the interest of one or other, sometimes of both, of the unhappy wedded pair. They scruple at nothing. They sneak, spy, lie and swear to a lie, nor will they hesitate to put temptation in the way of those against whom they are employed —in short, a divorce detective of the bad class does not scruple to do all he or she can to procure 'sufficient grounds for divorce' on the part of those he or she is commissioned to detect. There are estimated to be about thirty men and some fifty women in the city of New York who are almost constantly engaged in working up divorce cases, procuring or manufacturing evidence, etc. Of these some ten or twenty are credited with having accumulated considerable money, and of all the number there is said to be only five or six who are thoroughly to be relied on as honest. Several of these detectives have on several occasions taken pay from both sides in a divorce suit, have pretended to watch a husband in the interest of a wife, or to spy upon a wife in the interest of a husband, and have, of course, lied to and cheated both. As a rule it may safely be laid down that professional divorce detectives are about the meanest of all the people who live by their wits, though they are undoubtedly among the sharpest.

"In concluding this article, a number of make-shifts may be glanced at *en passant*, which are already familiar to the public, or which, though trivial in their nature, are curious. There is the bogus 'agent for charitable societies,' for instance, and 'the professional philanthropist'—the men and women who are supported, with their families, by the mistaken carelessness and lavishness of the charitable public; the 'shyster lawyer' who 'solicits' his own clients, and who fleeces them when he has got them ; the parties who compound those elixirs which make all who use them 'beautiful for ever ;' the men who make money by issuing bogus diplomas for doctors, and the charlatans who practice medicine under these diplomas ; the quacks who 'cure all diseases,' who have 'a magic touch ;' the people who pander to the vanity of other people by preparing 'coats-of-arms' and 'heraldic insignia' for grocers and butchers ; the people who hire 'wedding presents' for the occasion—who borrow diamonds and plate to display at parties ; the people who lend and hire dress coats ; the enterprising publishers of petty papers, who manufacture late at night or on Sundays bogus 'sensations' in order to sell bogus extras ; the ingenious parties who go round the streets and the ball-rooms, etc., picking up old cigar stumps, which they revamp into 'the best and most fragrant Havanas ;' the 'hangers on' at the market stalls, who pick up the 'scraps' and resell them again to poorer wretches who live upon them, after a fashion ; the thrifty people who sell 'bill-board tickets' to the theatre at half price (quite a recognized occupation, by the by), and the curiously-disposed persons who have a *penchant* for 'sitting-up' with sick people, or 'watching' insane patients or drunken men 'for a consideration.' Then there is a curious individual who makes a living by 'suggesting' styles of sign-boards and mottoes for tradesmen. He is really a clever fellow in this line, and as he gets from \$2.50 to \$15 for a 'suggestion,' he manages to keep quite a snug little place over his head. Some of his 'ideas' have really brought in a good deal of money to those who have adopted them.

"Then there is an equally clever woman, though in a very different line, who, as she phrases it herself, 'engineers beggars.' This remarkable female hires a number of children, sometimes an additional number of men and women, selecting with an artist's eye all the most wretched specimens of humanity she can procure—the halt, the maimed, the lame and the blind ; the dirty, the ragged, the sick and the sore. These wretches she stations singly or in squads, or distributes them around the hotels, churches, places of amusement and the like, and then takes her percentage or the greater part of the money they contrive to extract from the sympathies of the charitable. Of late years this woman's sphere of operations has been materially circumscribed by the police. Still she makes money even now, and in old times she was really 'getting rich.' Every night when there was a ball at the Academy of Music or Irving Hall, or an opera, she would station her 'wretched squad' along Fourteenth Street and Irving Place, and, hiding herself in some convenient place, would grin as her purposely hatless and shoeless beggars received whiningly the alms of the light-hearted, home-returning revellers. But, alas ! for this clever 'engineer of beggars.' The flush times of masked balls are over, and she can but mumble and grumble as she thinks upon the days, or rather the nights, of yore.

"This article might be expanded by reminiscences of the 'champion free-lunchers,' who know how to evade the eye or to mollify the wrath of the 'barkeeper of the period,' and by illustrations of the 'floaters' who are to be found all day haunting the reading-rooms or writing-rooms of hotels in which they never spend a cent, but whose seats, fires, papers, etc., they use with the utmost freedom and advantage—but *cui bono ?* From the details already given in this article, the substantial one-half of New York have doubtless obtained a vivid idea of how the other and less substantial half manages to exist."

OPIUM HABIT AND ITS CONSEQUENCES.

LIFE IN A NEW YORK OPIUM DEN.—ONE WHO KNOWS ALL ABOUT IT TELLS OF HIS STRANGE EXPERIENCES.

I HAVE read so many untrue and unreasonable articles about opium and opium smokers that I deem it a duty, as one who has had a thorough introduction to this habit, to write a true and unbiased account of all my experience, which will serve to enlighten your readers in all the details that have heretofore remained a mystery. It is no fault of the papers that they have been unable to get at the bottom facts, because those addicted to the habit are not noted for their veracity, nor do they wish their secret to become known. But I have been cured of the habit and so have no more interest in keeping the secrets of the United Order of " Dope " fiends.

One evening three years ago I met a friend whom I had not seen for some time. For one who professed to be so delighted to see me again, I thought it very strange he should be in such a hurry to leave, and I told him so. He then unbosomed his reasons for leaving. He was going to "hit the pipe." I demanded he should take me with him. He showed great reluctance, but after some persuasion consented, reminding me that if I ever had cause to repent the visit to a joint I should never blame him. I laughed at the idea of harm coming, except if the place were raided, and this I was willing to risk. So away we went, taking a car down-town.

Getting off the car we proceeded to Pell Street, where he led the way up several steps through a dark hall, and rapped at a door in the back part leading to the basement. Some one from the inside inquired " Who ? "

My friend replied *"En she quay."* (Chinese words meaning opium smoker.)

" Who *en she quay ?* " was asked.

" Little Doc," my friend answered again.

After a moment's waiting a bolt was withdrawn from the inside, and opening the door we proceeded down the stairs, which were lighted by a lantern hung from the ceiling. There were about six steps, then another door, in which a little wicket opened, and a yellow face appeared, scrutinizing us inquiringly.

" How many ? " the face asked on seeing us.

" Two," my friend replied, and another bolt was withdrawn. My friend opened the door, and we entered.

It was a small room, smelling like most Chinese laundries, only the odor was more pronounced. The room was about twenty feet long by fifteen wide. On one side, extending the whole length, was a platform raised two feet above the floor, and wide enough to permit a man to lie at full length. Four or five feet above this was another platform, only a few feet below the ceiling. At the further end of the room were two similar platforms.

The end of the room was partitioned off, having a door and a large window. This window had a number of wooden bars running across it. These were to prevent any one reaching their hands through to the counter behind. This little room was lighted by a single gas jet, and a couple of Chinamen were in there talking away in their own language. The platforms were occupied by men and women in little groups, lying around little lamps and smoking cigarettes and, I afterwards learned, opium. Several people were stretched out asleep.

My friend was evidently well acquainted with the smokers, for they nearly all saluted him and asked him what was new out in the world. Selecting a vacant place, my friend told me to take off my coat and place it on a little stool to be used as a pillow. He sat on the edge of the bunk talking to a man who had risen from the bunk when we entered.

He invited this man to smoke with us, and introduced him to me as " Frankie, the Kid." The Kid accepted the invitation and lay on the other side of us, my friend resting his head on my breast. A " lay-out," as my friend called it, was ordered, and one of the Chinamen brought it to us. The " lay-out " consisted of an ordinary little tin waiter, a knitting-needle flattened at one end and gradually receding to a point at the other, which he called a yen hock, a little glass lamp of peculiar pattern, a wet sponge in a china dish, a small tin dish to deposit cigarette stumps or ashes, and a pipe of very curious construction. A small clam-shell contained a black, tarry-looking stuff, and this was the opium.

The " Kid " prepared the pipe and my friend smoked, taking one long draw. Next was my turn, and I tried to do likewise, but it threw me into a fit of coughing. They told me to breathe through my nose whenever I felt the choking sensation. I did this, and got along pretty well, they said, for a beginner.

When I had smoked several times I began to have a dizzy sensation about my head and objects appeared very indistinct to my vision. I had an itchy feeling all over my body, which I tried in vain to relieve. I smoked a little more and there was a feeling of nausea at my stomach. I then decided to stop smoking.

My friend told me to lay perfectly still and try to go to sleep, but the more I tried the less sleepy I felt. My nerves became exceedingly sensitive, the least little noise causing me to tremble with fear, and my heart beat wildly. I also felt very thirsty and asked for a drink, but they told me that I must not, above all things, attempt to drink water. So I lay quiet a little while longer, getting all the more nervous, and then determined to start home.

My friend warned me not to, but I persisted and rose up. The moment I stood on my feet the room seemed to whirl around and around and strange noises buzzed in my ears.

This passed off in a few minutes and my throat felt so dry I could not resist the temptation of taking a drink from a bucket of water that stood on a table in the joint. The moment I drank it I was sorry I had not heeded my friend's advice, for the instant it was down up it came as bitter as gall; so, hastily bidding my friend good-night, I staggered out and started for home.

The fresh air revived me somewhat, but I vomited every few steps, pitching about like a drunken man, I was completely bewildered; everything appeared backward to my mind, and it was with the greatest difficulty I managed to find my way to a car.

But in some way, how I am unable to say, I succeeded in reaching home. I did not wait to disrobe, but threw myself on the bed just as I was, going to sleep instantly. I awoke in the morning, still very dizzy, undressed and got into bed; slept straight through till the next morning; awoke with a pale face, bloodshot eyes and a dull pain in the back of the head; felt like going to sleep again, but conquered this and started out to attend to my business for the day.

As soon as this sickness passed off I longed to smoke again, and did a day or two later.

This time I did. not smoke as much, lay quietly in the joint after smoking and drank no water. It was not till I reached the street that any unpleasant feeling arose, and then I had exactly the same experience as before, but was able to get up in the morning, only feeling very thirsty and dull.

For several other nights I had the same trouble, but each night I went it was less marked. A few more nights and I commenced to get the real enjoyment from the pipe.

After smoking I felt extremely easy and comfortable, lay indulging myself to the extent of my imaginative nature, indulging in the wildest fancies, that appeared at the moment so real, and no thought of worldly trouble entered my mind. Then the frequenters of the joint were always telling stories, cracking jokes. Sometimes we sang in low voices. Then we drank beer. Feeling hungry, two or three of us clubbed together and bought a kettle of hot coffee and sandwiches from a little restaurant near by. Again such refreshing sleep. How the time flew! Hours were only minutes and days hours.

My next step was to learn how to prepare my own opium for smoking, and before this I always had to get some one else to do it for me. This is termed cooking and takes months to become proficient in. To do this the needle or yen hock is grasped between the thumb and first two fingers of the right hand. The point is dipped into the opium, and on removing it a small portion, the size of a bead, adheres to the yen hock.

It is now held over the flame of the lamp and swells up to the size of a chestnut. Striking it against the globe of the lamp it bursts and a little confined steam escapes, leaving it all shriveled up. This is repeated until it ceases to swell.

The object of this process is to evaporate all moisture from the opium, changing it from a sticky substance to a solid, similar to sealing-wax.

The pipe is held in the left hand and the bowl warmed over the light. The opium, in a melted condition, is rolled over the face of the bowl until it is shaped into a cone, the apex being the point of the needle. This is termed chying. The cone is now heated until it is very soft, the needle is pushed into the small hole of the bowl and flattens the apex of the cone till it becomes a cylinder. The hole of the bowl is thoroughly heated, the needle is pushed entirely into the hole, melts the opium, which now adheres to the bowl; the needle is then twisted out, leaving a small hole through the opium to the opening of the bowl. This mass is termed a pill. To smoke this the bowl is held over the lamp, so that the pill is directly above the flame. The opium melts, giving forth a vapor or smoke. This is sucked into the bowl along with the melted opium.

It took me over a month to do this right. I now came to the joint every night, frequently lying in one spot two nights and a day. Some of the frequenters didn't leave the joint once a week, and then only for a few hours, having no home to go to.

They were the professional cooks, receiving so much for every twenty-five cents' worth of opium, that was brought in a shell. I hardly ever eat more than one meal a day. Sometimes I only took that because I thought it was best for me, and not because I cared for it.

Some nine months after my first introduction to a joint I was unable to get my usual smoke one night. I felt very bad when I got in bed, but immediately fell into a heavy sleep, from which I was aroused in the morning after much calling.

On becoming thoroughly awake I went through a series of novel sensations.

First, I began to gape and a pain in the back of the head started, then tears ran from the eyes, a catarrhal discharge from the nose, my teeth chattered and I trembled from head to foot, a cold sweat covering my body. I tried to eat some breakfast, but it would not stay on my stomach. Half an hour more and rheumatic pains shot through my limbs, cramps in the stomach. I took a dose of laudanum and in a few moments all the disorders ceased.

I now realized for the first time that I was a victim to the opium habit, or, as the Chinese have it, "*inyun fun.*" I was compelled thereafter to smoke at least once a day, sometimes oftener. When I could not smoke I used laudanum or morphia.

The misery I suffered is indescribable. Sometimes right in the midst of conversation I would be seized with this sickness, and must quickly get an opiate or be completely prostrated.

This went on for some time. My face became sallow; my eyes bright, the pupils contracted. I never passed a comfortable hour unless I was either under the influence of opium or liquor. My mind was filled with the darkest thoughts towards myself, and life became almost unbearable. It was then I determined to break the habit or die.

My treatment was this: I went to the country, away from my old associations, kept reducing my dose of opium every day gradually, at the same time taking nervines and tonics. It took nearly three months of unmentionable suffering before I was cured.

My advice is to keep away from opium in all forms, as no good comes of it. The opium used for smoking, called by the smokers "dope," is an aqueous extract of the ordinary commercial gum. The Chinese have a secret mode of preparing this extract, making it more palatable to the taste and easier to get ready for smoking. It is imported from China in an oblong brass box about five inches long, two and a half wide. The can is only half filled, as in warm weather it puffs up and would overflow the can if allowance was not made for this swelling. It is about the consistency of tar melted in the sun, and nearly the same color. The mode of measuring it when selling is by a Chinese weight called *fune*. There are about eighty-three *fune* in an ounce, and a can contains 415 *fune*, or about five ounces. This sells for $8.25 a can, best quality, and inferior grades as low as $6. In smaller quantities, eight to ten *fune* are sold for twenty-five cents.

The people who frequent these places are, with very few exceptions, thieves, sharpers and sporting men, and a few bad actors ; the women, without exception, are immoral. No respectable woman ever entered one of these places, notwithstanding the reports to the contrary. The language used is of the coarsest kind, full of profanity and obscenity. The old saying, " There is honor among thieves," applies equally well to opium fiends. They never steal from each other while in the joint. I have seen men and women come in the joints while under the influence of liquor, lie down and go to sleep with jewelry exposed and money in their pockets, but no one would ever think of disturbing anything.

As a general thing the men who are regular smokers have very little money, relying almost entirely upon the women, who spend their money freely upon the fiends. Beer and tobacco are generally sold, which considerably swells the revenue of the keepers.

Though a desperate set, fights rarely occur in a joint. In three years I can only recall one instance, and that was through a misunderstanding. A gambler struck " Sheeny " Sam across the arm with a pipe, breaking one of the arm bones. A fiend suffering with the *inyun* is a man to be avoided. His suffering renders him almost insane, and he is not responsible for what he does.

Few white men can run a " joint " successfully. A Chinaman is meek, pretends to not understand when anything insulting is said to him, and so long as he gets paid for the opium does not care what the patrons do. On the contrary, a white man will not stand insult, and wants to boss the place to suit himself.

Frank Webb, a well known west side character, opened a joint in a second-story room in Seventh Avenue. His patrons were of a better class of crooks. Among the frequenters of his place could be seen most any night such noted characters as " Kid " Miller, banco man ; " Kid " Fox and Raymond, swindlers ; our absent " Hungry Joe " (Joe did not " hit the pipe," but only came to see his associates) ; " Yen Hock " Harry, who earned his title by stabbing a man with a *yen hock*, and many other noted characters less known to the public. Women from the Haymarket, Tom Gould's, the Cremorne and other disreputable places in the immediate vicinity came there after these places closed, which was generally near morning.

At the present time there are no public joints in the city, most of the smokers owning a " lay-out " of their own, and smoking in their rooms, where the law cannot interfere with them.

The cost of a lay-out is from $5 up to $25, the value depending on the age of the pipe, it becoming more valuable the longer it is used.

THE EXPERIENCE OF AN OLD CALIFORNIAN WITH OPIUM.—REMARKABLE IN-
FLUENCE OF THE DRUG ON THE FACULTIES—A STRUGGLE TO OVERCOME
A TERRIBLE CRAVING.

"Oh, yes," he said, as we sauntered through Chinatown and were assailed by its unsavory odors, "I have smoked opium. I recognize the familiar smell."

"And still continue to do so?"

"No, thank God, my experience with the drug was short and decisive, but sharp while it lasted. The opium habit is like getting into a quicksand; once in its grasp escape is almost impossible."

"You got out, it appears."

"But not without a struggle. I feel the effects of the drug even to this day, and it is many years ago since curiosity induced me to try the first pipe. Of course, I had to give some excuse for my foolishness :—I wished to learn the secret of opium's control over the minds and bodies of its votaries. This is how it was, and I might as well make a clean breast of it. I'm not a De Quincey, but I'll tell you as clearly as I can my feelings while under the influence of the drug. I had become acquainted with a gambler, one of the most expert in the State, whether in front or behind the game. I noticed that he often left the table, when dealing, and after he returned, say in half an hour, his manner had undergone a change; he manipulated the cards with greater steadiness and ease. One day I asked him the plain question :

"'Why do you call on a substitute, and quit the table so often?'

"'Opium, my boy,' he said, in a feverish way. 'I can do nothing without it. Steadies the nerves. Deprive me of my periodical pipe and I'm like a fiddle minus strings. Ever try a whiff?'

"'No.'

"'Then you'd better take my advice and continue to let it alone.'

"But my curiosity was aroused, and after accompanying D—— to his favorite opium haunt several times, I resolved to realize the sensations derived from smoking, whatever they might be. I 'hit' my first pipe, as the slang goes, about four o'clock one afternoon, and shudder now as the remembrance of the terribly sickening experience I passed through recurs to me. It was hard work in the beginning to get the pipe-stem properly adjusted to my mouth, and the method of smoking is different from that when you are enjoying tobacco. In inhaling opium smoke you draw the fume into the lungs by a long pull, and then exhale it slowly. A pipeful will last about one minute, and then you have to roll a new pill, and so on, till the desired effect is obtained. Like most beginners, I smoked too much at the start, but hardly felt the power of the drug till I rose from the bunk where I had lain.

"Then I became comparatively helpless and staggered like a drunken man, zig-zagging toward a water-pitcher, of the contents of which I drank a cupful or more. Nausea followed and when I reached my wooden couch again my lower limbs gave way completely and I fell helpless and insensible. I lay in that state for three hours, or until my friend D——, who had missed me, and, suspecting where I had gone, found and brought me to myself. With his help I got to my room in the hotel, where I again fell into a sleep, disturbed by restlessness and horrible dreams. I would awake screaming and with the idea some one was in the room seeking my life. In fact I made such a racket that the night clerk threatened to send for the police and have me arrested for being drunk and disorderly and alarming the house. He summoned D——, who sat up with me until morning, when I still felt the effects of the drug, but was able to rise.

" ' Well, old fellow,' said he, in a bantering tone, ' how do you like it as far as you've gone ? '

" ' It's a pretty rough introduction,' I replied, ' and I guess I'll go no further.'

" ' That's right,' said he ; ' you'd better stop right now, but I'll bet a twenty you won't. Of course you smoked too much, and then drank water to make the matter worse. If thirsty after the pipe, all practised opium smokers drink only good strong tea.'

" ' Well, I'm done with the stuff, anyhow.'

" ' No, my boy,' he said, quietly ; ' you'll tackle it again—you·don't like to give up beat.'

" The time came when I did tackle the pipe again, thinking myself strong enough to smoke without getting sick. I pulled away for about three minutes, consuming three pills, and this time I got a glimpse of what is called the opium devotee's paradise. With my body and limbs completely relaxed, I dropped into a state of delightful dreamy half sleep, languidly knowing all that was going on around me, but caring for nothing. I was above and beyond all worldly considerations, all responsibilities. Then there came a change. Restlessness supervened, and the dream of delight was rounded off by horrible mental images that resembled the harpies of Doré, as he pictured them in the Inferno. Then I came back, in a dazed way, to real life again, drank the strong tea, as I had been advised, and went home with all my nerves in a state of protest, and I then, after a terrible struggle, left the drug alone."

PRISON COMMUTATION LAWS.

EXPIRATION OF SENTENCE.

FULL commutation time is allowed in all cases where the time of expiration of sentence is mentioned. To obtain the date of a prisoner's discharge, see the Commutation Laws of the State wherein he or she was sentenced.

NEW YORK STATE.

The provisions of Chapter 21 of the Laws of 1886 for the commutation of sentences for good conduct, and the rules formulated in compliance with its requirements, are as follows:

CHAPTER 21.—An Act providing for commutation of sentences for good behavior of convicts in the prisons and penitentiaries in this State. Passed February 23, 1886.

The People of the State of New York, represented in Senate and Assembly, do enact as follows:

SECTION 1. Every convict confined in any State prison or penitentiary in this State, on a conviction of a felony or misdemeanor, whether male or female, where the terms or term equal or equals one year, or who has a term the maximum of which is fixed by law, exclusive of any term which may be imposed by the court or statute as an alternative to the payment of a fine, or a term of life imprisonment, may earn for himself or herself a commutation or diminution of his or her sentence or sentences as follows, namely: Two months for the first year, two months for the second year, four months each for the third and fourth years, and five months for each subsequent year.

SEC. 2. Where any convict in any State prison or penitentiary in this State is held under more than one conviction, the several terms of imprisonment imposed thereunder shall be construed as one continuing term for the purpose of estimating the amount of commutation which he or she may be entitled to under the provisions of this act.

SEC. 3. For the purposes of this act, the term of imprisonment of each convict shall begin on the date of his or her actual incarceration in a State prison or penitentiary.

SEC. 4. On any day not later than the twentieth day of each month, the agent and warden of each of the State prisons in this State, and the warden or superintendent of each of the penitentiaries in this State, shall forward to the Governor a report, directed to him, of any convict or convicts who may be discharged the following month by reason of the commutation of his or her sentence or their sentences in the manner hereinafter provided, which may be written or printed, or partly written and partly printed, which shall be uniform as to size and arrangement, which size and arrangement shall be fixed by the Governor, and shall contain the following information, distinctly written, namely : the full name of the convict, together with any alias which he or she may be known to have, the name of the county where the conviction was had, a brief description of the crime of which the convict was convicted, the name of the court in which the conviction was had, the name of the presiding judge, the date of sentence, the date of reception in the prison or penitentiary, the term and fine, the amount of commutation recommended, and the date for discharge from the prison or penitentiary, if allowed.

SEC. 5.   In the cases of all convicts where the date of discharge from a State prison or penitentiary, as determined after the allowance of commutation for good conduct, falls on Sunday, or any legal holiday, it shall fall on the day following.

SEC. 6.   As soon as practicable after the passage of this act, the Superintendent of State prisons shall formulate rules governing the allowance or disallowance of commutation to convicts for good conduct in prison or penitentiary, which shall in all cases be strictly adhered to in all the prisons and penitentiaries in this State.   These rules may be changed from time to time, if necessary, in the discretion of the Superintendent of State prisons, and he shall, immediately on their adoption, or of any changes in the same thereafter, cause copies of the same to be forwarded to the agents and wardens of all the prisons, and the wardens or superintendents of all the penitentiaries in this State.   A copy of these rules shall be furnished to every convict entitled to the benefits of this act.

SEC. 7.   For the purpose of applying the rules mentioned in the last section for the allowance or disallowance of commutation for the good conduct of any convict, a board shall be constituted in each of the prisons and penitentiaries of this State, to consist of the agent and warden in each of the State prisons, and the principal keeper and the physician therein, and the warden or superintendent in each of the penitentiaries of this State, the deputy or principal keeper and the physician therein, or of the persons acting in their place and stead.   This board shall meet once in each month before the date fixed for the transmission of their report to the Governor, as hereinbefore provided, and proceed to determine the amount of commutation which they shall recommend to be allowed to any convict, which shall not in any case exceed the amount fixed by this act.   They shall have full discretion to recommend the withholding the allowance of commutation for good conduct, or a part thereof, as a punishment for offenses against the discipline of the prison or penitentiary, in accordance with the rules hereinbefore mentioned.

SEC. 8.   In all cases, however, where the board shall recommend the withholding of the allowance of the whole or any part of commutation for good conduct, they shall forward with their report to the Governor their reasons, in writing, for such disallowance, and the Governor may, in his discretion, decrease or increase the amount of commutation as recommended by the said board, but he shall not increase the same beyond the amount fixed by this act.

SEC. 9. In case any convict in any of the State prisons or penitentiaries in this State having a sentence or sentences which equals or equal four years, escapes or attempts to escape, he or she shall, for the first escape or attempt to escape, forfeit one-half the amount of commutation fixed by this act. For the second escape or attempt to escape, he or she shall forfeit all commutation for good conduct as provided for in this act. Any convict, however, having a sentence or sentences which equals or equal less than four years, who escapes or attempts to escape, shall forfeit all commutation for good conduct as provided for in this act. But where a convict has more than one term, the provisions of this section shall only apply to the term during which the escape or attempt to escape was made.

SEC. 10. The board hereinbefore provided for to fix the amount of commutation for good conduct shall, immediately on the escape or attempt to escape of any convict, meet and proceed to investigate the said escape or attempt to escape, reduce the testimony of all persons having knowledge on the subject to writing, cause the said persons to affix their signatures thereto and make oath to the same before any one of the members of said board, who is hereby authorized and empowered to administer such oath, and false swearing on such examination or in such statement shall be perjury. The said board shall thereupon make a full report in writing, and immediately forward the same to the superintendent of State prisons, who shall thereupon determine whether an escape or attempt to escape was committed, make an indorsement, in writing, of his decision, and return the same to the agent and warden of the State prison, or the warden or superintendent of the penitentiary where the escape or attempt to escape shall have occurred, where the same shall be recorded in a book to be kept for that purpose. But, if from newly-discovered evidence, or other just cause, there is reasonable ground to believe that an injustice has been done to any convict in his or her having been adjudged to have escaped or attempted to escape, the superintendent of State prisons may, in his discretion, make an order in writing directed to the agent and warden of the State prison or the warden or superintendent of the penitentiary from which such convict was adjudged to have escaped or attempted to have escaped, requiring that a re-examination of the former adjudication be had, and upon a report to him of such re-examination, he shall proceed to render a decision upon the same. And the proceedings on such re-examination, the decision and the proceedings had thereunder, shall in all respects be conducted in the manner above set forth in this section as upon a first hearing in the matter of an escape or attempt to escape. But the provisions of this section shall not apply to the case of any convict, the length of whose term or terms is less than one year.

SEC. 11. The provisions of section nine shall apply to all convicts who are now, or may hereafter be confined in any prison or penitentiary of this State.

SEC. 12. The reports of the various boards for the determination of the amount of commutation for good conduct of convicts in the prisons and penitentiaries of this State to the Governor, shall be personally signed by the members thereof.

Sec. 13. The Governor, upon the receipt of the report recommending the allowance of commutation of sentences of convicts for good conduct, as provided for in this act, may, in his discretion, allow the same, and place the names of all those convicts whom he may determine to commute upon one warrant, and direct the same to the agent and warden of the State prison, or the warden or superintendent of the penitentiary, wherein such convicts may be confined, who shall thereupon proceed to execute such warrant by discharging the convicts mentioned therein on the date fixed for their discharge.

Sec. 14. The Governor shall, in commuting the sentences of convicts as provided for in this act, annex a condition to the effect that if any convict so commuted shall, during the period between the date of his or her discharge, by reason of such commutation and the date of the expiration of the full term for which he or she was sentenced, be convicted of any felony, he or she shall, in addition to the penalty which may be imposed for such felony committed in the interval as aforesaid, be compelled to serve in the prison or penitentiary in which he or she may be confined for the felony for which he or she is so convicted, the remainder of the term without commutation which he or she would have been compelled to serve but for the commutation of his or her sentence as provided for in this act.

Sec. 15. The certificate of the agent and warden of a State prison, or the warden or superintendent of a penitentiary, that the period of imprisonment of a convict was commuted under the provisions of this act, and of the crime and the length of term for which such commutation was granted, shall be received in evidence as proof for the purposes mentioned and described in section fourteen.

Sec. 16. Upon the receipt of any convict in any prison or penitentiary in this State who shall be entitled to the benefits of this act, the provisions of the same shall be read to him or her, and the meaning of same shall be fully explained to him or her by the clerk of the prison or penitentiary.

Sec. 17. Upon the discharge of any convict by reason of commutation of sentence for good conduct, the provisions of sections fourteen and fifteen of this act shall be read to, and their nature fully explained to him or her by the clerk of the prison or penitentiary.

Sec. 18. The provisions of this act shall apply to any convict who may have been transferred to the State asylum for insane criminals from either of the prisons or penitentiaries, or from any reformatory of this State, to which he or she may have been transferred from any of the prisons or penitentiaries of this State, whose sentence or sentences aggregates or aggregate not less than one year. And the medical superintendent of the State asylum for insane criminals may and shall perform any of the acts which may or shall be done by any board mentioned in this act.

Sec. 19. The provisions of this act shall apply to any convict who may have been transferred from either of the prisons or penitentiaries to any reformatory of this State whose sentence or sentences equals or equal not less than one year. And the superintendent or chief officer of any reformatory in this State to which any convict may be transferred as aforesaid, may and shall perform any of the acts which may or shall be done by any board mentioned in this act.

Sec. 20.   In all cases where it is herein provided that any board shall or may do any act, a majority thereof may and shall perform the same.

Sec. 21.   All acts and parts of acts inconsistent with the provisions of this act are hereby repealed.

Sec. 22.   This act shall take effect immediately.

PRISON RULES.

Rule 1. § 9.   In case any convict in any of the State prisons or penitentiaries in this State having a sentence or sentences which equals or equal four years, escapes or attempts to escape, he or she shall, for the first escape or attempt to escape, forfeit one-half the amount of commutation fixed by the above act.   For the second escape or attempt to escape, he or she shall forfeit all commutation for good conduct provided for in the above act.   Any convict, however, having a sentence or sentences which equals or equal less than four years, who escapes or attempts to escape, shall forfeit all commutation for good conduct, provided for in the above act.

Rule 2.   Any convict who shall assault an officer with a dangerous weapon shall forfeit not less than one-half of the commutation fixed by the above act for good conduct.

Rule 3.   Any convict who shall assault another convict with a dangerous weapon shall forfeit not less than one-quarter of the commutation fixed by the above act for good conduct.

Rule 4.   For assaulting or attempting to assault an officer or assaulting another convict, not with a dangerous weapon ; for disobeying orders ; for resisting an officer ; for insubordination ; for feigning insanity ; for smuggling or attempting to smuggle letters or other articles in or out of prison or penitentiary, the convict offending shall forfeit not less than ten days of the allowance of commutation fixed by the above act for good conduct.

Rule 5.   Any convict who shall destroy or secrete property shall forfeit not less than five days of the allowance of commutation fixed by the above act for good conduct.

Rule 6.   For offenses not enumerated in the foregoing rules, but which in the judgment of the board constituted by section 7 of the above act require a penalty, the convict offending shall forfeit not less than three days of the allowance of commutation fixed by the above act for good conduct.

Rule 7.   If, while serving the remainder of a term as provided by section 14 of the above act, a convict shall commit any of the offenses enumerated in the foregoing rules, the forfeiture therefor shall apply on the term of the last sentence.

Rule 8.   The board constituted by section 7 of the above act may take into consideration the general average conduct of a convict, and recommend the withholding of such part of the commutation for good conduct as in its judgment may be just in accordance with the foregoing rules.

ISAAC V. BAKER, Jr.,
Superintendent of State Prisons.

Albany, March 15, 1886.

TABLES OF COMMUTATION ON SENTENCES FOR GOOD BEHAVIOR.

State of New York, Executive Chamber, }
Albany, March 26, 1886. }

The attention of all officers charged with the administration of the criminal law is directed to the provisions of section 697 of the Penal Code, as amended by Chapter 68 of the Laws of 1886, which is as follows :

" Section 697. Where a convict is sentenced to be imprisoned in a State prison or a penitentiary for a longer period than one year, the court before which the conviction is had must limit the term of the sentence, having reference to the probability of the convict earning a reduction of his or her term for good behavior, as provided by statute, and assuming that such reduction will be earned, so that it will expire between the month of March and the month of November, unless the exact period of the sentence is fixed by law."

This section, as amended, went into effect March 25, 1886.

The copies of commitments to the various prisons and penitentiaries and the reports of commutation received each month at the Executive Chamber, show that ninety-five per centum of convicts earn the reduction allowed under the provisions of the statute.

The wise and humane intention of the act above quoted, which aims at the release of convicts during the season of mild weather, and when the chances of employment are the best, should be strictly observed.

It is also proper that attention should be directed to section 2 of chapter 21 of the Laws of 1886, which provides that in estimating commutation, all the terms under which a convict is imprisoned shall be construed as one continuous term.

For the convenience of courts and others, the following tables, showing the amount of commutation which may be earned on a given number of years or fractions thereof, have been prepared and issued.

DAVID B. HILL, *Governor.*

TABLE SHOWING COMMUTATION ON SENTENCES FOR YEARS, FROM ONE TO THIRTY-FIVE INCLUSIVE.

SENT.	COMMUTATION.		SENT.	COMMUTATION.		SENT.	COMMUTATION.		SENT.	COMMUTATION.		SENT.	COMMUTATION.	
YEARS.	YRS.	MOS.	YEARS.	YRS.	MOS.	YEARS.	YRS.	MOS.	YEARS.	YRS.	MOS.	YEARS.	YRS.	MOS.
1	..	2	8	2	8	15	5	7	22	8	6	29	11	5
2	..	4	9	3	1	16	6	..	23	8	11	30	11	10
3	..	8	10	3	6	17	6	5	24	9	4	31	12	3
4	1	..	11	3	11	18	6	10	25	9	9	32	12	8
5	1	5	12	4	4	19	7	3	26	10	2	33	13	1
6	1	10	13	4	9	20	7	8	27	10	7	34	13	6
7	2	3	14	5	2	21	8	1	28	11	..	35	13	11

COMMUTATION ON SENTENCES FOR YEARS AND MONTHS, FROM ONE TO THIRTY-FIVE YEARS INCLUSIVE.

SENT'NCE		COMMUTATION			SENT'NCE		COMMUTATION			SENT'NCE		COMMUTATION			SENT'NCE		COMMUTATION		
YRS.	MOS	YRS.	MOS	DAYS	YRS.	MOS	YRS.	MOS	DAYS	YRS.	MOS	YRS.	MOS	DAYS	YRS.	MOS	YRS.	MOS	DAYS
1	..	..	2	..	5	4	1	6	20	9	8	3	4	10	14	..	5	2	..
1	1	..	2	5	5	5	1	7	2½	9	9	3	4	22½	14	1	5	2	12½
1	2	..	2	10	5	6	1	7	15	9	10	3	5	5	14	2	5	2	25
1	3	..	2	15	5	7	1	7	27½	9	11	3	5	17½	14	3	5	3	7½
1	4	..	2	20	5	8	1	8	10	10	..	3	6	..	14	4	5	3	20
1	5	..	2	25	5	9	1	8	22½	10	1	3	6	12½	14	5	5	4	2½
1	6	..	3	..	5	10	1	9	5	10	2	3	6	25	14	6	5	4	15
1	7	..	3	5	5	11	1	9	17½	10	3	3	7	7½	14	7	5	4	27½
1	8	..	3	10	6	..	1	10	..	10	4	3	7	20	14	8	5	5	10
1	9	..	3	15	6	1	1	10	12½	10	5	3	8	2½	14	9	5	5	22½
1	10	..	3	20	6	2	1	10	25	10	6	3	8	15	14	10	5	6	5
1	11	..	3	25	6	3	1	11	7½	10	7	3	8	27½	14	11	5	6	17½
2	..	..	4	..	6	4	1	11	20	10	8	3	9	10	15	..	5	7	..
2	1	..	4	10	6	5	2	..	2½	10	9	3	9	22½	15	1	5	7	12½
2	2	..	4	20	6	6	2	..	15	10	10	3	10	5	15	2	5	7	25
2	3	..	5	..	6	7	2	..	27½	10	11	3	10	17½	15	3	5	8	7½
2	4	..	5	10	6	8	2	1	10	11	..	3	11	..	15	4	5	8	20
2	5	..	5	20	6	9	2	1	22½	11	1	3	11	12½	15	5	5	9	2½
2	6	..	6	..	6	10	2	2	5	11	2	3	11	25	15	6	5	9	15
2	7	..	6	10	6	11	2	2	17½	11	3	4	..	7½	15	7	5	9	27½
2	8	..	6	20	7	..	2	3	..	11	4	4	..	20	15	8	5	10	10
2	9	..	7	..	7	1	2	3	12½	11	5	4	1	2½	15	9	5	10	22½
2	10	..	7	10	7	2	2	3	25	11	6	4	1	15	15	10	5	11	5
2	11	..	7	20	7	3	2	4	7½	11	7	4	1	27½	15	11	5	11	17½
3	..	..	8	..	7	4	2	4	20	11	8	4	2	10	16	..	6	..	..
3	1	..	8	10	7	5	2	5	2½	11	9	4	2	22½	16	1	6	..	12½
3	2	..	8	20	7	6	2	5	15	11	10	4	3	5	16	2	6	..	25
3	3	..	9	..	7	7	2	5	27½	11	11	4	3	17½	16	3	6	1	7½
3	4	..	9	10	7	8	2	6	10	12	..	4	4	..	16	4	6	1	20
3	5	..	9	20	7	9	2	6	22½	12	1	4	4	12½	16	5	6	2	2½
3	6	..	10	..	7	10	2	7	5	12	2	4	4	25	16	6	6	2	15
3	7	..	10	10	7	11	2	7	17½	12	3	4	5	7½	16	7	6	2	27½
3	8	..	10	20	8	..	2	8	..	12	4	4	5	20	16	8	6	3	10
3	9	..	11	..	8	1	2	8	12½	12	5	4	6	2½	16	9	6	3	22½
3	10	..	11	10	8	2	2	8	25	12	6	4	6	15	16	10	6	4	5
3	11	..	11	20	8	3	2	9	7½	12	7	4	6	27½	16	11	6	4	17½
4	..	1	..	..	8	4	2	9	20	12	8	4	7	10	17	..	6	5	..
4	1	1	..	12½	8	5	2	10	2½	12	9	4	7	22½	17	1	6	5	12½
4	2	1	..	25	8	6	2	10	15	12	10	4	8	5	17	2	6	5	25
4	3	1	1	7½	8	7	2	10	27½	12	11	4	8	17½	17	3	6	6	7½
4	4	1	1	20	8	8	2	11	10	13	..	4	9	..	17	4	6	6	20
4	5	1	2	2½	8	9	2	11	22½	13	1	4	9	12½	17	5	6	7	2½
4	6	1	2	15	8	10	3	..	5	13	2	4	9	25	17	6	6	7	15
4	7	1	2	27½	8	11	3	..	17½	13	3	4	10	7½	17	7	6	7	27½
4	8	1	3	10	9	..	3	1	..	13	4	4	10	20	17	8	6	8	10
4	9	1	3	22½	9	1	3	1	12½	13	5	4	11	2½	17	9	6	8	22½
4	10	1	4	5	9	2	3	1	25	13	6	4	11	15	17	10	6	9	5
4	11	1	4	17½	9	3	3	2	7½	13	7	4	11	27½	17	11	6	9	17½
5	..	1	5	..	9	4	3	2	20	13	8	5	..	10	18	..	6	10	..
5	1	1	5	12½	9	5	3	3	2½	13	9	5	..	22½	18	1	6	10	12½
5	2	1	5	25	9	6	3	3	15	13	10	5	1	5	18	2	6	10	25
5	3	1	6	7½	9	7	3	3	27½	13	11	5	1	17½	18	3	6	11	7½

TABLE SHOWING COMMUTATION ON SENTENCES.—*Continued.*

SENT'NCE		COMMUTATION			SENT'NCE		COMMUTATION			SENT'NCE		COMMUTATION			SENT'NCE		COMMUTATION		
YRS.	MOS	YRS.	MOS	DAYS	YRS.	MOS	YRS.	MOS	DAYS	YRS.	MOS	YRS.	MOS	DAYS	YRS.	MOS	YRS.	MOS	DAYS
18	4	6	11	20	22	7	8	8	27½	26	10	10	6	5	31	1	12	3	12½
18	5	7	..	2½	22	8	8	9	10	26	11	10	6	17½	31	2	12	3	25
18	6	7	..	15	22	9	8	9	22½	27	..	10	7	..	31	3	12	4	7½
18	7	7	..	27½	22	10	8	10	5	27	1	10	7	12½	31	4	12	4	20
18	8	7	1	10	22	11	8	10	17½	27	2	10	7	25	31	5	12	5	2½
18	9	7	1	22½	23	..	8	11	..	27	3	10	8	7½	31	6	12	5	15
18	10	7	2	5	23	1	8	11	12½	27	4	10	8	20	31	7	12	5	27½
18	11	7	2	17½	23	2	8	11	25	27	5	10	9	2½	31	8	12	6	10
19	..	7	3	..	23	3	9	..	7½	27	6	10	9	15	31	9	12	6	22½
19	1	7	3	12½	23	4	9	..	20	27	7	10	9	27½	31	10	12	7	5
19	2	7	3	25	23	5	9	1	2½	27	8	10	10	10	31	11	12	7	17½
19	3	7	4	7½	23	6	9	1	15	27	9	10	10	22½	32	..	12	8	..
19	4	7	4	20	23	7	9	1	27½	27	10	10	11	5	32	1	12	8	12½
19	5	7	5	2½	23	8	9	2	10	27	11	10	11	17½	32	2	12	8	25
19	6	7	5	15	23	9	9	2	22½	28	..	11	..	..	32	3	12	9	7½
19	7	7	5	27½	23	10	9	3	5	28	1	11	..	12½	32	4	12	9	20
19	8	7	6	10	23	11	9	3	17½	28	2	11	..	25	32	5	12	10	2½
19	9	7	6	22½	24	..	9	4	..	28	3	11	1	7½	32	6	12	10	15
19	10	7	7	5	24	1	9	4	12½	28	4	11	1	20	32	7	12	10	27½
19	11	7	7	17½	24	2	9	4	25	28	5	11	2	2½	32	8	12	11	10
20	..	7	8	..	24	3	9	5	7½	28	6	11	2	15	32	9	12	11	22½
20	1	7	8	12½	24	4	9	5	20	28	7	11	2	27½	32	10	13	..	5
20	2	7	8	25	24	5	9	6	2½	28	8	11	3	10	32	11	13	..	17½
20	3	7	9	7½	24	6	9	6	15	28	9	11	3	22½	33	..	13	1	..
20	4	7	9	20	24	7	9	6	27½	28	10	11	4	5	33	1	13	1	12½
20	5	7	10	2½	24	8	9	7	10	28	11	11	4	17½	33	2	13	1	25
20	6	7	10	15	24	9	9	7	22½	29	..	11	5	..	33	3	13	2	7½
20	7	7	10	27½	24	10	9	8	5	29	1	11	5	12½	33	4	13	2	20
20	8	7	11	10	24	11	9	8	17½	29	2	11	5	25	33	5	13	3	2½
20	9	7	11	22½	25	..	9	9	..	29	3	11	6	7½	33	6	13	3	15
20	10	8	..	5	25	1	9	9	12½	29	4	11	6	20	33	7	13	3	27½
20	11	8	..	17½	25	2	9	9	25	29	5	11	7	2½	33	8	13	4	10
21	..	8	1	..	25	3	9	10	7½	29	6	11	7	15	33	9	13	4	22½
21	1	8	1	12½	25	4	9	10	20	29	7	11	7	27½	33	10	13	5	5
21	2	8	1	25	25	5	9	11	2½	29	8	11	8	10	33	11	13	5	17½
21	3	8	2	7½	25	6	9	11	15	29	9	11	8	22½	34	..	13	6	..
21	4	8	2	20	25	7	9	11	27½	29	10	11	9	5	34	1	13	6	12½
21	5	8	3	2½	25	8	10	..	10	29	11	11	9	17½	34	2	13	6	25
21	6	8	3	15	25	9	10	..	22½	30	..	11	10	..	34	3	13	7	7½
21	7	8	3	27½	25	10	10	1	5	30	1	11	10	12½	34	4	13	7	20
21	8	8	4	10	25	11	10	1	17½	30	2	11	10	25	34	5	13	8	2½
21	9	8	4	22½	26	..	10	2	..	30	3	11	11	7½	34	6	13	8	15
21	10	8	5	5	26	1	10	2	12½	30	4	11	11	20	34	7	13	8	27½
21	11	8	5	17½	26	2	10	2	25	30	5	12	..	2½	34	8	13	9	10
22	..	8	6	..	26	3	10	3	7½	30	6	12	..	15	34	9	13	9	22½
22	1	8	6	12½	26	4	10	3	20	30	7	12	..	27½	34	10	13	10	5
22	2	8	6	25	26	5	10	4	2½	30	8	12	1	10	34	11	13	10	17½
22	3	8	7	7½	26	6	10	4	15	30	9	12	1	22½	35	..	13	11	..
22	4	8	7	20	26	7	10	4	27½	30	10	12	2	5					
22	5	8	8	2½	26	8	10	5	10	30	11	12	2	17½					
22	6	8	8	15	26	9	10	5	22½	31	..	12	3	..					

FUGITIVES FROM JUSTICE.

CHAPTER 442.—An Act to establish a Code of Criminal Procedure. Passed by the New York Legislature June 1, 1881. Title IV., chapter 1, provides as follows:

SECTION 827. 1. It shall be the duty of the Governor in all cases where, by virtue of a requisition made upon him by the Governor of another State or Territory, any citizen, inhabitant or temporary resident of this State is to be arrested, as a fugitive from justice (provided that said requisition be accompanied by a duly certified copy of the indictment or information from the authorities of such other State or Territory, charging such person with treason, felony or other crime in such State or Territory), to issue and transmit a warrant for such purpose to the sheriff of the proper county, or his under sheriff, or in the cities of this State (except in the city and county of New York, where such warrant shall only be issued to the superintendent or any inspector of police), to the chiefs, inspectors or superintendents of police, and only such officers as are above mentioned, and such assistants as they may designate to act under their direction, shall be competent to make service of or execute the same. The Governor may direct that any such fugitive be brought before him, and may for cause, by him deemed proper, revoke any warrant issued by him as herein provided. The officer to whom is directed and intrusted the execution of the Governor's warrant must, within thirty days from its date, unless sooner requested, return the same and make return to the Governor of all his proceedings had thereunder, and of all facts and circumstances relating thereto. Any officer of this State, or of any city, county, town or village thereof, must, upon request of the Governor, furnish him with such information as he may desire in regard to any person or matter mentioned in this chapter.

2. Before any officer to whom such warrant shall be directed or intrusted shall deliver the person arrested into the custody of the agent or agents named in the warrant of the Governor of this State, such officer must, unless the same be waived as hereinafter stated, take the prisoner or prisoners before a judge of the Supreme Court, of any superior city court, or the presiding judge of a court of sessions, who shall, in open court if in session, otherwise at chambers, inform the prisoner or prisoners of the cause of his or their arrest, the nature of the process, and instruct him or them that if he or they claim not to be the particular person or persons mentioned in said requisition, indictment, affidavit or warrant annexed thereto, or in the warrant issued by the Governor thereon, he or they may have a writ of *habeas corpus* upon filing an affidavit to that effect. Said person or persons so arrested may, in writing, consent to waive the right to be taken before said court or a judge thereof at chambers. Such consent or waiver shall be witnessed by the officer intrusted with the execution of the warrant of the Governor and one of the judges aforesaid or a counselor-at-law of this State, and such waiver shall be immediately forwarded to the Governor by the officer who executed said warrant. If, after a summary hearing as speedily as may be consistent with justice, the prisoner or prisoners shall be found to be the person or persons indicted or informed against and mentioned in the requisition, the accompanying papers and the warrant issued by the Governor thereon, then the court or judge shall order and direct the officer

intrusted with the execution of the said warrant of the Governor to deliver the prisoner or prisoners into the custody of the agent or agents designated in the requisition and the warrant issued thereon, as the agent or agents upon the part of such State to receive him or them; otherwise to be discharged from custody by the court or judge. If upon such hearing the warrant of the Governor shall appear to be defective or improperly executed, it shall be by the court or judge returned to the Governor, together with a statement of the defect or defects, for the purpose of being corrected and returned to the court or judge, and such hearing shall be adjourned a sufficient time for the purpose, and in such interval the prisoner or prisoners shall be held in custody until such hearing be finally disposed of.

3. It shall not be lawful for any person, agent or officer to take any person or persons out of this State upon the claim, ground or pretext that the prisoner or prisoners consent to go, or by reason of his or their willingness to waive the proceedings afore described, and any officer, agent, person or persons who shall procure, incite or aid in the arrest of any citizen, inhabitant or temporary resident of this State, for the purpose of taking him, or sending him to another State, without a requisition first duly had and obtained, and without a warrant duly issued by the Governor of this State, served by some officer as in this section provided, and without, except in case of waiver in writing as aforesaid, taking him before a court or judge as aforesaid, unless in pursuance to the provisions of the following sections of this chapter, and any officer, agent, person or persons who shall, by threats or undue influence, persuade any citizen, inhabitant or temporary resident of this State to sign the waiver of his right to go before a court or judge as hereinbefore provided, or who shall do any of the acts declared by this chapter to be unlawful, shall be guilty of a felony, and upon conviction be sentenced to imprisonment in a State prison or penitentiary for the term of one year.

4. Any willful violation of this act by any of the above-named officers shall be deemed a misdemeanor in office.   (New—as amended by chapter 638, Laws of 1886.)

SEC. 828. A magistrate may issue a warrant as a preliminary proceeding to the issuing of a requisition by the Governor of another State or Territory upon the Governor of this State for the apprehension of a person charged with treason, felony or other crime, who shall flee from justice and be found within this State.   (New—as amended by chapter 638, Laws of 1886.)

SEC. 829. The proceedings for the arrest and commitment of the person charged are in all respects similar to those provided in this code for the arrest and commitment of a person charged with a public offense committed in this State; except that an exemplified copy of an indictment found, or other judicial proceeding had against him, in the State or Territory in which he is charged to have committed the offense, may be received as evidence before the magistrate.   (Old.)

SEC. 830. If from the examination under such warrant it appears probable that the person charged has committed the crime alleged, the magistrate, by warrant reciting the accusation, must commit him to the proper custody in his county for a time specified in the warrant, to enable an arrest of the fugitive to be made under the warrant of the Governor of this State, which commitment shall not exceed thirty days, exclusive of the day of arrest, on the requisition of the executive authority of the State or Territory in which he is charged to have committed the offense, unless he gives bail, as provided in the next section, or until he be legally discharged. (New—as amended by chapter 638, Laws of 1886.)

SEC. 831. Any judge of any court named in section eight hundred and twenty-seven may, in his discretion, admit the person arrested to bail by an undertaking, with sufficient sureties and in such sum as he deems proper, for his appearance before him at a time specified in the undertaking, which must not be later than the expiration of thirty days from the date of arrest, exclusive of such date, and for his surrender, to be arrested upon the warrant of the Governor of this State. (New—as amended by chapter 638, Laws of 1886.)

SEC. 832. Immediately upon the arrest of the person charged, the magistrate must give notice to the district attorney of the county, of the name of the person and the cause of his arrest. (Old.)

SEC. 833. The district attorney must immediately thereafter give notice to the executive authority of the State or Territory, or to the prosecuting attorney or presiding judge of the criminal court of the city or county therein, having jurisdiction of the offense, to the end that a demand may be made for the arrest and surrender of the person charged. (Old.)

SEC. 834. The person arrested must be discharged from custody on bail, unless before the expiration of the time designated in the warrant or undertaking, he be arrested, under the warrant of the Governor of this State. (Old.)

SEC. 835. (Repealed by chapter 638 of the Laws of 1886.)

STATE OF ARKANSAS.

SECTION 4435. To encourage prisoners to conduct themselves with industry and propriety, it shall be the duty of the Governor, whenever it appears from the reports of the contractors, or keepers of State prison, that the conduct of a prisoner has been exemplary, and unexceptional, for a whole month together, to commute such prisoner's term of confinement, for any period of time, not exceeding two days for each and every month that he may have so conducted himself. (Act Jan. 31, 1867, sec. 8.)

STATE OF CALIFORNIA.

Following is a Table of Credits given by the Goodwin Act, re-enacted in the Statutes of 1880:

SENTENCE IN YEARS.	CREDITS IN MONTHS.	ACTUAL TIME WITH CREDITS DEDUCTED.		SENTENCE IN YEARS.	CREDITS IN MONTHS.	ACTUAL TIME WITH CREDITS DEDUCTED.	
		YEARS.	MONTHS.			YEARS.	MONTHS.
One	2	....	10	Twenty-one	97	12	11
Two	4	1	8	Twenty-two	102	13	6
Three	8	2	4	Twenty-three	107	14	1
Four	12	3	....	Twenty-four	112	14	8
Five	17	3	7	Twenty-five	117	15	3
Six	22	4	2	Twenty-six	122	15	10
Seven	27	4	9	Twenty-seven	127	16	5
Eight	32	5	4	Twenty-eight	132	17	....
Nine	37	5	11	Twenty-nine	137	17	7
Ten	42	6	6	Thirty	142	18	2
Eleven	47	7	1	Thirty-one	147	18	9
Twelve	52	7	8	Thirty-two	152	19	4
Thirteen	57	8	3	Thirty-three	157	19	11
Fourteen	62	8	10	Thirty-four	162	20	6
Fifteen	67	9	5	Thirty-five	167	21	1
Sixteen	72	10	....	Thirty-six	172	21	8
Seventeen	77	10	7	Thirty-seven	177	22	3
Eighteen	82	11	2	Thirty-eight	182	22	10
Nineteen	87	11	9	Thirty-nine	187	23	5
Twenty	92	12	4	Forty	192	24	....

STATE OF COLORADO.

Convicts are allowed for continuous good conduct: First year, one month off each year's sentence; second, two months; third, three months; fourth, four months; fifth, five months; for each succeeding year six months is deducted for good behavior.

All good time which may have accrued at time of escape, or attempt at escape, will be forfeited. For first breach of prison discipline two days are deducted. All subsequent breaches four days are forfeited for each offense.

STATE OF CONNECTICUT.

This State allows 5 days on each month, or 60 days on one year; 120 days on two years, 180 days on three years, 240 days on four years, and 300 on five years.

STATE OF GEORGIA.

Prisoners are allowed 4 days on each month, or 48 days on one year, 96 days on two years, 144 days on three years, 192 days on four years, 240 days on five years, for good conduct.

This law applies to any number of years, provided the prisoner does not escape or attempt to escape.

STATE OF ILLINOIS.

ACT OF 1872.

No. of Years of Sent'ce.	Good Time Grant'd Months.	Total Good Time Made. Yrs.	Mos.	Time to be Served. Yrs.	Mos.	No. of Years of Sent'ce.	Good Time Grant'd Months.	Total Good Time Made. Yrs.	Mos.	Time to be Served. Yrs.	Mos.
1	1	......	1	......	11	14	6	5	9	8	3
2	2	......	3	1	9	15	6	6	3	8	9
3	3	......	6	2	6	16	6	6	9	9	3
4	4	......	10	3	2	17	6	7	3	9	9
5	5	1	3	3	9	18	6	7	9	10	3
6	6	1	9	4	3	19	6	8	3	10	9
7	6	2	3	4	9	20	6	8	9	11	3
8	6	2	9	5	3	21	6	9	3	11	9
9	6	3	3	5	9	22	6	9	9	12	3
10	6	3	9	6	3	23	6	10	3	12	9
11	6	4	3	6	9	24	6	10	9	13	3
12	6	4	9	7	3	25	6	11	3	13	9
13	6	5	3	7	9						

STATE OF INDIANA.

The following law was passed by the General Assembly relative to the commutation of sentences in all penitentiaries in the State of Indiana, on March 8, 1883:

SECTION 1. Be it enacted by the General Assembly of the State of Indiana, that every convict who is now in or who may hereafter be confined in the penitentaries of the State of Indiana, or in the Indiana reformatory for women and girls, and who shall have no infractions of the rules or regulations of the prisons or laws of the State recorded against him, and who performs in a faithful manner the duties assigned him, shall be entitled to the diminution of time from his sentence, as appears in the following table, for the respective years of his sentence, and pro rata for any part of a year when the sentence is for more or less than a year.

No. of Years of Sent'ce.	Good Time Grant'd Months.	Total Good Time Made. Yrs.	Mos.	Time to be Served. Yrs.	Mos.	No. of Years of Sent'ce.	Good Time Grant'd Months.	Total Good Time Made. Yrs.	Mos.	Time to be Served. Yrs.	Mos.
1	1	......	1	......	11	12	5	4	2	7	10
2	2	......	3	1	9	13	5	4	7	8	5
3	3	......	6	2	6	14	5	5	......	9	......
4	4	......	10	3	2	15	5	5	5	9	7
5	5	1	3	3	9	16	5	5	10	10	2
6	5	1	8	4	4	17	5	6	3	10	9
7	5	2	1	4	4	18	5	6	8	11	4
8	5	2	6	5	6	19	5	7	1	11	11
9	5	2	11	6	......	20	5	7	6	12	6
10	5	3	4	6	8	21	5	7	11	13	1
11	5	3	9	7	3						

SEC. 2. In case any convict shall knowingly violate any of the rules or laws of the penitentaries of the State, as above provided, and who is entitled to any diminution of his sentence by the provisions aforesaid, he shall forfeit for the first offense (if he has gained that much) two days, for the second offense four days, for the third offense eight days, and for the fourth offense sixteen days; and for more than four offenses the warden shall have the power at his discretion to deprive him of any portion or all the good time gained; provided, however, should first or second offense be of a serious character, the warden may at his discretion deprive him of more than the time specified above, but not to exceed more than eight days for each offense.

SEC. 3. The warden, in computing the diminution of time for those convicts now in the penitentaries, shall allow them the good time granted for the years or year or part of a year of their unexpired sentence.

SEC. 4. The warden shall not be allowed to restore to the convict the time forfeited.

STATE OF KENTUCKY.

Convicts are allowed for good behavior five days off of each month, or sixty days off of each year.

STATE OF LOUISIANA.

Senate bill 99, which passed the Legislature in June, 1886, provides for commutation of sentences for good behavior of convicts in the penitentiary, and in the parish prisons of the State. Its principal provisions are the following:

A person convicted of a felony or misdemeanor, and under sentence for one year or more, may earn a diminution or commutation of sentence by good behavior, in the following proportions: two months for the first year, two months for the second, three months each for the third and fourth, and four months for each subsequent year. Where a convict is under sentence on more than one conviction, the several terms shall be continued as a continuous term.

The term shall begin with date of incarceration. On the 20th of each month the sheriffs shall forward to the Governor a report of convicts who may be discharged the following month by reason of commutation. The rules to govern the allowance of commutation are to be made by the Governor, Lieutenant Governor and Attorney General. For the purpose of applying the rules, a board shall be constituted in each parish; the Board of Control of the penitentiary to act for the penitentiary. They shall recommend the commutations. The Board of Pardons may increase or decrease the commutation recommended. A convict who may escape forfeits his right to commutation. If any convict commuted shall, between his discharge and the expiration of his full term, be convicted of a felony, he shall be compelled to serve the remainder of the term in addition to the new sentence.

Any person sentenced for life, and who has merited the approval of the Board of Control, may at the expiration of fifteen years apply for a pardon or commutation. If recommended by the Board of Control, it may be granted on certain conditions—that not more than one in every five persons sentenced for life shall be pardoned or commuted in any one year; if more than one person is recommended, the decision shall be by lot, and the commutation or pardon approved by the Board of Pardons.

STATE OF MAINE.

CHAPTER 140, REVISED STATUTES.

SECTION. 14. The warden of the State prison shall keep a record of the conduct of each convict, and for every month that such convict shall appear by such record to have faithfully observed all the rules and requirements of the prison, the warden may recommend to the Executive a deduction from the terms of service of such convict's sentence according to, but not exceeding, the following rule and proportion : for a convict under a sentence of two years or less, one day for each month of good conduct; three years, or less, and more than two years, two days; four years, three days; five years, four days; seven years, or less, and more than five years, five days; nine years, or less, and more than seven years, six days; ten years, and less than fifteen years, seven days; fifteen years, and less than twenty years, eight days; and for all other convicts, except those sentenced to perpetual imprisonment, ten days.

STATE OF MARYLAND.

Two months off of each year. For example : a convict sentenced to five years would be allowed ten months for good conduct, which would reduce his sentence to four years and two months.

STATE OF MASSACHUSETTS.

An Act relating to the release of prisoners for good conduct. Passed June, 1880.

SECTION 1. Section twenty of chapter two hundred and twenty-two of the Public Statutes is hereby amended by striking out the words following, to wit : [" Upon a sentence of not less than four months and less than one year, one day for each month; upon a sentence of not less than one year and less than three years, three days for each month ; upon a sentence of not less than three years and less than five years, four days for each month ; upon a sentence of not less than five years and less than ten years, five days for each month ; upon a sentence of ten years or more, six days for each month,"] and inserting in place thereof the following words : " Upon a sentence of not less than four months and less than twelve months, one day for each month ; upon all sentences of one year or longer, two months for each of the first two years, four months for each of the third and fourth years, and five months for each succeeding year." Every officer in charge of a prison or other place of confinement shall keep a record of the conduct of each prisoner in his custody whose term of imprisonment is not less than four months.   Every such prisoner whose record of conduct shows that he has faithfully observed all the rules, and has not been subjected to punishment, shall be entitled to a deduction from the term of his imprisonment to be estimated as follows : Upon a sentence of not less than four months and less than twelve months, one day for each month ; upon all sentences of one year or longer, two months for each of the first two years, four months for each of the third and fourth years, and five months for each succeeding year.   When a prisoner has two or more sentences, the aggregate of his several sentences shall be the basis upon which the deduction shall be estimated.   Each prisoner who is entitled to a deduction from the term of his imprisonment, as aforesaid, shall receive a written permit to be at liberty during the time thus deducted, upon such terms as the board granting the same shall fix.   Said permits shall be issued as follows : To prisoners in the house of industry, jail or house of correction of Suffolk County, by the board of directors for public institutions ; to prisoners in the other jails and houses of correction, by the county commissioners of the several counties ; to prisoners in the State prison and in the reformatory prison for women, by the commissioners of prisons ; to prisoners in the State workhouse, by the trustees of said workhouse.   The Board issuing a permit as aforesaid may at any time revoke the same, and shall revoke it when it comes to their knowledge that the person to whom it was granted has been convicted of any offense punishable by imprisonment.

SEC. 2.   Section twenty-three of chapter two hundred and twenty-two of the Public Statutes is hereby amended so that it shall be as follows : *Sec. 23.* Convicts in confinement prior to the first day of May in the year eighteen hundred and eighty-six shall be entitled to such deductions as were allowed by law for that portion of their terms which was before that day, and to the deductions hereby established for that portion of their terms which is after that day, but they shall be entitled to deductions as provided in this act for that continuous portion of their terms immediately preceding said day, during which their record of conduct shows a faithful observance of all rules and that they have not been subject to punishment for violation thereof.

STATE OF MICHIGAN.

The law is found in Howell's Annotated Statutes of Michigan, page 2328, paragraph 9704, section 41, and reads as follows :

" The warden shall keep a record of each and all infractions of rules of discipline by convicts, with the names of the persons offending, and the date and character of each offense, which record shall be placed before the managers at each regular meeting of the board, and every inmate who shall have no infraction of the rules of the prison or laws of the State recorded against him shall be entitled to a deduction for each year of his sentence, and *pro rata* for each part of a year when the sentence is for more or less than one year, as follows: From and including the first year up to the third year, a deduction of two months for each year; from and including the third year up to the fifth, a reduction of seventy-days for each year; from and including the fifth up to the seventh year, a deduction of three months for each year; from and including the seventh year up to the tenth year, a deduction of one hundred and five days for each year; from and including the tenth year up to the fifteenth year, a deduction of four months for each year; from and including the fifteenth year up to the twentieth year, a deduction of five months for each year; from and including the twentieth year up to the period fixed for the expiration of the sentence, six months for each year. The inspectors shall provide by rule how much of the good time thus earned a convict shall forfeit for one or more violations of the prison rules. The warden, in computing the diminution of time for those now in the prison, shall allow them for the good time made up to the time this act takes effect in accordance with the provisions of law previously in force, and thereafter it shall be computed in accordance with the terms of this section. Whenever a convict has been committed under several convictions, with separate sentences, they shall be construed as one continuous sentence in the granting or forfeiting good time."

STATE OF MINNESOTA.

For first month's confinement, if conduct is good, two days are deducted from each year's sentence; for the second month of good conduct, four days are deducted, and for every subsequent month of good conduct six days are deducted. Under this law a convict is allowed fifty-five days off the first year, and sixty days off every year after, and fractions in proportion.

STATE OF NEW HAMPSHIRE.

The general laws of New Hampshire allow a deduction of one day for every month's good conduct, if the party is under a sentence of two years or less; two days off a sentence of over two years and not exceeding three years; three days off a four-years' sentence, four days if for five years, five days if for more than five years and not exceeding seven, six days for more than seven and less than nine years, seven days if for ten years and less than fifteen, eight days if for fifteen years and less than twenty, and ten days off all above twenty, except a life sentence.

STATE OF NEW JERSEY.

For every month of faithful performance of labor, two days remitted ; for every month of continuous orderly deportment, two days remitted ; for every month of manifest effort at intellectual improvement and self-control, one day remitted. The whole matter of commutations is regulated by the State prison inspectors. They may declare a forfeiture of *part* or *all* of the remitted time as they may deem just.

STATE OF NORTH CAROLINA.

SECTION 3445 OF THE CODE OF NORTH CAROLINA.

Every prisoner who may have been sentenced for a term of years, who shall at the end of each month have no infraction of the discipline so recorded against him, shall for the first month be entitled to a diminution of one day from the time he was sentenced to the penitentiary ; and if at the end of the next month no infraction of the discipline is recorded against him, he shall be entitled to two additional days' diminution from his sentence ; and if he shall continue to have no such record against him a third month, his time shall be shortened three additional days, and he shall be entitled to three days' diminution of time from his sentence for each subsequent month he shall so continue on his good behavior during the first three years or less of his imprisonment ; four days during the fourth and fifth years, and five days per month for each subsequent month of his term of sentence, and for every ten days he shall thus become entitled he shall have a further reward of one dollar placed to his credit with the warden, to be paid to him on his discharge, or sent to his family, as he may elect ; and for every five dollars of commutation he shall be entitled to five additional days' diminution.

STATE OF OHIO.

LAW PASSED APRIL 14, 1884.

SECTION 7.   The Board of Managers shall, subject to the approval of the Governor, make such rules and regulations for the government of the prisoners as shall best promote their reformation, and, generally, as may from time to time appear to be necessary or promotive of the purposes of this act.   They shall make provision for the separation or classification of prisoners, their division into different grades, with promotion or degradation according to merit, their employment and instruction in industry, their education, and for the conditional or absolute release of prisoners sentenced to imprisonment under section five of this act, and their arrest and return to custody within the institution ; but in no case shall any prisoner be released, either conditionally or absolutely, unless there is, in the judgment of the managers, reasonable ground to believe that he will, if released, live and remain at liberty without violating the law, and that his release is not incompatible with the welfare of society ; and no petition or other form of application for the release of any prisoner shall be entertained by the managers. In order that good behavior may be properly rewarded, the board shall provide, in its rules and regulations, for a correct daily record of the conduct of each prisoner, and his fidelity and diligence in the performance of his work. A convict who shall pass the entire period of his imprisonment without a violation of the rules and discipline, except such as the board shall excuse, shall, upon his absolute release or discharge, be restored to the rights and privileges forfeited by his conviction, and he shall receive from the Governor a certificate, under the great seal of the State, as evidence of such restoration, to be issued upon presentation to the Governor of a certificate of such conduct, which shall be furnished to such convict by the warden. A convict who is not thus entitled to a restoration of the rights and privileges forfeited by his conviction, who has conducted himself in an exemplary manner for a continuous period of not less than twelve consecutive months succeeding his absolute release or discharge, and presents to the Governor a certificate of that fact, signed by ten or more good and well known citizens of the place where he has resided during such period, certified to be such by the Probate Judge of the county wherein they reside, and whose signatures are certified by such Judge to be genuine, shall be entitled, in consideration thereof, to a restoration of the rights and privileges forfeited by his conviction, which restoration shall be evidenced by a certificate of the Governor, under the great seal of the State. Each convict who is sentenced for a definite term, other than for life, shall be entitled to diminish the period of his sentence under the following rules and regulations : 1. (*a*) For each month, commencing on the first day of his arrival at the penitentiary, during which he has not been guilty of a violation of discipline, or of any of the rules of the prison, and has labored with diligence and fidelity, he shall be allowed a deduction of five days from the period of his sentence. (*b*) After he has passed one full year of his sentence, in which he has not been guilty of a violation of discipline, or any of the rules of the prison, and has labored with diligence and fidelity, the deductions shall be seven days from the period of his sentence, for each month. (*c*) After he has passed two full years of his sentence, as above provided, the deduction from his term shall be nine days for each month. (*d*) After he has passed three full years of his sentence, as above provided, the deduction from his term shall be ten days for each month. 2. For a violation of the rules and discipline, or for a want of fidelity and care in the performance of work, he shall not only forfeit all time gained for the month in which the delinquency occurs, but, according to the aggravated nature or the frequency of his offenses, the board may deduct a portion or all of his time previously gained, but the board may review the conduct record of a convict, and, if it appear that any violation of the rules and discipline was committed through ignorance, or circumstances beyond his control, or abuse of any officer, may restore him to the standing he possessed before such violation. 3. If a convict be prevented from laboring, by sickness or other infirmity not intentionally produced by himself, or by other cause, for which he is not responsible, he shall be entitled, by good conduct, to the same deduction from his sentence, each month, as above provided for ; and the board may, in its discretion, allow him a sum of money sufficient to defray all his necessary expenses to the county where he was convicted.

STATE OF PENNSYLVANIA.

No. of Years of Sentence	Commutation.		How Long to Serve.		No. of Years of Sentence	Commutation.		How Long to Serve.	
	Years.	Months.	Years.	Months.		Years.	Months.	Years.	Months.
1	....	1	....	11	11	2	5	8	7
2	....	2	1	10	12	2	9	9	3
3	....	4	2	8	13	3	1	9	11
4	....	6	3	6	14	3	5	10	7
5	....	9	4	3	15	3	9	11	3
6	1	....	5	....	16	4	1	11	11
7	1	3	5	9	17	4	5	12	7
8	1	6	6	6	18	4	9	13	3
9	1	9	7	3	19	5	1	13	11
10	2	1	7	11	20	5	5	14	7

STATE OF RHODE ISLAND.

PUBLIC STATUTES, CHAPTER 254.

SECTION 28.　The warden of the State prison shall keep a record of the conduct of each convict, and for each month that a convict, not under sentence to imprisonment for life, appears by such record to have faithfully observed all the rules and requirements of the prison and not to have been subjected to punishment, there shall, with the consent of the Governor, upon the recommendation to him of a majority of the board, be deducted from the term or terms of sentence of such convict the same number of days that there are years in the said term of his sentence. *Provided*, that when the sentence is for a longer term than five years, only five days shall be deducted for one month's good behavior ; and provided, further, that for every day a convict shall be shut up or otherwise punished for bad conduct, there shall be deducted one day from the time he shall have gained for good conduct.

STATE OF TENNESSEE.

CHAPTER 121, SECTION 14, ACTS OF TENNESSEE, 1883.

Be it further enacted, that the Superintendent of Prisons shall keep a correct register of the conduct of each convict, to be termed the "good time account," in which he shall faithfully record the exact conduct of each convict, and each convict who shall demean himself self-uprightly shall have deducted from the time for which he may have been sentenced, one month for the first year, two months for the second year, three months for each subsequent year until the tenth year inclusive, and four months for each remaining year of the time of imprisonment. *Provided*, that the reduction of time herein provided for is upon the consideration of continued good conduct; and such record shall be evinced for or against the convict in any of the courts of this State.

STATE OF VIRGINIA.

"An Act requiring the Superintendent of the Penitentiary to keep a record of the conduct of the prisoners," passed at the session of 1865–6, provides:

1. That it shall be the duty of the superintendent of the penitentiary to keep a record of the conduct of each convict, and for every month that a convict by such record appears to have faithfully observed the rules and requirements of the prison, and not to have been subjected to punishment, there shall, with the consent of the Governor, be deducted from the term of service of such convict, four days.

2. That the superintendent shall submit said record and deduction to the Governor, when required by him, that the same may be considered in the exercise of such executive clemency on behalf of any convict as he may deem conducive to the interest of the prison and promotive of the reformation and welfare of the convicts.

That the superintendent shall cause a copy of this act to be posted in the cell of each convict.

4. This act shall be in force from its passage.

CANADA COMMUTATION LAW.

Among the provisions of "An Act to amend and consolidate the laws relating to penitentiaries," assented to May 25, 1883, are the following:

10. It shall be lawful for the Governor in Council to appoint some fit and proper person to be inspector of all penitentiaries and of such other prisons, hospitals, asylums, and other public institutions as may, from time to time, be designated by the Governor in Council; the Inspector, who shall hold office during pleasure, shall be an officer of the Department of Justice, and as such Inspector shall act as the representative of the Minister of Justice.

11. The said Inspector shall, under direction from the Minister of Justice, visit, examine and report to him upon the state and management of all the penitentiaries, and all suggestions which the wardens thereof may have made for their improvement.

14. The Inspector shall have power, and it shall be his duty, to make rules and regulations for the management, discipline and police of the penitentiaries, and for the duties and conduct of the wardens thereof, and of every other officer or class of officers or servants employed therein, and for the diet, clothing, maintenance, employment, instruction, discipline, correction, punishment and reward of convicts imprisoned therein, and to annul, alter or amend the same from time to time, subject to the approval of the

Governor in Council,—which rules and regulations, so approved, the wardens of the penitentiaries, and every other officer and servant employed in or about the same, shall be bound to obey : Provided always, that until such rules and regulations are made as aforesaid, the rules and regulations existing in each penitentiary at the passing of this Act shall remain in force.

53. In order to encourage convicts to good behavior, diligence and industry, and to reward them for the same, it shall and may be lawful for the Inspector of penitentiaries to make rules and regulations, under which a correct record may be kept of the daily conduct of every convict in any penitentiary, noting his industry, diligence and faithfulness in the performance of his work, and the strictness with which he observes the prison rules—with a view to permit such convict, under the prison rules, to earn a remission of a portion of the time for which he is sentenced to be confined, not exceeding five days for every month during which he shall have been exemplary in industry, diligence and faithfulness in his work, and shall not have violated any of the prison rules : Provided always that when any convict shall have earned and have at his credit any of the several numbers of days of remission hereinafter respectively mentioned, it shall be lawful to allow him for every subsequent month during which his industry, diligence, faithfulness in his work and observance of the prison rules, shall continue satisfactory, the following increased rates of remission, that is to say :

a. When he shall have thirty days' remission at his credit, seven days and one-half day's remission may be allowed him for every month thereafter :

b. When he shall have one hundred and twenty days' remission at his credit, ten days' remission may be allowed him for every month thereafter.

If any convict be prevented from labor by sickness or any other infirmity, not intentionally produced by himself, he shall be entitled, by good conduct, to one-half the remission from his sentence every month to which he would otherwise be entitled.

LIST OF

STATE PRISONS, PENITENTIARIES AND REFORMATORIES

IN THE STATES AND TERRITORIES.

Alabama—State prison, Wetumpka. Penitentiary, Huntsville.

Arizona—Territorial prison, Yuma.

Arkansas—Penitentiary, Little Rock.

California—Prison, Folsom and San Quentin.

Colorado—Penitentiary, Canon City.

Connecticut—Prison, Wethersfield. Reform school, Meriden.

Dakota—Penitentiary, Sioux Falls.

Delaware — No penitentiary; jails at Newcastle, Dover and Georgetown.

District of Columbia—No penitentiary; those sentenced are sent to a State penitentiary, which is designated by the Department of Justice of the United States.

Florida—Penitentiary, Chattahooche.

Georgia—Penitentiary, Atlanta.

Idaho—Prison, Boise City.

Illinois — Northern penitentiary, Joliet; Southern penitentiary, Chester. Reform school, Pontiac.

Indiana—Prison. Michigan City and Jeffersonville; for women, Indianapolis.

Iowa — Penitentiaries at Fort Madison and Anamosa.

Kansas—Penitentiaries, Leavenworth and Lansing. Reform school, North Topeka.

Kentucky—Penitentiary, Frankfort.

Louisiana—Penitentiary, Baton Rouge.

Maine—Prison, Thomaston.

Maryland—Penitentiary, Baltimore.

Massachusetts—Prison, Boston. Penitentiary, Concord. Reformatory, Warnerville. Reformatory for women, Sherborne.

Michigan—Prison, Jackson. Reform school, Lansing. House of correction and reformation, Ionia.

Minnesota—Prison, Stillwater.

Mississippi—Prison, Jackson.

Missouri—Penitentiary, Jefferson City.

Montana—Penitentiary, Deer Lodge.

Nebraska—Penitentiary, Lincoln. Reform school, Kearney.

New Mexico—Penitentiary, Santa Fé.

Nevada—Prison, Carson City.

New Hampshire—Prison, Concord.

New Jersey—Prison, Trenton; Essex county Penitentiary, Caldwell; Hudson county penitentiary, Jersey City.

New York—Prisons, Auburn, Dannemora and Sing Sing.
Reformatory, Elmira.
County penitentiaries—Albany county, Albany; Erie county, Buffalo; Kings county, Brooklyn; Monroe county, Rochester; New York county, New York City; Onondaga county, Syracuse; Catholic Protectory, West Farms.
Houses of refuge, Rochester and New York City. (All female prisoners are committed to the penitentiaries.)

North Carolina—Penitentiary, Raleigh.

Ohio—Penitentiary, Columbus.
Reform school, Lancaster.

Oregon—Penitentiary, Salem.

Pennsylvania — Eastern penitentiary, Philadelphia; Moyamensing penitentiary, Philadelphia; Western penitentiary, Allegheny City.

Rhode Island—Penitentiary, Cranston Print Works.
Reform school, Howard.

South Carolina—Penitentiary, Columbia.

Tennessee—Penitentiary, Nashville.

Texas — Penitentiaries, Huntsville and Rusk.

Utah—Penitentiary, Salt Lake City.

Vermont prison—Windsor.

Virginia—Penitentiary, Richmond.

Washington Territory — Penitentiaries, Olympia and McNeil's Island.

W. Virginia—Penitentiary, Moundsville.

Wisconsin—Prison, Waupun.

Wyoming—Penitentiary, Laramie City.

ADDENDA.

RECORD OF NO. 1.—Rufe Minor, alias Pine, was last arrested in Brooklyn, N. Y., on June 19, 1886, for sneaking $102 from the drawer of a saloon kept by William Trott, at No. 224 Atlantic Street. He gave the name of John Reilly, and was discharged from custody on July 7, 1886.

RECORD OF NO. 12.—Edward Rice was discharged from custody by Judge Robertson, in Cincinnati, Ohio, on July 26, 1886, the authorities failing to convict him of the burglary at the silk house of J. W. Luhn, which occurred in 1883.

RECORD OF NO. 19.—William Kelly, mentioned in this record, was discharged from Sing Sing prison, New York State, on June 29, 1886.

RECORD OF NO. 26.—Augustus Raymond, in the rôle of a hotel thief, was arrested at the Monmouth House, Spring Lake, N. J. He was captured on the third floor of the hotel by the elevator man. While being detained in the office of the hotel, in the charge of a porter, he managed to get rid of a set of hotel workers' tools which he had upon his person, by dropping them into several convenient places. Raymond was committed to the Monmouth county jail, at Freehold, N. J., on August 2, 1886, and shortly after admitted to bail. At the time of this arrest he gave the name of Robert Ellison.

RECORD OF NO. 28.—John Tracy was arrested in Troy, N. Y., in July, 1878, in connection with William, alias Mush Reilly and four others, for assaulting and robbing a man named John Buckley in one of the horse-cars of that city. Through the intercession of friends and the assistance of able lawyers he succeeded in obtaining only a five years' sentence, in March, 1879. He was discharged from Clinton prison on October 13, 1882. Mush Reilly, the principal in this robbery, was arrested in Toronto, Canada, on July 14, 1878, brought to Troy, N. Y., tried, convicted, and sentenced to fifteen years in State prison on October 4, 1878. Tracy lived for a number of years on the east side of New York City. He is the man that made the arrangements with Watchman Shevelin (who was his friend) to rob the Manhattan Savings Institution, and it was during the progress of the scheme that he went to Troy, N. Y., and was arrested and sent to State prison as above stated.

RECORD OF No. 74.—Gilbert Yost, burglar, mentioned in this record, died in the Indiana State prison, at Michigan City, on July 10, 1886.

RECORD OF No. 74.—William O'Brien, alias Billy Porter, was admitted to bail in the sum of $20,000, at Troy, N. Y., on July 12, 1886. He was not taken to Brooklyn, N. Y., as expected. He arrived in New York City on September 22, 1886, from Europe, for the purpose of standing trial at Troy, N. Y., for the Marks jewelry store robbery.

RECORD OF No. 88.—Dennis Brady, mentioned in this record, was discharged from Sing Sing prison, New York State, on July 2, 1886. Larry Griffin, also mentioned, was discharged from Auburn prison, New York State, about the same date.

RECORD OF No. 116.—Mary Holbrook, alias Mollie Hoey, was last arrested on September 24, 1886, at Cleveland, Ohio, for the larceny of a shawl, valued at $450, from one of the dry-goods stores in that city. She was committed for trial.

RECORD OF No. 130.—Mary Ann Flynn, alias Annie Mack, alias McKenna, and Nellie Bond, alias Barnes, mentioned in this record, were sentenced to ten months in the penitentiary on Blackwell's Island, New York, on September 7, 1886, for shop-lifting.

RECORD OF No. 131.—Louise Jourdan (under name of Mary Johnson) and a tall, blonde woman, who said her name was Sarah Anderson, were arrested in Cincinnati, Ohio, on May 18, 1886, for picking pockets. They were both indicted. Admitted to bail, which they forfeited.

RECORD OF No 136.—Tim Oats, under the name of Charles Wilson, was arrested in New York City on September 10, 1886, in the company of Bernard Corcoran, alias Barney Rose, alias "Barney the Kid," and Mary Morton. They were charged with robbing two persons by the "panel game," at No. 16 Clinton Place. The complainants refused to prosecute, and the prisoners were discharged on September 12.

INDEX.